THE FUTURE
of
LIBERATION THEOLOGY

THE FUTURE
of
LIBERATION THEOLOGY

Essays in Honor of Gustavo Gutiérrez

Edited by
Marc H. Ellis and Otto Maduro

ORBIS BOOKS

Maryknoll, New York 10545

The Catholic Foreign Mission Society of America (Maryknoll) recruits and trains people for overseas missionary service. Through Orbis Books, Maryknoll aims to foster the international dialogue that is essential to mission. The books published, however, reflect the opinions of their authors and are not meant to represent the official position of the society.

Manuscript editor: William E. Jerman

ISBN 0-88344-421-6

To Gustavo

*On the occasion of your sixtieth birthday
these essays are a celebration of your fidelity*

In sending his Son, the Father "wagered" on the possibility of a faith and behavior characterized by gratuitousness and by a response to the demand that justice be established. When history's "losers" — persons like Job — follow in the steps of Jesus, they are seeing to it that the Lord wins his wager. The risks accepted in talking about God with the suffering of the innocent in view are great. But, again like Job, we cannot keep quiet; we must humbly allow the cry of Jesus on the cross to echo through history and nourish our theological efforts. As St. Gregory the Great says in his commentary on Job, the cry of Jesus will not be heard "if our tongues keep silent about what our souls believe. But lest his cry be stifled in us, let each of us make known to those who approach him in the mystery by which he lives."

This mystery is the one proclaimed by the dead and risen Son of God. It is the mystery that we come to know when his Spirit impels us to say "Abba! Father!"

— GUSTAVO GUTIÉRREZ
On Job

Contents

Acknowledgments   xiii

Introduction   xv
Otto Maduro

PART I
GREETINGS

1. *Luise Ahrens, MM, and Barbara Hendricks, MM*   3

2. *Cardinal Paulo Evaristo Arns*   9

3. *William Boteler, MM*   13

4. *Bishop Aloysius Jin Luxian*   16

5. *Cardinal Stephen Kim*   19

6. *Bishop Peter A. Rosazza*   23

7. *Bishop Desmond M. Tutu*   25

8. *Elie Wiesel*   27

PART II
GUTIÉRREZ: THE MAN AND HIS WORK

9. Gustavo Gutiérrez—A Friendly Profile   31
Frei Betto

10. The Originality of the Theology of Liberation   38
Leonardo Boff

11. Peru and the Mystery of Liberation: The Nexus and Logic of Gustavo
Gutiérrez's Theology   49
Curt Cadorette

12. Gustavo Gutiérrez: A Friend of Nicaragua   59
César Jerez, SJ

13. Gustavo Gutiérrez and the Originality of the Peruvian Experience   65
    Stephen Judd, MM

14. In Honor of Gustavo Gutiérrez   77
    Penny Lernoux

15. Gustavo Gutiérrez, the Person and the Message:
    Memories of an Encounter   84
    Teresa Okure, SHCJ

16. Gustavo Gutiérrez: A Historical Sketch   95
    Sergio Torres

PART III
INTERPRETING LIBERATION THEOLOGY

17. Women and the Theology of Liberation   105
    Ana María Bidegain

18. Love and Social Transformation in Liberation Theology   121
    José Míguez Bonino

19. Taking African History Seriously: The Challenge of Liberation Theology   129
    Marie J. Giblin

20. The Logic of the Christian Response to Social Suffering   139
    Roger Haight, SJ

21. Paganism and the Politics of Evangelization   154
    Nicholas Lash

22. Theology in the Struggle for History and Society   165
    Johann Baptist Metz

23. Religion and Society: Sacred Canopy vs. Prophetic Critique   172
    Rosemary Radford Ruether

24. The Religious and the Human Ecumene   177
    Edward Schillebeeckx

25. Jesus, Theology, and Good News   189
    Jon Sobrino, SJ

PART IV
DISPUTED QUESTIONS

26. Miriam and Her Companions   205
    Ana Flora Anderson and Gilberto da Silva Gorgulho, OP

27. **Community and Identity**   220
    Gregory Baum

28. **Seven Samurai and How They Looked Again: Theology, Social
    Analysis, and *Religión Popular* in Latin America**   229
    Harvey Cox

29. **The Ethnic, Peasant, and Popular in a Polycentric Christianity**   240
    Enrique Dussel

30. **The Exodus as Event and Process: A Test Case in the Biblical
    Grounding of Liberation Theology**   250
    Norman K. Gottwald

31. **Theoretical and Institutional Bases of the Opposition to Liberation
    Theology**   261
    François Houtart

32. **Dependency Theory, Marxist Analysis, and Liberation Theology**   272
    Arthur F. McGovern, SJ

33. **God and Society: A Response to Liberation Theology**   287
    Marie Augusta Neal, SND

34. **Human Rights Language and Liberation Theology**   299
    Aloysius Pieris, SJ

35. **The Politics of Otherness: Biblical Interpretation as a Critical
    Praxis for Liberation**   311
    Elisabeth Schüssler Fiorenza

36. **God's Pain and Our Pain**   326
    Dorothee Sölle

PART V
LIBERATION IN DIFFERENT CONTEXTS

37. **Christ and the World Religions: An Asian Perspective**   337
    Tissa Balasuriya, OMI

38. **Martin Luther King, Jr., and the Third World**   346
    James H. Cone

39. ***Mestizaje* as a Locus of Theological Reflection**   358
    Virgil Elizondo

40. **Critical Thought and Messianic Trust: Reflections on a Jewish
    Theology of Liberation**   375
    Marc H. Ellis

41. **Pakistani Women: Yearning for Liberation**   390
    Mariam Francis

42. **Doing Theology in a Counterrevolutionary Situation**   397
    Carter Heyward

43. *Mujeristas*: **A Name of Our Own**   410
    Ada María Isasi-Díaz

44. **Theological Perspectives of a Religious Woman Today**   420
    Mary John Mananzan, OSB

45. **Theology in a Prophetic Mode**   433
    Albert Nolan, OP

46. **Christian Feminism and African Culture: The "Hearth" of the
    Matter**   441
    Mercy Amba Oduyoye

47. **Wrestling in the Night**   450
    Samuel Rayan, SJ

PART VI
LOOKING TOWARD THE FUTURE

48. **Women in the Future of the Theology of Liberation**   473
    María Clara Bingemer

49. **Reflections of a North American: The Future of Liberation
    Theology**   491
    Robert McAfee Brown

50. **Liberation Theology: A Difficult but Possible Future**   502
    Pablo Richard

Contributors   511

Acknowledgments

This volume of essays came together with the support of the Maryknoll Fathers and Brothers, the Summer Justice and Peace program, and Orbis Books. Maryknoll provided the funding and setting for the month-long symposium acknowledging the importance of liberation theology and in particular the work of Gustavo Gutiérrez.

In the Maryknoll community, we are particularly grateful to William Boteler, Kenneth Thesing, and Ronald Saucci. Editorial assistance has been crucial to the focus and strength of this volume, and here Eve Drogin, Robert Gormley, and Robert Ellsberg deserve our special thanks, along with Matthew Lamb, Samuel Rayan, and Ana Flora Anderson, who were among our initial consultants. Clara Araujo and Geraldine DiLauro worked diligently in typing the manuscript and general correspondence; Robert Francescone and Paul Joly were instrumental in coordinating publicity and press relations for the symposium, at which many of these essays were first presented.

We are especially grateful to Jim and Jeanne Haster, Mary Jean Lindenger, Anne Marie Bucher, Laurie Brink, Karen Root, Curt Cadorette, Elizabeth Donahue, Maryann Hedaa, and Veronica McNally, all of whom served beyond the call of duty before and during the symposium. We want also to express our appreciation to the contributors to this volume, who responded quickly and generously to the call to honor a movement and a fellow worker in the global process of liberation.

Finally, we extend our heartfelt greetings and thanks to Gustavo Gutiérrez for agreeing to endure the sometimes painful process of congratulatory introductions and prayers, and who continually challenged our own faith through his humility and kindness.

Introduction

We have come a long way. The year of 1988 was marked by a number of anniversaries—whether obscure or noteworthy—that belong not only to the Christians of Latin America, but are already part of the struggles and hopes of the oppressed of the world.

Twenty years ago the theology of liberation received its name in an article published by a little-known Peruvian theologian named Gustavo Gutiérrez, an event overshadowed that same year by the historic meeting of the Latin American bishops at Medellín, Colombia. This conference, which was inaugurated by Pope Paul VI in the first papal visit to Latin America, concluded with a prophetic message that affirmed the essence of any theology of liberation: an understanding of the good news of Jesus Christ as a call for consistent commitment to "the least among ourselves," the poor, the hungry, the oppressed, who are the nameless majority of our population.

Last year, many scholars, theologians, and religious activists gathered in Maryknoll, New York, to remember and celebrate some meaningful anniversaries in the life and witness of one Latin American Christian, Gustavo Gutiérrez: his sixtieth birthday; the thirtieth anniversary of his ordination to a priesthood that he has lived and understood as a service to the poor; and last, but not least, the fifteenth anniversary of the translation and publication by Orbis Books of Gustavo's classic work, *A Theology of Liberation.*

The Summer Institute for Justice and Peace—at the Maryknoll School of Theology—was thus entirely dedicated to this joyous commemoration. With the support of Orbis Books and the Maryknoll Fathers and Brothers, more than one hundred people from all over the world assembled for five weeks with Gustavo and dozens of his theologians-friends. From Asia and Africa, from Latin America and North America they came, to join in a celebration that was at once a symposium and a summer course in theology, a press conference and a gathering of friends, a living dialogue and a spiritual feast. These guests and others were invited to submit essays for this present volume celebrating the life and work of Gustavo and the future of liberation theology.

In reality—both with this book and that memorable summer—we are celebrating life itself: the life of a church which, despite the efforts of the powerful, continues to voice anew the cry of the poor in her midst; and the life of the many persons, like Gustavo, who serve the oppressed in solidarity with their struggle for life in the Third World. This occasion is a celebration of the presence of the God of life in our midst.

Indeed, if there is something that we liberation theologians claim to have learned from the oppressed, it is precisely the challenge of upholding, esteeming, and joyfully celebrating life. Where the "wise" would find neither objective probability nor subjective motive for life to flourish, there the active faith of the oppressed creates myriad ways to save lives and a million forms of celebrating the sacrament of life.

This collection of essays honoring Gustavo Gutiérrez is thus nothing more and nothing less than another form of upholding, nurturing, communicating, and celebrating life.

THE COMING OF AGE OF LIBERATION THEOLOGY

In a way, too, we are celebrating the "coming of age" of liberation theology. This theology is no longer uniform. It is pluralistic and in process; more and more liberation theologies are being born among the diverse oppressed peoples of this earth. Feminist and black theologies; Jewish and Palestinian theologies of liberation; Minjung theology, "water buffalo" theology, "barefoot" theology . . . these are only some of the rich variety of theologies which owe some debt of origin to what was born twenty years ago in Latin America.

Liberation theologies can no longer be disregarded as minor religious movements. On the contrary, they are becoming the point of reference for all other discourse about God and religion. This is because liberation theologians are posing everywhere, in many languages and modes of expression, that eternal question which we believe is *the* biblical question: What are we doing for the children of God who are left in our care, those among our sisters and brothers who are suffering unjustly and dying before their time?

This is what the powerful and comfortable find most disturbing about liberation theology. It is not what liberation theologians might have to say about private property or about revolutionary struggle, but the troubling persistence with which they raise the biblical question: What have we done, what are we doing, what will we do about our sisters and brothers in distress? Moreover, the trouble with liberation theologians is that they are posing the biblical question in an increasing number of areas: from liturgy to spirituality, to church history. It is coming from the perspective of women; from the poor, the black, and indigenous peoples; from refugees, peasants, young people, and old. It has been taken up by Jews, Protestants, Muslims, and Roman Catholics. It is voiced in Korea, Sri Lanka, India, Israel, Palestine, Italy, Spain, Tanzania, South Africa, and Puerto Rico—to name only a few countries.

Unfortunately, the growth of this theology has reflected the intensification of the conditions that cry aloud for liberation. Over the past twenty years the victims of oppression have grown astronomically in Latin America, in the face of staggering inflation, cutbacks in public programs, capital flight, environmental destruction, and the effects of runaway debt. There are beneficiaries of these conditions—the international banking system, multinational corporations, and the most competitive sectors of the "national" business communities. But in the meantime, the number of children irreversibly damaged by malnutrition—or simply killed—are on the rise. Too many people are "dying before their time."

In the midst of these deteriorating conditions we have witnessed the awakening of much initiative, imagination, and commitment in the increasing solidarity of numerous middle-class persons, including Christian clergy and other professionals, who have opted for the life of the poor. Thus, we see projects developing low-cost dwellings on idle land; growing and sharing food; making health care and education available to the poorest; and organizing for the defense of their human rights.

It is in the heart of this process that basic ecclesial communities have flourished and liberation theologies have been born. Liberation theology is both an outcome and a source of this quest for life among the Latin American poor. It is the result of oppressed people searching out resources for survival and reflecting on this search from the perspective of their common faith in the God of life. Once this reflection begins, it becomes a source of "hope against all hope," a spirituality of joyful endurance and resistance-in-solidarity: a spirituality of liberation. In a sense, then, liberation theology is simply a by-product of the struggle of the poor for survival; but it is also a tool in that struggle.

Liberation theologies, as we have said, are raising uncomfortable questions, questions that some find intolerable. Thus, to the violence of economic, political, and social oppression must be added the violence of systematic repression. In a sense, both our Summer Institute and this volume are a commemoration of the martyrs of liberation theology. They include, in the last twenty years of Latin American history, two Roman Catholic bishops (Enrique Angelelli of Argentina and Oscar Arnulfo Romero from El Salvador) and more than one hundred priests, religious sisters, and religious brothers—all killed for becoming "the voice of the voiceless." Among these, two Maryknoll sisters—Maura Clarke and Ita Ford—and many other foreign missionaries have gone to Latin America in solidarity with the poor only to encounter violent death.

Sadly, these hundred-and-some martyrs are representative of thousands of lay pastoral leaders—Protestant and Catholic—who have given their lives in the struggle for peace and justice. And beneath these lie the bodies of the hundreds of thousands of ordinary peasants whose only crime was belonging to a co-op, a union, or a basic Christian community . . . or even simply being related to a member of one of those organizations, or merely living nearby. . . . And beneath them lie the millions of malnourished children and adults who were sacrificed on the altar of Mammon in the last two decades alone.

Gustavo Gutiérrez—the child of a humble family of native Peruvian descent; the medical student who wanted to serve suffering human beings beyond the level of mere individual physical health; the diocesan priest shaken by both the altruism of and the alienation from the church common to many of the young students with whom he worked as a chaplain; the European-educated theologian searching for a language to articulate the cry of the Latin American oppressed and struggling Christians—has lived most of his life among and for these martyrs, and this cannot but give a mournful note to this celebration of life. We could, of course, omit these unpleasant realities from this celebration and from this introduction. We could try to forget the massacre we are enduring in Latin America. In conscience, we cannot. In point of fact, what we are celebrating here is not merely life, but life despite, surrounded by, and over against the forces of death. What we are celebrating here and now is the God of life whose Spirit incarnated in Jesus animates our efforts to overcome the idols of death.

LOOKING TOWARD THE FUTURE

Gustavo Gutiérrez is, above any other consideration, a humble person of faith, love, and hope; a person full of caring concern for his sisters and brothers in distress; a priest who, moved by his faith in the God of life, has dedicated the latter half of his life to the task of the prophets. That is, he has heard the cry of the oppressed and has walked with them, listening to their questions, responding to their hopes and dreams, their prayers and grievances, their reflections and proposals for change. He has set himself the task of articulating a theological reflection faithful to the life and hopes of the oppressed.

This collection of essays in honor of Gustavo Gutiérrez is, therefore, not a collection of idolatrous praise of and sterile comments on Gustavo's life and work, but, rather, an effort to pursue that task of which Gustavo is one of the salient pioneers: to serve the cause of the oppressed by reflecting on the future role of liberation theologies for the ongoing struggles of the poor.

We have here the most recent and innovative production by the overwhelming majority of the most renowned liberation theologians from Africa, Asia, Latin and North America. New approaches, contexts, and themes, until now too often disregarded by most liberation theologians, are tackled here in provocative ways. Such is the case, among others, of the oppression and liberation of women—in the churches not less than in the larger society. But this is, too, the case of the reality and contribution of religions other than Christianity, the oppression of blacks by white Christianity, and the role of Marxism in regard to theology. Thus, beyond a thorough, multifaceted approach to the development of Gustavo's life and faith, and a commentary on the thrust of liberation theology, this volume attempts to raise many of the critical questions with which the diverse trends and regions of liberation theology challenge one another . . . and to point toward the many issues and directions for the growth and maturation of this rich religious movement that are today only on the horizon.

We do not know that these reflections will be successful in sustaining the life of the oppressed. We only hope and pray that it be so. There are many signs of hope; they are of course no guarantees that things are soon going to improve for the oppressed of the world, but they are the only lights we can count on to illuminate our path in these dark times.

One of these signs of hope, which we celebrated at Maryknoll and Orbis Books in the summer of 1988, is the life and work of Gustavo Gutiérrez: a lively, fruitful journey which has brought faith, hope, and strength to many human beings in distress. Let us only wish that the seeds of Gustavo's life and work continue to bear multiple fruit in fertile lands across the earth.

Shalom!

OTTO MADURO, MARYKNOLL

PART I

GREETINGS

1

LUISE AHRENS, MM, AND
BARBARA HENDRICKS, MM

It is indeed an honor to be invited to share in this celebration of such significant anniversaries—the CELAM conference at Medellín, the publication in English of *A Theology of Liberation: History, Politics, and Salvation*, and the sixtieth birthday of Father Gustavo Gutiérrez. For us Maryknoll sisters, the invitation has been an occasion to reflect on the influence Gustavo has had upon us as individuals, as a region in Peru, and in eight other Latin American countries, and as a congregation participating in mission in twenty-eight countries of the world. What has been the deeper meaning for us of a man, a conference, and a book?

In 1959, I was working in a poor barrio outside of Arequipa, called Cerro Colorado. At that time there were Maryknoll sisters working in Santa Rósa parish in Lima, in the archdiocesan Catholic Social Services, called Caritas and Misión de Lima, and in a slum area parish where we still work today, Ciudad de Dios. We also had Maryknoll sisters working in Puno town and in the prelature of Juli. I read in the newspaper from Lima that four Peruvian priests were being ordained after doing their theological studies in Rome and in France. I remember clipping the article and wondering what that might mean for the renewal of an old church struggling to become more alive. Within a year, I was assigned to Lima and would witness personally the impact of these priests, especially Gustavo Gutiérrez, and Jorge and Carlos Alvarez-Calderón, who became leaders in the rebirth of the church, not only in Peru, but also in other parts of Latin America. For us Maryknoll sisters, these priests soon became solid spiritual guides, pastoral leaders, and deeply loved and respected friends. It was clear to all of us, within a year or two, that the Peruvian church was producing its own leadership for ecclesial renewal, and that, for us missionaries, it was important to listen to these new voices, learn from them, and join them in reflection on our life and work among the people.

As the narration by Sister Barbara Hendricks, MM, indicates, the influence of Gustavo on theological method and praxis began in Peru long before the concretization of that influence took place in books and at high-level church conferences. Taking time to work with groups of persons—delegates of the word, pastoral agents, local religious, student groups, missionaries—became the modus operandi of these young Peruvian priests. And Maryknoll sisters were among the first of the foreign missionaries to recognize this at-first small group of men. But through the priests' organization (ONIS) and especially through the Peruvian Conference of Religious, many others—Peruvian, European, and North American church personnel—soon became aware of a breath of fresh air within the church and recognized the charism of these men, primarily Gustavo, who had remarkable gifts for recognizing the Spirit among the peoples' experience, articulating the reality, and developing new theological insights from the Peruvian experience.[1]

And what was the Peruvian experience? The church in Peru was an ecclesiastical structure, which, with a few notable and laudable exceptions, for hundreds of years had spoken with the voice of the colonial conquerors of Latin America. From its Spanish roots, the church arrayed itself with the attributes of the Roman empire—with wealth, with favoritism for the elite, with the trappings of power. The assumptions of domination of one class by another, of unequal distribution of the fruits of labor, and of privilege for the few, rested easily in the hearts and minds of those who led the church and the country.

The experience of Peru was not dissimilar to that of much of Latin America, to the Philippines, and in a somewhat analogous way, to all of Asia and Africa. Because of this, many movements were afoot in diverse countries of the world among reformers, among theologians, and among prophets who saw that all was not right with the status quo. Labor unions, utopian experiments, and farmers' groups were some of the secular responses to the social context in the developed world.

As the church read the signs of the times, and as scripture became available to the masses, movements also began on many church levels to address the questions presented by the varied realities around the world. The first of the social encyclicals, the exhortations on the use of the Bible, the rethinking of Aristotelian methodology as the sole philosophical pillar for Catholic thought, and the birth of phenomenology are just a few of the doors that opened in Europe in the early part of this century. It was in this milieu that Gustavo did his studies in Rome and France in the 1950s. He knew his own reality and he had heard the voice of his own people, but Europe gave him and others the distance and the tools to reflect upon and address the questions that surged within church and society.

Returning to Peru in 1959, the newly ordained priests entered a decade that would become one of hope in the midst of tumultuous activity, especially for those missionaries newly arriving from the North. New pastoral insights began to emerge among those who were working among the poor and marginated, but the most significant impact was made by the voice of the poor themselves. Gustavo and the Latin American liberationists interpreted the experience of the poor and faithfully articulated what this experience meant for the whole church—not only in Latin America, but universally, especially in the rich countries. It was Gustavo who, first and foremost, was able to proclaim this message from the poor, oppressed, and marginated. In a sense he helped restore to the silent masses their language. Gustavo was not alone in this renewal movement in Latin America; there were other Latin Americans who began to articulate their own experience of oppression and poverty. But Gustavo's genius was that he recognized the power of the poor in history, and that he developed a theological discipline that identified the most critical need of the contemporary church—to be a community of Jesus both of and for the poor.

Gustavo's insight that the poor were not simply objects of evangelization, but indeed the very subjects of the evangelizing mission of the church, was very significant for missionaries, because we had already begun to understand that we received more from the poor than we gave. Perhaps this experience of the poor helped us to realize and to affirm the authenticity of the theology of liberation. It reflected our own experience. This is true certainly of Maryknoll sisters.

In the Maryknoll regions of Latin America — Bolivia, Peru, and Chile — the influence of Gustavo and the as-yet unnamed theology of liberation, was already being felt. Maryknoll sisters had gone to China from .an original impetus in 1912 "to convert the pagans in heathen lands" (Constitutions of the Foreign Mission Sisters of St. Dominic — 1931) and we branched out in Asia in those first decades of institutional life. In many cases, the mode of mission was education, formal and informal. When China was closed to missionaries, thoughts and hearts turned to the then-known "dechristianized" areas of the world in Central and South America. Our institutions — educational and medical — were well-received, and we labored well "for the love of God and souls" in our schools and hospitals and social services.

As the 1960s began, Vatican II opened our horizons, and intimations of change entered all our Maryknoll regions. In Peru, the sisters and all the groups with whom they were working — local religious, young professionals, students, missionaries, workers — were strongly influenced by their contact with the reality of the poor and by the interpretation of this experience by Gustavo and the other liberationists, as well as by the growing amount of written theological reflection being circulated. Sisters have spoken unanimously of the devotedness of these priests to the people: no group was too small for them to attend, to lecture to; no gathering was too simple for them to be present. As we heard through a new voice the cry of the masses, we questioned our own commitment to the relatively few who could attend our schools, be attended to in our hospitals, and be served by our social institutions. If God indeed had a preferential love for the poor, how might we share this love of God and act within it for the poor?

It is this aspect of liberation theology that has resonated in our Maryknoll documents since the special Chapter of Affairs in 1968. The interplay of action for justice as integral to evangelization and a commitment to the poor and their cause is explicit and clear:

> The term "Kingdom of God" means a world as God really wants it to be, one of justice and peace. "For he is the peace between us, and has made the two into one and broken down the barrier which used to keep them apart. . . ." (Eph. 2:14). In our times the Kingdom of God means a world where men strive to bridge ideological gaps and break the great economic barriers that divide people so that the riches of the world benefit not a few persons or nations, but all; where the discriminatory social barriers — those between men and women, races, religions, etc. — are broken down. Jesus went about his mission of unity in a very concrete manner, going out to the poor, the outcasts, those considered excommunicated, sinners, to bring them more fully into the community of love. He took a definite stand on matters that brought about discrimination against some men or separation between them.[2]

And again in 1970:

5

Our task is to participate in the development of peoples, focusing on the realities of human dignity, the rights of man, freedom, responsibility, duty, work, and social harmony, in order to concretely proclaim the hope of man in the gospel of Christ. In carrying out this task, we choose to identify with the Church of the poor, not afraid of the risk and consequent insecurity this involves. It must be clear to all men that we take our stance unconditionally with the poor in the true gospel sense: the spiritually dehumanized, socially oppressed, culturally marginated, or economically deprived.[3]

More recent documents made the connection even more explicit: the poor are understood as evangelizers of a world without hope:

The salvific mission of the poor is becoming visible to the Church and offering hope to our world. SOLIDARITY WITH THE POOR is not an option but a sign of the Kingdom that must be made explicit in our day. We commit ourselves to the cause of the poor through the witness of our lives, our word, and our ministry. Our Sisters living among the poor experience more directly the transforming power of mutual evangelization.[4]

We know that the impetus for these statements originated with our missioners in Latin America. Discussion, tension, and interaction at our general assemblies of 1968, 1970, and 1974 brought the issues of justice and the poor into the heart of our documents. Delegates went back to their areas of the world with new insights and understanding, and found that the currents moving in Latin America were also awakening within the realities of Asia and Africa. The Medellín document was read by bishops throughout the world as the Church of Latin America announced: "We are on the threshold of a new epoch in the history of our continent. It appears to be a time full of zeal for full emancipation, of liberation from every form of servitude, of personal maturity and of collective integration."[5]

As James Scherer concludes about this theological moment in Latin America: "The three broad areas under study were human efforts toward justice and peace, the need for adaptation in evangelization and faith, and the reform of the church and its structures."[6]

In 1979 Pope John Paul II himself spoke at the CELAM conference at Puebla and expanded the notion of evangelization stated by Pope Paul VI in *Evangelii Nuntiandi* by including a plea for human rights, echoed again in the 1987 encyclical *Sollicitudo Rei Socialis*: "Nor would a type of development which did not respect and promote human rights—personal and social, economic and political, including the rights of nations and peoples—be really worthy of man."[7] These conferences were fruits of a confluence of influences, some of which have been noted above, chief of which was the work of the theologians of liberation, most notably Gustavo. The bishops at the synod on evangelization in 1974 shared insights and explored avenues for further regional development.

It has been our experience in Maryknoll that some of the most forward theological thinking and expression has been done within the missionary framework. This has been particularly true in Asia.

The Asian Missionary Congress in Manila in 1979 was a high point of theological development along with the meetings of the Federation of Asian Bishops Conferences in 1972 and 1976. All these meetings described the Asian context and pointed out that the vast preponderance of Asian peoples—two-thirds of the world population—lived in dire poverty. The notion of liberation was discussed and, though the language differed, the call to "solidarity and sharing with the poor and the advocacy of human rights" was articulate and clear.[8] And the Maryknoll sisters responded—with ministries among workers, with community-based health programs, with basic human community formation, with human rights promotion at all levels. But, more important, they responded as the sisters had in Latin America, by moving out of large, separated convents into the barrios, *kampungs*, villages, and favelas. Sharing a way of life became a dialogue of life—the needs and cause of the poor became our own.

In Africa, the Arusha Declaration in 1967 spelled out what Laurenti Magesa calls the crucial factor in the sequence of events that signaled the "death knell" of conventional Christianity, the Christianity that exists "withdrawn" from the world.[9] Vatican II and the changed stance of the World Council of Churches opened the door. But it was the Arusha Declaration that made it clear that religious experience for the Tanzanian was most clearly felt in the praxis of *Ujamaa*. The socialism that affects the socio-political-economic milieu, however, is not enough; it must, according to Laurenti, move into what Gutiérrez alludes to in *A Theology of Liberation*, "a new way to be human . . . *a permanent cultural revolution*."[10]

It is in this light of liberation that our sisters responded to the call of President Nyerere to move out into the villages, to share life with the ordinary people, and examine what it means to be truly free. Bishop Mwoleka of Rulenge established and was an integral part of a living, dynamic Christian community. He worked in the fields, walked the paths, carried his water, and in all ways shared the joys and suffering of his people. Paulo Freire went to Tanzania in the late 1960s and early 1970s, and his method of education revolutionized thinking as it stimulated movements for liberation within our sisters and the African peoples among whom they lived and worked.

To return to the immediate subject of this brief and somewhat superficial tribute, What aspect of Gustavo's large contribution has most clearly impacted the Maryknoll sisters? It appears that for us as a congregation, it is Gustavo's methodology that has shaped our thought and our response in mission. He constructed a theological methodology based on two essential contents and he links these two realities together in a continual dialogue: the experience (or reality) of the people—not only as story, but as analysis of causes; and the wisdom of their sense of faith and of the tradition of the church.

We, for our part, have moved in our missionary endeavors to modes that enable us to share and thus understand the experience/reality of the people as well as analyze with them the causes of their situation. We have been called to a new sense of theologizing from the events and people that are woven into the fabric of the day-to-day as well as from prayerful contemplation of the word of God in scripture. As Gustavo says so beautifully in his book, *On Job: God-Talk and the Suffering of the Innocent*: "Theologizing done without the mediation of contemplation and practice does not meet the requirements of the God of the Bible."[11] The Maryknoll sisters have affirmed by document and by deeds the validity of this seminal truth for mission and for life.

7

NOTES

1. Barbara Hendricks, unpublished manuscript, 1987, p. 1.

2. Maryknoll Sisters, *Missions Challenge*, Proceedings of General Assembly, 1968, p. 8.

3. Maryknoll Sisters, *Searching and Sharing*, Proceedings of General Assembly, 1970, p. 4.

4. Maryknoll Sisters, Proceedings of General Assembly, 1978, p. 8.

5. *The Church in the Present-Day Transformation of Latin America in the Light of the Council: Second General Conference of Latin American Bishops, Medellín, 1968*, vol. 2: *Conclusions* (Washington: National Conference of Catholic Bishops, 1979), p. 27.

6. James A. Scherer, *Gospel, Church, and Kingdom* (Minneapolis: Augsburg, 1987), p. 207.

7. Pope John Paul II, *Sollicitudo Rei Socialis*, no. 33.

8. *Toward a New Age in Mission: The Good News of God's Kingdom to the Peoples of Asia. International Congress on Mission* (IMC), Manila, December 1979.

9. *Christianity in Independent Africa*, Edward Fashole-Luke, Richard Gray, Adrian Hastings, and Godwin Tasie, eds. (Bloomington and London: Indiana University Press, 1978), p. 503.

10. Gustavo Gutiérrez, *A Theology of Liberation*, 15th Anniversary ed. (Maryknoll, N.Y.: Orbis, 1988), p. 21.

11. Gustavo Gutiérrez, *On Job: God-Talk and the Suffering of the Innocent* (Maryknoll, N.Y.: Orbis, 1987), p. xiii.

2

CARDINAL PAULO EVARISTO ARNS

When the Apostle Paul was talking to the community of Corinth, he introduced all the themes we ought to recall on this occasion, when we want to recognize the effort, the dedication, and the influential service of one of our brothers, an evangelist and theologian. The cross of Jesus is the fount of the Spirit's wisdom on the noble road of the praxis of love, in the poverty of Christ.

The whole church in Latin America must thank the Lord for the gift he chose to give us through the person and mission of our brother and friend, Fr. Gustavo Gutiérrez, the evangelist and theologian of the poor. His evangelical dedication has been shown often and in a variety of ways. The content of his books and articles, his lectures and courses, was born out of a proclamation of the gospel, taken directly to the poorest.

Fr. Gustavo Gutiérrez realized the urgency of taking the good news to the poor. From the beginning of his pastoral life he took up his position in the field of struggle and witness. Who is unaware of the value and influence of the *cursos populares* he organized in Lima? There the suffering of the poor, the cries of the oppressed, the generosity and struggles of women swelled and grew to become a clear sign of the kingdom of God and an appeal to discernment. The living water of the Spirit gathered and rose until the word shot dazzlingly forth, insisting that the task of witness and theological reflection consists in going to "drink from our own wells." It is the well of wisdom that plants its tent among the poor. And it is there that the prophets, evangelists, and doctors have to go to seek the newness of the gospel in our generation and in our society.

The evangelist's effort was matched by his charism as a theologian and doctor. In this capacity he saw, however, that his discernment would be fruitful and lively only if it was always rooted in the unity of the church. He saw that fidelity to the church was the prerequisite for the growth and maturing of a task full of new challenges and vitally important to the poor.

As a result the fruits were not slow in coming. Fr. Gustavo's ecclesial service and fidelity were shown most clearly and significantly at the conference of the Latin American episcopate at Medellín in 1968. Who does not remember the prophetic force of the young theologian during that memorable event, which has determined the direction of evangelization in Latin America over the last twenty years?

The seed grew. It became a tree that gave shelter to all efforts in a reflection taking into account the new phenomenon of the poor as the basic historical subject of Latin American history. And who does not also recall the faithful, humble, even hidden, efforts of our theologian brother at the Puebla assembly? The prophetic and pertinent sanction of the perspective of evangelization based on the preferential option for the poor found in Fr. Gustavo one of its warmest and most eloquent defenders.

I think that the pastoral and theological work of this friend of ours brought something new to our lives and mission. When the newness of the gospel touches us and penetrates to the very life of the churches, a common first reaction is reserve and, very often, fear. Those in positions of authority either keep silent or wait to see the results. They are not always the first to accept the offered newness.

One thing I should like to do here is to bear witness to the ecclesial quality of this newness, to which our theologian proclaimed and witnessed. What he was the first to say strongly and with conviction grew out of an overall ecclesial climate. At that moment he interpreted the signs of the times in Latin America and devoted himself with all his strength to make all this reach the heart of the church's life and mission. Happily, he succeeded. In this way, the theologian's principal role was to hear what the Spirit is saying to the church through the cry of the poor and oppressed, and to see all the energies of the people of God in the perspective of liberation, which is the effective name today for the transforming power of the gospel (cf. Rom. 1:16–17). It would be worthwhile to reflect on some aspects of this newness proclaimed to us with all the love and dedication of a disciple who discovered and experienced the power of the call to follow Jesus in the way of the cross so as to reach the fullness of communion with the God of life.

We all agree that the action of thousands of women and men changed direction and outlook once they were made aware of the irruption of the poor into the life of society and the church. The poor were always with us, and at our side. Nevertheless, it was a silent presence and very often an unnoticed presence. One of the great merits of liberation theology was to call attention to the situation and to the cry of the poor as a new historical phenomenon: the irruption of the poor into society and the church is a sign of a *new historical subject* that we are seeing emerge, take form, and search for alternatives.

This fact will not fail to have an effect on the way we analyze society, look for new social models, and also look for a new way of living the ever-demanding newness of the gospel. Indeed, this new historical subject is the bearer of the newness that provokes a deep conversion and change, not merely on the individual level, but also on the community and collective level both in society and in the church. The irruption of the poor into our history is a force that summons us to the urgent task of evangelical discernment. And this discernment points to the presence of the spirit of the kingdom of God, which is revealed in this "historical power of the poor, the little ones, believers and oppressed."

Another point that calls our attention is that the poor lead us to the core of the truth that sets us free. However, this truth cannot be a naively peaceful systematization, based on the false security of a system, however brilliantly constructed. Truth is found in a continuing search, and in the midst of a hostile world built on lies and slavery. Theological discernment starting from the struggle of the poor for liberation has shown us that the search for truth is not just a matter of clarity of ideas and concepts. This experience takes place and is validated in the practice of love for the "little ones."

In this perspective, theological discernment reaches the limits of radicalness because it starts from the experience of nothing other than the absoluteness of the

God of life. The hostile world of lies, which destroys the lives and liberty of the "little ones," manufactures a false image of God and constructs a set of ideas that turn into an ideal of death and disintegration.

Unfortunately, this stealthy activity of falsehood can even influence the way we seek to describe and proclaim the transcendence and the coming of the true God of life. To the extent that we keep our distance from the suffering and the struggle of the poor, we build up a particular image of God and a system of ideas that, in their certainty and assurance, are the projection of our own unjust and life-denying interests.

Fr. Gustavo Gutiérrez, in his profound meditation on the book of Job, drew our attention at an opportune moment to the fact that a radical experience of contemplation of the God of life and the prophetic power of his message will always be the product of the suffering of the innocent poor. This is the vocation, the task, of theology as the century draws to a close, to carry on looking for its strength in this experience of the God whose presence is revealed in the process of the liberation of the great majority of the peoples of our Latin American countries.

Only someone who has understood this dimension of theological discernment can appreciate, and see with pleasure, the unity of the venture of theology. Theology is one. It has one subject and central axis of judgment, the God of life, the God who comes to bring freedom and in the process is revealed as Father, Son, and Spirit of life, freedom, and love.

The unity of this judgment shows that we therefore need to practice an active and militant reading of the Bible. And the important thing in this reading is to go to the roots of the historical process in order to expose its most decisive contradictions and look for ways forward, which come from the very life of God and the historical praxis of Jesus Christ. And the unity of judgment, at this depth, shows also that the way we read and analyze the Bible as the sign and testament of the God who is coming is the same as the way we analyze the structures and contradictions of a particular social system.

Finally, the theological enterprise shines with full force when it presents itself courageously as the wisdom of the cross. Even today, many persons are still looking for signs and wonders. They want magical or mechanical formulas to transform nature. They put their trust in the logic of technology, of economics, of winning power at any price. But the person who has discovered the force of the gospel's newness from contact with the poor realizes that the wisdom that confounds the powers of the world is the wisdom of the cross.

The important thing, however, is to see how theology shows the unity and the connection between the cross of Christ and the cross of millions of poor and marginalized persons who continue to challenge us in everyday life and in the structures of our existing society. Wisdom is the image of the Son who is the word of the Father. Consequently, the task of theology is to read and reveal this image stamped by the Spirit of life on the process of the liberation of the poor. It then comes as no surprise that theology inevitably bursts forth in a rich and fruitful spirituality rising out of the communion and praxis of the poor in their search for life and freedom.

This spirituality is a call to conversion and a search for the real will of God. It is a search for the Spirit who leads us to abandon the idols of this world and wait for the coming and revelation of the Son of God in the twisting course of our present history.

The dynamism of this spirituality is found in the process of liberation itself. It is the Easter challenge of the passage from the world of law to life in the freedom of the Spirit. The experience of the Spirit and the experience of freedom occur in a single act. The Lord, we remember, is Spirit, and where the Spirit is, there is freedom.

The mission of spirituality is to proclaim and build the life of the new human person, the collective life in the alliance of freedom. To encounter the Spirit is to realize that it was for freedom that Christ set us free.

But life in the Spirit is life in the power of the gospel. It is the present force to transform and justify. The struggle for justice, to win dignity for our oppressed sisters and brothers, which is a common task, opens the paths to "justification": the transformation of the contradictions of history and society into transparency and into the calls of the Spirit. The same Spirit, united with the Son, is gradually shaping an egalitarian and friendly human race that continually cries out as a proclamation to the whole world, "Abba!" In this way this spirituality culminates in a life as sons and daughters, in a spiritual childhood whom the theologian we are honoring here stressed so much as a basis for an authentic theology and of the experience of life as a disciple of Jesus.

In a word, the great appeal that Fr. Gustavo Gutiérrez has been sending out over the last twenty years to the men and women of North and South is the word that he met among the Amerindians of Peru—*pachacuti*! We might translate it as: "Be converted, believe in the good news to the poor, and dedicate yourselves to changing our society to liberate the poor."

This is the revolution that comes from the gospel. And it is this which, enlightened and fired by the word that our brother proclaims to us, we wish to see accomplished, from hope to hope.

3

WILLIAM BOTELER, MM

> The Word became flesh, and made His
> dwelling among us, and we have seen His
> glory, the glory of an only Son coming from
> God, filled with enduring love [John 1:14].

We believers have witnessed that love in the prophets whom the Lord has raised
up among us. These prophets hold up to us a mirror reflecting back our reality and,
with special clarity and eloquence, they challenge us to change that reality to image
more the Son's enduring love.

We honor one such prophet now—Father Gustavo Gutiérrez. One who boasts
not of stature or status, but one who stands on the strength of his prophetic statements. For this he is judged grand and perceived as a giant. Our Holy Father, John
Paul II, in a recent first encounter with Gustavo, spontaneously remarked: "I would
have thought that you were taller!" Thus does the Lord surprise us through his
prophets.

For many, and certainly for Maryknollers, you, Gustavo, are of the line of Guamán Poma de Ayala and Bartolomé de Las Casas, those early missioners to the
native peoples of Latin America. You have been called to don their mantle and to
continue the task of exposing and changing the situations where the loving God is
going unimaged. You have called us to pause from our agitations to do good or
make good, and to prayerfully contemplate the reality around us, to listen and share
more, and then do actions that beget justice and promote the dignity of all. Guamán,
Bartolomé, and you, Gustavo, have caused an awakening in us, an ache to see the
loving God at work among the people. We thank you and humbly honor you for
the Spirit that works through you.

Liberation theology is not a new growth of Christian theological reflection, but
rather an outgrowth of long years of such reflection. It is intended by those theologians participating in its evolution as having application in circumstances like
those that prevail now in Latin America—circumstances analyzed and evaluated by
Medellín (1968) and Puebla (1979). It has helped to uncover what the Center of
Concern has called: "The Best Kept Secret—the rich heritage of Catholic social
teaching." This Catholic social teaching is the church's gift, as it were, to civil
societies. Archbishop Daniel Pilarczyk of Cincinnati states:

> The church must speak to the concerns of society. It must offer clearly ap-
> propriate contributions to those problems and challenges that face society—

13

namely, contributions that speak to social concerns in social ways, in ways that translate the truths of revealed religion into the language of the market place and the legislature.

[The Church] must take its place in society as a voice in social discourse.

We are dealing here not with imposing religious beliefs on reluctant fellow citizens, not with setting up a state religion, but with the translation of religious truths into social and political practice [*America*, 158/14 (April 1988)].

Liberation theologians like you, Gustavo, have provoked repercussions within other local churches that have resonated with your call to historical consciousness. They are now more explicitly aware of the impact of socio-political events and conditions, on how the church makes known and carries out its mission of salvation. You have made them aware that they struggle in common with other churches.

Mission education in the United States has been a vital part of Maryknoll since the beginning. Both of our founders, Bishop James A. Walsh and Father Frederick Price, were prophets in that respect. With the advancement in communications and transportation, and the world's growing interdependence, mission education becomes even more urgent. Inspired by what they experience in other churches around the world, today's Maryknollers continue to make known to our local church in the United States the struggle of others and the need to take up their cause wherever our concerns come together. Liberation theology contributes much to the content of that education by emphasizing the basic interconnectedness of the world's systems and by pointing out unjust situations in one area that are the result of decisions made in another area. I hope that the universal church is a better understood reality now, because of the felt coresponsibility among local churches.

The encyclical of Pope John Paul II, *Sollicitudo Rei Socialis*, speaks to this task and the entire document is a most welcome form of encouragement for all to become more engaged in the task of liberation:

The fact that men and women in various parts of the world feel personally affected by the injustices and violations of human rights committed in distant countries, countries which perhaps they will never visit, is a further sign of a reality transformed into awareness, thus acquiring a moral connotation. Recently, in the period following the publication of the encyclical *Populorum Progressio*, a new way of confronting the problems of poverty and underdevelopment has spread in some areas of the world, especially in Latin America. This approach makes liberation the fundamental category and the first principle of action.

It is fitting to add that the aspiration to freedom from all forms of slavery affecting the individual and society is something noble and legitimate. This in fact is the purpose of development, or rather liberation and development, taking into account the intimate connection between the two.

The principal obstacle to be overcome on the way to authentic liberation is sin and the structures produced by sin as it multiplies and spreads.

The freedom with which Christ has set us free (cf. Gal. 5:1) encourages us to become servants of all.

At stake is the dignity of the human person, whose defense and promotion have been entrusted to us by the Creator.... As many people are already

14

more or less clearly aware, the present situation does not seem to correspond to this dignity.

It is a dictum that the task of renewing civil societies and large institutions begins out on the edges where the bases are being impacted by newly emerging realities. Renewal starts when groups at the bases reflect on this reality. It develops and produces changes in less traumatic fashion if the centers of power listen, encourage, and accompany the bases without abandoning the center's concern for unity, continuity, and responsible growth.

John Fuellenbach, SVD, stated to the members of SEDOS, May 29, 1986:

> The real soil of liberation theology is the Basic Christian Communities where theology is done by constantly reflecting upon experiences in the light of the Gospel. Liberation theology would never have come into existence without these communities and will only remain a true theology if it continues to be rooted in this soil.

Unfortunately, some sectors of local churches, and not just in Latin America, had looked askance at the development of such communities. But a recent Vatican document has served to mollify the fears and to encourage the participation of all in these communities. The Instruction on Christian Freedom and Liberation (March 1986) states that basic Christian communities are a "treasure for the church as a whole" in their "commitment to the complete liberation of man" (no. 69).

Down through the eons of time, prophets have been withering in their contempt for those believers who would absolutize the "little beyonds" of human creation, while failing to search out and adore the final truth: a loving God. I finish, Gustavo, by thanking you for helping us to maintain a proper perspective in all that we do for the development and application of liberation theology. For our readers and listeners, I would recall your words from an interview for *Maryknoll* magazine when asked about the future of the theology of liberation:

> Well, first of all, I would like to say that for me the most important consideration is the future of the people and the future of the church. . . . I am also more interested in the presence of the church and its proclamation of the gospel than in liberation theology. I was a Christian and tried to be a Christian before the theology of liberation. . . . I believe in Jesus Christ, not in the theology of liberation. . . . In the future, I think the theology of liberation will touch on important themes. But it should always be in accompaniment with the church.

Well done good and faithful servant!

4

BISHOP ALOYSIUS JIN LUXIAN

On the day of Pentecost, as the apostles, full of the Holy Spirit, spoke, every listener—Jew or Gentile, Greek or Roman—understood them in their own language. This miracle, this symbolic event, means that the message of Jesus Christ, the message of love, was transmitted and understood by everyone, from each person's cultural, economic, and ethnic background. The influence of language and culture cannot and should not be an obstacle for understanding the teaching of our Lord Jesus. Evangelization cannot be limited to any one culture or one language. It cannot be monopolized by one nation.

Since the tower of Babel, humanity has always been divided by different languages. Today, we are still separated by social class and material possessions. We are also separated by money and property, which should really be for the use of everybody.

As you know, the message of Christ is addressed to all persons, but especially to the poor. Jesus, himself, always identified with the poor. Of course, his message is also to the rich. He knows how difficult it is for the rich to enter the kingdom of God and how necessary it is for them to help the poor.

Following the example of Jesus, the church must also identify with the poor and help the poor to be liberated from poverty. The danger that our church may encounter is to identify itself with the rich; to serve the rich and be indifferent to the poor.

I am honored to have the opportunity to make these simple comments in the company of theologians who are making so many efforts to liberate the poor from their poverty. I have the deepest respect for Father Gutiérrez and his many collaborators.

One may wonder how can I, a priest from China, from an already liberated country, praise and support the theology of liberation. I am indeed very much interested in the success of liberation theology. China is a liberated country, liberated from the oppression of feudalism and colonialism, but not yet liberated from poverty. We are a developing country, we suffer the pressures of poverty. To get rid of poverty and be liberated from it, we struggle for modernization. In the history of each modernization effort, there is a crisis, a challenge to traditional values.

We are now facing a crisis. Many younger persons look only for money, and are caught in consumerism, neglecting moral values. The crisis we face is the challenge of *having more* materially, while not *becoming less* spiritually.

We Chinese use two characters to express the word "crisis": the first character means "danger"; the second, "opportunity"—a danger that brings an opportunity:

16

danger for the past, for the traditional; *opportunity* for the future, for creation, for further becoming. A crisis is solved when one is not afraid to boldly face a challenge but instead grasps the occasion. We must learn to use the opportunities presented to us to conserve the quintessence of our traditions, while not fearing to assimilate good foreign elements.

In the effort to modernize China, our leaders decided on the open door policy; the open door to the Western world, to Japan, Europe, and especially to North America.

To liberate a population of over one billion persons is very difficult. The aim of revolution, of liberation, is certainly not to keep the people poor, but help one's people to have more of the world's goods.

What we have seen happening with this new policy in China is that a small number of Chinese are advancing economically much more quickly than others. Some farmers, some private enterprise owners, some merchants, became rich. These new rich think that money is all there is in life. They are becoming greedier and greedier. They want the American way of life. However, most of our people remain poor or have become, in fact, poorer. This is a challenge to our traditional values and virtues.

An ancient Chinese scholar, Zhang Zhu, has said, "Possessions are merely things." We should not be enslaved by them.

China is facing a crisis. Many Chinese were disappointed by the so-called cultural revolution. They have also begun to become aware that money does not necessarily bring happiness. They feel an emptiness in their hearts. They are looking to religion for truth. They are looking to Christianity for some of the answers to the problems of life. This is an opportunity for us.

We are trying to discover how to use the religious freedom that we now have in order to present Christianity to today's Chinese. The way of doing this is an important problem for us. We must find a way to inculturate Christianity into modern Chinese life.

In Taiwan, Hong Kong, and China more than four hundred years ago, Matteo Ricci and others attempted to inculturate Christianity into the society that was then greatly influenced by Confucianism. But China has changed and is still changing. The influence of Confucianism on the mainland of China has been replaced by Marxism.

Because China needs to be liberated from poverty, many have put their hope in Western thought. Our inculturation, perhaps, consists in a combination of some Chinese tradition, some Marxism "à la Chinese," and the essence of the message of Christ.

China has been politically liberated, but we are not economically liberated. We need a Chinese version of a theology of liberation.

We Chinese Catholics are a very small minority. We are less than half of one percent out of a population of more than one billion. We Catholics, along with all Chinese, must struggle for modernization. We Catholics must offer an example of high morality and be a witness of God's love by presenting Christianity in a "language" that can be understood by modern Chinese.

All of us priests and nuns in China are now old. To speak of the priests, we number only a thousand and our average age is over seventy. We need good theology and we need good thinkers.

I pray God that the day will come when we can invite foreign teachers to our seminaries and research centers to help us in the rethinking of theology from our own history and from our own culture.

We must create a theology of liberation for ourselves. We need to publish books fit and acceptable to most Chinese on the mainland. We must reeducate our clergy and laity who are still being formed in the Tridentine traditions.

The Chinese people must hear the message of Christ through us.

I have sung with you, "The Lord hears the cry of the poor, blessed be the Lord!" Now I ask you to pray for me, a poor old bishop from Shanghai, who, with sixty old priests and an equal number of old nuns are given a task that can be accomplished only with God's help.

Thank you, Gustavo Gutiérrez!

5

CARDINAL STEPHEN KIM

1988 is a year of many anniversaries: the twentieth anniversary of the Medellín Conference where the church of Latin America formally announced its preferential option for the poor; the fifteenth anniversary of the English translation of your book, Gustavo Gutiérrez, *A Theology of Liberation: History, Politics, and Salvation*, which introduced the insights, themes, and process of liberation theology to the rest of the world; and the sixtieth anniversary of your birth!

I congratulate you on all three events.

But above all, I wish to congratulate and thank you for what you and the theology of liberation have done for the entire Christian (and yes, even the non-Christian) world.

I should like to share with you what I, an Asian bishop, sense to be the most important effects the theology of liberation has had in Asia, and particularly in Korea.

With difficulty, I have limited myself to five areas:

1. Liberation theology has directed us back to the primary locus for theologizing.

2. It has helped to correct a distorted view of the church.

3. It has taught us a new way of reading the scriptures.

4. The grassroots communities have brought us back to our roots and proved the primacy of the Spirit.

5. Liberation theology provides a way to reconciliation.

1. Liberation theology has enabled us to rediscover a more realistic place (locus) of theologizing. We say theology is the study of God. But where do we go to study God, whom we can never grasp either with our senses or our intellects? We are like Elijah who felt God's presence in the whisper of a passing breeze. We find God, in a sense, only after God has passed by and we know God from "footprints" left behind. From this perspective, the unique *locus* for theologizing is the person of Jesus where the actions and the essence of God are most pronounced. But after this, the prime locus of theology is the "life-flow" of the *anawim*, for it is there that God's footprints are clearest.

2. The theology of liberation has helped to correct a distorted view of the church. In the past, for many of us the word "Church" called forth images of a building, or of the hierarchy, the clergy, religious sisters and brothers, or of some of the sacraments. Vatican II pointed us toward a more complete image when it spoke of the church as the people of God. Liberation theology proclaims the same—not so much in words as in action. Although the theological articulation of the theology

of liberation may have been done by professional theologians (either clerics or lay persons), liberation theology itself is mainly a product of the laity. This is particularly refreshing when one considers that approximately 99.9 percent of the church, the people of God, are lay men and women.

3. You, Gustavo, have taught us a new way to "get at" the meaning of the scriptures and how to narrow the gap between the secular and the sacred, between life and faith. When the oppressed, the *marginales*, bring their lives and the word of God together, amazing things happen.

Their eyes are opened and scripture is opened. They see the flow of their lives in a totally new light and at the same time they also see the word of God in a totally new light. When the word of God is brought down into the warp and woof of the lives of the poor, this very contact unlocks vast new riches and opens up whole new layers of meaning. It is in this meeting that we allow God to be and do what God wants: God is the one who said, "My delight is to be with the children of Adam." In the *process* of liberation theology, religion, faith, and God become a part of everyday life and cease being something reserved to an hour in church on Sunday.

4. Your grassroots communities, the seedbed of liberation theology, have brought us back to our roots, back to the heart of Christianity: community through the Spirit. Throughout history, it is true, the Spirit has been given in a fuller measure to certain individuals (in the Judeo-Christian tradition we call them patriarchs, prophets, and saints), and the Spirit of God is certainly at work in every person. But I think it is correct to say that the Spirit is more at home, more comfortable, more able to thrive and flourish, in community.

The Spirit, after all, is the bond of love that makes a community out of the Trinity. The fact that liberation theology begins with a few persons sharing their lives, reflecting, analyzing, discussing, and praying together — this says something very important to me: discernment in the Spirit is on much surer footing when "several are gathered together." These small groups of the oppressed point to and prove the primacy of community and the primacy of the Spirit. I think this is the greatest and most important achievement of the theology of liberation.

I should like to add here a small note about Korea. It has always intrigued me that around the same time liberation theology began to ferment in Latin America, there were similar seminal beginnings in Korea also. Around twenty to twenty-five years ago, lay men and women began living in small groups with farmers, laborers, and the urban poor. Some remarkable things happened. This sharing of lives developed into a real movement for justice. And when small groups (of Catholics, Protestants, Buddhists, but mainly persons with no religion) came together and discussed their lives in the light of the word of God, here also, there were startling results: persons with no religious background made statements and prayers whose content rivals the theology and spirituality of our greatest mystics.

What particularly interests me is the fact that we have, here in Korea, the "makings" of a theology of liberation. But, in fact, liberation theology came from Latin America — it never "happened" here. And I ask myself why.

Is it because your *marginales* have suffered more than our *minjung*? Is it a question of numbers — Christians in Asia are such a small minority? Or, more importantly, is it a question of culture? No matter how "un-Christian" your societies and cultures may have become on the surface, at least deep down there must have been some lump of leaven, some spark of the gospel, which was able to be ignited . . . . Is it that we had no Gustavo Gutiérrez to be a catalyst for these small groups, to foster and nourish their growth as communities, to synthesize and articulate their liberation?

Some or all of these factors may be involved—especially the last one. But the heart of the problem is that we have not been able to form many grassroots communities, let alone a network among them. Your success in this respect is your greatest gift to us, Gustavo. It is also the greatest challenge.

5. Finally, you have shown us the way to reconciliation as well as who the prime reconcilers will be.

Liberation theology is accused of being devisive, of making two churches: the church of the poor versus the church of the rich, the "official church" versus "the real (grassroots) church." It is accused of being exclusive, of concentrating only on the poor and neglecting the rich.

I think this accusation is unfounded. Let us look first of all at Jesus. Those imprisoned in ideologies of revolution are turned off by Jesus' frequent contacts with the rich and powerful. There is no evidence that he wrote them off as persons or gave up on the possibility of their eventual "salvation." There is evidence, however, that as his public life progressed, he did "give up" on the possibility of ever convincing them through arguments or words to renounce their dependence on their power and possessions so as to enter his kingdom. And it is obvious that, toward the end, he concentrated on the riffraff of society as the only chance to get His message through. It is clear he saw them as the vehicle of salvation; otherwise, why would he ever have said: "Happy are the poor"?

It is true that liberation theology begins with the oppressed who are only half (though numerically a vast majority) of the dichotomy between the haves and the have-nots. But liberation theology did not create this dichotomy. It was already a glaring, screaming reality in our world.

It is also true that this dichotomy becomes more sharply delineated as the *marginales* discover why they are poor, uneducated, sick, and oppressed. They also discover that injustice is firmly entrenched in all the (legal, political, social, economic, educational, medical, and, yes, even religious) structures of our society.

If the movement of liberation stopped here at this point where the poor realize the causes of their oppression, then perhaps liberation theology could be accused of being devisive. But it does not stop here. The poor also come to realize that most of the rich and powerful do not yet know that their riches and power are the fruits of unjust systems and structures; do not yet know that their excessive riches and power, which they think so essential to their being cultured and human, are in fact, dehumanizing them and distancing them from the riches of life. The poor come to see, as Jesus did, that the rich will never be convinced of this through words or logic. But if the poor are liberated, their freedom and joy will convince the whole world where true humanity lies.

I am convinced that the liberated poor of this world will liberate the rest of us, that they will be the sacrament of our salvation.

The *anawim* of scripture, the *marginales* of Latin America, the *minjung* of Korea, the poor and oppressed "little" ones of the whole world, are clearly the salt of the earth. Their unique quality is the tremendous lifeforce within them, which, in itself, shows how close they are to God—who is life. They are not the tree (of the Psalms) planted on the banks of the river; rather, they are floating along right in the middle of the river of life. They have no "distance" from life so as to look back on it and theorize about it. They are in life and all they can do with it is *live* it.

This lifeforce has enabled them to endure and survive years, decades, centuries, of oppression. And when they are awakened to their own dignity and rights, when they become conscious of the structures and mechanisms that have oppressed them, this same lifeforce becomes the strength propelling them to unbelievably heroic deeds—even sacrificing their own lives—to achieve justice.

The goal of their struggle—a just society where everyone is liberated from overdependence on power and things, and where all are able to be free and live with the same human dignity—may be a long way down the road. But once the poor are liberated, they have already won the war, and from then on their every step in this long journey to justice renews their own humanity and calls each one of us to our own liberation.

My dear confrere, Gustavo! This has become much too long and in places has turned into my own exposition of what I think liberation theology is all about. But it was the only way I could find to show you that your pains and joys, struggles and victories, and continued emptyings of self have reached across the world and touched us here in Asia, in Korea. I hope that my words here may sound like echoes of what you have said to the world.

I know you are the first to insist that liberation theology is not yours. You are also the first to emphasize that it is, first of all, the fruit of the Spirit and, secondly, the product of many, many laborers.

But in God's love, you were God's instrument to get it started and keep it moving. Let us all rejoice in this fact.

We turn glory back to God; we extend our thanks, congratulations, and prayers to you; and bow in silent respect to the *marginales* of Latin America.

6

BISHOP PETER A. ROSAZZA

My dear brother and friend, Gustavo:

May the peace of Christ be always with you.

What a great distinction you have given me to invite me to present one of the welcoming messages at this celebration in your honor. I am happy to be here with you and to listen to your words, which I always find filled with the power of God because they come from a heart given over to Christ and to the service of others, particularly the poor, with whom Jesus identifies in a very special way.

Sixteen years ago I began to work with Hispanics, mostly Puerto Ricans, in a very poor parish in Hartford, Connecticut, which is one of the most important economic centers in the United States, nicknamed the "insurance capital of the world," in the wealthiest state per capita. However, it is the fourth poorest city in our whole country. The contrast was very difficult for me at that time and continues to bother me and many others. One year after beginning my work I read your book, *A Theology of Liberation*, which helped me open my mind to the poor of the Third World and helped me make a connection between them and the economically poor Hispanics and blacks of Connecticut and the northeast of our country. Puerto Ricans, who make up the majority of our Hispanics in Connecticut, are often poor. They come here to seek a better life, but they suffer from discrimination and find a country undergoing profound technological change. Many Christians manifest a strong presence of the Holy Spirit, source of happiness and strength to keep one close to God despite the suffering experienced in another country and the attacks directed against them by those who do not wish to share substantially with others nor lose anything of their current standard of living.

Gustavo, with other modern prophets you are calling the whole church to renewal so that we might truly become the church of the poor. This is very difficult for most, myself included, to adjust to another renewal after Vatican II. Thanks to that council we are at least more accustomed to a church open to the world and we are trying to become the church in the modern world. However, you are convinced that this is not enough. We must also struggle to become the church of the poor. It is not enough to love God and neighbor. Our love must be at the same time prophetic, moving us to a preferential and nonexclusive option for the poor, the anonymous who die before their time. I also am grateful to you for telling us that aid or charity for the poor is not enough. As we become ever so slowly but progressively a world community, we must examine the structures that hinder development and which keep the poor in conditions of misery, such as the arms race and the international system of trade and finance. The statements of the popes, especially those of John Paul II, have affirmed you and have, I am sure, given you reason for greater hope.

Gustavo, I thank you because you have made the option for the poor by your simplicity of lifestyle and your perseverance in the prophetic line. This has cost you dearly because of criticism leveled against you from many fronts, both within the church and outside. However, please don't forget that you are a special gift to the church and that many persons in Latin America and here in the U.S.A. need your light, your theological clarity, your personal commitment, and the spirituality that is the élan of your writings and conferences. Please know that you inspire me and thousands of others who are struggling to unite ourselves with Christ under the force that comes from the Holy Spirit, to work for a world in which human beings will no longer be victims of other humans, and where the rights of every woman and every man will be respected. Gustavo, continue to encourage and prod us to be bearers of the hope that the risen Christ gives us, to persevere in the struggle for a world worthy of the great dignity of the human person. As you know, much better than most of us, the struggle is difficult, but Christ always gives us the grace to feel his presence and his love in that struggle.

7

BISHOP DESMOND M. TUTU

I recently had the great joy and privilege of reading Gustavo Gutiérrez's superb commentary entitled *On Job*. I read it in manuscript before its publication. God has blessed us signally in the gift of someone with the sensitivity and theological acumen and insights of Gustavo. Too many had thought that liberation theology was narrowly selective in the biblical paradigmatic passages that it used and that there seemed to be an inordinate obsession with the exodus motif. In his commentary on Job, Gutiérrez demonstrates that you could approach the question of God's bias from a different biblical perspective and still arrive at the same destination — that God has an extraordinary penchant to side with the suffering, with the marginalized, with those who have no one else to speak up for them.

And theodicy speaks about why God acts in this fashion. It is because these poor ones, these despised ones, know that they can lay no claim to the divine mercy or justice. They lack any credentials for laying such claims. They depend utterly on the divine mercy and righteousness that are gracious and unmerited. This is a tremendous assertion that fills the downtrodden with magnificent hope. It is precisely what Jesus said distinguished the religiously proper and respectable ones from the prostitutes, tax gatherers, and sinners who would precede them scandalously into the kingdom. Thus liberation theology is not just an aberration thought up by those who have a predilection for that sort of thing. It is biblical through and through, and utterly consistent with the God who is revealed to Moses. Jesus Christ has such a remarkable identification with those he came to save to the extent that for them and the world He was prepared to empty himself of his divine glory, to take on the form of a slave, and become obedient unto death, yes, even the death of the cross.

We who have the privilege of working in situations of injustice and oppression where God's children have their noses rubbed in the dust daily and where they have their God-given human dignity trodden callously underfoot with a cynical disregard for their human rights, are filled with an anomalous exhilaration. It is when we hear proclaimed so eloquently by such as Gutiérrez that this is the God who, when the Spirit anoints you, sends you out to preach the good news to the poor, the setting free of the shackled ones, and release for captives. We are filled with an indomitable hope and exhilaration because we know that ultimately injustice and oppression, evil and exploitation, cannot prevail, and that the kingdoms of this world are becoming the kingdom of our God, who shall reign forever and ever — Amen. This kingdom is a kingdom of righteousness, of compassion, of caring and sharing; where tears will be wiped away, and there will be no more weeping. God's

25

children—black and white and yellow and brown and red—will live as brothers and sisters, children of one Father, members of one family, the human family, God's family.

For me it is a great honor to write this welcome to God's stalwart champion of the poor and downtrodden—God's herald trumpeting forth the good news of God's love.

God be praised now and forever!

8

ELIE WIESEL

I feel very close to Gustavo Gutiérrez, even though we have not met one another. We share a common passion for Job—whose situation intrigues and saddens us at the same time—and a need to believe that God has not abandoned creation. Some theologians would describe our approach as "liberative." And indeed, why not? I feel at home with the term "liberation." Because we are created in the image of God, we human beings ought to be free just as God is free. And, like God, we should want to be vehicles of freedom for others. Or, to put it another way, those persons are truly human who recognize themselves in the freedom of others, and who measure the extent of their own freedom by its relationship to that of their fellow human beings. It was in order that we might be free that God chose to create us. Persons who live in fear, in oppression, in hunger, in misery, are not free. What remains free, however, is their thirst for freedom, their desire to free themselves— the part of them that God, as only God can do, loves to enlighten in the fulfillment of hope.

Yes, I feel very close to Gustavo Gutiérrez. Along with him, I believe that God is not an abstraction but a living presence. To the prisoner, God represents memory; to the starving, a smile; and to the wandering exile, a companion on the way.

The mystical tradition teaches us that even God is in exile. In the process of freeing the oppressed from their oppression, and the humiliated from their shame, we are likewise freeing God.

PART II

GUTIÉRREZ:
THE MAN AND HIS WORK

9

Gustavo Gutiérrez –
A Friendly Profile

FREI BETTO

Books, theses, articles, and reviews proliferate on the works of theologians like Gustavo Gutiérrez, Leonardo Boff, Hugo Assmann, Juan Luis Segundo, José Míguez Bonino, Elsa Támez, and countless others identified with the principles and methodology of the theology of liberation. The theology of liberation occupies the position of prima donna in today's theology. Thanks to Cardinal Ratzinger's instructions, theology of liberation has become a subject of interest to no less than the Academy of Sciences of the Soviet Union, as we found when a group of theologians visited the U.S.S.R. in June 1987. The two instructions issued by the Congregation for the Doctrine of the Faith and proceedings against the book *Church, Charisma, and Power* and the person of its author, Leonardo Boff, took the theological debate over the hallowed walls of ecclesiastical institutions and gave it ample space in the media, the universities, and political movements.

Theologians' works provoke much more interest than the personalities of their authors. This epistemological slant has its advantages: provided the work is rigorous by the criteria of its particular field, there is no need to disturb the author, safe in his well-earned privacy. However, the divorce between author and work has not always been a mere caprice of modern reason. At times it has served as an ideological tool—in the primitive sense in which Marx used the term "ideology"—precisely to cover up the contradiction between author and work. We need only recall the recent impact of revelations that Heidegger collaborated with the Nazi regime. In the case of dead authors, biographies are always of great interest to those who seek a better understanding of the text, in context. Who today reads Althusser with the same attention that his works provoked before November 15, 1980, when the Marxist philosopher strangled his wife? In contrast, Dietrich Bonhoeffer's death in a Nazi concentration camp gave his works a new character, just as the assassination of Archbishop Oscar Romero has ensured wide distribution of his sermons.

Although the main target is always the works they produce, the persons of the theologians of liberation have always aroused considerable polemic. Anyway, we are used to living in situations of conflict—whether it be the land invasion which took the brothers Leonardo and Clodovis Boff to prison in Petrópolis on March 4,

1988, or the censures and punishments imposed by our churches' rulers. A certain discomfort is created in some First World theological sectors by precisely this criterion, which give theology of liberation a new character: in it theological discourse cannot be separated from pastoral commitment. The liberation theologian is not an armchair intellectual, confined to libraries and lecture rooms, dedicated to an academic rigor antiseptically protected against current conflicts. And liberation theology is not written without getting one's hands dirty, because the liberation theologian's starting point is not his or her supposedly enlightened mind, but the pastoral practice of poor Christian communities, committed to the cause of popular liberation.

For that reason the theology of liberation does not exist without a link with its source, the liberating practice of oppressed Christian communities in the Third World. Gramsci helps us to understand this new status of theology with his concept of the "organic intellectual," which defines the theologian's relationship with the popular movement. This accounts for the degree to which theology of liberation is representative of popular groups through the support it enjoys from an immense network of basic ecclesial communities and countless martyrs and confessors, whose lives in the church and prophecy are a source for the theologians' thinking and production.

A BASTARD THEOLOGY

Being a bastard in Latin America does not necessarily affect a person's social image. We are all children of relationships between Spaniards and Amerindians, Portuguese and *caboclos*, whites and blacks, mestizos and mulattos. Our racism is only for social effect: it is diluted in the tropical heat, where sexuality is power and partying, bargaining and submission, fantasy and transgression. In these parts the family is as recent a concept as the constitution. To paraphrase St. Thomas Aquinas, here life extrapolates from thought. Not even theology escapes from the genealogical tree with uncertain roots and twisted branches. Interrogating theology of liberation about its legitimate ancestry is like asking a Mexican Indian or a Colombian coffee planter for the historical truth behind their family tradition.

Gustavo Gutiérrez can deservedly be considered the *father* of theology of liberation for he was the first to launch a book with this title, in 1971 with Ediciones Sígueme. But he himself does not deny the importance for his work of his visit to Brazil in 1969, when he made contact with our basic ecclesial communities and an episcopate confronting the military dictatorship, and experienced at close quarters the drama of the murder — still unpunished today — of Dom Helder Câmara's youth adviser, Fr. Henrique Pereira Neto, strangled and shot in Recife on May 26, 1969. Gustavo dedicated his *A Theology of Liberation* to him and to the Peruvian novelist José María Arguedas. Nonetheless there is no denying the European roots springing from Maritain's integral humanism, Mounier's committed personalism, Teilhard de Chardin's progressive evolutionism, de Lubac's social dogmatics, Congar's theology of the laity, Lebret's theology of development, Comblin's theology of revolution, or Metz's political theology.

The Second Vatican Council encouraged the conditions for cutting the umbilical cord that kept theology in Latin America dependent on the womb of mother Europe. As the 1960s began, the Cuban revolution, the failure of the Alliance for Progress, the crisis of the developmentalist model, and the rise of left-wing movements unconnected with the traditional communist parties were among the factors that led Latin American theologians to base their thinking on the ground they trod. Not that it was a matter of looking for categories that would allow a reinterpretation of social and political facts. The motor of the theory was the practice of the popular Christian communities rooted in the struggle; as they transformed the world they also altered the model of the church. Social change and ecclesiogenesis are ultimately connected. The construction of an alternative political project does not leave the church unaffected, as if it were a community of angels hovering above the contradictions which run through the fabric of society. The new element was the awareness, reached in the common life of the basic ecclesial communities, that the church is not just the pope or the bishops, but the people of God on the march in history. And the presence of this believing and oppressed people in Latin America's social movements stamped faith with a critical character that gave birth to the theology of liberation.

AN INDIGENOUS THEOLOGIAN

At the seventh international conference of the Ecumenical Association of Third World Theologians (EATWOT) in Oaxtepec, Mexico, in December 1986, the black North American theologian James Cone complained about the over-white appearance of Latin American theology of liberation. The odd thing was that beside him was Gustavo Gutiérrez, typically indigenous in appearance: brown skin, round face, short and stocky build, and slightly narrowed eyes revealing his Quechua ancestry. At home his father spoke that language of the ancient Inca empire. But more than the language and appearance, Gustavo inherited the style of the Andean Amerindians. It is just this that surprises anyone who makes his acquaintance: he combines—not without conflicts—a mind endowed with a quick and rational intelligence, magisterial, expressing itself in a language assembled like the parts of a precision instrument, and a sensibility that disarms all the models of modern rationality. In him there coexist the intellectual trained in Louvain—where he was a colleague of Camilo Torres and defended a thesis based on Freud—and the Amerindian of the Peruvian *altiplano*. It is this that enables him to enter a lecture room without being noticed—as though he was gliding over his own feet—or to visit his friend Miguel d'Escoto without anyone else being aware of his presence in Managua. It is as though he could travel, not just on the roads accessible to citified travelers, but on the trails and paths that only the inhabitants of the jungle know. This ancestral gift enables him to master a new language, a new field of knowledge, or to pass through New York, Paris, or Bonn like an Amerindian slipping through trees and leaves, observing without being observed, quick as a bird and discreet as a llama. This trait enabled him to work on the draft of the famous Medellín document, approved by the Latin American episcopal conference in 1968—a text that was to become fundamental to the practice and theory of the church of the poor of Latin America. On one occasion Gutiérrez arrived in Rome just as the Peruvian bishops were discussing his works with top dignitaries of the curia. Who can swear that the final text, more favorable to him than the initial draft, was not formulated by Gustavo's own pen?

Self-effacing as a Capuchin, he moves in the political realm of theological conflicts with all the finesse of a Jesuit. Though his expression sometimes betrays that metaphysical anguish characteristic of those familiar with the thin line that separates life from death, he never panics and his sharp intuition is able to present immediate solutions to intricate problems, as though he had meditated for months on a question just arisen. He can sit for hours on an airport bench, writing an article or listening to someone, all the time biting nervously on a toothpick with his strong, slightly separated teeth. His replies are almost always ironically amusing, in the manner of someone putting together a riddle. When he gives classes and lectures he follows a rigid pattern so carefully constructed that he gives the impression of having ornamented his text. His jokes give his words a flavor all their own, because he is always able to display that rare virtue that so much enchants him, humor. His sense of humor enables him to maintain a measure of critical distance from any fact. He never lets himself be betrayed by emotion, for he knows that nothing human deserves to be taken too seriously.

I lived with Gustavo Gutiérrez at Puebla in January and February 1979, during the third Latin American episcopal conference. On that occasion his name, in common with those of the other theologians of liberation, was excluded from the list of official advisors. He had no direct access to the bishops' meeting place, but many prelates came to him in search of his help, which forced him to spend entire nights formulating drafts and proposals. We were all precariously lodged in two apartments without furniture, which rarely had water and with no lights in the bathrooms. We lived on some manna that fell from heaven, for we had no kitchen and in the city's restaurants we would have been easy prey for the international press, always on the lookout for a theologian to decipher the ecclesiastical language of the texts or to give an exclusive interview that would confirm the rebellious or heretical nature of the theology of liberation.

After outmaneuvering all the foreign correspondents for days, on the afternoon of Sunday, February 4, 1979, Gutiérrez accepted the suggestion of CENCOS (the Mexican Centro de Comunicación Social) that he give a press conference in the El Portal hotel. In his remarks he stressed that theology of liberation did not set out to engage in reflection *on* the poor. The initiators of that theological reflection are the poor themselves, the agents of historical transformation. The aim of the theology of liberation is to give the poor the right to think and to express themselves theologically. The more the journalists pressed him to let slip something that would sound heretical, the more Gutiérrez showed himself faithful to the poor and to the church. He is a master of reconciling (conciliating) apparently opposite poles, putting forward syntheses that encourage us to reinterpret tradition and the world around us.

On several occasions I have met him in his office—the Rimac "tower," a poor district of Lima. It is definitely one of the untidiest studies I have ever seen. Scattered and mixed up together on the floor are Coca-Cola cans and books by Cardinal Ratzinger. Bottles lie on papal documents, stray wires wander between dusty papers. Not the slightest indication that any duster has been there since the arrival of Francisco Pizarro in Peru. Nonetheless this confusion has a logic for him. He knows exactly where to find each thing. It is amidst this mass of paper that he eagerly devours the books he receives. When he feels hungry he eats some indeterminate standard meal along with the unemployed and underemployed.

Gutiérrez has always preferred reading to writing. He has his own method of dynamic reading, as though he had an antenna that would tell him the quality of a work's content. Writing for him is a painful childbearing. And when he writes it hurts him to admit that he has reached the final version. He always regards a text as provisional, to be revised and improved. Because of this almost all his works have begun as mimeographed lectures. It is quite likely that he is the author of more unpublished texts, known only to a small circle of readers, than of published works. Usually he does not even sign the mimeographed texts, which include an excellent introduction to the ideas of Marx and Engels and their relationship to Christianity.

In January 1985, on the eve of Pope John Paul II's visit to Lima, I found him in the Rimac "tower" writing a series of articles connected with this important church event. While we talked, Gutiérrez tried to undo a tangle in a long telephone cord, which looked like a ball of wool in the mouth of a playful kitten. He always has to keep his hands occupied when he feels nervous, either twisting a rubber band or fiddling with a ball-point pen. And at that moment he had quite enough reasons to be tense, for Cardinal Ratzinger had announced for September a reply to Leonardo Boff's defense of his book, *Church, Charisma and Power*, against Rome's criticisms. Christmas had passed and the curia was still silent. The second instruction on the theology of liberation, based on consultation with the bishops of Latin America, promised for November or December, had also not appeared. Perhaps it had been decided that the pope should make a more official statement on the theology of liberation on the spot. Nothing would have been more opportune than a pronouncement during a visit to the homeland of liberation theology's *father*. Gustavo was afraid that the pope would say something that could be interpreted as a condemnation of his theology. It would be disastrous. Nonetheless he was ready to abandon the "tower" that protected him from the besieging press and appear at the pope's meeting with priests and lay persons in the square. Once more it seemed certain that, by dint of his native roots, as a person who can walk through the jungle without waking nature from its sleep, his presence would be as discreet as the drizzle that covers the terraces of Lima before dawn.

ADMIRERS AND INSPIRERS

En route for Cuba, the brothers Leonardo and Clodovis Boff and I passed through Lima on the evening of September 4, 1985. We met Gustavo in the working-class parish where, together with Padre Jorge, the director of Lima's ministry to workers, the theologian exercises his priestly ministry. We insisted that he come with us to Havana because Fidel Castro had shown a great desire to meet him. Gustavo was evasive, objecting that at that very moment a group of Peruvian bishops led by Bishop Duran Enriquez were preparing a textbook critical of his writings, which meant that he had to concentrate on producing a sort of advance defense. Some time later Gutiérrez confirmed that he had not gone to Cuba in response to a request from Fr. Carlos Manuel de Céspedes, the secretary general of the Cuban bishops' conference, who had been a fellow student in Rome. The Cuban priest was afraid that the Peruvian theologian's presence in Cuba would be exploited politically.

The night after our meeting in Lima, Leonardo, Clodovis, and I were with Fidel Castro in Havana. Fidel regretted Gutiérrez's absence. He read the letter the theologian had sent him and remarked that he had just finished reading *A Theology of Liberation* and had been impressed by its scientific basis and ethical impact. He mentioned especially the fairness with which Gutiérrez deals with the question of class struggle and the dimensions of poverty. He added, with emphasis, "We need to distribute books like this in the communist movement. Our people don't know about this. For you it's more difficult to write a book like this than it is for us to produce a textbook of Marxism." A few days later, Fidel was to say, in the presence of Bishop Pedro Casaldáliga, from Brazil, that "liberation theology is more important than Marxism for the revolution in Latin America."

But anyone who thinks that politics is what beats most strongly in Gutiérrez's heart is mistaken. He is above all a mystic. His most recent books, *El Dios de la Vida*, *On Job: God-Talk and the Suffering of the Innocent*, and *We Drink From Our Own Wells*, are fundamentally spiritual, intended to nourish the faith and prayer lives of Christians committed to popular struggles. For Gutiérrez theology is secondary. What is primary is doing the will of God in liberating action. And his keen theological eye captures the presence of the Lord in solidarity where he seems most absent, in the suffering of the poor. This suffering permeates Gustavo's own life, for his delicate health means he has to take constant care. But he does not complain on his own account. He prefers to cry out for the poor. On one occasion I spent a whole day with him at the Lima summer course, to which thousands of activists from the popular Christian communities come in search of theological grounding. I noticed that he was sad, although he had given his course with his usual vivacity. Nonetheless there was a shadow over the face that opens up with happiness when he is surrounded by simple, poor persons dedicated to the utopia of the kingdom. We talked and not one word of self-pity sprang from his lips. It was later that I learned that his mother had died that day.

The book on Job is a disguised autobiography of Gustavo Gutiérrez. From its pages emerges the deep conviction that all theology of liberation derives from the effort to give meaning to human suffering. In searching for this meaning, the theologian knows that, as Clodovis Boff says, everything is politics but politics is not everything. Solidarity with the poor is not exhausted in the cause of justice; it leads to the sphere of gratuitousness, where spiritual dispossession opens the way for communion with God. Just as in Latin America living the faith cannot be separated from the demands of politics, so the revolutionary project should be able to find in Christian mysticism a standard for the formation of new men and women. Consequently, the theology of liberation can only be accused of despising the spiritual dimension by someone who is unaware of the long list of publications springing from the contemplation and pens of Segundo Galilea, Arturo Paoli, Raúl Vidales, Elsa Támez, Pablo Richard, or Leonardo Boff.

The divine stigmata burn the entrails of Gustavo Gutiérrez. It is impossible to understand the full depth of his intellectual inspiration, his prophetic role, and his mystical soul without knowing those three Peruvians who are at the root of his genius: José Carlos Mariátegui, Cesar Vallejo, and above all José María Arguedas. From the communist Mariátegui, author of the classic *Siete Ensayos Peruanos*, Gutiérrez learned that technique of cultural cannibalism required to Latin Americanize all the theoretical baggage of his years of study in Rome, Belgium, France, and

Germany. From the poet César Vallejo, author of *Trilce*, poetry as important to modern literature as *Ulysses*, he inherited the nostalgic lament of the suffering creature at the creator's silence: "My God, if you had been human today, you would be able to be God" (*Los dados eternos*). "I was born one day when God was sick" (*Espergesia*).

However, the greatest influence was that of the novelist José María Arguedas, whose friend Gutiérrez was and to whom he pays tribute in many of his lectures and writings. It is that he should have chosen as the epigraph for his *A Theology of Liberation*, a page from *Todas las Sangres* by this Quechua author, specifically the place where the native sacristan of Lahuaymarca says to the priest:

> Your God is not the same. He makes persons suffer without consolation. . . . Could God have been in the hearts of those who tore apart the body of innocent Master Bellido? Could God be in the bodies of the engineers who are killing La Esmeralda? In the hearts of the authorities who have taken from its owners that cornfield where, at every harvest, the virgin used to play with her baby son?

In November 1981 I met Gustavo in Managua. There, among the theological discussions with the Sandinista leaders, in an attempt to help them to understand the different positions of Christians with regard to the revolution, was born what was later to become his book on Job. It takes up the fundamental question Gutiérrez asks himself: How can we talk about God amid so much oppression? If we want theo-logy, talk *about* God, he said, we must first be silent before God. Out of this silence, which covers the hearts of the poor, is born wisdom. And we must repeat with Job, among so many Latin American crosses and that deep thirst of love: "I once knew you only by hearsay; now my eyes have seen you." Everything in Gustavo Gutiérrez, his work and his life, converge on that vision.

—translated from the Portuguese by Francis McDonagh

10

The Originality of the Theology of Liberation

LEONARDO BOFF

The importance of Gustavo Gutiérrez transcends the borders of Latin America because what he has created possesses a universal theological significance. His achievement has been to have helped to create a new epistemological field within Christian thought. Creators of an epistemological break—that is, of a new possibility of interpreting reality—are rare. In modern Western philosophy such creators have included Descartes, Kant, Hegel, Marx, Heidegger. In theology there have been Thomas Aquinas, Luther, Bultmann, Rahner. Gustavo Gutiérrez has opened up a new and promising path for theological thinking; he has invented a new way of doing theology. The claim of the theology of liberation as a current within Christianity is to be a new way of thinking about God and everything connected with God. Liberation is not just one item on the theologians' list. It is a horizon against which everything is illuminated, a plane in which everything has a position and acquires new meaning. In other words, liberation is not just an entry in an encyclopedia alongside other entries. It is a perspective from which all the other terms are understood, analyzed, and explained. This basic claim of the theology of liberation was recognized by the papal magisterium in April 1987 in a letter to the bishops of Brazil, which contains the explicit statement that "the theology of liberation should constitute a new stage ... in theological reflection."[1]

In 1971, when he gave literary form to his intuitions about liberation theology, Gutiérrez wrote, quite deliberately:

The theology of liberation offers us not so much a new theme for reflection as a *new way* to do theology. Theology as critical reflection on historical praxis is a liberating theology, a theology of the liberating transformation of the history of humankind and also therefore that part of humankind—gathered into *ecclesia*—which openly confesses Christ. This is a theology which does not stop with reflecting on the world but rather tries to be part of the process through which the world is transformed.[2]

This is the new element introduced by Gutiérrez, a new task for Christian reflection: to examine critically, in the light of faith and revelation, historical action, to understand theology as one moment in a much larger process of the transformation of the world and its relationships.

THE CREATION OF A NEW EPISTEMOLOGICAL FIELD

In history Christians have provided themselves with the theology they needed and were able to produce. So, in the first centuries, they constructed a sapiential theology: confronting the word of God with life, they were able to draw lessons of wisdom and spirituality which sustained their existence and helped them to understand the challenges of culture. Later, when the demands of society were for rationality, Christianity developed a theology that was a form of rational and systematic knowledge. Now there was not just faith and life, but faith and critical and systematic reason. It is a permanent requirement of faith that Christ and the pursuit of the kingdom should be in the deepest sense human and therefore rational. Theology as rational knowledge deals with this permanent requirement. But it also takes up the challenge of the social process, which gives reason a central place. In this encounter between faith and reason, theology takes on the role of an organized form of knowledge, as critical and as systematic as possible.

In the present period Christians are associating themselves with the desire for social transformation, as embodied particularly in the aspirations of the oppressed. Human history is above all else "an opening to the future ... a task, a political occupation, through which we orient and open ourselves to the gift which gives history its transcendent meaning: the full and definitive encounter with the Lord and with other humans."[3]

In this context living and reflecting on faith means doing a theology of history, of human action, of social events, of politics, and of transformation. And if this transformation is produced from the position of and in the interests of the oppressed (who are the great majority of Christians) and by the oppressed themselves (and their allies), this theology will be a theology of liberation. The theology of liberation will therefore be the theory of a particular form of action. In Gustavo Gutiérrez's words: "Theological reflection would then necessarily be a criticism of society and the Church insofar as they are called and addressed by the Word of God; it would be a critical theory, worked out in the light of the Word accepted in faith and inspired by a practical purpose—and therefore indissolubly linked to historical praxis."[4]

To have identified this challenge, to have formulated its conscious and critical expression, this is Gustavo Gutiérrez's achievement. In doing so he has inaugurated forever a new way of doing theology, from the transforming action, from within the action, as a critique of and in support of this action for liberation. Now that this epistemological field has been opened, believing reason can put up its buildings and design its landscape. With this new grammar of interpretation and action, it incorporates other, older, forms of doing theology. This is another achievement of Gustavo Gutiérrez: he has succeeded in giving due weight to, and consciously and creatively incorporating, the other ways of doing theology, theology as wisdom and theology as rational knowledge. Not only that, but he has also shown that theology as critical reflection on historical action presupposes and needs the other two, because they represent permanent functions of any Christian thought. Nonetheless

39

he forces them into a fundamental redefinition. Now wisdom and rational knowledge take their starting point and context from historical action. The relationships between faith and life, on the one hand, and faith and science must now be placed within the context of the relationship between faith and society or faith and social injustice, which gives rise to the practice of liberation.[5]

This presentation of theological method will enable us to see the importance of theology in a Latin American perspective. In Latin America the need for social change is strongly felt: the oppressed—in their great majority, a religious and Christian throng—are crying out for liberation. Their faith can be a factor in historical liberation, and reflection on this action gives rise to the theology of the liberation— that which has been achieved and that which is still to be won. Perhaps the theology of liberation could only have emerged in Latin America, because only there could one find the cultural, ideological, ecclesial, and popular preconditions for such an occurrence. It required a huge faith, lived out by oppressed peoples, most of them Christian, who no longer accept oppression, because of their faith, because of faith in the biblical God, the God of Jesus Christ. All this was present in Latin America. Gustavo Gutiérrez learned this situation through his own commitment and formulated the requirements of a theology of liberation. Let us see how he articulates this new way of doing theology.

WHO HAS THE FIRST WORD?

Theology lives on something greater than itself. It is not the original datum. It is a result. It is the result of an attempt to express a primary and fundamental reality, spirituality. A point that repeatedly returns with emphasis in Gutiérrez's writings is the reference to spirituality. It is in spirituality that the true root of the theology of liberation is to be found. In Gustavo Gutiérrez spirituality has little to do with inwardness or individualism; nor is it based on the Greek concept of spirit. Spirituality is connected to spirit in the biblical sense. Spirit is the principle of life, of change, of the bursting in of the new. Spirituality implies walking according to the spirit in the spirit; that is, it is a form of action before it is a worldview.[6] Before talking *about* God it is important to talk *to* God. Prior to the talking that is the specific activity of theology is the being silent that belongs to contemplation and action. This is precisely what Gustavo Gutiérrez rightly emphasizes.[7]

First comes the silence of contemplation. We are absorbed by the gratuitousness of God and by God's saving and liberating plan. But this silence is not the silence of closed eyes that we find in some ancient and modern mystics but the mysticism of eyes open on the world, the mysticism of ears attentive to the cry of the oppressed and the demands of God that come from history and innocent suffering.

The second silence is that of action. This involves the hands rather than the lips. In action, in solidarity for liberation, we have to do with a political act. The relationship is not primarily prayer-action, but mysticism—politics, contemplation, and the desire to change society. Today's historical imperative moves in this direction: How, starting from faith and the subversive memory of Jesus, can Christians help in the immense process of bringing to birth a new society in which the oppressions suffered by the poor will be overcome? Rather than talking about God, what is important is to act in the light of God, to be an implementor of God's historical design, in which the oppressed undoubtedly have a central role. This silence, focused in contemplation and action, precedes any responsible speaking about God. "Theologizing done without the mediation of contemplation and practice does not meet the requirements of the God of the Bible."[8]

This God of the Bible sets one other prior condition for any Christian theology: listening to the cry of the oppressed. God is the God of the cry of the victim of injustice. God hears the cry. A theology deaf to the poor weeping for their innocent suffering is also dumb before God and before society. A theology which is dumb before the oppression of the majority finds it hard to escape charges of cynicism and triviality. This situation poses the central question of the theology of liberation:

How are we to talk about a God who is revealed as love in a situation characterized by poverty and oppression? How are we to proclaim the God of life to men and women who die prematurely and unjustly? How are we to acknowledge that God makes us a free gift of love and justice when we have before us the suffering of the innocent? What words are we to use in telling those who are not even regarded as persons that they are the daughters and sons of God?[9]

Gustavo Gutiérrez's book, *On Job: God-Talk and the Suffering of the Innocent*, has already become a classic. It does not speculate. It gives a commentary on the book of Job in a way which shows today's question to be the question of yesterday and of all times: Lord, why? God, how long? "The suffering of the innocent and the questions it leads them to ask are indeed key problems for theology—that is, for discourse about God. The theology of liberation tries to meet the challenge."[10]

After contemplation, after the silence of action and of listening to the cry of the victims of injustice, there can be speech. Theology is thus a second stage, derived from the first stage, which is contemplation and action as a response to the oppression of the poor.[11]

FROM WHAT PERSPECTIVE SHOULD WE DO THEOLOGY?

There are many perspectives from which theology has been done in the past and is done today. When I say "perspective," "horizon," or "viewpoint," I mean a set of vital social interests that is the motor of theological thinking. Under what conditions is theological work done? In First World conditions, where there are universities and abundant means of production? For whom is theology done? To whom is it addressed? Modern progressive theology has as its audience persons who have been educated and who have absorbed a considerable critical mass, a distinctive feature of the modern period. Their big question is how to combine faith and science, the church and democracy; how to justify religion in the face of the critiques of the masters of suspicion (Marx, Nietzsche, and Freud). The situation of the theological community in the Third World is different. Here the main features are desperate poverty and abundant faith. The masses are abandoned and semi-illiterate, and the theologians have few institutional spaces to do theology; for the most part they are tied by pastoral responsibilities in poor communities. The central question is how to combine faith with social oppression. How should the ecclesial community interact with the political community? The audience is not the critical and secularized man or woman, but the oppressed, the victims of social injustice.

This last question determines the social and epistemological locus from which Latin American theology finds meaning and is able to formulate an utterance that will have religious and political relevance. There is no theology of liberation that does not presuppose, in advance of all its work, this epistemological break. It has to take up its social and historical position; it has to reflect on faith at the heart of the suffering of an oppressed people, in contact with their hopes and starting from their struggles for liberation. This is the perspective of the theology of liberation. Gustavo Gutiérrez successfully developed this perspective in a text of extraordinary theological power, "Theology from the Underside of History" (1979).[12] Theology is done from the perspective of history's absentees, from the position of Las Casas's "scourged Christs of the Indies."[13] This theology makes its own the interests of the wretched of the earth; with its theological production it seeks to reinforce their cause, legitimize their struggles, and give their lives political weight. Faith confronted with the historical oppression of the great masses of our peoples can only result in a theology of liberation. This is the permanent dignity and evangelical mark of the theology of liberation; it has taken as the audience for its message the same persons who were the first audience for the gospel of Jesus. And it will always be a worthy aim to become one with the hopes and struggles of the least of this world in order to help them escape from their marginality into human and Christian communion.

A theology that makes its own the interests of the poor and their way of looking at the world, history, the church, and revelation will inevitably be a theology that provokes conflicts. It will clash first with theologies for which the poor are a subject, but not the perspective from which all theology is developed; these theologies feel themselves challenged as to their evangelical character, because of their ability (or lack of it) to evangelize the vast impoverished masses and in their function as sources of legitimacy for a society that creates poor persons and turns its back on them. It will also be a theology assimilated with difficulty by the ecclesiastical institution, whose historical interests have been and continue to be largely bound up with the dominant classes. The theology of liberation makes a vigorous appeal for conversion; this appeal is not always understood, and is quickly slandered as infidelity to the church and an obsessive desire to criticize institutional practices. Finally, the theology of liberation, because of its option for the poor, is misunderstood, distorted, and sometimes slandered and persecuted by the dominant powers in society because they see their interests opposed, delegitimized, and resisted. The theology of liberation presents itself, objectively, whether the theologian speaks or is silent, as a prophetic theology. And very often its members suffer the fate of the prophets.

In short, the theology of liberation, like any other theology, talks about God, the blessed Trinity, Christ, the Spirit, grace, sin, the church—about all the topics of theology; but that is not where its specificity and originality lie—it talks about all these topics from the perspective of the oppressed person who longs for liberation. Reading history from the position of the poor is the dominant (though not the only) perspective of the Bible. This methodological option gives the theology of liberation a strong biblical coloring and places it within the same field of activity as the message and activity of Jesus, who made the poor the arbiters of his messianic status.

HISTORICAL ACTION AS THE MATTER OF THEOLOGY

I remarked earlier that for Gutiérrez theology is fundamentally critical reflection on action. Let us try to understand how historical action is matter for theological reflection. This question is delicate, because it is the target of the main criticisms of the theology of liberation. These criticisms derive from a lack of attention to the specific perspective of the theology of liberation, and often from pure ignorance of the texts.

The very first task is to establish a minimal understanding of historical action. For the Christian the fundamental form of action is love. Whoever has love, as St. Paul sees it, has everything (1 Cor. 13:8): love is the nourishment and the fullness of faith, the gift of one's self to the other and, inseparably, to others. This is the foundation of the *praxis* of Christians, of their active presence in history.[14]

If God is love (1 John 4:8), all love has God dwelling within it. Love in itself is, by its nature, theologically significant. Whoever practices love is already within the sphere of salvation. This explains the identification that the New Testament itself makes of love of neighbor and love of God. It is the same movement, going in the direction of the other and also of the great Other. The challenge to us today in Latin America is not this perspective, which is classic in Christian thought. The challenge is macrolove—that is, love lived in the wider relationship of society, love that goes beyond the limits of the heart and reaches the structures of society. Love understood in this larger dimension means the ability to turn relationships of oppression into relationships of collaboration. It is out of love that we make an option for the poor against their unjust poverty, not to glorify poverty but to challenge it from within and to attempt, with the poor, to escape from it in the direction of justice, not of wealth.[15] This love is political and is translated by politics—that is, by the organization of critical consciousness, by giving structure to popular action in terms of a strategy and a project for society.

The theological question that now arises is: How far is the action of the oppressed in search of liberation directed toward the kingdom of God or, better, how far does it already imply the presence of seeds of the kingdom? In what way does it embody social grace? God is present in those who are the historical sacrament of the Son, in those who suffer, are naked and hungry, but not just in their persons, rather, fundamentally, in their struggles for justice, participation, and life. It is theology's task to carry out this interpretation with its arsenal of categories, drawn from revelation, from the church's tradition, from the reflection of theologians, and the life and witness of the faithful. As I said earlier, the theology of liberation does not remove the need for, or replace, theology as wisdom or theology as rational knowledge, which codifies our understanding of God and God's mystery in history. It requires and presupposes this work. In the light of the question asked by the oppressed, liberation theology is rediscovering the face of God as the God of life, enriching the understanding of Jesus as liberator, deepening the vision of the Spirit as consoler and strengthener of the poor (*consolator pauperum*), reinterpreting the mystery of the blessed Trinity as the communion and perichoresis of the divine three, which forms the perfect community. To make historical action the matter of theology means being able to see at the heart of that action the incarnation or rejection of the kingdom, of fidelity or infidelity to God. Only those who are secularized or who lack a mystical perspective could regard this interpretation as a politicization of faith. In other words, historical action is also the bearer of God and the kingdom or the rejection of them (but always related to God and the kingdom). Consequently, historical action is also an object for theological consideration.

Finally, ever since the incarnation of the Son and the presence of the Spirit as a person within history, God is in history, or rather, God has become history. From now on, history will never again be just secular; for a Christian it is pregnant with God, and so must be interpreted by theological reflection. Nothing that occurs in history can leave the Christian indifferent, especially the history of Jesus' weakest brothers and sisters, the poor (cf. Matt. 25:40). To reflect theologically on action implies reflection on the kingdom in the world, on the presence of the risen Lord, who may still remain crucified in those whom history crucifies, as we wait in hope for the new heaven and the new earth.

This reflection will always be prophetic. It denounces forms of behavior that are opposed to God's plan, in society and in the church, just as it proclaims signs that appear of the kingdom present in history, particularly in the poor.[16]

This theological concern was already present in 1964 when a meeting of Latin American theologians took place in Petrópolis (Rio de Janeiro) in which Gustavo Gutiérrez took part. At the meeting he proposed as an important task for theology in Latin America "to carry out an analysis of forms of behavior from the religious point of view, from the point of view of salvation, to analyze what are the underlying options of the various different types of persons."[17] Action, then, had a central place, interpreted in terms of the specific perspective of faith. But it was not just the forms of historical action of different social groups; in connection with them it was necessary to analyze as well the forms of action of the church to see how far it was carrying out its mission in the context of Latin America, visited by oppression and an urgent need of liberation.[18] Already present were the basic intuitions that later emerged in an explicitly formulated theology of liberation.

THEOLOGY AS CRITICAL REFLECTION

The last question raised above leads me to consider theology as critical reflection. By definition, theology—as rational, codified knowledge—entails critical reflection. But this criticism is not exhausted by theology's internal investigations. It extends to the presuppositions of theological activity, carried on within society and the church within its framework of socio-cultural, geopolitical, and community concerns.[19] Not to take account of such preconditions is naive and can mystify theological discourse. For theology to be critical therefore means that it has a capacity to analyze the forms of action of church and society in the light of faith and from the point of view of the oppressed. Without such analysis there is no guarantee of the *liberating* character of this action.

There are various forms of action, whether in society or within the church. The first task is to analyze forms of social action from the perspective of the poor. Here theology discovers that the predominant forms of action in society are not directed to serving the interests of the majority of the population, but those of the power elites. These forms of action highlight the system that oppresses the majority and therefore, in the light of faith, are wrong and, in the light of the aspirations of the poor, unjust and antipopular. In the context of this criticism of forms of social action, Gutiérrez has incorporated into his work the most valid and best-founded contributions of the critical and dialectical tradition of revolutionary and Marxist thought. He uses Marxism, not for its own sake, but as an instrument of clarification to unmask mechanisms of oppression and destroy illusions absorbed by the poor about the possibility of finding solutions to their problems within the capitalist system. The criticism also evaluates the effects of forms of action. There are ameliorative and reformist forms of action that bring about no more than an improvement within the system without touching its fundamental interests and privileges. These forms of action deceive the oppressed by perpetuating their relationships of dependency on the dominant classes. The whole of Gutiérrez's work is shot through with this criticism, which is an important aspect of his theological discourse.

At the same time, theology as a critical reflection on action has the task of identifying and acting in concert with liberative forms of action initiated by the oppressed themselves and their allies. These are forms of action that propose a real overthrow of the system of domination and make possible forms of freedom not previously tried. Theologically, they open the way for historical incarnations of the kingdom (always limited and subject to theological criticism), which lead forward toward eschatology.

Theology's second task is to analyze the church's forms of action, whether those of the church as a whole (of the church as the people of God) or those of the various segments within the church (of the bishops, the ecclesial communities, and the laity). Here it is necessary to discover what functional relationship the church's forms of action (theoretical and active) maintain with the forces in society, whether with dominant or subordinate classes. It cannot be denied that the church is divided by social conflict; its support is sought from all sides. It can, in important segments of its membership, work with the interests of that order which, for the majority of the population, represents social and moral disorder; so too, significant sectors of the church, and even whole bishops' conferences, can work in the interests of the oppressed and with them form the historical and social bloc of those who seek liberation and an alternative society. In both cases there is a difference in pastoral strategies and corresponding theological justifications. It is the task of theology to exercise discernment among these forms of church action. And not only that: it is the task of the theological ministry to reinforce those forms of action that proceed in the direction of the liberation of the oppressed and are initiated by the oppressed, for this purpose reflects the *ipsissima intentio Jesu* (Jesus' fundamentalism) and is inherent in biblical religion. A theology that does not help to produce life, justice, more human relationships, and greater happiness cannot call itself Christian or be an heir to the apostolic tradition, which preserves forever the liberating memory of Jesus and his Spirit.

THE MAIN LINES OF GUSTAVO GUTIÉRREZ'S THEOLOGY

Gutiérrez is a man of the silence of prayer and popular action. But when he speaks, we always have a spiritual experience, such is the depth of his feeling and

45

his extraordinary spirit of discernment. His great work is still *A Theology of Liberation*. Because it is a foundational work, it is always worth going back to read again; and every time new and relevant perspectives appear. This book presents the main lines of the theology of liberation. Today Gutiérrez's book has new relevance, as the Vatican administration, in collaboration with conservative groups in national and continental bishops' conferences (in Latin America, with CELAM in particular), is attempting to make the whole church return to the situation before Vatican II, introducing new theological foundations to support a clerical vision of the church: separation between church and world, new emphasis on the relationship between supernatural and natural, separation between the sacred and the profane, redemption and liberation, clergy and laity, stress on the church as mystery as against the church as people of God. The encyclical *Sollicitudo Rei Socialis*, equating development with liberation (par. 46), without realizing that liberation seeks to be an alternative to development, forces us to reread with interest chapter 2 of *A Theology of Liberation*, which deals precisely with the relationship and opposition between liberation and development. The fundamental importance of this book lies both in its method and in its content.

First, it demonstrates the transition from a modern progressive theology, characteristic of the First World, to a theology of liberation, typical of Latin America and regions that live under global exploitation. It indicates the moves by the official church which supported a whole pastoral approach directed toward liberation; it analyzes the crisis of the alternative models of Christendom and neo-Christendom, and the superiority of the liberation model. Secondly, it outlines the socio-political features of the process of liberation and the place of Christians and the churches within it. Finally it sets out the main elements of a theology of liberation: a theological anthropology and cosmology (faith and the new human being, the encounter with God in history), basic features of a christology of liberation, of a liberative ecclesiology and of the fundamental relationships between faith and politics. It ends by outlining a spirituality of liberation: poverty, solidarity, and protest.

Gustavo's style is always dense, concerned with correct formulation and the most serious information in the field, whether it be theology or social analysis. Through it all runs, like a conducting wire, the perspective of the poor—of the oppressed classes and humiliated races. In his writings can be heard the cry of the oppressed, which has gone up from Latin America for the last five hundred years.

Three other works of the same type by Gutiérrez deserve special emphasis. They all deal with spirituality: *We Drink From Our Own Wells* (1984); *On Job: God-Talk and the Suffering of the Innocent* (1987); and *El Dios de la Vida* (1982). Why spirituality? Because Gutiérrez is profoundly convinced that the roots of the theology of liberation are to be found, as described above, in a firm and decisive encounter with the Lord in the great throngs of the oppressed. The process of liberation involves a deep conflict. Clarity of aim is not enough; there is a need for a mysticism of resistance and renewed hope to keep on returning to the path in the face of the defeats of the oppressed. It is through spirituality that we have access to the oppressed and faithful people. As long as this spirituality exists, there will always be a commitment of solidarity with the weakest and, arising from that activity, theological reflection on liberation.

Lastly, there is another volume of diverse contextual essays: *The Power of the Poor in History* (1983). This includes one of Gutiérrez's most profound and innovative essays, "Theology from the Underside of History." In it he sketches the opposition between progressive theology, practiced on the social base of bourgeois democracies, and the theology of liberation, coming from the oppressed and the victims of capitalist models of development. He also explains why we Latin Americans talk about liberation and Europeans talk about freedom, a freedom paid for by others' sacrificing their freedoms. This very penetrating essay demonstrates the degree of autonomy and critical force attained by Latin American liberation theology.

Gutiérrez's work, seen in its totality, represents a genuine fundamental theology. It lays down the premises and axioms for a new discourse on faith. He has not had the time or opportunity to develop themes at length, to produce a complete system. Nor is that the way of the theology of liberation. It reflects specific forms of action; this emphasis on action for liberation requires a way of thinking that is free and always adequate to the needs of the moment, leaving for other circumstances a more distanced view of problems and, correspondingly, a greater possibility of systematization.

CONCLUSION: A MARTYR'S LIFE

It is not just the theology Gutiérrez produces that is important. His theology is linked at a deep level to theological existence itself. Classic and modern theology was developed in the academic world, at a distance from real events in society and the church. As a result it is a theology that includes very little of the conflicts of history or the cry of the millions of innocents who suffer. In Gutiérrez we cannot separate personal and community life from theology. He is an activist before he is a professor, committed to the fate of the oppressed. His own lifestyle is poor: he shares the hardships of the area he belongs to and out of which he develops his theological reflection. This reflection is not the product of his speculation. It is the product of the community of life and work with which he lives and whose destiny he shares. In his own flesh he experiences the oppression of illness and in his own skin the weight of discrimination against native peoples and those of mixed race. This personal existence is material for theological reflection. In the midst of immense historical and social challenges he has been able to confront personal challenges: the hostility of his own brothers in the faith and persecution by sectors of the church in his own country, Peru, and by the doctrinal authorities of the Vatican. On all these occasions he has shown himself to be a man of faith, attached to the sacrament of the church, in and through all its contradictions and structural sins, conferring credibility on the church that takes a genuine option for the poor and their liberation. Theology turns into martyrdom. Theology and martyrdom point to sanctity, lived in a new mode, appropriate to the new mode of being the church and to the new model of society developing in germ in the action of the poor. But of this there must be silence, for God alone is the faithful and true witness of the paths of divine love in the lives of individuals.

—translated from the Portuguese by Francis McDonagh

NOTES

1. Letter of John Paul II to the bishops of Brazil on the mission of the church and the theology of liberation, April 9, 1986; English translation, *Message to the*

Church in Brazil (Church in the World Series, New York: Catholic Relief Services; London: CIIR, 1987).

2. *A Theology of Liberation* (Maryknoll, N.Y.: Orbis, 1973; London: SCM Press, 1974), p. 15.

3. *A Theology of Liberation* (15th anniversary ed., Maryknoll, N.Y.:Orbis, 1988), p. 8.

4. Ibid., p. 9.

5. Ibid. (1973), pp. 13–14.

6. *We Drink From Our Own Wells* (Maryknoll, N.Y.: Orbis; London: SCM Press, 1984), pp. 54ff.

7. *On Job: God-Talk and the Suffering of the Innocent* (Maryknoll, N.Y.: Orbis, 1987), p. xiii.

8. Ibid., p. xiii; cf. *El Dios de la Vida* (Lima: CEP, 1982), pp. 63–88.

9. *On Job*, p. xiv.

10. Ibid., p. xv.

11. *A Theology of Liberation* (1973), p. 11; *We Drink From Our Own Wells*, pp. 35–36.

12. *The Power of the Poor in History* (Maryknoll, N.Y.: Orbis; London: SCM Press, 1983), pp. 169–221.

13. Ibid., pp. 193, 197.

14. *A Theology of Liberation* (1973), p. 7.

15. Ibid., pp. 299–302.

16. See the whole of chap. 10 of *A Theology of Liberation* (1973), pp. 189–212.

17. See the texts in R. Oliveiros, *Liberación y teología. Génesis y crecimiento de una reflexión 1966–1977* (Lima, 1977), p. 56.

18. Oliveiros, *Liberación*, pp. 56, 57.

19. *A Theology of Liberation* (1973), p. 11.

11

Peru and the Mystery
of Liberation:
The Nexus and Logic of
Gustavo Gutiérrez's Theology

CURT CADORETTE

RIMAC AND *EL VALS PERUANO*

Walking through the streets of Rimac, the working-class section of Lima where
Gustavo Gutiérrez lives, is not an experience that induces optimism about Peru or
the fate of the poor. A few kilometers from the Plaza de Armas with its presidential
palace, colonial cathedral, and mayoral offices, Rimac has absorbed none of downtown Lima's now tarnished splendor. Cut off by a polluted, garbage-laden stream
that gives it its name, Rimac is a world apart from the city center. On one side of
the bridge politicians and prelates go about their appointed rounds; on the other
side, countless ordinary Peruvians confront the daily battle of living. And given the
fact that only 40 percent of them have jobs, they face a never-ending challenge.

Rimac is a gray, dirty, noisy slum where residents are frantically trying to survive,
to find or keep a job, to feed and clothe their children. It is a place where struggle
is a common denominator and hope, however tenuous, is a thin thread that holds
human lives together. It is in Rimac that Gustavo Gutiérrez works as a pastor and
friend to the poor. Among decaying buildings and open sewers, in crowded single
rooms occupied by entire families, Gutiérrez has written almost all his theology. In
Rimac the poor of Peru struggle for hope and Gutiérrez puts that hope into theological language. He is their spokesperson and translator.

Walking through the streets of Rimac is sometimes an affront to the human ear.
The noise is often deafening—buses, trucks, and cars without mufflers blow their
horns. A multitude of radios in small stores and kiosks adds to the special cacophony
that Third World cities excel at producing. The music is often a dissonant blend of
imports from Europe, North America, and other Latin American countries. But on
occasion one will hear what Limeños, Lima natives, call a *vals*. The *vals* is a melody
characteristic of the Peruvian coastal region. Sung in a rhythmic Spanish, it speaks
of the triumphs and tragedies of life and the unfathomable mystery of love. The

vals criollo[1] is more than romantic music. Unlike foreign imports, it speaks about the Peruvian heart and soul. It is a narrative about the struggles of ordinary persons seeking love and meaning. The *vals criollo* is the music of Lima's poor sung in their own idiom and expressive of their deepest feelings.

Music and theology may seem like dissimilar entities, but reading the works of Gustavo Gutiérrez proves otherwise. With a bit of attention one can hear echoes of the *vals criollo* in the pages of almost all his writings. The joys and laments of the poor, their struggle for meaning and redemption sung with intense sincerity, surface in each of his works. The music of the poor, like Gutiérrez's theology, is an expression of longing for that which is not yet but should be.[2]

The *vals criollo* is the music of a people whose identity is still being formed. The people of Lima and most of the country's coastal cities are *mestizos*, the children of a turbulent marriage between Spain and Peru's native peoples forcibly contracted nearly five hundred years ago. The mestizos culture of Peru, Gutiérrez's own, is a product of conquest and violence, of Spanish and native Peruvian civilizations forcibly joined but never totally amalgamated. It is a culture of a people struggling with a history of oppression and a precarious sense of self. This is the human crucible in which Gustavo Gutiérrez lives and writes his theology.

THE PAINED SEARCH FOR IDENTITY

Gutiérrez is recognized throughout the world as one of the most original and articulate theologians of liberation. His reputation is surely well deserved. Few, however, give sufficient thought to the fact that Gutiérrez is a *Peruvian* theologian. That he is Peruvian, of course, is well known; but just what it means to be a Peruvian is sometimes overlooked. That Gutiérrez was born among the poor of Peru, that he knows their culture and language, that their hopes and aspirations are his heritage as well, are crucial factors in understanding him both as a human being and a theologian. The intimate connection between his context and his theology, between the daily sights and sounds of Rimac and his written words, is of the utmost importance. Gustavo Gutiérrez is far more than a renowned theologian. He is also a Peruvian thinker, one of many persons who have grappled with the complex drama of a people and nation known as Peru.

Peru is a land of striking physical beauty and complex socio-political problems. A former colony of Spain bled dry by mercantile capitalism, it is now besieged by neocolonial powers just as ruthless and violent as its old master. The sovereign powers of the crown now lie in the hands of the International Monetary Fund and World Bank. Contrary to European and North American perceptions, Peru is not a homogeneous country—not culturally, linguistically, or politically. It is, rather, a mosaic of many pieces, some of which are only loosely attached. The conquistadores, who savaged the Inca domains, never managed to totally conquer and replace the cultures and languages of the Quechua and Aymara, the tenacious inhabitants of the Andes who succeeded in putting together civilizations far more sophisticated and refined than that of Pizarro and his ignorant, illiterate troops. As conquered peoples they resisted the best efforts of the Spanish crown to destroy their self-understanding and way of life. On the coast, where ruthless oppression and Spanish diseases wiped out the native population, the *criollo* culture gradually took shape.

Indigenous emigrants from Peru's sierra and *altiplano* blended with Europeans to form a tenuous, mixed people that would come to call itself Peruvian. A short distance from the coast, however, in the chain of mountains that runs through the country, as well as in the immense Amazon basin, the "other" Peruvians continued to live and call into question the very nature of Peru. Although brutally exploited by Spanish-speaking *hacendados* from the sixteenth century onward, the tenacity of Peru's indígenas was, and is, remarkable. Turned into serfs and stereotyped as semihumans, they have still managed to maintain a sense of dignity, as well as their own languages and cultures. But the price of class and race division has been high. To this day Peru is afflicted by the twin disease of internal factionalism and external exploitation. Aymara and Quechua *campesinos* distrust the Spanish-speaking population. Peasants and urban workers are therefore cut off from each other, although they are natural allies. This fragmentation, of course, is duly capitalized on by native elites who manipulate group loyalties and interests for their own gain. At the same time, outside forces, predominantly multinational corporations, take advantage of a poorly organized labor force to pillage both the people and land. Wealthy Peruvians and rapacious foreign powers continue to divide and conquer just as the Spanish did nearly five centuries ago.

Peru is a nation struggling to free and know itself. Is it European, Andean, or perhaps an ill-defined mixture of both? To be Peruvian is to wrestle with this fundamental question of identity. It is to live in a land forged by conquest and violence. To be white, Spanish-speaking, and male is to have an enormous advantage over a bronze-skinned, Aymara-speaking woman. Both in the past and in the present, race, class, and gender determine who will flourish and who will perish in Peru. The legacy of colonialism is all too tragic: divisive, destructive stratification built into the fabric of the nation's history, immense disparity between rich and poor, male and female, and a painfully ambiguous sense of nationhood. This is the human, historical backdrop of Gustavo Gutiérrez's theology.

Many of the persons who inhabit Rimac have come as refugees trying to escape the class and racial violence that has marred Peruvian history since the arrival of the Spanish. Rimac is an old working-class section of Lima, but like so many of the city's slums, it is populated by new arrivals from other sections of the country, from Cajamarca, Ayacucho, and Puno, where cold, violence, and economic hopelessness leave no option but exile. Yet, all too often, the refuge Rimac offers proves illusory. The chances of escaping poverty, of finding a job, of "making it" in Peruvian society, are slim at best. The misery of the sierra becomes the misery of the city. Tragically, failed dreams often turn into self-hatred and violence.

Gutiérrez is one of many Peruvian thinkers who has agonized over the fate and identity of his own people. Since its inception as an independent nation in 1821, Peruvians have wrestled with a concept they call *peruanidad* — that is, what it means to be a member of this household divided between rich and poor, Spanish-speaking and Amerindian-speaking. Often Peruvians have looked outside themselves for an answer. They have fawned on European or North American cultures as if they were a model for their own development. Some have been equally uncritical and romantic about preconquest history, as if the Inca empire could somehow be magically revived and the corrupting influence of European and American culture made to disappear.[3] Gutiérrez's approach to this complex question of national identity is quite different. Instead of looking outward for a solution, he has looked inward. He is convinced that the answer to Peru's agonies can be found in Rimac itself. He has come to the unprecedented conclusion that poor and supposedly inarticulate persons, precisely because of their powerful belief in God and the future, have the most credible and saving vision of what it means to be both Peruvian and a human being. They embody "the great hope we feel"[4] and it is this very hope that pushes them along in the struggle for liberation.

Perhaps Gutiérrez's greatest accomplishment as a Peruvian thinker and an internationally recognized theologian has been his insight into the power and trustworthiness of the poor. Knowing them as he does, and viewing their world with the same eyes, he has recognized the deep thirst for liberation among them and their profound belief in the possibility of achieving it. Despite the bleakness of Rimac and the ever-present possibility of despair, Gutiérrez believes that hope is real. He believes this because he is convinced that God is present among the poor, by preference and in fact. It is this awareness that has made Gutiérrez's theology as revolutionary as it is. It is not so much the intellectual substance of his writings nor the incisiveness of his thought that makes his theology so unique and powerful, although these qualities are surely evident, but rather the fact that what he writes is suffering with belief, both in the poor and in their God.

Instead of looking outward for a theological and political solution to the Peruvian dilemma, Gutiérrez has looked inward. This simple reversal of focus has produced a Copernican revolution. Because of Gutiérrez, theology can no longer be done "from above." It has ceased to be an abstract discussion carried on by academicians. It is, rather, an expression of a people's struggle to live out the gospel in their society and lives. It is a song or narrative about the meaning and consequences of belief. Anything else is merely sterile God-talk.[5] Likewise, it is no longer a question of elites deciding what it means to be Peruvian or how best to run the country. Those decisions lie in the hands of the poor, for they alone understand the reality of oppression. What Gutiérrez has realized is that persons often characterized as ignorant and inarticulate actually have a powerful, eloquent vision of the future. The challenge they face is to make that vision real. It must shape their Christian faith while stimulating their political will. The challenge the nonpoor face is to listen to what the poor say—something theologians and politicians from the upper crust of society often fail to do. There is now only one valid locus, both for theology and politics; it is "from below."

THE GOD WHO REJOINS

Great insights, of course, are rarely the product of isolated genius. More often than not they are the result of collective effort and thinking. This is no less true of Gutiérrez's theology. It cannot be understood apart from the persons who surround him, those in Lima and those who have shaped his spiritual and intellectual horizons. Of the latter, none is more important than José María Arguedas. An anthropologist, novelist, and poet, Arguedas grappled intensely with the question of *peruanidad* even at the expense of his own life. Although few non-Peruvians realize it, the relationship between the thought of Arguedas and Gutiérrez is basic to understanding the evolution of the latter's theology.[6] Every major work Gutiérrez has produced contains Arguedas's name and thoughts, and *A Theology of Liberation* was dedicated to him.

That Gutiérrez and Arguedas would be attracted to each other's writings and thinking is quite logical, for both were passionately concerned about the self-identity of their people and the appalling violence and suffering that mars Peruvian history. That they would become close friends, however, was less likely, at least at first sight. When they first met, in the late 1960s, Gutiérrez was a relatively young, enthusiastic priest, whereas Arguedas was a depressed, exhausted man who had little use for institutional Christianity and took pride in his self-proclaimed agnosticism. Nonetheless, they met and became close friends. Their friendship coalesced in the city of Chimbote, a coastal fishing port to the north of Lima noted for its astounding stench and pollution produced by local fishmeal factories and steel mills. A small version of Lima, Chimbote harbors masses of exploited, impoverished workers who have come from the Peruvian sierra in search of work, only to find themselves unemployed and living in hellish, concentric circles of mat houses that surround the city. Gutiérrez was in Chimbote giving conferences on what would become known as liberation theology and Arguedas was finishing his last novel, *El zorro de arriba y el zorro de abajo* [The fox from above and the fox from below]. The agnostic was intrigued by a priest concerned about the poor, and the priest was fascinated by an agnostic poet intensely looking for God in the midst of the oppressed.

Arguedas was from a different world and social class than Gutiérrez, but they would find common ground and friendship in short order. Born to an affluent landowning family in the central mountains, Arguedas should have lived apart from the local Quechua campesinos his Spanish-speaking kin had exploited for centuries. Friction between his parents, however, left him emotionally orphaned and physically separated from both. He was reared by Quechua-speaking domestics and laborers who cooked and worked on his father's estate. Sitting in their quarters at night, they taught him their language and culture. White and privileged, he nonetheless experienced their world at first hand, seeing the exploitation, brutality, and humiliation of their lives. If he had been raised in a "proper" mestizo household, he would have been schooled in the selective blindness the children of oppressors learn at an early age. He would have accepted the caricatures of the poor as lazy, dirty peasants who deserved their lot in life. But because these persons had raised and provided him with more love than his natural parents, he could not accept his own social class's stereotypes of its victims. When he was eventually sent for by his father who had moved to Lima, he found himself pulled apart by conflicting loyalties. The painful dichotomies of his childhood wore at his mind like a fine, abrasive sand. He would spend his life trying to achieve some inner peace and self-understanding. Tragically, his struggle ended in self-inflicted death.

When Arguedas met Gutiérrez he was desperately struggling to find what he called "the God who rejoins," in himself and his own people. So, too, was Gutiérrez. Both were surprised to find that they were coming to the same conclusion, that God was present in the poor in Peru. Arguedas was beginning to see that below the surface of Peruvian history there was an intense subterranean current, a different history than that written by the conquering Spanish or the white, intellectual elites of the republic. There was a history in the Quechua songs and legends that he had heard as a boy and still ran through his mind. Disregarded by academic historians as insignificant or imaginary, this history was nonetheless a quickening, creative force for the poor. It had sustained the campesinos who sang their songs and taught him their legends in the servants' quarters of his father's hacienda. It gave them, and him, life. Arguedas began to realize that there was something of ineffable beauty in the world of his childhood. At the same time he realized that the creative, human beauty in and around him had been disfigured by his other self, by the world of the Spanish-speaking landowner. He knew that the beauty that gave cohesion and meaning to the life of the poor, that healed their wounds and sustained them, was God. He also realized that the same God was being slain by racism, sexism, and class hatred. Arguedas grasped a painful truth: that Peru was, and is, a crucified people.

Arguedas and Gutiérrez saw both the beauty and the destructive power of death in their own midst. As they talked together about their own lives and the complex challenge of undoing centuries of oppression and misunderstanding, questions about God and evil that both had wrestled with were addressed. They began to realize that in Peru such questions can be answered only in terms of the suffering and hope of the poor. To the extent that they might shed some light on the pain and joy of ordinary lives, then they could say something credible about God. Anything else would be a useless abstraction. In the words of César Vallejos, they came to the conclusion that "there is no God, no Son of God, without unraveling."[7] In effect, they set out to find God in the convoluted lives of persons in Rimac as well as in the peasant songs, a God hidden in human hearts and all too often made invisible by human evil. Searching for that God became their common quest and the foundation of their friendship. Arguedas wrote novels full of theological themes; Gutiérrez wrote theology shaped by the daily experience of the poor.

What started out as two Peruvian writers curious about each other's ideas became a friendship of tremendous significance, not only for Arguedas and Gutiérrez, but for the poor of Peru and believing peoples throughout the world. Indigenous peasants and urban workers were seen as real persons rather than as dehumanized statistics or benighted objects of pity. Discussing their own experiences and challenging each other to achieve deeper insights, Arguedas and Gutiérrez spoke *from* the world of the poor and *for* its liberation. They succeeded in speaking as a collective subject. They, the oppressed of Peru, could now be heard and their demand to shape their history could no longer go unheeded. The whole question of *peruanidad* was reframed and concretized as it never had been before. Likewise, the role of faith, both in God and human history, was recast in its long-forgotten prophetic guise. Belief in God meant doing justice, not performing rituals. Belief entailed faith in ordinary persons and a commitment to overcoming oppressive social structures that diminished God's creation. Arguedas and Gutiérrez have not only changed the history of Peru, they have also had a profound impact on the Judeo-Christian tradition.

SEARCHING FOR THE GOD OF THE OPPRESSED

Arguedas's death came as a profound shock to many Peruvians, but did not stop his friend and intellectual ally from pursuing their quest for a better understanding of Peru or the God present in its history. This has been Gutiérrez's prime concern for decades and, along with his pastoral work among the poor of Lima, the principal source of his theology. As a theologian Gutiérrez teaches and lectures, but such activities take up only part of his time. More often than not he can be found in his parish or in the Las Casas Center, which is also in Rimac. It is here that he normally writes. He receives his inspiration from the poor who surround him. He is convinced that they have something to say, that they are sources of revelation. The reason for this is not because the poor are innately better or more developed Christians, although many surely are good persons, but because God is present in their midst: not in spite of, but because of oppression and dehumanizing poverty. God is in Rimac because it is there that people must be rejoined. As Gutiérrez notes in *On Job*, one of his more recent works, "The ultimate basis of God's preference for the poor is to be found in God's own goodness."[8] God is present among the poor because they are most in need of the liberating spirit only God can provide. As victims of human evil, God is present to the poor as its antithesis and counterweight. It is up to them to choose. As Gutiérrez states with clarity, God has opted for the poor, but it is incumbent on the poor to opt for God:

> God wants justice, indeed, and desires that divine judgment (*mishpat*) reign in the world; but God cannot impose it, for the nature of created beings must be respected. God's power is limited by human freedom; for without freedom God's justice would not be present within history.[9]

Precisely for this reason Gutiérrez stays among the poor: to help them choose the God of life in their midst and reject the dehumanizing evil that threatens to engulf them. As realistic as he is committed, Gutiérrez knows that the struggle for liberation is arduous and that many pitfalls lay along the way. Only those with solid faith and strategic patience will survive its rigors.

Gutiérrez does not romanticize the poor. He is quite aware of their weaknesses as well as their strengths. To romanticize the poor would be equivalent to trivializing and treating them as objects. It would diminish their autonomy as active subjects, an oppressive trap Gutiérrez consciously avoids. Thus, those who accuse him of a type of "proletarian Pelagianism" have presumably not read his books. The point is this: only God can liberate the poor, but this can happen only if the poor choose God. We must bear in mind that to choose God in the midst of oppression, to make a conscious choice for creation and goodness, requires consciousness and courage. Deluged as they are by manipulative cultural and political propaganda, numbed by hunger, and hopeless, it is no easy task for the poor to see God among them, especially in their own lives. In a social system built on brutality, mistrust, and predatory behavior, to trust and love one's neighbor, as well as one's self, can seem like self-destructive folly. Protection of one's own interests, competition, and individualism—the cardinal virtues of capitalism—are attractive alternatives despite their ultimately destructive effects. To believe in the God of life without being able to foresee any immediate consequences or benefits is to take a monumental risk. What Gutiérrez asks of the poor, and of himself, is that they take that risk. Many have.

To opt for the God of life, to choose freedom over death, clearly requires more than verbal assent. If it were only that, it would be mere religious banter. Although Gutiérrez is convinced that only belief in God and in themselves will save the poor, he has no illusions about that belief being easy. It first requires struggle with oneself and then with society. "The wicked, those are both rejecters of God and enemies of the poor," will do their utmost to destroy belief. They will ridicule, persecute, and even liquidate those who refuse to worship the idols they set up. True belief is intolerable to the lords of death. For the politicians, magistrates, priests, and even the poor who have sold themselves to their oppressors, for all those who batten on the spoils of evil, belief in God is a capital offense.[10] This is not hyperbole. As Gutiérrez has pointed out, in many countries, including parts of Peru, to be a true Christian is to risk one's life.[11]

CONCLUSION: MYSTERY AND LIBERATION

In his struggle to understand his own people, Gutiérrez has become increasingly aware that he stands before a mystery. Exploited and despised, the poor nonetheless survive and continue to hope. According to the logic of their oppressors, they should simply acquiesce and accept their fate. But they refuse to. This refusal can only be explained by grace, by the spirit of God gratuitously present in their lives. God, the ultimate mystery that "cannot be pigeonholed in human categories,"[12] refutes the logic of those who inflict death by providing spirit and vision to the poor. Despite the poverty of Rimac, the persons who live there continue to believe, and because they do, they continue to struggle. They may not be able to articulate their belief in theological language, but that is immaterial. Talking *about* God is unimportant; talking *to* God is important. The fact that malnourished, mistreated persons can still believe, that they can talk to God and each other, is indicative of a mysterious, saving presence in Rimac.

In his more recent publications and books Gutiérrez has increasingly stressed the need for contemplation. Those involved in the struggle for liberation, especially the poor themselves, need to stand back and take stock of the process they are committed to. If their efforts on behalf of liberation are to be truly effective, they must be deeply rooted in belief, in God and in their own people. As Gutiérrez has pointed out, "contemplation and practice feed each other; the two make up the stage of silence before God."[13] Thus, the only liberating praxis that will have a real effect is that which flows out of a sense of reverent belief in the God of the poor.

Gutiérrez knows the history of his people like few other Peruvians. He is fully aware of the complex challenges that face his country. Those who propose glib solutions are only deceiving themselves and ultimately hurting others. The first step in the struggle for liberation is not to speak shallow and unfounded words, but to believe in what it means. Silence, action, and then words are the steps in liberative praxis. To put things more bluntly, it is rather easy to talk about liberation; talk, after all, is cheap. Understanding liberation, however, assenting to what it means and demands, is a more difficult task that must begin in silence and contemplation.

While listening to the songs of the poor in Rimac, Gutiérrez has become increasingly aware of just how mysterious God's ways are. The persons around him should be overwhelmed, but are not. They continue to struggle and take hesitant forward steps, being pushed by something greater than themselves. Much like Job, a biblical figure who has caught his imagination in the last few years, Gutiérrez has come to recognize and live with the fact that the God present in his own people defies description, and that the future course of the struggle for liberation cannot be foretold. To believe is to live with a certain amount of uncertainty. Yet the unknown is not some sort of "monster that threatens to devour things,"[14] but rather a stimulus to look deeper into the people and creative process called Peru. The unknown is a call to greater commitment. In many ways, that is precisely what his theology is, a continuing attempt to describe God's struggle to free the poor and oppressed, to give them life despite the intentions of those who deal them death. It is a narrative about the enigmatic power of the powerless. Written in a slum of Lima where optimism is a scarce commodity, it speaks of a God who will rejoin a fragmented people. It is the *vals criollo* of the poor.

NOTES

1. The coastal culture of Peru is generally known as *criollo*. Peruvians of the coast are often racially mixed and normally Spanish-speaking, whereas Peruvians in the sierra and *altiplano* generally speak Quechua or Aymara, two preconquest Andean languages.

2. The concept of futurity is fundamental to Gutiérrez's theology. His most important and demanding discussion of this theme can be found in the eighth chapter of *A Theology of Liberation* (Maryknoll, N.Y.: Orbis Books, 1973), pp. 213–50.

3. This tendency to romanticize Peru's indigenous past is evident in the propaganda of *Sendero Luminoso. Sendero,* of course, is more than an intellectual movement in contemporary Peru. It is actually an example of political pathology, the product of frustration and despair gone mad. It is nonetheless striking how members of this movement have exploited the symbols and myths of Peru's indigenous peoples in order to gain their allegiance.

4. Gustavo Gutiérrez, *On Job: God-Talk and the Suffering of the Innocent* (Maryknoll, N.Y.: Orbis Books, 1987), p. xi.

5. See *On Job*, p. 29, for a rather pointed treatment of traditional theology.

6. For further analysis of the role of Arguedas in Gutiérrez's theology, see my work *From the Heart of the People: The Theology of Gustavo Gutiérrez* (Oak Park, Ill.: Meyer Stone Books, 1988), pp. 67–75.

7. César Vallejos, a Peruvian poet who died in 1938, is noted for his intensely personal works, which often speak of the lives of the poor. Vallejos saw his own people as a source of revelation about both the human condition and the reality of God. Along with José Carlos Mariátegui, he too agonized about his country's identity and fate. In certain ways, these two figures can be seen as the precursors of Arguedas and Gutiérrez. All have carried on the search for *peruanidad* in their respective ways. Vallejos is quoted frequently by Gutiérrez, particularly in *On Job*. The text cited is from *Modern Poetry from Spain and Latin America,* Nan Braymer and Lillian Lowenfels, eds. (New York: Corinth Books, 1964), p. 14.

8. *On Job*, p. xiii.

9. Ibid., p. 77.

10. One can only speculate that it is for this reason that national elites, and those who direct the genocidal foreign policy of the United States in Latin America, are so intent on destroying the growth of base communities and the lives of those involved in liberative, Christian praxis.

11. Gutiérrez pointed out the possibility of persecution against the church in Latin America long before it assumed its current, systemic form. For a poignant

treatment of contemporary martyrdom, see *The Power of the Poor in History* (Maryknoll, N.Y.: Orbis Books, 1983), pp. 88–90.

12. *On Job*, p. 16.
13. Ibid., p. xiii.
14. Ibid., p. 91.

12

Gustavo Gutiérrez:
A Friend of Nicaragua

CÉSAR JEREZ, SJ

Living as I do in Nicaragua and trying to make a modest contribution to its survival, it is not possible at the moment for me to write a long essay. So I have written these brief pages in honor of Gustavo Gutiérrez's sixtieth birthday. But I could not write as a mere formality. Gustavo is a theologian of course, but also a pastor, Christian, and friend, and he deserves much more than an academic eulogy.

Gustavo's latest book *On Job* is about Job and his tremendous questions. He translates these into the lives of the poor in Latin America, innocent persons who suffer interminably. The triumph of the poor in Nicaragua in 1979 was like the first blessing Job experienced from God. Now the innocent Nicaraguan people is suffering from a war, which Gustavo foresaw even in September 1979. But he has behaved very differently from Job's comforters. He did not come to lecture; he came to see God passing through the history of the poor. He came in Nicaragua's hour of triumph and he returned when it was besieged and the hope of the poor once more threatened with death. He came as a friend who spoke about God from the standpoint of the poor. Above all, he came as a friend wanting to drink clear water from the well, which Nicaragua's poor had succeeded in digging. He was with it in victory and a comfort in hardship. In short, he lived what his theology preached, and he proved that his hope was the hope of the poor.

The inspiration given by his writings has been part of Latin American theology over the past twenty years. It has been an inspiration precisely because it has been backed up by the witness of his life. The same goes for most of the genuine theologians from this school. This is why in such a short time, this theology-life has become one of the richest contributions by Latin America to Catholicism—and beyond denominational barriers, to twentieth-century Christianity. In fact, together with our painting, architecture, literature, and the originality of our revolutionary politics, this theology has become one of the most important contributions by Latin America to the humanization of the world in our time. Gustavo called it "liberation theology" from the experience of living faith in Latin American poor communities. Another great Latin American theologian, Juan Luis Segundo, called it the "liberation *of* theology," because it also achieved for itself as a discipline the liberation it announced for the poor. As both one and the other, it has become one of theology's most creative forces.

Through it, theology has regained its roots in what has always been its most fertile soil, the following of Jesus. It has recovered the very same ground on which Jesus of Nazareth stood to announce the kingdom: the actual history of the people to whom the kingdom is being announced. And Gustavo's theology recovers, in Bartolomé de Las Casas, in José Maria Arguedas, and in the present-day communities of indigenous or mestizo Peruvians the historical memory both of the proclaiming of the good news to the poor, and the way in which it was perverted into bad news for them. That is why liberation theology is done from within communities of the poor, who live their faith in places like Chimbote or Quilali, Nicaragua or Peru. It is being done in the second half of the twentieth century, a time when Latin America's poor are trying to embrace what has always been their human vocation: to make their own history.

In Latin America the social sciences have been used to unmask the way history has been manipulated to make it fit a minority viewpoint with its logic and passions. The social sciences have read history from "the other side" — that of the majority, with its logic and passions. Gustavo Gutiérrez's theological reflection has had the courage to use the language of these social sciences, looking at human life "from the other side of history," the history that does not count or rather did not count, the history of the poor. Liberation theology had to give an answer in terms of Christian hope to the questions the poor asked when they analyzed their own lives. These analyses were given scientific vigor and the warmth of a story shared by social scientists involved in the historical projects of the poor. This is where to look for the interlocking of theology and social sciences, not in mistaken accusations of reductionism or false charges of theology's submission to the social sciences. Theology is always an answer given from the experience of living Christian faith to questions expressed in the different languages with which humanity tries to understand itself or simply roars out its pain. Using the questioner's language is a way of trying to give an answer that will be understood.

Gustavo Gutiérrez has been responsible for all this. He has been a friend in God who goes along with you and comforts you. He shows the humble friendship of someone able to get into his friend's own life and hope. He has made the theological effort to justify this God, who shines in friendship. He has also used language that has assured that the theological answer given is not just another hermetic secret kept by an elite group.

NICARAGUA: A SITUATION AND TIME OF GRACE

A large number of the "believing and oppressed" ones — as Gustavo Gutiérrez would call them — in Nicaragua welcomed the spirituality of liberation and gratefully absorbed the message from the meeting of Catholic bishops at Medellín (1968). Nicaragua had become a "foreign land" through a dynastic dictatorship supported in power for over forty years by its link with North American imperialism. The people's smoldering resistance burst forth at the end of the 1960s. After paying a very high price in struggle, suffering, repression, and death, Nicaraguans liberated themselves from this pharaonic dynasty on July 19, 1979. The victory was both the result of their struggle and an unexpected gift from God. This was the experience of the people, a small David taking on the gigantic might of the Goliath of dictatorship and empire.

A great light shone in Nicaragua, which lit up this tiny country and its neighbors, small peripheral countries of the Third World. This light kindled the hope in their hearts that they could reestablish freedom and construct an original model of self-governance. This model would be based on one of those new cultural syntheses of which young nations are capable: the synthesis between its national history with its heroic myths, the people's revolutionary tradition—Marxist or otherwise—and liberating Christian faith. Too soon, however, the empire, afraid that Nicaragua's example might spread, decided to quash its determination to be free and equal among the nations. Nicaragua needed to make major changes to meet the basic needs of the people after the long and heavy oppression. This was opposed by an economic blockade and a war. All this against a population of little more than three million. To tell the truth, we do not know exactly how many of us there are, because with the blockade and the war we have not had the time or money to do a census.

We should not confuse our terms, much less realities. The Nicaraguan revolution is not and never will be the kingdom of God, although it has taken justice very seriously, as well as the equality that is a right of peoples, the preferential option for and solidarity with the poor, the defense of life against death, the sharing by the majority in public life and responsibility, and other characteristics of joint human life, which Jesus in the gospels and faith in Jesus Christ in the primitive church designate as signs of God's kingdom. In the prolonged war of the Sandinista Front, in the people's insurrection, in the building of the new Nicaragua, many from among the poor and many who threw in their lot with the poor did it because of their Christian faith. And as Christians they met others who were unbelievers, except in justice and humanity's capacity for goodness. The process was violent but in Nicaragua nobody glorified violence. Ricardo Morales, a young university professor and member of the FSLN National Directorate, wrote from prison: "I do not believe that violence is a personal form of self-liberation."[1] One of the historically most improbable things that has happened in the Nicaraguan revolution has in fact been forgiveness and generosity to defeated enemies. This is not the least of reasons why this revolution has been a source of hope.

Ricardo Morales Avilés, later murdered by Somoza's National Guard, was also right when he said: "We must study our history and our reality as Marxists and study Marxism as Nicaraguans."[2] It was precisely this antidogmatic stance by non-Christian revolutionaries that enabled many Christians "as Nicaraguans" to adopt the revolutionary cause without fear, and build the Nicaraguan original model together with non-Christians. There was enough political will not to repeat the clash between Christian faith and revolutionary optimism.

Even during the struggle, this conjunction produced Christian contributions of continental, even universal, importance. We think, for example of the *Misa Campesina*, which sprang from our small, poetic, Christian, and revolutionary Nicaragua. Its theological and popular words and music were created in Nicaragua during its time of exodus. It fed a liturgical celebration of the eucharist, which was a subversive memory of Jesus and embodied the faith and yearnings of a whole people.

Nicaragua was the first country in Central America to have a triumphant revolution. This was not what was expected or calculated. The blood that was shed bore the fruit of freedom for Nicaragua before any other Central American country. But also in Guatemala, El Salvador, and Honduras—confining ourselves to Central America—faith as commitment to the struggle of the poor has become blood that was shed, producing heroes and martyrs.

The God of Jesus Christ passing through these countries has bestowed the painful blessing of martyrdom. "There is no greater love than to lay down your life for your friends" (John 15:13). In this love Central America, and Nicaragua within it, has become a privileged place for the theology that is trying to give an account of Christian hope in the following of Jesus Christ. With humility and simplicity we should remember what was written by the greatest of Central American poets:

> Throughout the fatal pages of her history
> our land is made of strength and glory,
> our land is made for humanity.[3]

The Lord has taken into account the littleness of this country, which serves him and he has put down the mighty. Nicaragua has spent nearly eight years resisting the overbearing determination of the empire to wipe this example of courage and hope for all peoples off the face of the earth. And all Central America resists with Nicaragua.

GUSTAVO GUTIÉRREZ'S PRESENCE IN THE NEW NICARAGUA

The allusion to Mary's Magnificat in the previous section gives us the right context in which to understand Gustavo Gutiérrez's presence in the new Nicaragua. Since the poor have irrupted in him, Gustavo is pregnant with desire for the liberation of all Latin America. The news of Nicaragua's revolutionary delivery made him set out, like Mary full of joy when she heard Elizabeth was expecting, to visit her and share her hope and happiness. Malice followed him even here. "They—it was said within the church itself about the liberation theologians—go to Managua now as if to their new Rome." However, Gustavo only came to Managua to share our hopes and wishes, filled with the Spirit that is "Father to the poor." He was present in Nicaragua's time of joy that it, a poor country, had received grace.

In Puebla, that same year, 1979, from outside the walls of the Palafoxiano Seminary, where the Third Conference of Catholic Latin American Bishops was taking place, Gustavo gave a friendly welcome to the Archbishop of Managua, Miguel Obando y Bravo, and honored him for his services to his people. When he arrived in Managua at the end of September 1979, it was to visit the archbishop, who told him of the plan to write a pastoral letter of the Conference of Nicaraguan Bishops giving a Christian comment on the triumphant revolutionary process. Gustavo was asked to be an advisor and he worked on a rough draft of the letter.

For their part, the then Vatican envoy in Nicaragua, Pietro Sambi, and a certain bishop, had asked the same of another group of Central American theologians, who also contributed their ideas in draft form.

From these joint efforts, which were a real cooperation between bishops and theologians, arose the pastoral letter *Christian Commitment for a New Nicaragua*, signed on November 17, 1979. Its salient points are the church's support for socialism with a human face, in which Christian faith and education play a part and are fully respected, recognition of the historical role of the Sandinista Front in the liberation of Nicaragua, the distinction in the class struggle between a dynamic transformation of structures—acceptable—and class hatred—unacceptable—and an exhortation to austerity during the time of scarcity accompanying a revolutionary process. Gustavo's mark is visible in the passage pointing out the historical opportunity for the church. It is worth quoting:

> Today we are experiencing in our country an exceptional opportunity to bear witness to and proclaim God's kingdom. It would be seriously unfaithful to the gospel to allow fear and suspicion, the insecurity some feel in any process of radical social change, the defense of large or small private interests, to prevent us from seizing this important moment to put into practice that preferential option for the poor demanded of us both by Pope John Paul II and the Episcopal Conference of Puebla.[4]

I am not giving away any secrets when I draw the eyes of the church to the contribution made at Puebla by Gustavo Gutiérrez to the text on the preferential option for and solidarity with the poor. It came through certain bishops asking for his help. The passage quoted from the Nicaraguan Bishops' pastoral letter shines with his joy as a Christian and churchman, because the circumstances of a country in revolution with a large Christian presence makes it possible to issue the challenge to "put the preferential option for the poor into practice."

Perhaps we might lament that this episcopal document has not had pastoral continuity. Undoubtedly, however, it will remain as one of the great church documents of our time, as a statement with which the church in Nicaragua identified, and gave joy to the people. Many non-Christians could agree here with the motivations of Christian revolutionaries.

Gustavo came to Nicaragua several more times. As I have already said, he came above all as the friend who goes with you along the road of faithfulness to the hopes of the poor. He came as one following Jesus' commandment to strengthen one's brothers and sisters in the faith, and in the right critical spirit toward every human endeavor. These contributions of his have been, if anything, even more important than his work as a theological advisor. Even in the midst of the difficulties he faced when he was under suspicion in his own country, and his faithfulness to the message of Jesus Christ was in question, he never forgot this small child, this little country under threat, as Nicaragua continued to be.

In the midst of a church divided by different political views, and marked by its inability to overcome intolerance, Gustavo always asked for patience to live together within the church in spite of painful conflict. His way has always been spiritual: be faithful to the following of Jesus; firmly maintain the preferential option for and solidarity with the poor; steadfastly show that the most convincing argument is humble, brave, and serene witness, to answer those who believe the solution to conflict is to exclude dissidents.

Gustavo has repeatedly insisted on a spirituality of liberation in a vigorous personal and communitarian following of Jesus. The battle during years when fear has tried to regain possession of Christians has never made him lose his sense of humor. With this, a genuine person can regard events in historical perspective, keeping one's feet firmly planted on the rock that is God who defends the cause of the poor—God who is greater than the word of theologians and the confabulations of inquisitors. What Gustavo has shown above all else is faithful tenacity with a gentle smile. He is determined not to separate faith and justice. He promotes faith in a preaching of the gospel that takes on the hopes of the poor being preached to, especially the indigenous of Latin America. All this bears the seal of the authentically Christian.

The horizons of faith indicated in Nicaragua by Gustavo, and affirmed by other companions like Leonardo Boff and Don Pedro Casaldáliga, are not indications of personal ambition. The human endeavors that have tried to reach them do not have the fullness that belongs only to the kingdom. The important thing is to continue with firmness, sincerity, and humility to live the faith within this revolutionary process, and make sure that the cause of the poor is not lost.

These brief pages, written in the midst of unending activity and the difficulties of a country still at war, where work is done under conditions of poverty and tension, are intended as a testimony of gratitude. Gustavo Gutiérrez has been the friend who has helped us live through this tension without losing our sense of humor. He has cheered us with his courage, his comfort, the witness of his life and of his theological and spiritual writing. His contribution has made our load lighter. The Spirit of Jesus will inspire him to go on offering Christian strength and clarity.

—translated from the Spanish by Dinah Livingstone

NOTES

1. Ricardo Morales Avilés, *Obras: No pararemos de andar jamás* (Managua: Editorial Nueva Nicaragua, 1983), p. 87.
2. Ibid., p. 83.
3. Ruben Darío, "Retorno, Poema del Otoño," *Poesías Completas* (Madrid: Aguilar, 1967), vol. 2, p. 783.
4. Bishops' Conference of Nicaragua, *Compromiso Cristiano para una Nicaragua Nueva*, part 2, para. 2.

13

Gustavo Gutiérrez
and the Originality
of the Peruvian Experience

STEPHEN JUDD, MM

COMMITTED INTELLECTUALS AND THE AGONY OF PERU

On the eve of the Socialist International Congress in June 1986 in downtown Lima, news of riots in three of the city's prisons began to circulate. Held in Lima with an impressive cast of internationally known leaders of the caliber of the West German Willy Brandt and the former Venezuelan president, Carlos Andrés Peréz, the congress aimed to recognize and bolster the standing of Peru's young and charismatic president, Alan García Peréz. The prison mutiny and riots quickly overshadowed the congress proceedings.

Inmates belonging to the *Sendero Luminoso* (shining path) terrorist movement staged the riots at the Lurigancho and El Frontón men's prisons and at the women's correctional institution, Santa Bárbara, that resulted in the deaths of approximately two hundred fifty inmates at the hands of the police and Peruvian armed forces. The mass executions of prisoners raised the level of violence and brutality to new heights and caught the attention of the world press corps assembled to cover the proceedings of the congress.

As the recently published and authoritative *Ames Report* indicates, President García acted precipitously in granting virtual free rein to the army and police to squelch the riots with violent means.[1] According to the findings in the *Ames Report*, he bears much of the responsibility for the prison massacres. Even in a country where the violence associated with *Sendero Luminoso* increasingly takes on the appearance of the commonplace, the prison massacres produced widespread indignation throughout Peruvian society and sent shock waves around the world. In the immediate aftermath of the tragedy, Peruvians of all social classes and political party affiliations attempted to examine the deep-seated causes of the violence that has brought the country to the brink of chaos and jeopardized its fragile experiment in formal democracy. The violence perpetrated by *Sendero* since 1980 plus the government's repressive antisubversion policy have generated both fear and outrage among people in the popular sectors committed to a process of peaceful transformation in Peruvian society through the strengthening of structures of democratic participation.

One of the first to respond to the prison massacres was the prominent theologian Gustavo Gutiérrez. On the editorial pages of the widely read Lima daily newspaper, *La República*, Gustavo took a somber look at the present situation in an essay entitled "Aún es tiempo".[2] In measured but impassioned language Gustavo protested the spiral of violence brought about in large part by the same kind of situation of "institutionalized violence" mentioned by the Latin American bishops at the Medellín Conference in 1968. At the same time, Gustavo's outrage—by no means interpreted as an apology for *Sendero*—was accompanied by expressions of faith in the capacity of the Peruvian people, especially the poorer classes, to find a solution for the chronic economic and social crises exacerbated by the violence.

Later, at a forum organized to analyze the causes of the violence and to look for alternative solutions, some intellectuals adopted a dim view of the prospects for peaceful change with at least a modicum of social justice. According to Luis Pasará, Peru is essentially a fratricidal society that derives from one of its founding myths dating back to the time of the Inca empire, that of the brothers Ayar, which "explains why we live in an authoritarian society, heading toward an inevitable bloodbath, the result of not being able to solve our problems in a democratic fashion."[3] On the other hand, Gustavo's intervention at the same forum typified a radically different response that reflected a progressive current of thought in Peruvian intellectual circles. Referring to the conclusion of one of the participants that the only alternative to dealing with the crisis and national malaise was to seek voluntary exile, Gustavo placed himself among those Peruvians who, if forced to choose between a *libreta militar* (one of the principal identification documents in Peru) or a passport, he would want to be included among those with the *libreta militar*.[4]

Coming from the widely traveled and internationally renowned theologian, the use of this metaphor substantiates the claim that Gustavo is an intellectual who addresses a world audience from the perspective of Peru, its people, and their conflictive social reality. His response to the tragic events of June 1986 confirms his declared position that the solutions to Peru's underdevelopment lie with the victims, the impoverished masses of campesinos and urban slum dwellers. Together with previous generations of progressive Peruvian intellectuals, Gustavo finds a deep identification in this conviction with Peru's and Latin America's foremost socialist thinker, José Carlos Mariátegui (1895–1930). Taking his cue from the Mexican intellectual José Vasconcelos, Mariátegui coined the phrase that symbolizes their perspective on the Peruvian reality: *pesimismo en la realidad, optimismo en el ideal* ("pessimism about the reality, optimism in the ideal—of a new society"). Mariátegui's thought informs and guides several generations of Peruvian intellectuals and social activists who assume the problematical situation of Peru as a life project, "organize intellectuals" in the mold of Antonio Gramsci, like the historian Jorge Basadre (1903–1983), who interpret the Peruvian experience as "problem and possibility."[5]

This intellectual movement approaches Peru and the quest for a new society from an identification with the plight of its people, agonizes over the disparities and contradictions in national life, and searches for the vital synthesis and alternatives for a country still in its formative stages. In the same vein as the *indigenista* novelist José María Arguedas (1911–1969), they discover in this conflictive "country impatient to be born, an infinite source for new creativity."[6] Like Mariátegui, the sole purpose of their intellectual endeavor is to create a vision of a just society based on what is original in the plurality of expressions of the Peruvian experience. Their life project hinges on the wager that the marginated masses of urban and rural poor will become the protagonists in the transformation of the present society and prepare the foundations for a new one. Clearly, Gustavo belongs to the latest generation of committed intellectuals who in the 1960s and 70s injected a new thrust into the Mariátegui legacy. In turn, he will contribute to the formation of a yet newer generation that in this decade has moved to the forefront of national life and challenged existing social conditions.

However, Gustavo's search to define the originality of the Peruvian character and experience does not remain exclusively or primarily within the confines of the world of ideas. Rather, his commitment is to discover this untapped reservoir of creativity and originality by means of a "spiritual and physical nearness to the world of the poor." His insertion into their reality requires more than an occasional visit. In this sense he identifies with a long line of missionaries and pastoral workers who draw inspiration from the sixteenth-century Dominican friar and "Defender of the Amerindians," Bartolomé de Las Casas (1484-1566). Gustavo's recovery of the Las Casas tradition is bound to mystify critics inside and outside Peru, as well as those who interpret his interest in Las Casas as either an inflated estimation of the friar or an unnecessary interruption in the further development of liberation theology. Why at this crucial stage in his theological development, they ask, would he choose to *remontarse* (to remount the cause) of Las Casas and re-create the conditions of the world of the sixteenth century?[7]

The answer to that question, as well as his place within a distinct current of Peruvian intellectual life organized around the followers of Mariátegui and Arguedas, provide the elements for a new approach to Gustavo's work. This approach is consistent with his challenge that "we drink from our own well." Moreover, his response to the prison massacres of 1986 is not an isolated case, but reflects the seminal ideas in the works and writings of Las Casas, Mariátegui, and Arguedas. This essay is an attempt to locate these currents of thought as the principal, if not the most overlooked and underestimated, sources for a new evaluation of the work of Gustavo Gutiérrez and for the future agenda of liberation theology. Finally, I will examine a concrete case study of a changed church presence in Peru, which provides the context for the convergence of these various sources in Gustavo's work. Within the pastoral praxis of the church of the southern Andes, Gustavo discovers the grounds to validate the insights of all three of his intellectual mentors.

"PERSONS WHO DIE BEFORE THEIR TIME": THE LEGACY OF BARTOLOMÉ DE LAS CASAS

What makes Las Casas relevant for Gustavo is the fact that in Peru and in many parts of Latin America conditions are in many ways similar to what Las Casas discovered in the sixteenth century—namely that they are places where "people die before their time."[8] That entire human races were dying a premature and unjust death affected the course of Las Casas's life, giving his writings their particular sense of urgency and polemical tone. The accounts of the violence of the Peruvian conquest that reached Las Casas through his missionary followers described a devastation that surpassed the earlier stages of the conquest in the Caribbean and Mexico. Gustavo's outrage at the prison massacres and the violence in Peruvian society today echo the sentiments expressed by Las Casas four centuries earlier.

Early in his American experience Las Casas underwent a conversion to the Amerindian that according to Gustavo "is the result of his having seen the Amerindian not just as a heathen to evangelize, but as a poor person, in the gospel sense—as an 'other' who is calling Western Christianity to account."[9] When we examine the entire trajectory of Las Casas's life, we discern a consistent pattern of conversion to the "other." In this case, the discovery of the Amerindian emphasizes the quality of human diversity beyond what the prevalent European currents of thought determined as the constitutive elements in human identity. Among other discoveries Las Casas demonstrated the importance of cultural relativity, and thus was one of the forerunners of modern anthropology.

Unlike many of the first missionaries, Las Casas recognized that one of the root causes of the violence against indigenous peoples derived precisely from a rejection of cultural plurality. Finally, at the end of his long and combative life this fundamental discovery led him to conclude that the solution to the Amerindian "problem" was to be found only in the affirmation of cultural plurality. The particular brutality of the Peruvian conquest, likewise, convinced him that neither appeals to the enlightened self-interest of the Spanish crown nor the church hierarchy would save the Amerindians from enslavement under the dreaded *encomienda* system. Only the guarantee of the right to self-determination could bring about a reversal of the evils associated with the conquest and colonization. In the later stages of his life Las Casas edged closer to the position that the Amerindians themselves were historical subjects in their own right and the only ones who could bring about a just social transformation.

The notion given wide currency in the *Puebla Documents* (1979) of the poor as the subjects of evangelization, "their evangelizing potential," is linked with Las Casas's original discovery.[10] Had it not been for Gustavo's pointed and timely critique of the Puebla Working Document on precisely this issue, the shift of emphasis to the poor as agents of evangelization would not have found its way into the Final Document.

For Gustavo to reappropriate the Las Casas legacy on the eve of the 500th anniversary of the Spanish discovery of America is to sensitize his readers not only to the historical evils of the conquest, but to pinpoint the need for a conversion to the "insignificant others" as the potential agents to bring about the transformation in Latin American society today. Neither those who approach the Columbus centenary with triumphalistic intentions nor those who seize upon it as the pretext for resurrecting the banner of the anti-Spaniard "black legend" will be pleased with the recovery of the Las Casas tradition. Gustavo performs a valuable service in drawing our attention to a prophetic figure that history and often the church would prefer to relegate to a secondary category so as to erase the subversive memory he evokes.

MARIÁTEGUI'S MYTH OF THE COMMON PERSON

Critics of Gustavo's work unfamiliar with the development of the history of ideas in Peru are likely to overlook the profound and lasting influence of José Carlos

Mariátegui. Gustavo's discovery of the poor as historical subjects links him with Mariátegui's school of thought. However, one eminently qualified Peruvianist conversant with this current of thought correctly places Gustavo and his collaborators in continuity with both Mariátegui and Victor Raul Haya de la Torre (1894–1979), Mariátegui's contemporary and founder of the oldest political party in Peru, APRA. Haya and Mariátegui, according to Frederick Pike, "were new men of ambition who reached down into their country's intrahistory so as to discover the vaguely formed desires and the gnawing fears that lurked among the lower classes."[11] Similarly, Peru's "increasingly assertive clergy," imbued with liberation theology, is intent on "providing the rationales both for revolutionary change and elite domination."[12] Although generally accurate in situating Gustavo within the principal current of twentieth-century intellectual life in Peru, Pike grossly misinterprets Gustavo's motivations for a greater insertion into the world of the poor. Had he known of Gustavo's tireless efforts to create spaces within church and society for the democratic participation of the poor, he would have altered his charge of elite domination.

At the same time, one must exercise caution in identifying a prominent figure like Gustavo with Mariátegui, for authoritarian groups with violent aims like *Sendero Luminoso* also stake a vague claim to Mariátegui's legacy. Clearly, Gustavo belongs to the intellectual movement attracted "to a constellation of more complex concerns in Mariátegui — the campesino, the indigenous world, the quest for national identity, cultural specificity, emotion, and the role of belief — what we today would call the popular and national movement."[13] Gustavo points out how Mariátegui's perspective has paradigmatic value for his own concerns:

As others I am interested in what it means to be a Christian in the life, struggles, and culture of the Peruvian people. Or, if you will, to borrow an expression from Mariátegui, the role of the religious factor in the historical process of the poor. Not starting with intellectual elites who rely on expressions from conservative Catholic thought, or in the best of cases, with isolated and qualified expressions [Christian Democracy]. I am referring to something much more profound that can only come from the oppressed and popular classes: How does a Christian enter into the process of popular liberation in the construction of a nation? There are things to explore here, a new area where creativity resides in an exploited people of deep Christian faith who are struggling for their liberation.[14]

By elevating the popular classes — *el pueblo creyente y explotado* (a believing and exploited people) — to a central place in his theological reflection, Gustavo captures a distinct feature of Mariátegui's thought — namely, the poor as the embodiment of the myth creating a new national spirit. For Mariátegui the myth originates in the sometimes disarticulated Andean world. His unfinished project was to bring that myth to a clearer and more explicit articulation, although he traveled a curious route in its pursuit. Influenced as much by the thought of Henri Bergson and his élan vital and the myth of the general strike in the writings of Georges Sorel, Mariátegui set out for Europe in the mid-1920s determined to drink from the intellectual wells of Western civilization. Instead, exposure to the decadent salon society of post–World War I Europe, combined with his growing disenchantment with the dominant philosophical schools of positivism and rationalism, convinced Mariátegui that Peru's future did not lie solely within the sphere of influence of the Western intellectual tradition. Written in this context in 1925, his celebrated essay *El hombre y el mito* pays homage to Bergson and Sorel, but at this point he has clearly turned his attention back to Peru to search for "the will to believe" in a world filled with skepticism, unbelief, and a lack of hope.[15]

Back in Peru, amid the world of indigenous peoples and the new masses of urban workers and students, Mariátegui discovers the embodiment of the mythic character, *el alma matinal* or "morning person," who rises every day before dawn to face a dismal and alien world with few visible prospects for a better life. Yet, this is the person in whom rests humankind's last best hope for creating a new society. Elsewhere Mariátegui describes this quality as a fundamental openness to life—*pesimismo de la realidad y optimismo del ideal*—or the willingness to struggle toward a better future even when surrounded by all the signs of despair.

Perhaps one of the sources for Gustavo's suspicion of the modern spirit reflected in the collected essays, *The Power of the Poor in History*, is Mariátegui's critique of Western civilization and its bourgeois revolutions. Like Mariátegui's *alma matinal*, Gustavo's absent ones and "insignificant others" provide hope for a new way of doing theology as well as the foundation for constructing a new society:

Any attempt to make progress in theology apart from the hope of the poor— a hope from within their world and in their own terms—could well gain a little here and a little there, perhaps, but would not give us the quantum leap we were looking for. The only way to come to a new theological focus and language was to sink our roots in the social life of the Latin American people—this people whose own roots are geographically, historically, and culturally so deep in this land: this lowly people who had so long kept silent and now suddenly wished to speak, to cry out.[16]

PERU AS THE SOURCE FOR NEW CREATIVITY

Mariátegui alone could not provide all the keys for Gustavo's interpretation of Peruvian reality. To complete his understanding of the role of the committed Christian in the complex Andean world, with its potential for "creating a different kind of society," Gustavo discovers in the novelist José María Arguedas another kindred spirit worthy of emulation. As with Mariátegui, campesinos had to play a major role as protagonists if Peru was ever to achieve the elusive goal of national construction and identity. Near the end of his life Arguedas explained the two major ideals that gave direction to his life and literary production:

It was in reading Mariátegui and afterward Lenin that I found a permanent order to things; socialist theory not only provided a foundation but a charge and a force in my life. However, *no mató en mi lo mágico* [it didn't extinguish in me a sense of the magical quality of life]. The other principle was that of always considering Peru as an inexhaustible source for new creativity.[17]

Through the medium of various literary genres, Arguedas, I believe, surpasses Mariátegui in portraying the Andean campesinos as well-rounded subjects and protagonists. As the Chilean novelist Ariel Dorfman reminds us in commentating on Arguedas's work: "Arguedas doesn't copy other portraits of the Amerindian's life, but neither does he cease to document every aspect; the sense is not so much to inform readers as to move them esthetically."[18] Moreover, according to Dorfman, Arguedas creates an epic by raising the ordinary day-to-day struggles and existence of indigenous peoples to new mythical levels. He does not try to dispel the old notions and impressions about the Amerindians, but creates "a new legend based on liberation." This coincides with how Mariátegui envisioned the poor as the carriers of the myth of the new Peru.

Curiously, Gustavo first became acquainted with Arguedas during a time of deep personal crisis for the novelist in the coastal industrial city of Chimbote far from the idyllic and pastoral setting of the Andean highlands that served as the principal backdrop for his literary production. Chimbote also served as the backdrop for the germination of much of Gustavo's critical thought. It was in Chimbote that Arguedas attended a lecture given by Gustavo and based on notes that later became the nucleus of *A Theology of Liberation*. Afterward a mutual friend introduced them. This brief friendship—one year prior to the novelist's tragic death by suicide in Chile in 1969—enriched both men in their visions of a new Peru. Arguedas's final and autobiographical novel, *El zorro de arriba y el zorro de abajo* (1971) contains numerous references to his friendship with Gustavo. Many credit their meeting as the source of Arguedas's changed views and positive appraisal of the role of Christianity in the Andean world.

Personally tormented by the changes and contradictions in Peruvian society of the late 1960s, Arguedas discovered, in the stark reality of Chimbote's steel mills and fishmeal factories, that his old ideal of nationhood based on a common Andean culture was perhaps flawed and unrealistic. From reading *El zorro de arriba y el zorro de abajo* Gustavo concludes that "it is obvious that ethnic identity loses ground to the progressive affirmation of class identity."[19]

Still, the Andean inhabitants he knew in Chimbote retained a sense of their identity managing to remain untainted and uncorrupted by the dehumanizing influences around them. Gustavo suggests that Arguedas was on the verge of expanding his notion of the myth of the common person, especially in the portrait he draws of Esteban de la Cruz, a transplanted Aymara fisherman. Before settling in Chimbote, Cruz had traversed the entire expanse of Peru and exposed himself to the problematic of a disarticulated country. Cruz emerges in the novel as the embodiment of Arguedas's revised historical myth, the common person as epic figure who remains anchored in the historical memory of a people. Significantly, Cruz also discovers common cause and an identification with the other exploited fisherfolk and factory workers in the human amalgam that is Chimbote.

In his short essay on Arguedas entitled "Entre las calandrias" [Between the Larks] Gustavo draws attention to the dialogue where Cruz, in his badly pronounced and ungrammatical Spanish, paraphrases quotes from Isaiah 41 and 65, announcing "new heavens and new earths." Cruz and others of similar backgrounds of struggle, hard work, and adversity represent the *calandrias*, and symbolize the two sides of the character of the Andean people in Arguedas's symbolic universe. One lark's song is a consoling melody that strengthens persons in their ties to the land and community, and prepares them for a new existence in a changed reality. But this lark's soothing song can lull one into a false sense of security, complacency, and a fatalistic outlook toward an uncertain future. In keeping alive the people's connection to the land and their Andean cultural traditions, the *calandria consoladora* awaits the song of the *calandria de fuego*, who symbolizes struggle and ultimate liberation after centuries of exploitation. This lark, according to Gustavo, holds the promise of opening up another cycle in Peruvian history where the faces of the new and old Peru converge to create a new synthesis.[20]

The encounter between the two larks will give birth not only to a new national identity based on the alliance of oppressed peoples in Peru, but to what Arguedas calls, *la fraternidad de los miserables*, a worldwide alliance of all exploited peoples. The meeting place of the two larks is the world of Esteban de la Cruz and that place of encounter becomes the site of a new revelation and image of God as the one who enters into reintegration as a liberating force in human history. God is reintegrated into the life of the poor who "feel God's presence in a different way."[21] Those who announce this new image of God are the epic characters like Esteban de la Cruz, Mariátegui's "morning person" reborn, the new men and women of Peru "without whom there is no authentic historical transformation."[22]

THE STRUGGLE FOR LAND AS HEROIC CREATION

Not only has Gustavo validated the insights of Las Casas, Mariátegui, and Arguedas on an intellectual level, but in the concrete accompaniment of church pastoral workers throughout Peru and Latin America he discovers anew their relevance for the present-day situation. One particular case within Peru illustrates well how Gustavo puts into practice his advice "to drink from one's own well."

In the southern Andes region of Peru encompassing the departments of Cusco and Puno and home to over two million Aymara- and Quechua-speaking campesinos, the church has adopted a unique approach to evangelization. Along with a sensitivity and appreciation for the cultural-religious values embodied in these peoples, the church in the past twenty years has repeatedly denounced the situation of extreme poverty and social injustice that marks life in this area of Peru. By their "spiritual and physical nearness to the poor" the bishops and pastoral agents of the four dioceses and prelatures actualize what Mariátegui and Arguedas continually emphasized in their writings—namely, the protagonist role of the poor as historical subjects in the transformation of Peruvian society. What underlines this particular appropriation of the Mariátegui-Arguedas tradition is a conviction that if Peru is ever to achieve national integration it must incorporate the values, traditions, and creativity of its previously marginated Andean peoples.

Gustavo's relationship with the southern Andes dates back to the early 1970s. There in that context he has witnessed to the originality and creativity of the Peruvian experience in terms of an evangelization project that takes as its starting point a people that is both "believing and exploited." Within that double condition are found the potentialities to overcome oppression and the elements on which to begin to construct a new society. Through various church programs the people have begun to exercise a participatory role in both church and society, a role that has helped in forming a vibrant popular movement composed of campesino organizations and produced mass mobilization to protest the prevailing conditions of structural injustice.

Moreover, the evangelization project in the southern Andes is in direct continuity with the missionary theory and praxis first espoused by Las Casas and his followers insofar as it advocates the people's perspective and recognition of its "evangelizing potential." Experiences of evangelization that integrate inculturation with the struggle for liberation like that of the southern Andes have shaped Gustavo's theological development in profound and lasting ways. Thus, as Juan Luis Segundo notes, Gustavo and other liberation theologians espouse a second variety of liberation theology where "the process of becoming the 'other' in the church occupies the theological position that the social sciences and their instrumentality for deideologization held in the first variety."[23] One distinguishing mark of this second current within liberation theology is its favorable evaluation of the role of popular religion, a position Segundo finds difficult to accept as valid grounds for doing theology.

Throughout the past twenty years one of the concrete mediations for this evangelization project has been the people's sustained struggle to regain their ancestral lands. Since the conquest, and in every subsequent period of Peruvian history, the indigenous campesinos suffered the loss of wide extensions of arable lands at the hands of landed gentry and local power elites, often with the silent complicity of the church. From 1880 through the 1920s Cusco and Puno were the scene of hundreds of popular rebellions as campesino communities supported by proindigenous intellectual movements demonstrated their resistance against further encroachment by avaricious *latifundistas*. These rebellions set the stage for a more organized popular campesino movement in the 1960s and 1970s.

The ambitious land reform program initiated by Peru's left-leaning military government in 1969 failed to redress the age-old problem of unequal land distribution that Mariátegui in the 1920s cited as the major obstacle to the achievement of national integration. Instead of redistributing land to the dispossessed campesino communities, the land reform program consolidated the expropriated lands into newly organized government estates, which excluded the people from direct participation in decisions affecting distribution. As a result of this failed experiment and the unfulfilled expectations it raised, campesino communities, with the support of the church, began to organize federations and labor unions to press their claims for lands incorporated into the government estates. When the organizations and communities exhausted all legal and administrative channels in Puno to recover their lands, the only recourse was to carry out a mass mobilization to invade the government estates in late 1985. This movement momentarily succeeded in pressuring the García government to initiate legislation for a restructuration of the estates, but progress has been slow and government officials adopt stalling tactics. Meanwhile, the communities and organizations continue to press their claims in a tense and conflictive context.

Throughout this most recent struggle to recover land, the southern Andes church, by virtue of its particular exercise of the option for the poor and a long history of insertion into the life of campesino communities, took an activist role in pressing the people's claims for land restructuration. Government officials quickly branded the bishops and pastoral agents as the "intellectual authors" of the land invasions. Besides the justice issue, the church bases its support for the movement on a theological reflection that land in the Andean cosmovision is more than a mere economic factor. Rather, it plays a highly symbolic and ritualistic role in forging the people's identity. Numerous church documents over the past twenty years attest to the relationship between the struggle for land and the faith praxis of the Aymara and Quechua peoples. The culmination of this pastoral-theological reflection is a landmark document published in the midst of the 1985–1986 land struggles entitled, *La tierra: Don de Dios, Derecho del Pueblo* [The land: God's gift, the people's right].[24]

Many of the theological warrants that underpin the document were introduced by Gustavo over the years during workshops and courses given to pastoral workers and campesinos. Chief among these warrants is the recognition of the people's right to full participation in church and society. The land struggles, as claims for economic justice and cultural self-determination, are seen as privileged moments in the evangelization project where the Andean people evangelize the rest of humanity to inherent values often overlooked in the church's theological reflection and social teaching. Considering the length and depth of Gustavo's involvement in promoting this accompaniment of the people and his subsequent theological reflection on land, John Cort's recent remarks merit an immediate rebuttal:

> I suggest that liberation theologians including Gutiérrez are doing precisely the kind of thing they accuse the European theologians of doing. They are imposing the European abstractions, or conclusions, of Karl Marx onto the Latin American peasant whose actual praxis cries out for his own land and by no means wants to be submerged in some collective farm owned and operated by the state, exchanging one landlord for another who is even more powerful and impersonal.[25]

Obviously, judging by these remarks, Cort knows little or nothing about Gustavo's involvement in questions relating to the Peruvian campesino. Otherwise, he would have discovered that Gustavo consistently has repudiated any form of collectivization in affirming the struggle for land as a legitimate life issue with roots in the Jewish and Christian scriptures.

Because of the southern Andes church's uncompromising position in favor of the people's right to land, Puno's campesino communities have thus far avoided the violent and authoritarian option advocated by *Sendero Luminoso*. For its part this church, with a liberation perspective on questions like the right to land, promotes democratic and peaceful alternatives to prevent the further spread of violence. Above and beyond any church intervention, however, is the dynamic faith praxis of the Andean peoples that validate struggle for land.

When Gustavo, by virtue of his experience and involvement in places like the southern Andes, employs expressions like the "irruption of the poor in history," he evokes the spirit of Las Casas, Mariátegui, and Arguedas. His journey to the southern Andes is, in a sense, a mission to retrace Arguedas's steps back to *el Perú profundo* where the church's liberating style of evangelization and "heroic creation" actualizes the vision of Mariátegui and Arguedas. At the same time, he challenges the church to intensify its insertion into the life of the campesino communities not to exercise any kind of elite domination, but to call them forth to identify with the plight of oppressed peoples around the globe and to exercise their rightful role in creating a new vision of church in a new and transformed society.

The future of liberation theology hinges precisely on the achievement of these kinds of connections. Its future agenda will be set in places like the southern Andes and elsewhere in Latin America where persons still "die before their time." In those peripheral settings we witness to a historical reversal of no small proportions when the poor, the "uninvited ones" of the gospel parable of the banquet, convoke the church back to its humble beginnings. There Gustavo and others who share his vision discover the same kind of hope expressed by the Colombian novelist and Nobel laureate, Gabriel García Márquez, in "a new and sweeping kind of utopia of life, where no one can decide on behalf of others how they will die, where truly there exists the possibility for love and happiness, and where the masses condemned to one hundred years of solitude may finally and forever have a second opportunity on earth."[26]

NOTES

1. *Informe sobre el caso de los penales*, December 1987. The Investigation Commission of the Peruvian Parliament was headed by Senator Rolando Ames. The commission's report is popularly known as the *Informe Ames*.

2. Gustavo Gutiérrez, "Aún es tiempo," *La República*, June 24, 1986.

3. Fernando Rospigliosi, "La democracia peruana: en defensa del futuro," newspaper report on the forum sponsored by the Instituto de Estudios Peruanos, *La República*, July 20, 1986.

4. Intervention by Gustavo Gutiérrez at the same forum.

5. Jorge Basadre, *Peru: problema y posibilidad*, fourth edition (Lima: Consorcio Técnico de Editores, 1984).

6. José María Arguedas, discourse upon receiving the literary award, Inca Garcilaso de la Vega, Arequipa, Peru, October 1968.

7. Alberto Flores Galindo, "Generación del '68: ilusión y realidad," *Margenes: encuentro y debate*, no. 1 (March 1987), p. 112.

8. Gustavo Gutiérrez, *Hablar de Dios desde el sufrimiento del inocente: una reflexión sobre el libro de Job* (Lima: C.E.P., 1986), p. 19; Eng. trans. *On Job: God Talk and the Suffering of the Innocent* (Maryknoll, N.Y.: Orbis, 1987). In many of Gutiérrez's works there are references to this phrase which originated in Bartolomé de Las Casas's *Rules for Confessors* (*El confesionario*).

9. Gustavo Gutiérrez, *The Power of the Poor in History* (Maryknoll, N.Y.: Orbis, 1982), p. 196.

10. *Puebla: The Final Document in Puebla and Beyond*, John Eagleson and Philip Scharper, eds. (Maryknoll, N.Y.: Orbis, 1969), paragraph 1147.

11. Frederick Pike, "Religion, Collectivism, and Intrahistory: The Peruvian Ideal of Dependence," *Journal of Latin American Studies*, 10 (1977) 250.

12. Ibid.

13. Tokihiro Kudo, *Hacia una cultura nacional popular* (Lima: DESCO, 1982), p. 101.

14. Luis Peirano, "Entrevista con Gustavo Gutiérrez," *Quehacer*, 3 (Jan.–Feb. 1980) 114.

15. José Carlos Mariátegui, "El hombre y el mito," *El alma matinal y otras estaciones del hombre de hoy* (Lima: Empresa Editora Amauta, 1985), pp. 23–29.

16. Gutiérrez, *The Power of the Poor in History*, p. 201.

17. Arguedas, discourse (n. 6, above).

18. Ariel Dorfman, "José María Arguedas y Mario Vargas Llosa: dos visiones de una sola América," Helmy F. Giacoman and José Miguel Oviedo, eds., *Homenaje a Mario Vargas Llosa* (New York: Las Américas, 1971), p. 152.

19. Gustavo Gutiérrez, "Entre las calandrias," in Pedro Trigo, *Arguedas: mito, historia y religión* (Lima: C.E.P., 1982), p. 251.

20. Ibid., p. 254.

21. Ibid., p. 263.

22. Ibid.

23. Juan Luis Segundo, "The Shift in Latin American Theology," lecture, Regis College, Toronto, March 22, 1983, p. 11.

24. *La Tierra: Don de Dios, Derecho del Pueblo*, documents of the Instituto de Pastoral Andina, Cusco, Peru, March 30, 1986.

25. John Cort, "Examining Liberation Theology: Christians and the Class Struggle," *Commonweal* (July 1986), p. 402.

26. Gabriel García Márquez, "La soledad de América Latina," text of the discourse on receiving the Nobel prize for literature, 1982, published in *Socialismo y Participación*, 21 (1983) 152.

14

In Honor of Gustavo Gutiérrez

PENNY LERNOUX

The first time I read Gustavo Gutiérrez's *A Theology of Liberation* was during Christmas 1977, just after the birth of my daughter. And I have always associated the book with birth and hope—the birth of the infant Jesus and the arrival of my own child, after many years of hoping; and the growth of a new faith among the Latin American poor in which the central vision is the hope of the resurrection, not defeat by death on the cross.

All birth is wondrous, but the emergence of such faith seems to me nothing less than miraculous. Latin American Catholicism, as I remember it in the early 1960s, was a narrow, stifling religion that encouraged fatalism. Rituals were somber, joyless; effigies spoke only of suffering and death—statues with multiple wounds, paintings of a profusely bleeding Christ, a weeping virgin Mary. If there was light, the Latin Americans did not perceive it. The poor believed it was God's will that they be downtrodden, for so they had been taught for centuries. "I'm a nothing"—a phrase heard frequently among the poor—summarized the widespread feeling of cultural and religious inferiority.

Consequently, when the Latin American bishops at their hemisphere meeting in Medellín in 1968 announced a preferential option for the poor, many were amazed and incredulous. Even before the Second Vatican Council in the early 1960s, changes had been occurring in some Latin American churches, notably those of Brazil, Chile, and Peru, but they were limited primarily to the middle classes. Similarly, Vatican II did not impact Latin America at the time of the council because it was seen as a European and hence middle-class event. Nevertheless, seeds had been planted among a small but influential group of Latin American bishops, such as Brazil's Dom Helder Câmara; the Chilean bishop, Manuel Larraín; and Cardinal Juan Landázuri Ricketts, the archbishop of Lima, as well as among young Latin American theologians studying in Europe, including Gutiérrez.

Vatican II produced numerous and far-reaching reforms, but perhaps the most important for future developments in Latin America was the redefinition of the church as a community of believers—the "people of God." The expression conveyed the biblical image of the Hebrew people in exodus, and for the church of Vatican II it symbolized a community on the move in search of a deeper understanding of faith. When translated into Spanish and Portuguese, however, "people of God" took on an even deeper meaning, for it became *Pueblo* or *Povo de Dios* — and *pueblo* has always been understood as the masses, the poor.

It was from this particular social location — *el pueblo* — that Gutiérrez and other Latin American theologians developed their original vision: a theology grounded in the reality of poverty. And it was this vision that prevailed at the Medellín Conference, particularly in the documents on justice and peace, which Gutiérrez helped write as an official *peritus* at the meeting.[1]

Like all others, theologians are a product of their environment. Most of them work in intellectual centers removed from the strivings and hardships of ordinary persons, and this is reflected in the sometimes esoteric quality of their writings. The first generation of liberation theologians was trained in such environments, primarily in Germany, France, and Belgium, but on their return to Latin America they found the real world in the slums and rural villages. So they put away their books in French and German, and began to learn a new theology based on the experience of the impoverished masses. This was no academic exercise but an awakening that came from actually living with the poor — being exposed to the hunger, smells, noises, and sickness that comprise the daily struggle for survival in an overcrowded Third World slum.

Gutiérrez, for example, began to compare the reality of the poor neighborhood where he lived in Lima with what he had learned in middle-class Europe, and found that the two worlds were as remote as different planets. His analysis of the causes of poverty and injustice in Latin America would have added little to the debate — the statistics of misery were well known — had he written as a social scientist, but Gutiérrez was a priest who felt passionately about the suffering he experienced in Lima's slums. He therefore focused on the religious dimensions of the issue, producing a new understanding of faith, truth, and grace from the perspective of the Latin American poor.

Looking at Peru's history, which was typical of Latin America's tragedy, he rejected the trickle-down theory of development that the United States had tried to sell the Latin Americans through the Alliance for Progress. It had not worked and would not work, Gutiérrez concluded, because the majority would continue in bondage to the rich. The only answer was economic and political liberation from a neo-colonial relationship with the United States and Europe and from internal structures of oppression. The basis for his analysis of liberation was not Marxist revolution but the exodus and Christ's good news to the poor of freedom and oppression. Therein lay its originality, for in the framework of Catholic Latin America the God of the exodus and the Christ of the poor were much more radical than the unintelligible dialectics of Marxist intellectuals.

Gutiérrez also reinterpreted classic doctrines of sin to include the sins of societies as, for example, the U.S. behavior toward Latin America and that of the Peruvian oligarchy toward the country's campesinos. It was not enough to seek liberation from personal sin, he argued, for faith also meant a commitment to work for social justice. Conversion demanded society's transformation, not just a change of heart.

The call to change unjust structures was clearly political, but then the Latin American church had always been political. Originally it had been the proselytizing arm of the Spanish empire, the Inquisition being its CIA. It took Spain's part in the wars of independence and afterward allied itself with the most reactionary

78

elements among the Latin American elites. Gutiérrez wanted the church to change sides; neutrality was impossible, he said, because of the church's historical influence in Latin America. Silence was also a political statement in support of the status quo.

Although it was not yet known as liberation theology, Gutiérrez's ideas received official sanction from the bishops' meeting at Medellín. Three years later his classic work, *A Theology of Liberation*, appeared, giving the new theology a name and winning worldwide attention as one of the most influential works of the period.

If there is a single message in Gutiérrez's book it is that God has historically been on the side of the poor. And it was this message that the impoverished masses gleaned from the bishops' declarations at Medellín—at first disbelieving, only gradually comprehending that poverty and repression were not foreordained by God but the result of man-made structures that could be changed.

In a culture imbued with Catholicism, such a message was political dynamite. Most poor Latin Americans had never heard of Marx or Lenin; many do not know the name of the president of their country. But most believe in God, and many families have a Bible, even if they cannot read it.

Many soon learned to do so through church-sponsored literacy classes, using the Bible as a primer and the adult literacy techniques of the Brazilian educational philosopher Paulo Freire, which teach the poor to understand their reality and the reasons for their oppression. In contrast to traditional rote catechism classes, the Bible readings emphasize the themes developed by liberation theology, showing the people that God has repeatedly taken the side of the humble and powerless.

Such education led to the creation of Christian base communities, in which small groups (20 to 30 families) of impoverished peasants or slum dwellers meet regularly, particularly in areas with a shortage of priests, to reflect on what it means to be a poor Christian in Latin America. In many parts of Latin America the communities have developed into local versions of the early New England town hall meetings. For the first time in their lives, persons are able to express themselves freely and without fear, and to take common action to alleviate their suffering—for example, through the construction of a health clinic or a road.

By the mid-1970s, when base communities had spread throughout Latin America, it had become clear to the upper classes and the military that they were a threat to their entrenched privileges. At the time, most of Latin America was under the boot of military dictatorships, and these regimes were determined to wipe out all dissent. They were able to destroy political parties, labor unions, a free press, and other opposition, but they failed to stop the growth of the base communities, because the institutional church gave them its protection. Hundreds of priests and nuns, and even some bishops, were threatened, arrested, tortured, murdered, or exiled, yet the church stood firm. Because of the church's institutional power—most dictators were Catholics, as well as 90 percent of the population—the military regimes did not close the churches, and the churches, particularly the base communities, became surrogates for democracy.

The experience of the 1970s, when tens of thousands of persons were assassinated or "disappeared" and when the poor became even poorer, indelibly marked the Latin American church. The Medellín documents had shown intellectual and pastoral vision, but only in the 1970s did the institution really become a church of the poor, through its suffering with and on behalf of the victims of repression. In such countries as Brazil the church's call for democracy in secular society was echoed in the church itself, which became more pluralistic, open, and dedicated to the priorities of the poor, such as agrarian reform and a more equal distribution of national wealth. At the start of the base community movement the Brazilian bishops had seen the communities as a means of converting the poor, but by the end of the 1970s the poor had converted the Brazilian church.

That conversion has given the church unprecedented influence in Brazil. For example, in the 1960s two-thirds of the Catholic university students polled in Rio de Janeiro called themselves "atheist" because the church "is on the side of an order that is unjust and antipeople." By 1978 three-quarters of the students declared themselves "believers" because the church had become the voice of the voiceless. Slum dwellers expressed similar feelings. "In 1978, seeing that the church was helping the people, I began to participate again," said a lapsed Catholic who is active in a popular movement. "It wasn't that I stayed away from the church for all those years, but rather the church that stayed away from the people."[2]

Although Brazil's church is more advanced than others in the region in its institutional commitment to a "people of God," bishops in other countries have also worked toward that vision, sometimes at the cost of their lives, as shown by the martyrdom of El Salvador's Archbishop Oscar Romero and Argentina's Bishop Enrique Angelelli, both assassinated by right-wing death squads. Indicative of such commitment was the regional meeting of bishops in Puebla, Mexico, in 1979, which not only reaffirmed Medellín but went beyond it by singling out the base communities as a model for the future and by making a more realistic assessment of the many obstacles that stand in the way of political and economic change.

Religious who work with the poor in Latin America often observe that they will not live to see the fruit of the seeds they are planting, for change in Latin America, Archbishop Câmara once noted, is measured in centuries. Twenty years of work having produced approximately 300,000 base communities—not much perhaps for the effort and blood expended—yet as pointed out by the Swiss Catholic writer Walbert Bühlmann, the miracle is that a seed should have been planted at all.[3]

Although the base communities are small in number relative to the total population, political scientists argue that the religious empowerment brought about by the communities is among the most significant political developments in Latin America in recent decades. The communities are primarily concerned with prayer, but because of their reflective reading of the Bible, and the application of such readings to their own reality, they have developed a new faith in themselves. The communal solidarity fostered by the communities and the living out of faith in daily life have had a multiplier effect on many slum neighborhoods and rural villages, where community members have been instrumental in the formation of other organizations, such as amateur drama groups, women's clubs, labor unions, and peasant federations. For the first time in the region's history, intermediate groups of poor persons have emerged to seek reforms at the local, regional, and national level. Unlike mass organizations manipulated by traditional politicians and populists, these groups are genuinely representative of and responsive to the poor.[4]

Indicative of the potential of such groups is the experience of Salvador, a sprawling slum in the sterile desert surrounding Lima. Salvador was founded in 1971 after the military government forced residents from the overcrowded inner city slums to what are euphemistically known as "young towns"—that is, outlying slums. The left-of-center regime was not a typical Latin American dictatorship, however, for it broke the stranglehold of the Peruvian oligarchy through a sweeping agrarian reform and labor reforms that enabled workers a share in the profits and ownership of industries. The regime also promoted grassroots organizations that became the seeds of self-government in the "young towns" and elsewhere. Although many of the reforms were halted after a takeover by more traditional generals in the second phase of the military government, the Peruvian church continued to carry the banner for social justice. Strongly influenced by Gutiérrez's ideas, it took the lead among the Latin American churches in upholding the preferential option for the poor in the years immediately following Medellín. In the first episcopal assembly after Medellín, for example, the bishops announced that the Peruvian church would look for ways and means of living out evangelical poverty, in order to become the "sacrament of union of the people with God and of the people among themselves." All social reforms, they said, should promote the idea of "elevating the way of being a human person" and of "announcing the liberation of the oppressed." To attain that goal, they proposed to encourage conscientization among the poor and to help them create new social structures that would fulfill the needs and aspirations of the people.[5]

Consequently, church persons were present from the time of Salvador's founding, including a group of teachers led by Salvador's current mayor, Michel Azcueta, a soft-spoken Spaniard who has worked for more than two decades with the Peruvian poor. The slum's first school, "Fe y Alegría," was constructed with church help, and socially concerned priests, nuns, and lay persons played a key role in the population's growing conscientization and in the promotion of base communities. "The church realized from the beginning that it had to become involved and accompany the people on their journey," said a teacher working with the Teresian Institute, one of several church groups active in the area.[6]

Early on, the people adopted a slogan: "Because we have nothing, we will make everything." They did so in the face of overwhelming odds, including widespread poverty and unemployment as well as the sterile site itself. Today the "young town" of 400,000 boasts several schools, in addition to popular libraries, a weekly newspaper, a radio station, four churches, and the beginnings of an industrial park. Many of the older homes have brick and cement walls instead of the flimsy reed mats used in the original construction. Even the poorest sections are shaded by trees in spite of the scarcity of water in the surrounding desert. The women, who lug cans of water from a distant well, first use the water for cooking, then recycle it for washing. Whatever remains of the dirty liquid is thrown on the saplings, which miraculously thrive.

The people's accomplishments reflect Salvador's block-by-block organization in which communal work is shared—for example, through neighborhood soup kitchens or Sunday morning building activities, such as the repair of a roof. Each neighborhood elects representatives to Salvador's local government, which holds regular assemblies to discuss problems of concern to the people, such as running water and road construction. Paralleling this civic structure is a network of base communities whose elected lay leaders set pastoral priorities. Like Salvador's schools, which encourage self-reliance and democracy, the communities are charged with preparing their children for First Communion and other important rites.

Building together has deepened the people's faith commitment; it has also made

81

Salvador one of the most politically effective neighborhoods in Lima. For example, Salvador has had electricity since 1975, but the nearby slum of Tablada, which is older than Salvador, obtained electricity only in 1983. Some of the most active lay leaders, such as Azcueta, have become involved in local politics through election to municipal office or have taken an important role in the development of labor unions. Such slum movements serve as a counterweight to the right-wing military and their allies in the upper classes as well as to the viciousness of the *Sendero Luminoso* guerrillas.

While the movement's main contribution is political, it is politics with a difference because, as Azcueta observed, religious values challenge the system. "I think one begins to change," he said, "when one goes back to the Gospels and discovers a small but very important difference. When one says that it is necessary to help the poor, I think everybody accepts that. But often we hide the causes of poverty — it's easy to say that someone is poor because he is lazy or a drunkard or squanders his money. But when one decides to serve the exploited, that's when it becomes clear that poverty just doesn't happen and that there are reasons for it. That's when a political commitment arises, but it's a commitment that originates in faith itself."[7]

As in Brazil, where the commitment to the poor converted the church, the experience of the Peruvian church in places like Salvador has had a profound effect on the institution. "The church of Peru has been revitalized because of its social commitment," said Bishop José Dammert Bellido. "Many Christians, lay persons as well as priests, have discovered a richness of the Gospels that perhaps before had been ignored because of merely spiritualist or ritualistic actions." For that, said Dammert, the church owes a debt of gratitude to Gustavo Gutiérrez, who "was the first Peruvian to make a contribution to Catholic theology. Before, we had some good imitators of European theological formulas, but it is now recognized that Gutiérrez contributed to something native." And it is the native — "the eruption of the poor onto the world scene," as another Peruvian bishop put it — that has proved both a gift and challenge to First World Christianity.[8]

Phillip Berryman, a popular American religious writer, points out that liberation theology was the herald of a large movement "of the excluded — women, nonwhites, the poor — onto the stage of history."[9] Just as women are asserting a new role in First World societies, Third World peoples seek their own cultural and political identification. The imperial powers, the United States and the Soviet Union, face a cultural explosion that promises to fragment spheres of influence, making the imposition of a single political, economic, or religious model more difficult. But that is also true of a centralized Roman order. Despite attempts to restore the old ways, such efforts are doomed, not only by the changes brought about by Vatican II but also by the demographic shift in Catholicism. With 907 million members, Catholicism now ranks as the world's largest religion. At home in every continent, it is culturally and ethnically more diverse than at any other time in its history. But if it were given a face, its color would not be white: more than half the Catholic population lives in the Third World. By the end of the century the figure will rise to 70 percent, with Latin America accounting for the largest number. Such a far-reaching change has occurred only once before in Christianity, wrote the late Jesuit theologian Karl Rahner — in the first century, when the primitive church, under the Apostle Paul, opened itself to the diverse cultures of the ancient world.[10]

Gutiérrez's gift was to announce this conversion and to give us a glimpse of the spirituality and community found among God's chosen—the poor. The experience of such poverty and the struggle with and for the Latin American poor "is our well," he says of the liberation theologians.[11] It is also a well for us to drink from in the First World—so rich in material goods but so barren in the humanity and solidarity that characterize daily life in the slums and villages of the Third World. Yet seeds have also begun to sprout here and there in the United States, just as they did in Latin America after Medellín. In such promise lies the fulfillment of the "people of God."

NOTES

1. *Medellín Conclusiones* (Bogotá: Secretariado general del CELAM, 1973).

2. Tarcisco Beal, "Brazil's New Church: Revolution and Reaction" (unpublished paper), n.d.; Scott Mainwaring, "Brazil: The Catholic Church and the Popular Movement in Nova Iguacu, 1974–1985," in *Religion and Political Conflict in Latin America* (Chapel Hill: University of North Carolina Press, 1986), pp. 124–55; author's interviews, São Paulo, Nov. 1984.

3. Walbert Bühlmann, *The Church of the Future* (Maryknoll, N.Y.: Orbis, 1986), pp. 26, 89–100.

4. On the political significance of religious empowerment by the base communities, see, for example, Daniel Levine, "Religion and Politics: Drawing Lines, Understanding Change," *Latin American Research Review*, 20/1 (1985) 185–200; Maria Helena Moreira Alves, "Grassroots Organizations, Trade Unions, and the Church," *IDOC Bulletin*, (Rome), 16/4 (Aug. 1985); Jane Kramer, "Letter from the Elysian Fields," *The New Yorker*, March 2, 1987; *Religion and Political Conflict in Latin America*, ibid.; José Marins and Teolide M. Trevisan, *Comunidades Eclesiales de Base* (Bogotá: Ediciones Paulinas, 1975); *Uma Igreja que Nasce do Povo* (summarizing the results of the first national meeting of base communities in Brazil) (Petrópolis: Vozes, 1975); Paul Singer and Vinicius Caldeira Brant, *O Povo em Movimento* (Petrópolis: Vozes, 1982); Frei Betto, *O Que e Comunidade Eclesial de Base* (São Paulo: Editora Brasiliense, 1981); idem, *CEBS, Rumo á Nova Sociedade* (São Paulo: Ediçioes Paulinas, 1983); Domingos Barbé, *Fé e Ação* (São Paulo: Ediçoes Loyola, 1980); and the Rev. Joseph G. Healey, "Comunidades Cristianas de Base," *Latin American/North American Church Concerns*, Monograph no. 1, Institute for Pastoral and Social Ministry, n.d.

5. Bishop Alban Quinn, "The Church and the Option for the Poor in Peru" (London: Catholic Institute for International Relations, 1982), p. 13.

6. *Vida Nueva* (Madrid), Nov. 7, 1987.

7. Ibid.

8. Interview by Mario Campos with Bishop José Dammert Bellido, *La República* (Lima), Sept. 9, 1984; Quinn, "The Church."

9. Phillip Berryman, *Liberation Theology* (New York: Pantheon, 1986), p. 215.

10. *Newsweek*, Dec. 9, 1985; *America*, June 13, 1987.

11. Robert McAfee Brown, "Drinking From Our Own Wells," *The Christian Century*, May 9, 1984.

15

Gustavo Gutiérrez,
the Person and the Message:
Memories of an Encounter

TERESA OKURE, SHCJ

In December 1986 I attended for the first time in Mexico, as a brand new member, the Second General Assembly of the Ecumenical Association of Third World Theologians (EATWOT).[1] During the first days of the assembly, expectation rose high as word went round the group that Gutiérrez would be coming; he would be coming with Leonardo Boff. This for me was a really good piece of news. I had never met Gutiérrez before, never read any of his works. Yet somehow, I had got to know that he was reputedly the leading liberation theologian in Latin America, and indeed in the whole world, also one of the living, dynamic inspirations behind EATWOT.

That I had never read any of Gutiérrez's works was not really surprising. I had just then completed seven years of biblical studies at Fordham University and the Ecole Biblique, Jerusalem. As is well known, the liberation theology approach had not yet penetrated to any great extent the mainstream of biblical scholarship in this century. Rather, scholarship had been dominated by the historico-critical method, with focus on discovering how the extant texts came to be put together by a given author (redaction criticism), what sources the author used (source criticism), and what influences an author might have been subject to from contemporary religious and philosophical movements of the time (*Religionsgeschichte*). Concern with what life-giving, liberating, and challenging message the biblical texts might hold for flesh and blood Christians today in their respective concrete socio-cultural and political life situations has largely been relegated to the periphery, if at all it has found a place in scholarship. The kind of approach applied by Gutiérrez in his study of Job is in many respects quite a novelty in the field.[2]

As I looked forward that December to Gutiérrez's arrival, I tried to form a mental picture of him based on the traditional image of a great scholar. I saw him as a tall, imposing character, of an aloof mien and reserved bearing, one who looked in every respect the world theologian that he was reputed to be. I wondered too what his voice sounded like, and thanked God that it would not be long before my curiosity on these scores was satisfied.

Then came the long-awaited moment. We were at a plenary session. Suddenly
there was a flutter at the back of the hall—the usual latecomers, I thought. But I
noticed that heads turned round more than was usual on such occasions, and faces
beamed with broad smiles. A new arrival, perhaps. It never crossed my mind that
it might be Gutiérrez; a person of his standing would not arrive that unobtrusively
by the back door. As I was trying to figure out what exactly was happening at the
back of the hall, the chairperson of the session came to my rescue. He interrupted
the session to extend "a very warm welcome to our brothers Gutiérrez and Boff
who have just arrived." Goodness me, I thought, surprised that it had actually
happened that way. Then I too turned round as quickly as I could, expecting to see
my tall, distinguished-looking character. To my even greater surprise, he was not
there! It was not only his height, the true nature of which I later discovered. By
the time I turned round, both Gutiérrez and Boff were already quietly seated, lost
among the other participants as though nothing had happened. One had the impression that they were embarrassed that the session had to be disrupted on their
account. I had to bear my disappointment till the end of the session when I could
meet Gutiérrez in person. But that moment of shattered expectations left a deep
impression on me.

When I did meet him after the session, I discovered how thoroughly wrong my
mental picture of him had been. He reminded me more of Paul of the New Testament than of Saul of the Old Testament. When I discovered later still that he
was popularly known as "the little man," I felt what an appropriate designation of
him that was. Here indeed was an ordinary human being: humble, simple, very
much in touch with his context and on fire with love for Christ's poor as he met
them in that context. It was a most happy discovery.

These first impressions of Gutiérrez grew and deepened throughout the assembly
period. A photo taken on the day of outing when we went to meet the people of
Mexico and the land shows him walking alongside Boff, shielding his head from
the sun, as simple country people are wont to do, with the only cardigan I ever saw
him wear throughout the assembly. I recall, too, that at a session on the revision
of the constitution, when we were spending much time debating the order in which
the articles should be expressed in the final draft, Gutiérrez passionately asked the
assembly how such a protracted discussion was benefiting the poor in his country.
He had figured out that for every minute we spent there, we were paying seven
dollars. The intervention had the effect of bringing the discussion down to earth
and moving it forward. Strangely enough, though Gutiérrez made a number of
interventions during the sessions, the only one that I remember very distinctly is
that intervention about the benefit to the poor of our protracted discussions on the
constitution. My last cherished memory of him in Mexico came on the day of
elections. After I had been elected as the new executive secretary of the association,
Gutiérrez came to congratulate me personally and promised to send me copies of
his books published in English. Was I touched by such a magnanimous gesture!

Such in general was the nature of my first acquaintance with this great "little
man" and theologian whose sixtieth birthday anniversary we are now celebrating.
Permit me at this point to express my deepest gratitude to the Maryknoll School
of Theology and Orbis Books for making this celebration possible in this fitting
manner, and to wish our most beloved friend and brother a very happy birthday
and many happy returns.

My next series of contacts with Gutiérrez came through reading his works. I am not going to attempt to offer even a brief synthesis of the many salient features and creative, innovative, and challenging aspects of his approach to theology. His works speak powerfully for themselves; so do their many appreciative reviews. Rather, I want to highlight just three points, which are related to my first impressions of him in Mexico and which, in my view, hold an important message and challenge for us theologians today.

The first point that struck me in reading Gutiérrez's works and the biographical notes about him was the correspondence between his dominant theological focus and his personal lifestyle as I had witnessed it in Mexico. A criticism often leveled against modern biblical scholars and theologians is that most of them lack faith and do not live their theologies. This perhaps explains why "scientific" biblical and theological scholarship in this century has been predominantly dry and devoid of life, the fruit of an approach that sees the doing of theology primarily as an academic exercise rather than as a way of life and as an endeavor to promote and consolidate Christian living.[3] Gutiérrez, on the contrary, lives his theology. That his approach to doing theology is person-centered and life-centered is well known; that it is life-centered with specific reference to the poor in the concrete socio-political and economic context of Latin America is also well known. Indeed, this concern with and for the poor constitutes in any reckoning the operative fundamental and raison d'être of his doing theology; even a cursory acquaintance with any of his works will reveal this.[4] What is likely to be missed, however, is that Gutiérrez's commitment to or option for the poor is not done purely theologically, academically, but also by his manner of living. For me the greatest message and challenge of his pioneering approach to theology lies here, as something that liberates and empowers to live.

Concern for the poor is not, of course, unique to Gutiérrez. We live in an age that talks much about preferential option for the poor, especially since after Medellín (1968) and before Puebla (1979) the 1971 Synod of Bishops popularized the concept.[5] But often one feels that in many cases this concern for the poor is no more than a fad, lipservicelike. The poor remain a nameless, faceless, abstract entity to be discussed in seminars, theological treatises and conferences. Often the theologian lacks personal contact with the poor, and personal experience of what it means to be poor. The same cannot be said of Gutiérrez. I have already mentioned the impact that his simple lifestyle made on me in Mexico. I have since learned, too, that while teaching theology at the Catholic University of Lima, he lives in a barrio in Rimac, a slum area of Lima, and works with the people. Hence he not only conducts a theological reflection on the socio-political and economic plight of the poor in Latin America, he not only endeavors to provide a theological basis for their struggle for liberation and for life, but he also personally shares their life in concrete solidarity with them. This, surely, is a new way of doing theology; it is by no means an enviable one. For as Gutiérrez himself observes, those men and women who identify with the poor and dispossessed in their struggle for life are regarded as "intruders," troublemakers, and outsiders, "simply because they think—and, be it said, live—differently."[6]

If the designation "little man" fits Gutiérrez, it is not merely because of his height. Littleness and poverty can serve as the locus where God's power to sustain and foster life as pure gift becomes most efficaciously and irresistibly manifest. Gutiérrez's involvement with the poor constitutes, in my view, a concrete response to 2 Corinthians 8:9, which invites us to imitate the enriching poverty of Christ. As a renowned theologian and writer, Gutiérrez is indeed rich, materially rich. But he has opted to be poor with the poor of his nation and church so that out of his poverty God may continue to effectively enrich both the Latin American poor with the courage to live, and the universal church with a theology that liberates and frees to embrace the gospel as a program of action. Gutiérrez's option for the poor expressed by his own way of life is indeed an "option in behalf of life."[7]

The second point I wish to highlight flows from the first. It is this: that by choosing to live and work with the poor, Gutiérrez has cogently demonstrated that living persons can provide authentic inspiration for doing theology. Traditionally, theologians operate and are expected to operate from theological schools and institutions. The material for theological reflection is provided primarily by books in well-equipped libraries. The main purpose of the research seems to be to contribute to learning and knowledge by publishing books, which in turn serve as inspiration for other researchers. But often there is little or no serious effort to draw from real life experiences, one's own or those of others, the basic inspiration and purpose for theologizing. I may recall here the remark of an M.A. student during a colloquium on marriage at the Catholic Institute of West Africa, Nigeria, where I teach, to the effect that often canon lawyers and theologians write copiously on marriage and advise authoritatively on marriage, themselves unmarried in most cases. But they hardly ever take time to find out whether there is any relationship between their treatises on marriage and the way married life is actually being lived out.

Although there is nothing wrong with the acquisition of scientific theological knowledge, it needs to be borne in mind that only living human beings can appreciate such knowledge and give it value. In Jesus' view, true knowledge is that which gives life, eternal life (John 17:3); and we know that in Semitic mentality, to know is to personally experience and to order one's life accordingly. Hence from the Christian perspective a theological knowledge that is not related to life, and does not seek to enhance Christian/gospel living, raises serious questions about its usefulness and the value of the energy spent in acquiring it. Indeed, the lack of personal commitment to the gospel message, which characterizes many of our Christians today, has largely been blamed on the fact that for a long time theologians have ceased to write from the perspective of life, and for living. Most modern theologians, especially those from the Catholic fold, do not consider themselves pastors; it is beneath them. Neither do pastors consider themselves theologians; it is beyond them. And in a number of instances theological categories lack meaning for the contemporary reader.

The same, again, cannot be said of Gutiérrez. He himself testifies that his "*daily* contacts [italics mine] with the experiences of some," constitute one of the generative impulses for his doing a theology of liberation.[8] And again, with specific reference to his living/working contacts with the poor, he states:

Our experiences in the framework of commitment to the poor and oppressed of Latin America are sending us back to the fundamental ideas in the gospels. It could not be otherwise. These experiences are suggesting new approaches and raising new questions. But at the same time, the biblical message is challenging our experiences and shedding light on them.[9]

I agree wholeheartedly with him that "it could" indeed "not be otherwise." For this issue of doing theology from the framework of commitment to the poor reminds me that the gospels present Jesus as someone who was very much in touch with the life experiences of the poor in his country, those considered as "the rabble" by the leaders (John 7:49). He shared their life in complete solidarity with them and thereby uplifted their hope—they learned that being poor made them special to God and possessors of the kingdom (Luke 6:20).[10] Moreover, he drew from their daily experiences the imagery and concepts he needed for revealing to them the nature of the kingdom (sowing, fishing, lost coin, and sheep). He in turn taught them to see in their daily needs concrete expressions of the manner in which the kingdom operates in their lives (the need to drink water and eat food). Similarly, Paul drew upon the social standing of his converts (cf. 1 Cor. 1:26–31) and upon his own lifestyle (1 Cor. 9) to teach and challenge them to embrace wholeheartedly their call to the Christian way of living.

Concrete manifestations and needs may be different in each age and context, but the call to theologize from life and for living remains binding for all times and persons. Our God became a human being in order to teach us that we can experience divinity only in our humanity in its different life situations, not in a theological vacuum. This is so because the whole purpose of Jesus' mission, which authentic Christian theology must needs seek to understand and promote, is to enable persons to live life in all its fullness (John 10:10). It seems to me that this is what Gutiérrez has endeavored to do by personally sharing the life of the poor in Latin America and drawing from their experiences the inspiration for his theological reflections, which theological reflections in turn seek to empower the people to persevere in their struggle for liberation from oppression, dispossession, exploitation, and repression, in the light of the biblical message and gospel values. Here again, Gutiérrez's approach serves as a message and a challenge for all of us to do the same in our different contexts.[11]

The third point I wish to highlight concerns Gutiérrez's intense commitment to and extensive knowledge of the Latin American situation to which he belongs. It is not possible to read any length of his works without knowing that he is from Latin America and writes primarily for Latin Americans. A reader who is not from Latin America may at first feel alienated by this intense focus on this particular continent. But this may be because he or she has been brought up to see theology as something concerned uniquely with the "spiritual," the findings of which can apply to anyone, anywhere, at any time, for all human beings are seen as "souls" that need to be saved. Gutiérrez, on the contrary, believes that theology, to be effective, must be related to the concrete life situations of a concrete people. But this does not mean that such a theology lacks universal, ecclesial value. For though the particular experiences of the Latin American countries may lead to the development of "a new and different way of following Jesus," one that is "stamped with the religious outlook of an exploited and believing people," this emerging Latin American spirituality is "a collective, ecclesial spirituality" that does not lose "anything of its universal perspective."[12] This is because the "major themes of collective Christian experience in Latin America are those proper to Christian existence in its entirety."[13]

To my understanding, this means that focus on the Latin American situation is necessary if the gospel is to really address this situation. Therein lies its power to transform concretely. The same gospel can also address and transform situations that may be stamped by experiences different from those of the Latin American countries. So rather than alienate, the focus on the Latin American situation challenges the reader to know his or her own context, and discover ways in which the gospel wishes to address and transform this context. It is useful to recall, too, that Jesus never left Palestine, and that Paul addressed the specific problems of the communities he founded (Galatia, Corinth, Philippi, Thessalonika); yet neither the Gospels nor the Pauline Letters lose their universal appeal today because of their focus on the particular needs and situations of the historical peoples addressed. Hence, here as in the two points previously considered, Gutiérrez's approach to theology is, in the last analysis, biblically inspired, and holds a message for all who would do theology after the manner of Jesus.

This manner of doing theology accepts that human beings are not only flesh and blood, but flesh and blood shaped and conditioned by experiences of life in a well-defined cultural, social, political, geographical, economic, linguistic (and so on) environment. It accepts that each of these distinctive environments is positively willed by God as part and parcel of human existence, and so takes it seriously into account in the doing of theology. It accepts finally that not only human beings but the environments themselves need to be liberated from structural sin and restored to God in Christ (cf. 1 Cor. 15:25–28; Rom. 8:19–23). In short, the approach is inspired by and rests on the mysteries of creation, incarnation, and redemption fully understood.

These, then, are three of the salient features of Gutiérrez's approach to theology, which, in my view, hold an important message and challenge to the modern theologian of whatever race or culture — the challenge of authenticity, to personally live one's theology, the challenge to do a life-inspired and a life-oriented theology, and the challenge to know one's context thoroughly well and bring this context into the doing of theology so that the context itself can be transformed by the gospel message.

At this point the reader or listener may be eagerly wanting to ask or to know how all this applies within my own African context. This, therefore, seems an appropriate place for me at least to raise the issue, which is often asked — namely, why liberation theology has not taken root in Africa, except, perhaps, for the black theology of South Africa. I say "at least to raise the issue," because the topic is one that requires a book on its own. Here I can only sketch in broad strokes the diverse contours of the problem.

First, it is not true that liberation theology has not taken root in Africa. What is true is that this theology takes a different form in Africa — it is called inculturation, especially outside South Africa. What is true, too, is that the liberational struggle in Africa operates very differently from that in Latin America. The reasons for this are pretty obvious — and herein, perhaps, lies the most summative answer that can be given to the question — that the situation in Africa and the liberational concerns are very different from those in Latin America. Critics, therefore, who expect to find in Africa the same liberational theological approach that obtains in Latin America have only themselves to blame for their disappointment. If I have understood correctly what liberation theology is all about, it is that this theology is directed to specific needs of a specific people in a specific context in terms both of content and method. Gutiérrez, for instance, emphasizes the need for Latin Americans to reject or "cease to be consumers of spiritualities that are doubtless valid but that nonetheless reflect other experiences and other goals."[14] It would, therefore, be ironic to expect African theologians to buy wholesale the liberation theology that grew out of the Latin American experience and is designed to address that experience.

I say that the liberational struggle going on in Africa is different from that in Latin America. I say, too, that the situation in Africa in general is different from that in Latin America. Both statements are closely related. Let me try to flesh them out briefly. First, the liberational struggle in Africa: the fact is that Africa spent a greater part of this century fighting for liberation, even if not with theological tools. I am referring to the struggle for political, cultural, and anthropological freedom. Politically, the struggle has been won in most African states. Namibia is still struggling for political independence. In South Africa, the struggle is not so much for political freedom, but for racial and human recognition, for both the white oppressors and the black oppressed are citizens of the same country. As in the case of black minorities in the U.S.A., and the poor majority in Latin America, theology becomes a primary tool for liberation.

Secondly, Africa is fighting for socio-cultural and anthropological liberation. The damage inflicted on the African psyche by the colonial movement is well known. Not only was the living continent carved out like a cake to European nations, but Africans themselves were considered as less than human. Mveng refers to this as *pauvreté anthropologique* (best rendered "anthropological impoverishment").[15] Their cultural values were summarily dismissed as "bush" and "pagan." This left them with a very poor self-image and a very poor regard of their own values, which they were ashamed to own, and so left to die out. But Africans have, since independence, woken up to the fact that their cultural values were indeed very precious, and that, although they were made to throw away gold, they were left with mud in some cases. They know, too, that their humanity was created by God and lacks in nothing which other human beings have. Hence great energy is spent in reviving its cultural heritage before all is lost. In short, Africa needs to recover its own lost self and values before it knows what to do with that self. On the theological level, the effort to revive the rich African cultural heritage and marry this with the gospel message is called inculturation or incarnation.[16]

Now a word or two about the differences in the general situation between Africa and Latin America. From reading the works of Gutiérrez and other Latin American theologians, I get the impression that Latin America is largely monolithic with regard to religion (Christian, mostly Catholic), culture (a dominant culture of the rich and a dominated, oppressed culture of the poor), and politics (the ruling class of the few rich and the ruled class of the poor majority). The situation in Africa, however, is extremely complex. Take Nigeria as an example. The country alone has over three hundred ethnic groups with corresponding languages and cultures. On the religious level the country is blessed (or cursed, as some would say) by a multiplicity of Christian sects and denominations, a multiplicity of traditional religions, as well as academic and professional atheists.[17]

On the socio-political scene, the situation is equally complex. After twenty-five years of independence, the country has not yet found the type of governmental structure that can contain or mold its three hundred ethnic groups into a nation. In addition to the federal government system with its subsidiary state and local government structures, there are the traditional rulers and village heads. The massive dispossession of the poor (especially the Amerindians) of their land in Latin America finds no correspondence in Nigeria. In theory, the entire land is said to belong to the government; in practice, individuals own, build, and plant on their ancestral or newly purchased lands. In terms of concern for social justice, the country does not lack its critics, even if these are not professional theologians. I am thinking, for instance, of the musician, Fela, and the atheist, Tai Solarin. Recently, too, the federal military government of the Babangida regime has initiated and budgeted for a nationwide program known as MAMSER (Mass Mobilization for Social Justice, Self-Reliance, and Economic Recovery). Then there are the individuals, women and church groups, who show a special concern for the poor and the disabled. The media, too, are continually raising the awareness of the nation to the needs of the poor. The country is not yet divided between the few ruling rich and the majority ruled poor.

On the specifically Christian level, the church in Latin America is much older than that in Nigeria or sub-Saharan Africa, taken generally. The first meeting of the Latin American CELAM, for instance, took place in 1955. The first indigenous bishop of Anglophone West Africa, the present Cardinal Dominic Ekandem of Nigeria, was ordained barely a year before that, in 1954. In addition, the Latin American church has more trained theologians and theological institutions (an estimated forty-six Catholic universities), whereas Africa is only just beginning to think in terms of setting up its first theological institutions against great odds.[18]

This is not even a sketch, let alone an analysis, of the socio-cultural, political, economic, educational, and religious situation in Nigeria and Africa. The point I am trying to illustrate is simply this: the context in Africa is far more complex than that in Latin America, and this complexity in turn influences greatly the way theology is being done, or not, in the continent. In addition to this internal complexity, Africa has always been and is still being subjected to great foreign pressures and interferences on the political, economic, and religious spheres, perhaps more so than it has received help in these spheres. Furthermore, though Africa is clearly one of the richest continents in terms of natural resources and the cradle of the human race, it is still the poorest, the one treated with most contempt, and regarded as less than human by the rest of humanity. Apartheid thrives only in Africa. And not only must the continent survive the memory of the slave trade, of the carting out of its wealth in terms of human, mineral, and agricultural resources; not only must it cope with the continuous brain-drain of its illustrious sons and daughters and with such natural disasters as drought and flood with the resulting famine — it must now in the latest development fight against the most ignominious, contemptuous, and inhuman act of dumping toxic waste on its soil and borders.

Often the cry "poor Africa" rises from the lips of her children. Yet if it is true that the God of the Bible and of Jesus Christ has a special predilection for the poor and despised, those held in contempt and treated as less than human, then God must reserve the greatest predilection for Africa and Africans, not because of their merit, but because of the goodness of God. In a number of respects, Africa is at the stage where Latin America was in the early sixteenth and nineteenth centuries when it first received the Christian faith and gained political independence, respectively. Yet liberation theology did not arise at this period in Latin America, even though the conditions that call it forth now were present then. So in its efforts at liberation its own way, Africa draws great encouragement from the successful struggles of its brothers and sisters in Latin America and other Third World regions. Gustavo Gutiérrez undoubtedly plays a major role in this struggle for liberation and for life.

Today we are celebrating sixty years of life of a great person and theologian, twenty of which, at least, have been spent in a passionate, courageous, and pioneering commitment to doing a people-oriented and life-enabling theology.[19] Both the life and the commitment to theology are gratuitous gifts from God, gifts to Gutiérrez personally, in the first place, then gifts to the poor and the church in Latin America, and finally gifts to the universal church. Today, therefore, we also render sincere thanks to God for having blessed the entire Christian community with the gift of our brother Gutiérrez.

But I do not imagine that either the life or the years of commitment to a theology that liberates and empowers to live were endured without much personal suffering, doubts, and questioning, as happens in any authentic Christian journey of faith through life. Moreover, Gutiérrez's pioneering approach to theology clearly involves a departure from the well-trodden paths of theological investigations. Such a departure necessarily calls forth severe criticism, if not attack, from those who have been used to drinking the old wine and who find the new wine unpalatable (Luke 5:39). It appears to me, therefore, that his most recent book that I have read, *On Job: God-Talk and the Suffering of the Innocent,* presents, not only a reflection on the biblical Job from the standpoint of the poor in Latin America, but a personal autobiography of Gutiérrez himself. One cannot read the section on the two types of theological reasoning (pp. 27–30) or the section on Job and the suffering of others (pp. 31–38) without thinking of his own struggle to do a new type of theology and his solidarity with the suffering poor in Latin America.

But what emerges most beautifully in this faith testimony of Gutiérrez, as I view it, is the full realization by Job that ultimately the answer to his problems and those of his co-sufferers lies, not in his being theologically correct against his opponents (which he undoubtedly is), but in his entrusting himself respectfully and trustfully to the mystery of God.[20] Ultimately, it is God alone who can save and liberate. We do our necessary part and our utmost to cooperate with God in this work of saving and giving life, but we know that without God we can do nothing (John 15:5), and that without the increase that God grants, both our sowing and the watering of others will not produce any fruit (1 Cor. 3:6–7). This position is indeed grounded in solid Christian theology. Such a faith testimony should lay to rest any doubts that one might entertain as to whether or not liberation theology as practiced by Gutiérrez belongs in line with authentic, orthodox Christian theology.

NOTES

1. The Second General Assembly of EATWOT took place at Oaxtepec, Mexico, December 7–14, 1986. Gustavo Gutiérrez and Leonardo Boff are cherished members of the association.

2. Gutiérrez, *On Job: God-Talk and the Suffering of the Innocent* (Maryknoll, N.Y.: Orbis, 1987). Part of the reason, perhaps, for the lack of influence of liberation theology on biblical scholarship is that liberation theology itself is a relatively new

concept. Gutiérrez's pioneer work, *A Theology of Liberation,* which was largely responsible for spreading knowledge of the concept in the West, appeared in English (Orbis Books) only in 1973.

3. On this issue, see my *The Johannine Approach to Mission: A Contextual Study of John 4:1–42* (WUNT, 2/31; Tübingen: Mohr-Siebeck, 1988), p. xvii.

4. In addition to the two works mentioned in n. 2, above, see, for instance *The Power of the Poor in History* (Maryknoll, N.Y.: Orbis, 1983); and *We Drink From Our Own Wells: The Spiritual Journey of a People* (Maryknoll, N.Y.: Orbis, 1984).

5. See "Justice in the World," Synod of Bishops, Convenientes ex universo, November 1971 in Austin Flannery, ed., *Vatican Council II: More Post Conciliar Documents* (Vatican Collection, vol. 2: Dublin: Dominican Publications, 1982), pp. 695–710.

6. Gutiérrez, *We Drink From Our Own Wells,* p. 12.

7. Ibid., p. 100. Our author believes firmly that "a commitment within history" must lead to "effective action within history," p. 93.

8. Ibid., p. 94.

9. Ibid., p. 93.

10. Jesus' teaching on the blessedness of the poor is, of course, a complete reversal of the Deuteronomic theology, which considered wealth a sign of God's special blessing, and poverty as a mark of God's displeasure, a result of personal sin. For Gutiérrez's own reflection on the beatitude of the poor, see *On Job,* pp. xii–xiii.

11. See further, Donal Dorr, *Spirituality and Justice* (Maryknoll, N.Y.: Orbis and Dublin: Gill and MacMillan, 1984), esp. chap. 3, "Challenge from the Third World," pp. 35–51.

12. *We Drink,* pp. 25, 29.

13. Ibid., p. 93.

14. Ibid., p. 28.

15. Mveng used the term in his position paper on Africa presented at the Second General Assembly of EATWOT in Mexico. The theme of the conference was "commonalities and divergencies in Third World theologies." Papers from the conference are in the process of being published by Orbis Books.

16. This focus on salvaging the cultural heritage from the wreck explains why most African theological literature south of the Sahara, with the exception of South Africa, centers on studying traditional African religions and beliefs. See, for instance, John S. Mbiti, *The Prayers of African Religion* (London: SPCK, 1975); *African Religions and Philosophy* (London: Heinemann, 1969); *Introduction to African Religions* (London: Heinemann, 1981); E. Bolaji Idowu, *African Traditional Religion. A Definition* (London: SCM, 1973); Kwesi A. Dickson and Paul Ellingworth, eds., *Biblical Revelation and African Beliefs* (United Society for Christian Literature; London: Lutterworth, 1969), a collection of essays by nine African Scholars; Aylward Shorter, *African Christian Theology—Adaptation or Incarnation?* (London: Chapman, 1975) [the term "adaptation" is now completely discarded by African scholars as being expressive of their type of theology]; K. S. Appiah-Kubi and S. Torres, eds., *African Theology en Route* (Maryknoll: Orbis, 1983); E. I. Metuh, ed., *The Gods in Retreat: Continuity and Change in African Religions* (the Nigerian experience) (Enugu: Fourth Dimension, 1986). The reader will notice that except for one or two entries this bibliography does not reflect the work done by African scholars in

the past thirteen years, and by such scholars as Jean Marc Ela, Mercy Amba Odu-yoye, and Justin Ukpong. This is explained by the lack of access to a theological library at the time of writing this paper. Furthermore, most of the doctoral disser-tations written by Nigerian and African students in theology at home and abroad center on the same issue of cultural revival and inculturation. See, for instance, E. O. Idem, *Inculturation of Leadership in the Nigerian* (Focus on the Laity) (Rome: Pontificia Universitas Lateranese, 1988).

17. See, for instance, David B. Barrett, *Schism and Renewal in Africa: An Analysis of Six Thousand Contemporary Religious Movements* (Nairobi: Oxford, 1968). If there were an estimated *six thousand* of these movements twenty years ago, the reader can guess how many there would be today.

18. In addition to the well known Institute in Kinshasa, Zaire, the more recent efforts are L'Institut Catholique de l'Afrique de l'Ouest (LICAO), Abidjan, the Catholic Institute of West Africa, Port Harcourt (CIWA), and the Catholic Higher Institute of East Africa (CHIEA), Nairobi. In Nigeria, for instance, most regions are yet to celebrate the first hundred years of the coming of Christianity. I am not aware that the situation is the same in Latin America.

19. Gutiérrez's pioneer work, *A Theology of Liberation,* was first published in Spanish in 1971; but the book was obviously the outcome of years of theological reflection and living.

20. See in particular, "Part III, The Language of Contemplation," pp. 51–92, esp. chap. 10, "My Eyes Have Seen You," pp. 82–92: "That is what Job did: he flung himself upon the impossible and into an enigmatic future. And in this effort he met the Lord" (p. 92).

16

Gustavo Gutiérrez:
A Historical Sketch

SERGIO TORRES

I am very pleased to be taking part in this project celebrating twenty years' work in liberation theology, which began in a country high up in the Andes, most of whose population is indigenous and which, like the gospel seed, has spread its branches through every continent.[1]

This homage today goes beyond the frontiers of Latin America. Gustavo has become a witness and spokesman for the whole Third World. This was said by the authors of a book published in 1983 on the contribution of liberation theology to current theological thought.[2] We share with Gustavo this vocation and this passion for the fate and future of the Third World, "for the oppressed classes, the despised races, and the marginalized cultures," as he put it. I join my voice to his to speak today.

I want to say loudly and clearly what a privilege my friendship with Gustavo has been. This friendship has been deep and uninterrupted for nearly forty years, since those far off days as students in the Pontifical Seminary in Santiago. It has been strengthened by countless meetings during the course of our common work in the service of the Latin American people and the church of Jesus Christ.

A SURPRISING SPIRITUAL JOURNEY

Those of us who know Gustavo will never cease to marvel at how much he has managed to do in so few years. In the course of one generation he has formulated a new model of theology, which has become a universal force for renewal and which history will judge as one of the most original contributions to this final part of the twentieth century.

In him we see the biblical theme at work: God working through the small and the marginal.[3] Gustavo was born of a family with close indigenous connections. He was attacked by a debilitating disease that made it difficult for him to walk. He was able to overcome his adversities and make his way in life to become a brilliant and committed thinker known throughout the world, the legitimate pride of Peru and of the church in pilgrimage in this country.

After beginning to study medicine, he decided to become a priest and join the

95

ministry in the archdiocese of Lima, so he entered the seminary in that city. His superiors' views of his qualities and the ecclesiastical mentality of the time sent him to Santiago, Louvain, and Lyons to complete a vast and very solid education in philosophy and theology.

On his return to his homeland he was ordained a priest in January 1959, and shortly afterward, he became an advisor to the National Union of Catholic Students (UNEC). This involved him in pastoral and theological work that meant traveling all over the country and taking part in meetings and courses all over Latin America.

From then until now he has always been connected with work at the base, taking part in all kinds of meetings, always listening, taking notes, learning, sharing, teaching. This has enabled him to practice what he preaches in his writing—that is, that spiritual experience and social and pastoral practice precede and enrich intellectual systemization.[4]

After a few years in the ministry his name began to be known and he was summoned by the Episcopal Council of Latin America (CELAM) to take part in its theological reflection team. In this capacity he worked hard and fruitfully at courses and conferences for bishops and pastoral workers all over Latin America.

With this competence and experience he took an active part in the Episcopal Conference of Medellín in 1968, which became the foundation of Latin American pastoral work. He shares with other bishops and theologians the title of "Medellín man." He is recognized as such in the history of Latin America because of the importance of this conference, subsequently confirmed by the Puebla Conference.

In 1971 the Lima Center for Studies and Publications (CEP) published his fundamental book *Teología de la Liberación, Perspectivas*, which became the foundation of the Latin American theological trend called "liberation theology." Here we find the first insights into this new way of doing theology, its method, content, and spirituality. Its successive editions and translations into different languages have made this book one of the most important works of present-day theology. It shares the stature of great historical works that shook the status quo and gave rise to qualitative changes in thought.

This theological trend was not slow in spreading to other geographical and cultural areas. It would be impossible to list the journeys, meetings, and conferences in which Gustavo took part, and spoke out in his indigenous Peruvian accent. No one but he could relate all these experiences.

I shall confine myself to a few occasions that I think are most significant or at which I was present myself. In 1972 the "Faith and Secularity Institute" of Madrid organized some study days in the Escorial under the title "Christian Faith and Social Change in Latin America." A select group of social scientists and theologians were invited to tell the Spanish public about the church's new experiences in Latin America. The Spanish theologian Alfonso Alvarez Bolado sums up thus the impact of the Peruvian theologian's contribution:

> Gustavo Gutiérrez gave us the feeling of experiencing together in the Escorial an intense new spiritual experience in common. He is not just the characteristic author of liberation theology. He is the shaper and the formulator in simple, sober, and expressive language of its fundamental insights.[5]

Between the years 1970 and 1973, Gustavo went several times to Chile to share the hopes and concerns of Christian groups facing huge challenges. His friendship with many bishops, lay persons, and pastoral workers, interrupted by the terrible years of the military dictatorship, is nostagically recalled by Gustavo himself and by many Chilean men and women.

In 1975 he went to the U.S.A. to hear at close quarters the principal exponents of Latin American theology. At a famous conference called "Theology in the Americas," held in Detroit, there was a long and fruitful dialogue between representatives of the two continents. Gustavo made a brilliant contribution, in spite of arriving late because he had been involved in dealing with conflicts in his own country.[6]

The impact of the theology of an underdeveloped continent, such as ours, quickly entered into dialogue with other Third World continents. This dialogue was not, as has sometimes been believed, the imposition of one way of thinking upon another. In Africa and Asia thinking is developing along parallel lines. They also see the need to define our continents' ecclesial and theological identity and are concerned with the influence of the historical, economic, social, and cultural context on theology.

Gustavo has taken an active part in many conferences with representatives from Africa, Asia, and Latin America and always contributed his lucid and committed thinking.[7]

In 1977 a book appeared called *Liberation and Change*,[8] a dialogue with Richard Shaull, a U.S. theologian who was one of the first to take an interest in Latin America. Shaull ventured into new territory and in the 1950s he proposed a theology of revolution. Liberation theology, and Gustavo in particular, parted from this tendency very early on. It did not have enduring influence.

Political and ecclesial events happened at great speed in Latin America. In 1979 the third CELAM Conference took place in Puebla, Mexico.[9] Through an exclusion procedure set up by Bishop Alfonso López Trujillo in Sucre in 1972, Gustavo and other Latin American theologians were not invited to take part as experts in the conference. With humility and in a spirit of service, these theologians accepted the invitation of various bishops to accompany them as personal advisors. This was not a "parallel Puebla," as it was sneeringly described, but a service to the church and an indirect but inestimable theological contribution.

In the same year, 1979, Gustavo's second most important book appeared, *La Fuerza Histórica de los Pobres*,[10] which traces the evolution of his thought and its particular contribution to new challenges. The book's title itself is one of the many characteristic expressions that he helped to create in the theological and social field.

During his journeys and meetings, new friendships arose as did invitations to courses and conferences. Curiously, in spite of his European education, Gustavo has taught more in the U.S.A. than in Europe. He pursued an ecumenical vocation, teaching in seminaries and Catholic and Protestant universities in New York, Boston, San Francisco, and other cities.

I should like to recall the period from 1973 to 1980, during which I lived in the U.S.A. We met many times to discuss at greater length the dramatic events taking place in our countries, and in particular in Chile after the bloody military coup. We also took part in many activities together and were able to make common friends. I should especially like to mention the Maryknoll fathers, Robert McAfee Brown, Virginia Fabella, James Cone, Rosemary Ruether, Nora Boots, and many other men and women friends too numerous to list here.

Contradiction and criticism have accompanied Gustavo throughout his life. He has also suffered defamation and persecution. But, worse yet, came suspicion and interrogation by the church itself, which he had served with such devotion and passion. In February 1983 a letter came to the Peruvian Episcopal Conference from the Congregation for the Doctrine of the Faith requesting a critical examination of Gustavo's theological positions. It was accompanied by a document entitled "Observations on the Liberation Theology of Gustavo Gutiérrez," which contained ten serious accusations concerning his doctrinal orthodoxy and questioning his commitment to the church, as a Christian and a priest.

Gustavo reacted, as always, with a sense of the church and with humility. At the same time, he began a long process of dialogue, clarification, and defense of his theological positions, which finally enabled him to prove his orthodoxy and receive the approval of the Episcopal Conference. He was always supported by Juan Landázuri, the cardinal of Lima, and was able to count on his friendship and confidence. However, he could not avoid attacks in the newspapers and the incomprehension of other theologians and some of the bishops in his country.

In this atmosphere of confrontation and judgment, on January 6, 1984, together with his lifelong friend Jorge Alvarez Calderón, he celebrated the twenty-fifth anniversary of his ordination to the priesthood. In the church of Santo Domingo in Lima, eleven bishops, 140 priest, numerous nuns, and thousands of lay persons from church communities and movements gave praise to the God of life and offered the thanks of the Peruvian church for the theological and pastoral work of these two committed priests.

Gustavo had no time to rest after this beautiful celebration. That same year the first instruction of the Congregation for the Doctrine of the Faith, *On Some Aspects of Liberation Theology*,[11] was published. This strongly criticized some forms of liberation theology, which pleased those who were hoping for its imminent condemnation. The second instruction, in 1986, *Christian Freedom and Liberation*,[12] and John Paul II's personal message to the Brazilian bishops that same year,[13] helped to create a more serene balance and a more positive evaluation of liberation theology. The second instruction says: "The Church, docile to the Spirit, advances faithfully along the roads of authentic liberation" (no. 57). Referring to the theology of Latin America it says, "Likewise, a theological reflection developed from a particular experience can constitute a very positive contribution, because it brings out certain aspects of the word of God, whose total richness has still not been fully perceived" (no. 70).

Pope John Paul II goes even further in his approval of liberation theology. He says in his text, "To the extent that [the Brazilian church] strives to find those just answers . . . we are convinced, you and I, that liberation theology is not only opportune but also useful and necessary" (Message, no. 5). It also charges the episcopacy of Brazil with the important mission of seeing that this theology develop and gather strength. In this same message he adds:

To fulfill this role there is no substitute for wise and brave action by pastors — that is, by you. God helps you to be continually on the watch so that this correct and necessary liberation theology should develop in Brazil and Latin America in a homogenous and not heterogenous way in relation to the theology of all time, faithful to the teaching of the church, attentive to the preferential, but not excluding or exclusive, love for the poor [no. 5].

HUMAN AND SPIRITUAL WEALTH

In this description we have been able to convey something of the deep reason for Gustavo's spiritual fertility—that is, his extraordinary personality in the service of the Spirit. He fulfills in himself what he wrote in his book on spirituality *Beber en su propio pozo:* "Reflection on the mystery of God (that is, a theology) can only be done by following Jesus. It is only possible in this way and in this spirit to think about and announce the Father's gratuitous love for every human person."[14]

All agree that he has an astonishing mind, which has enabled him to reach the deepest doctrinal and theological depths, and then speak and write about them with masterful simplicity. He has always written from the standpoint of his spiritual experience and practice. He himself has often repeated that he is more of a conference participant than a writer. Nevertheless his theological works, written in his free time from ceaseless action, have been decisive in formulating, expressing, and securing the Latin American trend of theology. Others have followed him and made valiant contributions, but he plowed the first furrow and planted the first seeds.

Gustavo is a model for human relationships and he has a gift for friendship. His rare spirit is nimble, intuitive, direct, with a subtle sense of humor. He has friends all over the world and he recognizes all of them at meetings and gatherings, thanks to his exceptional memory.

But above all, as has been said, he is a man of the Spirit. His personal life and his writings reflect this docility to the Spirit. From his first book onward he has stressed the theme of liberation spirituality.[15] His articles on "conversion to our neighbor"[16] and "the eucharist and human fellowship"[17] are powerful works of deep spirituality. However, critics and detractors try to reduce him to his political and social aspects, leaving aside the more theological aspect and his insights into liberation spirituality. By taking isolated texts out of context, they have tried to devalue his spirituality as a disciple of Jesus Christ and his deep feeling for the church.

In recent years he himself has tried to make this spiritual commitment more explicit and public. His latest works—*El Dios de la Vida;*[18] *Beber en su propio pozo; Hablar de Dios desde el sufrimiento del inocente: Una reflexión sobre el Libro de Job*[19]— are a clear testimony to this new emphasis in his theology. At the same time, he has not abandoned methodological and more conflictive aspects.

Finally, I should like to mention one of his more salient characteristics: his deep feeling for the poor. Everything he has said and written, everything he has suffered, his hopes and wishes, his whole life, can be understood only as a service to the poor. He has struggled all along to develop a theology whose point of departure is the person of Jesus, revealed in the face of those who are poorest.[20] In part, his efforts have achieved very positive results. Gustavo has been a constant strong presence on the road ratified by the Puebla Conference when it adopted the preferential option for the poor as the official position of the Latin American church.

This celebration of twenty years of liberation theology in the person of Gustavo has come at a very opportune moment. It is a symbolic occasion on which to give thanks to God and confirm our theological work. We must give due credit to its positive results and be open to correct its possible limitations.

With the approach of the celebration of the 500th anniversary of the arrival of the Spaniards in Latin America and the first preaching of the gospel, liberation theology will be able to contribute decisively to the process of discerning between the positive and ambiguous elements in this enormous missionary enterprise.

I am sure that Gustavo has agreed to take part in this celebration, not so much for his own sake, but in order to recall and celebrate the achievements of poor Latin Americans. They need moments of joy and hope in the midst of their lives of suffering and death.

Over the last twenty years, Gustavo has been a symbol of committed theology. We hope we can count on his presence and inspiration for many years to come.

—translated from the Spanish by Dinah Livingstone

NOTES

1. Matt. 13:31-32.

2. Gregory Baum and others, *Vida y Reflexión: Aportes de la teología de la liberación al pensamiento teológico actual* (Lima: CEP, 1983).

3. José Dammert Bellido, Prologue to Gustavo Gutiérrez's book, *La Verdad los hará libres. Confrontaciones*, (Lima: CEP, 1986), p. 2.

4. Gustavo Gutiérrez, *Teología de la Liberación, Perspectivas* (Lima: CEP, 1971), p. 28. See also *La fuerza histórica de los pobres* (Lima: CEP, 1979), pp. 64ff; Eng. trans. *The Power of the Poor in History* (Maryknoll, N.Y.: Orbis, 1983).

5. Alfonso Alvarez Bolado, Introduction to *Fe Cristiana y Cambio Social en América Latina* (Salamanca: Sígueme, 1973), p. 23.

6. Sergio Torres and John Eagleson, eds., *Teología en las Américas* (Salamanca: Sígueme, 1980), pp. 349-53; Eng. trans. *Theology in the Americas* (Maryknoll, N.Y.: Orbis, 1976).

7. There have been conferences organized by the World Council of Churches, universities or faculties of theology, and by the Ecumenical Association of Third World Theologians.

8. Richard Shaull and Gustavo Gutiérrez, *Liberation and Change* (Atlanta: John Knox Press, 1977).

9. There were three CELAM conferences. The first took place in Rio de Janeiro in 1955; the second in Medellín, Colombia, in 1968; the third in Puebla, Mexico, in 1979. A fourth conference has been announced to take place in Santo Domingo in 1992, the 500th anniversary of the arrival of Spaniards in the New World.

10. Lima: CEP, 1979.

11. Sacred Congregation for the Doctrine of Faith, *Instruction on Some Aspects of Liberation Theology* (Santiago, Chile: Paulinas, 1984).

12. Sacred Congregation for the Doctrine of Faith, *Instruction on Christian Freedom and Liberation* (Santiago, Chile: Paulinas 1986).

13. John Paul II, "Message to the Brazilian Bishops," in *Boletín de la Vicaria Pastoral del Arzobispado de Santiago*, June 1986, no. 3, pp. 3-12.

14. Gustavo Gutiérrez, *Beber en su propio pozo. En el itinerario de un pueblo* (Lima: CEP, 1983), p. 182.

15. Gustavo Gutiérrez, "Una espiritualidad de la liberación" in *Teología de la Liberación,* pp. 253–60.

16. Ibid., pp. 239–52.

17. Ibid., pp. 324–39.

18. Gustavo Gutiérrez, *El Dios de la Vida* (Lima: Catholic Pontifical University, 1982).

19. Gustavo Gutiérrez, *Hablar de Dios desde el sufrimiento del inocente: Una reflexión sobre el Libro de Job* (Lima: CEP, 1986); Eng. tran. *On Job: God-Talk and the Suffering of the Innocent* (Maryknoll, N.Y.: Orbis, 1987).

20. Matt. 25:31–46.

PART III

INTERPRETING LIBERATION THEOLOGY

17

Women and the
Theology of Liberation

ANA MARÍA BIDEGAIN

I should like to present a historical view of the role of woman in Latin America. I shall focus on the notion of sexuality propagated in society by the Catholic Church, which used as mediators, in the twentieth century, women themselves, through Catholic Action—the same women who would one day help to create the theology of liberation. By way of conclusion, I shall indicate our search for new horizons—the quest for the foundation of a human and Christian relationship between men and women in church and society.

PRESENTATION OF THE NEW WORLD

Michel de Certeau describes one of the first images to circulate in Europe of that continent's encounter with the New World:

Explorer Amerigo Vespucci arrives from the sea. Erect, cuirassed like a crusader, he bears the arms of his European experiences and beliefs. In the background are the ships that will bear to the West the treasures of a paradise. Before him is the Amerindian—nude, recumbent—nameless presence of difference, body stirring awake in a riot of exotic plants and animals.

After a moment of stupefaction in this antechamber of paradise, beside this colonnade of trees, suddenly the conquistador will write upon the body of this other, this female person before him. In her flesh he will carve his own history. He will make of her the storied body of his labors and fantasies. She will be called: Latin America.

This erotic, warlike image has an all but mythic value. It represents the inauguration of a new, Western purpose for writing. What is about to be scratched on this flesh is the colonization of a body by the discourse of power—the scripture of the conquistador. That conqueror will tear out this blank page, this untamed New World, and make use of it to mark down his Western desires and longings.[1]

Europeans arrived in America at the moment of the birth of the capitalist mode of production, and at the peak of their territorial, political, and military expansion.

For them, woman's sexuality was mainly a motive for uneasiness. And their only thought was to curb it.

They encountered other cultures—cultures unprepared to encounter them. Two cultures, two unequal fragments of humanity, had developed in parallel, without mutual interference. They came in contact at the end of the fifteenth century, by way of the expansion of the Iberian world. Western Christendom obviously bore the responsibility for this utterly fortuitous encounter.

Amerigo Vespucci had discovered a new world, a world with a new way of life. Vespucci learned that in this land—which he would present to Europe, which he would introduce to cartography, and to which he would give his name—persons lived in harmony with nature. There was no private property. All things were possessed in common. There were no kings or political authorities of any kind. All individuals were sovereign to themselves. The publication of Vespucci's *New World* inspired Thomas More's *Utopia* (1518).

Westerners failed to grasp the tenor of the relationship proposed by their lavish hosts. When colonial man was offered native woman, he failed to grasp the implied demand for reciprocal service. After all, the conqueror had come to the new world not to serve, but to reduce it and its natives to captivity.

In this confrontation of two unequal worlds, it was Europe that gradually gained the ascendancy. Thus native woman continued to be offered as woman and mother. But the Amerindians managed to impose their cultural matrix on the conquerors. After all, the sovereign of the land, of the age-old human tradition of the soil, was the native. The Hispanic and African newcomers only transplanted the topsoil of their European and African cultural matrices.

The apparent extermination of Amerindian social and economic structures does not militate against the fact of an ethical and cultural symbiosis between conqueror and native. Both the Spaniard and the African gradually adopted Amerindian tradition, and with it acquired a knowledge of nature that was thousands of years old.[2] It was woman who taught the European new eating habits adapted to the climate. She also prescribed thousands of hygienic recipes, like the daily bath, the use of natural elements in households, and the use of native drugs in the treatment of tropical diseases. She also served the white male by bearing him offspring to swell his labor force.

Amerindian material creativity is still very much alive today, in our practices and customs, in our culinary arts, in our handicraft. Amerindian artistic creativity is present in the melancholic, sensitive, emotional folklore of the first American cultures.

We can confidently assert, then, that the mother of America is native woman. We are her mestizo children. Our Amerindian mother has bequeathed to us her cultural womb. Our task today is to rescue and value it if we hope to stand erect before the white colonial.

Woman was a captive and a slave in a number of ways. She was used as slave labor. She was used as a woman: as the master's sex object, and as the mother who reproduced a labor force for toil in the mines or on the sugar plantations and ranches.

Enslaved many times over, the Amerindian, black, mulatto, mestiza woman prolonged in America the condition of the humiliated and wronged of the system down through the ages. Hence she was fertile soil for the gospel message of life that white woman, the dominator, could only communicate mechanically in the domestic chapel.

The Amerindian male, himself humiliated and exploited, frequently escaped his situation in drink, gambling, and an insanity that could culminate in suicide. It was the Latin American woman of the people who bore, firmly and stubbornly, subtly and tactfully, the burden of humiliation and subjugation placed on her shoulders by the colonial structure.

And therefore the gospel was handed down by successive generations of women—not so much from mother to child, but from female generation to female generation, just as in the Afro-American cults today.

Among the popular masses, the mother has always been the best catechist. It was mothers who handed on to future generations their own experience of the stubbornness and silence of faith, their hope beyond hope, and their totally gratuitous charity. Of course, the values of this captive, exiled Christianity were transmitted from generation to generation by humiliated women in a nonverbal way. Word was the property of the dominator.

The presentation of the new world, America, in the form of a naked woman, is a proclamation of the function of domination, in which, yesterday as today, sexuality is a key element.

The European allegory clearly expresses the invader's awareness that, in order to subjugate Latin America, he must first "tame" her sexually. On an unconscious level, this attitude expresses simply the underlying male fear of the unknown—an unknown represented so profoundly in the female biological process, especially motherhood, universally symbolized in soil and fertility. Here, woman is the secret dominator. Man is her subject. America is to Europe as the female to the male.

The same image recalls that woman's body is the locus of sexual domination. Hence the special urgency of her subjugation and domestication. Furthermore, sexuality is not autonomous. It is not a world apart from the world of politico-cultural and economico-social domination.

CAPITALIST BULWARK: PURITANICAL SEXUAL DOMINATION

Our Latin American historical experience demonstrates that sexuality is not an individual problem. It is a complex social and cultural reality. It maintains relationships with the prevailing economic system. A study of feminine Latin American religious process cannot be divorced from an analysis of European efforts, throughout the colonial process, to domesticate sexuality.

Of special importance in this process is the puritanical current in Christianity, championed by religious reformers in the sixteenth century. Puritanism dovetailed perfectly with the capitalist mode of production, which, like Victorian puritanism, reached the peak of its maturity in the nineteenth century.

Puritanism coincided with the sexual ideology of the Judeo-Christian sexual tradition, with its adventitious elements of Stoicism and Neoplatonism later reinforced by the moralistic rigorism of a William of Occam and the seventeenth-century Catholic Jansenist enlightenment.

Otto Maduro has shown that this rigoristic outlook conceives sexuality essentially as an evil energy, to be either repressed or orientated exclusively to the propagation

ANA MARÍA BIDEGAIN

of the species. It likewise coincides with a view of sexuality as an individual dimension, isolated from the rest of the personality.[3]

Thus viewed, sexuality seemed to have no connection with either economics or
politics or anything else in history—except that it had to be regulated according to
the norms laid down by society and church, norms that sacralized the fragmentation
and individualization of sexuality.

Christian puritanism installed sexuality at the center of its official pastoral ministry and practice, thus seeking to polarize the personal and collective energy of
the faithful. In the pastoral activity of the Catholic Church since the sixteenth
century, sexual morality has moved from the peripheral, secondary status it had in
the Middle Ages with an Albertus Magnus or a Thomas Aquinas, to constitute for
all practical purposes the principal focus of that activity. The resultant polarization
of sexual morality has meant the relegation of politico-social concerns to a secondary status. Hence we have the tendency, since that time, to identify "sin" all but
exclusively with a particular sort of sexual behavior.

This chronological process has coincided with the initiation and development of
the evangelization of Latin America and the worldwide expansion of capitalism. Its
contribution to the support of the capitalist system is based on two main factors:

1. It is the vehicle of a conception of sexuality that reduces the human body to
a means of the social production of surplus value, thereby reinforcing capitalism's
natural tendency to exploit the human being as the basic labor force of social
relationships of production.

The human body is not only the primary, indispensable material basis of a society's existence, but also the primary, indispensable means and principal element
of social production.

2. Inasmuch as evil is now most easily found in sexuality, it is no longer necessary
to judge the social structure in moral terms. Or at best, that structure will be judged
as a lesser evil. Individuals should bend their greatest efforts to overcome sin, which,
in the prevailing view of sexuality, is now almost entirely an individual concern,
hence no longer a subject for examination in terms of social relationships. Nor is
there any longer any reason for the faithful to direct their attention and energy
toward the struggle against human beings' exploitation of one another, which for
that matter is no longer the greatest sin, but a minor sin.

This outlook had another consequence, one of a socio-cultural order. It bolstered
the ideology of male supremacy and a cultural model according to which all personal
energy ought to be focused on the construction and reproduction of intrafamilial
relationships rather than being expended in the area of socio-political action.

A male-supremacist capitalism has tended to impose on women of the various
social classes the ideal of a total concentration of their energy on intrafamilial
relationships. But the male ought to dedicate only a part of his time to these
relationships, the part left over from the production of surplus value.

Thus woman appears as more religious, more family-oriented, less political, less
professional. However, this is not due to the nature of the feminine. Nor is it owing
to chance. It is due to the historico-social subjugation of women, as reinforced by
the view of sexuality propagated by a rigoristic, puritanical Christianity.

We must emphasize that the marginalization of woman from all public life has
been carried forward in two ways. First, she has been regarded as a minor, scarcely
more than an imbecile. Thus she must be placed under tutelage and guardianship.

Secondly, she has been exalted, by a kind of sublimation that renders activities outside the home somehow beneath her dignity. And so the only two vocations available to woman since the nineteenth century have been motherhood and consecrated virginity.

This has had another basic consequence, one of a religious nature. It has produced an aberration in Marian devotion—or rather a male-supremacist exploitation of devotion to the Virgin Mary. Mary is the synthesis of both aspects, virginity and motherhood. Thus she symbolizes the traditional ideal of woman (in a male-supremacist reading of her life).

This model of ideal femininity, in the tenor of an exaltation of the virtues regarded as proper to woman—modesty, a resigned acceptance of any and all reality as the will of God—has been of enormous service and satisfaction to males in the maintenance of their position of privilege. At the same time it has continued to demand of woman that she "accept her place" with humility and resignation, and leave the affairs of world and church to man.

This model marked the life of the church up until the middle of the twentieth century.[4]

WOMAN, SEXUALITY, AND CATHOLIC ACTION

In the middle of the nineteenth century a series of changes occurred. Although they were centered in the developed countries, they noticeably influenced Latin America, for Latin America implemented all the mid-century liberal reforms and structured itself in function of an internationalized market and political reality.

The politico-social transformations that produced the industrial revolution also influenced family life. A patriarchal society now entered a state of crisis. Women and children were suddenly in the capitalist marketplace as "personnel." Now their bodies were an additional article of merchandise. In the working family, the ideal of woman's place as in the home began to dissolve. The patriarchal family was weakened in certain ways. Various social classes now became the scene of a movement for "women's rights."

The urbanization process, jobs outside the home, access to education, the diffusion of birth control methods, changed family life, and with it the mentality of women's role in society, church, and home.

Certain individual figures—like María Cano, if I may be permitted to cite the example of a Colombian—fought in the political arena and the union movement, encouraging women's participation in these areas, taking advantage of women's presence in factories, and profiting from the dissemination of ideas like those of the socialist, anarchist, or liberal democratic movements.

Women of economic means began the fight for suffrage, matriculation in the universities, and admittance to the affluent and prestigious professions.

The church's first reaction to the "feminist" onslaught was to reassert the values of the traditional family and the role of woman in the home. The last flutter of this reactionary ecclesiastical movement occurred in the early part of the twentieth century, with the encyclical *Casti Connubii* (1931).

But historical development cannot be restrained by declarations, and the church itself had to adapt to the new reality. This is a fundamental moment in its history.

In order to perform its activity the church now had to avail itself of the weapons of its adversaries. And so lay organizations, rather like political parties, sprang into being. Now large masses of the Christian people could be encouraged to move toward the same ideological ends.

These permanent organizations of "militant Catholics" or Catholic activists eventually became a genuine mass movement. Antonio Gramsci regards them as a genuine church party. Their function was to provide the framework in which the Catholic masses could be used as a weapon—offensive or defensive as exigencies of the political, social, and especially cultural struggle might require.

The laity, male and female, was issued a call to participate in the apostolate of the hierarchy. Women took up the Catholic Action experiment, then in its infancy, and mounted a struggle for a place in evangelization and the pastoral ministry, the core of the life of the church. Woman had begun to emerge from her traditional role of wife in the home and consecrated virgin in the religious community.

Nevertheless, she was required to reinforce the traditional view of sexuality. To this end, she was kept in a sexless state, a kind of childlike innocence, instead of being helped to assume her sexual reality as woman.

The young unmarried women of Catholic Action were entrusted with forming leagues and conducting campaigns for moral behavior and good habits. The accent was on maximal control of the media (film, radio), amusement, and recreation. A great deal of insistence was placed on a rigoristic morality that eschewed flirting, dancing, the theater, novels, sports, and summer relaxation. The traditional view of sexuality as the capital sin, and woman as a near occasion of sin, prevailed.

This was the attitude adopted by the lay associations, pastors, bishops, and the Vatican itself, in the problem of women's dress. As woman's body was the supreme occasion of sin, it was important that it be covered as completely as possible. The model dress for the Catholic Action girl in our tropical countries consisted in high collars, long gray skirts reaching halfway from the knee and the ankle, thus hiding the legs, high button shoes, loose sleeves, and a sombrero!

Women's morality leagues exerted a great influence on Latin American cultural life, especially among young unmarried women, and especially in the middle and upper classes. Their moralistic outlook was accepted by all Catholic movements. More than ever before, celibacy was presented as the only model of holiness. Marriage was an inferior calling. Small wonder, then, that to militant Catholics the only true avenue to holiness seemed to be the religious life.[5]

The religious life was a reaction to the historical transformations set afoot by the massive presence of women in the factories at the turn of the century. Women cut their braids. They exchanged their long, heavy nineteenth-century clothing for short, light dresses. They emerged from the vigilance of their families into the new demands of their condition as paid laborers, with the freedom and independence of wage earners, and they adapted to these demands. Their attitude toward their bodies began to change. So did their carriage. They began to alter their world of affective relationships. New sexual conduct appeared.[6]

Like the rest of the population, nearly all Catholics hoped somehow to remain in the past. And so leagues of "decency" and morality were founded, constituted of the young ladies of Catholic Action, directed by the clergy, and functioning as guardians of feminine modesty.

But toward the end of the 1940s, certain young women joined the university student movement, especially in Chile and Brazil. In 1947 the Chilean Catholic Student Movement sent Olga de Cruz Grez to Potoise, in France, for the Second Conference of the JEC (Catholic Student Youth) International. In 1953 Maria de Lourdes Figuereido, of Brazil, participated in an international meeting of Pax Romana in Denmark, where she was elected vice-president of that worldwide organization—the first Latin American to hold office at the international level in an organization of Catholic students.

Beginning in 1950, due to the presence of women in the universities, all the Latin American movements gradually integrated. The old male and female branches of Catholic Action, composed almost entirely of university students, now joined forces. It was originally intended to have two presidents, so as to guarantee a female presence at the top level. This custom was abolished in many countries almost at once. But Gustavo Gutiérrez, then a young university chaplain in Peru, always insisted on the importance of respecting the female contribution to the organization by maintaining a female presence among the national officers.[7]

Students began to take their distance from the traditional Catholic Action outlook on sexuality. They sought to acquire a solid moral formation that would permit youth to live their sexuality with a genuine freedom and maturity. But sex, and male-female relationships—and still less the condition of women in society and the church—were never central to their discussions.

WOMEN AND THE BIRTH OF THE THEOLOGY OF LIBERATION

Thus a rigoristic, puritanical outlook on sexuality prevailed in Latin America in some form or other until the great upheavals of the 1960s. Then, amid such changes in the life of the church, and of our continent, we discovered that if we were to live a genuine Christianity, we should have to become involved in the construction and liberation of Latin America.

To this end it was considered essential to overcome our underdevelopment. Here the key points were agrarian reform, an autonomous capitalism, and a breach of our colonial ties—political, economic, and cultural—with the developed metropolises.

This posture was then influenced by the Cuban revolution, the dialogue between Christianity and Marxism, the political struggle of priests like Camilo Torres, the partial breakdown of the Christian Democratic parties, and the contribution of the developing social sciences.

The experience constituted a break with the spirituality of the age. Latin American Catholic youth now based their religious experience on the so-called Jocist methodology (JOC—Jeunesse Ouvrière Catholique): the *révision de vie*. Now the watchword was "to see, to judge, to act." Now our basic thrust, whether we were girls or boys, was an attempt to embody the gospel, the sacramental life, and prayer, in our own young lives through the witness we could give in the factories, at the universities, on the farm, and in our families. In the church itself, we became engaged in a struggle for the freedom and the rights of the laity, male and female, with a view to being able to act on society in the way that seemed correct to us as Christians.

It was in the youth movements of the 1960s, then, that young women and men joined forces to pass a point of no return. The movement we launched of course had ample theoretical support in the teaching of Vatican II. In practice, however, at least in Latin America, we could not depend on adequate support on the part of the bishops, and some years later our experiment was crushed by one sector of the episcopate.

We had found a new way of being Christian. But its authenticity was misunderstood by the majority of the clergy, and our movement had no church support. And so, in the 1970s, except in Peru and a few dioceses in the rest of Latin America, we were made to toe the line; or else our movements were watered down into political groups, so that they lost their effectiveness as a church experiment. Still, the religious lives of young persons, male and female, had been renewed, and a church committed to the popular sectors would be reborn.

It is to this Catholic youth experiment in Latin America that Gustavo Gutiérrez refers in the opening lines of his *Teología de la liberación* (1971):

This book is an attempt at reflection, based on the Gospel and *the experiences of men and women committed to the process of liberation* in the oppressed and exploited land of Latin America. It is a theological reflection born of the experience of shared efforts to abolish the current unjust situation and to build a different society, freer and more human. Many in Latin America have started along the path of a commitment to liberation, and among them is a growing number of Christians; whatever the validity of these pages, it is due to their experiences and reflections. Our greatest desire is not to betray their experiences and efforts to elucidate the meaning of their solidarity with the oppressed.

Our purpose is not to elaborate an ideology to justify postures already taken, nor to undertake a feverish search for security in the face of the radical challenges which confront the faith, nor to fashion a theology from which political action is "deduced." It is rather to let ourselves be judged by the Word of the Lord, to think through our faith, to strengthen our love, and to give reason for our hope from within a commitment which seeks to become more radical, total, and efficacious. It is to reconsider the great themes of the Christian life within this radically changed perspective and with regard to the new questions posed by this commitment. This is the goal of the so-called *theology of liberation.*[8]

At the same time as this effort was being carried forward by the Catholic Action youth of the 1960s, religious communities, especially those of women, were keeping pace, in their own work with the popular sectors. In communities with both a female and a male branch, like Maryknoll, it was frequently the sisters who more quickly intuited and understood what it meant to live the faith in a commitment of solidarity with the oppressed.

The students who had "been to the barrios" were unable to continue their labors of "conscientization" and evangelization. But women religious, especially, and some priests, who had understood the message of the Christian youth of the 1960s, took up the relays, and it was they who laid the foundation for a church of communion and participation in the following decade.

Priests who had been chaplains in the Latin American movements, along with certain bishops who had encouraged these same movements, were inspired to organize small communities and use the youth methodology to launch the comprehensive pastoral ministry proposed in the Medellín Final Document (Second Conference of the Latin American Episcopate, 1968).

In the 1970s certain sectors of the church, taking their cue from the documents of the Medellín Conference, as well as from their experience of a church that sought before all else to be the servant of the people, concentrated their efforts on creating base or grassroots communities. The membership and influence of these sectors grew, and it was on the basis of the reflections issuing from the communities they founded that they continued to develop the major themes of the theology of liberation.

The enormous contribution of Catholic Action youth to the history of the Latin American church is frequently ignored. It is said that this was only the work of a few elitist minorities. But as Pablo Richard states, to effect a sociological reduction of, and give a merely sociological significance to, theological reality is to forget the many little minorities in the history of the church who made a critical interpretation of history and the will of God, and communicated the result to broader communities.

I should like to emphasize that, just as men and women joined hands to make their commitment to the cause of liberation, so also both sexes were able to share all responsibilities involved. Their shared experience, together with the general social and cultural transformations underway, taught men—chaplains and lay militants—that women have a right to a place in society and the church not as minors, or indeed as children without the use of reason, but on an equal footing with men. Men learned that women, too, have a right to make decisions. However, there was still a long way to go. We women were entrusted with responsibilities, but, unconsciously, we were required to abandon our female identity. Anyone embracing the feminist theory, then being developed among European and North American women, was put in her place with the allegation that feminism was an imperialist theory calculated to divide and weaken the popular sector.

Those of us who were part of these movements, who were working for a transformation of society, saw the need to change woman's situation in society and in the church as part of that transformation. But we strove in this direction by our actions, not by discussion. We were certainly not about to proclaim ourselves feminists, if that was what feminists were accused of. Besides, feminism was seen as an antimale movement. Finally, and especially, as good Catholics we had internalized the ideology of abnegation and resignation to the point where it would have seemed altogether too forward, and hence morally wrong, to make any claims in our own behalf.

And because we had to perform our activity in a society like the church—an essentially male-dominated society, with a patriarchal ideology, accustomed to relegate women to subordinate functions—we had to, if I may say so, practically disguise ourselves as men. We had to reason like men, act with the same combativeness as men, use men's vocabulary, and live a man's spirituality. In a word, we had to become male, or at least present ourselves as asexual beings.

This was also the framework in which the theology of liberation came into being. Obviously, then, that theology was not going to address the situation of women in the church and society. Nor would it concern itself with the male-female relationship. Indeed, in a first moment, liberation theology was unconcerned to deal with the moral theology of sex.

I must say, however, that some community chaplains did insist on the need to take account of the feminine perspective and the importance of women's active participation in decision-making in the life of the church. Gustavo Gutiérrez is a particularly admirable case in point. Although he did not include the topic in his *A Theology of Liberation*, he was utterly aware of women's participation in the experiences he is systematizing. As we have seen, he explicitly states in his introduction that these experiences are those "of men and women."

In a second moment—when liberation theology had become a product of the systematization of a Christian experience immersed in popular reality—although religious women had been the first to intuit and assume this radically new way of being Christian, once again it was clerical males who wrote the books. Only one liberation theologian, Leonardo Boff, dealt with the subject directly, in his *The Maternal Face of God* (1979).[9]

Today, within the church itself, a battle is being waged for a new male-female relationship. Very timidly, a feminist theology is being sketched within the current of liberation theology, incorporating elements of feminist theory and today's moral theology.

In 1983 a group of historians of both sexes held a meeting in San Antonio, Texas, under the auspices of CEHILA. There we reflected on the subject of the poor woman in the history of the church in Latin America. In 1985 the topic of the Latin American theological conference held in Buenos Aires was "Theology from Woman's Perspective."[10]

An ever-growing group of women, lay and religious, in Latin America today are doing theology, and related disciplines like religious sociology or church history, from the same perspective, seeking to consolidate, within the popular movement in the church, a new kind of man-woman relationship.

IN QUEST OF NEW HORIZONS

The Latin American church has made a commitment to the quest for liberation. Therefore it is posing the question of sexuality. At the base, grassroots level, that church acknowledges the need to review and correct woman's position in the church and society. This need is felt in the hearts of men and women who experience the painful sexual unidimensionality of our society and our church. How could they not react?

Accordingly, I hold the urgency of (1) a review of the puritanical conception of sexuality as the ideological foundation, in the church as in Latin American society, of the patriarchal mentality on which all sexist oppression is based; (2) a prophetic denunciation of the process of feminization of poverty as the product of the capitalist system and of racism; and (3) a contribution on the part of Latin American women, and from our own female viewpoint, to the recovery of the liberating strength of Jesus and Mary.

Toward a Human, Christian Concept of Sexuality

We Latin American men and women have been calling for the actualization of a dimension that has always existed in Christianity, but which in the last centuries, for the reasons stated above, has been forgotten: human sexuality is something willed by God. It is God who created humanity sexed. Sexuality is a gift of God.

My outlook is traditional, then, and central to the Christian view of creation. And yet it has been forgotten. As we have seen, its place has been usurped by the tendency to regard believers who live their sexuality as somehow unfit for the divine life. This attitude is not the original Christian one. In fact, it has been reinforced by philosophical propositions alien to Christianity, such as Stoicism, Neoplatonism, and Victorian puritanism.

The concept of sexuality as something that estranges its subject from God, and hence something to be repressed, has not only motivated a repressive pastoral theory and practice, as we have seen, but has proposed asexuality as the only viable model of a Christian lifestyle and a monastic spirituality as the Christian ideal.

Today the only way to begin is to break with the traditional notion that reduces sexuality to an isolated area of the social relationship and an expression of sin, the latter being embodied essentially in woman.

It must be recognized that religious experience is neither essentially masculine, nor essentially feminine, nor essentially asexual. It is simply and fully a human experience. We must acknowledge that each of the sexes constitutes a way by which the human being reaches self-expression. Human beings achieve reality only as sexual beings, and they must be enabled to do this in all fullness, and in the possession of their rights. There are two ways of achieving this realization, then, and each of the two ways must be permitted to retain its originality through the adoption of continually new formulas.

Indeed, we have come to grasp that sexuality can contain a special experience of spirituality, or the encounter with God. Sexuality is expressed in love for one's partner, one's "con-sort" — the person with whom one shares a common lot. But the experience of God comes precisely by way of such an encounter with the "other," one's neighbor. Spirituality is a specific manner of self-encounter, of self-discovery, of the search for unification and oneness. In the love expressed in conjugal life, in the sexual life, appears the total, comprehensive encounter of two beings who give themselves up to one another fully and reciprocally. Here is a unique, privileged experience of horizons of transcendence. In sexuality, then, lived as the expression of love, we may find — have a living experience of — God.[11]

However, we shall not have this living experience, this empirical adventure, without a battle for the liberation of woman. That struggle cannot be separated from the struggle for the full realization of the human being. The former is a part of the latter. No wonder we men and women find it difficult to begin a journey whose starting point is a breach with the traditional notion of sexuality. But only thus can we begin the journey to a genuinely comprehensive liberation.

The Feminization of Poverty in the Modern World

Jesus criticized "stubbornness" — hardheartedness and thickheadedness. It is with this same thickheadedness that we conjure up an anthropological and sexual inequality between the women and men. Our sexual division of labor is dehumanizing for both.

Woman has traditionally been entrusted with the tasks of hearth and home.

Then that assignment has been belittled in comparison with the task of culture-building traditionally preempted by man.

Feminist studies have called attention to the worldwide process of the feminization of poverty. In 1980 the United Nations Organization reported:

1. Women constitute one-half of the world population.
2. Women spend twice as much time at work as men do.
3. They receive one-tenth of the world's income.
4. They possess less than one percent of the world's wealth.

This impoverishment of women is due in part to notions of motherhood, and to discrimination with regard to work and wages. That is, the feminization of poverty is a consequence of sexism (especially of sexist notions of economic processes) complemented by racial oppression.[12]

Racial discrimination, sexism, and capitalist exploitation in Latin America constitute the triad that keeps women in subjection. Latin Americans who dismiss feminism as a "bourgeois issue" are altogether off the mark. On the contrary, one of the basic tasks incumbent on Christians is to struggle against *all* discrimination—social, racial, and sexual.

Recapturing the Liberating Strength of Jesus and Mary

The life of Jesus is the Christian model par excellence. And so we women of Latin America never tire of reminding the community that Jesus' attitude toward women was never discriminatory, however radical a break with the traditions of his time he saw this to be. The figure of Mary—Mary poor, Mary committed and engaged—so central to our Latin American piety, is for us the power and model of liberation as the process of the feminization of poverty waxes apace.

Without having to use any rhetoric—but overturning, subverting the social order of his time—Jesus accorded all values, rights, and opportunities to all women of his time. In manifesting this humane attitude, he furnished us with a new model for the man-woman relationship.

From the first day of creation, God's plan has included the equality of man and woman. Both, male and female, are God's image. The image of God is that of mother-and-father. God is the synthesis of a sexed humanity:

God created humankind in God's image;
in the divine image God created them;
male and female God created them.
God blessed them, saying: "Be fertile and multiply;
fill the earth and subdue it [Gen. 1:27–28].

God, our Father and Mother, blessed the creature, and entrusted it, male and female, with one and the same mission: together, to be fertile and multiply and fill the earth and subject it to themselves jointly. That is, we are both responsible for the co-creation of home and society. Both of us, man and woman.

Today, in a culture and society of concrete challenges that tend to recast the role of woman and man in home and society, we face fears, perplexities, and anxieties. We have set aside the divine command. We have refused to accept the equality of man and woman, who, in complementarity, constitute the image of God, and to whom God gave the common task of filling and subduing the earth.

Jesus had to recall this to persons of his time when he spoke of the question of divorce:

[Moses] wrote that commandment [permitting divorce] for you because of your stubbornness. At the beginning of creation God made them male and female [Mark 10:5–6].

And still today our stubbornness and hardheartedness refuse to allow us to recall this absolutely basic fact: that from the beginning of creation God has made us male and female.

When we see woman's ability and maturity in undertaking the construction of society and culture (without abandoning her post in the home), we are awestruck. Women themselves are surprised at the breadth of their creative capacities. We forget that this is simply God's plan. It always has been.

We also forget that it is only the dynamics of the human historical process that have produced a society of male domination. What pertains to historical contingency is not carved in stone. It can be changed. By no manner of means must we allow it to be dogmatized. On the contrary, we must recover the attitude that the humanity God created is one, and that it is sexual.

Jesus calls women to set off down the road of their own liberation. After all, he has incorporated them into his church. There is no question of "feminism" in the sense of an insurrection in the cause of freedom. What is asked of us—men and women alike—is that we adopt a view, an outlook, that acknowledges the existence and condition of women. The advancement of women is only a particular aspect of the good news that Jesus proclaims to the poor, the privileged object of his liberation.

Those Jesus calls to build his reign are in the first instance the disinherited, the marginalized, the excluded. Among them are women, children, pagans, and sinners. Jesus prefers them because he discovers unknown, neglected values in them. It is a simple fact, attested by all four gospels, that the good news of Jesus includes women in the community called to build his reign.

We Latin Americans are becoming daily more conscious of the urgency of integrating the fight for women's rights into the struggle for the rights of society's other marginalized. We are not mounting a separate movement. Ours is but part of the one battle for a society of fellowship in which we can live the love of Jesus. The building of the reign is an affair of men and women together. Only united are we God's likeness and expression. But given the situation of women's historical oppression, it becomes absolutely necessary to accord a special interest to their advancement as part of the process of comprehensive liberation. Only thus—by incorporating women into the liberative struggle of the continent—shall we succeed in building a genuinely human society of brothers and sisters.

Mary in the Christian Community: Model of Liberation

Mary has been held out to Christians as a model of the feminine. But like the image of Jesus, so also that of Mary has frequently been utilized to justify a patriarchal mentality that marginalizes women. Mary has been simplified. She has become the model of self-denial, passivity, and submission as the essential (or worse still, the only) attributes of woman.

We are altogether accustomed to this predominantly patriarchal discourse. Despite efforts like those of Paul VI in *Marialis Cultus,* or of Puebla, Mary's genuine quality does not "come through" sufficiently to rescue the whole prophetic, liberative dimension that her mystery can offer the Latin American woman and man of today.

Jesus not only reminds us insistently that the female human being is God's daughter as much as the male is God's son. He not only incorporates this daughter of his into his church. He not only values her pedagogy highly enough to summon the people of God to hear her word and experience her prophetic role of proclamation. He actually takes a woman and makes her his mother, to fulfill God's plan by taking flesh within her.

From our Latin American viewpoint, the figure of the mother of Jesus helps us rediscover the role of woman and man, and calls us to be converted and sanctified by accepting her liberative dimension.

Luke 1:26–33 teaches us that the humility of Mary consists in the daring to accept the monumental undertaking proposed to her by God. At first Mary is in wonder. She is unsettled and disturbed, as a woman, at what God proposes to her. But the angel promises that the shadow of the Spirit will cover her. Then Mary says: "I am the servant of the Lord. Let it be done to me as you say" (Luke 1:38).

Mary's yes is a free, responsible yes by which she accepts being the vessel of the new creation to be embodied by her son Jesus. It is not the yes of self-denial, almost of irresponsibility, as it has been traditionally presented to us. Mary knows to whom she is committing herself.

We women of contemporary society, in all freedom, responsibility, and availability, hereby accept God's invitation to be part of the church that is to carry out the new evangelization. We accept God's invitation to share in the building of the new society.

We understand Mary's submission as a free act of surrender and self-bestowal for the purpose of co-creating, together with us, a new kind of humanistic and humanizing culture—one that will permit us to deliver ourselves from the rationalistic, inhumane, dehumanizing, hence discriminatory and utilitarian, culture of domination around us.

Like Mary, who receives God's invitation and accepts it freely and responsibly, so that the Spirit covers her and she becomes a servant "according to the word" ("according to your word" being the Greek idiom for the "as you say" of Luke 1:38), we accept the challenge of the third Christian millennium.

Mary is blessed because she bears and communicates life even though she knows the suffering her son will undergo in pursuit of the liberation of his people. What a blessing for our faith that she believed! Mary, a woman, is the model disciple for Latin American men and women performing the joint task of giving birth to a new society.

In a society like ours in Latin America, which has denied us the right to motherhood by sterilizing us psychologically (through the radical birth control campaigns) and economically (on a continent drowning in foreign debt)—where, politically, we are denied the right to life because dissent is silenced with prison, torture, and the threat of being put on a death list—where those who do their duty are murdered—where the use and abuse of drugs in the United States and the drug traffic in Latin America is killing our children, husbands, brothers, and friends— Mary, the prophet of the Magnificat, gives us the strength to fight, in solidarity and in community, for the right to life.

Mary's song sustains us in our quest for a bright tomorrow for our Latin American children. After all, her song proclaims to us that the promise is being fulfilled— that liberation, by God's mercy, is at hand:

He has shown might with his arm;
    he has confused the proud in their inmost thoughts.
He has deposed the mighty from their thrones
    and raised the lowly to high places.
The hungry he has given every good thing,
    while the rich he has sent empty away [Luke 1:51–53].

Mary the lowly servant of God—woman Mary—is God's decree of liberation, and the model of our action today. Woman—Latin American mother, eternal Eve, everlasting communicator of life—is also, like Mary, ever the first to communicate the good news, and thus to engender in her offspring a sense and feeling for their own life. The figure of Mother Mary helps us re-create woman's role, her identity and sense of belonging in the world. Man alone cannot create that world.

In today's world of sorrow and suffering, despair, war, and violence, where technological and scientific progress threaten to cancel life, the task of Latin American woman is to advocate, foster, further, and assume a commitment to the building of the new society and the new evangelization, so that she may never cease to give birth.

For now, she shares this dimension in precious few sectors of the Latin American church community. But little by little, she is coming into her own in the ministry and pastoral theology of the base communities. Feminist theology has called attention to the fact that the traditional oppression of women continues to be maintained among us at all levels of society, and that one of the great sins of the church is to have sacralized this oppression through its patriarchal discourse and the attitude of the majority of its leaders.

It is therefore incumbent upon us as Christian men and women to seek the genuine liberation of our peoples. It is our task to initiate a project that will permit the popular sectors (1) to assimilate Latin American history and the lot of women in that history, that by understanding our past we may understand our present and be able to transform it, building a genuinely human future; (2) to develop the capacity to submit to judgment by the word of the Lord, that we may make an irrevocable commitment to the building of the reign of God—the genuine reign of God, made up of male and female.

—translated from the Spanish by Robert R. Barr

NOTES

1. Michel de Certeau, *La escritura de la Historia* (Mexico City: Universidad Iberoamericana, 1985).

2. M. Zapata, "El hombre colombiano," in *Enciclopedia del Desarrollo Colombiano,* vol. 1 (Bogotá, 1974).

3. Otto Maduro, "Extraction de la plus-value: Répression de la sexualité et Catholicisme en Amérique Latine," *Liaisons Internationales,* 32 (1982), 18ff.

4. Jean-Marie Aubert, *La femme* (Paris, 1975), pp. 109ff.

5. Workers' leader and Brazilian Jocist director Angelina de Oliveira told us that up until 1956 the activists of the Brazilian JOC could not be engaged to be married, as this would mean not having enough time for the movement. See Ana María Bidegain de Uran, "Sexualidad, vida religiosa y situación de la mujer in América Latina," *Texto y Contexto* (Bogotá: Universidad de los Andes), no. 7 (Jan.-April 1986).

6. Magdala Velásquez, "Aspectos históricos de la condición de la mujer en Colombia," *Voces Insurgentes* (Bogotá), 1976.

7. Ana María Bidegain, "La organización de movimientos de juventud de Acción Católica en América Latina," thesis presented for the doctorate in historical sciences (Louvain: Université Catholique de Louvain, 1979).

8. Gustavo Gutiérrez, *A Theology of Liberation* (Maryknoll, N.Y.: Orbis Books, 1973), p. ix; first italics added. Originally *Teología de la liberación: Perspectivas* (Lima: CEP, 1971).

9. Leonardo Boff, *The Maternal Face of God: The Feminine and Its Religious Expression* (San Francisco: Harper & Row, 1987).

10. See CEHILA, *A Mulher pobre na historia da Igreja Latinoamericana* (São Paulo, Brazil, 1984); various authors, *El rostro femenino de la Teología* (San José, Costa Rica, 1986) [English edition: *Through Her Eyes,* Elsa Tamez, ed. (Maryknoll, N.Y.: Orbis Books, 1989)].

11. The group of laity called together by the Pontifical Council for the Laity to help prepare for the last synod (held at Rocca di Papa, May 1987), posed many of the themes that I am about to take up here. Although I was not elected by the bases of the movements or national churches (as we know, the organization of the church is not democratic), nevertheless the various tendencies and experiences of the Latin American church were represented, by and large, and their reflections seem to me to be representative of that very broad ecclesial spectrum.

12. Rosa D. Trapaso, *The Feminization of Poverty* (Latin American Press, May 1984); Thomas Kniesner, B. J. McElroy, and Steven Wilcox, "Family Structure, Race, and Feminization of Poverty," *Working Papers in Economics* (Duke University); see especially *Concilium* (Spanish edition), 1987, no. 214, *Las mujeres, el trabajo, y la pobreza.*

18

Love and Social Transformation in Liberation Theology

JOSÉ MÍGUEZ BONINO

Quite frequently, in North Atlantic theology, Latin American liberation theology is perceived as predominantly—or even exclusively—concerned with structural, macrosocial phenomena. It is a fact that the concern for the poor and poverty leads to assuming macrosocial analysis: the class structure, the phenomenon of dependence, the relationships of production, are indispensable tools for theological reflection. A more careful and discerning consideration, however, would have noticed from the very beginning that this analytical work was an instrument for a better understanding of "the human condition" of the people involved, at the service of that "salvific dialogue" that Gustavo Gutiérrez defined in the early 1960s as the mission of theology. When recent theological productions (Gutiérrez's last two books are a good example) develop the theme of spirituality, we are not witnessing a shift from an earlier concern with social, economic, and political liberation, but a deepening of the personal, subjective, and intersubjective dimensions that, from the very beginning, were constitutive of the spirituality that gave rise and made possible the emergence of a theology of liberation.

One way to explore this continuity is to track down one of the basic motifs which, in my understanding, has played and still plays a fundamental role in the language, experience, and spirituality of liberation theology: "the *love* motif."[1] Curiously enough, this has been even the case in liberation movements in Latin America outside the direct influence of the Christian or any religious inspiration. To anybody acquainted with Marx's harsh denunciation of Christian love in revolutionary struggle, it will be surprising that a confessed Marxist-Leninist like Ernesto "Che" Guevara gives love a central place in his thinking and even says that "a revolutionary is a person possessed by deep feelings of love."[2] Similar expressions can be found in the leaders of the Cuban and, more to be expected, the Nicaraguan revolutions. One could conceivably understand this vocabulary as a residue of a long established Christian tradition or even as a tactical use of language to evoke a positive response in religious persons. Both explanations, however, would witness to the persistence of a deeply rooted Christian consciousness.

Naturally, these expressions become more central and intentional in the discourse of Christians' participating in the struggles for liberation. In a mystic mood in the moving diary of Néstor Paz Zamora, killed in Teoponte guerrilla activities in Bolivia, or in a more articulated theological and ethical form in Camilo Torres. But it reappears continuously as a basic motivation for commitment. Hugo Assmann has framed, I think, the pertinent comment and question:

> With respect to the rich experience in which the personal need to love and be loved is realized, what is the meaning of giving one's life for one's brother in the wider context of the historical process? Is there not a need to enlarge the parameters of our experiential references in our understanding of the gratuitousness of love?

and a little later:

> Every attempt to discover a human motivation for the struggle for liberation sooner or later comes up against the need to inquire into the meaning of the radical praxis of dying for others. . . . This radical question is theological.[3]

Nevertheless, it is not my intention to follow these expressions in liberation theologians. Rather, I would want to suggest that this language corresponds to a primordial, decisive element in the experience of Christians and Christian communities committed to that struggle. It is this experience that demands the centrality of the love-motif in ethical and theological discourse.

THE GOSPEL FOR THE NONPERSON

Gustavo Gutiérrez has contended that, although evangelization means in the North Atlantic world to lead the secularized person to the acceptance of God's existence, in Latin America it is to help "nonpersons" to the awareness that God is their father. The first part of the statement may or may not be correct; the second is undoubtedly so. Nonpersons, the large masses of Latin American poor, however, are not an abstraction. Their present economic shape is determined by certain specific socio-economic conditions that, in greater or lesser degree and in somewhat different ways, affect most Latin American societies. Roughly since the First World War, a shift in the organization of production prompted a steady current of inter- and intra-Latin American migration, fundamentally from the rural to urban or semiurban areas. These displaced masses—a precarious industrial proletariat and much more common, a lumpen-proletariat, marginal populations around the big cities, displaced Amerindians from the forest areas—are the socio-economic matrix of the "nonperson," perhaps 60 percent of the total population.

These persons have always been "the poor of the land." As peasants in a semi-feudal system, or quasi slaves in the mines, or Amerindians in their reservations, they were never given or recognized to have full human status. But now the uprooting from their traditional social contexts has given a new face to their alienation. Sociologists call it anomie'—a condition in which the worldview, values, and norms that give stability to individual and collective life break down and persons are left without shelter. Self- and social-identity, social relationships, relationships to land

and country, ethical norms are shattered and have to be re-created. A resocialization, an adaptation or transformation of the person, has to take place, in coexistence, conflict, or syncretism with their traditions. But resocialization to which world? How? For what kind of society? What kind of life will this "new birth" produce?

This is the social and psychological locus where the question of evangelization has to be faced. In the new world into which this people are thrown, there are meanings, relations, roles, and self-understandings structured by the dependent capitalist societies. The market rules the exchange of work and commodities. Human beings are defined as producers and consumers in an arena of permanent competition. A few of the "newcomers" will become active participants in the race. But the great majority will be incorporated as passive "stuff" to be "used" or simply laid aside as "waste." This is the situation in which the emerging Christian communities (known as "base Christian communities") represent "another world" within this world, a new "socialization" with a different sign. Continuity with the old identity is preserved in a world of symbols and gestures deeply rooted in the people's consciousness. But the meaning and operation of these symbols and gestures is radically transformed. The center of this transformation is the experience of the community of mutual love and solidarity. This love is concretely lived in the common appropriation of the scripture and the church, the sharing of the sorrows and joys of everyday living, and the commitment to and organization for the solution of the problems and needs of the larger community.

Common celebration, reflection, and action are the cradle of a new personal identity. The nonperson claims and is given "the word," the right to speak and be heard. He or she becomes a subject of decisions. God announces the Word in this person's reading and responding to the gospel. The Holy Spirit builds the *ekklesia* as such persons come and celebrate together. Thus one's personal identity is not created over against "the others" but together with them. And social identity is not achieved by suppressing the individual (as in the mass) but by projecting and acting together in freedom. Of course, competition, conflict, envy, and indifference persist as in every human society. But the universe of meanings and symbols in which the whole ambiguous process takes place is conceived and approached as a project of love, an active, responsible, constructive, and lucid love in which the free reception of God's love and the openness in trust to the neighbor presuppose and implicate each other.

Can we recognize in this experience the New Testament account of "lostness" and "salvation"? It seems to me that we can. It is the transition from objective and subjective destruction (decay, corruption, death) to objective and subjective re-creation ("new creature"), an operation of the Holy Spirit bringing to life the Word of Christ in the mutuality of love, in the community of faith. This is precisely what liberation means—at the subjective level—for the nonperson. Liberation from defamation and scorn, self-hate and self-contempt, a reinstallation as active and responsible subject. How is the good news of God's unconditional acceptance historically mediated? We have almost exclusively relied on proclamation, understood as "oral proclamation." But we know today that words gain their meaning in terms of the language code and the accepted social relations and meanings. How can the message of unconditional acceptance be received unless a community of mutual free acceptance gives a sign to the meaning of the proclamation? Actually we are not speaking of two different realities but of a single event that needs to be accounted for in two sets of propositions (inseparable although not reducible to each other): "I am accepted by God" and "I belong in the community of love." New Testament studies have shown that Pauline formulas must be understood in this sense, not as a mystical, individualistic experience but "primarily as an ecclesiological formula."[4]

IDENTITY, MOTIVATION, AND COMMITMENT

This personal/communal process is of paramount importance when we think about the structural process of social transformation. Are we, in the struggle for change, forced to choose between the capitalistic, technocratic model where human life is sacrificed to the objective mechanisms of the universal market, or the captivity of a bureaucratic centralized society? The historical project, for which the Latin American liberation movements seek, could be characterized as a humanized, participatory society in solidarity.[5] But such a goal cannot be achieved automatically. In fact, the unavoidable harshness of the struggle for change under hostile conditions threatens to settle down as authoritarianism as the only self-defense. The only defense against it is the active participation of a people who assumes the sociopolitical project personally and collectively. In this sense the religious experience of which I speak is profoundly political: an experience of mutual love, which seeks expression in a political order congruent with the personalization-in-community that it has experienced.

In the language of Christians participating in the struggle for liberation, love as motivation for social change takes frequently the name of "solidarity." This notion has, of course, a long history, originating as a social and political concept probably among the forerunners of the French Revolution and taken up by the French socialists. It soon became a favorite among Christian socialists in England and men like Kutter and Ragaz in Switzerland. On the other hand it has also played a central part as one of the three basic principles (together with that of common good and of subsidiarity) in Catholic social doctrine. In ecumenical Protestant social teaching it has been central in the idea of "responsible society" and emphases such as "the unity of humankind," "the human community," and *Mitmenschlichkeit.* In Marxist thinking it has normally been restricted to class solidarity.

It is not difficult to discover the presence of all these influences in the Latin American use of the idea of solidarity as foundation and motivation of social and political action. But it would be a mistake to believe that it is merely the adoption of a concept taken over from an ideology or doctrine or a combination of several of them. What interests me is the way in which solidarity is lived, understood, and defined by groups of Christians under the conditions of the struggle for liberation in Latin America. In this respect I only want to suggest some points to be pursued.

1. It is a solidarity related to a specific historical situation. Medellín puts it in this way: "To commit oneself is to actively ratify the solidarity in which every human being is immersed, assuming the tasks of human promotion in the life of a specific social project," clarified later as "the peculiar circumstances of the present historical moment" (doc. 10, par. 9). Thus, we are not only speaking of an ontological structure but of a praxis. It is a "situated solidarity."

2. This means choices. Medellín again: "We must sharpen the awareness of the duty of solidarity with the poor, which love (charity) imposes on us. This solidarity means to make our own their problems and struggles" (doc. 14, par. 10).

Love, therefore, means a solidarity lived in the conflictive situations created by the struggle of the poor against injustice, exploitation, and alienation. We cannot simply adopt the notion of solidarity as developed within consensus models, which presuppose the existence of a fundamentally just situation and therefore deal merely with maladjustments within the system. As Denis Goulet has expressed it: "When underdevelopment prevails . . . existing structures are often unjust and devoid of legitimacy, despite a facade of legality. When this is the case, conflict may be necessary to challenge established order." In such cases, he adds: "authentic solidarity cannot be gained without serious conflict."[6]

3. Traditional doctrine tended to see solidarity as an ontological structure and consequently to base it theologically on a concept of human nature related to the doctrine of creation. This line is not to be rejected, but by itself it may result in a static and rather passive attitude. In Latin American spirituality—as expressed not only or mainly in formal theological literature but also in liturgy, poetry, and song—solidarity is seen more frequently in a christological and eschatological perspective. In the justly famous Medellín definition of peace, the concluding sentence says:

Peace is, finally, the fruit of love, the expression of a real fraternity among human beings, a fraternity brought about by Christ, the Prince of Peace, by reconciling all humankind to himself. Human solidarity cannot be fully realized except in Christ who gives a peace the world cannot give [doc. 2, par. 14c].

This is frequently articulated more specifically: Christ realized in his own life and death God's solidarity with the poor and oppressed. Thus, to follow Christ is to commit oneself to the cause of the poor. Eschatologically, solidarity is participation in a project that seeks to anticipate the universal unity in justice and love that is God's kingdom. While historically committed, and therefore engaged in the conflicts of history, solidarity with the poor is not a static thing but has an inherent tendency to universalize itself, overcoming the structures and conditions that disrupt social classes, peoples, races, or sexes, drawing into it the whole of humankind. "Class solidarity and the struggle that originates in it must not, therefore, be necessarily opposed to universal love but can be conceived as a condition for its realization."[7]

4. How does this tension between a committed partiality and the universal intention of the solidarity of love impinge on the struggle itself? I will not enter into the question of love and conflict or even love and violence, which has been frequently discussed.[8] But I want to underline one important aspect of this question—namely, How is personal and group identity perceived in a conflictive situation such as the present Latin American one? There is in such situations the natural tendency to define our identity by opposition, as a function of the existence of the enemy. It would be illusory to believe that such a tendency can be eliminated. But there is clear evidence that it is not dominant in the communities of Christians committed to social transformation. The image of the enemy is never absent—how could it be, when the enemy is constantly pressing his project of violence and death on the

poor!—but the deeper sense of identity is born in the encounter with the sister and brother who listen to me and speak to me, who sustain me in the struggle to the point of laying down their life for me.

Opposition to the enemy is not an end in itself but a temporary and necessary function of the solidarity with the brother and sister who suffer. Thus, the identity is not established as exclusive but as inclusive: of the poor and oppressed outside the community (in the larger society), of the poor and oppressed engaged in struggles of liberation elsewhere in the world, of the persons from other social groups and classes who make an option for the poor, and potentially for all as the conditions of oppression are overcome. The signs of this attitude can already be seen, not only in the different forms of religious expression but also in many concrete political actions.

5. The choice of the notion of solidarity represents also a theological perspective on political and social praxis. I would call it the perspective of "the greater good" as distinguished from that of "the lesser evil," which seems to inform much Protestant and some recent conservative Catholic approaches to politics (usually self-styled "realism").

In this view the doctrine of sin is made the decisive category for a theological anthropology and therefore the point of departure for understanding society. Moreover, the "eschatological reserve" is seen as limit in the assessment of human possibilities. Thus, the whole political order becomes primarily a negative endeavor, a way of preserving order against chaos, a salvage operation without eschatological future. If solidarity has any place in this scheme it is as "solidarity in sin," establishing the need for protection and thus for some form of balances and checks. There is no doubt that a certain motivation for political action and for social democracy and justice can be and has been built on this basis. The opposite perspective is usually characterized as "anthropological optimism," traditionally built on a restrictive view of the consequences of the fall of human nature.

Are we really forced to choose between an anthropological pessimism, which robs political life of all eschatological density, and an optimism resting on some precarious residue of "original justice" surviving sin? The theological shift I have indicated before opens a different perspective: the world and history are seen as encompassed and permeated by the presence of grace and the power of the Spirit. The love that motivates active and committed solidarity—which we can see in operation among the poor—is the love of the crucified Christ who, in the power of the Spirit, presses towards its fulfillment—"the all in all"—meanwhile opening in its way infinite new historical possibilities. Sin is thus seen not as a static quantity, an established blockage for human achievement, but as a negative force, with which a permanent struggle has to be waged. The quest for peace, justice, and freedom is therefore a permanent struggle until the end. The eschatological distance is not a predetermined limit to human creativity but an ever-moving target, or better, an absolute future that challenges us to discern the relative future striving to be born in the womb of present reality. Love, which is the only absolute future and the only absolute opposition to sin, is the power that gives an insight into new possibilities and motivates the struggle for "the greater good."

6. This unity of love (solidarity)/hope/commitment in the understanding of eschatology has another important consequence. It breaks the useless and misleading debate between a personal and a social eschatology. The question of personal

identity, which I discussed earlier, is here of fundamental importance. Personal identity is conceived in the bourgeois world as "privacy," a self-affirmation in permanent competition. Eternal life is the fulfillment of that vision: individualistic, privatist, and static: "A state of permanent satiety, from which every lack and anxiety have been excluded, heaven becomes a kind of 'eternal television.' "[9] In impersonal collectivism, personal identity is lost in collective identities. The future can, therefore, only be conceived as an ideal, utopian future society. There is no place for personal eternal life except as realized in the species.

In the experience of Christian community, one's personal identity and social commitment have become one single process: my personal future and that of the project of solidarity are interwoven. My personal identity is not "private property" but an interpersonal reality, a gift of the community. Those who "lose" their life in this project of love (the list is already long in Latin America) will "gain" it, not as a result of a divine adjudication of reward but because such life has entered into a fellowship of love with the crucified and risen Lord and his friends, which cannot be destroyed by death. Although we cannot expect much theological speculation at this very immediate base level, where the symbolic images of biblical eschatology are received immediately (though not literally), a deep conviction underlies the common gesture of naming the dead and having the community answer: "Present!"

7. Finally, it is interesting to note the absence of the apocalyptic evocation of the judgment and punishment of "enemies" in the eschatological language of the base Christian communities. The celebration of future freedom, the overcoming of exploitation and hunger, the victory over death and pain are celebrated in song and prayer. But there is scarcely a mention of the future of the enemy beyond their defeat. When the question is explicitly asked—mostly in historical rather than eschatological terms—the normal answer is that, once they have lost the power to oppress, they will be free (liberated) to participate in the common good. It seems to me that this attitude is the result of two things. On the one hand, the struggle is historicized rather than projected apocalyptically. Thus—in contradistinction to what happens in the reactionary religious rhetoric of the right—the enemy is not mythologized but kept at the human level where rational analysis can explain their attitudes (one frequently hears, from very simple persons, that the exploiters themselves have to be liberated). On the other hand, as I have insisted, the project is understood and lived as a project of love in solidarity, which is historically situated, but by its own nature universally open.

I must repeat that there should not be any idealizing or romanticizing of the "spirituality" I have tried to characterize. Together with all the forms of human weakness and sin, we find, however, a dominant "ethos" and a "project" that give coherence to the communities and this ethos and project can be best articulated around the "motif" of love. This, if we choose to put it in this way, is the subjective, personal, and communal side of the social and political activity just as the latter is the objective side of the ethos of love. To separate them is to misunderstand the whole movement.

NOTES

1. "Love" is one of the words that have suffered most from word-hyperinflation. The meanings of the corresponding words in biblical language are not simply

taken up adequately in either *charity* or *love*. Some biblical scholars have suggested "loyalty," "faithful solidarity," or "covenanted loyalty" as better equivalents.

2. Ernesto Guevara, *Obras Completas* (Buenos Aires: Editorial del Plata, 1967), vol. 2, pp. 19, 24.

3. Hugo Assmann, *Teología desde la Praxis de la Liberación* (Salamanca: Sígueme, 1973), pp. 69 and 76, respectively.

4. Rudolf Bultmann, *Theology of the New Testament*, vol. 1, pp. 130–132.

5. I have on purpose avoided a more direct political definition, not because I think it improper, but because it would require a more extended discussion than can be offered in this paper.

6. *The Cruel Choice* (New York: Atheneum, 1975), p. 140.

7. Girardi et al., *Cristianos y Marxistas* (Madrid: Alianza Editorial, 1969), p. 90.

8. Consult also G. Girardi, *Amor Cristiano y Lucha de Clases* (Salamanca: Sígueme, 1971).

9. Juan B. Libanio and Clara L. Bingemer, *Escatología Cristiana* (vol. 10 of the collection Teología y Liberación) (Buenos Aires: Paulinas, 1985), p. 290.

19

Taking African History Seriously: The Challenge of Liberation Theology

MARIE J. GIBLIN

In 1975, I was living in a cooperative village, called an Ujamaa village[1], in north-western Tanzania where about seventy-five families who needed land had gathered and were striving to make a new life for themselves on land that had been unoccupied except for a few homesteads. A school of one room was being constructed with plans for expansion. Besides the common fields, each family had private fields for cultivation. Another sister and I lived in a small house in the village, participated in common work in the village fields and other projects such as gathering rocks for the school foundation. We also worked with the women of the village and with the Christian community.

During the previous year, I had studied theology and had taken special interest in the tension that was evident between an existentialist theology (especially Karl Rahner) and the newer European theologies (Moltmann's theology of hope and Metz's political theology). Considering my involvement in Tanzania, it was not surprising that I was looking for a theology that would take into account African people's struggles for self-determination and search for new political, economic, and social models. I sensed a need for a theology that would reflect on human power to change oppressive situations while also taking into account our vulnerability as persons and as communities.

Life in the village was dominated by poverty, but that poverty did not eliminate the villagers' courage to fight it nor did it drive out their joy in relationships. Political arrangements pointed up the ambiguities of social change. Despite a well-articulated national goal of development from the grass roots, leadership was weak at the village level, and the next level of party and government officials told persons what to do instead of engaging them in a process of delineating what was wanted and needed to achieve genuine well-being within that impoverished community.

At the end of 1975, the village grew to two hundred fifty families when national government policy declared that all rural peasants must live in villages under government organization. Those living in the surrounding valleys were ordered to move into closer proximity on plots arranged by officials. In that area the plan went relatively smoothly, but in other areas of the country disorganization caused severe hardship, even deaths of children due to forced moves without preparation. These events provoked skepticism on the part of the people and new questions about the relations of the bureaucracy to the peasants.[2]

The church, as embodied in the local bishop (a Tanzanian, Christopher Mwoleka), was very much concerned about the concrete realities of peasants' lives together; he had asked us to live in the village to witness to the church's support for the people's cooperative effort. His hope was that if missionaries began living more closely with the people in the villages, then Tanzanian priests and sisters would begin to see that they need not be tied to the traditional parish structures that had been inherited from the colonial church.

My second year in the village, I read Gustavo Gutiérrez's *A Theology of Liberation*.[3] I had derived personal insight from studying Rahner, Metz, and Moltmann, but I began to see that those insights were individualistic and were not linked concretely to the world in which we live, when our horizons go beyond white middle-class Western culture. Their theologies had little relevance to my experience in the village. Reading Gutiérrez was different. Here was a theologian who knew about the problems of poverty and underdevelopment, and was willing to do the hard work of studying social science to search for explanations of oppression. Here was a person who could not conceive of our loving God without committing ourselves to those who suffer unjustly. Gutiérrez's theology dealt with our responsibility and capacity for social transformation and the revelation of God that takes place in our historical projects.

Read within the African context, the categories of Gutiérrez appeared quite Western. He did not put much emphasis on cultural liberation, an important issue in the eyes of contemporary Africans, nor did the struggles of women receive attention. Nevertheless, the book was enormously encouraging in providing sharper conceptualizations about salvation and liberation, economic dependency and conflict between classes, and the relationship between history and grace. These conceptualizations helped us to articulate better the theological depth and importance of the concrete struggles of the villagers to survive and provide a better life for their families.

Two insights of Gutiérrez struck me at that time. The first is the centrality of the commitment "to participate in the struggle for the liberation of those oppressed by others."[4] Especially meaningful to me in the village situation was his description of voluntary poverty as an act of solidarity with the poor and of protest against poverty.[5] This spelled out much more clearly what we were trying to live and had intuited but not yet been able to articulate so clearly. It was helpful to me as a white middle-class missionary, but in hindsight I see real difficulties in conceptualizing the persons with whom I was sharing everyday life as "the poor." One reason is that it turns persons into a mass of *others* and connotes a kind of objectification. Another reason is that Africans have been and continue to be so often portrayed in the West as poor and helpless that the use of this term risks reinforcing racist ideology. Africans themselves see "the poor" as those who do not have children (I am one of these), those who are chronically ill or severely handicapped. For this reason I will try to avoid the use of the term "poor" and use instead terms such as "African peasants and workers," which I hope will connote persons whose lives are constant struggles against poverty, but whose being is much more than "poor."

The element of protest as a result of solidarity was clarifying at the time and continues to be even more so today. Why should North Americans live for several years in an African village? The answer comes in terms of building a new shared future—a world where poverty is intolerable and shared well-being is the goal reflective of the dignity of human persons and our relationship with one another in God. The way to move toward that kind of world is through relationships of justice, of mutual respect, understanding, friendship, and love. Missionaries at their best seek to develop such relationships. Gutiérrez's notion of solidarity as a protest raises the question of what missionaries are to do with their experience. How are they to turn their solidarity into effective protest?

The second important insight of *A Theology of Liberation* is that all history is within the salvific process. Everyday lives and the struggles of whole classes like the peasants we were working with are all part of contemporary salvation history. History is one. Thus we must be willing to take historical reality with theological seriousness and seek God's word to us there.[6]

These two insights, the centrality of commitment to struggle against injustice and the unity of salvific history, are shared by African liberation theologians as well. Jean-Marc Ela, a Cameroonian priest, highlights the injustice of the cultural domination imposed on Africa as well as the politico-economic domination. The two issues cannot be separated. The church in Africa needs a more integrated notion of salvation that considers the church's role in the past and responds to people's situations today.[7]

These insights of liberation theology present fundamental challenges to the way missionary groups envision their role in Africa. In this article I would like to explore these insights and their implications for mission in Africa.

LIBERATION THEOLOGY'S CHALLENGE TO MISSION IN AFRICA TODAY

Commitment to Participate in the Struggle for Liberation

It is fairly easy for church persons in Africa quickly to assume that they have made an option for the workers and peasants, because working there for the vast majority of church workers (foreign and indigenous) means working within the context of these classes. But working *for Africans* is a different matter than working together *with Africans for their empowerment*. For this reason it may be better to think of the option we wish to make as an option to support the struggles of Africans for their own liberation, their own self-determination.

The approach of working *for* persons springs from a model of mission that sees some as senders, the religiously and materially wealthy, and sees others as receivers, those who are poor both religiously and materially. Even the incarnation can be badly used here to act as the model. Just as God took pity on poor human beings and sends the Son to rescue them, so too Christians of the First World take pity and send rescuers to the Third World.[8] This kind of approach can be not only a religious model but too often a model for humanitarian agencies as well. It is easily decried in principle, but in practice we have not yet seen the end of this approach.

The second approach, that of working together with African peasants and workers, is based on a model of mission that stresses the gifts of the people; the presence of God within persons, their culture and their efforts; and the ability of persons to unite together to work for the well-being of all in a new community more reflective of the reign of God preached by Jesus. This approach is not happy with focusing mission on the religious realm while attempting to ameliorate suffering via "development" assistance. Rather, mission is understood more in line with the 1971 Synod of Bishops' document *Justice in the World*, which stated that "action on behalf of justice and participation in the transformation of the world fully appear to us as a constitutive dimension of preaching the Gospel" (no. 6).

The reality is, however, that the combination of giving priority to the religious realm while maintaining a developmentalist mode of thinking is quite common in Africa. It is a safer mode than a transformational one, and one that bishops, priests, and sisters as well as many lay persons find congenial. The developmentalist mode, however, does not take history into serious account. It treats poverty at most as a result of past injustices, or an unfortunate fact of life, or blames it on natural causes, backwardness of particular ethnic groups, lack of education, and so on. Those holding a developmentalist view are unable to see that underdevelopment is an active historical process that began with the slave trade and colonialism, and continues even today via political, economic, and ideological measures that unite the interests of foreign and local elites.[9]

Some missionaries perceive avoidance of these questions as the best tactic. But this is far from being the overall picture. Other missionaries work diligently for justice and live in solidarity with African peasants and workers. It must be said that, in this regard as in so many others, white missionaries need African leadership. Most missionaries sense that they cannot be leaders in this area even when out of their solidarity they seek to take strong stands. When a crisis comes, missioners know that leadership in Africa belongs rightfully to Africans.

The protest element of solidarity must not be overlooked. Where does the missioner's responsibility lie when it comes to protest? A great deal of the responsibility of U.S. missioners lies in the United States when so many U.S. policies perpetuate the poverty and lack of self-determination in Africa.

Taking History Seriously

Being in true solidarity with African peasants and workers demands that we take their history seriously, relate our history in the West to theirs, and see that joint history in the context of God's saving plan for humanity. There are several historical facts that have massive implications for African peoples and for Western presence in Africa.

The first fact that missionaries in Africa have to take seriously is the history of the slave trade and colonialism, and the linkage between that history and the coming of Christianity to Africa. Most missionaries are intellectually aware of the linkage, but we have not come to grips with the results and the affective meaning of these historical facts for Africans.

We too easily exempt ourselves as unconnected to the slave traders and colonialists, not part of that history. In fact, it was Europe and the U.S.A. that profited from the triangular trade of West Africa. Our economies rapidly expanded at that time because of this exploitation. Africans taken from their homes as slaves provided huge profits to Europeans and Americans through their sale, their labor, and through the reproduction of labor power that slave women provided. Only in the late nineteenth century did Catholic missionaries step into the antislavery struggle in earnest. The Atlantic slave trade had already ended when in 1888 Pope Leo XIII encouraged Cardinal Lavigerie, the founder of the White Fathers (now Missionaries of Africa), to form a Catholic antislavery movement in Europe. Economic changes and pressure from the abolitionists had already ended the West African slave trade without moral leadership from the Catholic Church.[10] It is obvious that the church's entrance into the antislavery campaign occured in a context of fear of Islam in Africa. It was the *Arab* slave trade that Lavigerie campaigned against. Seeking to end the horrors of the trade, Lavigerie was preoccupied with the fear that Central Africa would become Muslim. In the European view of that time, and into which Cardinal Lavigerie fits, the slave trade had to be abolished so that Africans could be "raised to civilization" through the introduction of "legitimate commerce" and the "missionary enterprise."[11] This new interest in abolishing the slave trade followed immediately upon the partition of Africa by European powers in Berlin in 1884.

Colonialism followed with its own deleterious effects. African peasants were forced to grow crops for export by colonial demands for payment of taxes in cash. Hence African farmers were drawn into the world capitalist economy by raising commercial crops either on their own farms or on white settler estates where they served as migrant workers in poor conditions. Colonial administrations paid no attention to food production for Africans, which became more and more the responsibility of women, whereas cash crops and agricultural innovation became the domain of men. Families became subject to world prices and women became the subsidizers of these prices through their labor that kept the family fed despite low prices.

Mission schools were a mixed blessing. They provided education for new generations of leaders who would eventually lead their countries to political independence, but they were powerful tools for undermining traditional beliefs and social structures. In schools children learned not only to read, but look to Western leaders, values, and culture as the best, to disdain manual labor, and to look down upon their parents who followed traditional customs and religious beliefs.

A second important historical fact too easily overlooked is that Westerners and in particular white U.S. citizens were and are deeply affected by the history of slavery in the United States and continuing white racism. Both North Americans and Europeans go to Africa burdened with racial prejudice and ethnocentric value systems that yield only slowly and sometimes not at all to African intelligence, beauty, and values. With the best of intentions and a good deal of naivety we presume that through presence in Africa we are freed from the socialization processes in which we grew up and which instilled racial prejudice deeply within our worldview.

Racism, however, is not just a matter of prejudice, but of power. Racism has to do with control over standards of behavior, resources (money, education, personnel, etc.), definition of problems, and power to make and enforce decisions.[12] Here we have to face the issue of white power within the African church and more broadly within the African community.

Whites within the African church and within the African community wield tremendous power. I say whites because I think we need to see that white missionaries cannot be divorced as easily as we would like from the whites present as Western government representatives and as nongovernmental organizations' development and relief workers (NGO workers) such as Save the Children, Oxfam, and the like. We share too much in common. We have resources, vehicles, plane tickets home. We are all Westerners coming from nations that have benefited from the exploitation of Africa over the years. We have grown up in white cultures that have despised "blackness," while benefiting greatly from it. We are "a people" even though our culture pushes us to think of ourselves as individuals. In particular, as Americans, we have to face the fact that as a nation, we are supporting racist South Africa despite its death-dealing apartheid policies, its proxy wars in Angola and Mozambique, and its illegal occupation of Namibia. Indeed, through investment in South Africa itself and through aid to UNITA in Angola our nation strengthens South Africa.

The third historical fact is that we are living in the age of neocolonialism. Western media would have us believe that Africa is "naturally" poor. In fact, although some areas may be ecologically disadvantaged, this is not the case for the continent as a whole. Indeed, agricultural experts believe that Zambia alone is capable of feeding all of Africa. Southern Africa may be one of the potentially richest areas of the world. The continent is generously endowed with natural resources and peoples capable of managing them. But Africa is also the site of a new "repartitioning" by foreign governments and transnational corporations anxious for influence, trade, and access to resources on exploitive terms.

Prices for Africa's commodities have declined drastically in the 1980s and there is little hope for their rising. This has aggravated the debt problem in Africa and the two together have sent the economic spiral plummeting. The principal solution the World Bank and the IMF have suggested is to expand export crop production. But all countries in the South are receiving the same advice and the expanded world production is driving prices even lower. The result is increased impoverishment. This situation is what causes Africans to perceive the situation as living at the end of a pipeline of flammable gas—brush fires keep on igniting, and missionaries are there trying to assist those who are suffering, but missionaries are not addressing the question of what their responsibility is for shutting off the gas that originates in the capitalist economic system.[13]

If history is one and not separated into profane and sacred histories, then these matters are tightly woven within the history of sin and grace in Africa and in our world.

Questions That These Matters Raise

We have to ask ourselves if the role of missionaries now is really so different from that of missionaries in the colonial period. In the past missionaries thought they were serving a spiritual role in a completely different realm, though in fact they contributed to the overall acceptability and effectiveness of colonialism. Now we have to ask to what degree our presence contributes to the perpetuation of neocolonialism. We need to look beyond intentions to effects. To what extent does missionary presence serve to keep the West's conscience clear by providing the means to "help the poor," making psychologically possible the continuing exploitation—in other words, keeping the pipeline in place? What is the responsibility of missionary organizations for working diligently to shut off the gas and dismantle the pipeline?

To what degree is missionary work in Africa based on Western models that will require continued dependence? That is not a new question, but it is a continuously important one. In how many instances does our presence communicate lack of African competence? To what degree does our presence brake the taking up of responsibility by Africans? To what extent do church projects distract persons from facing more fundamental issues and drain the energy of those most equipped to grapple with these issues? To what extent do our works ameliorate situations just enough to demobilize persons—for example, providing services so that persons need not demand better services from the government?

On the other hand, to what degree do missionary work and relationships empower persons so that they realize their own communal strength and possibilities for effecting change? To what extent can whites and outsiders do this? Can we search out ways to do this more effectively with the local church and with local movements for justice?

Must missionaries give up hope of being constructive bridges between peoples, agents of a solidarity that leads to effective protest and growth to communion? I do not think the gospel allows us to give up hope on this. Feminist liberation theology has been very strong in showing Jesus as one who went out to others in *mutually freeing relationship*. This is what we need to emphasize today.

MUTUALITY IN MISSION—NEW POSSIBILITIES

Supposing we took seriously the possibility that all churches are missionary and each can learn from the others. Then we look at mission as truly a mutual process. Supposing, then, that every mission organization began to put its resources into mutual evangelization—that is, persons from one organization would go elsewhere, and persons from the "elsewhere" place came to the sending church. Brazilians might go to Mozambique and Mozambicans to Brazil. Mission could become an exchange among persons struggling as Christians against oppression.

Mission work in the U.S.A. would also then be taken seriously. For example, Maryknoll in the U.S.A. sends missionaries to East Africa. In this schema, Maryknoll would also bring East Africans to the U.S.A. to work for evangelization in the United States.

Efforts at mission education (sometimes also called "reverse mission") in the U.S.A. have usually been made by missionaries. This global education can serve as a vehicle for the "protest" that emanates from the solidarity that missionaries have lived. Missioners serve as a voice for the persons with whom they have shared life and daily struggles. Witnessing to the inspiration and life they have been given by Africans, missionaries can also protest against U.S. policies that continue the plunder of Africa.

With a mutual approach, missionary organizations would not be satisfied in letting their members be a voice for others, but would provide the resources so that, in our example, Africans can speak for themselves. Those of us who work cross-culturally know that we can only make attempts to represent others and that the best representative is a person from that culture who is committed to the liberation of her or his sisters and brothers. Teams of Africans and North Americans working together would witness to the mutuality that we are striving to achieve in mission.

It would be important that the style of mission education would also change. Now, most education efforts of this kind take place in white middle-class settings through the conventional channels of churches and schools. We should begin to think of the principles that have emerged in forming a church of basic Christian communities responsive to struggles for liberation. One principle is that change comes from below; hence one tries to reach the dispossessed who know what ought to change because they experience the injustice in their everyday lives. Another is that the experience of popular movements should be tapped and connections made with church groups when possible. These same principles should be applied to mission education, which might move from more traditional education to organization.

Representatives of oppressed African peoples could serve the evangelization of the United States in the following ways:

1. Share the richness of African culture and African Christianity—for example, perspectives on community and participation, on the meaning of salvation in the African context, and so forth.

2. Witness to the oppression of their people through the mechanisms of neo-colonialism and what those mean in the daily life of the people.

3. Learn about and witness to the interrelationships of the struggles of persons in the U.S.A. to those of African peoples. This would necessarily touch on racism (in the church as well as in society and U.S. foreign policy), economic issues (e.g., agriculture, labor, and trade), and the struggles of women in both places.

4. Urge action by citizens in this country, which is the "second front" for the struggle for liberation in Africa. When these African missionaries returned to their home countries, they would bring valuable experience and knowledge to their local church. They could serve as links joining the peasants and workers of Africa and low-income groups in the United States.

What might this approach mean? It could mean a step in the direction of a truly world church able to celebrate diversity and unity within the Christian community throughout the world. It could mean a world church that witnesses to the dehumanization process taking place because of economic, political, and cultural institutions that are not given from on high but can be changed to be responsive to human needs and aspirations.

For the United States church in particular, it could mean a shift in how we view the world. Already U.S. church connections in Central America in particular have helped the bishops to take stands that cut through the ideological morass fostered by the U.S. government that so distorts public understanding. This is already happening through existing solidarity groups and through the witness of those in sanctuary and the witness of missionaries. African presence in the U.S. church could bring apartheid, South Africa's proxy wars, economic exploitation, and famine into truer focus for U.S. Christians.

If a new style of mission education were used that highlighted the relationships between the struggles of oppressed and marginalized Americans with those of their brothers and sisters in Africa, then the U.S. church would be more truly missionary in this country by reaching out in a new way to those who suffer unjustly. It would be able to make connections with "the organized poor" and help to facilitate in further organization—even across national boundaries.[14]

CONCLUSION

All of this presupposes that the question of mission is not one of "servicing" Christians and initiating new Christians into a solely religious context. Rather, it presupposes that liberation and communion are the goals of the church, which is to be a sign and sacrament of the reign of God. The reign is one of love embodied in free, just, and mutual relationships between peoples and nations. Missionaries, persons enriched by the strength of African women and men, and drawn into their struggles through personal contact, are challenged by liberation theology to reshape mission into a truly mutual venture and together with Africans to reshape a joint history of oppression into a future of freedom.

NOTES

1. *Ujamaa* is Swahili for "familyhood" and is used to mean the Tanzanian form of African socialism. Julius K. Nyerere, president of Tanzania until 1985, developed *Ujamaa* as a political philosophy in the 1960s. See Nyerere's three volumes, *Freedom and Unity, Freedom and Socialism, Freedom and Development* (Oxford University Press, 1965, 1968, 1973).

2. Useful critiques of *Ujamaa* have been produced over the years. See, for example, Issa Shivji, *Class Struggles in Tanzania* (Dar es Salaam: Tanzania Publishing House, 1975); John S. Saul, *The State and Revolution* (New York: Monthly Review Press, 1979); Goran Hyden, *Beyond Ujamaa in Tanzania* (Berkeley: University of California Press, 1980); Andrew Coulson, *Tanzania: A Political Economy* (New York: Oxford University Press, 1982).

3. Gustavo Gutiérrez, *A Theology of Liberation* (Maryknoll, N.Y.: Orbis Books, 1973).

4. Ibid., p. 203.

5. Ibid., pp. 287–302.

6. Ibid., see esp. pp. 152–53, 177.

7. Jean-Marc Ela, "Le Role des Églises dans la libération du continent africain," *Bulletin of African Theology*, 6 (July-December 1984) 283; idem, "From Assistance to Liberation," *Lumen Vitae*, 36 (1981) 330–31. See also his *African Cry* (Maryknoll, N.Y.: Orbis Books, 1986).

8. Karla Koll, "Toward a Theology of Solidarity: Notes from Nicaragua," unpublished manuscript, Union Theological Seminary, New York, 1986, p. 37.

9. The title of the late Walter Rodney's famous book, *How Europe Underdeveloped Africa* is enlightening in showing that "underdeveloped" is an *active* verb.

10. John Francis Maxwell, *Slavery and the Catholic Church* (London: Barry Rose Publishers in association with the Anti-Slavery Society for the Protection of Human Rights, 1975), p. 119.

11. Richard F. Clarke, ed., *Cardinal Lavigerie and the African Slave Trade* (London: Longmans, Green, and Company, 1889), pp. 252–53, 274–84. The terms are those of Sir Samuel Baker, which Clarke used as evidence to back missionary arguments.

12. Brought out in a workshop on racism at the Maryknoll School of Theology in November 1987 by Nancy Richardson and Donna Bivens of Women's Theological Seminary in Boston.

13. A comment made in 1988 by Emmanuel Martey, a Ghanaian student at Union Theological Seminary in New York.

14. The Africa Peace Tours, month-long events annually since 1986, are an example of this approach. Informed African and American speakers, joined by educators and organizers, make presentations to groups in one U.S. region each year about conditions in Africa and U.S. policies there that are perpetuating a cycle of war and suffering. The aim is to show the relationships between the economies of the U.S.A. and Africa, to build support for counteracting militaristic policies in regard to Africa, and to strengthen connections among existing antihunger, antiracism, peace, justice, development, and human rights organizations in the United States. Hence, the tours attempt to reach those who are struggling for justice through movements in their local areas and to link these persons with the struggle for justice in Africa. This work requires research into the actual connections between militarism, racism, hunger, and poverty in the U.S.A. and warfare, hunger, and poverty in Africa. This is one of the frontiers of mission research for the future. The Africa Peace Tours are an example of ecumenical mission education. The tours are sponsored by the Africa Peace Committee, whose members include: Africa Faith and Justice Network, American Committee on Africa, American Friends Service Committee, Bread for the World, Church of the Brethren, Church Women United, Disciples of Christ, Maryknoll Missionaries, Mennonite Central Committee, Oxfam America, Presbyterian Peacemaking Program, Unitarian Universalist Service Committee, Washington Office on Africa.

20

The Logic of the Christian Response to Social Suffering

ROGER HAIGHT, SJ

How do Christians speak of God in the face of innocent social suffering? In his work, *On Job: God-Talk and the Suffering of the Innocent*, Gustavo Gutiérrez goes a long way in answering this question.[1] The book unfolds as an extended commentary on this classic work from the Judeo-Christian tradition dealing with the problem of the suffering of the innocent.

Several aspects of this work make this meditation of Gutiérrez of particular interest. First of all, the work tends to adopt a theocentric point of view. As the title indicates, the issue of the book is focused on God and "an appropriate language about God that does justice to the situation of suffering."[2] This does not mean that Gutiérrez has abandoned the christocentrism of Christian faith. Rather he treats Job—both the character and the book—as a kind of antitype of Jesus, and frequently points to how themes from Job have been recapitulated in the life and teaching of Jesus. But at the same time the explicit theocentrism of this work opens the thought of Gutiérrez both to a more universal perspective and an explicit dialogue with Jewish faith.

Secondly, the situation of Latin America, which presents us with a whole continent of persons who suffer innocently and unnecessarily, demands by its analogy with the situation of Job a reflective study of this canonical witness in the tradition of Christian faith. Gutiérrez explicitly locates his reflective commentary within the context of the liberation theology that itself responds to this situation. Although the work never relaxes its attention to the text of Job and dialogues with a tradition of other commentaries, Gutiérrez continually makes the relevance of this witness of faith come to bear on life in the concrete. "How are we to speak of the God of life when cruel murder on a massive scale goes on in 'the corner of the dead'?"[3]

The conclusion and thesis of the work is that in our understanding and speech about God "two languages—the prophetic and the contemplative—are required; but they must also be combined and become increasingly integrated into a single language."[4] "Without the prophetic dimension the language of contemplation is in danger of having no grip on the history in which God acts and in which we meet God. Without the mystical dimension the language of prophecy can narrow its vision and weaken its perception of God who makes all things new (Rev. 21:5)."[5] The key to the interpretation of Job lies in seeing what "the true relationship is between *justice* and *gratuitousness*."⁶

In the essay that follows I will enter into a dialogue with this thesis of Gutiérrez, which he has expressed in terms of biblical theology. My goal will be to uncover the anthropological dimensions and underpinnings of these "languages" about God. The intention here is not to negate the confessional stance of Christian theology but to transcend it by showing that beneath the Christian language about God there is also a logic or deeper grammar that can be uncovered by an analysis of common human experience. The apologetic intent here lies in the effort to show that religious and specifically Christian faith is universally relevant and appeals to dimensions of human experience as such. Although the point of departure of this essay is anthropological, its viewpoint is not anthropocentric; the point is to bring to the surface by analysis the common structure and transcendental dimensions of the human experience that underlies the languages that Gutiérrez has uncovered through his analysis of Job. To accomplish this I will bring into the conversation a number of other contemporary Christian theologians from different continents.

Christian language about God contains a great variety of themes and dimensions. Indeed, it would be somewhat arbitrary to limit in any exclusive way the languages about God in the face of human suffering to only two. In fact, I see a third prominent and distinct aspect of Christian language about God in Gutiérrez's treatment of Job, which he has included under the theme of contemplation—namely, the language of God's weakness in relation to human freedom and responsibility. In what follows, then, I will deal with four aspects of the language about God that provoke an anthropological analysis. These are (1) the language of prophecy, (2) the language of contemplation, (3) the language of freedom and responsibility, and (4) the language of faith as praxis. This last theme is more prominent in Gutiérrez's earlier work but remains implicit in his work on Job. For each of these "languages" I want to try to uncover an anthropological constant that helps to explain why these languages can correspond to a potentially universal experience. It should be clear that in what follows I shall not be engaging the Book of Job but Gutiérrez's theology.

THE LANGUAGE OF PROPHECY

Gutiérrez does not dwell on the meaning of the term "language," but allows it to unfold in the course of his work. For my part I take this term as having a very generalized meaning that refers to the major themes that characterize a set of words and statements used in a particular context. A language designates an intentionality that lies implicitly embedded in how persons speak in a certain situation and in what they say.⁷ Beneath the many words lies a truth, a conviction, a structured and discernible relationship to that which is spoken. It can be uncovered by analysis of the many things that are said. It should be recalled that in all of what follows, the language described arises out of the situation of an experience of innocent suffering. In that situation, some of the elements of the prophetic language of Christian witness according to Gutiérrez are the following three.

First of all prophetic language is most fundamentally a language of protest. "Those who suffer unjustly have a right to complain and protest."⁸ This complaint and protest unfolds at many levels and is directed at several objects. The language of prophecy protests against the situation as being unjust. By definition, when the innocent suffer, it is unjust; they find no justification for their suffering. The language of prophecy therefore also rejects every rationalization of the situation. Any received ideology that tries to make sense out of the situation and hence justify it becomes refuted by the situation itself. As it were, the language of prophecy allows the facts of history to contradict received theology. The language of prophecy even goes further to complain against God; Job's prophetic language becomes expostulation against God. "But my words are intended for Shaddai; I mean to remonstrate with God" (Job 13:3). The first characteristic of the language of prophecy, then, lies in this theme of reaction in protest.

A second quality of authentic prophetic language as it is analyzed by Gutiérrez is that it does not remain a private language; it is a generalized language. In other words, in terms of Job, although he began to protest his own personal suffering, it was not long before he realized that his condition was shared by many others. No one alone, as an isolated case, is the victim of innocent suffering. Theoretically even one case of innocent suffering would be an outrage. But in fact, the contradiction is magnified by its actual extent: whole groups of persons, masses of them in fact, find themselves in an identical situation. The identification with others grounds and solidifies the basis for the protest and complaint. In the case of Job, according to Gutiérrez, he "sees that commitment to the poor puts everything on a solid basis, a basis located outside his individual world, in the needs of others who cannot be ignored."[9]

Thirdly, insofar as the language of prophecy is the language of faith, it paradoxically both raises the question of God and at the same time makes an assertion of what God must be like. The mystery of innocent suffering will never cease to deeply challenge all faith in God. But by the very same token the prophetic language of faith insists that God is such that God too must stand against the situation. Because of the generalized condition of innocent suffering, then, this prophetic language itself becomes generalized; it appeals to a historical tradition that places God against innocent suffering as an advocate of those who suffer. In the prophetic tradition, the language of the prophets "has its historical roots in commitment to the poor, who are the favorites of God."[10]

In sum, prophetic language is the language of critical judgment that calls into question the historical situation of innocent suffering and all theologies that might in any way justify it. The force, the solidity, and the authenticity of this language depends on recognition of the generality of the situation and the conviction that at bottom God cannot accept it either and still be God.

The Logic of an Experience of Negative Contrast

Let me begin this dialogic response to Gutiérrez's presentation of the language of prophecy by a brief explanation of what I mean by the term "logic." As was said above, a given language motif has a theme or generalized meaning, the common elements of which can be found by an analysis of the language itself. But these themes are merely given; in itself a specific language does not contain an explanation of itself. The deeper rationale of the existence of a common language must come from the structure of the experience that it thematizes or that generated it. Such a view does not entail any separation of experience from language in human beings; all experience of human beings is somehow and in various degrees influenced by the languages we speak, for we are linguistic beings. But at the same time, the genesis of a common language, especially a common analogous language that transcends particular cultures, must have its deeper grammar in some common human experience. It is this level of experience that is aimed at with the idea of a "logic" of these particular languages of faith.

One can locate the logic of prophetic language in what Edward Schillebeeckx calls an experience of a negative contrast.[11] In a negative situation, such as one of innocent suffering, human beings commonly come to a realization that can be simply expressed by the exclamation, "This should not be." Behind this expression lies what looks like a kind of simple apprehension or direct perception that the objective condition is wrong and should not be. In fact, however, such a judgment is reflective, for it implies a distance and level of abstraction from immediacy without which there could be no judgment at all. But the conclusion is not reached by inference; the reaction is elicited out of an immersion in an objective state of affairs by the whole of a person. The statement reflects a negative value response and judgment that engages the whole person's response to a situation as a whole.

Such a contrast experience is not and cannot be wholly negative. The recognition of a negativity presupposes a positive horizon without which negativity would not appear. What is being experienced here is precisely a contrast. Without some intimation of what things should be, one could never perceive a negative situation as negative. This positive conception may be latent and not clearly imagined or conceived; indeed because it refers to a state of affairs that does not exist, it may be unknown in a concrete or specific sense, and thus the expression of an idea.

Finally, an experience of a negative contrast implies a desire that the negativity itself be negated, that things be righted. It may or may not imply the active desire to take on the responsibility to change them. One can have such an experience of negativity and at the same time feel powerless to effect a change.

This perception of negativity, which is so powerful in a situation of innocent suffering, especially on the part of those who are its victims, is a deep structure of common human experience. It is so elemental that some form of it can be seen at work in the basic datum of human perceptions of value. Without it one could not experience "oughts" and "shoulds," for ideals make no sense apart from a relationship to some contrasting state. It lies at the foundations therefore of all ethics. This does not imply that ethics and law have a merely negative function—against sin, for example, as was sometimes held in Christian tradition. But all ethics stands in contrast to some negativity, some lack of right order in human affairs, and a negation of such a negation.

So, too, an experience of contrast underlies all reinterpretation of truth, the retrieval of authentic meaning from the past expressions that do not fit present experience. The hermeneutics of suspicion, in the various forms it takes in Christian theology, such as demythologization and deideologization, rests on a deep perception that something is wrong, does not fit, does not correspond to the implicit perception of what should be.[12]

Prophetic language, then, rests on an experience of negativity as contrasted with the implied or searched-for ideal or right order of things. This negative experience and its prophetic language call into question reality as it is and how it is rationalized.

Thus, for example, in the case of Job, and generally in the situation of innocent suffering, the implicit and more truthful idea and ideal of God is appealed to in judgment of the situation, and at the same time the understanding of God that justifies or rationalizes this situation is negated. Without such a radical experience of contrast, one which deeply calls the way things are into question, there can be no continual movement toward more adequate understanding of truth, and no real openness to the reality of God.

THE LANGUAGE OF CONTEMPLATION

The second God-language that arises in the situation under the impact of unjust and innocent suffering Gutiérrez calls the language of contemplation. The motifs that thematize the language of contemplation stem from an encounter with God. In the words of Job: "I once knew you only by hearsay, now my eyes have seen you" (Job 42:5). The language of contemplation is still language about God, but the basis for it lies in an experience of personal encounter with a God who is also personal.[13] Because of this as it were direct encounter with God, Job "sees things differently now. God is present to him as an abiding newness."[14] The transition is from a general notion of God, from knowledge that is merely about God, from an ideology of God, to a personal encounter with God. The themes of this language of God can be summarized around the three characteristics it predicates of God: God's sovereignty, God's freedom, and God's gracious love.

First, the encounter with God reveals God to be truly God. God is sovereign, creator, and governor of the universe, who overwhelms anyone who comes in contact with this God. Thus God simply overpowers Job with the awesome and universal scope of God's laying the foundations of the cosmos, of reality itself. Before this God human beings cannot but experience their littleness.[15]

Secondly, God's sovereignty includes God's freedom; God is sovereignly free. Nothing from outside God binds God, for God is the very source of all that is, and everything emerges out of God's freedom. This freedom of God is best illustrated by the way it breaks open all anthropocentric conceptions that implicitly limit God. "God's speeches [to Job] are a forceful rejection of a purely anthropocentric view of creation. Not everything that exists was made to be directly useful to human beings; therefore, they may not judge everything from this point of view."[16] "God will bring [Job] to see that nothing, not even the world of justice, can shackle God."[17]

Thirdly, the language of contemplation recognizes that the total gratuity implied in God's sovereign freedom is not simply arbitrariness but graciousness and love. In a way this is the central characteristic of the Jewish and Christian languages of God; God is love and grace. God rules out of an intention of love. "The main idea has now been established: in the beginning was the gratuitousness of divine love; it—not retribution—is the hinge on which the world turns."[18] This is the language of grace and the freedom of grace; God's priority absolutely overrides every idea of merit in the face of God. "Nothing, no human work however valuable, merits grace, for if it did, grace would cease to be grace. This is the heart of the message of the Book of Job."[19]

Finally, Gutiérrez insists that the two languages of prophecy and contemplation should not be separated. The language of contemplation, rather, absorbs into itself the language of prophecy so that the two are always together and united. It follows that "the gratuitousness of God's love is the framework within which the requirement of practicing justice is to be located."[20] The prophetic concern, the practice of justice, and work at constructing a just society have their "value and ultimate meaning only within the vast and mysterious horizon of God's gratuitous love."[21]

The Logic of Revelation

What is the structure of revelation generally and the Christian revelation of God in particular that account for the language of contemplation? In the light of a general theory of knowledge of God, I will outline here a conception of Christian revelation that supports the language of contemplation as Gutiérrez has described it.

Because human life unfolds in the particularities of history, and because all human knowledge is bound to concrete sensible data, no human conceptions of reality escape the mediation of the world. The same applies to religious knowledge. It is true that the freedom that characterizes human existence is of itself a self-transcendence that reaches beyond itself, beyond its contingency and finitude, and toward an absolute. One can document and explain a universal religious sensibility that calls for and recognizes transcendent mystery. But there can be no concrete, positive, specific, or defined conception or knowledge of God without historical mediation.[22] All and every definable notion of God comes from revelation through a historical medium. In Christianity, that medium is Jesus of Nazareth. Although everything that Christians say of God does not come exclusively from this source, still Jesus remains the positive source and negative norm for whatever is specifically Christian. Without in any way trying to limit the fulness of this revelation of God in Jesus, some characteristics of this revelation will help to explain the language of contemplation, especially in relation to the structure of contrast.

The twentieth-century theologians of revelation have clarified the content of revelation and the way it is known. Christians affirm that God is and is one, that God is personal and benevolent, and that God is a God of salvation. But these affirmations do not represent the kind of objective knowledge that human beings have of the finite realities of this world. Christian revelation and the knowledge implied in it can only be explained in a language drawn from interpersonal knowledge and the encounter between subjects. In the logic of Emil Brunner, revelation does not communicate knowledge *about* God as about an object; revelation is rather an encounter with a subject analogous to the self-communication of one human subject with another.[23] The point here is not to provide an extended phenomenology of the dynamics of the revelatory personal self-communication of God in the medium of Jesus, but simply to name the distinctive structure and logic of revelation itself. As human beings freely communicate their inner selves to others through the media of bodily gesture and sign, so too God has made God's personal self present to and available in and through the life of Jesus. And just as one encounters another as subject within the bodily symbol, so too does the Christian encounter God in and through Jesus.

The effects of such a revelatory encounter dramatize its nature. A personal encounter with God is revolutionary and transforming. According to H. Richard

Niebuhr, who is dependent on Brunner and the whole Protestant tradition at this point, such a personal encounter with God through revelation when it is considered existentially cannot fail to turn everything upside down.[24] It is not that all natural knowledge is negated. It is not that everyday human knowledge, what human beings know to be true and right, is falsified. Rather it is transformed, seen in a new light, from a new perspective, given a new dimension, in view of a confrontation with God and the experience of the personal self-presence of God. To put it negatively, what is known within the context of our standing alone before nature and history is provided an entirely new horizon and context when one stands before the God who is creator, governor, judge, and redeemer of the universe.

Finally, this revolutionary reversal of all truth and value can be seen specifically in relation to justice. Within the context of Christian revelation one can no longer view justice merely from one's own or one's group's point of view. God's self-presence intervenes with a universal point of view.[25] It is true that in Christian revelation God is encountered as personal savior, as establishing *my* value and identity in divine love. But that gratuitous love for each person is impossible for me without being equally the love of all human beings. In the measure that one experiences the gratuity of God's love for oneself, in the same measure must one recognize that all human beings are God's own.

In sum, in the Christian view of things, the absolute ground for justice does not lie in a creaturely equality, which on inspection does not in fact exist. Rather justice has its ground in the revealed fact that all human beings are God's own and share in the value that God's love bestows on them. Human concepts of quid pro quo, of retributive justice, of measuring according to merit, of equality, are overthrown. God's perspective both levels and raises up. God's creative love fills up what is lacking, reestablishes what is missing, in all persons. In this sense are the poor the favorites of God in a special way, for the more one lacks in integral humanity and acquired power, the more powerful is God's love in reestablishing it. The very logic of justice is transformed by the God who is encountered in Christian revelation.

THE LANGUAGE OF FREEDOM AND RESPONSIBILITY

The third dimension of language of God arising out of the impact of innocent suffering is a minor theme in Gutiérrez's *On Job*. Indeed he does not treat the language of freedom and responsibility as a "distinct language," but it does merit a chapter within the context of the language of contemplation. Yet certain aspects that stand in paradoxical relationship to the sovereign freedom of God might encourage one to distinguish it from the former. These three characteristics are God's self-imposed limitation, God's respect for human freedom, and the idea of a collaboration of two freedoms.

First, Gutiérrez's analysis of the Book of Job yields the discovery of God as not only sovereign and all-powerfully free, but also as strangely weak. "In other words, the all-powerful God is also a 'weak' God."[26] This weakness or limitation of God's sovereign freedom does not come from outside God. It is rather a self-limitation of God. "Yahweh too has limits, which are self-imposed. Human beings are insignificant in Job's judgment, but they are great enough for God, the almighty, to stop at the threshold of their freedom and ask for their collaboration in the building of the world and in its just governance."[27]

Secondly, one can understand this self-limitation of God as being grounded in the graciousness and love that qualifies God's omnipotent sovereignty. God respects the inner nature and character of what God created. It may seem to make sense by human reckoning that God simply destroy the wicked and establish justice; but this is transformed in the light of God's revelation. "God wants justice indeed, and desires that divine judgment . . . reign in the world; but God cannot impose it, for the nature of created beings must be respected. God's power is limited by human freedom; for without freedom God's justice would not be present within history."[28] Precisely the contemplation of the mystery of divine freedom "leads to the mystery of human freedom and respect for it."[29]

Thirdly, the respect that God bestows on the inner nature and character of the human freedom that God created does not remain a passive noninterference. Rather God's gracious love reaches out to this freedom and asks for its cooperation. Thus the theme of collaboration seen in the words above falls into place. God asks for the collaboration of human freedom in the just governance of the world. In sum: "The correlate of the divine freedom that God revealed to Job is human freedom. The first calls to and establishes the second."[30]

The Logic of Faith

Can a fundamental theology of faith confirm the biblical language of freedom and responsibility? Does an analysis of the logic of faith, especially as a response to Christian revelation, support one of the implicit messages contained in the Book of Job? In responding to these questions I shall assume that faith may be understood as the human response to revelation. In a way, faith is a universal phenomenon; all persons live by some faith. But within this general structure, the specific qualities of Christian faith can be understood in relation to its object and the qualities that it possesses as these are known through revelation.

On this premise it would be impossible to reduce faith to a form of knowledge. Faith should not be understood either exclusively or primarily in terms of an assent to some objective truth. If Christian revelation is best understood in terms of interpersonal encounter, then faith also must be thought of as unfolding within a different context from believing or accepting an objective knowledge about God. This should not be taken to imply that faith lacks a cognitive dimension, for we are after all speaking of intentional human behavior. But an initial approach to faith within the context of objective or intellectual knowledge distorts the reality itself.

H. Richard Niebuhr is in agreement with the whole of modern theology when he speaks of faith in the existential terms of a response of the whole person to a center of meaning and value.[31] His analysis of faith shows that it has two fundamental dimensions or qualities. The first is passive or receptive. In the encounter with the object of faith, one recognizes that it bestows upon the self a value and meaning from outside the self. In Christian revelation this quality has been enshrined in the theology of faith in terms of grace. The object of faith comes to us; we do not create it. The whole history of the theology of faith witnesses to the initiative of God in its being awakened. Faith is not simply a product of a will to believe, but an accepting of God's action of self-disclosure and love. This surrender to and trust in God is not unconscious, but although it tacitly includes a knowing awareness of God, it also completely transcends objective knowledge.

The second essential dimension of faith confirms this transcendence of theoretical knowledge and unfolds within the sphere of a holistic and practical response to reality. All faith is also active; it contains within itself loyalty and fidelity to the object of faith. Implied within the object of faith is the value that it is for the self and what it stands for. Thus the response to the object of faith includes making it and its cause one's own cause. It becomes that for which one lives, dedicates one's life, guides one's behavior, directs one's action. A response of faith to the God revealed in Jesus means making this God's cause the central moving interest in one's life.

Two things flow from this fundamental theological understanding of the nature of faith that are relevant to the language of freedom and responsibility. First of all, this understanding of faith both presupposes human freedom and confirms it. Without a response of human freedom there would be no revelation and no faith at all. This intrinsic nature of faith is also reinforced in the experience of a personal God who personally encounters human beings as persons. The whole logic of faith unfolds within a context of a human freedom that responsively accepts and is responsible to and for what it accepts. Secondly, this response of freedom must also include an active dimension of commitment. Faith to be faith involves a dedication to God's cause, and such a practical response must involve action. This raises the question of what God's cause is and how it is known which will be the theme in what follows.

THE LANGUAGE OF FAITH AND PRAXIS

The language of faith in the end must be translated into the practical language of praxis. I will not spend a great deal of space analyzing this constant and familiar language from the earlier work of Gustavo Gutiérrez.[32] It represents a fundamental theme in liberation theology, which all liberation theologians have accepted. I will merely schematize this language in three themes that characterize it.

First, in this language of faith the term "faith" very nearly becomes synonymous with the term "praxis". Praxis not only reveals what faith is; both generally speaking and relative to any particular faith, praxis also tends to be understood as identical with faith. Thus theology arises after and on the basis of praxis, and is spoken of as reflection upon praxis, in a manner analogous to the way that traditional theology spoke of itself as reflection on faith. The logic for such language can be seen in the immediately preceding discussion of the logic of faith. Once one assumes that faith cannot be reduced to an objective mental assent to a truth about something but is also a commitment of the whole person to a cause, and once one assumes an existential and concrete historical point of view in responding to the question "What is faith?," it follows that one's practice will be closely associated with one's real commitment.

Secondly, the term "praxis" may be seen to add two dimensions to the more general term "practice". Praxis points to conscious, intentional, and thematized practice. Praxis refers to human action that is not simply blind, but which emerges out of critical reflection and theoretical thought. Moreover, praxis refers in Gutiérrez's thought to liberative action, action intending the overcoming of oppression in society. Both of these themes can be related to the ideas of God's desire for justice and God's invitation for the cooperation of human freedom that were seen in the languages of prophecy and freedom and responsibility. It follows that praxis is the actualization of the explicit or implicit intentionality of Christian faith in the God revealed in Jesus.

Thirdly, and on this basis, Gutiérrez can define Christian spirituality as "a concrete manner, inspired by the Spirit, of living the Gospel; it is a definite way of living 'before the Lord,' in solidarity with all human beings, 'with the Lord,' and before human beings."[33] Quite simply, faith plays itself out in action, and the specific way of life or praxis of the Christian is the actualized faith that unites a person to God.

In sum, in the language of faith as praxis the two are not logically identical, but are so inseparable that one cannot conceive the one without the other. Faith refers to the underlying intelligent acceptance of and commitment or loyalty to a cause that becomes real in praxis. Praxis is the enactment, realization, and actuality of an only logically prior faith. What has to be inquired into is the logic that guarantees that this commitment of faith in praxis is ultimately meaningful, valid, and real.

The Logic of the Ultimate Value of Faith as Praxis

The logic of faith involving freedom and active responsibility leads to the language of faith as praxis. But what is the ultimate logic of faith as praxis? What is it for and where does it lead? In the modern period human freedom cannot be reduced to a freedom of choice that so often dominated the discussions of grace and freedom. Today human freedom is understood in terms of creativity and novelty. In a historically conscious culture, where the rapidity of contemporary change and newness assaults and disorients the inner desire for security and order, one cannot avoid the question of the purpose of human freedom and the direction of human achievement. On the one hand, faith in God the creator requires the supposition that God had a reason and a purposeful intention in bestowing on human beings their power and inherent desire to create new things. And on the other hand, given this creative energy, human beings cannot avoid the question of its *telos*, its goal, that to which it should be directed. Another way to ask this question would be in terms of God's cause. What is God's cause?

In the Christian view of things, not only the nature and concept of God are mediated through revelation, but also any concept of the will of God too must come from the historical medium of that revelation—namely, Jesus of Nazareth. There are of course other sources for a discernment of God's general will, but they must come into congruent relationship with the central symbol of the revelation of God, the life and person of Jesus, as their negative norm and positive guide. Also, in the biblical symbols of Christian theology, the metaphysical question of teleology is transformed into eschatological terms. Thus the search for the will of God and the purpose of human action must enter into dialogue with the central message of Jesus' preaching, the kingdom of God. Although it is difficult to decipher exactly what Jesus meant by the kingdom of God, it represents Jesus' understanding of God's sovereign will both for this world and eschatologically for the absolute future. In sum, one must ask the eschatological question, and the Christian answer to that question is the kingdom of God.

But what role does human freedom play in fashioning the kingdom of God? In the theology of Juan Luis Segundo this question generates the response that the final kingdom of God is a work of God and God's collaborators. Something is pending relative to final reality, and it is dependent upon the work of human beings.[34] In Segundo's view, the works of love "will constitute a definitive service to the plan of God." "Only love is constructive, and constructive forever."[35] On the one hand, works done in love will be raised up on the pattern of the resurrection of Jesus to constitute a real dimension of final and absolute reality. On the other hand, what is not done in love is condemned to unreality, and God will not make up for what is placed in human hands to fashion in love.[36]

Is there a logic underlying this position, or is it a gratuitous assertion? And can it be reconciled with the language of contemplation and grace? The logic underlying this position appears to me to be twofold, at once negative and positive. On the one hand, one must say that the creative action of human freedom somehow contributes to the kingdom of God, for otherwise human action would in the end be meaningless. As Segundo puts it, "the values to which Jesus of Nazareth bore concrete testimony in his message and life can be realized only if the 'I' of each person has the power to accomplish a project that is both personal and definitive."[37] The sheer meaningfulness of life in history is dependent upon its ability to contribute to what Jesus called the eschatological reality of the kingdom of God. In terms of an experience of negative contrast, without some continuity between the history of human freedom and the eschaton, history itself is evacuated of real significance. But positively, on the other hand, in contrast to the negative experience of futility, this view corresponds exactly to what one encounters in a revelation of a personal God who is loving creator. The creativity of human freedom in history and into the future appears as the intentionality of the God who created it as meaningful and who respects it as creativity.

A continuous eschatology can and must be absorbed into the logic underlying the language of contemplation and grace, and the logic underlying the traditional idea of cooperative grace allows this possibility. Although originally conceived by Augustine in terms of freedom as free choice, and although developed by Aquinas in terms of teleology, the notion of cooperative grace equally illumines the exercise of freedom understood as creativity in the context of eschatology and a historically conscious age. There is no work of love that is not initiated and sustained by the totally gratuitous support of God's grace as Spirit. This grace, however, does not negate human freedom, but releases and empowers it. Thus God's final glory is not the negation but the transformation of what is accomplished in love by human freedom in history. In the words of Segundo:

The glory of God and the defense of the Absolute do not entail relativizing historical reality in order to make room for the irruption of God alone. The glory of God means seriously making human beings sharers in a joint construction project and giving them all they need to offer this cooperation, without which God alone will do nothing. The personal, creative stamp of each one of these human cooperators (*synergoi* in Greek) with God will be tested and verified in love, in "mutual service." Then it will be inserted in the definitive reality, in the only way that a finite freedom can do that: i.e., by hammering away, like the chisel of a sculptor, at the stubborn solidity of the resistant materials, but with the invisible hope that those materials will be overcome and to some extent turned into God's new heaven and humanity's new earth, the new creation as the joint work of Father and children.[38]

CONCLUSION

H. Richard Niebuhr has shown that every ethical vision, insofar as it is a system, rests on some fundamental faith in a center of value.[39] The very conception of a coherent organic set of values requires a dogmatic premise or confessional postulate that acts as the controlling value to which other values are relative. But this does not imply a complete relativism of ethical systems, for these centers of value can be objectified, analyzed, and compared among themselves and with the data of experience. The point of this essay has been to show that beneath the confessional language of biblical theology there lies a structured logic that can be brought forward and analyzed. The liberationist interpretation of the ethical vision implied in Christian faith is not arbitrary, but one whose logic can be rendered public and intelligible within the context of common human experience. Although the reduction of this logic to four elements scarcely does justice to the whole dynamics of either Christian faith or the liberationist view of it, at least it may serve as a schematic structure for discussion. To summarize, these four elements are the following:

First, every ethical vision of what should be rests finally against the background of some negative experience. One paradigmatic example of such a negative experience is that of innocent suffering. The Book of Job is a classic because it represents universal human experience. But this universality should not be used as a cover for the historical concreteness of human suffering that is scandalous only in its actuality. When unjust human suffering reaches the proportions of a general social condition, there must be protest.[40] There must also be a questioning of the fundamental values that underlie the situation. The deep negative contrast that is written into the actual situation itself necessarily calls for prophetic speech that calls for change. It also raises the fundamental question of finding once again the positive values upon which a proper order can be constructed.

Secondly, as was said, the most fundamental values upon which an ethical vision rests are a matter of faith that cannot themselves be demonstrated. In the Judeo-Christian tradition of monotheism, they find their ground and source in God. In Christianity, the specific nature of God is mediated to consciousness through the revelatory event of Jesus Christ. In the life, death, and resurrection of Jesus, Christians encounter a God who is personal and loving with a love that is creative, restoring, and salvific. In other words, the transcendence, awesomeness, and sheer power of God encounters human beings as that which would adopt and make God's own all human beings. The liberationist language of God's "being on the side of the poor" and of the church's "option for the poor," as inadequate as it may sound, has its deep logic in the sheerly creative love of God and God's will for the fulfillment of God's loving intent in creation itself. Innocent suffering is against God's holy will, which as loving fills up and restores what is lacking in human beings. In short, the logic of this dynamic love is such that it loves most what is most in need of love and care. This is the revolutionary and transforming character of encountering this God; it attacks the human logic of retribution and quid pro quo. God's will is rooted in God's love. The first dimension of a faith response to this revelation is sheer acceptance; and this acceptance becomes thematized in the language of contemplation. One can only surrender to this gratuitous power of cosmic love.

Thirdly, the response of faith, if it really be faith, also consists of fidelity and loyalty to the cause implicit in the object of faith. One cannot conceive of faith without this active response of freedom that commits and dedicates the self to the values that are the values of God. Faith includes a free and willing response to God's will.

This dimension of faith bears the logic that faith can only be authentic faith when it becomes transformed into praxis. Loyalty and commitment cannot be carried by any other medium. But it also bears within itself a profound paradox that somehow God not only wants but needs human action. The encounter with a personal God of sovereign freedom with human freedom takes on the character of a genuine dialogue between two freedoms. In its positive form it becomes a consortium. The God who created freedom respects it, and calls it forth to respond not to God's necessity and fatalistically imposed will, but to God's ideals and goals which are to become our own in freedom. This sovereign cause of God, as revealed through Jesus, is symbolized as the kingdom of God, a reign of justice and reconciliation.

This leads, lastly, to the final question of the ultimate value of the creativity of human action: Does it ultimately make any difference? Does this respect for human freedom, that seems evident in the immediate running of things in history, extend to the largest context of all, the end-time as described in terms of absoluteness and eternity? Once again, by both a negative experience of futility in contrast to a positive horizon of hope, the Christian must say that God has bestowed the possibility of real final value for human creativity. Ironically, in the logic of Segundo, the absoluteness of God does not relativize the human freedom that strives in love to actualize God's final will for the kingdom of God. Rather, the absoluteness of God's love draws human freedom into itself to bestow an absolute and eternal value on the works of love.

NOTES

1. Gustavo Gutiérrez, *On Job: God-Talk and the Suffering of the Innocent* (Maryknoll, N.Y.: Orbis, 1976).
2. Ibid., p. 93.
3. Ibid., p. 102.
4. Ibid., p. 94.
5. Ibid., p. 96.
6. Ibid., p. 84.
7. See the discussion of "language-games" and "forms of life" in Wittgenstein by Fergus Kerr, *Theology after Wittgenstein* (Oxford: Basil Blackwell, 1986), pp. 28–31.
8. Gutiérrez, *On Job*, p. 101.
9. Ibid., p. 48.
10. Ibid.

11. Edward Schillebeeckx, *Jesus: An Experiment in Christology* (New York: Seabury, 1979), pp. 621–22; *God the Future of Man* (New York: Sheed and Ward, 1968), pp. 153–54.

12. See the outline of the hermeneutical circle of Juan Luis Segundo in *The Liberation of Theology* (Maryknoll, N.Y.: Orbis, 1977), pp. 8–9.

13. Gutiérrez, *On Job*, p. 129, n. 5.

14. Ibid., p. 85.

15. Ibid., p. 76.

16. Ibid., p. 74.

17. Ibid., p. 72.

18. Ibid.

19. Ibid., pp. 88–89.

20. Ibid., p. 89.

21. Ibid., p. 96. This circumincession of language themes is at work in all four of the languages described here. They are distinct dimensions of one Christian language of God.

22. John Smith, *Experience and God* (New York: Oxford University Press, 1968), pp. 75–76. What Smith says here may be correlated with the distinction that Karl Rahner makes between transcendental and categorically mediated experience of transcendence.

23. Emil Brunner, *Truth as Encounter* (London: SCM Press, 1964), pp. 22–25; *Revelation and Reason* (Philadelphia: Westminster, 1946), pp. 24–28.

24. H. Richard Niebuhr, *The Meaning of Revelation* (New York: Macmillan, 1960), pp. 175–91. "It is true that revelation is not the communication of new truths and the supplanting of our natural religion by a supernatural one. But it is the fulfillment and the radical reconstruction of our natural knowledge about deity through the revelation of one whom Jesus Christ called 'Father' " (p. 182).

25. The theme of universalism is a major element in H. Richard Niebuhr's radical monotheism and radical monotheistic faith. God, the One behind the many and the creative source of all that exists, both relativizes all finite value-centers and sanctifies all beings with value. See Niebuhr's *Radical Monotheism and Western Culture* (New York: Harper Torchbooks, 1970), passim.

26. Gutiérrez, *On Job*, p. 77.

27. Ibid., p. 79.

28. Ibid., p. 77.

29. Ibid., p. 78.

30. Ibid., p. 80.

31. See H. Richard Niebuhr, "Faith as Confidence and Fidelity" and "Faith in Gods and God," *Radical Monotheism*, pp. 16–23, 114–26; "On the Nature of Faith," in *Religious Experience and Truth*, Sydney Hook, ed. (New York: New York University Press, 1961), pp. 93–102.

32. Gustavo Gutiérrez, *A Theology of Liberation: History, Politics, and Salvation* (Maryknoll, N.Y.: Orbis, 1973), pp. 6–15; "Liberation Praxis and Christian Faith," in *The Power of the Poor in History* (Maryknoll, N.Y.: Orbis, 1983), pp. 36–74.

33. Gutiérrez, *A Theology of Liberation* (15th anniversary ed., 1988), p. 117.

34. Juan Luis Segundo, *The Humanist Christology of Paul* (Maryknoll, N.Y.: Orbis, 1986), pp. 123–24.

35. Ibid., p. 124.

36. Ibid.
37. Ibid., p. 133.
38. Ibid., p. 157.
39. H. Richard Niebuhr, "The Center of Value," *Radical Monotheism*, pp. 110–11.
40. No criticism of liberation theology can even begin to be credible unless it too begins with the negative experience of contrast and maintains in its language a prophetic protest against the innocent suffering of the poor.

21

Paganism and the Politics
of Evangelization

NICHOLAS LASH

PAGANISM AND POLITICS

Paraphrasing Cardinal Pacelli's assertion that the church civilizes by evangelizing, Gustavo Gutiérrez remarked, some years ago, that "in the contemporary Latin American context it would be necessary to say that the church should politicize by evangelizing."[1] Is this also what it would be necessary to say in the context of contemporary Britain? Put thus abruptly, the question is too abstract. As a first step toward answering it with appropriate concreteness, it would be necessary to consider what, in practice, it might mean, in Britain today, to "politicize by evangelizing." And even on this preliminary question I can do no more than offer, in gratitude to Gustavo and in celebration of his work, a handful of reflections whose value is constrained by the context of their production: if not exactly an ivory tower, then something suspiciously like a dreaming spire.

In which same context, as it happens, Frei Betto spent some months in 1987. On leaving Cambridge, he recorded his impressions of the challenge confronting British Christianity:

It seems to me that there is a deep anxiety in Christian circles in Europe, including England. Something has come to an end: Christendom, of which the only thing that remains is the cathedrals, for visiting by tourists. The cultural and political hegemony of the church and the religious ideology, which once impregnated social values with a certain Christian viewpoint—these have gone. *And still nothing new has begun.* We are living in a time of impasse, a period of searching and perplexity. Some persons are rushing around, fighting strongly in defence of orthodoxy, like voices crying in the wilderness. Others are trying to create an alternate space where the faith can be lived outside the permanent control of the magisterium, outside ecclesiastical structures. The fact is that this anxiety is deep in the bowels of the church, which is afraid of losing its social privilege and at the same time does not want to be "the church of the establishment," legitimating an intrinsically unjust economic order, because it knows that the wealth of the First World is gained by the misery of the Third.

The church is an old woman always pregnant with herself: the new model of the church is always born from the old. Possibly liberation theology, which has aroused so much interest here in Europe, can contribute to this process, raising a central question: What precisely must Europe free itself from? What does it mean to follow Jesus Christ in this situation, which, materially speaking, is apparently quite satisfactory? It is, of course, evident that London, Liverpool, Manchester, Glasgow have many unemployed and poor. But in this country there is a more generalized problem than poverty, one which presents a big challenge to the mission of the church: this is a pagan nation![2]

If Frei Betto is right, if it is in fact paganism, more generally than poverty, from which we need to be set free, then the church, in the measure that it properly attends to its primary task of evangelizing, will provoke increasing hostility from those who at present dictate the form of British politics. To "politicize by evangelizing," in other words, entails arousing the antipathy of those whose politics is structured in paganism, in *deafness* to the gospel of reconciliation and the requirement of human community.

Notwithstanding their importance and complexity, I do not propose to consider the ethical issues raised by the charge of "deafness." From the fact that many of those operating an evil system may, for all we know or need to know, be guiltless before God, it does not follow that such a system is not the consequence of human choice and, as such, a proper object of ethical assessment. "A bad system," as John Milbank puts it, "is the incremental and sedimentation of lots of minor social articulations of selfishness and self-delusion."[3]

"The place of the mission of the church is where the celebration of the Lord's supper and the creation of human brotherhood are indissolubly joined."[4] The increasingly divided character of modern Britain, and the forces creating and reinforcing our divisions, eloquently illustrate the extent to which it is precisely this conjunction of the "holy" and the human, of eucharist and community, which modern paganism (not least in its "Christian" forms and guises) most strenuously resists. (In confining my remarks to Great Britain I am not being parochial, but simply trying to obey the injunction to respect the primacy of concrete situations.)

THE STRAWS IN THE WIND

In this period of (as Frei Betto put it) searching and perplexity, there are some interesting signs of changes in public perception. In February 1988 the journalist Richard Gott, who, for ten years had edited a weekly page of political discussion in the *Guardian* newspaper, reflected on what he called "the sunset rays of the great Modernist project, the idea that the world's problems might be solved by reason and electricity. It was a noble project that invoked socialism and economic planning, and the belief that the needs of society might sometimes take precedence over the rights of the individual." We still (most of us) have electricity, but if we remember how grim an epoch this has been for "enthusiasts of the rational (memories of Auschwitz and Hiroshima) . . . it is not difficult to see why the political philosophers of post-Modernism should have sought to throw reason out of the window." The evident fragility of reason, however, does nothing to render the studied irrationalism, opportunism, and cynical amorality of the ascendant authoritarianism any less destructive or disturbing.

Somewhat unexpectedly, in a newspaper traditionally inclined to be supercilious in regard to matters of religion, Gott ended his article: "And so, as this bleak intellectual era continues ... it is not altogether surprising that the best political writers today should be Catholics and Jews, Methodists and Marxists, people whose arguments are imbued with faith and a sharp sense of righteousness as well as informed by reason."[5] A straw in the wind, no more, yet challenging and, perhaps, an indication of our particular responsibilities.

Here is a second straw. The church, we are often told (especially by those whose preferred paradigms of power are aristocratic or oligarchic) is not a democracy. More generally, we are often warned that it is a mistake to seek, in the arrangements of secular society, analogues to aid our understanding of the mysteries of episcopacy. There is delightful irony, then, in finding a recent widely acclaimed analysis of the political predicament of modern Britain urging—beyond the "neoliberalism" that now strangles us and the "neosocialism" offered as its main alternative—a conception of politics as "mutual education," in the processes of which the political leader would be "a kind of pastor or moderator or chairman"[6] or, as we used to say, a bishop!

THE DESTRUCTION OF SOCIALISM

There is a passage in Robert Bolt's play *A Man for All Seasons*, in which Thomas More, lord chancellor of England, the perfect man of law, is arguing with his high-principled but romantically hotheaded son-in-law, Will Roper. The poles of the argument are, on the one hand, moral principle and, on the other, the protection of persons that the law affords.

"The currents and eddies of right and wrong," says More, "which you find such plain sailing, I can't navigate. I'm no voyager. But in the thickets of the law, oh there I'm a forester." The law, of course, affords protection to saint and sinner alike, or, as More puts it, he would let the Devil himself go free "until he broke the law."

This is too much for Roper: "So now you'd give the Devil benefit of law!"

"Yes. What would you do? Cut a great road through the law to get after the Devil?"

"I'd cut down every law in England to do that!"

"Oh? And when the last law was down, and the Devil turned round on you—where would you hide, Roper, the laws all being flat? This country's planted thick with laws from coast to coast—Man's laws, not God's—and if you cut them down—and you're just the man to do it—d'you really think you could stand upright in the winds that would blow then?"[7]

In Britain today there is the sound of woodchopping somewhere in the forest and the wind begins to blow. Consider the case of the "Royal Prerogative," the constitutional warrant, inherited from the days of absolute monarchy, for the non-accountable exercise of state power. "The conventional view of the Royal Prerogative," writes the professor of public law at the London School of Economics, "is that, following the Glorious Revolution of 1688, it was made subject to parliamentary control." It has therefore come as a surprise, to those who thought that absolute monarchy had been dead in Britain for three hundred years, to discover Mrs. Thatcher appealing to the Royal Prerogative as the justification for bugging and burgling by the security forces operating outside parliamentary control and countering not subversion by a foreign power but actual or anticipated internal opposition to the policies of the government over which she presides. Says Professor McAuslan:

> The present state of affairs is not consistent with any notion of constitutional democracy under the rule of law. The government's willingness to use prerogative powers to get its way and national security to block scrutiny of what it is doing is as much a threat to parliamentary control of the executive as ever was James II's use of prerogative powers. It is, indeed, alarming that exactly three hundred years after the Glorious Revolution, the executive is reviving the use of the prerogative to extend its powers over the citizenry.[8]

Such strong language from a constitutional lawyer suggests that it would be prudent to construe quite literally Mrs. Thatcher's repeated statement of intent to destroy socialism in Britain. This seems, indeed, to be the common thread linking the government's policies on education, housing, health, trade unions, the "poll tax," and the privatization of electricity. Directly or indirectly, in each of these cases the principal target of attack is those structures of municipal government in which the Labor Party continues to wield residual power.

And yet, it is perhaps not "socialism" that is the real target: that simply happens to be a term descriptive of the more important places in British society in which the government's authoritarian ambition is still, with diminishing effectiveness, withstood. But consider the undisguised exasperation with which *any* criticism of government policy is greeted. And, after exasperation, action: statutory instruments to place the universities more directly under ministerial control, and varieties of public bullying and private arm-twisting to "deal with" the Church of England or the BBC. The real target, in other words, is effective opposition, from whatever source and in whatever form.

Fewer and fewer persons, in Britain, have "faith in the political process. ... Parliament now stands alone, as a brightly-lit talking shop. And the State begins to be understood as a separate, not necessarily subordinate creature. Its central and repressive character swells. ... Political apathy spreads, and the remaining liberties of local government continue to be confiscated by the central State bureaucracy. ... An ice age of authoritarian government, a one-party glacier, is beginning to slither northwards from London."[9]

It is important to emphasize that voices such as those of Gott and Marquand, McAuslan and Ascherson, speak from what was, until less than a decade ago, the "extreme center" of the British political spectrum. It is a sign of how rapidly and dramatically the climate has changed that such voices should now sound radical or even (to some ears) subversive.

The energies unleashed by the present government are aggressively individualist, and the individualism is shaped or tempered by little else than a quasi-religious respect for market forces and what are perceived to be private virtues. Indeed, with the possible exception of patriotism, there are no public virtues left in a society in which the notion of "the common good" is becoming increasingly unintelligible as is the idea that "a political community is, among other things, a web of reciprocal duties and rights."[10] It would be difficult to express this socially corrosive individualism more succinctly than the prime minister herself has done: "There is no such thing as society. There are individual men and women, and there are families."[11]

Insofar as there is an ethic in the dominant ethos of Thatcherite conservatism, it is residually Social-Darwinist: if the fittest survive, then those who have survived must be the ones who are "fit" to do so, where "fitness" now has overtones of virtue or providential election. Thus it is that those who fail must be presumed to be not only responsible for failure ("workshy," perhaps, or gullible victims of "socialism") but a potential threat to the "health" of the rich and powerful. There are germs in poverty from which the wealthy must be quarantined.

Here is a parable of the divisions, physical as well as social, that are, increasingly, the outcome of present policies and their concomitant beliefs. (It is, as it happens, a true story.) There is a housing estate in one of our larger cities, a not untypically dreary expression of poor planning some thirty years ago, its seediness exacerbated by incompetence and underfunding in maintenance and repair. Before too airily expressing disapproval of the municipal socialism that produced it, we should, however, remember the appalling dwellings, so accurately expressive of Victorian values (as they actually were, and not as they have been reinvented in the theme park fairyland of Mrs. Thatcher's imagination), which it once replaced. Nevertheless, there is no doubt that this estate is now in urgent need of restoration and improvement.

Such improvement has, in some sense, begun. Recently, about a quarter of it was emptied of inhabitants on the discovery of asbestos. The newly Conservative local council then sold this portion to private developers who renovated the buildings to a very high standard. The occupants of its now desirable residences (and their sauna baths) are protected from their neighbors by a fence and guards. Instead of searchlights at the perimeter there are television cameras, and a piece of plastic (a kind of credit card) gains access to the promised land. (The irony, of course, is that the inmates of these ghettoes of privilege suppose themselves to have been set free.)

Through social engineering, a wide range of regressive taxation policies, and the systematic onslaught on intermediate institutions and the apparatus of the "welfare state," the British government has succeeded in creating, not merely new levels of poverty and long-term unemployment, but something like a permanent underclass. The deteriorating health and education of this underclass, together with the fact that, to a quite disproportionate extent, it is made up of those euphemistically (but increasingly inaccurately) described as "immigrants," can hardly fail, in the long term, to be catastrophically costly—in both economic and social terms.

In the short term, however, there are fences and guards to keep the underclass at bay. The function of these fences is, in part, symbolic: it is quite obvious to those in power that physical devices would not, in themselves, suffice for long (because, for example, of the escalating cost of maintaining an increasingly centralized, militarized, and politicized police force). It is, therefore, also necessary to get to work on the imagination of the poor.

In the United States, there is an ingenious device for doing this, known as "the American dream": the sustaining of the illusion that, if not you, then perhaps your child or grandchild may escape from deprivation and indignity into fame and fortune. The success of this device depends upon not many persons noticing how many backs get broken to keep the dream alive. For a variety of historical, geographical, and cultural reasons, the American dream is not available in Britain. Perhaps the next best thing to peddling ambitions unrealizable by the generality would (paradoxically) be the quenching of the fires of hope. As David Marquand puts it, in order to reduce the risk of "overload" to the economic circuits, "not only inflation, but inflationary expectations, must be squeezed out of the system."[12] The poor, in other words, must learn not to expect to be other than permanently poor. They must be educated to understand that it is no fault of the rich and powerful that things just happen to be the way they are. Or, as F. A. Hayek put it, in a passage whose idolatrous overtones are so evident as not to call for commentary: "The fundamental attitude of true individualism is one of humility towards the processes by which mankind has achieved things which have not been designed or understood by any individual and are indeed greater than individual minds."[13]

INDIVIDUALISM AND COMMUNITY

The "central thesis" of Marquand's study of the failures and contradictions of contemporary British political economy is that the roots of present problems are to be sought "in a coherent, though often unconscious, set of attitudes to politics ... and in the reductionist model of human nature which lies behind them." Of special significance is "the central Lockean assumption that individual property rights are antecedent to society."[14]

Marquand's critique of this pervasive, destructive, and (ultimately) illusory individualism is well done: "We are not egoistical calculating machines which decided to form a society, because, after careful scrutiny of the evidence, we came to the conclusion that it would be in our interests to do so. . . . We live in society because we are social creatures, genetically programed for sociability."[15] But how to do so fruitfully, how to be "sociable," is matter for continual experiment and education. Hence his view of politics as pedagogy of human community.

The assumption that "just as the world is made up of solid lumps of matter, so a society is made up of separate, sovereign, atomistic individuals," and its Benthamite development: "Politics is about reconciling conflicts between individually chosen purposes. It has no business with the choice of purposes."[16] These are not, of course, peculiar to Britain. As de Tocqueville (in the tradition of whom Marquand knows himself to stand) already perceived, they are also at work as a cancer threatening the American body politic.

Marquand is, moreover, surely correct in strenuously resisting the individualist assumption that the only alternative to individualism is "collectivism." Between the two, he speaks, quite properly, of "community," of which he has such sensible things to say as (for example) that "a flourishing political community will be a mosaic of smaller communities," or again: "I can only belong to a community if others belong to it as well; if the other members of my community question its reality, my membership in it will also become unreal."[17]

Nevertheless, it is just here, where, on both theological and political grounds, I find myself much in sympathy with him that my main disquiet concerning his analysis is also aroused. In his attempt to find a third way, under the rubric of "community," between the "neoliberalism" of the present government and the "neosocialism" associated with aspects of the Labor Party to which he once belonged, Marquand glosses over the ineluctability of conflict in the political arrangements of sinful human beings.

Thus, for example, in his remarks on "power-sharing," and on the "taming" of "class appetites," he writes as if class differences were simply differences of occupation or interest and not, in larger measure, differences constituted by inequitable distributions of social power. In similar vein, he runs into uncomfortably close conjunction the grammar of "community," "consensus," and "neocorporatism," without so much as a mention of those dark shadows of fascism that mention of the corporate state still conjure from the memory.[18]

It is at this point, perhaps, that we begin to need to differentiate between church and society, theology and politics. Christianity is about the gift, and fact, and promise, of *relationship*: relationship between God and the creature, and hence among creatures. To speak of relationship is, indeed, to speak of community, for communities are constituted by relationships. Christianity, therefore, is about the gift, and fact, and promise, of community. But, if this gives to Christianity, as to Judaism, a perspective from within which we enact (and not merely, in word or symbol, to proclaim) its prophetic critique of the dehumanizing and destructive mechanisms of both individualism and collectivism, it does not positively provide some other set of blueprints or proposals for our social arrangements. The gospel does not itself provide the program for the politics that it stimulates and engenders. Or, as I have put it elsewhere, there are no straight lines of inference to be drawn from discipleship of the Crucified to the construction of social policy.[19]

"The place of the mission of the church is where the celebration of the Lord's supper and the creation of human brotherhood are indissolubly joined."[20] But the manner of their conjunction is ironic, dialectical, attentive to the unexpected and unpredictable, sensitive to provisionality, and protective of the *openness* of the future.

The deterministic character of both individualism and collectivism renders them, as Marquand points out, strangely ambivalent "about democracy as a method, and even about politics as an activity."[21] To the collectivist, genuine debate about the purposes that society might pursue is precluded by the belief that those purposes have been laid down in the very structure of natural (including human) process. To the individualist, on the other hand, the freedom of the market overrides all other rights and freedoms; before it, as Hayek so eloquently indicated, we must all reverently bow down.

This would seem to leave the church, with its insistence on the openness of the future, on the nonidentity of history and kingdom, on the interim character of all our dreams, ideas, achievements, and institutions, among the last protectors and safeguards of genuine politics and effective democracy. This is not meant in jest, although I appreciate that the irony of it is likely to be lost, in just about equal measure, upon those burdened with either ecclesiastical or political power.

Collectivism is not a serious threat in Britain today (in spite of what the propagandists of the government, salivating over the scattered idiocies of the "loony left," would have us believe). Individualism, on the other hand, is increasingly our climate, our despotism, our disease.

The church itself, of course, is seriously infected with this sickness. It would be astonishing if things were otherwise. It is therefore to be expected that some of the most strenuous resistance that the bishops will encounter, in the measure that they find the courage to lead their people against the grain of the idolatries that oppress us, will come from within the church. One further anecdote or parable may illustrate this.

When the English bishops began to coordinate their opposition to government plans for allowing parents to withdraw schools from local authority control, they were criticized by the deputy director of studies at the Centre of Policy Studies (an influential conservative think tank). "Like many of the local authorities," she wrote, "with whose language and position on these matters it has become so closely identified if not confused, the church thinks in terms of planning and the 'community,' not of the different needs and dignity of individuals." She then went on to threaten the bishops: if they prevent Catholic schools from opting out of local authority control, "then Catholic parents may choose to abandon Catholic education altogether." When this day comes, the bishops (she claimed) will have driven Catholic children away from Catholic schools, and "will have done so in the spirit, if not the name, of the ideology of 'community' so espoused by the local authorities."[22]

And so, at a stroke, two thousand years of Christian teaching, from Ephesians to *Lumen Gentium*, is dismissed as the contemptible by-product of municipal socialism. Paganism runs deep.

THE POLITICS OF PRAYERFULNESS

How might the indissoluble connection between "the celebration of the Lord's Supper and the creation of human community" be most appropriately and effectively displayed in Britain today? The question concerns (among other things) the contribution the church might make toward "challenging [the] solidifying ideology of individualism and self-interest."[23] It is, of course, only too easy for a well-educated person with a home and a secure income to wave word-patterned paper at other people's wounds. Nevertheless, if "easy speech" would be one betrayal of fellowship, mere silence would be another. With considerable diffidence, therefore, I now propose briefly to comment on aspects of the church's "option for the poor" in Britain today. Paganism may, indeed, as Frei Betto suggests, be a more "generalized" problem in Britain today than poverty, but it is the poor who bear the brunt of our idolatries.

The first thing to notice is that the connotations of this option are very different in Britain from what they would be in any country of the Third World. Says the Labor member of parliament, John Battle:

Given the electoral geography of Britain, it is clear that even if the poor were to build up a solid amount of political support . . . the self-interested and rich could vote the poor out. Unlike in the Latin American world, where the poor banding together in solidarity could form an obvious majority to challenge democratically, and take power from, the ruling elite, and win on solidarity of numbers, in Britain the poor remain a significant but solid minority.[24]

In the second place, to cut a long and very complex sociological story short, the church in Britain will, for the foreseeable future, be for the most part at best a church "with," and "for," rather than "of," the poor.[25]

In the third place, even if the "mainstream" churches share a largely middle-class constituency, networks of ecumenical cooperation, collaborative leadership, and (increasingly) common theological and liturgical resources, it nevertheless remains the case, where the option for the poor is concerned, that they are each rather differently placed.

The Church of England, for example, is inhibited by the residual trammels of political establishment. This is more a matter of perception or imagination than of law. Not only do many of our rulers still *expect* the "national" church to give moral support to their projects and purposes (and it is to the credit of the Church of England that, with increasing frequency, it refrains from doing so), but established status, national responsibility, encourages a tone of voice, an angle of observation, that is (shall we say) more patrician than prophetic.[26]

There are, it would therefore seem, two reasons why the Catholic Church in Britain is better placed than the Church of England for finding ways of displaying prophetic solidarity with the poor. On the one hand, not being the national church, it is less implicated (in both fact and imagination) with the powers that be. On the other hand, it is at least arguable that it is, even now, not as uprooted from its base among the urban poor.

In the fourth place, British Catholicism has accumulated resources of dissent and exclusion upon which to draw. Until very recently, its spirituality was shaped by the experience of alienation, of suffering in nonconformity. It is perhaps time to put "devotion to the English martyrs" to new use as guidance for our solidarity with those on the margins of society.

In the fifth place, insofar as it is proper to apply the good word "community" to an association cohesive on the surface and in its official self-description but, beneath that surface, as deeply divided as the society of which it forms a part, then it is also appropriate to speak of the Christian community in Britain as already "a mosaic of smaller communities." My impression is that (inspired in part, no doubt, by what we have learned from Latin America about "base community") there is a great deal of growth and movement in this network or mosaic. And, more importantly, a deepening desire, often not quite acknowledged or clearly articulated, to find, in common prayer and practical reflection, ways of discerning the connections between eucharist and fraternity, faith and politics, the quest for earthly justice and the peace that only God can give.

In Frei Betto's view, contesting the prevailing paganism of British society will require of the church a redefinition of pastoral priorities and a profound declericalization of structure. This seems correct, but I also believe that the time is ripe: that a little leadership of the right kind and in the right direction would help a quite surprising number of flowers to bloom. This is not an intolerably paradoxical proposal: there is nothing in the office of a bishop that requires its occupant to be inhibited by "clerical" preoccupations with tidiness and power!

I am suggesting, in other words, that the resources (including, most importantly, the good will) lie ready to hand for mounting what we might call a program of continuous education in the politics of prayer. A church thus educated would discover new friends and powerful new enemies. It might even discover, to its own surprise, that it became something more like a sign of hope. This, were it to happen, would be the church's gift to Britain's poor.

But what would the church *receive* in return? (The question is important, because one-sided giving is patronage, not fellowship.) The answer, I believe, is joy. Britain has become (for most of its inhabitants) a richer place in recent years, but the laughter has departed, supplanted—from the City to the football terraces—by cruelty and fear. Ask any visitor from overseas what strikes them most about "Mrs. Thatcher's Britain," and you will not hear mention of joy or generosity, of gentleness or hospitality. These things are more securely stifled by egotism than by poverty and, though the rest of us have no right to them, we are, as Christians, entitled to pray that we might, perhaps, receive these gifts, for our redemption, from Christ's poor.

Nor should it be forgotten that the laughter of the poor, betokening their dignity, is a political weapon of a most subversive kind.

NOTES

1. Gustavo Gutiérrez, *A Theology of Liberation: History, Politics, and Salvation* (Maryknoll, N.Y.: Orbis Books, 1973), p. 269.

2. Frei Betto, "Comment: How Frei Betto Sees Us," *New Blackfriars*, 69/812 (January 1988) 2–3. I am grateful to the editor of *New Blackfriars* for permission to quote this passage.

3. John Milbank, "On Baseless Suspicion: Christianity and the Crisis of Socialism," *New Blackfriars* (January 1988), p. 11. Milbank was commenting on the point that, although it is true that "no one deliberately 'planned' capitalism" (p. 11), it does not follow that persons are not responsible for its production, operation, and continuance.

4. Gutiérrez, *Theology of Liberation*, p. 262.

5. Richard Gott, "Goodbye to All This," *The Guardian* (February 8, 1988) 24.

6. David Marquand, *The Unprincipled Society: New Demands and Old Politics* (London: Jonathan Cape, 1988), p. 233.

7. Robert Bolt, *A Man for All Seasons* (London: Heinemann, 1986), p. 39. The play was first performed in 1960.

8. Patrick McAuslan, "The Royal Prerogative as a Threat to the Rule of Law," *The Independent*, January 27, 1988.

9. Neal Ascherson, "Trotsky through a Tory Mirror," *The Observer* (February 28, 1988) 9.

10. Marquand, *Unprincipled Society*, p. 67.

11. Quoted from Douglas Keay, "Aids, Education, and the Year 2,000," *Womens Own* (Oct. 31, 1987) 10.

12. Marquand, *Unprincipled Society*, p. 79.

13. Quoted by John Battle, M.P., in "Pitching the Song in the Crack: The Option for the Poor and the Current Political Realities," *New Blackfriars*, 69/813 (February

1988) 77. The theme of this special issue of *New Blackfriars* was *The Church's Option for the Poor in Britain*.

14. Marquand, *Unprincipled Society*, pp. 213, 154.

15. Ibid., p. 217.

16. Ibid., p. 214.

17. Ibid., pp. 220, 223, 239.

18. See ibid., pp. 67, 160–65. It is, of course, possible that, in the extensive recent literature on "corporatism" to which he refers and with which I am not familiar, these ghosts have finally been laid to rest. It is possible.

19. See Nicholas Lash, "The Church's Responsibility for the Future of Humanity," *Theology on the Way to Emmaus* (London: SCM Press, 1986), p. 188; *A Matter of Hope: A Theologian's Reflections on the Thought of Karl Marx* (London: Darton, Longman & Todd, 1981), pp. 236–39. On the "eclipse of God" by individualism and collectivism alike, and on the continual requirement to be recalled into "relationship," see my discussion of Martin Buber in Nicholas Lash, *Easter in Ordinary: Reflections on Human Experience and the Knowledge of God* (Charlottesville: University Press of Virginia, 1988), pp. 194, 199–218.

20. Gutiérrez, *Theology of Liberation*, p. 262.

21. Marquand, *Unprincipled Society*, p. 65.

22. Sheila Lawlor, "An Answer to the Bishops," *The Tablet* (February 20, 1988), 206.

23. Battle, "Pitching the Song," p. 79.

24. Ibid., p. 77. That minority is not, of course, alone. Battle considers the possible emergence of a "clearer practical recognition of the need for solidarity between the poor in Britain and the poor in the rest of the world" (p. 79), but such speculation lies beyond the scope of this paper.

25. See Anthony Archer, *The Two Catholic Churches: A Study in Oppression* (London: SCM Press, 1986)—which argued that the practical outcome of the reforms initiated by Vatican II had, in Britain, so far been a triumph for the educated middle classes and a disaster for working-class Catholics whose religious needs have been neglected or misread. This provoked a lively debate: see *Class and Church: After Ghetto Catholicism*, a special issue of *New Blackfriars* (68/802 [February 1987]) devoted to this debate.

26. See, in this regard, some brief remarks of mine in "Ministry of the Word or Comedy and Philology," *New Blackfriars*, 68/810 (November 1987) 478–79, on the Church of England Reports, *Changing Britain: Social Diversity and Moral Unity* (London: Church House Publishing, 1987).

22

Theology in the Struggle
for History and Society

JOHANN BAPTIST METZ

The following reflections are dedicated to my friend Gustavo Gutiérrez. In his recent publications he has always stressed that liberation theology is not about a new social ethics for the church but about theology. It is this fundamental theological character of liberation theology that I wish to discuss here from various aspects that seem to me important.

I

Within the Catholic Church I find three principal concurrent theological models in operation. This does not cover everything but does single out three representative ideal types of theology. I mean neoscholastic theology, a transcendental-idealist theology, and a postidealist theology. Although they are very different, all three models fall within the scope of theology in the Catholic sense. They reflect the complexity and tensions of the present state of the church.

The *neoscholastic view* is still predominant in the church as a whole. Indeed, given recent developments in the church, which I see as reflecting and confirming neoconservative social trends, we may even speak of a "late summer" for this paradigm. Although in no way wishing to detract from the merits of neoscholasticism in the nineteenth and early twentieth centuries, we may describe this paradigm as mainly defensive and traditional, and unable to deal fruitfully with the challenge of modern Europe. Significantly, the principle work of nineteenth century neoscholasticism is called "theology of antiquity." This fixation on (scholastic) antiquity shows how Catholicism became spiritually and socially cut off in Europe, especially in Germany. Catholics barricaded themselves in a Catholic—and political—stronghold, a pale imitation of the great Christian stronghold—*corpus christianum*—of the Middle Ages. They adopted a strictly defensive position to the challenge of the modern world, in both social and political debates and interdenominational theological controversy. Church orthodoxy was more rigorous than radical; a defensive concern with security-minded pastoral theology—until Vatican II.

The transcendental-idealist view of theology stems from the most important and influential change in present Catholic theology. This is the attempt to use the church fathers and scholastics in a productive offensive confrontation with the challenges of modern Europe: the discovery of subjectivity as a crisis in classic metaphysics; the critico-productive confrontation with Kant, German idealism, and existentialism on the one hand, and the social processes of secularization and scientific civilization on the other. This theology found its ecclesiastical and social counterpart in new forms of church life. Taken as a whole, these can in fact be regarded as the impulse for the Vatican II Council.

Meanwhile theology was faced with crises and challenges that, in my view, could not adequately be dealt with by the two theological models so far described. Hence, I should like to mention a third theological model, which seeks to test and develop the church's theological legacy as it faces these crises and challenges. Somewhat at a loss, I call this model of Catholic theology "postidealist." It is recognizable in reflections on a new political theology in Europe and in the central thrust of liberation theology. This third theological model also has its roots in the last council. I should like to name three crises and challenges on which this theological model seeks to adopt a position:

1. Theology comes to the end of its historical and social innocence—that is, theology engaged in a dispute about its foundations in terms of ideological and social criticism. This amounts to an attempt by theology to establish a new relationship to history and society. Theological theories of world secularization and modernization have not yet fully clarified this relationship. And the problems cannot be solved simply by the usual division of labor between systematic theology and social ethics.

2. Theology comes to the end of a system that took no account of the individual situation or person—that is, theology concerned itself with the "irruption" of the poor, which does not permit the poor to vanish into an impersonal theory of poverty. Moreover the European version of postidealist theology has also been shaped by the "irruption" of the Auschwitz catastrophe. Nothing could show more plainly that the time for theological systems divorced from situation and person is over, because no one can possibly force this catastrophe into a "peopleless" system of meaning.

3. Theology comes to the end of cultural monocentrism—that is, theology relating to an ethnically and culturally polycentric world. Here a traditional Christian theology needs to overcome not only a great deal of social but also ethnic blindness. As well as the "option for the poor" it must adopt the "option for others in their otherness," for ethnic and cultural characteristics are not just an ideological superstructure based on economic problems, as Marxist theory and Western praxis would like to suggest.

II

History and society are and remain the place for Christian language about God— that is, for Christian theology. The crisis that has long confronted theology may also be formulated as an epistemological problem, a problem of knowing the truth. Therefore, it is a question of the relationship between knowledge and interest. From the time of the Enlightenment, religion and theology have had to deal with the axiom that all knowledge is governed by interest. This axiom is the foundation of the Enlightenment's critique of religion and theology, on the part of Voltaire, for example; religion and theology are deciphered in terms of their social interest context, but without any application of social criticism. Social criticism, of course, is applied by Karl Marx. Even if theology did not lose its innocence through the Enlightenment's critique of religion, it certainly has since Marx.

The attempt to take this situation into account and remain a proper theology capable of speaking the truth distinguishes postidealist theology's first phase of development. This tries to create the awareness that theology and church are never simply politically innocent and therefore one of theology's fundamental tasks is to consider political implications. But this is still not the main problem in theology's crisis. How can theology admit the connection between knowledge and interest without either giving up or perverting the question of truth? Is the question of truth not reduced here to a mere question of relevance, along the lines of "true is what is in my interest or in the interest of a particular group of persons?" No, it is just that the question of truth now takes a different form, which may be formulated thus: Are there any interests capable of truth? Of course, interests can only be capable of truth when they are universal or universalizable—that is, when they relate without exception to all human beings or could be so related. For truth is either truth for everyone or not at all. In this sense postidealist theology speaks of universal or universalizable interest, based on biblical tradition itself. This is "hunger and thirst for justice" and indeed, justice for all, for the living and the dead, present and past sufferings.

Thus, the question of truth and the question of justice are interrelated: *verum et bonum (iustum) convertuntur*. Interest in undivided justice belongs to the premises of the search for truth. Thus knowledge of the truth and speaking about God acquire a practical foundation. In my view this is the basis of the rightly understood axiom of the "primacy of praxis," which is criticized in Rome's instruction on liberation theology. The only interest that is appropriate to theology, because it is a universal interest, is hunger and thirst for justice, undivided justice, justice for the living and the dead. Hence questions about God and about justice, the affirmation of God and the praxis of justice, can no longer be separated. In other words, the praxis of Christian faith always has an interest in universal justice, and is thus both mystical and political. This is emphasized in talk about the one and undivided following of Jesus, mystically and politically understood.

Therefore, Christian theology is not political *because* it has surrendered Christianity to an alien political ideology. It is political because it tries to preserve the dangerous memory of the messianic God, the God of the resurrection of the dead and judgment. Theology's political root in this remembrance is much more than mere political rhetoric.

Christian speech about God is not subject to the "primacy of praxis" because it blindly submits to some present political praxis, but because the biblical idea of God, which it represents, is in itself a practical idea. The stories of setting out and hope, stories of suffering and persecution, stories of resistance and resignation, are at the center of the Christian understanding of God. "Remembering" and "telling" are therefore not just for entertainment; they are basic forms of Christian language about God. Thus, postidealist theology will always try to explain dogmas of the faith formulated under the influence of classical Greek metaphysics in terms of dangerous and liberating ideas. It treats these unhistorical and impersonal doctrinal statements as shorthand and tries to relate them back to the biblical stories of exodus, conversion, resistance, and suffering, and the synoptic stories of Jesus and his disciples. The result is that "simple believers" are now no longer merely being "talked at"; they become the active subjects of the language of faith and theology, a language in which individual life histories and faith histories are linked together.

If I am right, in its base communities liberation theology is trying to relax the usual division of labor in the church and to overcome the model of the church as "minder." This usual division of labor may be summed up thus: the bishops teach, the priests look after, the theologians explain and defend teaching and educate the minders. And what about the people? They are the recipients of this teaching and minding. Such a division of labor sees the church thus as a minding church and theology has to go along with the system willy-nilly. On the other hand, liberation theology works to change this minding church *for* the people into a church *of* the people—that is, a church with a community whose members are growing in personal awareness. It points out that besides the magisterium, the church's teaching office, there is also the authority of the faithful, to which theology (and not just theology but also the magisterium) is bound to listen. This view is the legacy of Vatican II. Finally, the church constitution of this council stresses the personal and subjective view of the church, in particular by its use of the biblical phrase "people of God" to designate the church. Hence, the council, at least in principle, underlined the active role of the faithful in the articulation and development of faith.

III

In my country, Germany, after the Second World War, there was a lot of theological talk about the "historicity" of human beings. I have a suspicion that with this general blanket term we were trying to retreat and get away as quickly as possible from the particular history of our own country, which, especially because of Auschwitz, was a catastrophic history. However, for the Judeo-Christian religion unlike all other great religions of the world, history has a specific importance. Christianity is dominated by the vision of "God and history," "God in history." There are several reasons why this is not fully clear to us today. One reason is that Christianity and theology—at least among us in Europe at this stage of evolution and technology—is under the anonymous pressure of a historical weariness, a tendency to posthistory. The less human beings are their memory, the more they are their own experience. Everything appears to be technically reproducible, finally even the human producer. Secondly, I think in present-day theology, Christianity's indispensable Jewish legacy, which has a thoroughly historical way of thinking, is overshadowed by its Hellenistic Greek legacy, which is more inclined toward an ahistorical dualism and therefore constantly threatening to transform Christianity into gnosticism, in which history is without salvation and salvation outside history.

I think theological talk of "two histories," one natural and one supernatural, falls into this danger. This is another dualistic undermining of the important adventure of our historical lives. And it cancels our history's final horizon, its ending in the parousia, the "Lord's Second Coming." In fact, there is not world history and, "after it" or "above it," salvation history. The history of salvation, about which Christian theology speaks, is that same world history, shot through with a constantly threatened and disputed but unshakably promised hope: the hope of God's justice, which also includes the dead and their past sufferings, and forces the living to be interested in justice for all. Faith in the messianic God, God of the resurrection of the dead and judgment, God before whom not even the past is fixed (before whom past sufferings do not disappear into the impersonal abyss of an anonymous, eternally indifferent evolution). This faith is not opium to lull us in humanity's historical struggle; it is the guarantee and measure of the dignity of every human person.

It shares with Marxism the discovery of the world as history, historical project, in which human beings are to be the enactors of their own history, and this challenge should be taken seriously. But, this, of course, raises two important questions for a postidealist theology orientated toward history and society. First, there is the question of the status and value of past suffering in the process of history and, secondly, the question of individual guilt. Although it is central to postidealist theology, I pass over here the first (very important) problem, the problem known classically as that of theodicy—that is, the justification of God in the face of the world's pain. Certainly in this context Gustavo Gutiérrez's reflections of Job are especially important.

However, I shall concentrate briefly on the second question, about the status and dignity of individual moral guilt. Unlike Marxism, postidealist theology stresses that this guilt is not an assumed but an authentic phenomenon in the historical process of personal lives. It cannot be regarded as an expression of pure alienation, even though theology and its preaching of guilt and sin have all too often been alienating and oppressive. Denial of this guilt is an attack on freedom, because the dignity of freedom includes the capacity for guilt. And acceptance of guilt before God does not prevent human beings from having full responsibility for their own history. On the contrary: where moral guilt is denied as an original phenomenon— that is, denounced as false consciousness—mechanisms arise to make excuses for the sufferings and contradictions in life. We get self-defense strategies for allegedly guiltless individuals. The historical responsiblity of the person in history is irrationally halved, and the horror and dismay projected one-sidedly onto the historical opponent. Thus, the question of guilt and nonguilt, right and wrong, cannot be reduced to a purely political opposition between friend and foe.

If and insofar as Marxist praxis of class struggle is mistaken about the abyss of human guilt and thus implicitly denies human moral dignity, it cannot be taken as a fundamental principle in the historical process of salvation. If and insofar as Marxist historical and social analysis is based on this premise, it cannot be accepted by theology uncritically as it stands. Of course, this is also true of all historical and sociological theories, which see themselves as metatheories for religion and faith, for whom Christianity is a historico-culturally necessary but now superceded phase in the evolutionary history of humanity. Theology cannot justify itself with regard to these theories by producing an even more comprehensive "pure theory." It can only do so by returning to individual believers and their praxis of a single, undivided discipleship, which must take effect in historical and social life. Of course, this theological claim must question its ecclesiastical basis, and the question will be particularly demanding where the usual ecclesiastical division of labor is in force. In my view this is shown in the exchange between theology and basic community life in the so-called poor churches.

The individual development of the believer in poor Third World churches is threatened at the moment by a danger that I think liberation theology fails to take into sufficient account. This is the threat of what I will call here "secondary colonization," through the invasion of the Western cultural industry and its mass media, particularly television, which increasingly holds persons captive in an artifical world, alienating them from their original images, languages, and history. Does this "soft" terror of the culture industry have more dangerous effects in poor countries than in Europe? Does it not threaten to paralyze the process of liberation? Finally, is not the opium of the poor no longer religion but mass media culture, which reaches even the most miserable slums? This mass media culture makes the poor and exploited feel overloaded even before they have achieved any personal liberation: it robs them of their memory, even before they have become aware of their own history; it threatens their language even before they have acquired this language and become culturally literate. An important amount of liberation work is taking on this "new immaturity," not only in Latin America but also in Europe.

IV

To conclude, I should like to turn back to Europe. In the present intellectual culture of Europe, often described as "postmodern," the usage I have adopted here of "history" (in the singular!) and "society" has been very strongly criticized. It is regarded as a suspiciously totalizing way of talking, which threatens the individual. It is regarded as language destroying the colorful multiplicity of life and leading to the dictatorship of a monolithic praxis. The scapegoat is often biblical monotheism. It is regarded as the godfather of a predemocratic, antipower-sharing autocracy, the father of an obsolete patriarchalism, the forerunner of totalitarian ideologies of history—in short, as a mania for uniformity in religious garb. In contrast to this monotheism, mythical polytheism is praised because it is said to guarantee an innocent multiplicity of life. God is sacrificed to the gods. There is talk of new mythologies: a new enjoyment of myths is spreading in secularized Europe; a new cult of innocence, deeply unpolitical, with a voyeuristic attitude toward social and political crises, a life on a reduced scale, private nest-feathering and new-age fantasies as a new religion. In the postmodern manner, what is proposed is the abandonment of all universities, and single-minded reason in the name of a praxis-free, colorful multiplicity of life and its unreconciled histories.

There are European theologians who see a chance for Christianity in this polymythic atmosphere. There is no theologico-political perspective I recognize here. I see only a calling into question of the substance of the Judeo-Christian religion and the danger of atrophy to our political culture. I distrust the promise of exoneration from the obligation to make choices and the promise of liberation for the sake of greater individualization. This latter is linked to the postmodern dismissal of the idea of unity and with the esthetic-mythical birth of a new multiple way of thinking. Will not new power settle down in a world of unrelated and "hands-off" multiplicity? In the history of my German people was there not a dangerous suspension of the idea of unity and equality of all human beings? Were not the Jews, before being sent to the gas chambers, excluded metaphysically and legally from this unity? Thus, politically and culturally can we allow ourselves that innocence we esthetically propose? Can we allow ourselves it in the face of the world's misery? The "new thinking" in Europe works toward the suspension of morality, it fascinates by its presumption of a new innocence for humanity. Friedrich Nietzsche is regarded as the new prophet. But is this new thinking not ultimately an excuse-making strategy, against the individual and against history? A bit like this: the excuse for the individual in the face of historical and social catastrophes in the world is that the individual does not exist as an individual person capable of guilt. If capacity for guilt belongs to the dignity of freedom, then this "new thinking" in Europe actually withdraws from the history of freedom that it claims to be saving. Here what is needed is Christianity's power of social criticism and historical imagination.

This Christianity and its theology do not derive from a guilt-free polymythic "spiritual wealth," but from the gospel "poverty of spirit," which does not take comfort in myths far removed from history and praxis. This Christianity compels us, against the mythical ban of a posthistorical world, to speak again and again of humanity and solidarity, oppression and liberation, and to protest against injustices crying to heaven.

—translated from the German by Dinah Livingstone

23

Religion and Society:
Sacred Canopy vs.
Prophetic Critique

ROSEMARY RADFORD RUETHER

Fifteen years ago, when Gustavo Gutiérrez's *A Theology of Liberation* was published in English, North Americans were in the throes of many social conflicts. American racism had been decisively challenged by the black civil rights movement, and other racial minorities, such as Amerindians, were making their voices heard. Women were challenging the patterns of patriarchy in society and in the churches. American foreign policy was being exposed as neocolonialist, and the United States was on the brink of ignominious defeat in Southeast Asia. Its claim to represent "democracy" against totalitarian communism was being questioned.

In the last fifteen years, particularly under the presidency of Ronald Reagan, there has been a concerted effort to reestablish the hegemony of the unself-critical pro-Americanisms that were being challenged in the 1960s. This has included an effort to delegitimate liberation theology in Latin America, and black and feminist theologies in North America. The Reagan administration recognized the political power of liberation theologies. It sought to vilify liberation theology by labeling it as simply a front for Marxism and to categorize the Sandinista government as "persecutors" of the true Christians—for example, Cardinal Obando y Bravo. It also sought to promote the wealthy right-wing evangelist as the normative expression of churchmanship in America.

We can evaluate this struggle between liberation theology and the Reaganite right-wing evangelism by putting this in a broader context. In the biblical and Christian tradition, there are two opposed ways of seeing the relationship of religion (and God) to society. One way I call "the sacred canopy," the other the "prophetic critique."

"Sacred canopy theology" assumes that the dominant social order is founded by God. Its social relationships are given by God as the order of creation. The king-ruler was seen as the divinely appointed representative of God on earth. To obey the king-ruler was to obey God. The social hierarchy of man over women, ruling class over subject classes, the election of a privileged nation to rule other nations as God's people — all this is seen as "natural," divinely given, and expressions of God's will.

The theology of prophetic critique, by contrast, locates God and the spokespersons for God on the side of those victimized or despised by the social and political elites. The word of God comes as a critique of these elites, calling them to reform their ways in order to be faithful to divine justice or else threatening them with a revolutionary intervention of God in history that will overthrow their power and bring in a new world, where justice and peace will be established. Prophetic critique also questions the way in which religion has become a tool of unjust social privilege, focusing on private and cultic ways of reconciliation with God, to the exclusion of God's agenda of justice.

In the 1960s and 1970s there arose a number of theological movements in the Third World, first of all in Latin America, and then in Africa and Asia, and also movements among disadvantaged groups in North America, blacks and women among others, who have challenged the dominant type of theology and religiosity as "sacred canopy piety." They have shown the way in which established theology and religiosity ignore the poor and the oppressed, and unconsciously make it appear that white ruling class males of the Western colonialist world are the normative human beings.

Black theology has shown how dominant theology is racist, both in its obliviousness to black suffering and in its assumption that the problems of the white elite culture are the normative problems of theology and ethics. Feminist theology has shown the way in which Christian theology has validated patriarchy as the "order of creation" and made male power over female subjugation seem both God's will and the metaphor for the rule of God over humanity and creation.

Latin American liberation theology has been about the challenging of two types of "sacred canopy theology"; the theology of colonial Christendom, which directly sacralized the ruling class as representatives of God, and neocolonialist theology, which does this indirectly by separating the sacred and the secular, and seeking to confine the purview of religion to private, nonpolitical matters. For liberation theology, the gospel is, first and foremost, "good news to the poor," whereas establishment theology creates a religion of "bad news" to the poor. God is present in history through Christ to create new social and political, as well as personal, relationships between human beings that will make for justice and effective love on earth. If Christians are to be a part of Christ's work on earth as the church, they must be about a struggle against unjust poverty and the creation of new social systems that equitably distribute the resources of the world.

Reaganite theology is basically about the reestablishment of "sacred canopy religion" as normative, and the vilification of any type of liberation theology as politics falsely garbed as religion. Reaganism thus continues the claims of privatized theology that true religion is purely individual and spiritual, and has nothing to do with politics, although this claim itself becomes, all too clearly, a political one. Underneath the split between private and public, religious and political, lies in actuality the conflicts between two types of understanding of religious faith, one that sacralizes the social status quo and another that challenges it.

I suggest that there are two main poles of Reaganite "sacred canopy theology": the family and the nation. On the one side, Reaganite theology seeks to reassert patriarchy as order of creation. Male headship is seen as the natural order for the family and for the whole of society. The Equal Rights Amendment was to be defeated because it challenged this divinely established order of male headship. It is assumed that if women get out of their place and seek equality with men, the whole fabric of society will come unhinged. Juvenile delinquency and homosexuality are but two of the social evils that are seen as flowing directly from the destablizing of patriarchal hierarchy in the family.

Implicitly it is also assumed in the Reagan ideology that the hierarchy of wealth in America is just and represents the merits of the righteous. Reagan and his friends are rich because they deserve to be rich. The poor are poor because they are lazy and want to live on welfare. If one helps the poor with social welfare, this just encourages their laziness. If they have to face the consequences of their laziness in starvation, they will get down to work. Wealth and prosperity are signs of divine favor, and so the wealth of Reagan and his associates are proof that they are doing God's will.

Reaganite theology has, as its second pole, religious nationalism. America is God's new Israel, God's elect nation. America is uniquely righteous and divinely favored. Its actions in the world are God's actions. Those whom America favors, God favors. Those whom America rebukes, God rebukes. Its military might is the expression of the righteous might of God. By contrast, communists, both in Asia and Eastern Europe, and in the Third World, and Arabs, are seen as enemies of God. To bomb Libyans and to arm counterrevolutionaries against Nicaraguan peasants is nothing less than God's righteous wrath against evildoers.

Reagan's world is divided into two camps, which are ultimately theological camps: the righteous empire, America, and the evil empire, communist Russia. All other divisions in the world are simply subdivisions of that fundamental dualism between the righteous America and the evil Russia. Reagan's God is a war God, a God of the holy war of America against its evil enemies, who are fronts for the great evil one, Satan.

Reagan's theology is basically optimistic, for divine favor and grace upon the righteous are assured. It is not necessary to bother one's mind with laboring details about particular countries and their histories, for all is determined in advance. This assurance of grace and divine favor lends itself even to an optimistic apocalypticism, in which nuclear war can be contemplated cheerfully on the expectation that it will be the final outburst of divine wrath against evildoers and the final establishment of the righteous on earth.

The Reagan revolution in religion has lent itself to a new emphasis on the corporate church as the counterpart to the business corporation. The millionaire evangelist becomes the living proof of divine favor upon those who "get right" with God. The Reagan administration has been characterized by more scandals of public corruption than any other administration in recent American history. Not accidentally, the new corporate church and millionaire evangelist have also been plagued by continual revelations of scandal. But it is characteristic of Reaganite theology that the sins of these evangelists are seen primarily as sexual. Their racism, sexism, and militarism, their readiness to bless South African apartheid, and racial and economic injustice in America, are not seen as scandalous. This is just religious business as usual.

Liberation theology unmasks this kind of religiosity as blasphemy, its god as an idol. It shows us that the real struggle of faith today, as in ancient times, is not the

174

conflict between theism and atheism, but between the true God and the idols. The idols clothe war and injustice, violence and oppression, in religious mantles and claim that these come forth from the hand of God. The true God of biblical faith speaks through prophets and prophetesses who break through the lies of idolatrous religiosity. We are called to conversion to God by being called to conversion to the poor.

How does one know the difference between true faith and the religion of the idols? By their fruits you know them. Those who truly believe in God distance themselves from social privilege. They live simply and work to bind up the wounds of the victims. The worshipers of the idols grow fat and bless the bombs and systems of violence. Their sins are many, and the least of them are one-night stands in motels with willing secretaries.

The theology of Gustavo Gutiérrez has allowed us to name authentic prophetic faith and unmask the idols for our times. Gutiérrez has been the key founder, not simply of a new "school" of theology, but of the renewal of Christian self-understanding in the context of the conflict between rich and poor nations. The preferential option for the poor has been the heart of his theological message. This call to solidarity with the poorest and most oppressed of the earth searches the conscience of the leaders of the church, who too often have allied themselves with the elites of society.

The challenge of Gutiérrez's theology is a church that starts at the base, identified with the poorest, rather than with those in power. The revolution it seeks is not one that would simply upend the pyramid, creating a new class of oppressors from the leaders of a revolutionary party. The church is called to witness to a society where justice and love are really and practically incarnate. This may never happen perfectly or finally, but the Christian must seek continually for new and better approximations of the just and loving society. Liberation can never be identified simply with ideologies or theologies about liberation. Nor can it be assumed to be the assured possession of any particular social system. Prophetic critique must be based on continual discernment of the realities of the times. Reading the "signs of the times" means asking about what is actually happening, not just discussing theoretical constructs that substitute themselves for reality.

A church that opts for the poor is one that must learn anew what it means to be baptized into the death and resurrection of Christ. For this church, the cross has ceased to be a golden and jeweled decoration on a church wall, and has become the living reality that Christians bear in their bodies. The option for the poor calls down upon the church the wrath of those powers and principalities that uphold the privileges of the rich. To opt for the poor is to risk suffering and death. The cry *presente*, by which the Latin American church remembers its martyrs, is the concrete, living expression of the presence of the risen Lord. In this living presence of the martyrs, one discovers once again what resurrection and the commitment to continue the witness of Christ really mean.

The churches and theological faculties of the First World would like to have it both ways. We would like to entertain Third World theologians, like Gustavo Gutiérrez, as "stars" in a new "field" of theology. We wish to bring them to give invitational lectures and prove thereby that we are au courant. But liberation theologians have sought to avoid becoming simply a new intellectual elite. As Gustavo Gutiérrez has repeatedly said, "the subject of liberation theology is not theology, but liberation." The criteria of its truth lies in praxis. The critical question is not whether one has the correct words, but rather how one commits one's life.

"What side are you on" is the challenge of Gutiérrez to those who profess to be Christian among the churches of the powerful and affluent. The future of Roman Catholicism in the world today rests very much on how it responds to that revolutionary challenge from a Third World Christianity, personified in Gutiérrez. Will the Catholic Church choose to stand for a new future for all humanity, through solidarity with the poor, or will it fall back on its traditional alliances with the ruling classes? The ambivalent response of church leaders to Gustavo Gutiérrez and their theological role signifies their ambivalence in the face of that call to commitment.

24

The Religious and
the Human Ecumene

EDWARD SCHILLEBEECKX

The history of humankind in past and present is marked by religious wars and the violence of religions. The coexistence of religions does not seem in fact to be favorable for the promoting of humanity, for the movement toward living together in community worthy of humanity. This is indeed a highly paradoxical situation, especially for Christians, for Vatican II declares solemnly the Christian church to be "the sign and the instrument . . . of the unity of all the human race" (*Lumen Gentium*, 1). But try saying this in Northern Ireland, where for years Christians have been doing everything to make one another's living impossible, in the most literal sense of the word. Or, look at Iran and Iraq, Lebanon, the Golden Temple of the Sikhs, and so on. If paying homage to the highest human values becomes imperialistic, such praise deteriorates into the worst enemy of concrete human dignity!

Gustavo Gutiérrez has brought the church "as sacrament of the world" into connection with "the option for the poor."[1] I should like to elaborate on that vision here.

THE PLURALITY OF RELIGIONS AND CHRISTIANITY

The history of humanity presents us with a collection of divergent ways of life, a multicolored proposal of "ways of salvation": monotheistic Judaism, Christianity, and Islam; Hinduism and Buddhism; Taoism, Confucianism, and Shinto; animism; African and Amerindian ways to salvation and blessing. We call all of these "religions"; that is, we are convinced that there is an essential agreement among all the divergent phenomena. That is why they are designated by a single concept: religion.

Likewise, *Nostra Aetate* (1), a declaration of Vatican II, says that persons "look to the various religions for answers to those profound mysteries of the human condition which today, even as in olden times, deeply stir the human heart." In other words, by offering a message of salvation and by showing a path to salvation, religions respond to a fundamental question about life. In a similar key, modern sociologists (such as H. Lübbe) say much the same thing, albeit in very general terms but nonetheless correctly, talking about religions as "systems of orientation to the ultimate" or "systems of dealing with contingency": comprehensive systems that give meaning or systems that help us to come to terms spiritually, emotionally, and especially existentially with our vulnerable, precarious existence in an ambivalent society.

However, students of culture and philosophers of religion have some misconceptions about all of this—in the dual line of either an essentialist or a nominalist approach via "general terms" ("universals") to what is meant by "religion."

In my opinion, we can say this better with a term of Wittgenstein: that there exists among the many religions "family resemblances." Then there is really no talk of one or more "common characteristics," or of "ideal types." Phenomena that show resemblances and are on that basis designated with the same term ("religion") are (just as the members of a family, so Wittgenstein would say) each really unique in their specific combination or configuration of characteristics. But on the basis of "family resemblances" they still can be compared with one another despite their uniqueness. As a socio-cultural phenomenon and system of meaning, Christianity is also a religion alongside other religions: one out of many.

And here the difficulties begin. How can religions as religions "live together" with another, despite their conflicting pretensions? We stand here before a particularly difficult and delicate problem regarding the question of how religious persons from a variety of religions might coexist.

For themselves, Christians find their only rescue in Jesus confessed as the Christ. Therefore they have kept asking (out of their own vision and orientation in life) in the course of history how non-Christians could work out their salvation. For their confession of Jesus' uniqueness was not merely an expression of a subjective conviction. According to Christian confession, that vision has to do with something real: that is to say, *it is true* (although it is an affirmative of faith and not a scientifically provable and verifiable truth; thus it can never be used in a discussion as a weapon against non-Christians).

On the basis of that faith conviction in Jesus' universal redeeming activity, Christians had to ask the question sooner or later about the possibility of salvation for non-Christians. This happened indirectly from the very beginning of Christianity: already the Second (or New) Testament says that God desires the salvation of "all" (1 Tim. 2:4), and that God wills it in a realizable manner, adapted to the situation of given individuals (even if they do not know Christ). The actual thematization of this problem—how individuals "could become blessed" if they had never come to know Jesus Christ—began especially in modernity and really only in our own time to become a fundamental and even crucial theological problem.

For we as Christians are confronted with biblical texts that do not fit easily with this problem and for which we must account. Jesus surely preached the reign of God as a reign of justice, peace, and wholeness of creation for all persons. But according to the witness of the New Testament, Jesus himself stands in a constitutive or essential relationship to this universal reign of God for all humanity. Christians say with the Bible that "there is one God, and there is one mediator between God and men," Jesus Christ (1 Tim. 2:5); "and there is a salvation in no one else, for there is no other name under heaven given among men by which we must be saved" (Acts 4:12). The Johannine Jesus also says: "I am the way, and the truth, and the life; no one comes to the Father but by me" (John 14:16). "For so the Lord has commanded us, saying, 'I have set you to be a light for the gentiles, that you may bring salvation to the uttermost parts of the earth.' And when the gentiles heard this they were glad" (Acts 13:47). Also a Paulinism directed in a different fashion but just as Christian, says: "For as by a man came death, by a man has come also the resurrection of the dead. For as in Adam all die, so also in Christ shall all be made alive" (1 Cor. 15:21–22). What happened to Jesus is a fact "once for all" (Heb. 9:12). That which has taken place holds for all nations, peoples, and cultures; it is universally relevant in time and space; it has world-historical significance. The post-Pauline tradition even says: "He is the image of the invisible God" (Col. 1:15). A similar sound is heard in all the gospel traditions. "He who sees me sees him who sent me" (John 12:45). The essential bond between the coming of the reign of God for all people and Jesus the Christ is confessed in all levels and traditions of the New Testament, also by the first Hebrew-Jewish interpretation of Jesus of Nazareth.

Those are texts that we cannot circumvent or dilute or act as though they were not there. Moreover, that would not be honest; a selective elimination of parts of the scriptures is also hardly an honest solution. To be sure: all these statements are statements of *belief*, of course; they interpret a confessing discourse, in no way a scientific-objectivizing or propositional and thereby verifiable discourse. But this latter has in no way an exclusive claim on truth. We cannot, however, disregard these absolute statements from the New Testament, or render them harmless by reducing them to exaggerated, elegant flourishes of rhetoric, such as when lovers say to one another "you are the most beautiful and the only one in the world." That is meaningful language, but it holds only for the two lovers, even though outsiders understand clearly its meaning. It is a sensible use of language.

Confessional language of faith, to be sure, also has something to do with similar expressions of someone's complete devotion to a loved one. It indeed says something also about one's subjective stance and complete surrender to another person. But confessional language is not exhausted by that. A certain confessional language also says something about that very person, about reality, a reality that actually calls forth this complete and radical surrender, and is worthy of it, precisely because it is real. Although the immediate basis for such language may lie in a personal or collective experience, that experience also mediates something more profound. The ultimate ground of Jesus' uniqueness spoken of in the scriptural quotation is, according to the New Testament witness, "for in him all the fulness of God was pleased to dwell" (Col. 1:19); or, according to the so-called Apostles' Creed, "He is the Christ, God's only beloved Son, our Lord."

The scriptural quotations refer clearly to Christian consciousness, that Jesus of Nazareth was considered by Christians as the definitive and decisive revelation of God, who nonetheless "desires all to be saved and to come to the knowledge of the truth" (1 Tim. 2:4), also therefore even if they have not come to know Jesus Christ. Whether that revelation then is normative for other religions is the next consideration. For all kinds of ambiguities can come about here if we use the word "normative" or "criterion," because those words are used extensively on the level of "scientific objectivity," whereas the assertion that in Jesus God's definitive and decisive revelation takes place is an affirmation of faith, something that is not accessible or evident on a scientifically objective basis.

In connection with the uniqueness of the Christian church, one can ask good and bad questions. And in the past many bad questions were asked, so that the answer to them shares in the meaninglessness of the question. In the history of the Christian churches it was generally accepted until recently that Christianity was the bearer of absolute truth. "In fact," the Christian churches have so comported themselves in the course of the ages. A proper claim to universality was twisted imperialistically into an ecclesiastical claim of absoluteness, to a monopoly or exclusive claim to truth. This imperialism became the cause of religious wars and of persecution.

A BRIEF OVERVIEW OF THE CONTEMPORARY THEOLOGICAL STATE OF THE QUESTION, ESPECIALLY IN CATHOLIC THEOLOGY

Vatican II broke with this imperialism of truth. In broad lines that was clearly a new path away from the previous centuries-old tradition. However, it was not a radical break, because both the First and Second Testaments and church traditions also recognized good things in the other religions.

Already before Vatican II Karl Rahner and other theologians went further than the already broad statements of this council.[2] They not only recognized the possibility of individual salvation of the adherents of other religions, but also ascribed to those religions themselves—as such, therefore as institutions—salvific value. They, too, were "ways of salvation" to God, institutions of salvation (something that Vatican II, despite urgings from theologians, did not yet dare to say). Even the already open statements of the Second Vatican Council in *Lumen Gentium*, *Nostra Aetate*, and *Ad Gentes* did not go so far, at least not expressly. It seems also that implicitly for the philosopher of religion from Bonn, Hans Waldenfels, that modern position (inspired by Rahner) goes too far, when he writes that if non-Christians likewise find their salvation, "that happens not *in spite of*, but in each case *in* their religion. The formula *through* (or through the mediation of) their religion is one Christians should rather avoid," he adds explicitly.[3] For myself, I do not understand this hesitation toward religion as a social system so well; apparently he fears that this touches a seed of the truth in the old claim to absoluteness of the "imperialist" Christianity.

One does have to concede with the theologian Max Seckler that the salvific value of all religions cannot be posited merely abstractly and globally.[4] One will have to look very concretely at each religion, one by one, regarding their own values and the image of humanity and the world implicit within them. How do you want to be and how do you see your own humanity? Although it was (unavoidably) schematic, Vatican II tried to express the proper value of Judaism, Hinduism, Buddhism, and Islam, and finally this council speaks in *Lumen Gentium*, chap. 16, even of the possibility of salvation of agnostics and atheists. With this we are already close by my personal theological position, which basically affirms the following: before one can speak historically of religions, there was the reality of God's saving activity in profane history: "outside the world, there is no salvation." God brings about in world history salvation through human mediation *and* persons bring about calamity. Religions are latecomers in the history of salvation coming from God in our profane history.

In recent years some have gone even further. Thus the philosopher of religion

180

Heinz Robert Schlette reverses the categories used earlier: for him, Christianity is not the "normal" or "ordinary way to salvation" to God; the other religions are that. Christianity is the "exceptional" or "extraordinary" way to God.[5]

With this we are still not through the bend in the road. Recently the American Catholic theologian Paul Knitter went even a step further than Schlette: he denies any form of claim to universality of Christianity.[6] In our times there indeed reigns among Christians a certain new form of modern "indifferentism," and some theologians have made themselves spokespersons for it: all religions are of the same value. Of course they are not, for even their visions about humanity are rather divergent, and a religion that, for example, sends the eldest son to death is certainly not of the same value as a religion that expressly forbids it. Criteria of humanity apply here too!

Even though one's own religion is involved in every comparison of religions with one another, one ultimately cannot avoid the truth question. But the truth question presents itself within a "hermeneutical circle." The question is not whether there are many open questions here that cannot be solved speculatively, and moreover whether one is asking the right question and not the wrong one (which can never be resolved). The question of truth with regard to one's own religion in no way need be discriminatory in itself vis-à-vis other religions. No single religion exhausts the question of truth. Therefore in religiosis we must put behind us both absolutism and relativism.

Our times have "liberated" themselves in many points from the peculiarly modern claim to truth and universality since the Enlightenment. Logically and practically, plurality has gained priority over unity. The ancient and neoplatonic Greek ideal of unity is in no sense still a norm for modern and postmodern persons. The claims made by a Jewish, Christian, and Muslim monotheism on all persons is perceived by many (or some) as something totalitarian. Some see in this the reason for the move of many Westerners to Asian religions. The statement "all religions are equal" is understandable to postmodern sensibilities, even though that statement is cheap and, to my mind, fundamentally wrong.

The question rather is whether monotheism with its claim to universality cannot be a critique or a challenge to those sensibilities. Current sensibilities are not normative in themselves either! The universal claim to salvation of Jesus and the human reason that remembers the suffering of humanity can also deliver a critique of that liberal pluralism of our time. For there is also a cheap form of toleration — indifference: laissez faire, laissez passer — I don't care! This is an attitude without the courage of the witnessing blood of martyrs.

To be sure, Christianity has often expressed its own truth, universality, and uniqueness (which are undeniable) as a claim to absoluteness, by means of which all other religions were considered inferior, whereas the good that was to be found in them was assumed to be present in Christianity itself in a preeminent fashion. One discovered "Christian values" in the other religions, but robbed them of their own identity by the fact. The consequence of this religious and cultural "imperialism" was that the modern history of colonialism and of mission has been in good measure also a time of oppression of foreign cultures and religions, both during and not less than before from the time of the abstract Enlightenment.

But Asia and practically all countries where Islam reigned shut themselves off from Christianity; these universal religions had their own claim to absoluteness.

Because of that in the public forum of the West, Christianity came to be considered more and more as one religion among many and moreover, historically, as a religion under which many non-Christian cultures and other religions had suffered severely. This climatic change in Western thinking was paired with a privatization of Christianity as religion: in one's own heart one could quietly praise Christianity as the one true religion, as long as it had no consequences for others and for the bourgeois public forum. At the moment Christianity is not dropping its claim to universality, but is letting both its exclusivist and inclusivist claim to universality go. "Exclusivist," in the sense of "only Christianity is a true religion," and "inclusivist" insofar as there is truth and goodness immanent in other religions, with their adherents being "anonymous Christians." In both cases this discriminates against non-Christians and this therefore is improper.

NEW THEOLOGICAL PERSPECTIVE

Given this prehistory, we shall have to seek in any case a direction that avoids both absolutism and relativism. To ask the truth question regarding Christianity, and simultaneously with that the question whether it is possible for Christians to live together with members of other religions and with atheists and agnostics, in no way presumes, as had been thought earlier, the superiority of Christianity in the sense of how can Christians, who as members of a particular religion consider themselves superior to other religious persons, live together with non-Christians? Rather, the question is about a Christian identity that respectfully acknowledges others' religious identity and allows itself to be challenged by other religions and challenges them in return on the basis of its own message. In short, we are being confronted with other questions than were asked in the past, questions that are more productive and fruitful for all parties concerned.

We are therefore asking other questions, even if it remains binding for Christian believers that they find salvation "only in the name of Jesus of Nazareth." And in this Christian perspective questions arise about whether and how, for example, can one be a Christian as a Hindu? In other words, is there a Hindu version of being Christian? This is not a question of a speculative approach to one another's religions, but of a probably centuries-long experiment to come to a "common experience." Only a common experience can lead to a consonant hermeneutical interpretation. That common experience is by no means here yet. Therefore it seems to me that the question is whether the pluralism of religions is a *factual* phenomenon that should be overcome as quickly as possible, or a *foundational* phenomenon that asks for a continuing humane coexistence. The consequences of this are rather important for one's own vision of the ecumene of the world religions and ultimately for world peace, which, through religious intolerance and through the pretensions to exclusive or inclusive claims to absoluteness, has been put severely to the test in the course of time and today in many countries through religious wars.

My concern here directly is the identity and therefore the proper self-definition of Christianity, in which this religion sees how it is to be situated vis-à-vis other religions: on the one hand, without absolutism or relativism; on the other, without discrimination or feelings of superiority.

PHASE ONE: THE HISTORICAL CONTINGENCY OR LIMITEDNESS
OF JESUS OF NAZARETH

In contrast to the earlier claim to absoluteness of Christianity, determined as it was by the regnant *Zeitgeist* of that time, lies the positive acceptance of the diversity of religions, which is, to my mind, inherent in the essence of Christianity. The problem is not so much that posed at the level of an earlier consciousness of the problematic: Is Christianity the one, true religion, or is it (in a more moderate version) a better religion than all the others? In these comparisons the concept "religion" is borrowed from the religion of the one doing the comparison (whatever religion that might be). For Christians, therefore, it is Christianity. Rather, the problem is this: *How can Christianity maintain its own identity and uniqueness and at the same time ascribe a positive value to the diversity of religions in a nondiscriminating way?* When posed in this way, it is not the common elements in the many religions, but precisely their respective differences that form their uniqueness and particularity, that is relevant for Christianity. If this is the case, one needs to indicate a basis in Christianity itself for this new Christian attitude of openness and nonintolerance toward other world religions.

This basis lies, to my mind, in Jesus' message and praxis of the reign of God, with all their consequences. For Christianity is in its particularity and uniqueness as a religion essentially bound to an insuperable "historical particularity" and thus to regionality and limitation. Thus Christianity, too, like all religions has boundaries: limited in forms of expression, and also in ways of looking at things and in concrete praxis. Christians sometimes have difficulty looking at this reality rationally. But this limitedness belongs to the essence of Christianity (even expressed especially when Christians use their "incarnation model" in their theology—which remains in this tradition the dominant paradigm).

The special, particular, and unique character of Christianity is that it finds the life and essence of God precisely in this historical and thus limited particularity of "Jesus of Nazareth"—confessed as the personal-human manifestation of God. Thereby is confessed that Jesus is surely a "unique" but nonetheless "contingent" manifestation (that is, historical and therefore limited) of the gift of salvation coming from God for all persons. Whoever ignores this fact of the concrete, particular humanity of Jesus, precisely in his geographically limited and socio-culturally recognizable and limited quality as "human," makes of the individual Jesus a "necessary" divine emanation or consequence, whereby indeed all other religions disappear into the void. This seems to be essentially in conflict with the deepest sense of all the christological councils and creeds, and finally with the very being of God as absolute freedom. Jesus' humanity is devalued in that vision to a (docetic) phantom humanity, while trivializing on the other hand all non-Christian religions. Nevertheless Christians have in the course of time absolutized without remainder precisely this historical and limited particularity of Christianity. This rang in the historical misery of empirical Christianity in opposition to the original evangelical authenticity.

However, the revelation of God in Jesus, as the Christian gospel proclaims it, does not mean that God absolutizes a historical particularity (be it even Jesus of

Nazareth). From the revelation in Jesus we learn that no single historical particularity can be called absolute and that therefore, because of the relativity present in Jesus, every person can encounter God outside Jesus, especially in our worldly history and in the many religions that have arisen from it. The risen Jesus of Nazareth keeps *pointing beyond himself to God*. One could say: God points via Jesus Christ in the Spirit to God as creator and redeemer: to a God of *all* persons.

The particularity of Jesus, which defines the origin, particularity, and uniqueness of Christianity, implies therefore that the differences between the individual religions remain and are not erased. The manifestation of God in Jesus does not close out "religious history," which is evident from, among others, the rise of Islam as a post-Christian world religion. And no one, not even in Islam, can deny that new world religions can and will arise after Islam. Despite all critical questions that can be addressed, certain contemporary neoreligious movements can support this hypothesis.

It is clear that there are convergences and divergences between all religions. Differences, however, are not to be judged in themselves as deviations that should be worked out ecumenically, but as positive values. God is too rich and too supersubstantial to be exhausted *in fulness* by one distinct and thus limited religious tradition or experience. Surely, according to the Christian view of things, "the whole fulness of deity dwells in" Jesus. New Testament texts witness to that for Christians (Col. 2:9; 1:15; Heb. 1:3; 2 Cor. 4:4). But it is precisely in "bodiliness" — or "this dwelling (of God's fulness) in Jesus' *humanity*" — that the *contingent* and *limited* form of Jesus' appearance in our history is drawn. (Otherwise one should proclaim the docetism condemned by all Christian churches — that is, that the divine could only appear in a phantom humanity in Jesus).

As a result of all this we can, may, and must say that there is more (religious) truth present in *all the religions together* than in one individual religion, and this holds also for Christianity. There exist because of that "true," "good," and "beautiful" — astonishing — aspects in the manifold forms of coming to terms with God present in humanity, forms that have not found and do not find a place in the specific experience of Christianity. There are divergent authentic religious experiences that Christianity has never thematized or brought into practice precisely because of its historical particularity, probably (I say it cautiously, but assertively) because of the specifically personal accents of Jesus himself, also cannot thematize *without undoing those particular accents of their jesuanic sharpness and ultimately of their specific Christianness.*

From all this I learn that (also in Christian self-understanding) the plurality of religions is not an evil that needs to be overcome, but rather a fructifying richness to be welcomed by all. This does not deny that the historically irresolvable plurality of religions is nurtured and fed interiorly by a unity within our history that is explicitly no longer thematizable and practicable: the very unity of God (confessed by Christians as a trinitarian one), insofar as this transcendent unity is reflected in the immanent family resemblances among the religions, something that gives us permission to give the unitary name of "religion" to all these divergent religious phenomena!

The particularity, identity, and uniqueness of Christianity vis-à-vis those other religions resides in the fact that Christianity is a religion that connects the relationship to God to a historical and thus highly situated and thereby limited particularity: Jesus of Nazareth. This is the uniqueness and identity of Christianity, but at the same time its unavoidably historical boundedness. Clear with this is that the God of Jesus (based on Jesus' parables and praxis of the reign of God) is a symbol of openness, and not of being closed. This gives a positive relationship of Christianity to other religions, at the same time nonetheless maintaining the uniqueness of Christianity and ultimately honoring the Christian loyal affirmation of the positive nature of the other world religions.

The truth question is not evaded by this, but what is true here is that no one holds a lease on the truth, and that no one can claim the fulness of God's richness for themselves alone. This insight, somewhat new for Christians, flows from the fact that we are also asking new questions now that could not have been asked earlier, purified as we are by past (and still new!) meaningless religious wars and unfruitful discrimination. In doing this we do not proclaim the cheap modern liberal principle that all religions are equal, or all are equally relative, or even equally untrue (as the atheists maintain).

Christology is an interpretation of Jesus of Nazareth: it states that Jesus is redeemer of all persons and is in that sense the universal redeemer. But that which redeems, which mediates liberation and redemption, is not the interpretation, but the means of redemption itself. In *Jesus: An Experiment in Christology*, I already referred to the fact that we are not redeemed by the christological titles of Jesus, but through the means of redemption itself, Jesus of Nazareth, in whatever framework of language that means is experienced and expressed. That is to say: "Jesus" redeems us, not "Christ," a christological title coming from a certain culture and often not usable in other cultures. Moreover, redemption in Christ is only unique and universal insofar as what happened in Jesus is continued in his disciples. Without a relationship to a redemptive and liberative practice of Christians, the redemption brought about at one time by Jesus is suspended in a purely speculative, vacuous atmosphere. The credal exclamation, "Jesus is Lord" (Rom. 10:9) does not of itself bring redemption, but rather "he who does the will of my Father" (Matt. 7:21). One has to follow the path Jesus did; then Jesus' way of life takes on concretely a universal meaning (Matt. 25:37–39, 44–46). An actual, albeit fragmentary, making persons whole is also the best proof of liberation!

The claim that Jesus is the universal redeemer implies that we are beginning in our history to bring forth the fruits of the reign of God. This christology receives its authenticity from the concrete praxis of the reign of God: the history of Jesus' path through life must be continued in his disciples; only then is there meaningful talk of the uniqueness and particularity of Christianity. There is also a coredemptive function of the "body of Christ," specifically, the historical Christian community. The path through life, following after Jesus, is marked by two essential characteristics: the way of denial of any messianism of power, coming from a seigneurial-human interior freedom (resisting oppressive powers is the basis for the human voluntary commitment to poor and oppressed persons: a solidarity of love), *and* this path includes the *via crucis*, the cross. Jesus was indeed the expected messiah, but he was that in an "unexpected way," perceived only by a few. In this is the uniqueness of Jesus; the "proof" is this: throughout the centuries Christians have witnessed to this path through life by going through him to a witnessing martyrdom. "In my flesh I complete what is lacking in Christ's afflictions" (Col. 1:24), as it was expressed in ancient times. Resistance and surrender. This brings us to the following concretization or second phase, without which that first phase of reflection remains still abstract.

PHASE TWO: THE UNIVERSAL RIGHT OF THE POOR

The *universality* of Christian faith means that the Christian faith community is an open community. Sadly enough, the institutional church has had the inclination to universalize precisely its nonuniversal, historically inherited peculiar characteristics bound to a certain culture and time, and to impose them uniformly upon the entire Catholic world: in catechesis (think of the "universal catechism"), in liturgy and church order, also in theology and until recently even in a uniform language (Latin). Universality—in Greek it is called "catholicity"—means rather that the Christian faith places itself open (critically) for each person, for each people and each culture. "Universal" means: what holds equally for all. That universal must incarnate itself then in all and in each one, without exhausting all the potentialities and virtualities of the universal in those given incarnations. Thus, in the contemporary context of aching structural world poverty, the universal openness and universal invitation of the gospel message receives a socially very concrete dimension and a new location, as it were. In that way especially Latin American, but also African and Asian forms of liberation theology inspire me.[7]

In the West we used the concept "universality" often in an abstract and nonhistorical fashion, in the sense of "valid for all persons." In itself, a correct usage! But, we said rather nonchalantly that something is valid for all persons while forgetting that humanity is divided concretely into "poor" and "nonpoor" persons, and that what was valid for the nonpoor, historically and concretely was not valid for the poor and oppressed. Structurally they are excluded. Talking about universality is therefore only meaningful and concrete if, in our fundamental theological concepts, we express at the same time the distinction between nonpoor and especially the structurally poor. It is not a matter of speaking of a pastoral predilection of the church for the poor in the sense of the duty to universal love means always a preferential love for individual, certain persons, as the church also can speak of pastoral priorities—for example, in connection with the church's option for youth. No, the option for the poor is a *datum of revelation*. The basis for that option is the Christian faith in the God of Jesus Christ, who himself gives witness to this partisan option. That option for the poor is thus a question of Christian orthodoxy; it touches all the belief statements of the Christian credo. The option for the poor, the indigent, and the oppressed is a partisan, free choice of the God of Jesus of Nazareth, as well as an option for the not always in fact "nonpoor," socio-culturally, psychologically, and religiously marginalized persons. The incarnation of God in Jesus of Nazareth is not a "becoming human," but an identification of God in Jesus with the poor, oppressed, and finally executed innocent individual, for whom Jesus stands as a model. Only within this perspective can we now speak of the concrete universality of ecclesiastical Christianity, insofar as it walks in the footsteps of Jesus.

It is therefore a matter of a "concrete universality" through which Christian believers take upon themselves the aspirations of those who are deprived of their rights in this world and are in solidarity with the cry for justice of the poor and disenfranchised. The cause of justice is the cause of all. Freedom, the rights of humanity, are there for all; and if this is not the case (in other words, if there are only rights for those who demand them), there are no human rights! If rights are valid only for a part of humanity, this part of humanity would thereby legitimate and sanction the lack of rights. In the measure that the church chooses the side of the poor and those deprived of rights and is in solidarity with human rights, it takes up that concrete universality, for the "Catholic universality" is not only a given from the very inception of Christian faith, it is a contextual charge to be achieved historically.

In the contemporary socio-political and economic time-bind of structural deprivation of rights for the majority of humanity, not only the *caritative diaconia universalizes* the Christian gospel among all people (as Mother Teresa benevolently practices it), but also the *political diaconia* that wishes to remove the causes of this structural deprivation. It thereby recognizes the universality of human rights and human dignity, and does not cover up poverty theologically and prolong it ideologically. The active presence of the Christian churches with poor and deprived persons, adding its voice to the cry for redemption of the oppressed, has therefore a universal meaning: a *meaning for all*—also for the rich and powerful as a summons to solidarity. The transformation of the world toward a higher humanity, toward justice, peace, and wholeness of creation belongs therefore essentially to the "catholicity" or universality of Christian faith, and this is a nondiscriminatory universality par excellence.

That Christianity is a universal message to all people means therefore that Christianity is only universal if Christians are concerned to reach all of humanity in its being lacerated into "poor" and "nonpoor." "To the poor is preached the good news": that is the essence of the Christian gospel! And this message is also practiced toward the poor (without Christians being able to view this as a Christian exclusive right or monopoly). The sending of Christians in solidarity to the poor in all the world belongs then also to the essential aspects of what we now call "mission." For Christians it comes down to this: by Christian praxis—in the footsteps of Jesus—to witness to the one whom they confess as their God: the God of Israel, father of Jesus Christ, who is called a defender of the poor, creator of heaven and earth, who cannot be claimed by any single religion for itself. But then we must keep clearly before our eyes with this the peculiar accent of Jesus' conception of God (if we wish to preserve the evangelical accents).

Critique of certain images of God, especially of conceptions of God that threaten our humanness, is also an essential aspect of the evangelical message of Jesus of Nazareth; it is even a focus in that message. And it was from a religious source and, for that matter, from a Christian insight of faith (otherwise therefore than in the Enlightenment) that God is personally involved with persons in their history, that Christianity is, from a theologal or mystical source, originally and simultaneously an impulse toward liberation and emancipation. On the basis of Jesus' message, parables, and his praxis of the reign of God, we see how the biblical concept of God is essentially bound up with a praxis of persons who liberate their fellow human beings, just as Jesus did before us. Precisely because in the course of church history the bond weakened and was even forgotten, and God was thereby "objectified" as the capstone and guarantor of all human knowledge, order, and behavior, and thus was declared the legitimation of the status quo—an enemy of any change,

187

liberation, and emancipation, therefore—the crisis of the Enlightenment was historically not only possible, but even "unavoidable."

This all had, on the other hand, the consequence that in Enlightenment deism (and in its direct and indirect aftereffects) the biblical "calling upon God" disappeared and left only a secularized and diminished liberation and emancipation process—a diminished freedom movement. From a Christian point of view it is, however, a matter of an unbreakable connection between revering God (let us say: prayer and mysticism) *and* emancipatory liberation in the fullest and multifaceted sense of this word—in that a theologian such as Gustavo Gutiérrez goes ahead of us all with conviction!

This mystical and liberating message, accompanied by a consonant evangelical praxis, following after Jesus, proclaiming loudly to all who will hear, is the good right of Christianity. But Christians must remember in this a word of the prophet Amos: "Did I not bring up Israel from the land of Egypt, and the Philistines from Caphtor and the Syrians from Kir?" (Amos 9:7). Suffering humanity is evidently *the* chosen people of God. If that is so, living together with the "human ecumene," seen religiously, and the "ecumene of suffering humanity," is indeed possible.

—*translated from the Dutch by Robert J. Schreiter*

NOTES

1. Gustavo Gutiérrez, "Twee perspectieven op de kerk. Sacrament van de wereld—keuze voor de armen," in Hermann Häring, Ted Schoof, and Ad Willems, eds., *Meedenken met Edward Schillebeeckx* (Baarn: H. Nelissen, 1983), pp. 221–45.

2. Karl Rahner, "Christianity and Non-Christian Religions," *Theological Investigations*, vol. 5, pp. 115–34; see also "Church, Churches, and Religions," ibid., vol. 10, pp. 30–49; "Anonymous Christianity and the Missionary Task of the Church," ibid., vol. 12, pp. 161–78; "Jesus Christ in the Non-Christian Religions," ibid., vol. 17, pp. 39–50; "Über die Heilsbedeutung der nichtchristlichen Religionen," *Schriften zur Theologie*, vol. 13, pp. 341–50.

3. Hans Waldenfels, "Der Absolutheitsanspruch des Christentums und die grossen Weltreligionen," *Hochland*, 62 (1970) 202–17; "Ist der christliche Glaube der einzig Wahre? Christentum und nichtchristliche Religionen," *Stimmen der Zeit*, 112 (1987) 463–75.

4. Max Seckler, "Theologie der Religionen mit Fragezeichen," *Theologische Quartalschrift*, 166 (1986) 164–84.

5. Heinz Robert Schlette, *Toward a Theology of Religions* (New York: Herder and Herder, 1966); idem, *Skeptische Religionsphilosophie* (Freiburg: Herder, 1972).

6. Paul Knitter, *No Other Name? A Critical Survey of Christian Attitudes toward the World Religions* (Maryknoll, N.Y.: Orbis, 1985).

7. Among those to be cited are Gustavo Gutiérrez, Leonardo Boff, and others. For Africa and Asia, especially Jean-Marc Ela, *African Cry* (Maryknoll, N.Y.: Orbis, 1986); Aloysius Pieris, *An Asian Theology of Liberation* (Maryknoll, N.Y.: Orbis, 1988).

25

Jesus, Theology, and Good News

JON SOBRINO, SJ

Many subjects would be appropriate for a book in honor of Gustavo Gutiérrez, himself and his theology, because this Peruvian theologian has brought depth and inspiration to so many themes. In this article I offer some brief reflections on one particular subject: Christianity's essential reality as *eu-aggelion* (gospel, good news) and the consequences this has for theology. I have chosen this subject because— apart from its intrinsic importance—it figures largely in liberation theology. Liberation theology stresses the good news in what it says and its own work has a *eu-aggelion* or gospel mode, as well as a historical, practical, and prophetic mode. To all this Gustavo Gutiérrez has made a powerful contribution.

In this article I concentrate on analyzing the relationships between theology and good news in two of its aspects: the precise presentation of Christ as good news and the gospel mode of theology. Both aspects are dialectically related because a proper understanding and presentation of Christ as good news will tend to give theological work a more evangelical mode or style. And vice versa, if theology does its work in an evangelical way, it will tend to bring out the reality of Christ as good news. I begin with the second point because here I see the ultimate theologal horizon that allows a radical treatment of the *eu-aggelion* in theology.

THE "EVANGELICAL" MODE IN THEOLOGY

First we must recall, however schematically, the theologal framework within which Christian reality is set. It is essential for this Christian reality to adhere to the fact that its central core is something positive—good and supremely good. On God's part this is expressed as self-donation to humanity, and on the part of humanity. it is expressed as accepting God's welcome, responding and giving back accordingly. Hence, to describe this central reality, we must always use positive terms, as the final expression of the event of revelation received: love, justice, salvation, redemption, liberation. By any of these words we state formally that the essence of Christian reality is good and the supremely good.

This is the general framework within which we can systematically understand the term *eu-aggelion* as expressing what is good and positive in Christianity, but with specific characteristics. *Eu-aggelion* stresses that the good and the positive break into time, they happen as something real in human lives, and are clearly announced, so that equivalency is broken between two possibilities: that God might be either salvation or condemnation for human beings. And furthermore, the way in which the *eu-aggelion* is in fact proclaimed suggests a messenger who brings good news addressed directly to particular privileged recipients. In fact, although there are other terms to express what is good and positive in Christianity, the term *eu-aggelion* has been reserved as *the* specifically Christian term to sum up Christianity's positive whole as the "gospel of Jesus Christ." (As we shall see later, it is used with a number of meanings.)

First and foremost, this means theology must make the good news — gospel — its central content. And if this content is really central, it also means that the good news must be the hermeneutic principle for understanding any theological content at all, and the verificatory principle of whether theology is Christian — that is to say, whether or not and to what extent a theology communicates its content as good news. What I want to analyze here is what it also means that theological work must be informed with this good news, with what I have called the evangelical or gospel mode.

Perhaps this evangelical "mode" is not easy to put into words. It is felt when it is there, and missed when it is not. Perhaps it could be compared to a tone or quality of voice, which may be clear or equivocal, strident or serene, passionate or calm. Even at the same volume and with the same intonation, the timbre or tone of voice can communicate something specific. The same goes for theological work; even when it is formally dealing with the same subject, the "tone" may be different. It can communicate what it is saying in a way that is just routine or that carries conviction; it may sound resigned or hopeful; it can be abstract or more personal. To give an example, the theology of Karl Rahner, which is speculative and transcendental, has a religious, mystical tone of venturing into mystery, which other equally speculative theologians lack.

By evangelical "mode" I mean a theology with a certain "tone." In the way it goes about its work and in what it says, theology with this tone conveys the conviction and joy of being good news. The truth it holds — which has to be analyzed and presented with the full rigor required by its logos — is good for human beings.

To avoid misunderstandings from the start, let me make clear that this mode has nothing to do with optimistic and naive attitudes that are purely a matter of temperament. It has even less to do with escapism from unpleasant realities. It does not soften, sweeten, or bowdlerize history's tragedy or the painful and costly efforts needed to transform it. Liberation theology knows all this very well. Nevertheless the question remains about the evangelical way of doing Christian theology and the requirement that this mode have formal coherence with its contents. (It is also required to be historically and pastorally fruitful.) Put simply, good news cannot very well be communicated, even in theological language, without conviction, without hope, or without joy. For Christianity a theology is deficient if it is incapable of communicating something at least of the joy of the good news at the same time as it communicates its contents.

Theological activity has to be in tune with its central content, ideally both in those who engage in it and those who receive it. If, hypothetically, the evangelical mode of theology disappeared, then theology would cease to be formally Christian; it would be reduced to giving information about certain truths and doctrines that Christianity states are true and important. Or to put it more radically, if Christianity totally ceased to be good news, it would simply cease to be Christianity. This is all a way of saying that good news belongs to the very identity of Christianity, and is therefore what makes it relevant. So on both counts theology must treat Christianity as good news and do so in an appropriate evangelical mode.

All this might seem obvious and not in need of repetition. But I do not think so. I think it does need saying because of an important, perhaps crucial, theoretical and pastoral problem facing us now. In his monumental work *Jesús, la historia de un viviente,*[1] which appeared in the original fourteen years ago, E. Schillebeeckx makes this grave statement: "The main reason why our churches are emptying appears to be that we Christians are losing the capacity to present the gospel to our contemporaries with creative fidelity and . . . as good news." In this paragraph Schillebeeckx mentions as a serious problem the lack of creativity, and then goes on to added difficulties for societies that have been through the Enlightenment: "the authoritarian tone" with which the gospel is preached, insisting that the message "*must* be accepted out of respect for the *authority* of the Old Testament."[2] Obligation and authority present difficulties for societies that, theoretically at least, value or overvalue freedom and rationality. But what I want to stress is that in Schillebeeckx's text these serious difficulties are *additional* ones and appear in inverted commas. The chief difficulty is the inability to present the gospel as good news—that is to say, as what it is. Accordingly, if there is an obvious crisis of relevance—"the churches are emptying"—it derives from an identity crisis: not knowing what to do with the *eu-aggelion* as such.

All this is said about the church in general, but we should also think about it in relation to theology. We should ask ourselves if and to what extent theology is responsible for the empty churches because it lacks the power to communicate the gospel as good news. There are a number of reasons for this.

In my opinion, over the course of history a change has taken place, subtle in its formulation but decisive for the direction of theology. From theological activity whose core was good news and whose aim was to communicate it—even though as theo*logy* it made use of rational reflection—we have arrived at theological activity having as the aim of its logos assenting to the truth. The theology of the early centuries had good news at its center—good news that was *true*—but little by little over the centuries theology turned its attention to establishing the truth. Thus theology has changed modes and now concentrates on the rational, a dangerous concentration, not for what it embraces but for what it excludes. Of course I should not oversimplify the complex relationship between "truth" and "good news," or be unaware of the challenges presented by changing situations during the course of history. But for reasons to be mentioned below, it does not seem idle to affirm that theological work has come to be thought of more and more in terms of assenting to the truth (the magisterium, tradition, scripture), instead of communicating the central content of this truth: that it is good news.

The reasons for this development are understandable.

1. In places where until recently the vast majority of theological work has been done, Christianity has been questioned as to its truth, both at the historical level (historical criticism of its sources) and, above all, at the transcendental level (questioning of transcendent reality, God, Jesus as the Christ, etc.). There has been a kind of methodological change to theology as a whole. If Christianity is not true, it is simply of no interest (or should be abolished, according to the more radical).[3]

Hence it is very understandable and praiseworthy that theology should devote itself to showing the truth of Christianity, and should maintain a first-class apologetics, in the case of its best representatives, with some of them retaining a certain gospel mode (in my experience, for example, Karl Rahner, de Lubac, and Chenu). But all in all, it seems undeniable that the process I have described has taken place. Perhaps without intending to, theology has started thinking of itself as a way of assenting to the truth of Christianity, showing the possibility of combining faith and intellectual honesty. But at the same time good news has retreated to the background, and with it the evangelical mode.

2. Another reason for the loss of the evangelical mode in theology is that good news is intrinsically related to gratuitousness. Christianity affirms that God is good and is the good for human beings, but not as an abstract truth or as a mere attribute to divinity, discoverable a priori or comprehensible a posteriori. God is good as a historical truth, which becomes known when God reveals it freely and gratuitously. Although what is good about the good news is reasonable, and therefore analyzable by reason, the good news as such is not attainable by reason alone, but is given to us. One of its elements is the fact that it is a gift, grace. Here is another difficulty for today: what is good about the good news is what is given (either in transcendental form in creation and consummation or in historical form in the liberation from Egypt, the message of Jesus, etc.). Of course neither scripture nor present-day theology as a whole takes this to suggest passivity toward the good news; it requires an accompanying praxis. But this praxis cannot be our whole attitude toward the good news, because this still has its aspect of gift and grace. And this is what the Western world with its present-day attitude questions, although, on the one hand, this world wants a lot of good things and, on the other, it is becoming disillusioned with what it has. The difficulty for the modern Western world about what is gratuitous (grace) goes beyond theological, qualified anthropology and concerns anthropology in general. The modern Western world finds it difficult to accept that, in order for us to become human, we need not only exercise our own activity, or even just give and serve others; we also need to let others do things for us and give things to us. This difficulty is reflected in theology. There are still treatises on grace, but the mode of gratuitousness is becoming rare and with it the evangelical mode in theology.

3. A final difficulty, perhaps not fully resolved by referring to New Testament texts, resides in the addressee of good news. To simplify things we can say that in Paul's view the *eu-aggelion* is destined for all, whereas in Jesus' view the *eu-aggelion* is good news directly for the poor of this world and them alone. In my opinion, the theologies of today that work on the assumption that the good news is for all find it difficult to have an evangelical mode. This is a historical statement about what seems to happen apart from the biblical texts and the subjective intentions of theologians. What happens is that when the good news is related to all human beings, this good news tends to concentrate on universal hope or the transcendent hope of eschatological salvation—sometimes spuriously translated into mere survival after death—and it is difficult to combine this with historical hope and joy, which can be visibly attained here on earth. But when theology is addressed to the poor of this world, it talks about historical hope. Then, visibly, what theology communicates brings *actual* hope, joy, gratitude. It also demands action. This in return has an effect on theological work and helps it to become more evangelical in tone. Thus

if, for whatever reasons, theology suddenly becomes universal in its scope and moves outside the reality in which faith is understood today as good news, then it is difficult for theological work to be done in an evangelical way.

However difficult it is to do theology in an evangelical way, nevertheless it is essential. In order to help this evangelical mode exist as something real, rather than speculating a priori on the conditions in which it would become possible, I want to reflect on what already exists. In my opinion, there is no doubt that Latin American liberation theology, in various forms and at various levels, possesses an evangelical mode and this mode—together with its historical, practical, and prophetic mode—distinguishes it from other theologies. The two Vatican instructions on liberation theology did not take this into account.

Above all, it should be noted that liberation theologians share this evangelical mode without having made a conscious, common decision to do so. They share it, in spite of the fact that in general they have come from, and even partly depend conceptually on, theologies that have much less of this mode. Sharing the evangelical mode is therefore not something that can be explained purely subjectively, because these theologians are all very different persons. Neither can it be attributed to naivety, because normally these theologians have been trained in critical theologies more orientated toward assent to the truth. Neither can it be attributed to lack of interest in intellectual rigor, because even though this needs developing, it is not disdained a priori, and there are signs of it a posteriori.[4] It certainly cannot be attributed to naivety about the historical reality, because Gustavo Gutiérrez, for example, makes Job's question, the question of how to speak about God in this world full of misery and horrors, the fundamental question for theology. Finally it cannot be attributed to mere opportunism—that is to say, depicting Christianity in an attractive way when Christians still have unquestioned religious expectations.

The reason why these theologians share the evangelical mode is a structural one: they have found a more adequate place for the realization of the Christian faith and thus also for Christian theology. Faith and theology also have their own ecological problem requiring answers: where and how can· they take root and grow. And the answer is known only too well: in the poor and oppressed of this world. Out of them grow faith and theology, and grow as good news.

Theology's evangelical mode in Latin America is helped by the fact that on the one hand the world of the poor has not been subject, as a massive phenomenon, to the three difficulties mentioned earlier: questioning of the truth of faith, hubris and rejection of gratuitousness, and the undifferentiated universalization of expectation for the good news. In Latin America the way the poor live, their faith and religiousness, make it easy for theology to work naturally in a certain mode. That in the Third World this mode should be historical, partial, practical, and concerned with hope, seems obvious. What needs adding is that this helps it to be evangelical. A priori we can say that in the poor there exists the primary correlation with the *eu-aggelion;* a posteriori we can say that they represent the place where there is faith in this good news, and the joy this *eu-aggelion* contains is theirs. It is not enough to speculate on this fact in conceptual, scriptural, dogmatic, or even sociological terms. It happens when it happens and what we must recognize is that it does happen (in different ways of course). We can adduce that the poor are naturally prepared to accept the good news as such because of the suffering they have in their actual lives. But this does not explain everything, because they could react

193

to this suffering with resignation or with a purely transcendental hope. The poor are experts on suffering, but they can keep up the joy of the good news, because, as Gutiérrez says, quoting a peasant, the opposite of joy is not suffering but sadness. The poor can have suffering and joy at the same time, and thus they affirm in the most radical possible way that they grasp and live their faith as *eu-aggelion*.

The poor and oppressed are therefore the place for theological epistemology and also the right place for doing theology in the right way. A theology whose natural place is the poor of this world can drink from their well. From them it can draw many things—suffering, and failures, and limitations—but also the primordial joy brought by the good news.

Of course a theology deriving from this source does not ignore or soften the cruel injustice, the terrible suffering in history, the conflict and the hard requirements of following Jesus. It does not pretend not to see the failings and sins of the poor. Nor does it ignore the transcendental questions that arise from these realities: Job's question, God's silence when Jesus was on the cross. In fact, precisely because liberation theology does not claim to give an answer to these problems purely in the abstract but in real historical terms, this questioning becomes sharper than it is in other theologies. Nevertheless liberation theology maintains its evangelical mode; it does not become disillusioned with faith or fall into paralyzing doubt and speak with resignation about God and the Christ. It keeps its own language, its *parresia*. It does not consciously or unconsciously build a wall against real problems and take refuge in all kinds of historical investigations, necessary and important though they may be, but falling short of what is fundamental in faith. The fact that theology in Latin America should have an evangelical mode is really surprising, as is its *parresia*. The only possible explanation for it is that this theology is done in the historical home of the *eu-aggelion:* the poor and oppressed of this world.

To express this in a more conceptual way, liberation theology takes seriously what it affirms is its fundamental object: the kingdom of God. And because it takes the kingdom seriously, it allows its work to be shaped in accordance with what this kingdom is. Hence obviously this work will be hopeful, partial toward the poor, practical and constructive of justice, prophetic and denouncing injustice. It also takes seriously an aspect of God's kingdom frequently overlooked, misinterpreted, or relegated to spiritual rhetoric: "The kingdom of heaven is like a treasure hidden in a field, which a man found and covered up; then in his joy he goes and sells all that he has and buys that field" (Matt. 13:44). We have not understood this parable properly if we think it is only talking about the relentless demands made by the kingdom (which is of course completely true in other respects). The stress here is on something else: the joy that the kingdom of God produces. As J. Jeremias comments, "The good news of the arrival of the kingdom of God is overwhelming and brings great joy."[5] Something of this must be present and communicated in a theology that takes God's kingdom seriously. But, I repeat, this joy and happiness do not appear in theological work through conceptual analysis of this aspect of God's kingdom. It comes from the real experience of becoming a practical theory (theo*logy*) in the service of building the kingdom. It comes from being involved in this work by those for whom the kingdom is directly intended: the poor and oppressed.

To conclude this first section, what is at stake is the evangelical mode of theology. I believe that liberation theology possesses this mode. This is what gives it its potential and shows the crucial importance of the place where it is done in shaping its content, methods, and also its mode. This mode is not the private property of liberation theology. In my opinion, to give two examples, the work of Karl Rahner, so sophisticated in his more scientific writings and so full of devotion in his more pastoral-spiritual writings, is also charged with the conviction and joy that God is good, and that it is good for human beings that God exists, and this "the sacred mystery" has come radically closer to humanity. The work of J. I. González Faus increasingly communicates good news, perhaps partly because it is also affected by the reality of Latin America. So there is no need to exaggerate the link between the evangelical mode and liberation theology. This mode can have other roots, which are not just the lives and faith of the poor. But this does not affect the fact that there are places structurally more suited to doing theology with an evangelical mode, as liberation theology shows.

JESUS AS *EU-AGGELION*

What I have said so far has been formulated against a fundamentally theologal background: it is good for God's reality to be communicated to humans and God's will to be done in this world. Now I want to analyze in what precise sense Christ is good news. First I make a preliminary comment, which we have developed more fully elsewhere.[6]

In the economy of salvation the following appear:

1) God's *reality;*
2) the *mediation* of God's will (the kingdom);
3) the *mediator* of God's reality and God's will (Christ).

In scripture it is evident that both God and God's mediation are the good (whether or not the term *eu-aggelion* is used), and the conviction that God is good is arrived at through the goodness of God's mediation. Although it says in Genesis that God saw that "it was all good," or in Exodus that God came down "to liberate the people from oppression," or after the exile that God says "comfort ye, comfort my people," the fundamental point remains the same: there are mediations that occur historically in this world and that are good for human beings; through them human beings arrive at the proclamation of the goodness of God from whom they come.

But together with the mediation of God who is good, the mediator starts appearing. This already happens in the Old Testament (liberation from Egypt, Moses, and messianic kingdom, the anointed one) and very clearly in the New Testament (kingdom of God and Jesus, salvation and Christ). The point to stress is that now the good news also includes the mediator, and when the good that is God and God's mediation is expressed by the term *eu-aggelion,* then the mediator is an intrinsic part of it.

This is evident in the New Testament. The terms *eu-aggelion* and *eu-aggelizomai* are intrinsically related to Jesus Christ the mediator, in two fundamental ways: Jesus the mediator announces and initiates the *eu-aggelion* (the kingdom of God) and he himself is *eu-aggelion,* good news, because through his incarnation, death, and resurrection God accomplishes the world's salvation. This is well known, just as is the discussion on the different meanings of the terms, and their possible reconciliation. What I want to analyze now is in what precise sense Jesus the mediator is related to the *eu-aggelion* in Latin America and its theology, and what are the consequences of this relationship for faith, theology, and its evangelical mode.

In my opinion, the way the *eu-aggelion* is related to Jesus Christ in Latin American faith and theology is primarily through what Jesus of Nazareth announces and initiates: the kingdom of God for the poor. In the terminology commonly used, good news is the *mediation* announced and initiated by Jesus. But the *eu-aggelion* is also related to Jesus Christ himself. That is to say, the *mediator* himself is also seen as good news. However, in my opinion, this does not happen in practice and theological theory only, or chiefly in the Pauline sense that what happened in him is good news. It happens in a more basic and historical sense: it is good news that Jesus, the mediator of the kingdom, is as he is. As pure speculation, it would be possible to dissociate the goodness of the mediation from the goodness of the mediator; that in Latin America God's kingdom announced was good news but this did not mean that the mediator also was in any necessary or important way good news. But this is not what happens: the kingdom of God announced by Jesus is good news and it is also good news that Jesus announces it. The kingdom of God is good and so is Jesus good. This does not mean ignoring the more Pauline sense of *eu-aggelion* applied to Jesus Christ, but merely insists that Jesus' *being* as he is is a good thing and good news in itself.

From this grasp of Jesus' reality we can reread the New Testament from the viewpoint—trivial in its formulation—that Jesus of Nazareth in himself was good news—and not just for a priori dogmatic reasons requiring the postulation of goodness and virtues in Jesus, without which it would be logically contradictory to declare him to be the Christ, the Son of God, and the like. The reason is more basic, that this was the real impact Jesus caused in this world (and goes on causing). A summary, like that in Acts 10:38, can say that Jesus "went about doing good," turning God's goodness into historical fact in this world. But in the New Testament it also says *in what way* he went about doing good. In systematic form the Epistle to the Hebrews shows Jesus as a man faithful to God and merciful to weak human beings. At the same time it shows him as a real human being, close to others and in solidarity with them because "he was not ashamed to call them brothers" (2:12). The fact that the mediator is like this is already good news. It is good news—the epistle argues—because thus he can effectively bring salvation (fulfil mediation); but he is also good news in himself. The fact that the mediator is one of us, "a little lower than the angels" (2:9), that he shares our weakness, that he can share our infirmities, that he has to learn obedience and experience suffering and tears—in a word, that he is in real solidarity with his human brothers and sisters—is something good, something that in itself is an encouragement, brings hope and joy. He is not just the theoretical possibility that salvation can come about, which is what all the Anselmian proofs tend to reduce Jesus to. In the epistle, the author can think of nothing better to say to his readers to inspire them in their lives than: "Keep your eyes fixed on Jesus" (12:2).

The Epistle to the Hebrews says in systematic and concentrated form what is spelled out in more detail and at greater length by the narratives that are aptly called "gospels." Whatever the various theological and pastoral intentions of the gospel narratives may be, it remains clear that in order to explain the kerygma—

Christ's cross and resurrection—they are obliged to tell the actual story of Jesus the mediator as he was. And the way he was is shown to be good.

In my opinion this is still a reality today in Latin America. The mediator in himself goes on being good news. The "turning back to Jesus" asked of Christians— sometimes even by nonbelievers—is more than a rhetorical demand. It expresses the intuition that the way Jesus is is still good news today. He is good news, of course, because of his liberating message. But he also is good because in him we grasp—with a certain aura of the miraculous—the appearance of the truly human. And this goes on being good news.

There are of course historical details involved in grasping Jesus' human appearance. There may be some debate about the choice of Jesus' characteristics that make him good news, but we cannot get away from history and its risks. I pick out here what seem to be the salient characteristics of Jesus for the poor and those who opt for the poor. This is necessary in order for Jesus to go on being good news *today*. These characteristics are also those best borne out in the New Testament, so that the good news is really *Jesus* and not a manipulated construct.

Fundamental integrity. Jesus was born, like all human beings, into a particular reality, but what the New Testament shows is his decision to live in the true reality of his time, a world of the poor. In transcendental language this is saying that in order to come into this reality, Jesus had to lower himself, *kenosis*. In transcendental language again, this self-emptying is expressed as "being rich he became poor." In historical language, the gospel narratives show Jesus actively entering the lives of the marginalized (lepers, publicans, prostitutes, the poor). This intimacy is already good news for the marginalized. But it also shows Jesus' fundamental integrity, living in the real human world. From this point of view, Jesus' option for the poor is first and foremost an option for reality.[7] The fact that Jesus is like this is good news in itself. He appears as truly human and his fundamental choice is the real world. This was in no way a self-evident option: it is natural for human beings to escape from reality.

The primacy of pity. The reality in which Jesus comes to live is an oppressed reality. His primary reaction to it is pity. Jesus reacts with pity to a reality that oppresses and causes unjust suffering, because it affects him deeply and moves him to eliminate it. He finds the suffering of the oppressed truly intolerable. We know how Jesus behaved and this behaviour is absolutely fundamental for liberation theology: he reacted with signs to overcome this suffering (miracles, casting out devils, welcoming sinners); denunciation and unmasking of the socio-politico-religious reality that caused the suffering; demands for change. From this point of view Jesus' praxis is simply his pity in action.

This in itself is good news: the appearance of the man of pity, the man of mercy. Even better news is that this pity is Jesus' first and last reaction, and is motivated and conditioned by nothing but the suffering of others; and this is not so obvious. In history there can be various manifestations of pity, but it is uncommon for this to be pity for its own sake, with no ulterior motive. It is normal, in the exercise of pity, that the church, for example, should seek the good of others, but "over and above" it also seeks its own good as an institution; and the same thing happens with other movements, and political parties, including liberation groups. That pity should come first and last, that everything else is subordinated to it and not vice versa, that institutional risks are run for it, that love is given to others, just given with no ulterior motive, does not happen very often. This, however, is what appears in Jesus: pity comes first and last with him; it is for its own sake, and everything else has to be subordinated to it. Even religion is subordinated to it (and must be unmasked when it is opposed to it). Even our own lives must be subordinated to it. Pity in this sense is so fundamental for Jesus that in Luke he describes the just man as the man who shows pity: the Samaritan is the just man because he showed pity; God, the prodigal son's father, was one who showed pity.

Wanting the truth. Seeking, getting to know and speak the truth, the whole truth and nothing but the truth, is not common in history but this is what happens in Jesus. He shows no signs of faking the truth or converting it into propaganda to his own advantage. He is determined to proclaim it whatever it is. And vice versa, Jesus does not tolerate lies, cover-ups, distortion, and manipulation of the truth. He makes the whole of it good news. Its content is good news: he proclaims a truth in favor of the poor and against their oppressors. It is also good news because he shows he believes in the truth, responds to its demands, and is convinced that the truth humanizes everyone.

Jesus appears as a truthful man, someone whose word can be believed, someone who is required to be truthful, because without it the essence of being human is vitiated. But over and above this he appears highly reasonable and rational in communicating the truth when it has to be argued. Jesus speaks with authority without being authoritarian; he speaks with conviction but not dogmatically. For him the truth does not oppress but sets free. Therefore he does not inveigh against the ignorant but against those who oppress the truth out of self-interest, and thereby oppress others. Jesus offers the truth as intrinsic light that sets all persons free, and in particular is on the side of the poor.

Historical fidelity. Jesus does not withdraw from historical changes, not even from those that have the most effect on his mission and himself. Quite the contrary. Jesus goes through crises, temptations, and darkness and thereby makes himself what he is. His attitude is not to hang on to what is his own (in transcendent language, "he did not count equality with God a thing to be grasped" [Phil. 2:6]), but to be open to change, the "apprenticeship" of Hebrews 5:7, conversion. And all this not just in little things but in the things most fundamental to him: his mission, the way he carried it out, the day of the coming of the kingdom, his vision of the Father. However new, unfamiliar, and opaque reality became for him, Jesus faithfully remained with it.

In theologal language, Jesus let God be God. If his trust in God let him rest in the Father, his openness to the Father made him maintain God's mystery. Jesus realizes to the full God's final demand expressed by the prophet Micah: "walk [in history] humbly with your God" (6:8).

Freedom from and for goodness. Jesus was a free man, as we hear so often today. This was not in the narcissistic sense, according to a kind of asthetic anthropology. Neither was it in the liberal sense as if claiming and exercising one's own rights were the most important thing. Nor was it in the personal-existentialist sense, as if the ultimate meaning of existence consisted in fulfilling oneself, in independence of others and in total autonomy, creating one's own life and death. It is not that these anthropological visions find no support in Jesus, but I do not think that what was deepest in Jesus' freedom is to be found there.

Jesus' freedom is a freedom with a very precise context. Both where it comes from and where it is going, its origin and its aim, are goodness. It is a freedom that derives from goodness (God's) and is exercised for the sake of goodness (love for human beings). The particular expressions of his freedom—cursing oppressors without mincing his terms; sitting down to table with Zaccheus; choosing among his followers pious Jews and also publicans, zealots, and women; welcoming and encouraging his disciples, mercilessly upbraiding Peter—all this is more than a pure exercise of freedom. It is a freedom directed toward the good of others and freed by its conviction of God's goodness. It is a liberating freedom to make this goodness of God real in history for others. At the last it is a supremely free freedom, to surrender it to God and to give his own life for love of others. "No one takes my life from me, I give it freely," as he says in John.

Joy that God is good. To conclude, Jesus has the conviction that God is good and *the* greatest good for human beings. Jesus believes it is good that there is God and he is glad that God exists. Therefore Jesus can celebrate reality now in history, in his meals, in his gladness, that the mysteries of the kingdom are revealed to the poor, in his joy at being able to call God "our father." And what is said here in theologal language is also translated into history. Jesus believes that, in spite of everything, reality is ultimately positive and good; he knows only too well that reality is limitation, oppression, and malediction, but he believes that its ultimate possibility is also justice, fellowship, grace, and blessing. Jesus appears to be set in the stubbornly hopeful current of humanity because he truly believes and is glad that God is good for human beings.

This Jesus, with these characteristics, is the one who is still good news today, certainly in Latin America. We may discuss theoretically whether these characteristics are well presented and selected; but what is above dispute is that, Jesus as a whole, in himself, appears as the good. The mediation, God's kingdom, is good news and it is also good news that the mediator of this kingdom should be Jesus. To deepen this point I conclude with three final remarks.

1. This presentation of Jesus has not been made for dogmatic reasons that this is how Jesus *has to be.* Neither has it been to elaborate an anthropological doctrine based on a doctrine about Jesus. And, although this can never be avoided completely, it has not been made in order to present an attractive Jesus according to the desires of a particular time (Jesus as model of spirituality or morality, Jesus as the model bourgeois citizen, or even the revolutionary Jesus). It has been done this way because that is how Jesus is and how he is experienced. I have not tried to construct a doctrine about Jesus but to grasp Jesus as *eu-aggelion,* because in him the utterly human appears. If Jesus can be spoken of as *eu-aggelion,* this is because of the real weight with which the truly human is manifest in him, always hoped for and finally realized.

In order to deepen this point, perhaps it is convenient to recall something that is frequently overlooked. When we analyze Jesus as he actually was, what also appears is his limitation. If we compare Jesus with other historical figures, we may think that prophets like Amos and Jeremiah were more forceful in their denunciations of oppressors. We may think that Ezekiel or Isaiah expressed the feeling of God's tenderness better. We may think that Jesus' physical and psychological sufferings were not as great as some ancient or modern tortures. I say this in order to insist that proclaiming Jesus as *eu-aggelion* is a matter of reality and not just a theoretical construct for the creation in a laboratory of the unimprovable and unsurpassable human being. The way Jesus actually was, his characteristics as a whole, the way they fit together—sometimes historically it is difficult to fit them together— is what made and still makes him appear as the miraculous apparition of the truly human. Jesus is *eu-aggelion* as a happening, not as a doctrine or theoretical projection.

2. To all this we may add—and object—that without his pascal destiny, without that which in the New Testament makes him properly become *eu-aggelion*, the good news of Jesus would not be anything definitive. From a certain viewpoint this is so. But this is no objection to what I have said. In the first place in Latin America, neither in faith as it is nor in theology is the resurrection ignored as the definitive sanction of the person of Jesus. The resurrection is believed in and it functions as the ultimate horizon of the good news. But in the second place, this does not alter the fact that historically and existentially Jesus of Nazareth is grasped as good news in himself, even independently (logically) of his resurrection. And moreover, in my view, Jesus' life has more real weight than his resurrection for the grasping of what is good news in the faith. Thirdly, although this always happens dialectically, what there is of historical *eu-aggelion* in Jesus of Nazareth is what in fact makes possible the radical act of faith in his definitive transcendent resurrection and what gives us the courage to shape history in accordance with the final transcendental ideal. Thus there is no opposition between Jesus of Nazareth as *eu-aggelion* and the crucified and risen Christ as *eu-aggelion*. They mutually reinforce each other, but in historic-existential experience, the first is a necessary road to the second.[8]

What happens, it seems to me, is that the first is the real impact of the appearance of God and the truly human on earth. "God's loving-kindness has appeared," it says in the New Testament. "With Bishop Romero God passed through El Salvador" (I. Ellacuría), it is said today. We may question its truth, and the only final answer is the affirmation of the resurrection, but this is what has real evangelical weight.

3. Finally, stressing that Jesus of Nazareth is *eu-aggelion* in himself does not mean—either in theological intention or in reality—concentrating reductively on his person at the expense of his cause. And it certainly does not mean falling into mellifluous and spiritualizing considerations about the mediator. What it does mean is that the mediator himself is important for faith and cannot just be dissolved into his cause. It also means—as experience shows—strengthening his cause.

All this adds up to saying that the good news of Christianity is doubly good: the mediation is good and so is the mediator. As an empirical fact, there is no doubt that those who see Jesus as we have presented him are more, not less, likely to promote his cause. The mediator does not distract them from the mediation; on the contrary he encourages us to work at this task, overcoming the difficulties and keeping joyful. Once more the example of Archbishop Romero is an illustration of this: there is no doubt that he encouraged many to go ahead with the work of transforming the reality of El Salvador. The Christian task is to go on promoting Jesus' cause and do it in the way that Jesus did. Both are required today and it is encouraging that both are good news: *eu-aggelion*.

I believe this is one of the contributions Latin American theology has made to christology: stressing that Jesus in himself is gospel, good news, because in him appeared the miracle of the human. He encourages us to realize this humanness in ourselves. L. Boff, discussing Jesus' "originality," concludes simply "Christ

...was original. Not because he discovers new things, but because he says things with absolute simplicity and mastery. Everything that he says and does is transparent, crystalline, self-evident. Others see it at once. In contact with Jesus each of us meets our own self and what is best in ourself: each of us is brought to what is original in us."[9]

To conclude, let me briefly draw some conclusions for what theology now needs to do. Fundamentally it comes down to introducing the *eu-aggelion* into the *vere homo* and *vere Deus* proclaimed in Christ, showing that in the truth of his being human and being God lies the *eu-aggelion*. From this we can deduce important consequences for anthropology and theology. Consequences can also be drawn for the treatment of the *vera ecclesia*, in the way it understands itself, in its mission — called evangelization for good reason — and in the historical verification of its mission. There are consequences for the treatment of church ministries, including the presbytery, episcopacy, and papacy, especially for what needs to be made actual *in persona Christi*; for spirituality, personal and apostolic, and so on. If these are the consequences for what concerns the content of theology, the *eu-aggelion* should also make itself felt in the way of doing theology, as we saw in the first part of this essay. The work of theology, although specific, is one of various kinds of Christian work. It too therefore must be done in Jesus' way. As specific discipline it must be rational, critical, and rigorous. As a Christian discipline it must also be imbued with Jesus' way of doing things — honest, merciful, faithful, scandalous, and, finally, evangelical.

— translated from the Spanish by Dinah Livingstone

NOTES

1. *Jesús, la historia de un viviente* (Madrid: Christiandad, 1981), p. 103.
2. Ibid., italics in the original.
3. This is reinforced, of course, if Christianity is seen as alienating, whether it is true or not. In my opinion, liberation theology's fundamental theology is very rigorous (e.g., in J. L. Segundo, I. Ellacuría). In the treatment of systematic theology, limitations in biblical or historical scholarship may appear, but this does not signify a lack of interest in intellectual rigor or that the evangelical mode claims to be able to do without it.
4. See J. Sobrino, "La centralidad del 'reino de Dios' en la teología de la liberación," *Revista Lationoamericana de Teología*, 9 (1986) 247–81.
5. *Las parábolas de Jesús* (Estella: Verbo Divino, 1970), p. 244.
6. Ibid., pp. 266ff.
7. Saying that the option for the poor is an option for reality is in itself an option, a wager, as J. L. Segundo points out. What I wish to stress here is that this option is necessary in order to be in the real world and that the true option, which is ultimately faith's vision of reality, consists in being in the real world with and for the poor.
8. Schillebeeckx, *Jesús*, p. 101, asks the following question: "Should we not say that without faith in Jesus Christ as risen, glorified, and alive forever, Jesus' life and work are more a reason for sorrowful resignation or despair than for hope,

given that his message was rejected and he himself executed?" At the conceptual-existential level this is an important question. But we do not think Jesus becomes *eu-aggelion* only because of a fact that could be considered extrinsic to his life—as if the resurrection were something arbitary with regard to his actual life. The resurrection should be seen as the confirmation of his life. For the hermeneutics of the resurrection and for real faith in the resurrection I think it very important—because this is what happens in practice—to see Jesus as he is in himself and his life as an "anticipation" of the final good news in the resurrection, the appearance of the ultimately human, although this humanity is subject to historical conditions.

9. *Jesucristo y la liberación del hombre* (Madrid: Cristiandad, 1981), p. 122.

PART IV

DISPUTED QUESTIONS

26

Miriam and Her Companions

ANA FLORA ANDERSON AND
GILBERTO DA SILVA GORGULHO, OP

It is more than a pleasure for us to pay homage to the work and the effort of discernment in faith that characterize the theologian Gustavo Gutiérrez. His work is a seed and a leaven embodying a prophetic force of the kingdom of God.

In truth, Gustavo Gutiérrez fanned the flickering flame of the life, struggle, and voice of the oppressed. He has revealed the dimension of their cry and shown the presence of the God of life in the process of liberation. From the beginning, the theologian we are honoring has made a point of demonstrating that theology is faith-discernment within the historical action of the poor for liberation.

In a first stage, the situation and the struggle of the poor, oppressed, and believing filled the stage as the theology of liberation grew and matured. This stress served to clarify the overall content of liberation and to develop the analytical connections. The task of theology, as discernment applied to action, consists in speaking about God from the basis of the suffering of the innocent poor.

Gutiérrez has also shown that the cry and the cross of the poor in Latin America are a theological locus of the first order. In them is unveiled the content of the Christian mystery: the revelation and communication of the presence of the God of life in the exodus and in the following of the way of Jesus of Nazareth:

1. The "poor who die before their time" are those to whom theology talks. They raise questions that make it possible to articulate in a relevant way the central subject of reflection: the God of life who is the *Goel* (the liberator, redeemer, savior) of the poor. The experience of Job—contemplative and prophetic—continues to be the primary source for theology conceived in these terms (Job 19:25).

2. The exodus is the hermeneutical key to the process of liberation. It is there that we see revealed the presence of the God who comes to form a people free and united in solidarity. The exodus is the experience that gives rise to reflection.

3. The God who is coming, the exodus, and the liberation of the poor are a single reality based on the person and mission of Jesus of Nazareth. Thus discerning the new situation created by the gospel is based on following Jesus' way. That is where we find the *method* and perspective of the new form of action for freedom in the power of the Spirit (Gal. 5; Rom. 8).

Our tribute is to record the fruitfulness of this seed. It has already borne fruit.

We are certain that it will bear even more fruit in the future for the liberation of millions of the poor in Latin America.

It is in this context, and following in the path opened by Gustavo Gutiérrez, that we wish to present the following reflections. What we are interested in is the hermeneutical perspective of the place of the "female" in the liberation of the poor. We focus on the women who figure in Exodus 1–15 and on the figure of Sara in Genesis 12:10–20.

THE POVERTY OF THE SERVANT WOMAN (LUKE 1:48)

The theology of liberation was born and grew as a reflection centered on the poor. They are the partners in the dialogue, and the hermeneutical key to discourse.

This analytic horizon broadened. It was realized that the original focus had to include the oppressed races and marginalized women. The task of theology developed into the discernment of the forms of liberative action devised by the poor, Amerindians, blacks, and women. There was an anthropological clarification. Two significant events show the development of this process.

The first was the Tepeyac seminar in Mexico.[1] The domination under which Latin American women live led to a structural analysis of the female role in this society, in which women are "nonpersons" — dominated and alienated — as a result of the totalizing effect of the economic, political, and ideological system.

The value of this first event was to show that the hermeneutical problem of the "female" in action for liberation has a character of its own, and cannot be treated in a merely idealist or academic way. The problem of the "female" in this society is a matter of life and death, domination and freedom, for millions of women, believing and oppressed.

First and foremost, the oppression and domination of the "female" by a capitalist and macho society brings to light the roots of a system of death structured by "maleness," with an iron logic of domination and destruction of the woman as an active subject of the production and reproduction of common life.

The other significant event was the progress of feminist theology.[2] There was a notable hermeneutic advance, which identified the blockages and challenges facing the interpretation of history and society in terms of the subjugation of the female. It became clear that this subjugation had a threefold structure deriving from a woman's class, race, and sex. As a result the specifically "female" element emerged, in both a theology of liberation and the construction of a new type of society.

This gave rise to a basic theological reference point, the historical and bodily relationship between the "female" and life. The liberation of the "female" is rooted in the relationship with the God of life who is revealed in the process by which the people is formed:

1. The situation in which the "female" is dominated is presented in the Magnificat, where the *poverty of the servant woman* (Luke 1:48) indicates the full depth and range of the hermeneutical and theological problem.

2. The God of life lays bare the roots of the evil and injustice of this oppression. God establishes the correlation between the *female, liberation, and the formation of the people*.

3. The scope of this life of sisters and brothers is measured by the realization

of the Father's will. This is the new family of Jesus, the sign and germ of the new world. The liberation of the female must be seen as heralding the coming of the kingdom of God.

4. This is equivalent to saying that the role of women can be understood only in the context of the new creation (Gal. 3:28). The free woman is an embodiment and prototype of the new human being, the covenant of freedom (Gal. 4).

HE WILL RULE OVER YOU (GEN. 3:16)

The Tepeyac seminar focused on the situation of women in a capitalist system with roots in patriarchal and macho structures. This is the specific focus the female element brings to the discernment of liberation.

The domination of the female is the product of a long history. It flows from the logic of an economic and political system whose continuation requires the exclusion and subordination of women.

In fact, since Medellín, 1968, sociologists have shown that the violence of the economic and political system in Latin America falls first on the poor, Amerindians, and blacks. However, all researchers have found that this violence has the heaviest impact on women—within these subgroups and within the social structure as a whole.

The situation of dominated women is thus the source of an understanding of the evil, the untruth, and the injustice that pervade an economic and political system created and maintained for the benefit of the male. The oppression and marginalization of the female are permanent, structural signs of the antikingdom, whose structure is based on violence and death—the destruction of the life of the people.

The historical root of this domination goes back to the change introduced by colonization. This was argued by Dom Bartolomé Carrasco Briseño, archbishop of Oaxaca:

> In America's pre-Colombian cultures women had a predominant role, not just as bearers of children, but also as the source of organic and ideological unity for the human groups of the period, and as a proponent of a social model rooted in a harmonious relationship between human beings and "Mother Earth."
>
> The movement's great leap forward was adopting a stable base for settlement, and it continued from there into agricultural and urban development, which took place thanks to the deeply significant contribution of women to this process. Women were undoubtedly the prime agents of this incredible genetic transformation of the primitive *teozintle* into domestic maize, which came to be the fundamental basis of all food and culture in Mesoamerica.
>
> This contribution to the development of indigenous cultures was so important that the concept of God remained closely linked both to maize and to the female principle. There were peoples who knew God only as Mother. Others, the majority, combined male and female in God: God *Teotl* and *Ometetl*, the dual God or God of duality, father and mother, master and mistress of life and death, of closeness and unity of day and night. It was impossible for the ancient—as it is for the present-day—native peoples to conceive of God only in a male mode.[3]

Colonization destroyed this harmony. It became a mechanism for establishing a male-dominated capitalism. Violence against women became part of the process of the economy, politics, and ideology.

The anthropological root of this exclusion is the affirmation of the man and the negation of the woman as person and initiator in the social structure. The whole system and its mechanisms were planned and maintained in function of the man. It was the affirmation of the male through the subservience and death of the female. The structural domination was rooted in and transmitted by the relationship of the *domination of the man over the woman* (cf. Gen. 3:16).

It is interesting to record here the results of some recent surveys on the domination of women by men in Latin America:

1. It is difficult for the man to admit his machismo: "it is difficult for men to recognize their machismo, to see it. Something similar exists in any relationship between oppressor and oppressed. If you ask an employer, he'll always tell you he treats his employees wonderfully. Between man and woman things are more complicated because, as well as the power relationship, we have bonds of deep feeling and attachment."

2. It is necessary to confront the "logic" of a whole system that excludes the female: "I mean that for a man it's very difficult to appreciate all the subjective power inherent in man-woman relationships, which gives men privileges. What has become established in this society is male logic. Female logic is different. It's not that one is better than the other. What happens is that one is absent, in this world!"

3. The political structures are influenced by machismo. "Dictatorship is the supreme expression of machismo. The dictator is the patriarch of patriarchs. Why should it be surprising that there should be a 'Mr.' who dominates us with his power? That's simply the tip of the iceberg."[4]

There are various types of response to this situation. A vague explanation in terms of individualistic egoism is not enough. Nor is a response in terms of evolution: the weaker at the hands of the stronger, who is the bearer of life in society.

Nor is there an explanation in the argument that women's situation in society is inherent in the nature of the female sex, made to be submissive and at the service of man. This sort of reply insists on the difference between the sexes and on the limited and predetermined role of women in the construction of society as a whole, and it is undoubtedly the one most heavily imbued with the ideology of domination and discrimination.

This type of explanation derives from an idea of power, the social order based on and organized in terms of the difference of the sexes and so rooted in human nature itself. The present situation is inevitable, and will inevitably continue. The female's role may simply improve to maintain the balance of the underlying structure, but that has to remain the same. This fundamental structure for the benefit of and under the supremacy of the male is allegedly in accordance with the natural order. It is therefore legitimate and may not be changed.

The solution lies in the female task of liberation. The subservience of the female shows the extent reached by the process of negation and the situation of the "nonperson" in a macho-capitalist system. The solution lies in a new birth, and not just of individuals. It lies in the emergence of the new collective creation (Gal. 3:28).

The prospect of a solution lies in women as active agents in the whole system of social relationships. In this perspective attention should be drawn to the new dimension of the church's social teaching that appears in John Paul II's encyclical *Laborem Exercens*. This way of analyzing society in terms of the subject working in community has implications for the way we analyze the role of women in the formation of a free people. Franz J. Hinkelammert has shown the novelty of such an outlook in the church's social teaching. It should also affect the hermeneutics of female liberation: "the core of this outlook is the circle running from the subject in community to the common good, as a subsidiary interinstitutional equilibrium of the subject in her or his autonomy, creating a human being with full subjectivity as a person."[5]

This means that the liberation of women requires, and is only really possible through, a change that goes to the root of this system and of its mechanisms of domination. We have to uproot structural violence and move toward a new type of social relations. We need a *new exodus*, in which the female role is fundamental and determining.

WOMEN ARE FULL OF LIFE (EXOD. 1:19)

Interpreting the exodus in terms of domination of women by a male-dominated economic system opens the way for an anthropology of female liberation. But what was, or what is, the role of women in the liberation of the people? The sagas of women in Exodus 1–15 take us some way toward an answer.

The Role of Women

From the beginning of the text the frequency and importance of female roles are striking. It is all the more surprising when we recall that traditionally—in the Semitic world—war, forced labor, and the liturgy were areas reserved for men.

In Exodus 1–15, however, female figures occupy prominent positions. There is no other part of the Bible that contains so many references to the role of women in the liberation and the creation of a free people.

Here women's roles are fundamental and crucial to the success of the exodus. These female sagas have their origin in the participation of women in the liberation struggles. These histories (her-stories) point to elements of an anthropology of the female that came into being with the origins of Israel. Archeologists and anthropologists suggest that it was in the period of the liberation of the slaves from Egypt (Exod. 1:11; 14:5) and of the farmers and shepherds dominated by the city-states of Canaan that the social and political position of women, and their position in the organization of religion, changed.[6]

The female sagas are the record of this memory. They were incorporated and developed in a narrative of persecution.[7] And it is here that we find an indication of the criteria for understanding and evaluating the role of women in the formation of the people. Israel, generation to generation, saw in this episode its identity and its future destiny as a liberated people (Exod. 3:15; 12:2–28).

The Memory of Women's Struggle

The social origin of these stories goes back to the lives and struggles of the peasants and shepherds who passed on the memory of the exodus (cf. Exod. 5:17–

18; 14:5). They are rooted in the sociological fact of the domination of the families of the "Hebrews" by Egypt and by the city-states of Canaan, and in the struggles of the peasants, in which women had a crucial role (cf. Exod. 15:21; 1 Sam. 18:6). The memory of the role of women in the exodus—the escape, the crossing of the sea, the battles for liberation—has its roots in a tradition dating from before the formation of the tributary state with David and Solomon.

In fact, the exodus of the group from Egypt and the withdrawal of various groups in the Sinai peninsula and in Canaan come at the end of the Bronze Age and the beginning of the Iron Age. This period was crucial for the situation of women, as C. L. Meyers has shown:

In social life the active role of women was essential to the survival and continuity of the people. The new position of women was connected with their participation in the defense of life, and in the defense of the land ravaged by constant disasters. It was necessary to defend the homes and families against the effects of these hazards and to increase the number of children to ensure the very survival of the population. It is therefore understandable that popular memory should have preserved one of the characteristics of "Hebrew women": *they are full of life* (Exod. 1:16–19).

In religious matters the status of the cult also affected the position of women. The cult of Yahweh, bound up with the memory of the exodus (Exod. 3:15, 18), came into conflict with the gods and goddesses of fertility. Women as servants of the cult disappear, and worship is gradually concentrated around the male figure of the levite. But the active role of women in the socio-religious integration of the people could not be obliterated (Exod. 4:25). This led to the subsequent development of an ambiguity in relations between men and women in the organization of the people.

The creation of the tributary state under David and Solomon had a deep effect on peasant households. The "families who work the land" (Gen. 12:3) were now threatened by new forces of domination. The structures of the state, and patriarchalism, began to appear as a new force by which males dominated females (Gen. 3:16; 12:10–20).[8]

This new position of women, and the ambiguity that grew up in these historical conditions, are the sociological background to an understanding of the function of the female sagas in the anthropology of the exodus. The sagas took root in the lives and struggles of those who handed down the memory of the liberation: fighting peasants (Exod. 13–14), levites and shepherds (Exod. 2–4), exploited workers (Exod. 5), and "Hebrews" under domination (Exod. 1).

The Liberation and Integration of the People

These sagas were taken and inserted into the themes of the "historical credo." This credo became the central element of the paradigmatic account of liberation in Exodus.[9]

What interests us here is to see which ancient roots were used to link and unify the different traditions (the escape from Egypt, the Sinai experience, and the promise to the fathers). The female sagas turn out to be a means of integrating the anthropology that emerged from the process of liberation.

It would be necessary to analyze in more detail the social origin of these traditions and the process of composition that lies behind the present form of Exodus 1–15.[10] We suggest that the anthropology of Exodus in its present form is focused on the unity and integration of the liberated people in terms of the active role of women. The female figures are to be understood in relation to *the defense of the home, the fight against the plagues, the liberation of work,* and *the family passover liturgy.*

The Anthropology of Liberation

The different traditions were unified and structured to present an anthropology of liberation. The memory of the manifestation of Yahweh in the process of liberation is the basis and continuing underpinning of this anthropology (Exod. 3:15).

The *defense of the house of the "Hebrews"* and *the peasants' holy war* are the basis and introduction to the narrative as a whole: the exodus is the manifestation of Yahweh's war against the dominating power of the pharaoh (Exod. 1).

The integration of the people as a social and religious unit is explained in terms of *ties of kinship.* The combination of the experience of the different groups is effected through the memory and the sense of liberation of the group from Egypt, and for the Sinai groups through the role of the mountain of God and the function of the levite Moses. The reality of kinship and the unity of the people are woven and structured by the figures of the women, who unify traditions deriving from shepherds and levites (Exod. 2–4).

The *situation of forced labor* and the exploitation of the workers indicate more sharply the condition of the people of the land (Exod. 5:5). Liberation from the servitude of labor thus acts as a parameter to articulate the meaning of the mission of Moses and Aaron, and to root the covenant in the fact of the exodus (Exod. 5–6).

The memory of the *struggle against the plagues,* and infant mortality, acquires political and liturgical meaning. The plagues that threatened farmers and shepherds are now directed against the pharaoh, the chief source of the people's oppression and disintegration. This part of the narrative takes on the characteristics of an elaborate liturgy preparing for the celebration of passover, in which the blood of the lamb is the sign of liberation from the power of the destroyer (Exod. 7–12). The account of the plagues is a prelude to the celebration of passover and to the consecration of the firstborn, symbols of a liberated people.

The triumph of liberation is once again announced in the forms of the *holy war.* Yahweh's victory over the power of the pharaoh is manifested in a war that brings liberation and is celebrated in song by the liberated people (Exod. 13–15).

In this movement the sagas of the women are a determining factor in the understanding and constitution of the people. The place of the women in the formation of a free people must be understood in relation to the lives of the children, dominated by work, the plagues, the passover sacrifice, and the struggle for liberation.

In this way the resistance of the midwives in Exodus 1 acquires its full significance in relation to the escape, which is presented as a victory in a war of Yahweh (Exod. 1:10; 13–14). The mysterious gesture of Moses' wife Zipporah can be understood only in relation to the threat of the plagues, and in relation to the liberating significance of blood, which is given its full expression in the passover ritual connected with the departure from Egypt (Exod. 4:26; 12:13).

WOMEN IN THE STRUGGLE FOR LIBERATION

Miriam (Exod. 15:20–21)

We shall seek to understand the person and role of Miriam in relation to two titles under which she is presented to us.

THE PROPHETESS

In an ancient prophetic tradition, Miriam appears alongside Moses and Aaron in the context of the exodus (Mic. 6:4). In an old story Miriam and Aaron challenged the authority of Moses (Num. 12:1; it is interesting to note that Miriam comes before Aaron!). We have here indications of the prominence and the leadership of women in peasant struggles. Hereditary and centralized leadership was being questioned. Everyone, men and women, exercised leadership and took part in the struggles for liberation.

The title "prophetess" brings the figure of Miriam into association with that of Deborah. Deborah stimulated a liberation struggle in the villages. She was a leader who gave orders (Judg. 4:6). This very comparison with Deborah, the prophetess who sang the victory song (Judg. 4:4) explains the position of women in the battles for liberation and indicates the importance of her victory song (Judg. 5:3).

Miriam has an active role as prophetess and leader, and in carrying out that role gathers other women to defend the people and ensure its survival. There is no reason to restrict or reduce the status of leader given to her and preserved by popular tradition.

In this role Miriam also acts as a "theologian." Her victory song is a celebration of the act of liberation that preserves the life of the people. In fact, Exodus 15:21 is regarded as an ancient war song. It is an ancient formula that unites the escape with the event at the sea. The holy war, or the peasants' defensive struggle, is, as in the case of Deborah (Judg. 4–5), its sociological context and one in which women play a crucial role (1 Sam. 18:7ff.).

AARON'S SISTER

The problem of the texts that refer to Miriam as "sister" is well known. This way of presenting Miriam reflects the situation of women in the life of the tribes and, subsequently, shows their position in the monarchic state and in the community organized around the "sons of Aaron."

Miriam cannot be identified with the anonymous sister of Exodus 2:4. There has been a concern, in both ancient and modern times, to prove that Aaron and Moses were brothers (Exod. 4:14; 7:1). The text of Exodus 6:20, which is much more recent, says that both are the sons of Amram and Jochebed. The same background produced Numbers 26:59: Miriam is the daughter of the same parents and sister to Aaron and Moses.

The title "the sister of Aaron" in Exodus 15:20 certainly preserves an ancient link in this process, the origin of which is to be sought in the levitic circles that regarded Aaron as a levite prophet. The title given to Miriam is part of the levitical concern not to give undue prominence to the leadership of woman, and to subordinate her to Aaron, in the context of a struggle against the role of women in the cults of the fertility goddesses (Deut. 13:7; 22:5).

The Hebrew Midwives

This is made up of a popular stratum with a theological expansion. We will leave on one side vv. 21–22, which are a link with the scene of Moses' rescue and examine the levels of composition and transmission.

The Hebrew Women

The narrative has the picturesque flavor characteristic of popular tales. It is a story of poor and oppressed persons laughing at their oppressors. The women and the midwives are Hebrews, and not Egyptians, as some authors claim. The story is set in the households of the "Hebrews," who are subject to and exploited by the city-states. It must have been told as a memory of this oppression, and of the active role of the women.

The setting suggests a constant feature of these defensive struggles. Leadership and strength do not come from above or from individuals. Resistance comes from inside the households, where women have an irreplaceable role. The midwives go into all the houses. The women unite to defend the households and to protect the future of their sons. The unity of the households and the women's struggle were the base of a resistance designed to ensure the survival of the population, threatened as it was by endemic plagues and burdened by an oppressive, exterminating social structure.

At this level the story shows the role of Hebrew women in resistance. It highlights their role in the procreation of children as the main factor in the growth of the population in families and villages.

The tyrant king is presented as close to the Hebrew countrywomen. The retention of the significant names of the midwives, "Beauty" and "Splendor," shows that this is a popular village story.

The story comes from a female environment that contrasted the vitality and robustness of the Hebrew women with the delicacy of the ladies of the city and the palaces. The contrast in v. 19 should be compared with that made in relation to warfare, with women who are mere palace ornaments, as in the comparison between Jael and Sisara's wife (Judg. 5:24–30).

Work and War

The use of the figure of the king of Egypt indicates that the popular tale has been taken up into the tradition. The king is a symbol illustrating the extent of oppression.

This presentation is associated with the ancient description of oppression in terms of forced labor (Exod. 5:7–9). In its present form the description has overtones of criticism of the Salamonic corvée, which was detrimental to the rural households and affected the role of women as bearers of children and free workers (Gen. 3:16–19; 1 Sam. 8:13–16).

The theme of war in Exodus 1:10 makes the connection with the rest of the story. The story is part of the "escape from Egypt." This is a battle between Yahweh and the oppressive power of the pharaoh. Yahweh's war is directed against the pharaoh's obstinacy. The women's resistance prepares the ground for the victory that results in the Hebrews' escape (Exod. 1:9–10; 13:17).

THE FEAR OF GOD

The story was taken up by the levitical circles and the rural prophetic movement. They introduced the notion of the "fear of God" as a dominant theme. The action of the midwives is now seen from a prophetic point of view. The midwives' action acquires overtones of the levitical and prophetic view of God's action in the history of the people (Exod. 1:17; Gen. 20:11).

The Mother of Moses the Levite (Exod. 2:1–10)

The role of the women is once again given great prominence. There are now three women whose function is presented in relation to the main mediator of the exodus, the levite Moses. The women's role has to be interpreted in relation to the narrative of Exodus 2–4, which contains the central point of the anthropology of the exodus.

MOSES THE LEVITE

Exodus 2–4 is the result of a combination of traditions. The most striking feature is that the Sinai event now takes place in connection with the situation of the Hebrews in Egypt. There is a close unity between the groups in Egypt and the groups from the Horeb-Sinai region.

The function of these stories is to indicate the relationship between these groups and to demonstrate their social and religious unity. The link is made in terms of *kinship* and the *common basis of religious faith in Yahweh*. This is the reason for the stress on Moses' *father-in-law* and on the expression *bridegroom of blood* (Exod. 4:25), and, in the story of Moses' birth, for the stress on the fact that he was nursed by his own mother.

The original source of these stories is probably a pastoral society and the circle of the wandering levites. The text gives a number of indications of this. Aaron is the levite who speaks for Moses (4:14). The name of Moses' son, Gershom, explains the origin of the wandering levites (cf. Exod. 2:22 and Judg. 18:30; the levites of Dan regarded themselves as descendants of Moses).

The function of the story of Moses' birth is to show the significance of his mediation for the formation of the unity of the people in the process of its liberation. His meditation is legitimate. He is a "Hebrew" and a "levite." His delivery from the water is a prefiguring of the liberation of the whole people (Exod. 2:1,9,10).

The story uses the stereotypes of birth scenes of heroes and also of persecution stories. Nonetheless its principal role is to highlight *the role of women in the creation of this meditation and of the unity of the people.*

214

THE WOMEN'S ROLE

The importance of the women appears in the division of labor and in their *unity in action*. Without this action on the part of the women, the particular mediation which was to snatch the people from the pharaoh's violence and oppression would not have come into being.

The active role of the anonymous sister makes the connection between the imperial household and the oppressed Hebrews. This role is indicative of the march of history and the linking of the different types of women who unite in defense of life and oppose the oppressive state. The central role is that of the mother. The pharaoh's daughter thinks that caring for the infant is just a job, but in fact it is his real mother who looks after him. The levitical tradition is seeking to explain the legitimate origin of the Hebrew leader. Moses has to be a Hebrew, and above all a levite. The legitimacy of his mediating role derives from his being a levite.[11] And he is these because he has been nursed by his own mother. Here the story uses an ancient concept of parenthood and ethnic solidarity established by suckling.

The pharaoh's daughter is introduced to complete the idea of the legitimacy of Moses' mediation. The princess integrates him among the Hebrews and among the oppressors as well. Her role is indicated by her naming of the child. The popular interpretation of Moses' name has a particular intention (v. 10). The name is Egyptian in origin and means "son." But Moses is not the son of a foreign god (like Thutmoses, Amoses). The whole story suggests that he is the legitimate son of a levite mother. His rescue from the waters heralds his liberating mission.

FEMALE MEDIATION

This division of female labor contains the anthropological perspective of the story: the establishment of the mediating role is based on *a reciprocity of compassion brought about by the action of the women.*

It is this reciprocity that constitutes the mediator and liberator of the Hebrews, crushed by the pharaoh's violence. And it is the action of this mediator that will make the violence of the plagues turn back on the pharaoh to liberate the children of the Hebrews. The reciprocity of the women's action shows the direction and the means for escaping from violence.

The mediation of Moses the levite emerges in function of a liberation from violence. Here the narrative uses stereotypes of the struggle against the violence that destroys the people. In this connection René Giscard suggests that the underlying narrative is a persecution story:

> The figure of Moses is an example of the legislator who is a scapegoat. His stammer is the sign of a victim. Elements of mythical guilt can be seen in him: the killing of the Egyptian, his sin resulting in his prohibition from entering the promised land, his responsibility for the ten plagues of Egypt, which are indiscriminate scourges. All the stereotypes of persecution are there.[12]

ZIPPORAH AND THE BRIDEGROOM OF BLOOD (EXOD. 4:24–26)

The story of Zipporah continues the theme of women in the anthropology of Exodus. Her marriage to Moses explains the unity of the people by kinship. The scene of the circumcision is the commissioning of Moses for the struggle against the stubborn pharaoh.

MOSES IN MIDIAN

The story begins with a shepherd narrative. This link between the Egyptian and the Sinai-Horeb groups explains the fundamental unity of the people. The Sinai experience is inserted and incorporated into the kinship relationships with the shepherds of Midian (Exod. 3:1).

This shepherd story was taken over and told by the wandering levites. The levitical movement took over and transmitted the story because of the account of the birth of Moses' son (Exod. 2:16–22). The function of the story therefore lies in its explanation of the son's name. The name, in fact, has a double function: it explains the connection between the wandering levites and Moses, and explains the condition of being strangers in Egypt. The latter is the typical feature of the whole people, considered as a unit in its social organization (Exod. 22:20).

THE BRIDEGROOM OF BLOOD

Zipporah's significance lies in the mysterious circumcision scene. Here too we have a pastoral tradition, closely linked to the meaning of the passover. It will certainly have been the shepherds who first developed the meaning of the passover in relation to the escape from Egypt: they saw the parallel between the "destroyer" of their flocks and the threat hanging over the households of the enslaved Hebrews. The pastoral ritual was incorporated and enriched with the sense of the historic liberation of the Hebrews.

From this point of view the meaning of circumcision—a ritual focusing on the *protective role of blood*—has to be explained in this pastoral context. The blood ritual supposedly kept away threats and dangers from the flock and from the couple. Underlying it may be an ancient attitude that the red color of blood drives away plague and spirits that threaten the flocks and the safety of the family. There is a correlation between Zipporah's action and the meaning of the passover blood (Exod. 4:26; 12:13).

This pastoral tradition enables us to understand the implications of the circumcision rite performed on Zipporah's son. Thus the Hebrew expression "bridegroom of blood" (*hatan dâmin*) may have had originally the sense of "protected by blood." Circumcision was a measure of preventive medicine and protection against hazards. It was a ritual to defend the lives of sons, who were especially vulnerable to the hazards and the diseases responsible for the high rate of infant mortality. The blood kept the "destroyer" away.

Zipporah's action has a more direct relationship with the success of the exodus. It is presented as Moses' investiture as liberator of the people. He is to take up the fight to liberate his kinsfolk; he has to turn the violence of the plagues back on the power of domination and make the force of liberation manifest in favor of the oppressed people.

Thus the gesture with the blood transforms the threatening figure of Yahweh into a force of liberation for the oppressed people. Exodus 4:24 alludes to this by mentioning a *meeting* between Yahweh and Moses. This meeting is decisive: the force of death weighing on the people is to be transformed into a force of liberation and life. Yahweh is not a force of death. Yahweh is a force of life and freedom. This meeting is the pivot of the change.

Zipporah's action also has an explanation in terms of the power of kinship. She acts in the name of the extended family. This is why she has an active role here as a woman. She performs an act that defends the family, which explains why the genital organ is the focus of the symbol. She is defending the lives of the sons and keeping at bay the threat of death and violence, which destroys them. Zipporah, in her activity as a woman, has a priestly function in the deepest sense.

This action, then, was taken over and presented in the larger context of the anthropology of the exodus:

1. The threat in 4:23 hangs over the pharaoh's son. The purpose of this is to show that the story of the plagues will be a battle against the power of domination and to *save* the people, God's firstborn.

2. Zipporah's action as the investiture of Moses with his mission is incorporated into a set of symbols (the snake, leprosy, blood: Exod. 4) to show that his mission will be a superhuman battle (Exod. 4:27–31). This is the scale of the marvels that Zipporah's action foretells.

The liberative process of the exodus begins with the significance and power of a woman's action. She removes and destroys the conception of a violent and destructive deity, and reveals the liberating dimension of the God of life who comes to destroy the violence hanging over the enslaved people.

Sara: the Liberated Woman (Gen. 12:10–20)

The figure of Sara/Sarai has to be understood in relation to the women in the exodus. It reflects the situation of women in the ancient context of families retreating from the cities or living in the steppes. The figure of Sara is also an example of the situation of women in the new form of patriarchal domination after the organization of the tributary state.

AN EXPERIENCE OF DOMINATION

The story of Sara is told three times (Gen. 12;20;26). This repetition indicates the oral origin and transmission of the story. We have the memory of the situation of women in the context of the patriarchal family. Sara is an example: she is dominated by the pharaoh and by her husband Abram. She remains silent. This silence contains the memory of her resistance and a critique of the domination she suffers.

This may confirm the suggestion that Genesis 12 is the oldest form of the story. It was reworked in Genesis 26 and 20. The subservience of women is the initial model for the history of the patriarchal families, which are used and instrumentalized by Solomon's tributary state. This state leads families to instrumentalize women as mere means of production to protect and enrich men (Gen. 3:16).

THE SILENCE AND THE PLAGUES

The narrative's simplicity contains a deep meaning. Claus Westermann regards it as a carefully worked out reflection.[13] Walter Brueggemann calls attention to the centrality of Yahweh's action in the narrative.[14] Yahweh acts in support of the woman dominated by the pharaonic state and by the astute and ambitious patriarch. The structure of the narrative is as follows:

v. 10, introduction: Abram's action
vv. 11–13, first scene: Abram's statement
vv. 14–16a, second scene: action at the Egyptian court
vv. 17–19, third scene: the pharaoh's statement
v. 20, conclusion: the pharaoh's action

The introduction and the conclusion concern the two main characters, Abram and the pharaoh. The first and third scenes contain their words. At the center is Yahweh's surprising action on behalf of the reified woman.

We have here a story that comes from a dominated or threatened minority. The story seeks to arouse courage, identity, and dignity in these oppressed groups. It is an ironic critique of women's situation both under the domination of the state and under the "astuteness" of her male partner.

A TASK OF LIBERATION

The structure of the narrative highlights the action of Yahweh, Sarai's silence, and the plagues threatening the pharaoh. These motifs are the recollection of the fact that, in the struggle for liberation carried out by various groups since the time of the fathers, there was an equality between men and women in the defensive struggle and in the cultivation of the land.

Once the period of the great dangers (war, plagues, possession of the land) had passed, the patriarchal household tried to return to the old patterns. The man was to be the head. Women found themselves in continual danger of being reduced to objects and instrumentalized by the tributary state and the structures of the patriarchal household.

The scene shows that Yahweh is on the women's side. That is why the story reduces Sarai to silence. It makes Yahweh in person bring the pharaoh and Abram to understand that women cannot be used and treated as objects. The husband makes his wife an instrument of protection and enrichment. Yahweh's action once again indicates that liberation has to be understood in terms of the exodus (v. 17). The plagues here turn against the powers that try to dominate women.

Historically this struggle—represented by Sarai's silence and Yahweh's intervention—was carried on by the women themselves. They resisted patriarchal domination for many, many years. The historicity of this story lies in the subversive memory of the women who struggled for their dignity and freedom as human persons and essential agents in the formation of the community. The figure of the patriarch's wife is presented as a model and as an appeal: a woman cannot be treated as an object either by structures (the pharaoh) or by the position of her male partner (Adam or Abram). The woman, Sarai/Sara, is a free wife and an heir to the promise.

Sarai/Sara is the model of the free woman who overthrows the thrones of the powerful. In this sense, the best commentary on Genesis 12 is still the Magnificat. The whole song is a theology of woman in terms of the exodus. And the position of the liberated woman, fruit of Yahweh's action and promise, is incorporated into the covenant of freedom, which she foreshadows, as the apostle Paul realized (cf. Gal. 4:21–31).

—translated from the Portuguese by Francis McDonagh

NOTES

1. See *Mujeres para el Diálogo*, seminar "La mujer latinoamericana, la praxis, y la teología de la liberación," Tepeyac, Mexico, October 1–15, 1979, text from the

papers of the *Congreso Internacional Ecuménico de Teología* (São Paulo, 1980).

2. See E. Schüssler Fiorenza, *In Memory of Her. A Feminist Theological Reconstruction of Christian Origins* (London: SCM Press, 1983); T. P. Fenton and M. J. Heffron, *Women in the Third World. A Directory of Resources* (Maryknoll, N.Y.: Orbis Books, 1987); *A Mulher na Igreja* (Portuguese), *Concilium*, 111 (1987); M. L. Marcilio, *A Mulher pobre na história da Igreja*, CEHILA (São Paulo: Paulinas, 1984); *Women, Work and Poverty* (English), *Concilium*, 194 (1987).

3. Bishop B. C. Briseño, "María de Guadalupe: modelo de mujer creyente y solidaria con su puebla," *Páginas*, 87 (November 1987), 3ff. See Pamela Jiles, "Reportaje al Machismo-Leninismo," *Análisis*, 10/107 (Dec. 28, 1987) 32–37.

4. See Jiles, "Reportaje."

5. F. J. Hinkelammert, *Democracia y totalitarismo* (San José, Costa Rica: DEI, 1987), pp. 69–88.

6. Cf. N. K. Gottwald, *The Hebrew Bible. A Socio-literary Introduction* (Philadelphia: Fortress, 1985), pp. 224–27.

7. On the structure and meaning of the persecution narrative, see the analysis by René Girard, *El Chivo Expiatorio* (Barcelona: Anagrama, 1986), pp. 39, 172, and 232. In his book *Violence and the Sacred* (Baltimore: Johns Hopkins, 1972), chap. 3, Girard outlined for the first time the hypothesis of a victim and reciprocal violence warded off by unanimous violence against this victim: this could be the origin of the myth and of the persecution narratives.

8. See C. L. Meyers, "The Roots of Restriction: Women in Early Israel," in N. K. Gottwald, ed., *The Bible and Liberation* (Maryknoll, N.Y. Orbis, 1983), pp. 289–306.

9. Cf. M. Schwantes, "O êxodo como evento exemplar," *Estudos Bíblicos*, 16 (*A Memória Popular do Exodo*) (Petrópolis: Vozes, 1988), pp. 9–18.

10. M. Schwantes, "A origem social dos textos," *A Memória Popular do Exodo*, pp. 31–37.

11. Cf. N. K. Gottwald, *The Tribes of Yahweh. A Sociology of the Religion of Liberated Israel, 1250–1050 BCE* (Maryknoll, N.Y.: Orbis, 1979), pp. 35–36, 39–40, 53–54.

12. Cf. Girard, *El Chivo*, p. 232.

13. Cf. C. Westermann, *Genesis 12–36. A Commentary* (Minneapolis: Augsburg, 1985), pp. 159–73.

14. Cf. W. Brueggemann, *Genesis. Interpretation.* (Atlanta: John Knox, 1982), pp. 126–32.

27

Community and Identity

GREGORY BAUM

There are many ways of looking upon liberation theology. It is possible to understand it as a theological methodology. Gustavo Gutiérrez takes us through several distinct steps in his famous *A Theology of Liberation*. The starting point is solidarity with the oppressed. It is out of this solidarity that all subsequent questions are asked. Commitment and action here precede theological reflection. The first question asked is: Why this suffering? What is the cause of the increasing misery and powerlessness of the majority in Latin America? To reply to this question theology must enter into a dialogue with the social sciences. With many Latin American searchers, Gutiérrez found the theory of dependency a convincing explanation of the poverty in Latin America. In a generalized form this theory has since been used in many ecclesiastical documents.

The next question that arises is: Why have these structures of oppression had such a hold over the whole of Latin America? They were not only imposed by the powerful, they were also legitimated by the dominant culture and the religious tradition. What is required, therefore, is a critique of ideology. To what extent has the church, its organization, its teaching, and its piety, contributed to the stability of the structures of oppression?

After such an analysis some Christians turn their backs on religion altogether. But the Christians whose option for the poor has been a response to the gospel realize that the biblical tradition contains elements that promise liberation. The question they now have to answer is how they can formulate, after the critique of ideology, the liberating message of the scriptures. Christians realize that they cannot speak of Jesus Christ truthfully unless they first analyze the character of social sin in their place and then present Christian teaching as the message of liberation for that place. In this sense, liberation theology is always and inevitably contextual.

Juan Segundo has called this methodology the hermeneutical circle of liberation theology. The methodology is indeed circular because new historical experiences may reveal that the solidarity with victims must be extended to sectors of the population—for instance, women or racial minorities—that were previously overlooked. Calling the methodology a circle assures us that liberation theology never offers a once and for all theological theory but always comes back upon itself to examine whether its own critical proposals are truly liberating or whether they have unintended and at first unrecognized implications that legitimate new forms of oppression. Calling liberation theology a circular methodology brings to light its affinity with critical theory, which has been so influential in European and North American political theology.

In this article I wish to ask a question often posed by conservative thinkers but not only by them: What are the implications of preferential solidarity for community and identity? The secular left has left this question unattended. Solidarity with victims produces a conflictual perception of society: society is seen as divided between oppressor and oppressed. From this perspective, expressions that praise the unity and harmony of society appear as political ideologies that disguise the class conflict. Socialism has seen itself as an internationalism. It has opposed nationalism as an ideology that creates the illusion of social solidarity. Solidarity, socialists argue, must first of all be preferential—that is to say, there must be identification with the exploited sector.

In order to promote solidarity among workers and constitute them as a class, socialists have had little sympathy for the ethnic and religious heritages of these men and women. Workers were to define themselves simply in terms of their economic location. Attachment to ethnicity or religion was seen as divisive and an obstacle to class unity. In many countries workers faithful to their religion or their ethnic heritage were disappointed by the socialist movement because it seemed to rob them of the values that in their situation of powerlessness gave them a sense of personal dignity. Cornel West records that blacks in the United States were repeatedly put off by Marxism because the purely economic analysis of oppression proposed by socialists made insignificant the ethnicity through which blacks defined their own collective identity.[1]

Socialists in colonized nations have been well aware of this unresolved ambiguity. In nineteenth-century Eastern Europe, socialists in nations that had become part of the Russian, Austrian, or Ottoman empires were debating whether they should be internationalists and identify with the struggles of the entire working class in the empire or whether they should be nationalists, join the national independence struggle led by the bourgeoisie, and then, after national independence, pursue the struggle for socialism in their own country. In contemporary Quebec this continues to be an important debate.

Liberation movements tend to break up existing unities by unmasking them as structures of domination. The conflictual perception of society puts a question mark behind national identity. Preferential solidarity threatens to undo community. Is the family the small social cell built upon love that renders possible a just and harmonious society? Or is the family, as Marx and Engels believed, the matrix of oppression? Does the women's liberation movement leave any ground for bonding in the family?

One of the reasons why political conservatism and, in the 1930s, European fascism attracted so many ordinary followers, including workers and the marginalized, was that the socialist movement of economic liberation did not seem to protect the values these persons cherished, especially identity and community. At a recent conference on social democracy today, held at the University of Ottawa, democratic socialists from Europe and North America discussed the present success of neoconservative values in the societies of the West and concluded that the exclusive emphasis of the economic factor often made the political left overlook the fact that individuals were attached to community and their collective identity.[2] From these, even the poor derived their sense of dignity. This neglect on the part of the left allowed neoconservative politicians to mobilize the public around these values.

The reason that social thinkers and political scientists are so fascinated by liberation theology is that here they see a social theory of the left that gives those who struggle for justice a tremendous sense of identity and community. Liberation theology does not say to the people, you have nothing to lose but your chains. It assures them, on the contrary, that they have inherited a religious tradition that is the bearer of radical values. Liberation theology gives them an extraordinary sense of historical continuity, reaching back to the exodus community whom God delivered from oppression in the land of bondage. The identity and community that liberation theology communicates is of course that of the Christian church.

The question I wish to raise in this article is what liberation theology might say regarding community and identity of the wider society.

Sociologists tend to argue that a nation preserves its historical identity not simply through its political structure but also through a collective myth or a set of symbols that blesses and legitimates these structures and the values they express. The national myth allows persons to internalize the dominant values. This theory is upheld by many sociologists who do not regard themselves as functionalists. If this theory is true, the following question poses itself. Should a liberation struggle unmask and demystify the national ideology as an illusion of unity aimed at disguising class division? Or should those who struggle against oppression unmask a certain national self-understanding and in its stead propose an alternative interpretation of national identity and national purpose?

This question is so important that some liberation theologians have argued that it may not be useful at all to use the word "ideology" in a purely pejorative sense as legitimation of injustice. Radical social theories must not only reject the distorted values of the past but also bless and legitimate new values, partially derived from the past, that are to constitute the new society. The Canadian political theologian, Harold Wells, has recently drawn attention to the work of Paul Ricoeur and Juan Segundo to defend a wider definition of ideology, one that includes the negative and the positive sense.[3]

Reading the work of Latin American liberation theologians from a distance, I have the impression that they say very little about national identity. However, they do have a very strong sense of the historical unity of Latin America. They see the multitudes of Latin America, of all regions, subject to the identical forces of oppression, and thus they propose a social liberation project that involves the whole continent. Their contextual theology is Latin American. In the Puebla Document the bishops entitled their pastoral message "God's Saving Plan for Latin America."

Latin American liberation theology is not concerned with the nation, but it does communicate a sense of collective identity beyond the religious realm. It promotes a collective self-understanding of Latin America. The conflict sociology adopted by Latin American liberation theology is not used to explode all secular symbols of collective identity. The community promoted by liberation theology directly and immediately is the religious one. But beyond this, liberation theology offers an interpretation of Latin American history that provides a collective myth, an ideology—if the word is used in the wider sense—that reinforces the unity of Latin America and grounds the continental social project of liberation.

The secular left has been so suspicious of myth and symbols that its social theories offer only critiques of ideology and hardly ever spell out the set of symbols and values that ought to pervade the imagination of those who struggle. It will eventually be institutionalized and reritualized in the liberated society. Marxist theorists understand the role of myths in such a negative way that they do not even analyze the symbolic power exercised by their own movement. Even the critical theory of the Frankfurt school, which has criticized the economics of Marxist orthodoxy and recognized the political power of culture and myth, was quite unable to define a set of symbols that would insinuate the just society, legitimate socialist struggle, summon forth energy, and intensify the yearning for emancipation. Because the secular left was so uncomfortable with symbols of identity, its social theories easily gave the impression that while promising economic liberation, the socialist struggle would take away from citizens many of the values they treasured, especially community.

The religious left, by way of contrast, has a strong sense that the ever-necessary, ongoing critique of ideology must not be allowed to explode all symbols of unity and identity. It is precisely the task of liberation theology to criticize collective identities that legitimate oppression and to redefine them in accordance with collective stories that (1) bind persons together in the struggle for justice and (2) reveal the nature of the liberated society.

It is instructive to examine the famous debate involving sociologists and theologians over the "civil religion" of the United States of America. In an article written in 1967, Robert Bellah, a distinguished sociologist in the tradition of Emile Durkheim, argued that examining American political culture over two centuries, including the inaugural speeches of the presidents and other texts of the public liturgy, the social scientist discovers the existence of a myth relating to God and the destiny of America, a myth that deserves to be called religion, though a religion different from Christianity and Judaism.[4] It is the "civil religion" of the United States of America. Bellah's article was not without its ambiguity. In an explanatory note added later, Bellah explained more clearly that the civil religion he examined referred to a set of "transcendent values" by which Americans evaluate and judge the government's domestic and foreign policies.[5] He suggested that the student movement of the late 1960s represented an exercise of America's civil religion because the students supported the civil rights movement in the South and opposed the involvement in Vietnam in the name of traditional American values—democracy and freedom from colonial control.

Bellah's critics understood this civil religion in a variety of ways.[6] Some argued that Bellah's civil religion referred to the religious ethos of church-going persons, the sanctification of the American way of life, with little reference to the biblical message. Others feared that Bellah's theory fostered an exaggerated nationalism, a quasi-religious devotion to America as the first of many nations. Some Christian theologians argued that if the civil religion is made consistent with Christian self-understanding, then this civil religion may be the contextual form of Christianity in the United States. By contrast, other theologians denounced Bellah's civil religion as a form of idolatry leading America astray.

This celebrated debate clearly reveals that the national myth of the United States, whether it is called religion or not, exists in a variety of forms and is capable of being interpreted in several ways. The task of liberation theology is here to critique forms of the national myth that legitimate oppression and exploitation, and

223

to reach out for a possible interpretation of the civil religion that would promote the cause of justice.[7] If, for the moment, we return to the strict (pejorative) definition of ideology, we may say that liberation theology, following its proper methodology, must reject the ideological collective self-definitions of America and in its stead search for a national myth with utopian possibilities.

Writing during the period of the student movement, Rosemary Ruether insisted that it was a fatal mistake of the American left to allow the symbols of nationhood to become representative of the right and to define itself by the rejection of the flag and other symbols of the republic.[8] What was demanded instead, she argued, was to replace the ideological meaning of the national symbols by a radical interpretation of America's mission, based on its struggle for independence and democracy.

These critical reflections on collective identities fit perfectly into the methodology of liberation theology. Solidarity with the oppressed—the starting point—calls for social analysis, including an ideological critique of the dominant culture. Such an investigation creates suspicion in regard to various collective identities. To what extent do these disguise the conditions of oppression? At the same time, collective identities play an essential part in the cooperative action of men and women building a stable society. This is an insight derived from the social sciences, from philosophy—and from scripture. Collective identities must therefore be negated dialectically: this means that the repudiation of their ideological meaning must be followed by a reconstruction of a collective self-understanding oriented toward emancipation.

In this context it may be useful to retain the strict (pejorative) definition of ideology, for this enables us to differentiate collective myths defined as ideologies from those constructed as utopias.

It is perhaps no accident that it was a Canadian political theologian who pleaded for a wider definition of ideology. He was probably afraid that a purely pejorative concept of ideology would make critical Canadians overlook the political importance of a national myth. Because Canada is an unlikely confederation of former British colonies, including one the British took from the French in 1759, Canadian society lacks symbols and stories that define its collective identity. It is this absence of ideology, understood here in the wider sense, that weakens Canada in its resistance to the growing influence of the United States. The lack of a strong collective identity makes Canada vulnerable to increasing economic and political dependency on the United States. At this time, the Canadian government is negotiating a free trade agreement with the United States, an agreement that promises higher profit for the major corporations, yet that frightens workers and farmers who anticipate increasing unemployment and deterioration of the conditions of employment. Afraid of this free trade agreement are also Canadians, English and French-speaking, who treasure the Canadian social democratic tradition and Canada's greater sense of society's collective responsibility, expressed for instance in socialized medicine. Many of us fear that the cultural impact of this free trade agreement will weaken the Canadian socialist heritage. Canadian churches and church groups have joined the movement against free trade. In the Canadian situation, the interests of class and nation tend to coincide.[9]

Let me mention that left-wing secular political scientists do not agree in their analysis of Canadian capitalism. There are political economists who try to understand the Canadian economy by analyzing the structure of capital and the social relations it creates in this country. There are other political economists who argue that the Canadian economy is a dependent capitalism and for that reason can be understood only if this dependency on the center of the system is taken into account.[10] In the light of this second analysis, the interests of class and nation tend to coincide. It is worth noting that the recent Canadian church documents on the demands of economic justice in Canada have used this dependency theory to understand the plight of the Canadian economy and the marginalization of an ever-increasing sector of the population.[11]

Yet this "economic nationalism," supported by labor groups, farmers, and churches, has only a faint echo in the Canadian population. Why? Because of the weak sense of collective identity. Because of the absence of a national myth. The task of Canadian political theologians is not to institute a critique of the national ideology—for there is none—but rather to tell the stories of Canadian struggles for emancipation and the creation of a socialist tradition in English and in French Canada. Out of these efforts, joined by similarly oriented efforts of secular groups, may well emerge liberating symbols of national identity.

Although these theological reflections are contextual, they have universal implications. It may possibly be the task of liberation theology to help the secular left in various parts of the world to arrive at a positive evaluation of identity and community. Similarly it is often religious women in the woman's movement who reach for an emancipatory theory of marriage that negates inequality and yet affirms new forms of bonding in the service of love and of the community.

The Canadian collective identity raises other questions that deserve attention. Canada as a political entity has a weak sense of itself, but many regions in Canada have a fairly strong sense of their collective identity. This applies above all to the French-speaking community of Quebec, which understands itself as a people or a nation. English-speaking Canadians tend to look upon Quebec as an ethnic minority that, though entitled to its heritage, must fit itself into the political structure of confederation. Quebecers, on the other hand, see themselves not as a minority but as a people with the moral right to self-determination. Even Quebecers who favor remaining in the Canadian confederation see themselves as members of a nation: they understand Canada as a binational country. Many English-speaking Canadians oppose the binational understanding of Canada.

Let me mention in this context that church documents published by the Catholic Church and by the United Church, the largest Protestant church in Canada, have acknowledged the peoplehood of French Canadians and recognized their moral right to self-determination.[12]

Faced with these difficulties, the task of political theology in regard to collective identities is not only to distinguish between the ideological and utopian dimensions of the national myth but also to provide critical insight into the relationships of one collectivity to the other.

I wish to explore a startling idea taken from a long, as yet unpublished essay, written by an Iranian scholar, Modj Sadria, residing in Montreal, which tried to deal with the question of how the Orient should define its own collective self-identity. Let me lift this idea out of the essay's particular historical context. In general it can be said that it is politically dangerous for a collectivity to define itself out of its own tradition and only afterward, as a second step, turn to the other collectivity facing it. If a community creates its identity and produces its national myth by relying exclusively on its own experience, it will never be able to make room for the other as other. It will eventually look upon the other as stranger, as opponent, as rival, as enemy. To overcome this inner dynamic of hostility, a collectivity must define itself dialogically from the start. In constituting its own self-understanding it must simultaneously make room for the self-definition of the other. This respect for the other does not imply that one collectivity necessarily accepts the self-understanding another collectivity has of itself. No, it may indeed be necessary to reject this present self-understanding. What is always possible, however, is to imagine a possible self-understanding of the other collectivity that would facilitate dialogue and respect. There may, in fact, exist minority movements in the other collectivity that are critical of the present national myth, movements that actually strive for the reconstruction of that other collectivity and its culture so that respect and dialogue with a neighboring collectivity is possible. Persons involved in the definition of their own collectivity must simultaneously make room for the self-identity of the other collectivity and the easiest way to do this is to be in solidarity with minority movements among the other collectivity, which themselves strive for a dialogical self-definition.

If these reflections are valid, then we must humbly admit that the Christian churches have erred over the centuries. For the churches have always defined themselves nondialogically, in exclusive reliance on their own heritage, and for this reason they had to look upon other religious communities as stranger, opponent, revival, and eventually enemy. It was only the ecumenical movement of the twentieth century that taught the churches to define themselves anew, this time in dialogue with the ecumenical aspirations of the other communities.

If these reflections are valid, Canadians—by which I here mean mainly English-speaking Canadians—must try to define the collective identity of Canada by leaving room for the self-determination of Quebec and learn to do so by extending their solidarity to the movement in Quebec that also struggles for a dialogical self-definition.

Conversely, to avoid the political danger of projecting the other as opponent and enemy, Quebecers (whether or not they seek sovereignty) must also seek a collective self-understanding that makes room for an appropriate self-understanding of English Canada. The only way Quebecers can do this is to extend their solidarity with those groups in English Canada that are committed to social justice and a dialogical collective self-understanding.

Applying the same principle to Canada's presence vis-à-vis the United States, we recognize immediately that it is politically dangerous for the Canadian left to look at this powerful country simply as empire. There are of course many Canadians who like to think of Canada as junior partner in the American empire, just as many Canadians at the turn of the century wanted Canada to be junior partner in the British empire. But the Canadian left that strives for an economy beyond capitalist contradictions must avoid defining America as an enemy and instead make room in Canada's own self-symbolization for an appropriate collective identity of the United States. Again such a dialogical self-definition becomes possible if we extend our solidarity to those Americans who in their country wrestle against political and economic empire and envisage American culture based on social solidarity.

Nationalism has often been an ideology (in the wider sense) in the struggle for a people's self-determination against the remnants of the feudal order and, later, against crumbling colonial empires. Nationalism of this kind has been inspired by the quest for justice. The symbols of nationalism have tried to unite the social classes in a joint historical project to overcome national oppression. But nationalisms, however valid, have always been politically ambiguous because they tended to define national identities in a nondialogical way, making no room for an appropriate collective identity of ethnic minorities nor for a dialogically defined national identity of the other collectivity. A Zionist philosopher in Israel recently said: "When we were young, we thought we could pluck the raisins out of the poisonous cake of nationalism; now that we are old, we have discovered that even the raisins were poisonous."

In this paper I understand liberation theology as a critical social theory of the left that appreciates the values of identity and community. I regard this as an important service rendered by the religious left to the human struggle for emancipation.

In his remarkable book, The Socialist Decision, published in 1932, a few months prior to the victory of Nazism in Germany, Paul Tillich distinguishes two sets of political theories. The first, "the myths of origin," relates a society to the great moments of its history, especially its genesis, and the second, "the myths of destiny," relates a society to its evolution in the future. Myths of origin, be they religious or ethnic, are politically conservative; they hold up the past as a model and raise up barriers against outsiders. Myths of destiny, by contrast, look toward the unfolding of the rational possibilities in society. They dream of the future society defined in terms of equality and justice. Liberalism and socialism are myths of destiny. Socialism, Tillich argued, wants to overcome the unresolved contradictions of liberalism. Socialism wants to transcend the individualism and utilitarianism created through liberalism by constructing a society based on social solidarity. Yet, Tillich continues, socialism is as rationalistic as liberalism and hence has been unable to inspire values of community and identity. The contradictions of instrumental rationality cannot be overcome by a new application of the same instrumental rationality.

To inspire community and identity, socialism must be willing to turn to the myths of origin. This is a dangerous undertaking. Political philosophies guided by a myth of origin remain indifferent to rational definitions of human progress. Under certain critical circumstances, a myth of origin may even give rise to fascism. Still, if a myth of origin remains strictly subordinated to the principle of justice, it may be joined to a socialist project, and then it could teach the socialist movement how to create community and strengthen collective identity.

Tillich wrote his famous book when his own movement of religious socialism had hardly any political presence in Germany. Yet he appealed to communism and social democracy to abandon their scientific rationalism, to incorporate a myth of origin, strictly controlled by justice, in its social theory and by doing so find support beyond the working class in the entire lower sector of society, including farmers, crafts people, and village and small town populations. Tillich recognized that the name "national socialism," adopted by German fascism, was fraudulent: there was no subordination of the myth of origin to the principle of justice. Here a romantic return to the past made the people vulnerable to an outburst of barbarism. In The Socialist Decision Tillich continued to believe in the historical mission of socialism.

He thought that in the future socialism may be able to overcome the exploitation and alienation of workers and the poor, if it learned to promote, within this context, the spirit of community and identity. This is why Tillich created the movement of religious socialism. Yet in the Germany of the 1920s this movement represented only a small circle.

Liberation theology in Latin America and equivalent religious movements in other parts of the world are movements with a popular base. Their originality lies in the fact that they offer a left-wing, critical, social analysis and at the same time create symbols of community and identity.

NOTES

1. Cornel West, *Prophesy Deliverance!* (Philadelphia: Westminster, 1982), p. 100.

2. See G. Baum, "Social-démocratie et engagement éthique," *Relations* (January-February 1988) 25–27.

3. Harold Wells, "The Question of Ideological Determination in Liberation Theology," *Toronto Journal of Theology*, 3/2 (Fall 1987) 209–20.

4. The article was first published in the winter issue of *Daedalus*, 1967, and republished in *The Religious Situation: 1968*, D. R. Cutler, ed. (Boston: Beacon, 1969) and R. Bellah, *Beyond Belief* (New York: Harper & Row, 1970), pp. 168–89.

5. See Bellah, *Beyond Belief*, p. 168.

6. The entire debate is presented and analyzed in *American Civil Religion*, R. E. Richley, ed. (New York: Harper & Row, 1974).

7. See *Civil Religion and Political Theology*, T. Rouner, ed. (University of Notre Dame Press, 1986).

8. Rosemary R. Ruether, *Liberation Theology* (New York: Paulist Press, 1972), p. 163.

9. Cf. Duncan Cameron.

10. For an analysis of this controversy, see Daniel Drache, "The Crisis of Canadian Political Economy: Dependency Theory Versus the New Orthodoxy," *Canadian Journal of Political and Social Theory*, 7 (Fall 1983) 25–49.

11. Christopher Lind, "Ethics, Economics and Canada's Catholic Bishops," *Canadian Journal of Political and Social Theory*, 7 (Fall 1983) 25–49.

12. Canadian Conference of Catholic Bishops, "On the Occasion of the Hundredth Year of Confederation," *Do Justice!*, E. F. Sheridan, ed. (Toronto: Jesuit Centre of Faith and Social Justice, 1987), pp. 122–34; The United Church of Canada, "Brief to the Joint Committee on the Constitution of Canada," in *Canadian Churches and Social Justice*, John Williams, ed. (Toronto: Lorimer, 1984), pp. 189–97; The Catholic Bishops of Quebec, "The People of Quebec and Its Political Future," in *Canadian Churches*, pp. 181–88.

28

Seven Samurai and How They Looked Again: Theology, Social Analysis, and *Religión Popular* in Latin America

HARVEY COX

Twenty years ago an unlikely combination of actors surveyed Latin America and saw a specter haunting the land. The specter was *religión popular* and the odd coalition that descried its threatening visage was made up of seven fierce warriors who normally viewed each other with considerable suspicion. It included (1) pre-Vatican II Roman Catholic integralists intent on holding the line; (2) post-Vatican II liturgical and theological reformers intent on changing it; (3) Protestant missionaries from North America and the local clergy they had trained; (4) Pentecostal preachers, nearly all of them Latin Americans; (5) liberal developmentalists from agencies such as IMF, AID, and the World Bank; (6) Marxist activists; and (7) liberation theologians. These seven samurai agreed on virtually nothing else. But they could—and did—join hands in common opposition to popular religion. They could—and did—form a united front against unauthorized cults of the Virgin, "patronales," and raucous fiestas, against the use of holy water to cast spells, against pre-Christian healing rites and scapulars designed to ward off evil. The specter, it appears, bore many faces, but its presence was so menacing and so manifold that this heterogenous cohort of ghost busters set aside other differences to track it down.

Of course the different members of the alliance opposed popular religion for their own quite different reasons:

(1) *Integralists* saw in the local cults remnants of pagan piety and the subversive syntheses of official saints with pre-Columbian deities. Undiscouraged by four hundred years of spotty successes, they were still pursuing the "cut and burn" policy initiated by the Franciscans at the time of the Conquista.

(2) *Post-Vatican II reformers* longed to gather congregations around the altar (newly moved out from the wall), which now became the table of the family of God.

229

They did not look kindly on worshipers saying beads during Mass or siphoning off energies in individual devotions at side chapels. Christians were to become (in Vatican II terms) a "people of God," and popular religion—the reformers thought—worked against this goal.

(3) *Protestant missionaries and local evangelical leaders* saw popular religion as yet another example of the debased Roman Catholicism that had been disparaged since the Black Legend first appeared in the sixteenth century: superstition and magic blended with popery and ignorance. For them, to embrace Protestant faith obviously required eschewing all that.

(4) *Pentecostal preachers*—mostly Latin Americans themselves—railed against devil worship, and the drunkenness and lusty excess that often accompany fiestas and patronales. In their opposition to popular religion they seem—if anything—more zealous than their other Protestant colleagues.

(5) *Liberal developmentalists* saw popular religion as an unfortunate obstacle to the introduction of modern agriculture, education, and especially health care, for *curanderos* were often key leaders in popular religion.

(6) *Marxists*—rarely masters of nuance in making judgments about religion—dismissed popular religion along with all religion as one more opiate of the masses. Like other rural idiocies it would evaporate once capitalism was abolished.

(7) *Liberation Theologies*—most of them at least—tended to see popular religion as a fundamentally alienated expression of religiosity, a form of false consciousness that prevented Christians from responding to a gospel that called them to become aware of their role as subjects and agents of the historical project of building the kingdom of god.

Thus the seven samurai harbored their own peculiar *causae belli*, but for each the struggle against the perversions of popular piety was one they took up with enthusiasm.

This grim catalog of reasons why so many different actors showed so little sympathetic interest in what has accurately been called "the religion of the poor" seems remarkable given the "preferential option for the poor" some of the same parties trumpeted so widely at the same time. Yet, in retrospect, what now seems equally remarkable is that during the same period the "high" forms of scholarly and academic theology displayed equally minimal interest in the religion of ordinary persons. Protestant theologians were busy refining historico-critical methods and reappropriating the theologies of the Reformation, most of which were not sympathetic to popular piety. Catholics were absorbing the impact of Vatican II and reveling in their newfound freedom to engage in critical biblical studies. With the possible exception of a few French Catholics who were still interested in "spirituality," and of an even smaller handful of "liberal" Protestants who continued to be intrigued by "religious experience," most of theology simply ignored religion, popular or otherwise.

This benign neglect of the phenomenon of religion by most theologies was even more evident with reference to the non-Christian religious traditions. One can hardly locate a memorable paragraph in Gilson or Maritain about the other religions of the world. The same lapse is true of Barth, Bultmann, and Bonhoeffer. Hendrik Kramer, the only neo-orthodox theologian who addressed himself to the issue, argued, in effect, when it comes to world religions, the less said the better.

But by the late 1960s this picture was changing. The Vatican had established secretariats for dialogue with Jews, Protestants, and non-Christian religions. In his last book published just before he died, Paul Tillich declared that the vexing question of the relationship between Christianity and the non-Christian faiths of the world now loomed as *the* most important theological issue, one he had scarcely addressed at all in his fifty years of scholarly theological production. By the early 1970s other Protestant theologians followed suit, and "theology of the religions" became a central preoccupation. Even so, it has taken years for theologians to recognize that in order to deal with this issue they must move beyond old comparativist methods (which had focused largely on the scriptures of other faiths) and learn something from more recently developed approaches to religious studies, including the need to study both "high and low," both official and popular versions, of world religions.

This brings us to the threshold of the 1990s where, due in no small measure to the vast influence of the theology of Gustavo Gutiérrez and his co-workers, the entire situation vis-à-vis attitudes both of activist parties and of academic theologians toward *religión popular* has shifted dramatically. What I wish to do now is to chart briefly how parallel changes occurred in each of the seven samurai, focusing especially on liberation theologians. In doing so I want to suggest why this change signals a possible quickening of the sometimes limping conversation between theologians and those who study religion from the perspective of psychology, anthropology, and sociology. After that I wish to hazard some tentative hunches about what all this might mean for the more general question of the "theological problem of religion."

CHANGES: THE FIRST SIX SAMURAI

How did the seven samurai come to look at the ever-present reality of popular religion in Latin America in a new way? In each one the change came about both because of internal developments within the party itself and also because of changes in the functioning of popular religion itself.

1. *Pre-Vatican II integralists* continue to play some role in the Catholic Church, but their influence is waning. Admittedly, Pope John Paul II has appointed conservative bishops nearly every time a vacancy has occurred in Latin America. But the men he appoints cannot usefully be described with the old-fashioned term "integralist." Rather, they represent the school of thought within Catholic ecclesiology that holds that the reforms of Vatican II have gone too far, and that the time has come for retrenchment and consolidation. The most articulate spokesman of this line is of course Cardinal Joseph Ratzinger, prefect of the Sacred Congregation for the Doctrine of the Faith, who declares repeatedly that the most pressing need in the Catholic Church today is for what he calls *recentrage*. He uses this French term to refer to a tendency he welcomes, in particular within the French church, to look more to Rome and to deal sternly with the various forms of democratization and decentralization that have crept in since the 1960s.

When it comes to popular religion Cardinal Ratzinger is hardly an exclusivist or integralist. During a visit to Canada a few years back, he responded to a question about the prospects of Christianity with characteristic comprehensiveness by dividing the battlefield—as a previous dweller by the Tiber once did—into three parts.

In the First World, he declared, consumerism and moral decay are the main challenges to the church. In the Second World—countries with communist governments—he found a growing disillusionment with Leninist ideology and a hunger for faith. He was most enthusiastic, however, about the Third World, including Latin America, where he suggested that "the natural piety and deep religiousness of the people present a genuine opening for christianization." This telling remark of the prefect parallels the position taken by Cardinal López Trujillo, the president of CELAM (the Latin American Bishops' Conference), who frequently declares that in time of rapid social change and jarring cultural dislocation the simple piety of ordinary persons should not be disturbed since it is what enables them to survive the traumas of history. This idea represents a conservative, in fact "functionalist," view of the role of religion, which differs from integralism in that virtually any faith that performs this role can be viewed with sympathy.

2. *Post-Vatican II reformers* who once swept through the churches of Latin America removing statues of saints, relics, and the accumulated detritus of previous waves of popular devotion, have now begun to take a second look at *religión popular*. The conviction is emerging among them that much of the enthusiasm for liturgical renewal that sprang from Vatican II had a certain elitist cast and that for liturgy to become the "work of the people" it has to incorporate elements of the local folk heritage. A good example of this rethought strategy can be seen in the history of the cathedral in Cuernevaca, Mexico. There, Bishop Don Sergio Mendez Arceo (now retired), first zealously removed all the saints' images and the traditional trappings from the church. But then, sensitive to popular tastes, he initiated the famous Mariachi Mass, using the instruments not so much of folk culture but of the regional music tradition of his people. A form of popular devotion was thus readmitted.

3. *Protestantism* of the "mainline" variety has not officially altered its abiding suspicion of popular religion. But this form of Protestantism appears to be one of decreasing vitality in Europe. On one wing its youngest leaders are drawn toward liberation theology and therefore toward a form of cooperation with Catholics, which their grandfathers—most of whom were converted from folk Catholicism— would have rejected. A decade ago the North American sponsors of the Baptist Seminary in Mexico reacted with deep dismay when the local leaders of the school began including Roman Catholics not only in the student body but on the faculty as well. On the other level, mainline Protestantism is beginning to merge with pentecostalism. Indeed, it is often difficult for a visitor to a Protestant congregation in Latin America to detect its denominational affiliation. All these developments suggest that the Protestantism introduced by missionaries in the nineteenth century will probably not continue to nurture its animus against popular religion as ardently in the future.

4. *Pentecostal* changes in attitudes have also taken place but more as a result of the actual structure of pentecostal worship than as the fruit of theological analysis. With the exception of Afro-Brazilian spiritism, pentecostalism represents the most thoroughly indigenized expression of non-Roman Catholic religion in Latin America. Nearly all its preachers and leaders are themselves Latin Americans (this in contrast to Catholicism, which still relies on a high proportion of foreign-born priests and religious.) This, along with the highly decentralized organization of pentecostalism, means that hierarchical forms of social control are less workable,

so the censoring out of the folk elements that persons bring with them to worship is more difficult. Also pentecostalists encourage the use of indigenous musical instruments and melodies, and this inevitably allows elements of popular religion to sift in. Finally, the explicitly emotional tone of pentecostal worship and the "speaking in tongues" phenomenon permits images from what might be called the "cultural unconscious" to come to expression. Pentecostal leaders still vigorously discourage their members from taking part in most popular rituals and fiestas, but there is considerable evidence that at another level pentecostal spirituality may be preserving elements of folk piety that might otherwise have been eradicated by urbanization and other types of social change.

5. Among *developmentalists* who are interested in stimulating changes in societies, especially in matters such as food production, health care, and education, again the attitudes toward religion have begun to change. Though they once saw popular religion as the primary obstacle to any form of change, developmentalists now tend to be much less sweeping and judgmental in their assessment of religious practices and institutions. The general shift in attention among developmental theorists away from more technological fixes and toward questions of culture has brought this concern into an even sharper focus, and developmentalists now try to cooperate with religious movements in the areas in which they are working. Some even look at them not as obstacles to innovation but as the main source of values and hopes by which persons may be motivated to make any changes at all.

6. One of the most dramatic changes has come in the *Marxist evaluation* of the significance of religion. Confronted with a continent where the only promising revolutionary activity seemed to be coming from Christian sectors, Latin American Marxists and their colleagues elsewhere were eventually forced to reassess some of the standard Marxist analyses of the role of religion in society. The most visible example of their new attitude toward religion is the one demonstrated by none other than Fidel Castro himself in his widely read book *Fidel and Religion* (Simon & Schuster, 1987) in which the *comandante* not only does not condemn religion out of hand, but in fact insists that for large numbers of persons faith may provide the principal motivation for their participation in revolution. When the leader of the communist country, who has the longest claim to longevity in office, thus speaks, many listen:

Basing themselves on their faith, believers can take a revolutionary stand and . . . there need not be any contradiction between their being believers and revolutionaries. As I see it, that phrase [that religion is the opiate of the people] cannot be, nor is it, a dogma or an absolute truth; it is a truth in specific historical conditions. Moreover, I believe that this conclusion is perfectly in keeping with dialectics and Marxism.

I believe that, from the political point of view, religion is not, in itself, an opiate or a miraculous remedy. It may become an opiate or a wonderful cure if it is used or applied to defend oppressors and exploiters or the oppressed and the exploited, depending on the approach adopted toward the political, social, or material problems of the human beings who, aside from theology or religious belief, are born and must live in this world.

From a strictly political point of view—and I think I know something about politics—I believe that it is possible for Christians . . . to work together with

Marxist Communists to transform the world . . . even though, in the case of the Christians, their starting point is a religious concept.

At the more theoretical level, Latin American Marxists who were once dazzled by Lenin's rather idiosyncratic views about metaphysical materialism, have now begun to study religion more from the perspective of the Italian theoretician, Antonio Gramsci. As they do, they make their judgments more on a political rather than on a metaphysical basis. Consequently their attitude toward all forms of religion tends to be much more nuanced.

LIBERATION THEOLOGY

In the case of the seventh samurai, liberation theology, the story is both more complex and more immediately significant for the larger issue of "the theology of religion." The fact is that even at its inception there was an active discussion in the liberation theology movement about the significance of *religión popular*. Liberation theologians after all did not appear out of nowhere. Many had been trained in some form of pre-Vatican II integralism. Most were understandably intoxicated by the reformist currents of the council. Some were touched by various expressions of Protestant theology. All, as Latin American intellectuals, had had to come to terms with one or another type of Marxism. They were men of their time and of their region, and as one follows their early debate about *religión popular* and notes the course it has taken more recently, two things become evident. First, the positions various of the theologians took were deeply influenced by their theological and even confessional commitments, and secondly, the present, more positive, appreciation of popular religions emerged as a result of ideas that were there from the beginning. Both these observations can be confirmed by a brief examination of some texts from an earlier stage of the discussion.

In 1976 José Míguez Bonino published a widely discussed article entitled "La Piedad Popular in América Latina" in the journal *Cristianismo y Sociedad* (no. 47, Buenos Aires, 1976, pp. 31–38). Relying on the earlier work of Aldo Büntig and on the declarations of the Medellín Conference of Latin American Bishops (CELAM) Míguez Bonino drew a very grim picture of popular religion. Referring to a report by the director of the CELAM Instituto Pastoral, Míguez Bonino quoted as follows: "The religiosity of poverty does not work to change life. It is well known that such Catholicism strengthens a dualistic vision of reality and, therefore, a religious attitude alien to the tasks of this world." In Latin America, he insisted, such popular Catholicism reinforces the social system with all its injustices, contradictions, and forms of oppression.

But Míguez Bonino was hardly alone. A paragraph from the international catechesis weekly published in Medellín in 1968 makes—if anything—a more severe judgment:

The manifestations of popular religiosity—even if they sometimes show positive aspects—are, in the rapid evolution of society, the expression of alienated groups—that is, of groups that live in a depersonalized, conformist, and noncritical manner and do not make efforts to change society.

This document, reflecting as it did the enthusiasm of the post-Vatican II era, did not withhold its indictment of the church for allowing such popular piety to continue. "This kind of religiosity is maintained and encouraged," the report said, "by the prevailing structures of which the church is a part. . . . The expansion of this type of religiosity slows down changes in the structures of society."

Five major elements appear in the harsh post-Vatican II liberationist critique of popular religion. The first pointed to its alleged *fatalism*: it encourages persons to accept the situation in which they find themselves as the will of God or as according to the order of creation. The second criticism, directed especially at pentecostal forms of popular piety, focused on *individualism*, on the attempt to "save my own individual soul" at the expense of corporate or cooperative action in society. The third had to do with what might be called *substitute satisfaction*, finding spurious solutions to genuine human dilemmas: lighting a candle before a saint's picture when a child is sick instead of summoning whatever health care is available. A fourth critique had to do with the *blessing of intergroup and interclass harmony* through an emphasis on love and reconciliation—a "false universalism." It was often noted that this universalism is gladly seized upon by those in power to maintain the status quo. Fifth, there was the critique (mainly of developmentalists) that immersion in the popular religious mind-scape *prevented persons from "integrating,"* from participating in the development of the wider society.

Reading these critiques in historical perspective, it becomes evident, however, that both Bonino's widely read article and the Medellín catechetical material were written to attack other positions. Thus Bonino sounded an alarm about romanticism, and warned those who look for liberative potential in popular religion that it can never be found in a pure state. Folk religious expressions exist *within history,* he argued, and therefore in a context of class conflict and oppression. The Medellín paper echoed the same caution, adding that such movements are always to some extent misshaped by the distortions introduced by ruling elites in order to make use of religion to perpetuate the prevailing system of privilege. But both Bonino and the authors of the Medellín document realized that popular religion could not simply be ignored. It was present everywhere and had a special appeal for precisely the persons whom liberation theology was supposed to liberate. What was the answer?

Replies to the challenge of popular religion often followed theological positions in a remarkably predictable way. A Methodist, Bonino suggested that the only solution was that of conversion—*metanoia*. In order to encourage such a conversion, he said, popular religious movements needed to be brought to a point of crisis. The poor and marginated who participate in them had to be made to see the contradiction between the picture of the world religious movements project and the actual world in which they had to live. Out of the resulting breakdown would come a transformation not just of the person, Bonino hoped, but of the *tradition itself.* Its rudiments could be then redirected toward the proper historical task of human beings.

Míguez Bonino does not delineate more specifically what these rudiments might be, but his prescription drawn from the lexicon of Wesleyan theology is an understandable one: like individuals, religious traditions must also be brought to the mourner's bench, to a point of crisis, in order for a genuine conversion to occur. The resurrection comes only after the cross.

Similar prescriptions were advanced by many Catholic writers at the time, especially Juan Luis Segundo. Perhaps some of them were more influenced by protestantizing theological currents than they themselves were aware.

Still, neither Bonino's voice nor the Medellín instruction were the only sentiments being articulated. At about the same time Míguez Bonino's article was published, Juan Carlos Scannone, who like Míguez Bonino wrote from Buenos Aires, took a quite different position about what the appropriate attitude of liberation theologians toward popular religion should be. Scannone believed the Second Vatican Council had brought to Latin America two different forms of postconciliar theology. One was shaped by the European liberal enlightenment and its more rational way of thinking. Scannone criticized this stream for viewing popular religion with a thoroughgoing "hermeneutic of suspicion." It signaled a deep distrust of what he called the "sapiential wisdom" of ordinary persons, a wisdom embedded in their religious beliefs and ritual practices.

The other stream of postconciliar theology that Scannone noted was the one he himself represented. It is a theology that allows popular culture to provide what used to be called *locus theologicus* or *Sitz im Leben*, what Scannone calls the "hermeneutical locale." He argued that only this second theological approach could in the long run make a genuine contribution to the authentic liberation of Latin American peoples. "Without denying its ambiguities," Scannone wrote, "it [popular religion] is an expression of authentic Christian faith inherited from the past and received from the preaching of the first missionaries. It should continue to be evangelized but in terms of its own proper cultural values."

The heart of Scannone's argument lay in what Alisdair MacIntyre has since called the "tradition specificity" of any mode of reasoning. Scannone rejected outright the notion that universalistic and scientific modes of discourse were the only valid ones and argued forcibly that there are *different* traditions of reason. He further argued that incarnate in the religious practices of the Latin American peoples, there is a deeply symbolic mode of reasoning, which not only needs to be preserved in Latin America but has an invaluable contribution to make to other parts of the world. Scannone's point coheres well with the ideas advanced more recently by C. S. Song (*Theology from the Womb of Asia,* Orbis, 1986) about theologizing in the context of local symbolic codes.

Scannone's main argument with Bonino and the other liberation theologians who looked with suspicion on popular religion is posed by his most basic question: Who is the real subject of liberation theology? Granted that theologians make such theology explicit and critical, and that they reflect on it, who is the *original subject* of this discourse? Furthermore, who is the genuine addressee? Is the addressee of theology all persons of faith or is it mainly elites—religious or nonreligious—who have been conscientized into the process of social change and historical responsibility?

Scannone views the "hermeneutic of suspicion" with suspicion. He suspects that it is informed by a scientistic bias that prevents it from fathoming the full potential of popular religion. He calls for a radical incarnation of the theological enterprise into the "culture-specific" religion of a particular people. He asked for a hermeneutic of appreciation, one that would be open to the significance of symbolic modes of thinking and would recognize that mythic thought is not merely a stage to be outgrown but a permanent component in any thinking that is essentially human.

Scannone's approach to popular religion, it seems, is just as "Catholic" as Bonino's is "Methodist."

In the past twenty years it can be said with a considerable degree of accuracy that the old argument between Bonino and Scannone has moved more in Scannone's than in Bonino's direction. Such influential figures as Gustavo Gutiérrez have published significant works on the necessity for drawing on the spiritual resources and traditions of the people for the project of liberation. Gutiérrez's book *We Drink from Our Own Wells* is a particularly good example of this thesis. Nevertheless the argument is not over. Other theologians, such as Jon Sobrino, when they adumbrate a spirituality of liberation, rely heavily on a reinterpreted version of the classic European Catholic tradition itself. Sobrino for example refers hardly at all to popular religious devotions and movements in his work, *The Spirituality of Liberation.* Leonardo Boff, for all his difficulty with the Vatican and his radical criticisms of Catholic ecclesial forms, makes few references to popular religious movements in his writing. Still, a consensus seems to be appearing that those who do not take the religions of the poor with utter seriousness have fallen somewhat short of a genuine preferential option for the poor.

THE "THEOLOGY OF RELIGIONS"

What does all of this mean for the "theology of religion"? In the work that lies ahead on this vital subject, it seems clear that a deepened conversation between theologians and social scientists is required. In order to do their work theologians need to become students of religions not just in their classical scriptural expressions but in their *actual local* manifestations. Theologians, Marxists, and others have been forced to take another look at *religión popular* in part because, empirically, it has not conformed to the mental images they held of it. The revolutionary Christians of Central America and the Christian advocates of democracy in Brazil often came from the sector of *religión popular.* This suggests that the discussion, among theologians and others, about religion must move outside the abstract level on which it has often been lodged. It must also focus on highly particular expressions of popular religion. Only then can informed theological judgments and evaluations be legitimately made.

There can be no doubt that the religions of marginated and oppressed peoples frequently serve an absolutely indispensable positive function. Such religious expressions preserve a *mythic past,* which then can become a source of what Metz calls the *subversive memory* that can bring a critical perspective to the present world around them. Popular religion also nurtures the *values* and *moral practices* that hold together a culture under siege and without which a people collapses into anomie. As has been pointed out frequently, popular religions also to some extent *protect cultural minorities* from the intrusive domination of cultural and religious majorities, and in some measure inoculate them against the narcotizing effect that hegemonic religions (of elites) exert on those on whom they are imposed. Finally it has been pointed out that popular religions nourish a *Prinzip Hoffnung* (Ernst Bloch); they project the *hope for a better time,* a future redemption, a utopian realm. Without such hope any people becomes cynical and defeated. These are all persuasive reasons that are advanced to suggest why harsh judgments about popular religions are often inappropriate. In short, it is held, popular religion serves a genuine function and should not be tampered with until that function is clearly understood.

Theology, however, is an *evaluative* discipline and must eventually make judgments. It asks questions not only about the *functionality* of religious beliefs but about their truth and their value for life as God intends it. Theology has various ways of asking these questions but at least these ways—albeit "traditional specific"—are *explicit*. Theologians have much to learn from the empirical specificity of students of religious phenomena. But perhaps theology's value-explicitness should evoke from social scientists on the other hand a more candid clarification of the values and commitments that underlie their work. We can no longer accept the premise that social science is merely descriptive, while theology is normative. Both are both normative and descriptive, and their specializations must be seen to lie elsewhere.

A Christian theology of popular religion will be informed by an explicit and value-conscious anthropology. Therefore Christian theologians will probe specific expressions of popular religion with some of the following questions:

What is the *nature* of the mythic past preserved in ritual and legend? Does it sacralize oppressive patterns of rank and gender discrimination? Does it stigmatize certain groups within the society in a degrading way? Is it, to use a theological category, "idolatry"?

What about the values it perpetuates? *Which values* are they? How does one judge *among* values especially at a time when the word "values" itself has become a cliché. The mere "preservation" of values is surely not an ethically positive function. Which values should be nurtured? Which subverted?

In protecting minority groups against cultural domination, do popular religions sometimes erect an obstacle to that minimal degree of recognition and coping with the dominant culture needed to ward off extinction or lethal marginalization? What is the optimal form of human community and how can it be attained?

Finally what about transcendent hope? *How* transcendent is it? Is it so otherworldly as to undercut constructive action within the society? Is it individualistic rather than corporate? How does the kingdom of God impinge on the kingdoms of this world?

There are many questions to be asked from a theological perspective of any popular religious movement. This is how a positive and appreciative engagement must take place. After all, Christian theology itself projects a mythic past, a set of prescribed values, a circumference that delineates who is in and who is out, and a hope for the coming of a reign of peace and justice. Christianity is not completely asymmetrical to other religious movements in these regards. But in its prophetic mode Christianity is also highly critical of the dehumanizing and oppressive components of religious practices and institutions. Both Judaism and Christianity emerged initially as religious protest movements against a dominant sacral system. Both began as "liberation theologies." Still if this theological engagement is to be specific rather than merely general, if it is to be concrete rather than abstract, some of the tools of observation and modes of analysis that have heretofore been the monopoly of social scientists will need to become part of the tool box of theologians as well.

We may be entering a new and fruitful place of the sometimes troubled relationship between theology and the social scientific study of religion, one in which the latter can help the former to be more concrete, while theology can challenge social science to be more explicit about its value commitments.

If there is anything to be learned from the story of the seven samurai it is that history is open and that no theological or ideological judgments are final. Things change and persons change, even religiously. So in the matter of what "popular religion" is and what it might contribute to the liberation of women and men in the future, it is always useful to take another look.

29

The Ethnic, Peasant, and Popular in a Polycentric Christianity

ENRIQUE DUSSEL

About twenty years ago, I wrote an article in *Concilium* about the way Christianity has been identified with Mediterranean culture.[1] Twenty years later, last July 29–31, we held a CEHILA (Commission for Church History Studies in Latin America) symposium in La Paz, Bolivia, "Peasantry, Land, and Church."[2] We studied the historical and social centrality of the peasantry (and the indigenous ethnic groups within it: the Aymara, Quechuas, Zapotecas, Mayas, Chibchas, Guaraníes, etc.) to the whole history of Latin American religion. I want to turn again to what we have been observing over more than two decades, to try to make some progress with this question, which is also so important to the revolutionary process that Latin America is at present undergoing. In particular, there is Nicaragua, where the "peasant question" and the ethnicity of the Miskitos are key factors in the war confronting the Sandinista process, which is so vital to a liberating Latin American Christianity.

THE CHRISTIAN EXPERIENCE IN THE FIRST THREE CENTURIES

As is well known, Christianity began to take shape within the Roman empire—it spread little outside into the Persian empire to the East, for example—in the culture of the Mediterranean Sea area (*mare nostrum*). Christianity, a Jewish sect that arose in Palestine, was formed from the "faith" taught by Jesus to his disciples, and necessarily embodied partly in the religion inherited from Israel and partly in the "religions" of the Mediterranean world. Christianity is not just a "faith" (in fact it is essentially a "praxis," a "reality" in Christ). It is also a conjunction of rites, symbols, cultural elements (which act as institutional "mediators"), making the faith understandable and practicable in a particular cultural context. If "the Word became flesh," likewise "faith became culture"—that is to say, *religion*. This is why we say plainly that Christianity always has been and always will be a religion.

And certainly the "Christian religion" took many elements from the Mediterranean religions. Few know, for example, that for the important "Christian" festival of Christmas the Christian "faith" took up and took over—"subsumed"—the sun-birth festival from Mediterranean culture (and its service in northern Europe). Jesus certainly was *not born* on the shortest day of the year (really December 21), and from then on grows until June 21. On the other hand, Easter, the pascal festival celebrating the rebirth of life, was already a festival in the Jewish religion and as such (being Mediterranean) it had analogies in other cultures. The pascal festival belonged to the Jewish *religion*, in which the historical "faith" of the prophets (or later of Christians) relived the exodus that freed them from Egypt or the death and resurrection of Christ. A cosmic-agricultural festival became *historified*.

It is also true that primitive Christianity of the first three centuries, through the *practical experience of a faith lived in small, poor communities*,[3] involved, on the one hand, the "evangelization" not just of individuals or communities but also of Mediterranean culture as a whole. A "religion" was born, which succeeded in taking—up and over—all that was most worthwhile—in Christian eyes—from ancient religions, which thus in some way lived on in Christianity *as religion*. It was not a destruction but a subsumption (*Aufhebung*). On the other hand, Christianity identified itself with this cultural result of its own preaching of the gospel. Never again—at least until the present day—did it accomplish such a feat of cultural transformation. This is a limitation we must overcome, if at all possible, now at the end of the twentieth century.

IMPOSITION OF THE MEDITERRANEAN EXPERIENCE UPON OTHER CULTURES

"Christendom" is what we call the phenomenon of the identification of the Christian faith and religion with Mediterranean faith and culture from the fourth century onward.[4] The generative nucleus of the Christian faith expressing first and foremost the *practice of a community*,[5] which grew out of the Jewish religion, gave rise, through its evangelizing of Mediterranean culture, to a new religion, which became identified with Christianity itself. From the south of Europe began the expansion of a "fixed" Christianity, set in a particular way, which would never again be aware of its real historical constitution. Faith and religion became equally Christian: the birth of the Word (the essential moment of faith) was identified with Christmas (a moment belonging to Mediterranean Christian religion). From then on it became impossible to take up any other culture through the preaching of the gospel (these were considered to be by definition "pagan," "anti-Christian": unsubsumable).

The only possibility remaining for the Christian religion was to "impose itself" or dominate other cultures (and this is what happened in what were called "mission fields") or simply be "driven back," unable to penetrate (as happened in the Arab world over the last thirteen centuries). This has been Christianity's sad experience from the fourth century until today. The cultures with the least resistance to Christendom's aggressiveness (Mediterranean or European) have become "converted" to Christianity; those with greater resistance (like the Muslim, Chinese, and Indian) are not Christian to this day.

From Mediterranean Christendom toward the North and East of Europe

With the establishment of "Christendom" from Constantine to Theodosius, "established Christianity" spread toward the North: to Gaul, Britain, across the Rhine to Germany, arriving centuries later in the Nordic countries of Denmark, Sweden and Norway. "Latin" Christendom also became "German" and even "Polish" (a slave people who were still "Latin"). And to the East Christianity spread through Constantinople to Moravia and then to Russia—with Moscow as a "third Rome." The countries that received this already established Christianity added little or nothing to its essentials and were able to express their creativity only through a burgeoning popular religiosity, rich in popular devotions (especially those to the Virgin Mary, rooted in agricultural cults to the Earth Mother, not only Latin ones, but also German, Polish, and Russian deriving from popular Byzantine religiosity). Nevertheless the "official" cult had been established in the South, the Mediterranean, and the Council of Trent was a savage reminder of this.

From European Christendom to Latin American Christianity

In the continent of Europe as far as the Urals or Vienna occupied in the fifteenth century by the Turks, the expansion of Christianity at least had a certain continuity: its geography slowly spread North and East, and as the centuries passed its processes became set. There was an imposition but the medieval world accepted it as its "own." In contrast, the conquest of America was aggressive, violent, instantaneous and much more painful and destructive because it was far away (both geographically and historically). It was not softened by the passage of time: in one generation everything was over (the ancient religious elites and the process of "evangelization"). From 1519 (when the destruction of the Aztec empire began) to 1551 (which accomplished the occupation of the core of the Inca empire to the south of Santiago, Chile), in just thirty years, the whole American "backbone" (the Andes, which contained more than 60 percent of the population of the American continent, and up to Alaska) was dominated, conquered, and "evangelized."

All who resisted the Christian presence (members of European-Latin-German Christendom) were eliminated. Those who resigned themselves to living in slavery and oppression were "converted" to Christianity. Such "Christianity" (expressed as Christendom) came "full blown" from the other side of the Atlantic in good Renaissance Latin (incomprehensible both to conquerors and conquered)—that is to say, "fetishized." It was imposed by force (or for the best of reasons, which did not alter the result), destroying any previous culture or religion: *tabula rasa*.

Thus, the "Christendom of the Western Indies" was born, Latin American, Hispano-Portuguese, colonial, dependent, imposed from outside by "European intruders."[6] Christian faith was identified with European religion, fossilized in Counter-Reformation Christendom. This created a religious dualism in Latin America between the "official" religion and the survival of the "ancient" religions, which demand respect, as Father Domingo Llanqui, a believing Aymara and Catholic priest, told us.[7] Any kind of triumphalism, such as the celebration in 1992 of the fifth centenary of the "discovery" or "evangelization" of America, is profoundly ambiguous, even wrong.

What is certainly true is that Christianity did not "convert" the pre-Columbian cultures, ethnic groups, or religions; it destroyed them. Something of them remains in imitation form in present-day peasant and marginal cultures, even among the urban working class. Only the ethnic groups such as the Mayas, Zapotecas, Otomíes,

those in Central America, Chibchas, and others in Colombia, the Aymaras, Quechuas, Calchaquíes, and Guaraníes, as well as those in the great Amazon basin,
have resisted, although they are on the brink of extinction. And even though they
were not all destroyed, in no case did a religion arise through the Christian faith's
adoption of these cultures—as it did in the Mediterranean and as the Inca Garcilaso
de la Vega insisted it should.[8] Indeed, some of these cultures had attained classical
perfection.

Resistance of Africa and Asia

Africa and Asia were closer to European Christendom—they were connected
by uninterrupted land masses. They were able to defend themselves better than
Latin America or the Philippines against the European Christians, simply because
they possessed almost the same military technology. It proved impossible to "conquer" the Chinese or the Mogul empire or the Arab world. The Europeans had to
resign themselves—first the Portuguese, then the Dutch, English, and French—to
occupying ports for trading purposes and thus "expanding Christianity." They never
succeeded in a military occupation of these strong autonomous cultures. The genuine intention to preach the gospel (without violence or weapons) of Nobili in
Madurai or Ricci in China failed finally because of the identity that had been
established between the Christian faith/religion and European culture. (Catholic
Christendom of Southern Europe was not all that different from the Protestant
Christendoms of the North: Anglican England and Evangelical Holland were Christendoms just as much as Spain and Portugal, or even more so.) Rome condemned
Ricci in China for much the same reasons that it condemns liberation theology or
African theology today. And as we shall see, Rome of today has also identified
capitalism with Christianity and condemns socialism, just as in the past it condemned Chinese culture as intrinsically perverse. Ricci strongly denied this. He
believed that Chinese customs, even *religious* ones, could be used, as long as they
were not contrary to a de-Westernized Christian faith transcending not only Chinese
culture but also Roman, Greek, and the European culture of his day.

It was not until the nineteenth century (at the Congress of Berlin in 1885) that
Europe was able to "conquer" Africa and Asia. The industrial revolution and the
phenomenon of imperialism had given Europe an incontestable military supremacy.
Now they were able to do to Africa and Asia what they did to Latin America in
the sixteenth century: occupy the continent. The Protestant pastors Livingstone and
Stanley, "explorers" (who "looked after" the empire: a sort of nineteenth-century
CIA) "discovered" Africa from within. Now "capital" could expand and with it, in
a disgraceful but historical partnership, the "gospel."

In Africa Islam resisted solidly. The animistic religions with their music and
rhythm, legends and "spirits," resisted less. Something of them was "saved" in
paraliturgical adaptations, but no fundamental modification took place in the "religion" already firmly established in Mediterranean culture. The Christian "faith"
of the first three centuries had the "right" to do something the Africans could not
do. It imposed an alien Christian experience on them.

The same thing happened in Asia but here religions thousands of years old
(Hinduism, Buddhism, Taoism, etc.) were much more highly structured than Af-

rican animism. They resisted much more strongly than in Africa and demanded at least that the Christian "faith" should evangelize them from within (as had happened within the Roman empire), so that new Christian cultural forms could arise. However, this was not allowed until today and Christianity remained a culturally alien minority.

Religious Destruction in the Southern Hemisphere

For thirty years I have been crying in the wilderness. In the Southern hemisphere—in cultures south of the equator—religious destruction has been the most devastating. In Cuzco every year on June 21 the Incas used to celebrate the birth of the sun, Inti. The imperial authorities met in the temple of the sun and prayed the gods to intercede for the human race, so that the sun would give them one more year. Obviously, in the Southern hemisphere (most of South America, Africa, Australia, etc.) the agricultural year (and therefore the liturgical year of all the religions) is the opposite to the Northern. The "birth" festival (Christmas) is on June 21, the "Easter" festival of the renewal of life (when sowing takes place) is on September 21, etc. Members of European Christendom, both Catholic and Protestant, arrived in these countries and as they had dehistorified their religious calendar; they imposed it in a fetishistic, magic, and destructive way. They abolished the winter festival of "birth" and forced it to be celebrated in the middle of summer (December 24 in the Southern hemisphere). All ancestral religious life was destroyed on behalf of a "Christian religion" established and fossilized twelve centuries earlier in the Northern hemisphere.

I remember the sadness of Holy Week in my city, Mendoza, Argentina. It was in the middle of autumn. We were supposed to be celebrating "life" and I saw the yellowing leaves falling from the trees as we were getting ready for winter. The ethnic cultures were destroyed because the "calendar" was the sacred order of things, stars in the sky, plants, animals, humans. Let us hope that one day the Christian communities of the Southern hemisphere get the right to change round their liturgical year! I mentioned this to some Aymara and Quechua brothers in Bolivia and they were very enthusiastic.

CHRISTIANITY'S FEUDAL AND CAPITALIST IDENTITY

From the fourth century onward Christianity became identified with Hellenistic Roman culture. On this foundation—which did not even keep its Georgian, Armenian, and Coptic versions—two new identifications took place in European Christendom (Latin-German and Polish, Russian in this case).

Even though they were very different, the European Christendoms were, from the eighth century onward, feudal Christendoms. The German barbarians were accepted first as brothers, then as fellow Christians, and finally as "the nature of things." For St. Thomas himself the "feudal lord" is a member of the political society *simpliciter* (whereas the serf is only a member *secundum quid*).[9] The church "becomes feudal." The "princes of the church," such as the abbots of Benedictine monasteries, were true feudal lords (and first the lay brothers, and then the peasants, were their "serfs"). They converted Christendom into a European feudal culture.

The capitalist revolution (under the leadership of the "burghers" or members of medieval cities) arose from the working arrangements of masters and apprentices, loans from Jewish moneylenders, and the organization of work in guilds with a patron saint. It spread through the Renaissance cities in the sixteenth century and later throughout Protestant Northern Europe. In fact Protestantism took shape in accordance with newly emerging capitalism, whereas in the South Catholicism found it more difficult to dissolve its identification with feudal, monarchic, precapitalist society.

With *Rerum Novarum* (1891) we see a Catholicism that has finally adopted the fundamental principles of capitalism (defining the three factors of production as capital with its profit, land with its rent, and labor with its wage). These three factors have become "fetishized."[10]

That is to say that the Christian religion, which is culturally Mediterranean and European, has now become politically and economically capitalist. "Private property" has become the fundamental guarantee of the absolute dignity of the human person.

Moreover modern Protestant fundamentalism or the Catholic charismatic movements often identify U.S. culture (and the transnational economy) with Christianity. A partial exegesis of scripture enables them to identify "Western," "democratic" and "capitalist" with the gospel itself.[11] This is a new kind of Christendom (twentieth century U.S. Christendom).

THE "POOR" AS THE ETHNIC, THE PEASANT, AND THE POPULAR

We have a Christianity that confuses the church with the kingdom (under institutional obedience to the ecclesiastical hierarchy as an absolute condition of holiness). It does not clearly distinguish itself from capitalism (and therefore indiscriminately supports Christian Democracy where this party exists). It is therefore wrongly committed to the dominant classes and the richest and most developed countries (like the United States and West Germany). But the irreducibly, utterly "other," "outside" all its tactics in the modern world, are the poor. The "wretched of the earth," as Frantz Fanon called them, are those whom the system cannot feed, cannot clothe, cannot house, or give them health or freedom. It has no work to give them (if by "work" is meant capital's capacity to subsume the creative potential of the poor by means of a wage, which gives them less than the value of what they produce and thus robs them). The "poor" in the "poor" countries—the majority of the present human race, more than 50 percent of the whole—remind "established" Christianity of its unfaithfulness to the gospel of Jesus and the need to take into account the "church of the poor."

But who are these poor persons? Primarily they are those in capitalist societies (countries of the "center" or the "periphery") who are "outside," even outside the dominant capitalist system. Hence we see why numerous ethnic groups (Mayas, Zapotecas, Aymaras, Quechuas in Latin America; entire tribal and village nations in Africa and Asia with their own language, religion, traditions, etc.) are the poorest of these poor. They demand respect for their own way, and respect from established Christianity. Thus the FSLN has given the Miskitos ethnic autonomy in Nicaragua (language, religion, regional political organization, etc.). It is necessary to rethink the preaching of the gospel, so that it becomes creative and not destructive for these cultural "nations," which express humanity's richness.

In the same way the peasants (a "social block" of the oppressed who work the land directly) are the face of the poor in the world today. I am not talking about U.S. or Dutch farmers who exploit the land capitalistically. I am speaking about the exploited (that is to say, those who transfer the value of their labor and their lives to the dominant classes and urban populations) who work the land directly in Africa, Asia, and Latin America. They are still the majority of humanity; although the urban populations are slowly overtaking them in numbers, the peasants will always be the qualitatively poor.

To the peasants we should add those who, through extreme poverty and the impossibility of gaining a livelihood, are forced to leave the countryside and go to swell the marginalized masses of the unemployed in the cities of the Third World. They are merely "available for work" (not free to work but merely workless workers, who by their very existence and availability lower the wages of those in work), unorganized masses (who can also become revolutionary).

These three groups (the ethnic, peasant, and marginalized) are the "poorest" of the people (meaning the whole "social group" of the oppressed in any society).[12] The working class in the Third World can be a privileged group, forming a constitutive part of "the people" but not always the vanguard in revolutionary processes. In fact the peasants are the "social block" among which creative contradictions are generated.

The presence of the church in this "social block" is of crucial importance for the future of world Christianity and its life in the Third World. Capitalist, urban, elitist Christianity—identified with Western culture—cannot arouse any hope in this people of the poor. Only a "church of the poor," in which the poor are not the objects of the church's labor, but the subjects of the church's evangelizing action, could be the solution to long-standing problems in now secular Christianity.

A POLYCENTRIC CHRISTIANITY

The obsession with unity, centralization, and even absolute uniformity, so common today in certain Vatican circles, where everything is seen from the strategic viewpoint of a conservative "restoration," has no clear awareness that this church "image" or model is purely Western, European, urban, elitist (because it is identified with the dominant classes), and even capitalist (in the values it supports). Attempts at decentralization, such as that made by the Latin American Bishops' Conference (CELAM), founded in 1955, were regarded very unfavorably and hence from 1972 onward a movement arose to lessen its autonomy (in the Sucre Assembly). Analogous conferences in Africa and Asia were annulled, and also in Europe. Likewise, especially in Latin America, the systematic nominating of anti-Medellín bishops from 1968 until now, shows the determination of certain groups in Rome to "retake" control of a single, homogenous European church whose ethos is pre–Vatican II.

But what is really needed by the world of the "poor," the ethnic groups or nations with their own personality, the utterly different peasant world, peoples living their way within the peripheral nations, is the chance to re-create Christianity "as it was in the beginning," consisting of small base communities with the creative capacity to take on their customs, cultures, ancestral religions (if they have not already been destroyed), their own ethos. This would be a "polycentric" Christianity. It would be decentralized and go beyond the confines of European or North American experience to meet the needs of "outsiders." We know that everything goes to show that this is becoming more and more difficult to bring about in the near future, at least in the Catholic Church. Nevertheless, it is a fundamental need of our time. Decentralization or polycentrism would allow the churches of Asia and Africa freedom to make their own decisions (an autonomous Bishops' Conference for Asia and Africa with genuine freedom). Freedom for the church in Latin America to nominate its own bishops would follow in the tradition of Medellín.

This would be a Christianity that would listen to the needs of the impoverished peoples, who are suffering a crisis in their lives for which they are not responsible but for which they must pay heavily. Liberation theology is the theoretical expression of these aspirations of peoples who have the same right as Mediterranean culture in the first three centuries to create a Christianity that is a true expression of themselves.

CHRISTIANITY AND POSTCAPITALIST SOCIETY

Last but by no means least, the identification of Christianity with capitalism is an error that causes the oppressed (ethnic groups, peasants, the marginalized, workers in peripheral countries) to suffer in a very special way. The capitalist system in many cases is the expression of an unjust social relationship of domination.[13] Peasants transfer value and their life to world society; paid workers also transfer their life, which is given to the service of capital; poor countries transfer value to more developed countries. It is a giant "circulation of blood," the life of the poor nourishing the abundance of the rich, the powerful, the rulers (the sinners). The identification of Christianity with this type of society ("Western Christian civilization") condemns "the world's poor" to bearing their poverty in the name of their Christian faith. Rebelling against the system that oppresses them is seen as going against the gospel, against the church. The "Christian God" is identified with "capital," "private property," "democracy" (as the bourgeoisie understand it). The same thing happens as happened to our nineteenth-century heroes. When they took up arms against the king of Spain in 1810, they were condemned for having rebelled "against their God and against their king."[14]

The "outsiders" who today are suffering grave injustice—the ethnic groups, peasants, the marginalized urban populations, the workers, all the oppressed of the Third World—are beginning to glimpse the possibility of rebelling against this injustice in the name of their faith. The 1987 Nicaraguan Constitution speaks of the God who impelled Christians to take an active part in the revolution in response to the cry of the oppressed people.[15]

When Christianity, Christian faith, allows and inspires Christians to take part in the revolutionary processes at work in the Third World against the capitalist system as a whole, then the process of evangelization, which began almost five centuries ago, will have begun to approach its goal. When the oppressed and Christian people are inspired by their Christian faith to become a liberated people (freed from the domination of national and world capitalism), then we will be able to say that they have been fully evangelized. Once they were the passive recipients of teaching; now they must become the active creators of their history.

All the people (ethnic groups, peasants, marginalized, workers) in their base communities will defend as active creators the right to a religion expressing all that is best in their own traditions and thus bring their Christian faith to its full flowering. This may seem like utopia but it is the hope that inspires heroes and martyrs, such as Carlos Fonseca Amador—a political saint—or Rutilio Grande—an ecclesial saint.

—translated from the Spanish by Dinah Livingstone

NOTES

1. "De la secularización de la ciencia, desde el Renacimiento a la Ilustración," *Concilium*, 47 (1969) 91–114. Here I use the word "religion" in a more restricted sense, as a structure of symbols and rites, rather than as "practical relations."

2. Fourteenth Symposium, which took place July 29–31, 1987. To be published shortly.

3. Cf. Eduardo Hoornaert, *The Memory of the Christian People* (Maryknoll, N.Y.: Orbis, 1988).

4. See my work *Historia General de la Iglesia en América Latina*, Introduction (Salamanca: Sígueme, 1983), I/ 207. I elaborated this concept in my work *Hipótesis para una historia de la Iglesia en América Latina* (Barcelona: Estela, 1967).

5. See my work *Ethik der Gemeinschaft* (Düsseldorf: Patmos, 1987).

6. Expression used by the Incan Tupac Amaru (Peru and Bolivia) in a manifesto he was carrying in his pocket when he was killed by the Spaniards in 1781. See B. Lewin, *La rebelión de Tupac Amaru* (Buenos Aires, 1967), p. 421.

7. In the La Paz symposium (see note 2, above): "Ritos agrícolas y producción alimentaria" (unpublished), we heard: "The potatoes that you eat every day have been harvested by force of prayers, fasting, and incense."

8. In his *Comentarios Reales* the sixteenth-century Peruvian author shows clearly that the name *Dios*, the god of the day, of the Indo-Europeans was Pachacamac in the Inca language. Likewise, little by little he demonstrated the meaning of many Christian rites and beliefs in the Inca religion.

9. *Summa Theologica*, II-II, 57, 4.

10. *Laborem Exercens* (1981) defetishized economics by showing that *work* is the single foundation of capital (and of the assumed value of the earth). Moreover work is not wage (which is just objectified work, whereas work is *lebendige Arbeit*, i.e., "living work").

11. See Michael Novak, *The Spirit of Democratic Capitalism* (New York: Simon and Schuster, 1982).

12. See my work *La producción teórica de Marx* (Mexico City: Siglo XXI, 1985), chapter 18.4: "La cuestión popular."

13. See my work *Ethik der Gemeinschaft*, chap. 2.

14. Text written on the breviary that the liberator of Mexico, José María Morelos, a priest shot in 1815, was holding in his hand when he died.

15. The new Nicaraguan Constitution says in its Preamble: "in the name . . . of those Christians who through their faith in God committed themselves and took part in the struggle for the liberation of the oppressed" (*La Gaceta*, January 9, 1987).

30

The Exodus as Event and Process: A Test Case in the Biblical Grounding of Liberation Theology

NORMAN K. GOTTWALD

It is characteristic of liberation theology to seek its biblical rootage in broad themes that it takes to be constitutive and regulative of Christian faith and practice. Among these preferred themes, the exodus of Israel from Egypt has held paramount sway.

In his ground-breaking *A Theology of Liberation*, Gustavo Gutiérrez underscored the biblical exodus as one of the keystones for constructing an "integral" notion of salvation capable of cancelling out and transcending the older "distinction of planes" model, which left Christians ineffectually torn between "profane" this-worldly and "sacred" other-worldly preoccupations. The exemplary status of the exodus is described by Gutiérrez in this way:

> The liberation of Israel is a political action. It is the breaking away from a situation of despoliation and misery and the beginning of the construction of a just and comradely society. . . . The Exodus is the long march towards the promised land in which Israel can establish a society free from misery and alienation. Throughout the whole process, the religious event is not set apart. It is placed in the context of the entire narrative, or more precisely, it is its deepest meaning. . . . The liberation from Egypt, linked to and even coincid-ing with creation, adds an element of capital importance: the need and the place for human active participation in the building of society. . . . The Exodus experience is paradigmatic. It remains vital and contemporary due to similar historical experiences which the People of God undergo.[1]

It would not be difficult to find similar statements of the foundational significance of the exodus in the work of other liberation theologians. In particular, the centrality of exodus has been elaborated by J. Severino Croatto[2] and George V. Pixley.[3]

IS LIBERATION THEOLOGY SUFFICIENTLY BIBLICAL?

At first glance, liberation theology's appeal to the Bible may seem straightfor-ward and unproblematic, for it unquestionably draws upon central scriptural themes and has recovered a vivid sense of biblical faith as praxis in the service of justice. Nonetheless, the use of the Bible in liberation theology has not gone uncriticized, not only as we might expect by its opponents, but likewise by its supporters. Those dismissive of liberation theology find its employment of the Bible either too "arbitrary" or too "political." There is no point in detailing or responding to these hostile criticisms, for my own orientation is supportive of the perspective of liberation theology. It is appropriate, however, to evaluate liberation theology's deployment of scripture in terms of its thoroughness and adequacy, and in the process of doing so, to clarify some matters that may ultimately help to blunt the force of criticism from the detractors of this theology. My chief interest in this assessment is to deepen and enrich the work of liberation theology exegetically so that its already enormously productive influence will be extended and multiplied into the future.

For my point of departure, I refer to the work of the Spanish theologian, Alfredo Fierro, who argued more than a decade ago that, in order for the noteworthy promises of liberation theology to grow in explanatory power and to fuel social change in church and society, they must be developed in a more comprehensive, self-reflective, and rigorous manner.[4] Although Fierro's criticisms are by now somewhat dated, it is nonetheless my conviction that the fundamental challenges in his evaluation are still valid and that liberation theology can only profit in the future by paying heed to his sympathetic strictures.

Fierro claims that liberation theologians have tended to waver between "first order" statements of faith and "second order" reflections on faith, and, when brought into question, have been inclined to shift from one level of discourse to the other without answering sufficiently to the criteria of consistency and coherence of discourse. This shows up especially, he believes, in the way that liberation theologies typically regard Marxism, on the one hand, and the Bible, on the other. Although appealing to Marxism as a more or less suitable, even necessary, method of analysis, liberation theologians have frequently refused to engage Marxism as philosophy, social theory, and political strategy and, to the degree that they shrink from doing so, they lapse from being theologians, in the judgment of Fierro. Similarly, although invoking biblical symbols and liberation, these same theologians seldom plumb those symbols all the way to their socio-historical foundations—or at least they do so incompletely—so that we miss a concrete analysis of the inner-biblical strands of oppression and liberation in all their stark multiplicity and contradictory interactions.

Consequently, the danger to which Fierro appears to point is not that liberation theologies will be too radical or too critical and thus lose a hearing, but that they will not be as radical and critical as they claim and intend to be, and thus will lose the interest and respect that they initially awaken. He laments that a thinness of social structural analysis and theory and a thinness of biblical analysis combine to give many articulations of liberation theology the look of devotional and polemical tracts. In effect, he fears that shallowness of penetration into the subject matter may issue in an "*un*hermeneutical circle" in which neither the biblical "then" nor the contemporary "now" is adequately illuminated.

Of course I recognize that to summarize Fierro's criticisms so briefly lends them an excessive and pontificating ring, whereas proper justice can be done them only by reading his entire text in which he is at pains to cite and quote particular works rather than to issue untargeted broadsides. In any event, Fierro's own constructive contribution toward deepening and sharpening liberation theology is devoted to the programmatic sketch of a materialist theology that would engage Marxism and anticommunism head-on. He has far less to say about strengthening the biblical dimension of liberation theology, and it is precisely the biblical aspect of his criticism that I wish to take up in this essay.

In the liberation theology of Latin America, Fierro observes, the main biblical approach is to dwell upon certain "exemplary" themes such as exodus, the prophetic criticism of society, and Jesus' confrontation with authorities.[5] Critical exegesis is tapped rather meagerly in most cases, and there is virtually no effort to penetrate biblical social structure and social history in detail. Although this lack of depth in biblical exegesis is being gradually corrected, it seems to me that Fierro is basically correct in his discernment: because liberation theology vociferously claims that the Bible has been misread by dominant theology, it has an obligation to offer specific, detailed corrections of these misreadings. Moreover, the very cogency of liberation theology, in considerable measure, depends upon its being able to demonstrate, and not merely to premise, more socially precise and accurate readings of the Bible than "unliberated" biblical exegesis has been able to produce. Why, we must ask, in contrast to materialist exegesis in Europe and feminist theology in North America, has Latin American liberation theology lagged behind in this important work of "setting the exegetical record straight"?

It seems to me that there may be three contributing factors to the sparseness of in-depth biblical exegesis in liberation theology. First, there is the strong appeal of this theology to a devotional regard for scripture in the ecclesial base communities that displays a predisposition to accept the Bible as authoritative for liberation without extensive demonstration. This, in turn, seems to contribute to overstatements of the liberative dimensions of scripture, without adequate attention to its reactionary currents. Secondly, Latin American biblical scholars have been for the most part only marginally involved in liberation theology. Doubtless one reason for this is that, in spite of its intentions otherwise, liberation theology has not been able to overcome the curricular divisions of the academy that maintain a radical separation between biblical studies and theology. Another factor in the relative marginalization of biblical scholars from liberation theology is the apparent reality that post-Vatican II attitudes toward the Bible are not as widely represented among Latin American biblical scholars as among Latin American theologians. Thirdly, because of the suspicion of Latin American liberation theologians toward First World theology, there has been a concomitant "blocking out" of the recent contributions of First World biblical scholars from the consciousness of Latin American theologians when they do their biblical appropriation. This means in practice that, against their own wishes, the liberation theologians are at times working with an older and inadequate biblical exegesis that weakens, or at least fails to do full justice to, their own case.

It is striking that the literature of liberation theology, with some notable exceptions, is largely uninformed by socio-critical biblical scholarship stemming from North America. As a case in point, it is symptomatic that my *The Tribes of Yahweh*[6] has rarely appeared as a biblical resource in the major works of Latin American liberation theologians, at least in those so far translated into English. This oversight of the theologians is all the more curious since *Tribes* is used in Portuguese translation[7] as a resource in the teaching programs of the Brazilian base communities and a mimeographed Spanish translation[8] circulates among liberation-oriented biblical scholars in Latin America. This neglect of highly pertinent socio-critical biblical analysis leads to anomalous and contradictory social and cultural accounts of early Israel, which are often oddly "out of step" with the theological outlook brought to the biblical text as well as with the theological conclusions purportedly drawn from the text.

To illustrate my point, alongside claims about the liberation of slaves from Egypt, one finds naive remarks in liberation theology about the Israelites as "nomads" or about the "conquest" of Canaan that proceed as though the initial biblical social revolution broadly posited by liberation theologians does not require us to reformulate our views of the socio-cultural formation of the Israelite tribes and of their connectedness with the people of Canaan. In other words, a careful critical reconstruction of the political economy and social organization of tribal Israel is largely lacking at the very point in their work where the method of liberation theologians mandates that it be present, for how are we to make sense of the religious ideas of early Israel if they are not integrally grounded in the praxis of the actual Israelite communities that took shape in Canaan? Likewise, the imprecision of liberation theologians about tribal Israel is duplicated in frequently sketchy or erroneous social descriptions of monarchic, exilic, and postexilic Israel.

EXODUS AS HISTORICAL EVENT AND AS SOCIO-HISTORICAL PROCESS

The exodus may be understood as event, or a series of events, or it may be understood as a process—as a complex of events exhibiting certain recognizable features. As *event*, the scope of the exodus may be more or less broadly defined. Narrowly, the term is used to designate the exit of the Israelites from Egypt in their crossing of the sea. More extensively, exodus designates the whole complex of events described in the Book of Exodus, from oppression in Egypt to law-giving at Sinai, and—even beyond—to encompass the events of Numbers through Joshua, as far as the relocation of the Israelites in Canaan. As *process*, exodus refers typologically to the movement of a people from a situation of bondage to a situation of freedom, from a collective life determined by others to a collective life that is self-determined, and this movement is understood to be a venture in the face of risk and uncertainty as to the consequences of making "a break for freedom." This entails the possibility and, in appropriate circumstances, the actuality of social and political revolution.

The exodus events are set forth in the Bible in a mixture of literary genres that include sagalike narratives, theophanic descriptions, instructions, lists, and laws. The extent to which we can locate "historical facts" within this melange of mythico-symbolic origin stories is a matter of great dispute. It can be safely said that at no stage in the development of the single units and complexes of traditions was there any intent of rendering a coherent account according to historiographic conventions. Our hope of recovering the reality of the exodus must be a modest one that respects the nonhistoriographic nature of the traditions, their ultimate unity as a compiled text in late exilic or postexilic times, the prior anchorage of the compiled traditions in a number of different preexilic social horizons, and the indirectly social referential character of literature of this folkloric and instructional type. In short, we must be wise practitioners of "hermeneutical circulation" if we are to discern the socio-historical contours of the exodus in order to give warrant to our reflections on a theology of exodus.

Nevertheless, there is definite truth to the claim that the exodus is "a fact of history," and this truth has several facets. Most obviously it is a "fact" in literary and theological terms. The reports of these events of exit from Egypt and entrance into Canaan are a given of world literature and, moreover, a given of sacred literature for Jews and Christians. The entire edifice of the Jewish and Christian religions may be said to rest upon the foundation stone of these reports. But can we say more? Is there any way of knowing what relation these reports have to events that actually occurred in Egypt, Sinai, and Canaan sometime between the fifteenth and twelfth centuries B.C.E.? I believe that the answer to this question is a cautious but deliberate yes, but this yes, far from being a simple assertion of facticity, must be a complexly nuanced historical judgment that takes into account the whole field of Israelite origins and not merely some presumed happenings alluded to in the Book of Exodus. It must be emphasized that the entire exodus process encompasses much more than a possible escape of slaves from Egypt insofar as it alludes to the incontestable reality of the birth of Israel out of "bondage in Canaan." Whatever happened in Egypt, Israel sprang to birth in Canaan in the approximate socio-historic manner attested in the exodus traditions: by resistance to state oppression and by a bold bid for self-determination.

FOUR BIBLICAL HORIZONS FOR VIEWING THE EXODUS

An analysis of the Book of Exodus strongly suggests that the exodus is recounted from the perspective of at least four successive social "horizons" or "moments" that clearly correspond in part to a division by sources and also, more subtly, to "levels" of the text, inasmuch as we can often detect traces of earlier horizons that have been retained in later horizons. To my knowledge, the only interpreter of the exodus who makes an attempt to hold the literary sources, textual levels, and social horizons in systematic correlation is Pixley.[9] Because it is a commentary, however, his study does not provide a format for bringing the widely scattered observations on the text into a final synthesis.

The literary source, textual level, and social horizon discriminations operative in the Book of Exodus are as follows:

Horizon no. 1 is that of the hypothetical participants in the events reports. No continuous source exists that speaks consistently and coherently from this horizon, precisely because of the liturgical and instructional mythico-symbolic shaping of the traditions. If such a source once existed, it has been so totally excerpted, reworded, and subsumed by traditionists of later horizons that it is irrecoverable. For this reason I refer to "the hypothetical participants in the events reported."

Nevertheless, continuous sources from later horizons now and then display features that do not jibe with the overarching conceptions of those later horizons and thus have the marks of being "literary survivals." For example, when the J source says that "the people of Israel set forth. . . a mixed multitude went up with them" (Exod. 12:37b, 39), this innocent-looking aside explodes the source's presupposition that the Israel that departed Egypt was an already ethnically cohesive and self-contained entity of twelve well-defined tribes. And when *all* the later sources refer to the exodus Israelites as a people under arms, this surprising concurrence shatters the apparent presumption of the final postexilic horizon (one not necessarily shared by earlier horizons) that Israel did not have to engage Egyptian forces inasmuch as Yahweh saved the people miraculously.[10]

In addition to the glimmers of horizons no. 1 in later sources, the so-called Song at the Sea in Exodus 15:1–18 (short variant in 15:21) contains a poetic celebration of the exodus that could have been composed by the first, or at most, second generation of exodus Israelites.[11] Because it tells not only of crossing the sea but of a leading of the people into Canaan, the date of the finished whole implies horizon no. 2 (see below), but vv. 1–12 may well have been composed earlier and, in any case, the events underlying the poetry do not seem to correspond to those delineated in later sources. Thus, exodus 15:1–12 enjoys a certain independence uncontaminated by influence from the narratives in the major pentateuchal sources. Although we tend to read the poem's recounted "churning" of the sea through the lens of the miraculous walls of water in the postexilic account, the text of Exodus 15:1–12 actually implies no more than a severe windstorm that whipped up gigantic waves in which the Egyptians drowned. Very possibly the poem may also imply that the Egyptian charioteers and archers were crossing a body of water in boats when they were overwhelmed by a sudden storm, so that they "went down like a stone . . . sank like lead" in the deep waters (Exod. 15:5, 10).[12]

On the basis of the foregoing data from horizon no. 1, I do not think that we have enough bona fide firsthand information to posit categorically a historically verified exodus, if only because the data are so meager. Moreover, the role of "the sea" as a symbol of primordial chaos is so patent that we cannot even be certain that a body of water was involved in the historical events at all. In fact, the sea itself may possess no proper name, for it is now plausibly argued that the so-called Sea of Reeds (*suph*) is preferably rendered as Ultimate Sea or Distant Sea (*soph*), and is thus more symbolically than geographically identified.[13] What we can conclude, I believe, is that, when joined to our broader knowledge of the conditions of captive peoples in pharaonic service, these data do accord with the genuine possibility that the "historical kernel" of the exodus traditions was a motley group of state slaves who employed stealth and cunning, along with stolen and captured weapons, and even an assist from elements of nature, to make good their escape from Egypt. This possibility is so tenuous, however, that it is unwise to try to build any large-scale socio-historical or theological conclusions based on it.

Horizon no. 2 is that of the Israelite social revolutionaries and religious confederates in the highlands of Canaan in the twelfth and eleventh centuries. As with horizon no. 1, this perspective on the exodus is not preserved in continuous narrative sources but in certain accents and details in the later narrative strands, some of which are of significance in helping us to correct "quietist" and "pacifist" interpretations of the exodus.

Of particular interest in this regard is the picturing of the Israelite rescue at the sea in terms of holy war ideology, which stressed "having no fear," "standing fast," and "being still" before battle (Exod. 14:13-14), with the result that Yahweh energizes and empowers the meager Israelite forces and at the same time augments and multiplies them with elements of nature opportunely wielded against the foe (cf. hail in Joshua 10:11, a wadi swelled by rain in Judges 5:21, and snow in Psalm 68:14). It is probably in this sense that the J source tells of the sea being driven back by "a strong east wind all that night" (Exod. 14:21b) and even of "the column of cloud" (Exod. 14:19b–20) that intervened between the Egyptian and Israelite forces. A "naturalistic" reconstruction of the battle is not possible on the basis of the terse, disjointed, even nonsequential, way the story is told, but the immobilizing of the chariots (with "locked" or "clogged" wheels; Exod. 14:25) may allude to their entrapment in treacherous sand along the seashore. Interestingly, this J version has nothing to say about the Israelites crossing the sea or about the Egyptians trying to cross it, for the Egyptians perish, not because they are pursuing the Israelites into the sea, but because they flee into the waters out of sheer panic (Exod. 14:27b).

It is solely the fourth and last horizon on the exodus that speaks of a crossing of the sea. Although the absence of the crossing motif in J and E might be explained by editorial excision in favor of P's dramatic description, the lack of the crossing motif in the early poem of Exodus 15 should give us pause. It is, I think, a more reasonable interpretation that JE simply does not conceive of the sea as a barrier that has to be crossed in order to continue the route of march, but strictly as a point of entrapment from which the Israelites, at first tactically "hemmed in" by the surprise Egyptian attack, extract themselves by "turning the table" on the enemy.

Although we cannot make a secure separation between horizons no. 2 and no. 3 on this issue, it is likely that the practices and ideology of holy war among the citizen militia of the premonarchic tribes have shaped this J version of events at the sea rather than the more professionalized military practices of the monarchy. The import of the holy war influence on the exodus accounts in J is to heighten the agency of God in directly aiding the Israelites, such that a literal reading makes it look as though Israel was utterly passive in the conflict. Yet it is precisely this one-sided impression that is corrected by a look at the holy war traditions of Joshua and Judges, for in those traditions, although their forces are invariably smaller and more poorly armed, the Israelites are definitely active on the field of battle. This means that horizons no. 1, no. 2, and no. 3 remember an exodus deliverance in which Israel used such military weapons and stratagems as it could muster and in which God fought on the people's behalf, but not in their stead.[14]

The horizon of the early Israelite social revolution is not confined, however, to narrative details in later sources. It shows up in other ways. For instance, the final version of the Song at the Sea closely links exit from Egypt and victory over pharaoh (Exod. 15:1–12) with entrance into Canaan and victory over the Canaanites, Philistines, Moabites, and Edomites (15:13–18), and it is characteristic of early Israelite poems celebrating victory over enemies in the land to describe events in the revelatory and theophantic language of Exodus (see Deut. 33 and Judg. 5). Moreover, although compiled during the early monarchy, there is a core of social legislation in the Covenant Code (Exod. 10:22–23:19) that presupposes the communitarian agrarian practices and judicial system of the confederated tribes prior to the monarchy, and thus attests to the growing formation of an alternative society in Canaan. This developing Israelite society "sees itself" in the exodus, magnifies and creatively "distorts" the exodus memories, in order to give scope and dimension to its own comparable project of liberation.

Horizon no. 3 is that of Israelite traditionists in monarchic times who conceive Israel of the exodus experience as an essentially national entity in transit toward its secure establishment as a state of Canaan. The J and E traditionists have retained, as we saw above, features of the earlier horizons, but the overarching conceptual frame they employ is that of the relatively secure identity and institutional forms that Israel attained under its own kings. Because the destination that J and E have in mind is the establishment of the nation-state of Israel, they visualize the Israelites of the exodus as embracing all the people of Israel whose descendants went on eventually to occupy Canaan. At the same time, they stress the exodus deliverance as the wonderful action of Israel's God. It is not, as I argue above, that they rule out Israelite military action in the exodus experience, for in fact they seem to presuppose an armed exit from Egypt, but rather that they put their predominant stress upon the divine source and enablement of whatever actions Israel took.

In any case, the telling of the exodus experience by J and E is pervaded by two major emphases: the marvelous work of God in delivering Egypt and the presentation of Israel as a sharply defined national entity set off from other peoples. This means that our attention is taken away from *the instrumental actions of the people on their way to liberation,* although of course many of these actions are mentioned, and no consideration is given to *the process by which Israel was formed and came to a distinct identity* in the time before it had monarchic definition, even though there are fragments from earlier horizons that hint at the process of Israel's self-composition.

Why was it that, although possessing some earlier traditions about the self-determining actions and mixed origins of the early Israelites, J and E so strongly stressed the transcendent source of the events and the unified, fully-formed status of the people? No doubt two major influences converged to produce this result. One was the liturgical setting in which the exodus traditions had taken shape before J and E put them into connected written form. After all, we can see the impress of liturgy on the poem of Exodus 15, which was composed prior to the monarchy. Liturgy, beginning in the tribal period and continuing on into the monarchy, celebrated the founding of the people under its sovereign God. It did not seek to trace the immanent and instrumental developments of the people's formative history. The other factor at work was that Israel, at the time of J and E, was still a relatively young national state whose leadership and institutions called for explanation and legitimation. The liturgical mode, emphasizing stability and order under a protective God, was well suited to the ideological needs of the new state(s). Even though there are indications that J and E were not simply exponents of monarchic rule, but have shaped the traditions so as to present monarchy with certain cautions, perhaps even warnings, they nonetheless functioned in the first instance to show how the prestate beginnings of Israel prepared the way for the appearance of the monarchy, which aspired to be the conservator of the older traditions.

Horizon no. 4 is that of the late exilic and postexilic restorers of Judah as a religious and cultural community that had lost its political independence. The priestly traditionist has the challenging task of recording the exodus experience as a charter for the rebuilding of Jewish community in the wake of the loss of political independence due to the destruction of both Israelite kingdoms by foreign conquerors. The JE emphases upon the transcendent source and empowerment of Israel and upon the distinctive unity of Israel are taken up and carried to still greater lengths by P. Whereas in the earlier sources, pharaoh "stiffened his heart" by his own choice, P reports that Yahweh "hardened his heart," virtually against pharaoh's own better judgment. The terse and obscure allusions in J and E to "a strong east wind" and shifting waters give way in P to a cleft sea with a canyon of dry land between towering walls of water through which the Israelites safely march but into which the Egyptians plunge compulsively to meet their watery death. In JE the Egyptians rush into the sea because they flee from Israel in panic, but in P they pursue Israel into the sea with reckless abandon, goaded on by an obsessive single-mindedness.

The measured narratives of P, together with its great corpus of ritual law, give the picture of a worshiping community going forth in religious procession, a kind of "Salvation Army" on the march. The exodus Israel of P is not so much the national state, which had perished at the hands of Assyria and Neo-Babylonia, as it is the law-observant community of Jewish believers who are defined not by territory or political structure but by a set of religious and ethical norms and practices, which are set forth in the Torah revealed during the exodus march from Egypt to Canaan.

In this horizon on the exodus we observe a decided separation between "religion" and "politics." Whereas in all the preceding horizons, the political dimension of the exodus is very clearly present or presupposed, for P it recedes into the background in favor of the delineation of a religio-cultural perspective. Deprived of political autonomy, and dependent on Persian overlords for the success of Jewish restoration in Palestine, the restoration traditionists make the most of their restricted situation and highlight the conditions of intercommunal "law and order" among the exodus Israelites on the basis of which they hope to shape a contemporary Jewish identity that can outlive the loss of statehood. This completely understandable tendency in P's version of exodus joins with the heightened stress on the initiative of God to further separate religious ends and means from the contingencies of political and social history.[15]

THE PROVOCATIVE MULTIVALENCY OF THE EXODUS

With this postexilic outlook on exodus, we have reached the dominating hermeneutical tradition through which the exodus has been viewed by Jews and Christians: the marvelous and exceptional deliverance of a people from slavery to a new religious identity in which the palpable political purport of the founding events of Israel is "played down," dismissed in some cases, muted in others, and at times delayed or postponed into a messianic future.

Yet, just as the changing socio-political Israelite/Jewish horizons for viewing the exodus significantly shaped what the various biblical traditionists saw it to be, so in subsequent Jewish and Christian history the socio-political, ethnic, or class positions of interpreters have had a decisive bearing on what was "picked up" as the informing meaning of those delivering events. The protean exodus symbol refuses to be "laid to rest" in the nationalist and ecclesial securities of the horizons of monarchy and religious restoration. Insistently, hermeneutical suspicion reaches back to the originative revolutionary event/process of the first exodus, but only in circles where new exoduses are striven for. Reformist and revolutionary religious and political groups and movements throughout postbiblical history have "latched on" to the exodus as a paradigm for religiously inspired and religiously based reorderings of church and society.[16]

258

Liberation theology is one such "recuperation" of that political dimension of exodus that is normally silenced by religious and political establishments content with pharaoh's rule. The contemporary recovery of the exodus as a divine-human collaboration in social revolution, already well begun in liberation theology, will be actualized in all its illuminative and energizing power only as the biblical root-metaphor is grasped within the entire spectrum of the biblical social horizons and with discriminating reference to the social horizons where we live and work today:

It should by now be evident that efforts to draw "religious inspiration" or "biblical values" from the early Israelite heritage will be romantic and utopian unless resolutely correlated to both the ancient and the contemporary cultural-material and social-organizational foundations.[17]

NOTES

1. Gustavo Gutiérrez, *A Theology of Liberation: History, Politics, and Salvation* (Maryknoll, N.Y.: Orbis, 15th anniversary ed., 1988), pp. 88–90.

2. J. Severino Croatto, *Exodus: Hermeneutics of Freedom* (Maryknoll, N.Y.: Orbis, 1981).

3. George V. Pixley, *On Exodus: A Liberation Perspective* (Maryknoll, N.Y.: Orbis, 1987).

4. Alfredo Fierro, *The Militant Gospel: A Critical Introduction to Political Theologies* (Maryknoll, N.Y.: Orbis, 1977).

5. Ibid., pp. 129–81, and especially on the exodus, pp. 140–51.

6. Norman K. Gottwald, *The Tribes of Yahweh: A Sociology of the Religion of Liberated Israel, 1250–1050 B.C.E.* (Maryknoll, N.Y.: Orbis, 2d corrected printing, 1981).

7. *As Tribos de Iahweh: Uma Sociologia da Religião de Israel Liberto 1250–1050 A.C.* (São Paulo: Paulinas, 1986).

8. *Las Tribus de Yahveh: Una Sociología de la Religión del Israel Liberado 1250–1050 A.C.* (Bogotá: Seminario Teológico Presbiteriano, 1986).

9. Pixley, *On Exodus*, pp. xiii–xx.

10. Lewis S. Hay, "What Really Happened at the Sea of Reeds?," *Journal of Biblical Literature*, 83 (1964) 397–403, shows convincingly that the biblical account presupposes armed conflict between Israelites and Egyptians, although his speculations about the particulars of the battle are less persuasive.

11. Gottwald, *Tribes*, pp. 507–15; Frank M. Cross, *Canaanite Myth and Hebrew Epic: Essays in the History of the Religion of Israel* (Cambridge: Harvard University Press, 1973), pp. 112–44.

12. David N. Freedman, "Early Israelite History in the Light of Early Israelite Poetry," in *Unity and Diversity: Essays in the History, Literature, and Religion of the Ancient Near East*, H. Goedicke and J. J. M. Roberts, eds. (Baltimore: Johns Hopkins University Press, 1975), pp. 3–35.

13. Bernard F. Batto, "The Reed Sea: *Requiescat in Pace*," *Journal of Biblical Literature*, 102 (1983) 27–35.

14. Under the rubric, "In What Sense Did Yahweh Bring Israel Out of Egypt?," Pixley, in *On Exodus*, offers some wise remarks within the framework of process theology, pp. 76–80.

15. Gottwald, "Social Matrix and Canonical Shape," *Theology Today*, 42 (1985) 307–21 analyzes the way canonical criticism can be misled if it takes an ostensibly "apolitical" posture of postexilic redactors and canonizers at face value.

16. Michael Walzer, *Exodus and Revolution* (New York: Basic Books, 1985); Ernst Bloch, *Atheism in Christianity: The Religion of the Exodus and the Kingdom* (New York: Herder and Herder, 1972), esp. pp. 84–105.

17. Gottwald, *Tribes*, p. 706.

31

Theoretical and Institutional Bases of the Opposition to Liberation Theology

FRANÇOIS HOUTART

From the very beginning of its developments, the theology of liberation has been a cause for worry, warnings, and even head-on attacks. Its approach was unusual: instead of defining the locus of its development within the religious field, it saw itself at the very heart of the society, thus turning society into the starting point of the systematization of its thought about God. That was not merely a social ethic with religious references, but quite definitely a fundamental theological approach. And it dealt with all the aspects of the Christian faith, from a concern with Christ and the church to the meaning of the kingdom. It must be said that the social analysis of Latin American reality was that of a society marked by class contradictions, and that on the basis of active liberation, the social practice of a believing people took on—as had been the case of Jesus' own practice within the society of his time—a central significance. Thus Marxist analysis was seen as an adequate mediation insofar as it was used to grasp a conflictive reality and practices of liberation. We will first study the various Roman stands and then those of CELAM (*Consejo Episcopal Latinoamericano*) in the action undertaken against the new theology.[1]

THE ROMAN STANDS

In March 1983 Cardinal Ratzinger sent to the bishops of Peru "ten observations" issued by the Roman Congregation for the Doctrine of the Faith, concerning the theology of Gustavo Gutiérrez, asking the bishops to take a stand on the matter (DIAL, no. 925).[2] The document starts by stressing the "appeal" of the author whose theology is, however, characterized by "an extreme ambiguity," both features resulting from the prioritization of attention given to the destitution of the masses and to the uncritical acceptance of Marxist interpretation. The text goes on to state that Gutiérrez uses such a perception to reinterpret the Christian message: a selective and reductionist rereading in which the exploited peoples of our time are put in the same category as the poor of the Bible and in which events, such as the

261

exodus, for instance, become episodes of political liberation. Gutiérrez is also blamed for slipping into a temporal messianism that would mistake the growth of the kingdom for the progress of "justice." Also, among the "shortcuts" chosen by the theology of liberation, Cardinal Ratzinger points to a restrictive conception of sin, which would be limited to "social sin."

Moreover, Marxist influence—according to the Congregation—is manifest when it comes to the primacy of orthopraxis as opposed to orthodoxy. To state that the experience acquired in the struggle of liberation is an encounter with the Lord and that it is marked by the presence of the Spirit is to go against the transcendence of revelation and its normative value, as well as against the specific character of theological faith. Besides which, any rereading of the Bible, at any time of history, amounts to questioning the unity of meaning of God's word and the reality of tradition.

Lastly, as the document explains, since the theology of Gutiérrez posits that the kingdom is built through the struggles of liberation, it sees the church as a mere sign of unity and love, a fruit of such struggles. This negates the reconciliation that has already been achieved through the sacrifice of Christ and the fact that salvation is already given in Jesus Christ; on the contrary, future salvation (liberation) is thus seen as eschatological.

Also, in the liberationist perspective, class struggle is to be found within the church too, and the opposition between the churchmen who are on the side of the powers that be and the church of the poor logically leads to a rejection of the hierarchy and of its legitimacy. This church of the poor is said to be present in the basic communities that are committed to social struggle, and therefore the danger is not a purely theoretical one. As to eucharistic celebrations that announce liberation, one must question their correspondence with the true nature of the sacrament.

In its conclusion, the document affirms that the purpose of such a theology is to use Christianity as an agent of mobilization for the sake of the revolution, for class struggle is seen as an objective reality. Such a theology, by resorting to Marxism, can thus pervert evangelical inspiration, the meaning of the poor and of their hopes.

To put it briefly, the Congregation for the Doctrine of the Faith considers that to start with class analysis would have as a consequence a triple theological reductionism: it is opposed to the transcendence of revelation expressed in God's Word, it is opposed to the redemption, which has already been achieved, and it is opposed to the concept of the church as mystery, the consequence being quite logically a rejection of the hierarchy.

If we read Gutiérrez carefully, such a reductionism cannot be found. In fact, the text of the Congregation of the Faith clearly makes two points. On the one hand, it notes a confrontation between an ahistorical and metaphysical conception of God's salvific action in humankind and a vision that replaces it in human history. On the other hand, it reveals a concern to safeguard the exclusivity of those who speak for the magisterium as well as of the controlling function of the hierarchy, which is obviously in keeping with the logic of the first vision. The study of the second document will provide a few additional details.

In the course of a lecture he gave in Rome in September 1983, Cardinal Ratzinger dealt with the epistemological structure of the theology of liberation (DIAL, no. 930). In the first place, he said, there is an opposition between Jesus, the historical character, and the Christ of faith.[3] For the liberation theologian, referring to history brings in a scientific dimension that makes new research possible, and this goes against tradition and implicitly brings the magisterium into disrepute, for it would appear as bound to theories that are untenable in the modern world.

The second element is that of the hermeneutics on which the new theology is based. It is accused by the cardinal of wanting to actualize Christianity according to a historical given. It is on this level, says he, that Marxism and its class struggle make their presence felt. They make Christianity into a political doctrine. Their predilection for the biblical "poor" incorporates a confusion between historical imagery and Marxist dialectic. The proletariat of the capitalistic society is seen as following in the footsteps of the biblical poor, and when faced with class struggle — a fact seen as objective — a Christian cannot remain neutral. To ignore the struggle is to conform with the will of the ruling class. Thus, said Ratzinger, the magisterium cannot intervene anymore, for if it rejects such an interpretation of Christianity, it takes a stand against the poor and therefore against Jesus himself.

Such a choice, Ratzinger said, though it seems to be a scientific one, is obviously hermeneutic. It determines a path that leads to a later interpretation of Christianity. We may ask what are the interpretive authorities. The key concepts are as follows: people, community, experience, and history. In liberation theology, the "community" interprets events thanks to its experience and is able to discover an orientation for its "praxis." The people, in its socio-religious dimension (the community of belonging) is thus opposed to the concept of "hierarchy," which is — in classical theology — the only interpretive authority. Moreover, the same people is also involved in class struggle. And here we see that the popular church is against the hierarchical church. In such an opposition, the concept of history becomes the decisive hermeneutic authority. The popular church is reasoning in terms of salvation history and therefore only in an antimetaphysical mode. It considers history as the locus of revelation.

Thus, as far as Cardinal Ratzinger is concerned, the concept of history absorbs that of God and of revelation. It also becomes a way of legitimizing Marxism's materialistic philosophy. If the magisterium insists on permanent truths, because its way of thinking is metaphysical, it will be considered not only as an authority set against progress but also as an institution that uses oppressive force.

I will not analyze here the other parts of the document, that in which the author points to the spread of liberation theology to other continents of the Third World, as well as to its ecumenical features or that in which he studies how it came into being. Let me only mention that he credits German exegetes and philosophers with an important influence. He also attacks directly the idea, which was voiced by Vatican II, of reading "the signs of the times" and using the social sciences for that purpose. Above all he accuses the Marxist interpretation of history as a critical instance of theological thought.

Most of the theologians of liberation have a difficult time recognizing themselves adequately in such a document, and some of them have already said so. Though it is a private text, it does have a great importance because it expresses an absolute rejection of liberation theology and concludes that urgent measures must be taken.

CRITICISMS AND THE STRATEGY OF CELAM

The documents that I analyze here are the result of a relatively long history in which CELAM played a very active role. It was indeed particularly concerned because that school of thought had started in Latin America. While theologians working on those themes had played an important role in the pastoral agencies of CELAM, and even in the preparation of the Medellín Conference at the end of the 1960s, the situation was progressively reversed as early as 1972. During a meeting held at Sucre in Bolivia, CELAM started to revise the functions of its various agencies and appointed as Secretary General Alfonso López Trujillo, who was at that time auxiliary bishop of Bogotá. Before studying the strategies of action, I will take a brief look at the arguments used by CELAM against the theology of liberation and against all the pastoral methods inspired by it or that it had inspired.

Criticisms of the Theology of Liberation and of New Pastoral Methods

In the course of those years, such criticism centered around four points: the use of Marxist analysis, christology, ecclesiology, and social doctrine. On the first one, López Trujillo leaves no doubts. In his opening speech to the eighteenth Assembly of CELAM in 1981 he said about the theologians of liberation: "The problem is not that they speak loudly when talking about the poor, but that they make an ideological use of a Marxist instrument of analysis ... and this is in contradiction with the magisterium of the church." This is a serious danger, he added, because nothing can be safe from the theological and pastoral consequences of such a use: "neither christology, ecclesiology, nor a certain conception of the basic ecclesial communities ... could CELAM remain silent about ... when one knows to what extent the church structure is endangered by the indiscriminate use—and I would even say the ascientific use—of an analysis that is 150 years old and is presented by some persons today as a novelty."

The CELAM texts refer frequently to "ideologies." Even though the latter are never specified, it is quite clear that the concept refers mostly to Marxism. Thus does the secretary general say when talking about the basic communities: they represent "the inrush of dubious ideologies and ecclesiologies" and the global pastoral plan for 1983–1986 includes a section entitled: struggle against sects and ideologies. In his speech at Puebla, John Paul II indicated the distinction that must be made between "a Christian liberation" and "a liberation nurtured by ideologies destroying the coherence it must have with an evangelical vision of humankind, things, and events." He took up the same theme forcefully in his homily at Managua on March 4, 1983. The meaning became even more obvious when Bishop Quarracino, the new president of CELAM, referred to "ideological manipulations" in a report to the conference of CELAM in Port-au-Prince, Haiti, in 1983. He gave as an example "Marxist analysis as a working tool."

In short, the accusation is clear. What is less clear is what persons mean when they talk about Marxism, Marxist analysis, "ideologies." Cardinal Aloisio Lorscheider, archbishop of Fortaleza, Brazil, did not hesitate to clarify the matter. In an interview published by the newspaper of his diocese, he stated: "When I hear people talking about a Marxist infiltration in the church, I ask them what they mean by Marxism. Most of the time, I don't get an answer. . . . Many when they talk about Marxism do not mean Marxist philosophy but Marxist analysis . . . [the latter] endeavors to be a means of understanding the society in which we live."⁴ Such a declaration should be enough to show that there is no unanimity among the bishops of Latin America.

As to theologians, they answer with the Boff brothers: "Marx is not the godfather of liberation theology. The tool of Marxist analysis is a mediation. It might be dangerous, but it is useful in order to understand social reality."⁵ Thus it seems quite clear that the CELAM position amounts from the start to a lack of distinction—in the Marxist approach—between the use of social analysis and philosophical option. According to CELAM, the analysis necessarily originates in and leads to the philosophy. Then CELAM stresses the essentially atheistic character—thus contradictory to faith—of that same philosophy. In such a logic, social analysis can only bring about the destruction of religion. It is therefore necessary to oppose it forcefully. An examination of the theological writings of liberation and of the practices of the basic communities does not easily lead one to such conclusions, and so the question that remains is this: Why such an amalgam? I will come back to this point.

The second part of the argumentation against the theology of liberation concerns christology and even more generally redemption. It is accused of showing "the incarnate Word as an eminent example of charity and socio-political commitment."⁶ "The Christ of the Gospels is reduced to the Christ of temporal liberation only."⁷ According to López Trujillo, the Lord is not shown "as the one sent by the Father, but as a tool of class struggle; the rebel of Nazareth." Moreover, according to this theological school, the good news would only concern the poor. Such a choice is "to be understood as a class option."

Also in the argumentation about redemption, the secretariat of the bishops of Central America and Panama was even more explicit when preparing the papal visit: "Those who are hoping that the pope will come only for 'the poor' have not read *Redemptor Hominis*" (John Paul II's first encyclical). The pope is not "a class pope."⁸ He clarified his own thought when speaking at the opening of the meeting of CELAM in Port-au-Prince, in 1983, pointing out, among the serious problems to be faced by the church in Latin America: "the bitterness of many who, because of an erroneous option for the poor, feel that they are abandoned and forgotten in their aspirations and their religious needs."⁹

In other words, the reproach concerns a characterization of the poor seen as being inspired by "criteria that are only political and ideological,"¹⁰ whereas the biblical message is more global and salvation in Jesus Christ is more than a simple liberation from economic and social oppression. Such an option, "exclusive and excluding," begets inevitably "feelings of hatred and struggle between brothers."¹¹ But, once again, is this not a rather shallow reading of the theology of liberation, which for most of its authors, such as Gustavo Gutiérrez, the Boff brothers, or Jon Sobrino, insists on the universality of salvation and its nonreductibility to social processes? On the other hand, it remains true that it stresses the concrete character of the poor, who are not only suffering and living in destitution, but above all oppressed by the economic, social, and political practices of the classes that exploit them. And, again, we are faced with the question: Why was this forgotten in the presentation of their theological reflection?

Before answering this question, I will examine the last two issues: ecclesiology and the social doctrine of the church. In the first case, the main problem is that of "the popular church." According to Bishop Quarracino, elected president of CELAM in 1983, it is unacceptable to talk about a "church born from the people." Indeed, "we must warn our churches against this danger, which leads to a theory about two churches, and this calls for a vigorous work of clarification and unitary action."[12] As far as López Trujillo is concerned, the theology of liberation introduces on the one hand a popular church, for it opted for the poor, and on the other hand a bourgeois church, thus inserting class conflicts within the church itself.

Such a presentation of the ecclesiological thought of the theology of liberation and of the reality of the basic communities seems, at first sight, to be more adequately in keeping with what is generally said. There is, however, a fundamental difference. Never did the basic communities or theological reflection about them speak about two churches. On the contrary, they insist on their genuine membership in the one church of Jesus Christ, while also stressing the fact that there are various options within that church. They point out, in particular, that political choice, social and cultural practices, a preference for certain Catholic movements, a type of spirituality, and even theological positions on the part of some Latin American Christians as well as most of the hierarchy put them in fact, if not intentionally, in a correspondence of interests and mentality with the ruling classes. Does not such a fact call for a critique of the gospel?

Bringing differences to light is not acceptable in a concept of the church based above all on obedience and authority. This was summed up in a letter of John Paul II to the bishops of Nicaragua on June 29, 1982. It would be "absurd and dangerous to imagine next to—not to say against—the church based on the bishops . . . a popular church—that is, without reference to the legitimate shepherds" and "infiltrated by ideological connotations."[13] In his homily in Managua, the pope returned to that theme even more vigorously, talking about "parallel teachings" that weaken the church and demanding that doctrinal concepts and pastoral projects be subject to the magisterium of the church, represented by the pope and the bishops.

We, therefore, witness two parallel discourses, though they are not necessarily in contradiction. The first perceives the church in its concrete reality, though not denying in any way its eschatological character. The second favors the reality of the church as a sign or sacrament of unity, according to the words of Vatican II. But it precludes any possibility of seeing the hierarchy as so placed in social reality as to give it a precise meaning, thus crediting it with an ontological character, therefore, an indisputable one. Once again, the dialogue comes to a dead end. But in this case, the stakes seem clearer.

As to the social doctrine of the church, it is questioned by the theology of liberation. "As happens in puppy love, many were blinded by the scientific analysis of reality, class struggle, the theory of dependency, revolutionary praxis"; thus wrote Bishop Quarracino, then secretary general of CELAM, "and they did not perceive anymore the viability of the church's social doctrine."[14] Now, John Paul II said in Managua, the principle of subjection applied to doctrinal concepts and pastoral projects "must also be applied in the field of the church's social doctrine, developed by my predecessors and by myself."[15]

The perceptions of all the above are therefore very different. In the first case, class analysis brings to light the antagonistic character of economic interests, an opposition expressed in the reality of a class struggle that has repercussions in the political, social, cultural, and even religious fields. The resulting social ethic seeks to implement structural changes that go beyond mere interpersonal relationships. The goal is to establish a logic of the majorities, which means a break from the capitalistic economic system and a start on the socialist way. On the other hand, in the second case, though social differences are seen as a given, the various social categories must coexist in harmony. Thus, there is a need for cooperation between the various classes for the sake of the common good. Such an ethical norm, obviously, calls for doing away with abuses and injustices, correcting all excesses and, therefore, appealing to the sense of justice and generosity of the ruling classes but also to the patience and nonviolence of the oppressed classes. And in the end, this results in the condemnation of class struggle, considered as unacceptable behavior in interpersonal relationships and leading necessarily to violence. Such is the meaning of John Paul II's intervention in his speech to the campesinos of Panama.

This brings us back to the first point concerning Marxist analysis. To oppose its adoption in this field is justified by what is seen as a contradiction between such an analysis and an understanding of social reality inspired by Christianity, the one implicitly adopted by the church. Once more the question is raised: Why would one favor an interclass understanding of reality in the name of Christian faith?

Do we not find again and again in the reproaches addressed to the theology of liberation a logic linking all its various elements? That is what we may ask ourselves in order to formulate some interpretive hypotheses. Is there not, in fact, a double rejection? First, that of history as a dynamic part of the work of redemption, a history built by human beings. Taking it into account does indeed relativize a view of faith conceived as a deposit guarded by the magisterium and seeing the hierarchy at the top of the entire religious structuring. It also rejects class analysis because it calls for a stand. This puts the institution—in this case, the hierarchy—in an impossible situation, because it defines itself as having to rule unanimously without even mentioning the socio-political space that it would lose if it became partial. Such a double rejection would be all the more radical in that it refers to the defense of a revealed truth regarding salvation, a function considered essential by religious authorities.

What is probably not perceived is that in the concrete situation of the Third World, such a position leads to a choice that is also political and facts are a far more eloquent proof than theological writings: this choice is made against the poor insofar as they take into their own hands their own liberation and when they raise their voices without the church.

The CELAM Strategy

The year 1972, when Cardinal López Trujillo was elected secretary general of CELAM, can be seen as a watershed: it was then that the activities of CELAM started in this field. The first step was, in 1973, a meeting in Bogotá about the theme of liberation. The idea that obtained at the time was that there are two concepts of liberation, one that is spiritual and of Latin American origin, and the other stressing politics, and coming from Europe. The review *Tierra Nueva*, founded in Bogotá, specialized in refuting the theology of liberation. The first strategy was therefore at the intellectual and strictly theological levels.

It went on during the following years. A working group was set up in cooperation with German theologians, the "Church and Liberation" study circle meeting in 1973, 1974, and 1975, and leading then to a colloquy in Rome. During the latter, an important report on the "world propagation of the theology of liberation" described it as a "contagious virus" and denounced in rather violent terms the persons and institutions spreading it.

During the preparation for the Puebla Conference (1979), which brought together the bishops of Latin America for the tenth anniversary of the Medellín Conference, there was an intense activity, devoted among other things to bringing back in step the theology of liberation and the basic communities. The result was quite moderate; there was no condemnation, thanks to the intervention of influential bishops and especially of several Brazilian cardinals. Cardinal López Trujillo became president of CELAM at the beginning of 1980, and organized in 1982 two important meetings: one on ecclesiology and especially on the basic communities, and the other on christology. Father Hamer, O.P., of the Congregation for the Doctrine of the Faith (the former Holy Office), took part in the first meeting. The second one, held in Rio de Janeiro barely a month after, saw Cardinal Ratzinger, president of that same congregation, in attendance. The second meeting, described by CELAM as pluralistic, was aimed at a refutation of liberation theology, and no theologians of that school were invited.

A second aspect of the strategy consists in reorganizing the agencies of CELAM according to the objectives described above and in practicing a policy of nominating "safe" persons for the key positions. It would be too long to describe all the stages of this cleverly planned action. Persons invited to the various colloquies and meetings wind up at the key posts of CELAM, thus insuring a continuity of action. This was done in close cooperation with the Holy See where Cardinal López Trujillo has a great influence on the CAL (Committee on Latin America), the head of which is also the prefect of the Congregation of Bishops, formerly nuncio in Latin America, Cardinal Baggio. CELAM is also very active in the preparation of the pope's tour of Latin America both in the field of topics and that of orientations.

Lastly, the third part is pastoral action through pastoral projects, the third of which was implemented from 1983 to 1986, offering a logistical support to local ordinaries for the formation of religious personnel, organization of study sessions, and support for lay groups. It will be recalled that an emergency plan for Nicaragua was set up after the Sandinista revolution. All these strategies are, of course, calling for considerable funds that CELAM obtains from various sources, notably from German Catholic foundations and private American entities.

Even though this is not the topic of this article, I think it important to mention that all those actions met with some opposition. For instance, the Brazilian Episcopal Conference, the largest one of Latin America, was clearly reserved about the CELAM policy. However, new appointments of bishops might progressively erode this resistance. Moreover, the basic communities of Latin America organized themselves in 1980 during a meeting in São Paulo under the aegis of Cardinal Arns. CELAM exerted tremendous pressure to minimize the effects of the meeting. Cardinal López Trujillo also intervened with the Catholic development organizations providing aid in order to bring an end to their support of pastoral and social initiatives of groups and persons connected with the church of the poor. Lastly, in his letter to Philip Potter, Secretary General of the World Council of Churches, in early 1982, he blamed that organization for giving help—especially of a financial nature—to groups and centers "trying to hide under the ecumenical label" and "carrying ideologized forms of theological expression which are radically critical of the church, its shepherds, and even the very basic principles of the faith."

After his two terms as secretary general and one as president, having thus spent eleven years with CELAM, Cardinal López Trujillo, ordinary of Medellín, was appointed a cardinal on February 2, 1984. In a private audience, the pope expressed his appreciation of the cardinal by stating: "His contribution to the study and clarification of theology, particularly of the so-called theology of liberation, has been and remains an eminent service to the church."[16]

Controversies outside the Catholic Church

It might be useful to mention here that opposition to the theology of liberation and to new trends in the Latin American church did not only come from the church itself. In 1982 a working group met in Santa Fe, New Mexico, to prepare the outline of a U.S. policy toward Latin America in case Reagan were to be elected president. A paragraph of the confidential text, which was published anyhow, mentioned the necessity to fight the theology of liberation. At the same time, the Institute for Religion and Democracy was founded in Washington, D.C., under the direction of Peter Berger, a Protestant sociologist, and Michael Novak, a Catholic journalist and author, for the purpose of attacking the aid given by North American Christian groups to the theology of liberation and to "the popular church" in Latin America, more particularly in Central America. This institute is financed by several foundations, some of which are close to the Republican Party.

Among arguments voiced outside the church, we can mention in particular an article published by the CELAM newsletter and written by Rabbi Leon Klenicki, entitled "Theology of Liberation, the Viewpoint of a Latin American Jew."[17] After denouncing the alliance with leftist ideologies and the politization of the biblical message that he perceives in the theology of liberation, the author affirms that the latter strengthens the anti-Jewish trend in Christian theology because it does not make any reference to "the return to the Promised Land after twenty centuries of exile, through the foundation of the state of Israel . . . nor to Zionism as a process of liberation."

A First Reply

As soon as the text of Cardinal Ratzinger came out, the Boff brothers published a reply, which I already mentioned. They admit that there are dangers in the theology of liberation, which can appear as a form of reductionism. But this comes precisely from the awareness of the dramatic situation in the Third World. They add that what is new has not always had the time to be perfectly harmonized and that this is in itself a normal occurrence. Such a situation does not, however, justify an attitude tainted by the presumption of perversity. We cannot recognize ourselves in what Cardinal Ratzinger said, state the two Brazilian theologians.

The theology of liberation is, on the contrary, a creative broadening of traditional theology. To start from liberation means to read the signs of the times in the light of faith. Such an approach includes the transcendental dimension of faith, liberation from sin, and gratuitous communion with God. It is developed in a living contact with reality, and not in an academic universe. Unlike Bultmann, it stresses the historical Jesus Christ. As to Marxist analysis, it is a tool for grasping reality, perhaps a dangerous tool "but the best we have to account for concrete situations."[18]

The text ends with a reproach: that of lacking sensitivity with regard to the cause of the poor: it is not simply a factor, a mere concept, but an ethical, mystical, and theological experience. A position such as that of Cardinal Ratzinger can also become a political tool.

WHERE ARE WE GOING

The dynamics of the process now in development will lead to a confrontation if church authorities go to the very logical conclusion of their position. Should we read a sign in the fact that Clodovis Boff was deprived of his canonical mission of teaching theology at the Pontifical University of Rio de Janeiro by Cardinal de Araujo Sales, its Great Chancellor, just as the academic year was about to start in March 1984? In any case, a parallel with the crisis of modernism seems to be justified because the controversy is at least partly about similar elements.

However, the stakes are bigger this time. They are located at the very heart of the struggle of the Third World people, particularly in Latin America. There can be another parallel, that of the church in the face of the working-class problems in Europe, and this time the consequences can be foreseen. To entwine a new form of antimodernism with a struggle against popular emancipation in the Third World is an intellectual and social challenge that might become very costly in terms of human lives and religious vitality. On the other hand, to accept theological and pastoral pluralism within today's church might perhaps enable us not to be forced—within a few decades—as has already happened in many cases, to a rehabilitation of those who have been rejected.

—translated from the French by Nelly Marans

NOTES

This text of François Houtart was published in *Le Monde Diplomatique*, no. 363 (June 1984), under the title, *La peur d'une contagion marxiste* (fear of a Marxist contagion).

1. A more detailed document about the theologies of liberation in Latin America and about the countertheologies was published as a dossier by the Tricontinental Center, 5 Avenue Sainte Gertrude, B-1348 Ottignies-Louvain-la-Neuve, Belgium.

2. *Diffusion de l'Information sur l'Amérique Latine*, 47 Quai des Grands Augustins, F-75006, Paris.

3. According to Cardinal Ratzinger, it was the influence of the German exegete

Bultmann that obtained in this field, an assertion contested by several liberation theologians who are precisely stressing the central character of Jesus' practice within his society.

4. Interview given to the diocesan bulletin of the archbishopric of Fortaleza, *Páginas* 7/46 (August 1982).

5. Leonardo Boff and Clodovis Boff, "The Cry of Poverty Coming from Faith" *Folha de São Paulo*, published by *DIAL*, no. 931 (April 26, 1984).

6. Speech by Bishop Quarracino, secretary general of CELAM, at the Port-au-Prince meeting.

7. Article by His Excellency Quarracino in the CELAM Bulletin.

8. Declaration of the secretariat of the episcopacy of Central America and Panama, *CELAM Bulletin*, no. 180 (February, 1983).

9. Discourse of John Paul II at Port-au-Prince, to the general assembly of CELAM.

10. Ibid.

11. Ibid.

12. Bishop Quarracino, see n. 7.

13. *CELAM Bulletin*, no. 176 (September, 1982).

14. Bishop Quarracino, (n. 7, above).

15. Homily of March 4, 1983, in Managua.

16. *CELAM Bulletin*, no. 181 (March-April, 1983).

17. Rabbi Leon Klenicki, "La teología de la liberación: Una exploración judia latinoamericana," *CELAM Bulletin* n. 185 (Nov.-Dec. 1983).

18. The Brazilian episcopacy did not make known that between 1979 and 1983 drought had cost some ten million lives in northeastern Brazil, because the social structures in place prevented an adequate response to the climatic conditions.

32

Dependency Theory, Marxist Analysis, and Liberation Theology

ARTHUR F. McGOVERN, SJ

Over the past twenty years no theological movement has stimulated more writing or engendered more controversy than has liberation theology. Liberation theology has drawn attention dramatically to the plight of the world's poor nations and it has challenged the church to question its political alignments and its very presentation of the Christian message. While liberation theology seeks first of all to articulate the meaning of faith for a particular context, most of the criticism has centered on its political implications, especially on its use of Marxist analysis. It was this use of Marxist analysis that first drew my attention to liberation theology.

This present essay constitutes an "interim" investigation of the use of Marxist analysis and dependency theory by Gustavo Gutiérrez and other liberation theologians. It will become part of a more comprehensive book on liberation theology and its critics, following some more extensive studies in Latin America. In this interim study I should like to consider first the role that dependency theory has played in liberation theology: its main theses, how it developed, what liberation theologians have said about dependency, and some issues about its use. The second part of the essay will deal with Marxist analysis: what it involves, what liberation theologians have said about its use, how in fact they have made use of it, and finally some comments about its use.

The social sciences have played an essential role from the outset in liberation theology. Clodovis Boff and José Míguez Bonino both assert that the social sciences form a "constitutive part" of liberation theology, the first of three essential "mediations" according to Boff.[1] Other socio-scientific theories figure in the analyses used by liberation theologians, but dependency and Marxist analyses have played very prominent roles in considering the major problems faced by Latin America.

This last point—major problems—merits special emphasis. Liberation theology operates at two very different, though interrelated, levels. In practice, most of the social analysis used by base communities and Christian programs of popular education focus on very specific problems: agricultural development, violations of human rights, health care, land reform, and so on. In most instances this type of analysis relies very little (and often not at all) on Marxist analysis or dependency theory.

Liberation theologians have, however, addressed issues about the root causes of problems in Latin America, and at this level dependency theory and Marxist analysis do come into play. We will see, in the course of the article, various reasons given by liberation theologians for accepting these methods of analysis as "useful tools." But one initial point stands out: most liberation theologians view Latin America's situation as one of "dependent capitalism." They judge this combination, dependency on an exploitative world capitalist system, as the major source of Latin America's problems. One could, then, present a unified view of liberation macroanalysis focused on a common target: dependent capitalism. One could also group the forms of analyses used by liberation theologians under the common heading of "dialectical" methods (methods that view conflict rather than functionalist striving for equilibrium as necessary for understanding Latin American reality). But liberation theologians distinguish between the uses of dependency theory and Marxist analysis, and their uses raise quite different issues, as we shall see. Hence I have treated them separately, while acknowledging from the outset their convergence on a common problem.

DEPENDENCY THEORY

I begin with dependency theory because it played an instrumental role in the very articulation of a theology of liberation. The new theology rejected "developmental" policies and called explicitly for "liberation" from dependency. I will discuss how liberation theologians used dependency theory in their initial formulations of liberation theology, but I need first to recall briefly some key points about dependency theory itself.[2]

Prior to the development of dependency theory, conventional economic wisdom proposed a "modernization" model for underdeveloped countries like those in Latin America. Latin America, according to this model of analysis, faced the same problems that Europe had faced before its industrial revolution: scarcity of capital, undeveloped technology, and a lack of entrepreneurs seeking to make profits through more efficient production. To achieve development, underdeveloped nations must break out of traditional mores, adopt a profit incentive, and discover newer ways to become productive. Advanced countries, from this perspective, could play an important role in supplying some of the missing components needed to "prime the pump" of development. Foreign companies (multinationals) could help by bringing in needed capital, new technology and managerial know-how.

In the first decades after World War II, Latin America sought to pattern its development according to this model. But one aspect of conventional wisdom soon came under attack by Raúl Prebisch and the United Nations Economic Commission on Latin America (ECLA). They challenged especially the conventional view that international trade was mutually beneficial for all trading powers. ECLA studies indicated that Latin American countries suffered from short-term instability caused by fluctuating prices and from long-term deterioration in terms of trade. This resulted, ECLA argued, from Latin America's reliance on export of primary goods (bananas, coffee, minerals, etc.) to provide income to finance the buying of imported industrial goods. Far from being mutually beneficial, Latin America continued to run a deficient balance of payments. The "center" nations profited; the "peripheral" nations suffered. Prebisch and ECLA still retained much of the modernist model for development, but they introduced a framework of analysis that would become an essential part of all dependency theory: the division of the capitalist world into dominant "center" nations and subordinate "peripheral" nations such as those of Latin America.

The dependency theorists of the 1960s (Cardoso, Frank, Dos Santos) focused on the influence of foreign trade and investment on Latin America. Using Prebisch's "core-periphery" framework the new analysts sought to show that weaknesses in Latin American economy resulted in large measure from policies controlled by the "center," from the United States and Europe. Dos Santos defined dependency as "a situation in which a certain group of countries have their economies conditioned by the development and expansion of another country's economy."[3] The relationship between countries becomes dependent when the dominant center countries alone have a power of self-starting and expansion, whereas the dependent, peripheral nations can only act in reaction to the dominant countries' policies and development. In this relationship, the dominant countries impose their dominant technology, commerce, and values on the dependent countries who find themselves easily exploited and subject to loss of revenues produced in their own countries.

This dependency theory took different forms. The strongest form, enunciated by André Gunder Frank, argued that capitalist countries in the North created and have maintained underdevelopment in Latin America. According to this position, development in the North and underdevelopment in the South represented "two sides of the same coin." Europe and the United States financed their own development by exploiting poor nations and draining off profits (surplus value) from them. They thus keep Latin America (and other Third World countries) from developing, by drawing off the capital needed for development, and imposing their own technology and controls. A more nuanced form of dependency analysis, proposed by Fernando Henrique Cardoso, gave far more attention to internal factors. It accepted the detrimental influence of foreign investors as an important factor, but tried also to show the social and political forces within Latin America that shaped its economy and socio-political systems.

Early works in liberation theology show the close connection between the concept of liberation and the fact of dependency. Gutiérrez proposed the concept of liberation to the bishops at Medellín (1968), precisely as a needed alternative to the failed policies of development. He spelled out his arguments in the early pages of *A Theology of Liberation*. Developmental policies, Gutiérrez judges, had obviously failed in Latin America. Not only did poverty and oppression continue but the gap between the poor countries of the world and the rich had widened. More importantly it was becoming increasingly clear that the continuing misery in Latin America was in great part *caused* by the dependency that developmental policies encouraged. Latin Americans were realizing that their own development would come about only through a struggle to break the domination of rich countries and their own native oligarchies. True development would come only through the struggle for liberation.[4]

Other liberation theologians echoed the same convictions. Hugo Assmann stated that the major contribution of the social sciences to liberation theology came from their critiques of developmentalism, critiques that pointed to dependence as the central problem. "Underlying liberation theology is the historical experience of the actual nature of *under*-development, as a form of dependence."[5] Marxism exercised an influence, Assmann continued, but the major influence was a new awareness that Latin Americans are "not merely underdeveloped peoples . . . but peoples 'kept in a state of underdevelopment.' "[6] José Míguez Bonino concurred: "Northern development is built on Third World underdevelopment."[7] Leonardo Boff spoke in similar terms: "The affluence and advanced scientific and technological development of the Northern hemisphere . . . has meant the impoverishment and marginalization of the dependent, underdeveloped nations."[8] Each of them spoke not only of the fact of dependence but used André Gunder Frank's formula that blamed Latin American underdevelopment on Northern development. A closer look, however, at the thought of Gustavo Gutiérrez and Leonardo Boff will indicate some important qualifications in the use of dependency theory.

Even in *A Theology of Liberation* Gutiérrez noted some important qualifications made by Fernando Henrique Cardoso about dependency theory. Latin American countries are constitutively dependent on rich nations, but Gutiérrez adds, "we are not dealing with a purely external factor."[9] He cites Cardoso's warning that "one can have recourse to the idea of dependence as a way of 'explaining' internal processes of the dependent societies by a purely 'external' variable."[10] Gutiérrez makes a similar point in his *The Power of the Poor in History*. "External dependency and internal domination are the marks of the social structures of Latin America." Although the early theories of dependency were beneficial, they sometimes failed by focusing too much on the conflict between nations (center versus periphery) and not enough on internal factors requiring class analysis.[11]

Gutiérrez added still further qualifications in a 1984 essay, "Teología y ciencias sociales." He stressed the provisional and transitory nature of all social science studies. To say these disciplines are scientific "does not mean that their conclusions are definitive and beyond discussion." Liberation theology, says Gutiérrez, needs to be attentive to the many variations of dependency theory and to criticisms made of it; it should avoid generalizations and be enriched by other types of analysis. He considers Cardoso the most important figure in dependency analysis and he notes also that Cardoso considers his theoretical attitude as situated at the "opposite ends" (*antipodas*) from Marx.[12]

Leonardo Boff, in *Liberating Grace*, affirmed the fact of dependency and used the strong formula of André Gunder Frank: "Development and underdevelopment are two sides of the same coin."[13] But he also voiced serious reservations about its use: "It is only a theory, not an established truth. It is one stage in an ongoing investigation and has its own intrinsic limitations. It offers a good diagnosis of the structure of underdevelopment, but it does not do much to offer any viable way out."[14] Expanding on this last point, Boff expresses skepticism about the revolutionary type of breakaway advocated by Frank. "More moderate advocates of the theory of dependency showed a greater historical sense" and recognized the need for work for change within the system.[15] Citing José Comblin, Boff says that one cannot choose both complete autonomy *and* development. Compromise is necessary. If development is the goal, says Boff, one has to work within the international system.

We have from liberation theologians, then, statements that seem to "blame" foreign countries and their companies for Latin America's problems, and more nuanced statements that affirm dependency but treat its causes and resolution as more complex. By distinguishing between the fact of dependency and the causes of its creation and continuance, we can better assess how much and in what way dependency causes or contributes to underdevelopment in Latin America. The points that follow constitute a necessarily brief and tentative assessment of this issue.

The Fact of Dependency. One important dependency analyst, Fernando Henrique Cardoso, claims that he never intended to create a special "theory" of dependency. He sought rather to challenge and correct existing models of development by investigating more fully what Latin Americans had experienced and discussed for years—the fact of dependency.[16] Indeed historians wrote about Latin American dependency well before dependency theory came onto the scene. Thus, for example, a history of Latin America written in the 1950s subtitled one of its chapters "Latin America's Decided Dependence on Foreign Trade and Foreign Capital." Moreover it described the Latin American situation in language that anticipated dependency theory as well. "Latin America became a weak outlying segment of the great industrial economies of the West."[17]

A more recent study, aimed explicitly at assessing dependency theory, questions the tenability of several theses proposed by some dependency theorists, for example that dependency necessarily impedes economic growth in poorer countries or necessarily results in authoritarian political rule. But the same author argues that at least two theses from dependency theory are "easily defensible": (1) "Because of their dependence on the developed 'core' countries, the peripheral countries are experiencing a growing loss of national control over their economic, political, social, and cultural life"; and (2) "The current economic growth in less developed countries is unevenly distributed among sectors of the society. . . . Because income distribution is badly skewed, the poorest half of most societies is left relatively untouched by economic growth."[18]

Reports by the International Monetary Fund and the World Bank—hardly suspect sources—give contemporary evidence of the dependence of Latin American countries on the United States and other First World nations. When the United States and its allies experienced recession in the early 1980s, the economies of every Latin American nation suffered even greater losses. An IMF report noted that growth rates in Latin American countries, which had averaged 5 to 7 percent annually from 1967 to 1980, fell dramatically to 2.3 percent in 1983. The reasons given by IMF are consistently *external*: "a major factor" in the problems faced by developing countries has been "the recession in industrial countries." Weakness of foreign exchange earnings and indebtedness made developing countries "particularly vulnerable" to interest rate increases in 1980. The weakness of economic activity in the industrial world had a "substantial adverse effect" on the terms of trade in countries not involved in oil developing. "Faced with an abrupt change of external finance, many developing countries had *no option* but to cut back sharply their current account deficits."[19] A World Bank report reflected this same causal relationship. Restrictive monetary policies used by the United States to control inflation had a "profoundly adverse effect" on the rates of growth of many developing countries. "Enormous pressures" have been exerted on the positions of countries in Latin America.[20]

Dependency affects not just a country's economy, but the poor in that country especially (as argued in the second "easily defensible" thesis noted earlier). Even in times of growth, income distribution in Latin America has remained extremely skewed. Of all countries listed by the World Bank in its *World Development Report 1987* Brazil shows the worst record in the world for disparity of income distribution. The lowest 20 percent of the population in Brazil receives only 2 percent of the national income; the top 10 percent account for over 50 percent of the income.[21] The poor suffer most, however, when the economy declines. Another World Bank study (1986) asserts that the poorest sectors of society in Latin America were hit hardest by the 1980 recession. The rural poor in Mexico, for example, suffered a 31.3 percent wage decline.[22]

The Causes of Dependency. The fact of dependency and its sharply negative consequences in recent years do not, however, explain how such dependency developed or how much dependency causes underdevelopment. The strong form of dependency theory articulated by A. G. Frank, and supported by some statements of liberation theologians, focuses on external forces primarily. This strong form tends to read the history of Latin America as successive epochs of domination and exploitation by foreign powers: by Spain and Portugal from 1500 to 1800, by England and other European nations in the nineteenth and early twentieth centuries, and then by the United States in more recent decades. But such an explanation, if neatly simple in theory, overlooks some important causal factors. In contrast, the type of analysis done by Cardoso studies internal and external factors and avoids targeting any single factor as a primary cause.

Most historians would certainly hold Spain and Portugal accountable for Latin America's original dependency and for creating severe impediments to development. The conquistadores subjugated the native peoples, forcing them to labor in fields and mines. The Amerindians became and remain "oppressed" peoples. The Spanish and Portuguese made vast fortunes from the gold and silver resources of Latin America. And, as some Marxist analysts have noted, this wealth often passed from Spain and Portugal into the hands of the English and Dutch, helping to finance the industrial revolution. Thus one reading of Latin American history would emphasize these factors of plunder and exploitation.

The same colonial heritage, however, points to other factors that help to explain why Latin America failed to follow the path of industrial development — and agricultural development — that occurred in Northern Europe and the United States. The Spanish brought with them a disdain for manual work, and Spanish mercantilist policies prevented Latin America from producing manufactured goods for itself and from open trading with other nations. In striking contrast to the United States, where four of every five white Americans owned their own land or trade prior to the civil war, property ownership in Latin America was concentrated in the hands of a few and the vast majority were left propertyless. In the United States, free enterprise developed and agricultural industrial development met domestic needs (though it did so by ruthlessly excluding Amerindians and enslaving blacks). Latin America, though subordinating these groups in rigid class structures, at least included them in society. But concentration of ownership and failure to invest profits into new domestic markets crippled Latin America's efforts to build a productive economy. The concentration of land ownership begun in colonial times continues into the present with 1.3 percent of landowners in Latin America controlling 71.6

percent of all land under cultivation.[23] This structure of concentrated ownership deprived the great masses of the population access to their own land and trades. One could characterize this legacy in Marxist terms as lack of control over the means of production; but one could also describe it in terms of the absence of any real experience of free enterprise.

As for the Spanish conquerors' disdain for manual-industrial work, even the liberationist philosopher Enrique Dussel acknowledges its devastating consequences:

> Spain chose the easy way: exploiting the American mines with the Indians rather than taking the narrow road that England chose, namely, the hard work of an industrious people. The Spanish lack of economic vision was catastrophic for Spain and also for the Latin American countries. Spain could easily have had coal and steel in Europe, but this would have signified an austere, simple, daily industrial effort. Spain preferred to mine only gold and silver, which in the short run produced ephemeral splendor, but in the long run produced economic catastrophe from which Spain as well as Latin America has never recovered.[24]

With the coming of independence in Latin America (the 1820s), British and other foreign investors did move in and accounted for much of the commercial-industrial development that did emerge. But here again one can attribute blame as much to the failure of Latin American elites who lacked the capital and motivation to build up an industrial economy, and who remained content to gain wealth from massive *latifundios* devoted primarily to supplying crops for export to Europe and the United States (e.g., bananas, coffee, sugar).

Latin Americans have good reasons for resentment against the United States and transnational influence. Often in the past U.S. companies literally dominated the economies of some Latin American countries—for example, United Fruit in Guatemala and U.S. copper companies in Chile. Often these companies have taken out millions in profits and done so with exorbitant profit rates. When Chile nationalized U.S. copper companies in 1971, the Allende government claimed that the companies had taken out of Chile wealth estimated at $10.8 billion dollars over a sixty-year period. Chile refused compensation on the grounds that the copper companies had already been compensated by exorbitant profit rates. Kennecott, Allende claimed, had an average annual profit rate of 52.8 percent from its Chilean operations from 1955 to 1970; Anaconda averaged 21.5 percent in profits from Chile during the same period, as opposed to 3.6 percent from their investments elsewhere.[25]

Political interventions by the United States have also blatantly violated the autonomy of Latin American countries, with interventions in most cases aimed at overthrowing democratically elected governments (Guatemala in 1954, Brazil in 1964, the Dominican Republic in 1965, Chile in 1970–1973, and Nicaragua in the 1980s).

One can easily overstate, however, the causal relationship between U.S. and foreign investment and the problems of underdevelopment in Latin America. Complete withdrawal of U.S. business and political influence would not solve the problems created centuries before by concentrated local ownership and consequent failures in internal development. Statistics showing that transnationals take out more in profit than they invest do not of themselves prove that underdevelopment has been caused by "draining off of surplus value," for the transnationals do at least create new wealth. Chile might not have developed a copper industry, at least not at the same level of productivity, without the capital and technology invested in it from without. One can still criticize, however, the fairness of the terms involved in transnational investment. Thus although U.S. copper companies paid Chile more in taxes, after World War II, than it took out in profits, they also so aggravated Chileans by their profit rates, by not investing profits from Chilean copper in Chile itself, and by U.S. government restrictions on trade and control of copper prices, that the Chilean assembly called *unanimously* for nationalization in 1971.[26]

Dependency analysis does help to explain problems in Latin America, but Gutiérrez's cautions should also be heeded. Liberation theology does need to note variations within dependency theory and it needs to weigh legitimate criticisms against those dependency arguments that oversimplify causes and solutions.

MARXIST ANALYSIS

Dependency theory has its critics, but it does not begin to generate the militant opposition (or support) that one connects with Marxism. The reason for this is clear. Dependency theory may prompt various strategies of response, some reformist and some more radical, but it has not led to the creation of political parties and popular movements committed to a specific program of change. Marxist analysis, on the other hand, has become linked with concrete tactics, strategies, and goals, as well as realized embodiments of Marxist ideas in many countries of the world. Hence, though liberation theology has more explicit ties with dependency analysis, the strongest criticisms against it have focused on its use of Marxist analysis.

Marxist analysis includes various components. It involves first of all a method of studying societal changes in history (historical materialism). This method considers modes of production and economic structures as far more determinative in shaping history and society than the political figures or ideologies that historians had tended to focus upon. This method views the class struggles generated by divisions of labor and ownership as driving forces in history. It includes also a critique of religion (with religion seen as pacifying the poor and justifying the status quo) and of other dominant ideas or ideologies in a given society.

Related to this general view of history, Marx developed a more pointed and specific critique of the capitalist system. Marx believed that capitalism systematically alienated workers from their work, their products, from nature and from other humans. Capitalism exploited workers by paying wages that did not reflect the true contribution of workers, but were based on what they needed to subsist. The difference between what workers actually received in wages and the real value of their work constituted a "surplus value," which owners expropriated as profit. Concepts like alienation and exploitation provide Marxism with much of the moral power it generates, but Marx sought also to show "scientifically" how various contradictions within the capitalist system would create its downfall: overproduction and underconsumption, falling rates of profit, crises leading to mass unemployment and ultimately to workers' revolution and the overthrow of capitalism.

When capitalism did not collapse, new Marxist theories were developed to explain its continuance. The theory of capitalist "imperialism," made prominent by Lenin, argued that the creation of industrial and banking monopolies created greater price and market stability, whereas the development of colonies created new markets for investment as well as supplying cheap labor and raw materials. This analysis of imperialism concurs with dependency theory in their common perception of a capitalist center dominating poorer peripheral colonies. But Marxists and dependency theorists also disagree on numerous other points.[27]

In the early years of liberation theology especially, many Latin American theologians spoke positively about Marxist analysis as a "useful scientific tool" for understanding conditions in Latin America. Many critics of liberation theology focused on Gutiérrez's discussion of class struggle in his *A Theology of Liberation*. Even in these pages, however, Gutiérrez does not "call for" class struggle or view it as the "driving force of history" (as later Vatican critics implied), but only affirms that the church should recognize the "fact" of class struggle and should place itself on the side of the poor.[28] Throughout the rest of the book Gutiérrez has only a handful of short comments about the contributions of Marx and Marxist analysis. For example, he writes: "Marx created categories which allowed for the elaboration of a science of history."[29] Gutiérrez felt that Marxist analysis could be separated from Marxism's atheistic worldview. In making this separation he appealed to José Carlos Mariátegui, a Peruvian religious-minded Marxist, who viewed historical materialism as a flexible "method" of interpreting society not dependent on philosophical materialism. Gutiérrez referred also to Althusser's distinction between Marxism as a science and as an ideology.[30] His only other notes on Marxism in this first book dealt with its influence on modern theology (showing the need for transforming the world) and on the challenge of Marx's critique of religion.[31]

Gutiérrez speaks directly to the issue of Marxist analysis in his 1984 essay on the social sciences and theology. He stresses that the presence of elements of Marxist analysis does not mean identification of social science with Marxism. He notes the conflicts between Marxist analysis and dependency theory on many issues; he insists that liberation theology involves no use of Marxism that would deny human liberty; he agrees with warnings made by the magisterium about uncritical use of Marxism; and he asserts that there has never been any proposal in liberation theology to synthesize Marxism and Christianity.[32]

José Míguez Bonino wrote extensively about Marxism in the mid-1970s. One would hardly classify his own writings as Marxist, but he did speak of the "unsubstitutable relevance of Marxism" for Christians concerned about social change.[33] If Christians are serious about the commitment to the poor, Míguez Bonino asserted, they need some instrument for analyzing society, and Marxism offers "a scientific, verifiable, and efficacious way to articulate love historically."[34]

Hugo Assmann's early writings seemed the most Marxist. He noted that liberation theology confronts problems arising from dependence, exploitation, and imperialism. Assmann then adds: "For most of those who use this language, this implies the use of a sociological analysis derived from Marxism."[35]

The most militant statements in favor of Marxist analysis came from the Christians for Socialism groups in the early 1970s. They called not only for Marxist analysis but for the realization of a Marxist socialism: "In this matter, our Movements recognize the contribution of Marxism, insofar as the latter aims at a scientifically rational history, connected with a praxis that constructively transforms the project of a new and different society." "We accept Marxism as a theory and praxis that are indispensable if our Christian love is to take concrete form."[36]

If one concentrates on Christians for Socialism documents and the period of the early to mid-1970s, one can find a strong influence of Marxism. But such a focus gives a very incomplete picture of liberation theology overall. In a collection of essays, *Frontiers of Theology in Latin America*, none of the thirteen theologians affirms Marxist analysis as a necessary or integral tool for liberation theology.[37] One could read Jon Sobrino without knowing that Marxism constituted even an issue in liberation theology. Juan Luis Segundo uses Marx (critically) as only one source among many social theorists. José Comblin has written strong criticism of Marxist analysis and especially of Marxist socialism. He warns against ideologies that "appear" scientific but impose their own values and programs, and against philosophies that replace free human activity with some underlying "movement" shaping history.[38] Comblin speaks with even sharper critique of Marxist regimes, comparing the Soviet Union to Latin American military dictatorships, which seek control over all parts of society. "Consequently, in Marxist revolution there is no freedom for the people, only for the Party."[39]

Liberation theology remains, however, profoundly and rather uniformly "anti-capitalist." Consequently, while references to Marxism have become more muted and nuanced and the framework of liberation analysis has broadened, some use of Marxist analysis remains precisely because it serves as the most prominent instrument of criticism against capitalism. Thus Leonardo and Clodovis Boff's comments about Marxism, in their *Introducing Liberation Theology*, probably represent positions held by the majority of liberation theologians. The Boffs state that liberation theology uses Marxism "purely as an instrument" and that it "maintains a decidedly critical stance" in relation to Marxism. Marxism can be a companion, but never *the* guide — a position reserved for Jesus Christ.[40]

Nearly all the references one finds in liberation theology, however, affirm only that Marxist analysis *can* be a useful scientific tool for understanding conditions in Latin America. But liberation theologians do not tell us much about *why* they find Marxist analysis useful, *how* they adapt it, and *what* specific works of Marxist analysis have proven helpful. Exploring these questions about "why, how, and what" use of Marxist analysis one finds in liberation theology proved insightful to me.

Why do liberation theologians find Marxist analysis useful? Some liberation theologians have said that the very pervasiveness of Marxist ideas in Latin American political and intellectual movements make some use almost inevitable. But this would not explain the generally positive assessment attributed to Marxist analysis. Others have stated that commitment to the poor means commitment to the "popular movements" that struggle with and for the poor, and that such movements use Marxism as a guide. This justification, however, raises a serious problem. Marxist ideas, as Lenin noted, do not arise spontaneously in the working class or the poor; revolutionary theory must be brought "from without." The historical record of Marxism does not lend great assurance that Marxist ideas represent the true desires or the needs of the poor.

When liberation theologians stress the usefulness of Marxist analysis as a scientific tool, the most fundamental reason, in my judgment, is that they believe that Marxism has correctly identified the basic root of Latin America's problems — the capitalist system. And Marxist analysis does offer a penetrating criticism of capitalism. But the usefulness of Marxism depends on its correctness in naming and analyzing capitalism as the central problem.

For many Americans and others the "scientific" claims made in behalf of the social sciences, and of Marxism in particular, seem greatly exaggerated. In the natural sciences we have methods of testing that lead to clearly verified results. Social sciences rarely produce conclusive results. Even in conventional economics, which uses the most quantifiable testing, economists differ sharply in their assessments of a given situation and often prove far wide of the mark in predicting outcomes. Americans lend more credence to positions that build upon extensive empirical data, but they recognize even then that the data used can be very selectively chosen to support a given position. They view Marxism as especially suspect in this regard. Its "scientific" record of predictability appears quite weak. In each new period over the past century and a half, Marxists have pointed to crises of overproduction that would "soon" bring the downfall of capitalism. Most of Marx's predictions about the increasing pauperization of the working class and about continual decreases in the middle class proved to be almost the reverse of what actually occurred in industrialized countries.

There exists a striking difference between the strong sense of scientific truth, which many Latin Americans associate with the social sciences (and Marxism), and the skepticism expressed by many in the North. The difference arises in great part from very different views about what scientific theory means. Phillip Berryman states this difference well:

> A discussion of theory and practice reveals clear cultural differences between the intellectual milieux of North America (and often Western Europe as well) and Latin America. In our everyday usage "theory" is often contrasted pejoratively with "reality." We tend to take as normative the "scientific method" in which theory is the result of an empirical, self-correcting trial-and-error process.
>
> Among Latin American intellectuals, on the other hand, "empirical" is most often a pejorative term, denoting superficial appearance rather than the deep reality of things. Theory is regarded as a tool for cutting through appearance to get at the heart of things. Many essays by Latin American social scientists, for example, seem to be focused largely on constructing a "theoretical framework." Concrete data often seem to take second place. What Latin Americans understand as "praxis" is poles apart from Yankee "practicality."[41]

How do liberation theologians use Marxist analysis? One line from Berryman's quote goes far in explaining both the "how" and the "what" in the liberation theology use of Marxism: "Theory is regarded as a tool for cutting through appearances to get at the heart of things"—and the very genius of Marx's mode of inquiry is precisely its dialectical method questioning "appearances" to get at the reality of things. For all the controversy over use of Marxist analysis in liberation theology, I have yet to find (at this stage of my investigation) *any* specifically Marxist studies of Latin America that serve as guides to liberation theology analysis. One finds in Gutiérrez and others many references to dependency theorists and the use of *ideas* from earlier Marxist writers (Mariátegui in Peru, Gramsci and Althusser from Europe, and of course Marx). But at this point I have not found in liberation writings any references to detailed contemporary works of analysis by Latin American Marxists. One does find, on the other hand, Marxist concepts and insights used as "heuristic" principles (the Boffs refer to methodological "pointers" in Marxism) to challenge prevailing, traditional ways of thinking.

This use can be illustrated with numerous examples. Liberation theologians place great stress on the idea of "praxis" borrowed from Marx. The idea of praxis emphasizes the need for "transforming the world"; it stresses also the need for changing unjust "structures." (On this point and the following ones as well, liberation theologians reacted against what they saw as a weakness in traditional Christian thought with its emphasis focused on personal, moral conversion.) The Marxist critique of religion seemed too often accurate in its description of prevailing Christianity as an ideology used to pacify the poor and justify the status quo. The concept of "ideology" and the method of studying the use of ideologies by dominant sociopolitical groups have been broadly and frequently used by liberation theologians. Many liberation theologians see their own position in reference to the poor as that of "organic intellectuals." They take this idea, along with the struggle to win "hegemony" in society, from the Italian Marxist Antonio Gramsci. Franz Hinkelammert's *The Ideological Weapons of Death* constitutes a prolonged reflection based on Marx's concept of the role of "fetishism" in capitalism. Otto Maduro's *Religion and Social Conflicts* offers a lengthy and modified use of Marx's sociology of religion to explain the involvement of religion in the conflicts that have occurred in Latin America.

Along the same lines, concepts of "exploitation," the theft of "surplus value," the dominant influence of "imperialism," and the moral critique of capitalist "profit-seeking" have all been used by liberation theologians. Again these indicate a "heuristic" use of Marxist concepts, but they do not constitute what many U.S. social scientists would view as the "scientific"—that is, empirical—side of Marxism (studies of overproduction, falling rates of profits, etc.). For all the criticism of Gutiérrez's use of the *concept* of "class struggle," I have yet to find in liberation theology any detailed class analysis, or even less any program directed against a certain class or classes in Latin America.

A longer study would be needed to assess the validity of Marxist charges. Certainly "exploitation" is obvious in Latin America. But its clearest expressions lie in concentrated landownership that predated the development of "capitalism" in Latin America. The predominance of "state ownership" of industries in many Latin American countries has also created a situation far different from the capitalism criticized by Marx. Sweeping and generalized critiques of capitalism often fail to distinguish what structures create injustices (for example, exclusive concentrated ownership) and what structures may prove healthy for Latin America (for example, widespread distribution of private property, including workers' cooperatives, as opposed to Marxist state control). The importance of free, independent political organizations needs also to be stressed.

A fuller study would also need to take up the issue of whether Marxist analysis can be "separated" from Marxist ideology and tactics. (I believe a separation can be made, but it requires a very cautious and critical discernment, for the still dominant "classic" Marxism does not make such a separation and builds its analysis on an atheistic, materialist philosophy.)

Liberation theology has undergone significant developments in recent years. Many of its critics still focus on statements by activists of the early 1970s. The great effort to build up base communities has given the poor themselves greater voice and active participation in determining their own praxis and goals. Many liberation theologians have already incorporated the cautions and self-criticisms noted by Gutiérrez in his 1984 essay on the use of the social sciences. Liberation theology has provided a much needed voice in Latin America, as Pope John Paul II, encouragingly affirmed in his letter to the bishops of Brazil: "We are convinced, we and you, that the theology of liberation is not only opportune, but useful and necessary."[42]

NOTES

1. Clodovis Boff, *Theology and Praxis: Epistemological Foundations* (Maryknoll, N.Y.: Orbis, 1987), p. 30, and José Míguez Bonino, *Toward a Christian Political Ethics* (Philadelphia: Fortress, 1983), p. 45.

2. This summary of dependency theory and of its development is drawn from several studies. A word about each may be helpful. (1) Gabriel Palma, *Dependency Theory, A Critical Assessment* (London: Frances Pinter, 1981), first published in *World Development* (July-August 1978), is the best source I found, especially in relating dependency theory to Marxism. (2) Philip J. O'Brien, "A Critique of Latin American Theories of Dependency," in Ivar Oxaal, Tony Barnet, and David Booth, eds., *Beyond the Sociology of Development* (London: Routledge and Kegan Paul, 1975), gives a useful account of ECLA, and of A. G. Frank and Cardoso. (3) Ronald H. Chilcote has edited or co-edited several helpful studies dealing especially with the debate between Marxism and dependency. See his *Dependency and Marxism* (Boulder, Colo.: Westview, 1982); Chilcote and Dale L. Johnson, eds., *Theories of Development* (Beverly Hills: Sage, 1983); Chilcote and Joel C. Edelstein, eds., *Latin America: The Struggle with Dependency and Beyond* (New York: John Wiley, 1974). (4) James L. Dietz, "Dependency Theory: A Review Article," *Journal of Economic Issues,* 14/3 (September 1980), compares Frank and Cardoso. (5) Míguez Jorrin and John D. Martz, *Latin American Political Thought and Ideology* (Chapel Hill: University of North Carolina Press, 1970); chap. 14 deals especially with ECLA and the early dependency theorists in Brazil.

3. Theotonio Dos Santos's definition (brief form) from a work he co-edited, *La dependencia política-económica de América Latina* (1971) is cited by Michael J. Francis, "Dependency: Ideology, Fad, and Fact," in Michael Novak and Michael P. Jackson, eds., *Latin America: Dependency or Interdependence?* (Washington, D.C.: American Enterprise Institute, 1985), p. 89.

4. Gustavo Gutiérrez, *A Theology of Liberation* (Maryknoll, N.Y.: Orbis, 1973), pp. 26–27.

5. Hugo Assmann, *Theology for a Nomad Church* (Maryknoll, N.Y.: Orbis, 1976), p. 37.

6. Ibid., p. 49.

7. José Míguez Bonino, *Revolutionary Theology Comes of Age* (London: SPCK, 1975), p. 16.

8. Leonardo Boff, *Liberating Grace* (Maryknoll, N.Y.: Orbis, 1979), p. 29.

9. Gutiérrez, *A Theology of Liberation*, p. 85.

10. Ibid., p. 87.

11. Gutiérrez, *The Power of the Poor in History* (Maryknoll, N.Y.: Orbis, 1983; the original articles written from 1974 to 1978), pp. 45, 78.

12. Gutiérrez, "Teología y ciencias sociales," appeared originally in *Christus* (Mexico City), October-November 1984; it will be published also in Gutiérrez, *The Truth Shall Make You Free* (Maryknoll, N.Y.: Orbis, forthcoming).

13. Leonardo Boff, *Liberating Grace*, p. 66.

14. Ibid.

15. Ibid., pp. 77–78.

16. F. H. Cardoso, "The Consumption of Dependency Theory in the United States," *Latin American Research Review*, 12/3 (1977) 8.

17. J. Fred Rippy, *Latin America, A Modern History* (Ann Arbor: University of Michigan Press, 1958), pp. 389–90.

18. Francis, "Dependency," pp. 92–95.

19. *International Monetary Fund Annual Report, 1984* (Washington, D.C.: IMF, 1984), pp. 9–11; quote, p. 31.

20. *The World Bank Annual Report, 1984* (Washington, D.C.: The World Bank, 1986), p. 32.

21. *World Development Report 1987* (New York: Oxford University Press, 1987), Table 26, pp. 252–53.

22. *Poverty in Latin America, The Impact of the Depression* (Washington, D.C.: The World Bank, 1986), pp. 16–17.

23. Michael P. Todaro, *Economic Development in the Third World* (New York: Longman, 1981, 2nd ed.), p. 260.

24. Enrique Dussel, *A History of the Church in Latin America* (Grand Rapids: Eerdmans, 1981), pp. 77–78.

25. From a summary of a speech given by Salvador Allende before the General Assembly of the United Nations, December 1972.

26. Theodore H. Moran, *Multinational Corporations and the Politics of Dependence, Copper in Chile* (Princeton: Princeton University Press, 1974), p. 55 on taxes paid by the copper companies; pp. 87–94 on trade restrictions and price-setting; pp. 102–15 on ways profits were used (and the mounting discontent in Chile).

27. On the differences and debates between Marxists and dependency theorists, see Chilcote, *Dependency and Marxism*.

28. Gutiérrez, *A Theology of Liberation*, pp. 272–79.

29. Ibid., p. 30.

30. Ibid., on Mariátegui, p. 90; on Althusser, p. 97, n. 40.

31. Ibid., pp. 9, 220.

32. Gutiérrez, "Teología y ciencias sociales."

33. José Míguez Bonino, *Christians and Marxists: The Mutual Challenge to Revolution* (Grand Rapids: Eerdmans, 1976), p. 19.

34. Ibid., p. 115.

35. Assmann, *Theology of a Nomad Church*, p. 116.

36. The Christians for Socialism statements cited by Bonaventure Kloppenburg, O.F.M., *The People's Church; A Defense of My Church* (Chicago: Franciscan Herald Press, 1978), pp. 72–73.

37. *Frontiers of Theology in Latin America,* Rosino Gibellini, ed. (Maryknoll, N.Y.: Orbis, 1979).

38. José Comblin, *The Church and the National Security State* (Maryknoll, N.Y.: Orbis, 1979), pp. 66, 140–42.

39. Ibid., p. 132, and quote, p. 220.

40. Leonardo Boff and Clodovis Boff, *Introducing Liberation Theology* (Maryknoll, N.Y.: Orbis, 1987), p. 28.

41. Phillip Berryman, *Liberation Theology* (New York: Pantheon, 1987), p. 85.

42. Pope John Paul II, to the Brazilian bishops, 1986, published in part in the *National Catholic Reporter,* May 9, 1986.

33

God and Society:
A Response to Liberation Theology

MARIE AUGUSTA NEAL, SND

There are in our society clearly different approaches to the reality of God. Some of these operate to achieve strong resistance to change in social structures; others, to assist toward effective change in those same structures. Although the actors involved are individuals, their approaches to God are common, for they are culturally embedded and rise out of shared experiences. Emile Durkheim was perceptive when he explained that the God whom many individuals worship is the society that nurtures them. What liberation theology does for the modern world is to direct our attention to where God dwells. Through liberation theology, we can come to discover that God is with the poor as they organize themselves to claim their rights as human beings. This is a great gift to a world, which has been struggling with atheism in its various forms since the eighteenth-century Enlightenment.

Our beliefs about what is of God are closely linked to our beliefs about what constitutes the good society or at least the society with which we deal. That is why the concept of listening to the Spirit means such different things to different persons. Some assume that all that can happen does so only within the fabric of the social structure. For others, the structure itself is potentially an object of reform. Some pray for miracles because they are convinced that only divine intervention can change the conditions they find intolerable. Others, addressing the same reality, entirely ignore the possibility of supernatural life. They seek, instead, a clear and scientifically replicable model for change that adheres to the laws of logic, because they believe that all that happens is organically related or spiritually determined by an infinite force that does not yield to charismatic petition. They seek to understand the existing social structures, the better to use them as they are. Neither of these points of view includes a belief in planned social change.

But there are some who do believe in planned social transformation. Here again, however, there are several recognizable approaches. Some, facing the same intolerable conditions, prepare in advance to try to change the situation. First, they assess the causal links among the known elements of existing social systems and then devise possible pathways to change. They know that such pathways must first lead to shared control: of power, wealth, and social constructions of reality (Berger), as presented through the major media of communication and internalized by the interacting communities. These persons believe that social structures can be changed. They know that agents of change have to get control of the power of the state, the wealth of the economy, and the influence of the media, and have to have the skill and knowledge to do what they think needs to be done. This group includes a whole range of religious believers and nonbelievers. Some of these persons include prayer among their methods: praying for the courage to see, to judge, and to act: praying to control their own psyches and to participate effectively with other actors and reactors in each specific situation. Believers in divine intervention work together with nonbelievers in this model with the believers exercising the hope that comes with their faith in God's presence among them. Their hope is a powerful factor in the outcome. It also provides the energy to risk death in the process. Some of these persons really believe that all the members of the human community can share in that control.

Another classic approach to social analysis and social change rests in the belief that the charism for social transformation, in its historical specificity, resides in the social consciousness of an organized worldwide work force. This work force, in revolutionary enthusiasm, stands firmly against the organized owners of the means of production. Freed by persuasive results of social analysis from the influence of cultures created by their powerful adversaries and imposed on them as definitions of the situation, they throw off the control the oppressors have over socialization. They then responsibly take decision-making into their own hands and, through new relationships to the means of production, redefine the rules. In so doing, they create a new culture and, in some cases, rediscover whatever divine reality exists for human beings to know. They thus set the world on a new course that makes the state ultimately unnecessary in its present form, for the new classless society, now completely socialized, manages itself into the future. This, of course, is the Marxist dream of a new reality. It is as faithful as either of the first two positions described above. In fact, all these points of view from which action or reaction stems are rooted in some kind of faith, whether it be in God, the self, the process, the people, or some or all of these.

My analysis takes the third position—namely, that social structures are knowable through careful and critical social analysis: there is no hidden hand—of God or of the universe or of philosophical reason—that directs societies totally independently of human choice and action. It holds that changes can be directed by an informed public will and it recognizes that drift, along with controlled power, accounts for some of what happens in society. To take this position is to be aware that, at present, complex networks of drift, manipulation, focused altruism, and other factors influence change and help to shape the public will. In other words, God's grace acts through human choice and human initiative, even as other factors of physical and biochemical origin, as well as of entrenched culture, act as forces of resistance and of change. It seems clear, however, that neither God nor the devil intervenes with miracle or malice at the social level and that here God acts through us, the human community. This places an enormous responsibility on us as we gather to determine God's will in these times.

These many approaches to social analysis are grounded in and derived from religious and social philosophies: biblical fundamentalism, social Darwinism, Hegelian idealism, existentialism combined with Christian socialism and theoretical Marxism. We can come, therefore, to at least one valid conclusion: that whatever is defined to be the truth will prevail as a standard to test its validity, until a new understanding of reality or some social disaster brings persons to new reflections to account for unintended consequences of their purposive social action. From that point, they will move to other interpretations that seem more reasonable to them in view of the new realities that they must now face or they will bring them to death. The world currently faces one of these new social realities. We are willing to come together at this moment, therefore, to reflect, lest we die. The present social realities that move us to action today include: the immanent possibility of nuclear disaster; an environmental threat from toxic waste; the possibility of the failure of disease control; and, most especially, the unnecessary poverty of two-thirds of the world's peoples. This latter reality is the result of the inequities in the use and distribution of world resources for food, shelter, literacy, health, and human freedom, a maldistribution manifestly unjust and intolerable.

For too long, our social analyses have been grounded in premises of natural personal self-interest (Adam Smith), national self-interest, scarcity of resources (Thomas Malthus), and inevitable development toward some ideal end (Herbert Spencer). At present, it is essential to review these arbitrary assumptions to enable us to make an adequate response to the compelling call of liberation theology as it comes to the First World from the Third World and announces the joyous news of the liberation of peoples from every oppressive situation (Bishop's Synod, 1971, p. 2). In the meantime, both of these worlds must also interact with the Second World with its own utopian assumption in place.

Today, not philosophical ideologies but rather systematic social analysis, applied to the new data of population size and available resources, should subsume our understanding of society and its capacity to provide for the needs of all. The skill to estimate present and future population trends, technology to find and develop resources, and the analytic tools for interpretation are sufficiently refined to yield credible conclusions. Our hopes for the future and our plans for social change can be supported by testable hypotheses now resting on ever-more reliable factual data about resources and persons. With this grounding in place, our theological reflections can concentrate on what God is asking of us today, given the signs of these times. We can discover that providing for human need is no longer a Malthusian problem but a solvable one. We can assess the weakness of a lifeboat ethic, used to legitimate the violent destruction of unneeded peoples and their neglect of the environment where they live. We can object to the accumulation of concentrations of wealth and services. At a time when millions are homeless and without adequate health or educational means, this privilege is a violation of basic human rights. Hence, from a religious perspective it is an unacceptable solution even though it seems tolerable to a laissez-faire economics. We can reject claims that the hidden hand of the market provides adequately for human need by demonstrating that, in fact, it does not do so. So, too, we can reject the principle that national self-interest legitimates interference in the internal affairs of other nations. On the contrary, it becomes increasingly clearer that all international relations should operate on the principle of the common good, with the dominant nations yielding to the rights of the developing nations as they strive to get control of their own destiny.

The fundamental statistical realities that change the situation for our times are the facts that the world population is reaching a peaking point of about 10.5 billion and that the world's resources are sufficient to provide adequately for such a population (see Neal, *The Just Demands of the Poor* [Paulist Press, 1987]). The will to provide, however, is not yet part of our public ethic. The assimilation of this will is not the domain of social science but of culture. Just as slavery, formerly considered by some an efficient means of cheap labor, is no longer an acceptable or legal option, so too is exclusion of the poor from access to necessary resources no longer a human option. How the world goes about eliminating forms of human exploitation as viable choices is part of the record of history but that it does so is recognizable by all. Liberation theology is a major factor in the current historical moment addressing the exploitation of the poor of the world and taking action to eliminate the causes of their poverty.

The Second Vatican Council recommended the use of critical social analysis for addressing the social problems of the day. It did so because the world was witnessing the struggles of Third World countries emerging from the burdens of colonialism only to be exposed to the hostile challenges of imperialism. The developing peoples, seeking liberation from want in the mid-1960s, were feeling the impact of resistance, phrased in the ideologies of competing world powers: those of liberal capitalism on the one hand, and of communism on the other. Various new movements of the contemporary period—of civil rights groups within the First World, of peasants seeking land in the Third World, of women seeking equality in the work place, in the state, and in the church—joined the organized workers and other cultural groups of an earlier era also acting to shape their futures. These movements urged the reexamination of the assumptions undergirding many firmly entrenched analytic systems that were preventing the liberation of peoples. Church persons were not the only concerned groups addressing this reality with the altruistic intent of standing with the struggling poor. They were a major and powerful witness to the legitimacy of the claims of the organizing poor with whom they took their stand on the moral basis of a biblical mandate to do so. The church's mandate to be involved was necessarily strong because among its functions is that of the prophetic calling to account of a society when it fails to provide for its people.

In 1965 a group of social scientists, fifty in all, funded by the United States Department of Education came together at Tufts University in Medford, Massachusetts. They assembled at the invitation of Jerrold Zacharias, a physicist at MIT, Andrew Gleason, a mathematician from Harvard, and an educator, Jaqueline Grennan then a Sister of Loretto and president of Loretto College in St. Louis, Missouri. They had received a grant from the United States Department of Education for this venture. By way of background, in the previous decade a small group of physicists, recognizing that their disciplines had been used to generate the H-bomb and aware of the consequences of this use, had developed a more critical way of teaching physical science and mathematics. Their objective was to educate toward an acceptance of social responsibility for such inventions. Then, in the 1960s, perceiving the centrality of the social sciences to the new historical challenge of developing peoples, they wanted to provide an opportunity for their colleagues in the social sciences to bring a more critical stance to their teaching and research. Those invited to the 1965 meeting included social scientists from the disciplines of history, anthropology, political science, economics, education, and sociology.

We social scientists were challenged to examine the supposed neutrality of the assumptions underlying the theories of the disciplines that guided our research and, most especially, our educational techniques. We were urged to reassess our textbooks and other materials used for teaching, to determine in whose interests we dedicate ourselves when we systematize knowledge and apply it to life. The lack of adequate education for minorities in the United States was a motivating factor in funding this assembly. Who was invited? Colleagues present at the meeting had made reputations for being open and concerned about the quality of life developing unevenly for peoples of different heritages and locations. This group of fifty lived an intense week of searching study. Its objective was that of developing more critical modes of teaching so that education could include the challenging of premises not always true to the experience of some peoples. The goal was not that of a theoretical exercise but that of changing, where needed, the presuppositions of our teaching methods and of our disciplines—that is, if found to be ideologically adverse to developing peoples. The problem specific to the social sciences was twofold: the assumption of political science that a foreign policy of natural self-interest is a natural course of action; the dictate of economics that scarcity of resources is a market reality legitimating an abstract formula to determine prices, production, and wages. These theories had not been challenged within the disciplines themselves, even though the descriptions of social realities, constructed on the basis of the accuracy of their premises, actually rested only on the acceptance of their validity. First World resistance to the development of Third World peoples suggested to the social scientists that their validity needed review.

The stimulus to this initiative came from our having witnessed the struggle for self-determination that strained the societal rules of First and Second World hegemony. The civil rights movement, the Third World movement, and the women's movement were the cases in point. The rules that justified keeping the oppressed peoples subjugated were now being questioned. One small group at that meeting of social scientists decided to experiment with teaching a social science course—across the three disciplines of political science, economics, and sociology—that began with the question of why there are poor persons in a rich society like the United States. We did this to develop, from the very beginning of the teaching experience, a critical stance toward the social structures we would describe and explain. We believed that students would care about that question as about a problem that ought not to persist. In time, we found that, in fact, many did care. We found too that many more did not. Furthermore, formal education provided ample legitimization for alternate explanations of the same reality, thus providing rationales for a whole range of public action, as well as for resistance to action. Today, I begin my introduction to sociology course by asking: Why is it that two-thirds of the world population live at or below subsistence, when we have technology that could be used to provide adequate production, but does not do so? I then demonstrate with data that there are resources sufficient to supply for human need and that world population is not exceeding what the world's resources could supply with adequate planning. The data challenge the assumption of scarcity in economic models (Neal, 1987). They raise basic questions about the functional usefulness of the international banking system and its links with First World governments. What is lacking as part of this approach is the corporate enthusiasm to respond effectively to this new reality. The acquisition of that enthusiasm is a function of the cultures learned in the socialization process. More specifically, it is a function of religion as taught and lived.

The reason for recalling this 1965 gathering of physical and social scientists is to locate a social event, chronologically simultaneous with the Second Vatican Council, indicative of the altruistic concern of some academics and parallel to the social analysis of the council. Those men and women perceived as morally wrong the movements of technology and science into the accelerated production of weapons so destructive that they could easily threaten the whole human race. The physicists saw that their special competencies were being so used. The social scientists recognized that now the evidence of their disciplines could and was replacing that of philosophy, which once grounded the motivating disciplines of ethics and theology. We were shedding old tenets of social Darwinism. We were convinced by the social behavior of the organizing poor that, although they too could think, judge, and act responsibly, something more was needed: the formation of public will to welcome new peoples as peers.

By the early 1970s news began seeping into the United States that experiential learning was already going on. It was being used in Latin America through methods like those of Paulo Freire, who introduced the process of conscientization, a literacy learning method richly rooted both in social analysis and in biblical reflection. (Missionaries on home visits communicated to us the fact that whole villages were becoming literate in from six weeks to six months. Working in the remote villages of Brazil's northeastern region and in crowded *barrios* in Chile and elsewhere, they could tell us what remarkable progress in literacy learning, social awareness, and basic Christian community development was taking place.)

In 1971 I visited villages in the interior of northeast Brazil, in Coroata, as well as in the environs of San Luis. I heard and watched as villagers, gathered from twenty-two surrounding areas, reflected together on pressing social problems they were experiencing, and planned actions to change those conditions. In dialogue homilies at the liturgy, in marriage and baptismal preparation classes, and, then, in late-night political planning meetings, they linked gospel readings, prayer, and planning. In 1973 I met Paulo Freire, who was giving formal lectures at Harvard University and living as neighbor of friends of mine in the Boston area. I read his *Pedagogy of the Oppressed* and discussed with him how this method of literacy learning worked so effectively in rural enclaves and crowded city ghettoes to develop effective organized action for change of unjust social structures. When, then, I read Gustavo Gutiérrez's *A Theology of Liberation* in 1973, I knew it was an analysis of those same realities that I had personally witnessed. I was convinced that it was not just one more of many theologies. It was naming a spiritual social process set in motion in our world, a process in which persons prayed and worked, aware that God was with them as they reached out to claim what was rightfully theirs. Later, in South Africa, where I went from my Brazil experience, I visited township after township, where the same growing awareness of unjust structures was forming the understanding of black South Africans living under the apartheid system of discriminatory laws.

By that time, I had been teaching sociology for seven years, using the new, more dialogical, method developed by a small group of those present at that 1965 meeting. It became clearer to me, with each year of teaching, that the method generated in many an inquiring attitude toward learning the social sciences. Further, it fostered a desire to work with others for change that would confront social injustices. Those who critically evaluated existing social structures were often rejected by many of their colleagues. Choice of career inevitably became a problem for those who came to a growing social awareness. They realized that the careers chosen in accordance with their new awareness were not ladders to wealth and power. One had to think seriously whether or not to join a crusade defined as deviant by one's peers, those with whom one continued to live and work within family, community, religious community, and friendship groups, as well as in the wider society. Furthermore, one was moved to question the role of religion in a society that is resistant to the struggle of the poor for liberation. Persons with this new understanding of the social realities of the organizing poor also sought new religious experiences and a new theological foundation for their own developing consciousness. They also experienced, in some places, alienation from the reluctant local church.

Liberation theology became known in theology schools in the 1970s in North America. Some of those who received it with enthusiasm and who simultaneously had learned of the pedagogical methods of Paulo Freire tried immediately to adapt the method to their own personal experiences of oppression. For the nonpoor to think of themselves as oppressed rather than as oppressors posed a problem. Groups of learners who were studying Freire raised to consciousness in discussion groups the oppressions of their own lives in order to change those situations. Their oppressions as nonpoor persons, however, were quite different from those of the residents in the little villages of northeastern Brazil and urban *favelas*. Furthermore, channels for action to change these conditions were much more immediately available to them, even if difficult of access. Almost immediately, their own agenda as the nonpoor preoccupied the learners, who thereafter began to set aside or obscure the agenda of the organizing poor, for whom Freire's method was originally intended. The poor in oppressed areas use this method to challenge the legitimacy of the social order itself. The method uses decisive language of class conflict and struggle for liberation. It demonstrates the reality of unjust political, economic, and class structures, legitimated by such cultural givens as religious services, patriotic songs, and classic literature. As used by the nonpoor, however, it was and is, in fact, co-opted. The disconcerting ease with which First-World culturally established thinking can divert even a tool most effective for discovering social injustices became manifest in this theology school experience. The students and scholars alike were identifying themselves with the experience of the poor but they were assuming the role of victims rather than of colleagues. Despite the disparity in access to resources they had as the advantaged nonpoor, they presumed to enter their own competing claims.

To clarify this point, let us shift briefly to 1988. In February *Sollicitudo Rei Socialis* (social concerns of the church) Pope John Paul II's encyclical marking the twentieth anniversary of *Populorum Progressio* was published. It moved the church's decisive option for the poor a step further by calling the rivalry between liberal capitalism and collectivist communism for world hegemony social sin. Denouncing ideologies that accept the operation of uncontrollable social mechanisms acting in human interests, it urged the transformation of political, economic, and social structures that currently oppress the developing peoples of the world. It put the moral force of the church on the side of the struggling poor and loosened its link with established law and order. The judgment that current social structures prevent human liberation led the present pope to define some of them as sinful. By way of definition, social sin refers to unjust rules of social behavior in those institutional areas in which work gets done, governance is carried out, meanings are made and shared, and social behaviors reinforced or rejected. Included are economic, political, social, cultural, and religious systems. The immediate reaction of some Catholic conservatives to the papal encyclical was to denounce the document as uninformed. Consider, for example, the televised discussion on Firing Line, February 13, 1988, a week after *Sollicitudo Rei Socialis* was published. William Buckley and his two guests, ethicist Michael Novak, of the American Enterprise Institute, and Rev. Richard McBrien, ecclesiologist from Notre Dame University, all agreed that the description in the encyclical of the present world system, as controlled by two powerful blocs that resisted the Third-World poor, was naive. They could recognize the structured evil of the communist world but could not equate it with the same degree of evil in the capitalist system, because their perspective was not that of the affected poor (see William Safire, *New York Times,* Feb. 22, 1988, p. A19).

It is useful to review, in summary, the sequence of church teaching that culminated in the papal judgment of social sin in 1988. In 1967 *Populorum Progressio* applied the decisions of the Second Vatican Council to the dispossessed of the world. It expressed the option for the poor that the council concluded to be the new position of the Catholic Church in the world. By that time, the church in Latin America, urged on from the time of *Mater et Magistra* to look critically at the link of Catholic life to the political and economic power systems of Latin America, questioned its own close alignment with centers of wealth and power. It actively struggled to link itself to the cause of the dispossessed poor.

Having concluded that human development could not advance under existing social structures, the church in Latin America loosened its historical association with established states and economic systems. As is widely known now, the position papers prepared for the Medellín Conference (1968) provided the background work for a major leap of faith. That leap began to be evident to us in North America when we recognized that not only was that church hearing the cries of the poor but it was also standing at their side as they organized themselves to seek their just due. Others who write in this volume can recount and interpret the struggles and the sequence of events that became known to us in the publication of Gustavo Gutiérrez's *A Theology of Liberation*. It is a landmark volume that made it possible for others to reflect on the biblical and historical roots of the church's option for the poor and the causes of the current conflict within its own membership in the struggle to respond to God's call at the present time.

At this point, I should also mention the earlier factors influencing the faith response of the institutional church in Latin America. Those were the nineteenth-century faith challenge of Marxism to all churches that preached to the poor to be patient and long-suffering in expectation of an eternal reward in the next world; the new support brought to Latin America by the worker priests exiled from a Europe that feared the worker-union organizing of the 1930s; and the incentive of the priest worker movement, itself inspired by the earlier social encyclicals *Rerum Novarum* (1891) and *Quadragesimo Anno* (1931), and realized in the "think, judge, act" formula of Catholic Action of depression days. The 1960s further added the sophisticated skills learned from Paulo Freire's biblically based literacy learning methods toward conscientization. Finally, the formalization of this whole process is what we call today liberation theology—that is, the living church finding God with the organizing poor seeking social justice.

Ongoing research is discovering, reporting, and interpreting the precedents of liberation theology, within both narrow and broader frames of reference, depending on the experience of the researchers. The theoretical links of movements and countermovements since the emergence of eighteenth-century Enlightenment philosophy—Marxism, the labor movement, and the development of peoples—all need to be seen in their proper perspective to understand whence we gather our strength and vision, feel resistance, and are called to respond to the efforts of the poor in the late twentieth century. The political culmination of all these phenomena can be seen in the United Nations Bill of Human Rights. I do not intend to review here all the elements cited but simply to name them to frame the setting for a response to liberation theology.

My purpose is to highlight an emerging response to the productive influence of liberation theology and conscientization in the developing poor nations. It is a response that is biblical, guided by the church's social teachings, and compelling as a call to mission in the United States. This response is already alive but is in need of systematization and celebration to sustain it and increase its influence. It celebrates the same good news proclaimed by liberation theology: that God is with the poor as they claim their rights as human beings. God's presence is experienced in the struggles of base communities in Latin America. It is a continent peculiarly suited to initiating these grassroots movements of Christianity because it received the faith as a part of the colonialism brought to it. It is fitting, therefore, that it should be the locale of the struggle for new freedom in the church and in the world.

The historical reality we face today underscores the struggle in the Third World of the poor who claim the land. They are resisted by powerful landowners, allied with military forces that use violence against them in the name of the state. It includes the struggle, in the cities of the First and Third Worlds, of the homeless who claim the same right as the rural poor to housing and who organize for legislative action to secure shelter, food, health care, literacy, and a share in the planning for these resources. In those struggles, the Catholic Church announces that the claims to the land and the priority of labor over capital are just and are in line with biblical teaching (see *Laborem Exercens, Sollicitudo Rei Socialis,* and the Bishop's Pastoral on the Economy). The historical reality of the day also includes huge indebtedness of the developing nations to the banking system of the First World countries, especially in the United States and Western Europe. An unfortunate factor in this reality is the witness that the Catholic Church presents of division within itself over the biblical claim to the land and the degree of holiness of the demands of the poor. But the teaching and pastoral church stands firm in recognizing the right of the poor to take what they need in their poverty (*Gaudium et Spes,* no. 69).

Conflict and misunderstanding have been endemic to issues of social justice. The poor and the nonpoor often divide in their perceptions and exemplify the need of the nonpoor to be educated to the experiences of the poor in the context of social justice rather than in the relatively modern tradition of the rightness of profit (Weber), private property, and power through control over the use of weapons. As a result of action and reflection around biblical themes and as a response to the signs of our times, the poor are declaring that they are not eternal slaves to the nonpoor. They are persons who now, with the development of literacy, can read the Bible, reflect on the oppressions of their lives, discover their human rights, and experience the presence of God sufficiently to believe they are called by God to eliminate unjust structures. In our times, that means for them challenging structures that prevent the sharing in those resources necessary for their human existence: food, shelter, health care, education, and participation in decisions that affect their lives. The development of the world now makes available, through human invention and technology, resources fully adequate for human need. The theology of liberation addresses this reality from the perspective of the poor. It notes that, currently, despite plentiful resources, they are still withheld on the basis of the rules of the enculturated operating system. Accordingly, liberation theology stirs the people to respond. This means that it does what, in essence, Jesus did, and hence stimulates the same threat—death from the establishment.

When Juan Luis Segundo was visiting professor at Harvard Divinity School in the early 1970s, we discussed the physical dangers experienced by the Latin American poor. They had learned Paulo Freire's methods of conscientization and held the belief, derived from liberation theology, that they had rights to the land. In their organizing they claimed rights long dormant under the law. This was because, although they had felt the oppression, as illiterate peasants they had lacked a social awareness and social analysis sufficiently articulate to name the causes of their poverty and dispossession. When they finally did so, they threatened the status quo. Segundo concluded, at that time, that their new consciousness endangered their lives as long as the government was a dictatorship. This led him to recommend not using the method of conscientization while those with power could inflict violent injury on those who attempted to create the awareness of oppression and who organized to make just demands. Although I could appreciate the danger, I felt that the conclusion not to teach was pointing to an incomplete evangelization, explaining the meaning of the gospel today in the lives of the nonpoor. They/we are being called to respond to the just demands of the poor. However, we are reinterpreting the call as if we were those poor. (Poor is best defined in this discussion as peoples with high infant mortality, low life expectancy, and low gross national product per capita.)

The villagers I met in Brazil in 1970, in the interior of the northeast, were planning how they could further their claims to the land on which they had worked as tenant farmers for over thirty years. They knew the danger because, at that very time, two of their members had already been imprisoned for refusing their "X" for a signature on documents they could now read and sign. Why were they in prison? Because they had become literate. The action was defined as a communist act. Picture-based copies of *Populorum Progressio* had been confiscated there as communist literature. The villagers with whom I met were deliberating how they could send some of their members to the trial, which had been moved to a military court in the next state, and take care of the families of the absent farmers at the same time. A heavy task for poor farmers. One of the distasteful factors in this situation was that the case against them was being brought by the local landowner with the support of the local church. What was wrong? The whole country was Catholic. Why were the farmers defined as atheistic communists? They had never even met a communist. The label was sufficiently effective, nevertheless, to jail their comrades at the order of landholders who shared the same religion but not the same beliefs about ownership, even though the church was officially affirming those beliefs since the council. Yet, to claim rights against those who controlled the land was defined as communism. It permitted curtailment of human rights, even with the support, in some cases, of local church authorities. A new struggle, then, was now in progress, one that divided the church from within. It needed, therefore, a new theological reflection or persons would not be able to find God in their lives.

When I left Brazil in 1971 I was on my way to South Africa to do a study of the Catholic schools of South Africa for the Southern African Bishops' Conference. When I arrived there, I found that one violated the Anti-Communist Act, promulgated in 1927, merely by criticizing the government. It is a government that defines itself as Christian and anticommunist yet, at the same time, it practices a unique form of racism called apartheid. This ideology states that peoples of different races can develop only if they develop separately. Only one of the races, moreover, the white one, names the rules for the separation. Nevertheless, this state enjoys acceptance by other modern states that repudiate communism as a social evil yet tolerate the social evil of apartheid. Happily, we see the living church today addressing this evil in South Africa and standing with the oppressed poor. However, we also see the church being co-opted by the state. In 1988 in South Africa, when blacks organize to claim their rights, they too are defined as communist, a label that rallies a white majority to vote and act against them, even though that majority is 93 percent Christian.

What is the perspective from which liberation looks communist and why is the misnomer so successfully used to kill the initiative of conscientized poor persons? Furthermore, why is it that the spirit that moves the organized poor to believe that God is with them is described by some of the non-poor as atheism? Clearly, God is perceived to be linked to the state in the progression of its history. When President Reagan ended his talks with "God bless you," he conveyed his belief in that link. It is disarming. The American flag in church and the prayer before Congress mean something in that respect too. The indignation of the American Civil Liberties Union at these acts has to be deliberated. A good, however, is involved, a good that is susceptible to manipulation. In fact, manipulation is obviously occurring. This reality needs to be understood theologically and to be analyzed socially. We call on God to be on our side in public life, in the life that is supposed to reflect the common good.

What liberation theology is doing with the poor is to provide for empowerment in a biblical context, creating and furthering the church of the future. What is lacking is a theologically sound response to the liberation initiatives of the poor, also biblically derived and authentically taught. We are not going to be able to rejoice in the liberation struggles of the poor if, as a result of the powerful resistance they receive from many of the nonpoor, they themselves are destroyed and all those who struggle with them are denounced as atheistic. Surely, the gospel speaks to the nonpoor today with some inspirational and compelling content that allows us to enter enthusiastically into the new awareness of the dispossessed as they stand up and cry freedom.

What is it saying? How are we recommended to act? What is the most relevant formulation of the question to the Christian nonpoor as liberation theology guides marginalized peoples to claim their rights as human beings? The question then is this: When the poor reach out to claim what is rightfully theirs, what does the gospel mandate the nonpoor to do? Suppose we try as a tentative response: to let go our grasp on the things the poor need in order to survive.

Before we can shape that response, we need to come to a clear understanding

MARIE AUGUSTA NEAL

that this is indeed what the times call for. That response supposes that what the poor need, the nonpoor possess. We know that the poor need, in addition to food, clothing, shelter, health care, and education, the right to participate in plans that determine their production and distribution. These things we purchase with money, or provide for through taxes—that is, with our common wealth. The response also implies that there is enough of these goods for all. Further, there are good reasons for the nonpoor to take the demands of the poor seriously and to share existing resources. That, in turn, suggests that the poor have prior claim to the existing resources, one that is ethically persuasive and biblically based. The response accepts the fact that the poor are capable of and are needed for making wise decisions about production and distribution. Pragmatic reality demonstrates that the nonpoor, for the most part, tighten rather than release their grasp as the poor reach out to take what is theirs. This fact indicates that no adequate theology operates in the larger society with sufficient force to prevent an ensuing struggle. Finally, the response suggests that the struggle is caused more by the nonpoor resistance than by the violent initiatives of the poor. We have yet to elaborate the theology that reflects these realities. However, we can begin with one certain proposition:

> Inherent in our developing understanding of mission is the belief that God who speaks to us in diverse ways, today, calls to us with special insistence through the voices of the poor as they organize themselves to claim their rights as human beings [*Probe* Sisters' Survey, item 395].

I did not critique here the assumptions about social class as used in sociological analysis. But, as the poor continue to organize and to claim their place in world society, to share in resources and to participate in decision-making, the division into classes with distinct cultures, as we have known them in the past, will change. Beliefs, practices, and lifestyles too will change. Hierarchy may yield to democracy, as capitalism, whether private or of the state, yields to planning boards, which represent many interests. And what will happen to war? We do not know. All we know, at this juncture, is where God is. Even this is still a mystery, which, for some, is beyond belief.

298

34

Human Rights Language and Liberation Theology

ALOYSIUS PIERIS, SJ

The cloud of incomprehension that surrounded recent discussions on liberation theology in the official churches in the West cannot be dispelled fully without acknowledging that the two parties in dispute were using two theological languages, albeit within the same orthodox Christian tradition. Many First World theologians committed to social justice follow their pastoral magisterium in using *human rights language* as a theological discourse whose primary addressees could only be the wielders of power and the accumulators of wealth, including the governments of rich nations. Third World theologians on the contrary take *human liberation as God's specific language* primarily addressed to and easily understood by the poor and the oppressed.

Unfortunately, this language difference is not respected. Thus certain First World theologians tend to universalize and absolutize their paradigm, unmindful of its contextual particularity and ideological limitations. On the other hand, many activists and some theologians in Asia fail to make a "paradigm shift" when perusing the plethora of literature issued by human rights advocates from the West and liberationists from Latin America.

This essay is occasioned by this confusion, over which therefore, I wish to reflect aloud in the hearing of my colleagues both in the First and Third Worlds. With their critical response, I hope to arrive at some clarity, some day.

THE HUMAN RIGHTS TRADITION: A BRIEF HISTORY

In origin and development, "the human rights tradition represents an almost Anglo-American phenomenon."[1] This movement reached its climax with the incorporation of the so called Bill of Rights in the American Constitution. It was, undoubtedly, the most revolutionary event in constitutional history. The very idea that certain *individual* human rights should be invested with constitutional inviolability is said to be unprecedented in the history of political thought.

However, "without prior English development, *individual* rights could scarcely have developed to the level they did in the American law," says the American constitutional historian, Bernard Schwartz.[2] Historians find the Magna Carta of medieval England (1215) a convenient starting point. The next convenient milestone would be the Petition of Rights (1628) followed by the English Bill of Rights (1689), which gave its name (not its contents, which were too meager) to the American Bill of Rights. For brevity's sake I omit here other intermediary events.

The Magna Carta was a monarchical document saturated with the language, the concerns, and the spirit of feudalism. It merely *conceded* certain rights to the barons in return for obedience. It was a royal bargain with feudal chiefs rather than the outcome of a common people's struggle for liberation. The English playwright Arden's play, which commemorated the 750th anniversary of this great charter in 1965, was aptly titled *Lefthanded Liberty*! Yet in some of its provisions, the phrase "any baron" seems to alternate with the more generic term *liber homo* (any free human). Such elements give these provisions an elasticity that the monarch may have never intended but that later human rights advocates found helpful. Thus the charter happened to contain "the germ of the root principal that there are *individual* rights that the state—sovereign though it is—may not infringe."[3]

The Petition of Rights of 1628, in contrast to the Magna Carta, was not a feudal claim of privileges. The battle for parliament's independence from the crown was the context that gave rise to it. It started with the "Protestation of 1621," and this struggle climaxed with the fundamental rights of English persons becoming a positive law by way of a parliamentary enactment. Herein, "the almost superstitious reverence Englishmen feel for their law" and their "legal conservatism" were made use of by a group of "common lawyers who rewrote the history on parliamentary lines in the House of Commons and who built up the body of rights and precedents alleged to be the immemorial heritage of the English People."[4]

History showed that superstitious reverence for the law was not effective even among the English. A law-enforcing machinery was never built into the parliamentary acts, which therefore remained merely declaratory. Charles, the king of England, did not bow down to this act of parliament. It is the crown that ruled. Thus the achievements of 1628 were null and void from a constitutional point of view—a lesson the Americans learned to avoid in *their* declaration of rights.

It is true that the so-called levelers—religiously motivated radicals in the parliament—tried to bring out a more fundamental concept to the fore: (what we might anachronistically call) the people power as the primordial source of authority to which even the parliament should bow and which alone can countercheck any form of arbitrary government. Their document—the "Agreement of the People"—after a series of debilitating amendments, succumbed finally to the fate of all previous written declarations. It had no binding power. The whole exercise was no more than a mere dream. And there was Cromwell who would not let it become history.

Only against this background could one recognize the revolutionary character of the English Bill of Rights of 1689. King James II had dissolved the parliament in July 1688 and five months later fled from the kingdom after throwing the Great Seal (the symbol of constitutional continuity) into the Thames. In the absence of a crown to legitimize a new parliament, a body of responsible persons assembled in an unprecedented manner to form a self-legitimized parliament and offered the throne to William and Mary, subject to the conditions laid down in the "Declaration of Rights"—better known as the "Bill of Rights"—which passed as a regular act of legislature. According to the bill, the parliament was to be freely elected by the people, and was to enjoy complete freedom of speech uninhibited by court or crown.

The revolutionary nature of this document has earned it the title: the Second Great Charter.

Yet, the English Bill of Rights, Schwartz warns us, was rudimentary compared to the American one; for the former contained much fewer rights than the latter, and was ever subject to interference by the legislature.[5] The American Bill of Rights, with its more complete list of *individual rights*, succeeded in immunizing itself constitutionally against any such interventions from successive governments or courts whereas the English Bill of Rights did not have enforcement machinery built into it. Thus, the American Constitution has immortalized the inviolability of the human person in terms of a series of basic, "God-given" rights.

THE "SECULAR HUMANIST" AND "RELIGIOUS-CHRISTIAN" CONTRIBUTIONS TO THE HUMAN RIGHTS THEORY

The major influential factor in the development of the American Bill of Rights is what Garrett calls the *Human Rights Tradition*, which, he complains, is too easily confused with something quite different, the *Natural Rights Tradition*, as he names it. In presenting Garrett's valuable insights,[6] I am compelled to make use of his terminology. In the subtitle above, I have called these respectively, the *secular-humanist* and the *religious-Christian* streams of the one human rights tradition. I shall switch back to this terminology after allowing Garrett to make his point.

The movement that climaxed in the American Bill of Rights could be viewed as a confluence of these two streams of thought. But a sociological analysis has convinced Garrett that the natural rights tradition is overrated as an influential factor, whereas the human rights tradition was also largely responsible for the development of the American ideal.

Garret's analysis of the natural rights tradition begins with medieval Europe. The immediate context was the phenomenon of papal absolutism, which tried to absorb secular monarchy into its own hierocratic structure. The defensive posture adopted against this papal hierocracy was twofold. The first reaction produced the "dualist school." It revived the ancient "divine right theory of monarchy." It saw both pope and king as two independent recipients of divinely conferred authority in their respective spheres of competence, spiritual and temporal. The other defensive posture was adopted by the "Natural law school" with leanings toward the Aristotelian theory of nature and society, a theory gaining currency among intellectuals. It looked for a secular basis for political authority, to free it from all ecclesiastical interference. Their appeal to "reason" and "natural law" was equally aimed at the dualist school in order to safeguard humans from the dangerous consequences of the state claiming God-given, inalienable rights over persons.

There was, in the course of time, a *populist view* emerging from these conflicts. In the divine rights school, this meant that God bestows political power to the king through the people. This same theory, applied to the papacy, resulted in the "conciliar movement." In the natural law school, however, it took the guise of a social contract theory, which received a more sophisticated articulation later in Locke and Rousseau.

The "human rights tradition" differs from this European ancestor on many counts, Garrett maintains. First of all, it was an exclusively *Anglo-American* phenomenon. In England, it was associated with the lower-status levelers (as opposed to the Independent Party, which was made up of the gentry); in America, the main actors were Roger Williams and Issac Backus, with the Baptists and Separatist Congregationists serving as the social carriers of the tradition.

Secondly, it was essentially a *religious* movement in neat contrast with the natural rights tradition, which had a clearly marked secular thrust. It was particularly nurtured by a piety expressed through a variant form of Calvinistic theology. To me the implication seems to be that, here, the inviolability of human rights is based on a "divine origin," so to say, and this makes the individual the only "sacred" component of any given society.

The third difference, in Garrett's list, is that the human rights tradition was a *populist* movement, both in England and in America; its social carriers were the "lower status folk" and its ideologues, for the most part, were not even university trained. This explains the widespread support that the American Bill of Rights received from the common folk in the colonial states. The natural law theory, by contrast, was a movement of intellectual theoreticians, from the lawyers and philosophers of medieval Europe to the founding fathers of the American dream.

Finally, the motivational points of departure are diametrically different in the two traditions. The natural law theory aimed at protecting the sovereignty of the secular state from ecclesiastical encroachments, whereas the human rights tradition, especially in America, began as an effort at safeguarding the "freedom of conscience"—that is, *individual religious liberty* against a secular state trying to impose an official religion (in this case, the Church of England) on the consciences of all. In fact, almost all the rights (speech, assembly, property, and the like) were derived from this basic concern for religious liberty.

Obviously, the two movements, despite radical differences, converged in the demand for total separation of church and state. The "experts" who framed the Bill of Rights and the "people" who greeted it with an overwhelming approval arrived at the same conclusion from divergent points of departure. The two streams have joined together to form one river: a great human rights tradition. It has flowed beyond the confines of the North American continent thanks to the UN Charter of Rights.

THE HUMAN RIGHTS LANGUAGE AS A PARADIGM OF HUMAN FREEDOM IN WESTERN CHRISTIANITY

The human rights movement—I am now shifting back to my original nomenclature, leaving that of Garrett—has been shown to be a convergence of a secular-humanistic and a religious-Christian tradition. In appropriating this tradition as a theological discourse on social ethics, both the radical reformed movements in Protestantism and the progressive thinkers, including popes, within Roman Catholicism, were merely yielding to an ancient Christian propensity to combine humanistic reason with biblical revelation—that is, a universally valid and transcendent *theoria* with the concrete tenets of Christian faith.[7]

In fact, according to one scholar, " 'human rights' is not a biblical construct"; it is one of the "nonscriptural categories" that, in confrontation with the scriptures, gave rise to the Christian discourse on human freedom. "The biblical communities functioned with a conception of rights, though they would not recognize the terminology of natural rights or human rights," for the manner of stating universal human claims in terms of a comprehensive and compartmentalized list of rights reflects a typically Western mode of perception.[8]

The human rights movement is, in other words, the West's specific contribution to the understanding of human liberation. It is the spiritual nucleus of Western culture, the quintessence of the Western ethos. It is the ideological substance of which the Western democratic order of social relationships is constructed. Understandably, therefore, all political organs of the West—both governments and the NGOs—could hardly perceive, proclaim, or promote the values of freedom and fellowship except in terms of individual rights.

The Western church absorbed this language in the very process of contributing to its development and to its eventual refinement. This Church gave the human rights tradition a solid biblical basis, by rooting it in the revealed doctrines of creation (every human is created to the *image of God*) and redemption (every human is an object of God's redemptive intervention through Jesus' *atonement*). Accordingly, it is God who has *gratuitously* endowed each individual with a transcendental and inviolable dignity so that the "autonomy," which the secular-humanist tradition (of the natural rights school) claimed for the human person in terms of inalienable rights, takes the guise of a "theonomy" in the social teachings of the church.[9]

With this type of theological reasoning, the Western patriarchate tried to refine the rights tradition in three interconnected areas. The first revolves around the phenomenon of "individualism," which has now come to be the hallmark of Western spirituality and is the most pernicious outcome of enthroning individuals where formerly kings ruled with divine authority. A team of North American sociologists, led by Robert N. Bellah, have monitored "the classical polarities," or more bluntly, the contradictions of American individualism, one of which is described as "the commitment to the equal right to dignity of every individual combined with an effort to justify inequality of reward, which, when extreme, may deprive people of dignity."[10] The church resolved this contradiction—theoretically, of course—by presenting the human person not as a self-enclosed unit dissociated from the human community, but as a dynamic member of society intrinsically related to other members of that society even in the exercise of rights.

The other inadequacy springs from the close ideological nexus that this individualism maintains with the liberal democratic tradition of the West. The church consciously steered clear of both individualism and collectivism by distancing itself from this liberal democratic ideology—as well as from Marxism, which rightly insisted on the inseparability of personal freedom and social solidarity.[11] Although it repudiated Marxism, the church was certainly influenced by the Marxist critique of liberal democracy and of individualism, and also by the Marxist thesis that economic freedom is basic to political freedom.[12]

Thus we come to an important distinction that Christianity's "public theology" introduced: the distinction between *economic* rights (to food, shelter, work, health care, social security), which Marxists lay stress on, and *civil* and *political* rights, which are the foundation of Western democracies (freedom of speech, belief, assembly, association, habeas corpus, due process, etc.).[13] By affirming them both as inseparable and as equally essential, the Catholic social teachings in particular have not only critically accepted the Marxist distinction, but also partially appropriated its critique of the Western tradition of rights—namely, that this tradition concentrated on political rights, without basing them on the foundation of economic rights. This is the third area in which the Christian rights theory corrected the human rights tradition of the West. The most powerful statement of recent times in this direction is the North American Catholic Bishops' Pastoral, "Economic Justice for All."[14]

As Hollenbach has argued, social doctrine still continues to be developed in the Christian community and he has himself suggested "three strategic moral priorities" that all liberation theologians would endorse, though from quite another perspective: (1) the needs of the poor take priority over the wants of the rich; (2) the freedom of the dominated takes priority over the liberty of the powerful; and (3) the participation of marginalized groups takes priority over the preservation of an order that excludes them.[15] This is indeed a revolutionary stance; if carried out, it would overturn the ideological framework of Western democracy. For such a shift in policy implies a radical structural change that goes beyond the "social democratic conception with the welfare role of the state" as advocated by other Western theologians who wish to combine the "freedom rights" of liberal democracy with "benefit rights" of socialist systems.[16] Liberation theologians too are asking for a structural change in opposition to the Western democratic model. Can the Catholic human rights tradition, even in the radical form envisaged by Hollenbach, meet the demands of liberation in Latin America and other Third World countries? This is the issue I take up next.

THE LIBERATIONIST THESIS VERSUS THE HUMAN RIGHTS DISCOURSE OF THE WESTERN CHURCH

I was intrigued to note that there is no entry on "individualism" in the extensive index of the Hollenbach classic—*Claims in Conflict*—which is the most comprehensive and critical exposition of the Western church's social teachings. I was equally intrigued to note Hollenbach's own surprise at the absence of any entry on "human dignity" or on "human rights" in the extensive index of the Gutiérrez classic, *A Theology of Liberation*. As Hollenbach suspects, the liberation theologians abandon the rights language because that language, in their minds, is associated with "the static and individualistic notions of the human person."[17] These omissions in Gutiérrez and Hollenbach are a clear index of the language difference between the First World theologians concerned with rights and the Third World theologians steeped in the liberation struggle.

The two paradigms differ primarily in the way they combine the secular-humanist and the biblical-religious components of their respective theologies. In the West, the human rights theologians not only ground their natural rights language in the doctrine of the human person extracted from the Bible, but they also employ that language as a *critique on the Bible*, detecting the absence of scriptural references to many rights, such as freedom of religion or freedom for women, even though such rights could eventually be deduced from the biblical principle of "the dignity of the human person."[18]

In the liberationist paradigm, the secular humanist contribution comes from socialism, which includes the reality, if not also the ideology, of class struggle,[19] whereas the biblical foundation it seeks for its praxis is not a transcendental principle extracted from the Bible—as is the case with human rights theology and Catholic social teaching—but the *foundational experience* that forms the axis of biblical revelation: the election of the oppressed as God's covenant partners in a liberation praxis initiated by God. This foundational experience is the "canon within the canon," which is the critical principle that judges the biblical contents internally. Unlike the human rights theologian who "critiques" the Bible from a human rights perspective, the liberation theologians subject the whole corpus of Catholic social teachings and human rights theology to this critical principle of biblical revelation (and would perhaps question the right of anyone other than the oppressed to speak of human rights!).

Thus, according to Gutiérrez, even *Populorum Progressio* seems to be entrenched in the Western developmental model of human growth. The first comprehensive use of the language of liberation, according to Gutiérrez, is found in the message delivered by eighteen Third World bishops in response to that same papal encyclical; this language resonated in Medellín and became its central and all-pervasive concern.[20] And, if Puebla was a step back from Medellín, was it not because the Catholic social doctrine permeated by the human rights language was trying to regain lost ground in Latin America?

I find it quite significant that Gutiérrez not only makes absolutely no use of the human rights language, as Hollenbach has already noted (see above), but has also ignored the whole human rights movement, as if to say that it has no relevance in a Third World context. This movement, as I described it in the earlier part of this paper, began from an elitist concern, not from the underside of history, as is made evident by the nature of the major events that contributed to that movement from the Magna Carta to the American Bill of Rights.

The implication of this observation is not that the human rights movement has no global message but that it constitutes the mood and method of a theology that continues to speak from elitist and conceptual heights, and presupposes Western democratic structures, whereas liberation theology is born out of a struggle that in some way is directed against those same democratic systems and their domination in the Third World. Hence, one cannot gloss over the contextual, ideological, and methodological discrepancies that separate the two theologies.

This may be why the American Bill of Rights has not merited even an adverse comment in the pages of *A Theology of Liberation*. The United States of America is mentioned there only about three times; and in each instance, this gigantic paragon of Western democracy is made to appear as the major hindrance to Latin America's sovereignty! In Gutiérrez's references to liberative initiatives recorded in history, the great American independence struggle is conspicuously absent, whereas the French Revolution (which was, in fact, inspired by it) receives an honorable mention, as does also Russia's October Revolution. He counts these two among "the great revolutions," which, at least tentatively "wrested the political decisions from the hands of the elite"—that is, from the "elite" who claimed they alone were "destined" to rule.[21]

Does this mean that for Gutiérrez the American Revolution was not really an example of a "people's struggle" as it had not "wrested the political decisions from the hands of the elite"? I would hardly contest the fact that the social carriers of the human rights movement (the religious, populist stream of it) in the British colonies of North America were the lower-status folk, as Garrett (quoted above) has cogently argued. But in the wider context of colonization and in the perspective of liberation theology, it was a battle of the elite and not a *colonized* people's struggle against the domination of *colonists*; indeed it was a case of colonists wrenching for themselves the "privileges, liberties, and immunities" of English citizens— that is to say, the colonists' acquisition of "Englishmen's rights."[22] The colonists were (European) "emigrants" who—according to John Adams's boast—were the real "author, inventor, and discoverer" of American independence.[23] Neither the *black slaves* imported by the colonists, nor the *colonized natives* marginalized by the same colonists were the immediate beneficiaries of this revolution. Thus, to the liberationist it is not a meaningful model even though it remains the crown and glory of the human rights movement in the Western democratic tradition.

And yet, no liberationist would deny the fact that the human rights language is the West's own indigenous way of communicating the gospel of justice to the rich and the powerful. Nor would Third World theology stand in the way of Western theologians forging a third way between capitalism and communism, even if that might sound abstract.[24] For that abstract idea has crystalized into a "public theology," which has, at least *theoretically*, corrected three major defects of the human rights tradition—individualism, liberalism, and neglect of economic rights, as indicated above.

Although one would be skeptical about a mere idea generating a change in social structures, one would still respect the great philosophical tradition of Western theology that succeeds in clarifying issues conceptually. Hence when the church appropriates radical ideas as basic to Christian message, it is bound to express them with prophetic clarity. When this happens, a sigh of relief is heard in Third World churches. That certainly was the case when the news of the U.S. Bishops' Pastoral Letter on Economic Justice reached our ears in Asia! Though reformist and tame,[25] it is the only language the Western church knows to speak.

As long as this theology speaks to the rich and the powerful in the West and in the westernized enclaves of the Third World, it is within its own right and the only enemy it will encounter will be political liberalists and Christian fundamentalists. But it draws the wrath of liberation theologians only when it becomes a tool at the service of the Western church's ecclesiastical colonialism in the poor countries. This is the concluding argument of my analysis.

HUMAN RIGHTS THEOLOGY: A TOOL OF ECCLESIASTICAL IMPERIALISM IN THE THIRD WORLD?

Ecclesiastical imperialism is the tendency of one church to regard all others as its extensions, and to make its "particular" theology "universally" obligatory. This is but an ecclesiastical version of the ethnocentric dogma: "my culture is the modern universal culture." The human rights theology as it appears in the social teachings of the Western churches tends to be used in this manner.

Eminent and much respected theologians join the official church in this campaign, though not with bad faith. They criticize black, feminist Latin American and Afro-Asian theologies for being mere particularized perspectives claiming to be theologically comprehensive, but quite firmly believe that the human rights theology is based on transcendent universal principles valid for all situations.[26]

Although this universal principle ("dignity of the human person") is invoked against all other theologies, the ultimate criterion, I suspect, is a matter of *ideological* preference.[27] The human rights theology is ideologically tied to the Western democratic model of social organization; but liberation theology accepts critically the socialist paradigm, which includes also the *reality* of class struggle. Therefore, at the root of the argument against liberation theology there is more ideology than theology at work.

The history of the Roman Church's social doctrine can be cited in support of this. For instance, two popes who laid the foundation for the church's social doctrine, Leo XIII and Pius XI, may have had many biblical, theological, and philosophical arguments against the Marxist theory of class struggle. But, as Hollenbach observes with scholarly candor, their rejection of the class struggle idea, in reality, came from "the close links between the church and the classes which were the targets of Marxist attacks." Moreover, "these links prevented the papal tradition from understanding important aspects of the Marxist social analysis."[28] It is such ideological links that prevent both the pastoral and the academic magisterium of the Western patriarchate from respecting the particularity and therefore the validity of another local church's theology.

The Vatican's reaction to liberation theology cannot be explained otherwise, as a careful analysis of this excerpt from Ratzinger illustrates. Explaining his own Congregation's second instruction on liberation theology, he says:

> Catholic social teaching accordingly knows no utopia but it does develop models of the best possible organization of human affairs in a given historical situation. It, therefore, rejects the myth of revolution and seeks the way of reform, which itself does not entirely exclude violent resistance in extreme situations, but protests against the recognition of revolution as a *Deus ex machina* from which the new man and new society are one day inexplicably to proceed.[29]

Here one local theology posing itself as "Catholic social teaching" refuses to recognize that the shift ("conversion") from sin to grace in the order of social relationships is a qualitative jump; the "myth of revolution" is rejected in favor of "reform." But the scripture scholar and Ratzinger's collaborator in *Communio*, Norbert Lohfink, has inquired into the biblical roots of liberation theology and come to quite another conclusion: the revealed notion of liberation is distinguished from the nonbiblical approaches to social questions (1) by treating the poor as *the* poor—that is, a people oppressed as a class—and therefore also (2) by advocating a radical opting out of that oppressive system rather than resorting to reformist solutions, and (3) by believing that God takes full responsibility for this radical change[30]—(not withstanding Ratzinger's suspicion of deus ex machina). In that case, "Catholic social teaching," which, according to Ratzinger, is called to "develop models of best possible organizations of human affairs in a given historical situation," cannot a priori preclude a Third World church's option for a social system that conforms to the biblical principle enunciated above, or impose on a Third World church the West's reformist model of human rights theology as if it were "catholic" (universal). That would be an ideological imposition of the Western church on other churches.

It is this "ecclesiastical imperialism" that liberation theologians wish to combat, and not necessarily the human rights theory or the public theology that appropriates it, or the ideologically ambivalent principle about social models that Ratzinger enunciates.

The most critical area of conflict, therefore, revolves around the ideologically interpreted biblical foundations of the two theologies. Liberation theology does not speak of a "transcendental principle" extracted from the Bible and then "applied" to concrete situations. Such a manner of theologizing is indigenous to a Christian culture that employs philosophy as *ancilla theologiae*. Liberation theology does not explain reality philosophically; it analyzes reality sociologically. Hence, it is not concerned about a "transcendent principle" (biblical or otherwise) that "integrates" various conceptual diads such as "individual and society," "economic freedoms and political freedoms," "liberal democracy's anticollectivism and Marxist socialism's anti-individualism." Liberation theology is engaged, not with reconciling conceptual opposites, but with resolving social contradictions between the classes.

Let me, therefore, reiterate that the biblical basis of liberation theology is not a transcendent principle derived from reason and confirmed by the Bible but the *very foundational experience that gave birth to the Bible*, a canon within the canon, by which the Bible itself is criticized internally. This foundational experience is the *election of the oppressed class* as God's equal partners in the common *mission* of creating a new order of love, a mission that can be shared by anyone who becomes one with God by being one with the oppressed class. Each concrete situation that reveals a new class of oppressed—women, minorities, and the like—is a continuation of this biblical revelation.

In this scheme, the transcendental and universal principle of "the dignity of the human person" fades away into a larger picture: God's *election* of the oppressed as God's co-creators of the kingdom and God's co-redeemers of the world; it is not an ontological status conferred by grace through creation and atonement, as in human rights theology, but an *elevation* of the oppressed, insofar as they are a class, to the status of God's covenantal partners engaged in God's project of liberation. Thus in partnering God, they have learned to use the language that the rich and the powerful refuse to speak or understand, the language of liberation, the language that God speaks through Jesus.

The human rights language is a language that may persuade the rich and the powerful to share their riches and power with the poor and thus gain access to this covenantal partnership. In that sense, the human rights language has a pedagogical value for liberation theology. In fact, Sobrino seems to use it as a means of communicating this message to the churches of the rich nations.[31]

When the secular humanist tradition, which discovered the role of the proletariat in the construction of the new order, coincides with the aforementioned biblical foundation of liberation theology, then "socialism" appears to be "the best possible organization of human affairs in the given historical situation"—to use Ratzinger's words. The past failures in the socialist experiments could serve as guideposts rather than as barriers, if only the powerful ideological blocs of either side do not interfere—as Russia does in Vietnam and the U.S.A. in Nicaragua—and if the church does not side with one or the other of these superpowers, but allows the "foundational experience" of the Bible to become a social reality.

This theology is diametrically different from the human rights theology of the Western patriarchate, but considers itself as a local theology, which, however, confronts the human rights theology on ideological grounds. This healthy confrontation is neutralized when the human rights theology parades itself as the universal theology valid for all churches. The tendency in the West to extoll Christian institutions that follow the human rights tradition,[32] and to condemn missionaries who opt for the liberation schema,[33] contributes to this species of ecclesiastical imperialism. Most episcopal peace and justice commissions in Asia stay at the human rights level; if they change their stance in favor of the liberation scheme, they could be disbanded by the hierarchy, as the Australian experience warns! This way, human rights theology is *used* as the tool of ecclesiastical imperialism.

My concluding remark is directly addressed to the human rights theologians in the very language they have created: respect the God-given inalienable *right* of every local church, especially in the Third World, to evolve its own theological discourse. Any tendency to universalize the social teaching of the Western patriarchate and impose it on others is a violation of the autonomy of the local church. Even in the struggle for justice, let justice be done to the creativity of the Third World theologians who have initiated a "neat break" from the cultural domination of the Western church even in social ethics; it is the *caesura* (radical rupture from the West) that Karl Rahner, voicing our concerns, advocated fearlessly as the conditio sine qua non for the birth of a truly universal church.[34]

NOTES

1. William R. Garrett, "Religion, Law, and the Human Condition," *Sociological Analysis*, 47 (1987) 21.

2. Bernard Schwartz, *The Great Rights of Mankind: A History of the American Bill of Rights* (New York: Oxford University Press, 1977), p. 25; italics added. This is the source I follow in writing this section of the paper.

3. Ibid., p. 3.

4. Ibid., p. 9, referring to Pocock, *The Ancient Contribution and the Feudal Law* (1957), p. 48.

5. *The Great Rights*, p. 1.

6. Garrett, "Religion, Law, and the Human Condition."

7. Max L. Stackhouse, "Public Theology, Human Rights and Mission," *Human Rights and the Global Mission of the Church* (Cambridge: Boston Theological Institute, 1985), pp. 13–21.

8. Stephen Charles Mott, "The Contribution of the Bible to Human Rights," in *Human Rights and the Global Mission of the Church*, pp. 5–6.

9. Ibid., pp. 7–8.

10. Robert N. Bellah, et al., *Habits of the Heart: Individualism and Commitment in American Life* (Berkeley: University of California Press, 1985), p. 150. See also pp. 28–35.

11. David Hollenbach, *Claims in Conflict* (New York: Paulist Press, 1979), p. 21.

12. Ibid., p. 83.

13. David Hollenbach, "Both Bread and Freedom: The Interconnection of Eco-

nomics and Political Rights in Recent Catholic Teaching," in *Human Rights and Global Mission*, pp. 31–34.

14. "Economic Justice for All: Catholic Social Teaching and the U.S. Economy," *Origins, NC Documentary Service*, 16/24 (1986) 410–55.

15. Hollenbach, *Claims*, p. 204.

16. Mott, "The Contribution," p. 11.

17. Hollenbach, *Claims*, p. 179, n. 2.

18. Mott, ibid.

19. Gustavo Gutiérrez, *A Theology of Liberation* (Maryknoll, N.Y.: Orbis Books, 1973), pp. 26, 27, 30, 90, 91, 111–13, 274.

20. Ibid., pp. 33–35.

21. Ibid., p. 46; see also p. 28.

22. Schwartz, *The Great Rights*, p. 27.

23. Ibid., p. 29.

24. But Hollenbach ("Both Bread and Freedom," p. 32) argues against the accusation that human rights theology is abstract.

25. See Leonardo and Clodovis Boff, "Good News of US Bishops' Economic Pastoral and Bad News Left Unmentioned," *National Catholic Reporter*, 23/38 (Aug. 28, 1987).

26. Eg. Stackhouse, "Public Theology," p. 17.

27. Here I understand ideology as I have defined it in chap. 3 of my *An Asian Theology of Liberation* (Maryknoll, N.Y.: Orbis Books, 1988).

28. Hollenbach, *Claims*, p. 52.

29. Joseph Ratzinger, "Freedom and Liberation: Anthropological Vision of the Instruction 'Libertatis Coscientia,'" *Communio*, 14 (Spring 1987) 70.

30. Norbert Lohfink, *Das Judische am Christentum. Die verlorene Dimension* (Freiburg: Herder, 1987), pp. 132–134.

31. Jon Sobrino, "The Divine Character of Human Rights," *COELI Quarterly* (Brussels) 43 (Fall 1987) 19–27.

32. Max L. Stackhouse, "Militarization and the Human Rights Tradition in Asia: Implications for Mission Today," in *Human Rights and Global Mission of the Church*, p. 86.

33. Ibid., p. 87.

34. Karl Rahner, "Toward a Fundamental Theological Interpretation of Vatican II," *Theological Studies*, 40 (Dec. 1979) 716–27.

35

The Politics of Otherness: Biblical Interpretation as a Critical Praxis for Liberation

ELISABETH SCHÜSSLER FIORENZA

Gustavo Gutiérrez, whose life and work we celebrate in these pages, has placed in the center of theological reflection the poor, the "others," the nonpersons who are absent from history. He has insisted over and against Euro-American "progressive" theology that the point of departure for Latin American liberation theology is not the question of the modern *nonbeliever* but the struggle of the *nonperson*[1] for justice and freedom. However, Latin American liberation theology has not sufficiently attended to the fact that the majority of the poor in the world are women and children dependent on women. This realization requires not just an incorporation of "women's questions" into the framework of liberation theology[2] but calls for a different analysis and theoretical framework.

Since Simone de Beauvoir, feminist theory also has focused on the "other." Therefore feminist theory and theology predominantly has understood patriarchy as the domination of men over women.[3] Yet feminist theory has not sufficiently attended to the fact that most women in the world are not just the "others" of white Euro-American men but are the "others" of "the others." This insight asks for a transformation in the self-understanding of feminist analysis and struggle that must address not only sexism but also racism, classism, and colonialism as structures constituting women's oppression.[4] I have therefore proposed that we understand patriarchy as a differentiated political system of graduated domination and subordination that found its classic Western legitimization in the philosophy of otherness.

The Canadian writer Margaret Atwood has given us a political novel that displays the discursive practices constituting the politics of otherness. Atwood's narrative articulates the interstructuring of sexism, racism, class differences, and colonialism on the one hand and the availability of the Bible as language and legitimization for totalitarian ends on the other. *The Handmaid's Tale* decodes the history of a future totalitarian society whose structures and language are modeled after the Bible.

The speaking subject of the novel is a woman whose real name and identity is not known. She is a Handmaid called Offred who lives in the Republic of Gilead. Gilead has replaced the United States of America and is ruled by a group espousing an ideology similar to that of the Moral Majority in the pre-Gileadean period in the late twentieth century. After the president and congress of the U.S.A. have been massacred, the regime of this modern biblical republic is established. Women lose their right to property and employment, the black population, the children of Ham, are resettled in segregated national homelands; Jews are repatriated through the Jewish boat-plans. In this biblical republic, reading and writing are outlawed, the news media censured and controlled, and everyone is required to spy on everyone.

The stratifications of Gileadean society are marked by dress and color developed by the secret Think Tank of the Sons of Jacob. White women, for example, are classified according to their functions: the wives of the Commanders of the Faithful are blue-clad and their daughters white-veiled. Those who do household work are called Marthas and have to wear a dull green. The wives of poor men, the Econowives, wear red-, blue-, or green-striped dresses, because they have to fulfill all functions divided among different women in the elite households. Unwomen are those women who have been shipped to the Colonies, because they are childless, infertile, older women, nuns, lesbians, or other insurrectionary elements.

Handmaids are chosen because of their reproductive capabilities. Their dress is red topped by a white headdress. The Handmaid's role in the *Ceremony* and her whole rationale of being is patterned after that of Bilhah, the maid of Rachel in Genesis 30:1–3. Handmaids and Wives are under the control of Aunts who as female overseers are to control women in the most cost-effective way.

I have chosen Atwood's narrative to indicate the political context of U.S. scholarly discourse on the Bible as well as of the discourses of liberation theologies. For theological discourses that remain unconscious of their rhetorical functions and abstracted from their political contexts are in danger of "squandering the word." Atwood's futuristic projection of a totalitarian state re-creating classic-biblical patriarchy in modern technocratic terms underlines that liberation theologies cannot afford to engage in a purely apologetic reading of the Bible or to relegate a critical biblical interpretation to "bourgeois" scholarship addressing the question of the nonbeliever. Rather, a biblical interpretation for liberation has to engage in a critical analysis that can lay open the "politics of otherness" inscribed in Christian scriptures. By making feminist theoretical discourse central to my hermeneutical explorations, I invite not only biblical scholarship but also malestream[5] liberation theologies to attend to the conversation of the "others" on the patriarchal politics of "otherness."

ISSUES IN FEMINIST BIBLICAL INTERPRETATION

Because the Bible is the foundational document for the Republic of Gilead, it is reserved for the elite and only to be read by men in power:

The Bible is kept locked up, the way people once kept tea locked up, so the servants wouldn't steal it. It is an incendiary device: who knows what we'd make of it, if we ever got our hands on it? We can be read to from it, by him, but we cannot read. Our heads turn towards him, we are expectant, here comes our bedtime story. . . . He has something we don't have, he has the word. How we squandered it, once.[6]

312

Atwood's narrator not only discloses the dehumanizing horrors of the totalitarian patriarchal state but also alludes to the potentially "incendiary" character of the Bible if it were given into the hands of "the subordinate others," the nonpersons of Gilead. In the awareness that reading can be subversive, elite men have kept the key to biblical interpretation in their own hands. It is mostly elite men who still read their Revised Standard Versions to us in liturgical celebrations and academic lectures. In the past thirty years women have entered theological schools in significant numbers and have begun to produce biblical scholarship. Yet replacing men with women and other nonpersons in pulpits, universities, the Supreme Court, or Buckingham Palace does not guarantee that the word read to us will no longer be a bedtime story legitimating situations of oppression.

Although still a marginalized minority in academy, church and synagogue, contemporary feminist theological scholarship and studies in religion have begun to claim the theological word and religious symbol-systems of biblical religions in the interest of women. However, the more feminist articulations are in circulation, the more it becomes pressing to ask how we can prevent our readings functioning like the Aunts of Atwood's Gileadean Republic who manipulate and adjust women's intellectual and spiritual needs in order to survive by serving the patriarchal system. For women's readings of androcentric texts and patriarchal traditions are always in danger of recuperating the "Commander's readings to us," of using the "biblical bedtime-story" for quieting women's and other nonpersons' anger and rebellion. Finally to own "the word" could mean in the end to own a word that legitimates the totalitarian regime of Gilead.

How, then, can a feminist biblical hermeneutics situate its readings of the Bible in such a way that they do not support the totalizing discourses of Gilead but empower women and other nonpersons in struggle for justice and freedom? In order to minimize the possibility of such a co-optation in the interests of Western patriarchy, I suggest that feminist biblical interpretation must reconceptualize its act of critical reading as a moment in the global praxis for liberation. In order to do so, it needs to decenter the authority of the androcentric biblical text, to take control of its own readings, and to deconstruct the politics of otherness inscribed in the text before it can positively retrieve biblical language and visions of liberation.[7]

Insofar as feminist biblical interpretation has been motivated by an apologetic retrieval of biblical authority, it has focused on biblical texts about women, on male injunctions for woman, on the biblical teaching on womanhood, on the great women of the Bible, or on feminine biblical language and symbols. By using "woman" or "the feminine" as a hermeneutical key, such gynecentric biblical interpretations, however, are in danger of recuperating the totalizing discourse of Western gender dualism.

Moreover, in its academic forms feminist scholarship has not only adopted diverse historical, social, anthropological, psychological, or literary critical methods of interpretation, but also the academic posture of "detached" inquiry. For the sake of scientific objectivity, such biblical scholarship often masks its own political location and forecloses theological or ethical evaluation. Although it focuses on "women" or the "feminine," it cannot but reproduce the whitemale[8] androcentric discourse.

Finally, feminist biblical interpretation seems to remain caught up in the same

313

"logic of identity." Feminist critics have elucidated the indebtedness of modern political theories to the classic patriarchal discourses of Plato and Aristotle, and especially criticized the theories of Rousseau and Hegel, which understand the civic public expressing the "impartial and universal point of view of normative reason," on the one hand, in opposition to the private realm, which encompasses the family as the domain of women, on the other. *Ratio* as the "logic of identity" "consists in an unrelenting urge to think things together, in a unity," to formulate "an essence that brings concrete particulars into unity."[9]

To achieve theological unity, feminist hermeneutics has attempted to reduce the historical particularity and pluriformity of biblical writings to a feminist "canon within the canon" or a liberating "organizing principle" as the normative center of scripture. Feminist biblical and liberation theological scholarship has inherited this search for an interpretative key or authoritative "canon within the canon" from historico-theological exegesis that has recognized the contradictory pluriformity of scripture.

Although liberationist biblical discourses have rejected the value-neutral, objective, apolitical rhetorics of academic biblical scholarship, they have not avoided its "drive to unity and essence." Just as male liberation theologians stress God's liberating act in history, single out the Exodus as "canon within the canon," and focus on a "new reading of the bible," or stress the liberating "biblical recollection and regathering of God's salvific deeds," so also feminist liberation theologians have sought to identify a liberating theme, tradition, text, or principle as the hermeneutical key to the Bible as an androcentric-patriarchal book in order to reclaim the authority of scripture. In this search for a "canon within the canon" or the "unity" of scripture, biblical theological interpretation engages in the universalist "logic of identity," which eliminates the irreducible particularity of historical texts and the theological differences among biblical writers and contemporary interpreters.

A debated question in feminist liberation hermeneutics remains: Must such a feminist critical hermeneutical key be derived from or at least be correlated with the Bible so that scripture remains the normative foundation of feminist biblical faith and community? Or—as I have argued—must it be continually articulated and called into question in the contemporary liberation struggle?[10] The Bible is to be understood as formative root-model rather than to be obeyed as a normative archetype of Christian faith and community. Whereas a feminist apologetics locates authority formally if not always materially in the Bible, a critical feminist reading derives its theological authority from women's experience of God's liberating presence in today's struggle to end patriarchal relationships of domination. Such divine presence, for instance, is at work today in the emerging Christian recognition that the systemic oppressive patriarchal contextualizations of our readings—sexism, racism, economic exploitation, and military colonialism—are structural sin.

My own work, therefore, has sought to shift the focus of feminist liberation discourse on the Bible away not only from the discourse on "women in the Bible" to the feminist reconstruction of Christian origins,[11] but also from the drive to construct a unifying biblical canon and universalist principle to a discussion of the process of biblical interpretation and evaluation that could display and assess the oppressive as well as liberating functions of particular biblical texts in women's lives and struggles. Concern with biblical positivity, normativity, and authority is in dan-

314

ger of too quickly foreclosing such a critical analysis and feminist evaluation of particular biblical texts and traditions. It neglects the Bible and its interpretation as the site of competing discursive practices.

A critical feminist theological hermeneutics of liberation positions itself at the intersection of three theological discursive practices—historical and literary biblical criticism, liberation theologies, and feminist critical theory—practices that question the Western totalizing "logic of identity." However, this positioning can only be appreciated when the interrelation of all three critical discourses is not seen as correlative but as mutually corrective interacting in the matrix of a feminist commitment and struggle for overcoming the patriarchal politics of otherness.

THE PATRIARCHAL POLITICS OF OTHERNESS

The Euro-American "classic" form of the politics of otherness is rooted in the practices of the andro-social Greek *polis*, its politico-philosophical subtext is democracy, and its social formation is patriarchy, the governing dominance of elite propertied male heads of households. Freeborn propertied women, poor women and men, slave-women and -men, as well as barbarians, women and men, were excluded from the democratic government of the city-state. This exclusion required ideological justifications as to why only freeborn propertied Greek male heads of households could be full citizens if, as the Sophists maintained, all are equal by nature.

The articulation of human-animal/male-female dualism, of androcentrism fostering the marginalization of Greek women and the exclusion of barbarians, as well as the articulation of the "natural" inferiority of freeborn women and of slave-women and men, of nonpersons, are ideological constructs of difference formulated by Plato and Aristotle. They continue to define relations of dominance and submission in Western culture and philosophical discourse today.[12] They were reproduced not only in early Christian writings and malestream theology but also in the modern democratic discourses of political philosophy, in the Enlightenment construction of the *Man of Reason*,[13] as well as in colonialist articulations of racism.[14] This political and philosophical rhetoric of otherness masks the oppressive relations of domination and exclusion in systemic patriarchy. However, it must be recognized that it does not simply elaborate the *generic person* but the Sovereign-Father or, in black idiom, the Boss-Man, as the universal subject. Its totalizing discourse of male-female dualism masks the complex structuring of patriarchal domination in Western societies and religions.

Insofar as feminist theory has focused on woman as the "other" of man, it has tended to identify patriarchy with sexism or gender-dualism. It has not focused on the complex interstructuring of patriarchal domination in women's lives. Although one of the earliest manifestos of the women's liberation movement in the U.S.A. categorically states: no woman is free until and unless every woman is free, feminist analyses and strategies generally have not taken their political measure, standpoint, and strategy for change with the women on the totem pole of patriarchal oppression, with the "others of the others." Instead Euro-American feminist discourse has tended to take its measure from an idealized version of the Man of Reason, the sovereign subject of history, culture, and religion. Its oppositional discourse has been in danger of reproducing the cultural-symbolic construction of masculine-feminine polarity and heterosexual antagonism that is constitutive of the patriarchal "politics of otherness."

Women's studies in all academic disciplines have greatly enriched our knowledge *about women* but have not been able to undo the marginalizing dynamics of the androcentric text and its institutions. In order to dislodge the androcentrism of Western metaphysical discourse, feminist theories or theologies of femininity, whether they have as god-fathers Jung, Tillich, Lacan, or Derrida, have valorized woman—body, sexuality, maternity, nature—as feminine archetype, essence, or divinity. Yet in this attempt to construct an oppositional discourse on woman or on gender differences, feminist theory has kept in circulation the discourse of classic Western philosophy and theology on gender-dualism or gender-polarity that understands man as the subject of history, culture, and religion, and woman as the other.

This universalist Euro-American feminist discourse on "woman as the other of man" is more and more interrupted by the diverse resistant discourses of an emerging global feminist movement coming-into-consciousness. In an anthology of the international women's movement entitled *Sisterhood Is Global*, Robin Morgan has compiled statistics and collected reports on the worldwide struggle of women for liberation.[15] The global character of this movement is displayed in its very particular and concrete political struggles that are not to be universalized, for the configurations of patriarchy are different in different historico-cultural formations. The voices of this movement insist that feminism requires a political commitment not only to the struggle against sexism but also to the struggles against racism, classism, colonialism and militarism as structures of women's exploitation and oppression. Feminism's self-understanding and analysis must therefore shift from a preoccupation with gender-dualism in order to attend to the interstructuring of sex, race, class, culture, and religion in systems of domination.[16] This insistence of black, Hispanic, Jewish, Asian, African, or Palestinian women asks for a new analysis of the patriarchal "politics of otherness." For, only when patriarchy is understood not as a universal transcultural binary structure but as a historical political system of interlocking dominations, can it be changed.

The rhetoric of the feminist movement that is emerging around the globe, therefore, is directed not only against male supremacy but also against the totalizing discourse of Western universalist feminism. Insofar as this rhetoric elaborates racial, political, cultural, national, ideological, sexual, religious, age, class, and other systemic differences, and discriminations among women, it challenges the essentialist definition of woman and female culture as "the other" of man and male culture. However, because of its commitment to the political liberation struggle, its insistence on the perspectival character and historical particularity of knowledge does not degenerate into an endless play of deconstruction and negative reaction nor lead to a determinism and nihilism that denies women's subjectivity and historical agency.

Unraveling the unitary otherness of woman from man in Western philosophico-political discourse, the emerging discourses of global feminism insist on the specific historical cultural context and subjectivity as well as the plurality of women. By deconstructing the ideological construct "woman," such global feminist discourses also elucidate how the identity of women of subordinated races, classes, cultures, or religions is constructed as "other" of the "other," as negative foil for the feminine identity of the white Lady. For instance, with her analysis of lynching, Ida B. Wells has elucidated the patriarchal manipulation of race and gender in the interest of political terrorism, economic oppression, and conventual sexual exploitation.[17] The variety of feminist discourses emerging around the globe thus enjoins middle-class feminists in the First World not to reduplicate the whitemale universalistic discourse of gender dualism and at the same time cautions Third World middle-class feminists not to reproduce the colonial discourse on woman and femininity.

The differences and often irreconcilable contradictions among women and within women are always concretely embedded in power relationships. To collapse them into a unitary identity, homogeneous image or totalizing discourse of universalist feminism — be it Euro-American or Afro-American, lesbian or straight, activist or academic, or any other feminism — would mean to reproduce the androcentric discourses of universalist abstract humanism on woman or to reinscribe differences and contradictions among women as patriarchal divisions and oppositions.[18]

However, if just as race, nationality, or social status, so also gender is a social-cultural-historical construct and not a feminine substance or universal female essence, then the question arises: How can women transcend our being socially constructed as *women* and at the same time become historical subjects as *women* struggling against patriarchal domination? If subjectivity is seen as totally determined by gender, one ends up with feminine essentialism; if it is understood as genderless, then one reverts to the generic human subject of liberalism for whom gender, class, or race are irrelevant.

This theoretical either-or posed by cultural and poststructuralist feminism[19] can be negotiated — I would suggest — if we attend to the patriarchal politics of otherness in Western culture. The totalizing ideologies of sexism, racism, classism, or colonialism that make the patriarchal oppression and exploitation of "the others" of elite white men appear to be "natural" and "common sense," produce at the same time contradictions and fissures in the social psychological identity construction of the nonperson. Far from being irrelevant to human subjectivity, the experience and articulation of gender, race, class, cultural, or religious alienation and exploitation motivate the nonperson to struggle for human rights, dignity, freedom, and equality:

> What is emerging in feminist writings is, instead [of the posthumanist Lacanian white male subject], the concept of a multiple, shifting, and often self-contradictory identity, a subject that is not divided in, but rather at odds with, language; an identity made up of heterogeneous and heteronomous representations of gender, race, and class, and often indeed across languages and cultures. An identity that one decides to reclaim from a history of multiple assimilations, and that one insists on as a strategy: "I think," writes Elly Bulkin, "of all the women [of mixed heritage] who were told to choose between or among identities, insist on selecting all."[20]

In short, in order to sustain a global feminist movement for ending patriarchal oppression, all feminist discourses must engage at one and at the same time in a continuing critical deconstruction of the politics of otherness, in reclaiming and reconstructing our particular experiences, histories, and identities, as well as in sustaining a permanent reflection on our common differences. The subordinated others must reject the rhetoric of self-lessness and articulate the "option for the oppressed" as an *option for ourselves*. Self-identity *as women* cannot be assumed but must be chosen in the commitment to the struggle for ending patriarchal structures of oppression. Moreover, the "politics of otherness" can be displaced only when identity is no longer articulated as unitary universal identity and established either by exclusion and domination of the others or by the others' self-negation and subordination.

The hermeneutical insights and theological challenges of the heterogeneous voices emerging from the global movements of liberation must, therefore, become central to a differentiated theological discourse on biblical interpretation and evaluation. A historical and global contextualization of biblical interpretation has to deconstruct the totalizing biblical rhetoric of Gilead and to generate new possibilities for the communicative construction of self and world. Christian identity grounded by the reading of the Bible must in ever-new readings be deconstructed and reconstructed in terms of a global praxis for liberation. Insofar as the Bible still is used in Western public discourse for reinforcing an Euro-American identity formation based on the exclusion and subordination or vilification of "the others," it becomes important to deconstruct the "politics of otherness" inscribed in its pages.

THE POLITICS OF OTHERNESS INSCRIBED IN THE FOURTH GOSPEL

If feminist biblical interpretation should not continue to reproduce the patriarchal politics of otherness, it has to reconceive its task as critical consciousness-raising or conscientization that can explore the functions and patriarchal contextualizations of biblical discourses, and replace them with a diversified public biblical rhetoric[21] and feminist frameworks of reference.

In the following cursory discussion of the fourth Gospel[22] I will indicate the complex process of such a critical feminist reading understood as a strategy and process of conscientization. Such a focus on the contemporary reading process does not replace historical text-oriented readings but presupposes an evaluative analysis of their textual interpretations and of their reconstructions of particular historical contexts. My focus on certain Johannine problems and my theological emphases indicate my subject position as a white German Christian feminist biblical scholar and theologian living in the U.S.A. Such a particular reading invites other readings that begin from a different subject position in the liberation struggle.

Whereas historical critical exegesis attends to the text in its historical contexts, but not to its ideological formation and textual "politics of otherness," rhetorical analyses and reader response criticism seek to make conscious how the text "works" in the complex process of reading as a cultural or theological praxis. By elucidating how gender determines the reading process feminist reader-response criticism underlines the importance of the reader's particular socio-cultural location.

Every reader brings cultural (grammatical principles, social customs, cultural attitudes, historical experiences) and personal contexts (personal experience, social location, education, beliefs, and commitments) to the act of reading. "Contextualization" is often assumed but not articulated; it is often masked in order to produce an "unbiased" objective reading. Such contextual knowledge operates as "a kind of grid that obscures certain meanings and brings others to the foreground."[23] However, whereas feminist biblical scholarship has become skilled in detecting the androcentric contextualizations in malestream biblical interpretation, it has not paid sufficient attention to its own inoculation with gender stereotypes, racism, sexism, or theological confessionalism.

In recent years New Testament scholarship has elaborated the social world and symbolic universe of the fourth Gospel. It has highlighted the leadership role of women in the Johannine community, its sectarianism and anti-Jewish polemics, as well as its dualistic worldview and religious exclusivism. In all three instances of inscribed Otherness, a certain tension or contradiction in the text has been elaborated.

First, the fourth Gospel presents the Christian community as a circle of friends, an egalitarian community of the children of God, that does not exclude the leadership of women, but appeals to the apostolic women disciples of Jesus for its legitimization of this practice. Nevertheless, its symbolic language and universe is not only androcentric but patriarchal because it stresses that the Father is revealed only through the Son and at the same time co-opts the language of sophia-theology and masculinizes it.

Secondly, although the language of the fourth Gospel is very "Jewish," the term "the Jews" is predominantly a negative term. It does not include Jesus and his followers as Jews but distances them from the Jews. The expression can also be used in a neutral sense, in order to mark that not all Jews have rejected Jesus but many have believed, or even as a positive theological affirmation in the dialogue with the Samaritan woman: "Salvation comes from the Jews" (4:22). However, anti-Jewish language is predominant in the Gospel. It bespeaks not just fear of expulsion but aggressive sectarian affirmation.

Thirdly, this anti-Jewish polemics is generated by a cosmological dualism of light and darkness, spirit and flesh, life and death, above and below, "the world" and the believer, God and satan. One could say that the whole narrative of the Gospel is woven within a framework of dualism. However, the cosmological dualism of the fourth Gospel is not absolute: God has sent the Son not for the condemnation but for the salvation of the "world."

This dualistic framework engenders not only anti-Judaism but also christological absolutism that breeds religious exclusivism, although the Gospel's intent is universal — namely, to present Jesus in an idiom that reflects the profound interests of the Greco-Roman world in religious syncretism and with religious symbols that have the widest appeal. In light of the Gospel's dualistic framework and its religious exclusivism, it is remarkable that its dualism does not include the pair male and female. Nevertheless, the Gospel exhibits a patriarchal identity formation characterized by the politics of otherness.

In the last twenty years historical critical scholarship has moved away from a gnostic or antignostic interpretation of the fourth Gospel's *Sitz im Leben* toward an understanding of its anti-Jewish polemic as an expression of the socio-religious alienation of the Johannine community because of synagogue expulsion.[24] Although Jewish scholars have disputed that such an official synagogue ban had existed at the time of the Gospel's redaction, Christian scholars maintain that explicit references to the expulsion from the synagogue of those who believe in Christ testify to the strained relationship between the Jewish leadership and the emergent Jewish-Christian movement. However, scholars do not reflect critically that such a reconstruction of the historical subtext of the Gospel reinforces the anti-Jewish Christian identity formation today.

Just as historical-critical exegesis so also liberation theological interpretations have explained away the Johannine "politics of Otherness" if they have it addressed as a theological problem at all. José Miranda, for instance, seeks to "undo" the traditional spiritualistic interpretation of the Gospel by stressing that belief in Jesus Christ (John 20:31) means that the kingdom has arrived in Jesus of Nazareth, the messianic kingdom that "consists in justice being done to all the poor of the earth."[25] Luise Schottroff in turn rejects the term "anti-Judaism" for the interpretation of the fourth Gospel by pointing to the oppression under which Jews and the emerging Christian community lived. "To accuse the Jewish leadership as it is portrayed in John's Gospel of opportunism vis-à-vis the Romans, or to accuse the Christians ... of anti-Judaism, is to apply labels which are inappropriate to the historical situation."[26]

Stress on the prophetic principle or the prophetic activity of Jesus also makes it possible to explain the anti-Jewish statements of the Gospel historically as a remembrance of Jesus' "prophetic renunciation of a corrupt religious establishment" or as prophetic call to conversion and renewal. A feminist apologist reading in turn has proposed to dissolve the tensions in the text by claiming that the Gospel contains its own critical principle, when it says that salvation comes from the Jews, that believers are children [not sons] of God, and that "God loves the world." Such liberation theological attempts of characterizing the Johannine text positively as a liberating text is not able to unravel and critically reject the patriarchal Christian identity formation inscribed in it.

Literary critical studies on the other hand have shown that the gospel narrative integrates these apparent tensions and contradictions of the Gospel into a realistic unitary story. Since the masculine figure of the Son as the revealer from above is the narrative axis of the Gospel, the stories about women, for example, function to harness the affection of the historical women readers for the masculine revealer of the Father. Further, the "Jewish" language of the Gospel in its positive or neutral use serves to reinforce the conflict of the revealer Son with "the Jews" whose Father is the devil, a conflict which climaxes in the passion narrative. Finally, the Gospel's relative cosmological dualism aims at a radical theologico-ethical dualism. Those who do not believe—the world, the Jews, and their leaders—will continue in darkness (15:18–16:4).

According to Culpepper, the Gospel's characterization, plot, comments, misunderstanding, irony, and symbolism "all work together in leading the reader to accept the evangelist's understanding of Jesus as the divine revealer."[27] As a reader-response critic, Culpepper does not shirk the question as to the function and impact of the Gospel's rhetoric today when he points out that the reading experience of the original reader was quite different from that of the contemporary reader, for the world of the text is quite different from our own. Insofar as modern readers distinguish between empirical and fictional narratives, between history and literature, they assume that they must read the gospels as "literally true."

Culpepper thus shares the concern of modern "progressive" theology when he insists that the real question and issue for contemporary readers is whether John's story can be true if it is not history. In response he suggests, if contemporary readers no longer would read the text as a window to the life of Jesus but with openness to the ways it calls "readers to interact with it, with life, and with their own world," they will again be able to read the Gospel as the original audience read it. The rhetorical effect of the Gospel is then profound:

> The incentive the narrative offers for accepting its world as the true understanding of the "real" world is enormous. It places the reader's world under the providence of God, gives the reader an identity with a past and secure future, and promises the presence of God's Spirit with the believer, forgiveness for sin, and an experience of salvation which includes assurance of life beyond the grave. The gospel offers contemporary readers a refuge from all the unreliable narrators of modern life and literature.[28]

Culpepper's summary appropriately underlines that the fourth Gospel narrative engenders Christian identity formation today, but he does not attend to the fact that such Christian identity is articulated in terms of androcentric dualism, religious exclusivism, and anti-Judaism. Moreover, he does not problematize the political effects of the Gospel's narrative that according to him offers "a refuge from all unreliable narrators" of contemporary society and life. Assuming that this characterization of "what the narrative offers" is adequate, the whole narrative of the fourth Gospel and not only elements in it must be problematized and assessed if we want to unravel its anti-Jewish Christian identity formation, which is shot through with racism. Although in classical and New Testament times "darkness" was not associated with race, and therefore the original readers would not have interpreted the dualistic matrix of the Gospel in racist terms, a long history of racist interpretation provides the contextualization for racist readings today.

Whereas historical and literary criticism focus attention on the text and its historical context but does not explore and critically assess the textual inscription of the patriarchal "politics of otherness," a critical feminist hermeneutic for liberation seeks to make conscious the complex process of reading as a cultural and theological praxis. Feminist reader-response criticism has shown that reading and thinking in an androcentric symbol system produces reader *immasculation*. It requires identification with men and therefore intensifies women's feminine socialization and internalization of cultural values that are self-alienating and often misogynist.

The androcentric text of the fourth Gospel derives its seductive "power" from its generic aspirations that play on women's authentic desires and liberative aspirations in order to harness them for the process of *immasculation*. The Gospel's christological focus and attention to "the love of the Father for the Son" reinforces theologically the linguistic and cultural process of *immasculation* and establishes Christian identity as male identity in a cultural masculine-feminine contextualization. Focusing on the figure of Jesus, the Son of the Father, when reading the Gospel, "doubles" women's oppression. Not only is our experience not articulated, but we also suffer "the powerlessness which results from the endless division of self against self, the consequence of the invocation to identify as male while being reminded that to be male — to be universal — ... is to be *not female*."[29] Conversely, the androcentric scriptural text communicates that to be female is to be *not* divine.

However, such a conceptualization of the first moment of reading in feminist-reader response criticism is in danger of recuperating the totalizing discourse of gender dualism when it insists that one read "as a man" or "as a woman." Reading as a woman does not necessarily mean to activate solely the ideological context of gender and femininity. Women readers can read from a feminist, black, Asian, or any number of "contexts." The identity of the reader is not a fixed gender position maintained by the exclusion of other contexts. The reading subject is not unitary but as the agent of her reading can activate different subject locations and positions. In the process of reading, identity is always assumed and then discarded, it is decentered and reassumed.

This means that we have to learn in a series of readings from different contextualizations to unravel the full dynamics of the Christian identity formation produced by the Johannine text and elaborated in its subsequent interpretations. A feminist biblical interpretation for liberation that understands its task as ongoing conscientization engages in an ongoing process of reading that deconstructs the politics of otherness inscribed in the biblical text without getting lost in the endless play of textual deconstruction and undecidability. Different starting points in the reading process will result in competing readings of the Gospel. Nevertheless, all such feminist readings must be assessed in terms of the liberation of the women on the bottom of the patriarchal pyramid of domination.

A feminist analysis of the politics of otherness and commitment to the liberation struggle of all nonpersons also will avoid the liberal pitfall that declares race, gender, class, or cultural differences insignificant for the reading process, because in essence we are all human and the same. Empirical studies have documented that so-called generic masculine language ["man"; pronoun "he") is read differently by men and by women. This is possible because of the ambiguity of generic masculine language. In the absence of any clear contextual markers, a statement such as "all men are created equal" can be understood as generic-inclusive or as masculine-exclusive.

Insofar as a feminist analysis elucidates the function of androcentric language in different contexts, it challenges the presumption that such language functions as "generic" language in patriarchal contexts. Inasmuch as women's reading tends to deactivate masculine/feminine gender contextualization in favor of an abstract de-genderized reading, such an analysis makes a conscious discrimination between patriarchal and generic-inclusive language contexts possible. Moreover, reading experiments have provided evidence that men report a higher incidence of male imagery when completing neutral sentences with generic pronouns. Women in turn associate virtually no images with generic masculine pronouns in such cases probably because we are required to suppress the literal meaning in order to be able to understand ourselves as included in the values of freedom, self-determination, and human rights.[30] Therefore, Christian women have read and still read biblical texts without attending to the fact of Jesus' maleness or the masculine images of Father-Son. As Virginia Fabella insists: "In the Asian Women's Consultation in Manila, the fact that Jesus was male was not an issue, for he was never seen as having used his maleness to oppress or dominate women."[31]

Catherine Belsey elaborates this contradictory ideological position of women reading unmarked generic male texts: "We (women readers) participate both in the liberal-humanist discourse of freedom, self-determination, and rationality, and at the same time in the specifically feminine discourse offered by society of submission, relative inadequacy, and irrational intuition."[32] However, I submit, only if this ideological position becomes conscious in a process of feminist conscientization are women readers able to become readers resisting the *immasculation* of the androcentric, racist, classist, or colonialist text. If this contradiction is not brought into consciousness, it cannot be exploited for change but leads to further self-alienation.

For change to take place, women and other nonpersons must concretely and explicitly reject an abstract reading. For instance in reading the fourth Gospel we should not too quickly resort to abstract God language such as God is love or God is light, without deconstructing the structural dynamics of the Gospel's Father-Son language and replacing it with images of God gleaned from the concrete contextualizations of women's life. Or, if as liberation theologians we insist that God is on the side of the poor, we need to spell out theologically what it actually means that God is on the side of poor women and children dependent on women.

However, we can appropriate as our very own only those "human" values and "Christian" utopias that can be reasoned out in a feminist process of conscientization as liberating not only for Euro-American white elite women but also for those women who suffer from multiple oppressions. Only after having deconstructed the politics of otherness, which constitutes the dualistic frame and theological identity formation of the fourth Gospel, will we be able to reclaim its vision of life and love in the context of the global movements for liberation. Christian identity that is grounded by the reading of the fourth Gospel's inscribed patriarchal politics of otherness must in ever-new readings be deconstructed and reconstructed in terms of a global praxis for the liberation not only of women but of all other nonpersons.

NOTES

1. For this expression, see for instance G. Gutiérrez, *The Power of the Poor in History* (Maryknoll, N.Y.: Orbis, 1983), p. 93. See also C. Cadorette, *From the Heart of the People. The Theology of Gustavo Gutiérrez* (Oak Park, Ill.: Meyer-Stone, 1988).

2. See the interviews of leading male Latin American liberation theologians by E. Tamez, *Against Machismo* (Oak Park, Ill.: Meyer-Stone, 1987); see also Schüssler Fiorenza/Carr, eds., *Women, Work, and Poverty* (*Concilium*, 194; Edinburgh: Clark, 1987).

3. See the overview and discussion by Sylvia Walby, *Patriarchy At Work. Patriarchal and Capitalist Relations in Employment* (Minneapolis: University of Minnesota Press, 1986), and the definition of the term by G. Lerner, *The Creation of Patriarchy* (New York: Oxford University Press, 1986).

4. See especially B. Hooks, *Feminist Theory. From Margin to Center* (Boston: South End Press, 1984).

5. I owe this expression to the feminist sociologist Dorothy Smith.

6. Margaret Atwood, *The Handmaid's Tale* (New York: Ballantine, 1987), pp. 112–13.

7. For the fuller development of a model for a critical feminist interpretation for liberation, see my book *Bread Not Stone. The Challenge of Feminist Biblical Interpretation* (Boston: Beacon, 1984).

8. For this expression, see K. G. Cannon, *Black Womanist Ethics* (AAR Academy Series, 60; Atlanta: Scholars Press, 1988).

9. I. Young, "Impartiality and the Civic Public: Some Implications of Feminist Critiques of Moral and Political Theory," in Benhabib and Cornell, eds., *Feminism as Critique* (Minneapolis: University of Minnesota Press, 1987), p. 61.

10. For this discussion, see the essays in L. Russell, ed., *Feminist Interpretation of the Bible* (Philadelphia: Westminster, 1985).

11. See especially the methodological chapters in *In Memory of Her. A Feminist Theological Reconstruction of Early Christian Origins* (New York: Crossroad, 1983).

12. See also Page duBois, *Centaurs and Amazons. Women and the Pre-History of the Great Chain of Being* (Ann Arbor: University of Michigan Press, 1979).

13. See G. Lloyd, *The Man of Reason. "Male" and "Female" in Western Philosophy* (Minneapolis: University of Minnesota Press, 1984).

14. See, e.g., the essays in Jan Mohamed and Lloyd eds., *The Nature and Context of Minority Discourse*, which have appeared as special issues of *Cultural Critique*, 6 (1987) and 7 (1987).

15. R. Morgan, *Sisterhood Is Global. The International Women's Movement Anthology* (Garden City, N.Y.: Anchor Books, 1984). See also V. Fabella and M. Amba Oduyoye, eds., *With Passion and Compassion: Third World Women Doing Theology* (Maryknoll, N.Y.: Orbis, 1988).

16. See, e.g., the dialogue between G.I. Joseph and J. Lewis, *Common Differences. Conflicts in Black and White Feminist Perspectives* (Boston: South End Press, 1981).

17. This is pointed out by H. V. Carby, " 'On the Threshold of Woman's Era': Lynching, Empire and Sexuality," in H. L. Gates, Jr., ed., *"Race," Writing and Difference* (Chicago: University of Chicago Press, 1986), pp. 301–28.

18. See E. W. Said, "An Ideology of Difference," in Gates, *"Race," Writing and Difference*, pp. 38–58.

19. See also N. Hartsock, "Rethinking Modernism: Minority vs. Majority Theories," *Cultural Critique*, 7 (1987) 187–206; L. Alcoff, "Cultural Feminism Versus Post-Structuralism: The Identity Crisis in Feminist Theory," *Signs*, 13 (1988) 405–36.

20. T. de Lauretis, ed., *Feminist Studies/Critical Studies* (Bloomington: University of Indiana Press, 1986), p. 9.

21. See my "The Ethics of Biblical Interpretation: Decentering Biblical Scholarship," *JBL*, 107 (1988) 3–17.

22. For an overview see R. Kysar, "The Gospel of John in Recent Research," *RSR*, 9 (1983) 314-323; see also D. Moody Smith, *John* (Philadelphia: Fortress, 1986, 2nd ed.) and the commentary by R. Schnackenburg, *The Gospel According to John*, 3 vols. (New York: Crossroad, 1968–82).

23. S. S. Lanser, "(Feminist) Criticism in the Garden: Inferring Genesis 2–3," *Semeia*, 41 (1988) 77.

24. See the very influential work of L. J. Martyn, *History and Theology in the Fourth Gospel* (Nashville: Abingdon, 1979, 2nd ed.).

25. José Miranda, *Being and the Messiah. The Message of St. John* (Maryknoll, N.Y.: Orbis, 1977), p. 88.

26. L. Schottroff, "Antijudaism in the New Testament," in Schüssler Fiorenza/Tracy, eds., *The Holocaust as Interruption* (*Concilium*, 175; Edinburgh: Clark, 1984), p. 59.

27. R. A. Culpepper, *Anatomy of the Fourth Gospel: A Study in Literary Design* (Philadelphia: Fortress, 1983), p. 226.

28. Ibid., p. 235.

29. P. P. Schweikart, "Reading Ourselves: Toward a Feminist Theory of Reading," in Flynn and Schweikart, eds., *Gender and Reading. Essays on Readers, Texts, and Contexts* (Baltimore: Johns Hopkins University Press, 1986), p. 42.

30. M. Crawford and R. Chaffin, "The Reader's Construction of Meaning: Cognitive Research on Gender and Comprehension," in *Gender and Reading*, pp. 14–16.

31. Virginia Fabella, "A Common Methodology for Diverse Christologies," in *With Passion and Compassion*, p. 116.

32. C. Belsey, "Constructing the Subject: Deconstructing the Text," in Newton and Rosenfelt, eds., *Feminist Criticism and Social Change. Sex, Class, and Race in Literature and Culture* (New York: Methuen, 1985), p. 50.

36

God's Pain
and Our Pain

DOROTHEE SÖLLE

The religious question of suffering is not the one we so often hear: "How could God allow this to happen?" but rather the one we have yet to learn: "How does our pain become God's pain, and how does God's pain appear in our pain?" I would like to try here to go a few steps along the path from the easier to the more difficult question.

The first question poses God as the almighty ruler of history and of each individual's life. God stands, figuratively speaking, at the summit of the universe, as the great ruler, the one who knows everything, who is really responsible: the one who can, at least, step in and end human torment, assuming God wants to. In this context, we often speak of the suffering of the innocent, of children who are tormented, for example. But in a deeper sense, all human beings are innocent: no one deserves to starve. Not a single one of the six million Jews killed during World War II—even if they had lied, stolen, or been bestial—ever "deserved" the suffering inflicted upon them. An "almighty" God, who inflicts suffering, who looks down from above upon Auschwitz, must be a sadist. And a theology that thinks up such a chief ruler, producer, responsible originator, mastermind, reflects the sadism of its creators.

Here, in a word, I want to criticize and straighten out this wrong thinking, and, what is worse, wrong feeling: I speak of "God's pain." I am not speaking of something that God could avoid or do away with. If we speak of God's pain, then we have another conception of God than the purely masculine one. This God is our mother, who weeps over the things that we do to each other and to our sisters and brothers, the animals and plants. God comforts us like a mother: God cannot make the pain go away by magic (although that occasionally happens too!) but she holds us in her lap until we stand up again with renewed strength.

God could not comfort us if she were not connected to us in pain, if she did not have this wonderful and rare ability: to feel another's pain in her own body. To have compassion means to suffer with, to be present with. The Gospels describe Jesus as one who has this ability. If he is there when someone is slapped in the face, he winces and feels the blow on his own cheek. If someone is lied to, he is

326

there with his need for truth. If a whole people is trampled down by the brutal might of the empire, he weeps over his city Jerusalem.

I have just said, in a realistic and limited way, "if God is there when these things happen." But we can remove this limitation. All who suffer are in God's presence. There is no longer any "if." God does not forget. The *praesentia Dei* is not a mere observing presence, but is always the pain or joy of God. Without God's pain, God is not really present, but only turns up from time to time like a president who occasionally visits the people. But God takes part in our suffering. An American feminist communion liturgy by Carter Heyward puts it like this:

> ¿DONDE ESTA DIOS?
> Where is God?
> God is with the people of God.
> ESTA CON EL PUEBLO DE DIOS.
> ¿DONDE ESTA EL PUEBLO DE DIOS?
> Where is the people of God?
> It is in the struggle for justice.
> ¡ESTA EN LA LUCHA POR JUSTICIA!
> ¿DONDE ESTA LA LUCHA?
> ¡ESTA AQUI!
> Where is the struggle?
> It is here.

God is here and she struggles with us. Really? Each time we suffer, each time of injured vanity, each toothache, each frustration that life inflicts upon us? I think that before we can think of God's pain and our pain together, we must learn to distinguish between them. The New Testament is very clear on this point. In his second letter to the Corinthians, Paul distinguishes between "worldly grief" and "godly grief" (2 Cor. 7:10).[1] Worldly grief, Paul says, produces death. It knows no hope, and leads to nothing. When I think about "worldly grief," I think of these dreadful diseases of affluence that are spreading among us, like alcoholism, anorexia nervosa, and workaholism, to name only a few. These diseases arise in a climate of affluence, which ignores our nonmaterial needs and manipulates them so they are transformed into addictions. Human beings are sacrificed to an apparently rich, well-ordered world, and bear in their bodies and souls the dreadful disorder and spiritual impoverishment of the whole of society.

Paul contrasts this "worldly grief" with another kind: "For godly grief produces a repentance that leads to salvation and brings no regret, but worldly grief produces death" (2 Cor. 7:10). What is this "godly grief" or "sorrow as God wants it"? What is this other pain, which does not just revolve around itself but calls forth conversion? How is our pain, which so often expresses only worldly grief, different from God's pain?

Is not each pain, each heavy suffering, each kind of torture and torment, such an unbearable misfortune that we should combat it with all means available to us, if possible do away with it, or at least make it invisible and repress it? That is the response of an atheistic consumer culture, which says: "Away with it! Take a pill! Get rid of it right away!" Suffering is pushed away like a bothersome shadow. In this life model, human beings are thought of as machines: they function, they produce, they run, or they are broken, they do not work anymore, and need new parts or must be replaced completely. This technocratic machine model dominates our thinking. A machine feels no pain. There are some theologians who seem to me to conceive of God as an indestructible giant machine, which will presumably continue to function even after a nuclear war and the destruction of creation. I can see how such fantasies of God perfectly express God's might, greatness, and independence, and yet I cannot find in this way of thinking any hint of God's pain and God's connectedness. Therefore, I find it difficult, within such a system of thought, to believe in God's love. The totally transcendent God is not bound to us through pain, and Paul's distinction between worldly grief and godly grief loses its meaning if there is no sorrow dwelling in God. But it is precisely this godly grief which I would like to learn to understand.

Paul mentions to the Corinthians the fruits that God's grief has called forth in them: "For see what earnestness this godly grief has produced in you, what eagerness to clear yourselves, what indignation, what alarm, what longing, what zeal, what punishment!" (2 Cor. 7:11). Luther even speaks of "revenge," an expression that is unfortunate for us. But that the guilty are called to account is certainly one aspect of this blessed grief. Then would the Argentine "Mothers of the Plazo del Mayo," who are calling today for the punishment of those who have tortured and murdered their family members, partake in God's pain? And would all those, in Argentina and in West Germany, who want to let the past rest in peace, close themselves off from the pain of God? Yes, this is what the Bible means. If we do not participate in God's pain, then we do not partake of God, we let God rest in peace. Like West German Chancellor Helmut Kohl, we invent the "grace of having been born too late"[2] and thereby evade responsibility for the sorrows of our times.

In the context of Paul's epistles, grief, *thlipsis,* usually means the kinds of adversities the apostle encounters as the proclaimer of liberation: official chicanery, poison, threats to his life, torture, and death. Paul measures both kinds of grief, worldly and godly, by what they bring about. Godly grief arises from God's pain over a barbaric world filled with injustice and the destruction of life. To participate in this pain of God means to become aware of the grief of God. "You have understood its meaning. What eagerness it has awakened in you! You have engaged in resistance, putting up a fierce struggle. You were outraged and shocked, you longed for a change, and forced it to come about, and have called the guilty to account" (2 Cor. 7:11, translated by Jörg Zink). We must read Paul's letters as documents of resistance against the Roman state, which proceeded from faith in the liberating Christ. Accordingly, signs of godly grief, or the sorrow that God wants, are: to become outraged, to engage in resistance, to long for change, to force it to come about, to call the guilty to account. This grief does not just turn around in circles or brood over itself. It is the kind of grief we find in the hearts of those who resist the extermination of creation and the plundering of the poor. It is the grief that was in Martin Luther King and in Dag Hammarskjold, the outrage that cannot be lulled to sleep, over the brutality of a system that wishes to function but does not participate in God's pain and refuses to believe in God's vulnerability.

In John's Gospel, as well, the situation of the Christian community is that of persecution by the Roman empire. The Christians of this little community at the end of the first century in Palestine experienced their day-to-day lives as a prison of fear. The word "world" here no longer has its ancient Greek meaning of cosmos, order, ornament, beauty; rather, it expresses above all enmity toward God, a world full of dangers and lies, a world that hates God, that destroys light and life, in which the community is afraid. "In the world you have tribulation" (John 16:33). Life is hopeless; perhaps Mary Magdalene, weeping over Jesus' murder, is the clearest witness to the pain that characterizes the Christian minority's feeling about life in this world of persecution and the triumph of injustice. Mary Magdalene neither accuses God nor defends God; she weeps, which means she is far deeper in God than accusation or defense can be. To accuse—or to defend—she would have to have a distance from God; she would have run away like the male disciples. But she is *in* God's pain and surrounded by it. "Truly, truly I say to you," says the Johannine Christ, "you will weep and lament, but the world will rejoice" (John 16:20). The ones who rejoice are those who cheer the triumphal marches of the Roman Caesars when yet another conquered people is forced to its knees, pillaged, raped, and sold into slavery. The world will rejoice—these are the glittering gladiatorial combats and sports shows the Romans hold to distract persons from the misery of hunger. "You will weep and lament," because, in a world of legalized violence, each word that speaks seriously of justice and peace is clubbed down and mocked. The Romans knew exactly what a threat the Christian community posed to the politico-religious state consensus.

Visiting El Salvador at the beginning of 1987 helped me to understand the New Testament better. In this tiny country, under the military boot of the empire, the poor weep and lament, when their harvests are burned, their teachers and trade unionists abducted and made to disappear, when the secret service and security forces arbitrarily and undisturbedly torture all prisoners for two weeks long under decree number 50. "You will weep, but the world will rejoice." Meanwhile, the television, firmly in the hands of the empire and its local collaborators, broadcasts sports programs and fashion shows. Every day, one and a half million dollars flow into this tiny country, primarily as military aid, allegedly for pacification, but in reality for the ever-more extensive "low intensity warfare." One and a half million dollars daily for napalm and electrical torture equipment, for low-flying strafer planes that force the population to flee, for watchtowers and barbed wire, for military boots and blood.

God's pain and our pain—in El Salvador, the pain of the poor is also God's pain. God suffers with them and God transforms their pain. God will liberate them, and God will heal the land. The most important image the Bible uses for God's pain in the world is an image from the experience of women, the image of giving birth:

> You will be sorrowful, but your sorrow will turn into joy. When a woman is in travail she has sorrow, because her hour has come; but when she is delivered of the child, she no longer remembers the anguish, for joy that a child is born into the world. So you have sorrow now, but I will see you again and your hearts will rejoice, and no one will take your joy from you [John 16:20b–22].

How does this transformation happen, from fruitless, senseless pain, to the pain of God? How do persons move from the pain that crushes their hearts to the labor pains that lead to birth? How is our pain connected with God's pain? And how does God's pain bring light into our pain?

Late one evening, I was walking down an isolated street in Manhattan. A beggar was squatting on a pile of rags, and I was afraid of the old black man. As I gave him some money, he looked at me and said, clearly and with great dignity, "God bless you." I was moved, but I was not quite sure why. Today I would say that God's pain was visible in the old man's pain. Insofar as I took part in it, my own pain was transformed: my fear left me. My rage returned. Everything that Paul told the Corinthians about the sorrow that comes from God was present in that experience: I was outraged and horrified over this everyday picture of street life. "You have engaged in resistance, you have longed for a change and have called the guilty to account" (2 Cor. 7:11, Jörg Zink). I knew once again why I want to convert to peace the persons I meet, why I am no longer willing to tolerate the hatred, and the terrorism called "deterrence," of those who tremble in fear of their stereotypes of the enemy. The old man who has no shelter in the richest country on earth, the richest country in history, evangelizes me; he calls forth my pain for his country, which I love and despise. But I also grieve for my own country, for West Germany, which has sold its soul in its greed for more weapons, in its addiction to more security. I am overcome by disgust with the world in which I live, with its brutality and its greed for more death. Yet in the midst of this world of ever-more elegant and more open advertising for the beauty of fighter-bombers and tanks, in the midst of unchecked economic growth that profits from the murder industry and has learned nothing from Chernobyl, in the midst of this shimmering and perfect lie, I am no longer alone with my grief: God's pain surrounds my pain, and the grief in which we live today becomes the power of struggle and solidarity that connects us.

My power grows out of my grief. My entire endeavor is to transform "worldly grief." I do not believe it is possible to transform "worldly grief" into joy. That would be too much to ask, as though we could simply "rearrange" a grief deep as an abyss. It would also be too little to ask, because it would only replace "worldly grief" with worldly joy, which is essentially the joy of having, possessing, using, consuming. I think our task is to transform "worldly grief" into the pain of God, and with God's pain I have experienced something unusual. Without soothing, dulling, or lying about the pain, I have been brought into a deep joy. It is as though I had touched the power of life that is also in pain, the pain that, after all, is biologically life's protest against illness and death, which indeed hurts us so much for the sake of life itself. I am not speaking of an automaton God who after pain sends joy and after rain sun; rather, I see the sun *in* the rain. I do not want to look for this power outside pain, for that would mean to separate myself from God and to betray God's pain. "The people who walked in darkness have seen a great light; those who dwelt in a land of deep darkness, on them has light shined" (Isa. 9:2). Where does such a sentence come from, if not out of the pain of God? How can we see darkness and light together, if not in the one who embraces both?

What I am trying to say sounds mystical, but we all know this sense and we have heard it often before, for example, in the D-minor piano concerto of Johannes Brahms, because great music deals with God's pain, immersing us in it.

Someone might object, "I hear the music that you speak of, but why should I connect the pain it expresses with what you call God? I have no use for this concept." To this friend, I would respond, "If the pain were only pain, I could not call it 'God's pain.' But because it points toward joy, because it is carried by joy, therefore I call it 'God's pain.' "

This union of contradictions, joy and pain, this *coincidencia oppositorum*, can be expressed only with great difficulty in our language; we must use a different language than our usual one. The experience of such pain is in fact very close to the overwhelming inner experience of birth. To "bring a child into the world," to bear it, is a primal experience in which we come very close to the secret of life. It is an experience that we both suffer and accomplish; we participate in it both passively and actively. It is an experience that challenges and can deeply change body, mind, and soul. It is one of the great experiences of the creation of which we are a part. It is a mystical experience, for in its presence we stand before the secret of life itself. This secret of life is what the religions call "God," and my religious tradition includes pain in the secret of life, placing pain in God's very heart. The legacy of theologian and martyr Dietrich Bonhoeffer is the understanding that Jesus calls us to "participation in God's powerlessness in the world."

The question of suffering upon which West European Christians must reflect today is not only: "How shall I bear my pain? How shall I deal with my loneliness, my fear, my illness?" These individual human questions can be answered entirely within the framework of the capitalist world. The self-help boom, in which individuals whirl from group to group, from personal growth experience to personal growth experience, from encounter to encounter, speaks for itself. The task of theology is not to follow the wisdom of this world, pastorally useful though this may be. If we want to move from worldly grief to godly grief, the sorrow that God wants, then we must learn to become aware of God's pain. Then our question will also be: "How do I conduct myself toward the nameless suffering that I cause? What stand do I take toward the business deals my bank carries out in cooperation with torturers and racists? How do I deal with the large-scale destruction of foodstuffs? How am I tied in with the war industry (which nineteenth-century pacifist Bertha von Suttner called in clear German "the murder industry")? How much energy do I consume, and at whose cost? How much longer can I stand to be an accomplice in a system of injustice? All these questions belong within the question of suffering. We cannot afford to stick these questions in a "political" box, and our personal questions about suffering in a different box, as though we could keep our entire relationship with God in a little box marked "private." If we think this way, then we take away from God the possibility of drawing our pain into God's pain; we make ourselves incapable of taking part in God's pain and experiencing it as the labor pangs of birth.

We do not want to relieve the grief of this world and our pain with the methods of this world, with tranquilizers. For God calls us, in the midst of our pain, to God's kingdom. God wants to bind up our personal history in God's great, good history. How can this happen?

Father Alfredo is a priest in a base Christian community in Brazil. While lifting two full canisters of water, his back gave out under the weight; he ruptured a disk. Terrible pain overwhelmed him, and no painkillers were to be had for many miles around. The priest lay in his bed, twisted from pain, for five days and nights. He told his friends he wanted to "offer up" this pain to Christ. This is a pious custom in Catholic tradition whereby the suffering are taught to "offer up" their suffering to Christ. A sick woman who is in great pain is instructed by her pastor not to curse the suffering but to bear it patiently, because she can then add the fruit of her suffering to the treasure store of the church.

In my enlightened Protestantism, I used to smile at this custom and the theology behind it, and later I criticized its terrible abuse, by which the poor and above all women were kept in eternal subjection. Now, when I am trying to overcome middle-class, individualistic understanding of suffering, this thought is much closer to me. I understand Alfredo better. It seems to me he is saying that it is not technology that makes suffering bearable, but rather a changed approach to suffering; it is not technological hope—for the right medicine, a good doctor, a new method—that helps us, good as these things are, and much as Padre Alfredo, in his revolutionary work, fights to bring them to his community. But really to deal with suffering, we need theological hope, which connects our pain with the pain of God.

In many human traditions, suffering freely borne has a cleansing, reconciling, saving power. The nonviolent movement has always believed with Mahatma Gandhi and Martin Luther King, Jr., in the power of such suffering. And our little beginning efforts, in the West German peace movement, among those who blockade, let themselves be arrested, and are fined or sentenced to imprisonment, draws on this faith in the persuasive power of suffering freely borne.

In the Catholic pious practice of offering up one's suffering, this basic thought is alive and carried further, in that we can transform even pain inflicted or forced upon us, turning it into something freely taken on. We add it to the church's treasure store of grace, which is cared for by Christ. Two elements of this practical theology of suffering are clear to me: the elements of freedom and solidarity. Suffering is not only borne, but is made one's own. Thus it becomes a part of my life, a part of my freedom. I am free to deal with my suffering in a grim, frustrated, despairing way, or to "offer it up to Christ." Father Alfredo chose a life for and with the poor, who have no painkillers. Now, on his bed of pain, he makes impersonal, brutal suffering into an element of his freedom, by seeing it in the light of Christ, by giving it as a gift to Christ. He does not simply live as a failure and a torment to himself, and a burden to others, but experiences much more God's special preferential love for the poor. His personal pain becomes a part of God's pain.

The second theological element that becomes visible here is community. Suffering is deprivatized. It does not belong to one oppressed, tormented body. It becomes part of everyone's life. In that it is given to God, it benefits everyone. You do not suffer for yourself alone, or for the pedagogical ends of your self-realization, as is often thought in Protestant theology.

"And of what use is that to anyone?" we may still ask, in our rationalistic obsession with success. I believe it is useful to Alfredo, because it allows him not just to write off these days and nights of pain as senseless, unproductive failure. It helps him to live now as a human being, not as someone who has been cut off from everything. "If my suffering is in God, and God suffers with me, then how could suffering make me suffer?" asks Meister Eckhart.

Father Alfredo's suffering is also of use to those who see and hear him. Perhaps it changes them, perhaps they become more aware, perhaps they will pray and work to get a health clinic in their region. Father Alfredo helps God to bear God's pain. He shares God's pain.

— translated from the German by Victoria Rhodin

NOTES

1. All citations are from the Revised Standard Version of the Bible unless noted.

2. This refers to a comment made by Chancellor Kohl during the controversy surrounding U.S. President Reagan's proposed visit to the Bitburg military cemetery in 1985. Kohl contended he could not be held responsible for the events of 1933–45, because of the *Gnade der späten Geburt* — the grace of having been born too late — and thus having been too young to share responsibility for the Nazi crimes.

PART V

LIBERATION
IN DIFFERENT
CONTEXTS

37

Christ and the World Religions: An Asian Perspective

TISSA BALASURIYA, OMI

As a contribution to the tribute offered to Gustavo Gutiérrez, I should like to present some thoughts on the further development of liberation theology in relation to the Asian context.

Gutiérrez's *A Theology of Liberation* is a most important contribution to the development of Latin American theology of liberation. Liberation theology is the greatest change in theology that has taken place since the time when the Christian church came to terms with the Roman empire under Constantine. Since that time theology had been done, as it were, from the side of the powerful. This is true particularly of the modern period when the European countries expanded into other continents.

Latin American theology of liberation is the first school of theology that clearly reflected the side of the oppressed. They, therefore, were able to perceive many changes necessary in Christian theology for it to be faithful to the liberative message of Jesus. Fortunately, the entire church is now becoming more conscious of its significance and importance.

All the same, we can note that the Latin American theologians in their first phase of theologizing were particularly conscious of the opppression of class and of capitalism. This was what impinged on their consciousness, given their own background. It is only in subsequent decades that they began to open themselves to the issues of liberation from the domination of sex and of race. This has been partly due to the influence of the dialogue within EATWOT and other movements, such as that of feminism and black liberation.

In this article I wish to deal with the need for developing Christian theology in relation to the other religions. Here, too, there is an element of domination and oppression in which Christianity and Christian theology have been on the side of the powerful. Hence, there is a need of a certain liberative purification of our theology in this connection, too.

REASONS FOR CONCERN

We need to rethink our theology from the point of view of religious plurality in the world. In Asia, fortunately, the other religions have not only survived the onslaught of Christian colonizers, but are also undergoing a revival, especially since the independence of formerly colonized Asian countries.

The first reason that calls for a reassessment is the tragic history of the European Christian missionary collaboration with European armed forces and merchants in colonizing the African, Asian, and American continents. It is very difficult to speak of this to Europeans who feel that their ancestors thus carried out a "civilizing" mission. Or they argue that the missionaries were on the side of the poor natives. They give examples such as those of Bartolomé de Las Casas as persons who championed native rights.

What I wish to stress is that the great evils of colonization were linked to a Christian theology that legitimized the European expansion and the missionary enterprise. This theology was based on the premise that all human beings were trapped in original sin and condemned to eternal damnation unless they were saved by Jesus Christ. This salvation had to be obtained by becoming a member of the Christian church. The church was the vehicle of God's grace essential for salvation.

This theology had a christology, an ecclesiology, a soteriology, a missiology, and a way of thinking about other religions. It all came down through the centuries, including the times of the Crusades. The christology was from the early councils of Nicea and Chalcedon. It held that Jesus Christ is true God and true man; two natures united in one person; Jesus Christ is the universal redeemer of all humanity, the unique Son of God. Acceptance of Jesus as Lord and God is essential for eternal salvation.

This Christianity was the source of the concept of the church as the unique barque of salvation. The mission of the church was the preaching of this message and the conversion of all human beings to this message. Otherwise, they would suffer eternal damnation. This doctrine is revealed in the Bible and confirmed and developed by the tradition of the church. The church is the infallible teacher and moral guide of humanity.

Today this seems too simple. In fact, many will protest on being reminded of this, saying that the church has long since given up these extreme positions. This is true to a great extent. The point is that it was such a theology that prevailed in the time of Columbus and Vasco da Gama and up to about the middle of this century. In fact, even today there are quite a few Christian fundamentalists who hold and loudly propagandize similar views.

This theology had the impact of legitimizing the European colonizers in their cruel approach toward other religions. They went about Asia, Africa, and the Americas destroying the sacred places, literature, and traditions of other religions. They despised these religions as pagan, the work of the devil and leading souls to eternal damnation. They found in this theology some justification for their own colonial expansion and even the extermination of some unbelieving peoples. This went so far that in continents like the Americas and Oceania, the memory of other religions hardly remains.

The peoples of Asia have a historical memory of this reprehensible behavior of persons who claimed to be civilized and called themselves Christian. Hence, even today there is a deep suspicion of Christians as persons who have been against the Asian religions, cultures, and peoples.

They do not think that Christians have really rethought their theological positions. Even new, forward-looking ideas are regarded as a ruse for further conversions and for debilitating the ancient religions and cultures. The European linkage of Christians and the new colonial economic policies of Western Europe and North America gave further support to their suspicions.

Although modern Christian theology has brought about a certain rethinking in ecclesiology, soteriology, and missiology, it has not gone far enough for a genuine dialogue of Christianity and the other Asian religions. It is only gradually that the opening of Christianity is taking place, beginning with a recognition of some spiritual values in the other religious traditions. The Vatican Secretariat for Other Religions, after the plenary assembly of 1987, went further in affirming the salvific potential of other religions. It states:

> Interreligious dialogue is thus a dialogue of salvation. It does not aim at converting others to Christianity, but at mutual understanding, collaboration, and mutual enrichment. It leads the partners "to work together towards truth" to a deeper conversion among people of the kingdom of God [art. 45].

Pope John Paul II took a very positive initiative in inviting leading personalities from all the religions to pray for peace at Assisi in October 1987. It broke new ground in interreligious dialogue, but the participants have not yet advanced to the position of being able to pray together for peace, and much less to consider together issues concerning world peace. Such a process is likely to lead the religions further in this common quest.

In the Asian countries interreligious collaboration is essential for meeting the issues of communal harmony, peace, social justice, modernization, culture, and the like. For genuine collaboration on such issues, the church needs to clarify beyond doubt its stand concerning "proselytization" or attempts at conversion by using unfair means. Any sense of superiority or privilege of Christians has to be purified by a deep theological reflection and contemplation. In this we have not gone far enough. And even as the more long-standing churches are gradually moving forward, new groups, such as different pentecostal or charismatic communities, are pushing an "evangelistic" approach of promoting conversions to their churches, using questionable methods: threat of eternal damnation or the favors of financial assistance.

We need a theology that will positively motivate toward common action for the human good of all without any fears and inhibitions concerning one another.

TRADITIONAL POSITIONS IN CHRISTOLOGY

Traditional christology was based on the definitions of the church concerning Jesus Christ. He was defined as God-man, the incarnation of the second Person of the Trinity. He was regarded as the unique and only Son of God; God in person. He is the source of all things; for him and in him were all things created. It is through him and in him alone that there is redemption and salvation. He alone is to be worshiped and adored as God. He is, above all other human beings, the source of all truth.

Traditional theology tended to deduce the rest of Christian theology from the premise of Jesus as God-man. For this it used the philosophy that was in vogue in

Europe at the time. The Church came to conclusions about the nature of Jesus, the value of his life, the meritoriousness of his death, the "satisfaction" given to God by his death. Hence, also conclusions about the divinity and infallibility of the church. Jesus was said to give divine powers to the church. Hence, the sacraments were thought of as communicating divine grace because of the divinity of Jesus defined in dogmas.

The other religions find this unacceptable. Islam sees this as contrary to monotheism. How could a human being be God? How can we worship a human being? Buddhists can think that this is the absolutizing of a human person. It also means that the Buddha is regarded as secondary and subordinate. Buddhism is considered incapable of leading persons to their eternal happiness. To Hinduism this christology would mean the absolutizing of one particular manifestation or avatar of God.

Thus, although the members of other religions respect the person of Jesus as shown in the New Testament, this christology makes interreligious dialogue rather difficult. Christians can hardly accept the other religions as valid ways for spiritual growth and eternal salvation. On the other hand, other religions can see Christianity as seeking to possess God so exclusively as to be incapable of dialogue with others.

The Asian context raises deeper theological questions concerning doctrines and dogmas that have been held for many centuries. This is because here we face not only the reality of social and economic exploitation, as is in fact dealt with in Latin American theology; but we also have alternative ways of thinking about the human and the universe and God. There are different founders of religions, different sacred scriptures, and different views of the origin and destiny of human life. There is a great similarity in the moral teachings of the religions, or at least their implications for the important issues of personal and social life. The fundamental differences are in what we consider the dogmas of the churches. It is from these dogmatic teachings that the powers and rights of the church have been deduced, concluded, enforced, and in a sense entrenched.

The relationship with the other religions in the Asian context, therefore, demands a much deeper rethinking of the total reality of the church. Its position and role concerning human salvation are called into question. Latin American liberation theology brought up the issue of how authority in the church is to be exercised and what its role can be with respect to the liberation of the oppressed. This in itself is a very valuable contribution to theology and spirituality. The Latin American study of Jesus Christ, as it were, in an ascending manner, taking into account how he lived in a given social context, is itself an innovative contribution to Christian theology—along with related studies in Europe and North America. Theologians like Jon Sobrino and Leonardo Boff reflect deeply on the real story of Jesus seen from the New Testament. They discuss the knowledge of Jesus, his prayer, his death as that of a human person intimately united to God. The motivation for their reflective study is the need to bring back the memory of a truly human and historical Jesus. The emphasis on the dogmas of Chalcedon had tended to see in Jesus more the Son of God who had divine knowledge from the beginning of his life. As Sobrino notes, Jesus did not pray to himself but to God the father.

The issues of Christian dogma on which there is profound difference of opinion between Christianity and the other religions are ones that cannot be proved by human reasoning or comprehended by the human intellect. Nor are they clearly borne witness to in the Christian sacred scriptures in the manner in which they are proposed now as dogma. Thus, the New Testament does not say clearly that Jesus is the unique Son of God. There is no teaching concerning the two natures of Jesus attributed by later theology. Nor is there certitude about the specific redemptive role assigned to Jesus. The divine foundation of the church hinges on our understanding of Jesus as God.

All these are based on some fundamental assumptions or presuppositions: that we can know the nature of the divinity, that we can make certain propositions concerning God. The story of the fall, and the condition of humanity before and after it, are also largely theological elaborations about which we cannot have historical evidence and we do not have even biblical certitude. The view that Jesus is a God-man who brings about such a redemption is dependent on such presuppositions. If the proposition of two natures in one person is accepted, what would be the nature of the consciousness of Jesus? What merit would his actions as a human being have if his personality is divine?

Many questions arise from these presuppositions. What would be the position of a Father who agrees to, demands, or condemns his beloved son to such a death? If Jesus was so divine as to have the fullness of knowledge from his birth, then his whole life would be a mere role playing or a theatrical performance in which he knew how everything would evolve. What would be the merit of a death in which Jesus knew that in three days he would rise from the dead by his own power and confound all his enemies? How could such a death be really painful or difficult and meritorious? It is difficult to see how such a concept of a "hypostatic" union of two natures in one person does not gravely reduce the value of the actions of Jesus the human being. In fact, this was the result of long centuries of Christian theology when the human agony of the life of Jesus in the context of his society was largely neglected. The Latin American theologians try to revalorize this by developing a theology of Jesus that does not begin with his divinity, but takes the historical data from the scriptures and builds around them an understanding of Jesus.

THE NATURE OF DIVINITY OF JESUS CHRIST

In the understanding of Jesus Christ in the Christian scriptures, we can distinguish:

1. Jesus who was born of Mary, at Bethlehem at a given time;
2. Christ as an anointed person, or the one awaited by the Jews as the Messiah, "the King of the Jews"—to restore the kingdom of Israel (Mark 15:26,32; Acts 1:6f.);
3. The second Person of the Trinity—the Logos, the Word also identified as Jesus Christ or Christ Jesus. The Word was at the beginning—before all things and all things were created in and for the Word, as John says;
4. Those who are baptized in Christ put on Christ (Gal. 3:27); Christ is formed in them (Gal. 4:19); to live in Christ (Phil. 1:21), the Christian is incorporated into the church (Rom. 6:11).

Against this background, the term "Jesus" is not necessarily synonymous with that of "Christ." Jesus is Christ; but the whole of Christ is not Jesus. It can also be said that Jesus is God, but God is not limited to Jesus.

A problem in our background is that these senses are all used without adequate distinctions: Jesus is called the Son of Man, Son of God, Messiah, Prophet, Christ, the Word, the second Person of the divine Trinity. The second Person, Logos, is prior to the historical Jesus, is uncreated, and cannot die.

Though there are many senses in which the terms "Jesus," "Christ," "Son of God" are used, subsequent Christian teaching and life have identified Jesus the human being with the second Person of the Trinity. Accordingly, philosophical explanations and theological dogmas were developed as in the Council of Chalcedon. In countries where the population is, at least nominally, Christian (as Europe was until recent decades), this did not present much of a problem. But the situation is quite different in Asian countries. This poses issues for our theological reflection. We are compelled to deal with it for we cannot have a deep and genuine dialogue with the other living faiths without discussing and discerning this issue.

In our context, especially in the Indian subcontinent, we can say that Jesus is God, provided it is not understood in an exclusive sense of Jesus monopolizing the divine. In fact, in the Hindu perspective there is a spark of the divine in all beings; some may be closer to the divine than others. Therefore, we do not say that Jesus is not divine. On the contrary, we can affirm that the life and teachings of Jesus are most divine. He is the one in whom we may find no fault, and in whom there is every perfection. But what we cannot affirm is that Jesus is so unique that he alone of all human beings is divine, that God could not reveal to others and through others a message of similar significance to other peoples, that God could not be present in other persons in similar manner.

This makes it difficult for us to express our theological teachings in terms of some of the classical definitions of the councils. Christians do recite and chant the Nicene creed at the liturgy, but this is hardly intelligible to persons of other faiths: "consubstantial with the father."

This is another reason why we have to be cautious of these theological definitions: because they have helped Christians to develop a theology, ecclesiology and missiology that have been devastating for others. It has led to the genocide of several peoples. Therefore, we can ask whether a theology that has had such an iniquitous and nefarious impact on Asian peoples can be correct, true, and from God. The basis of the theological approach to other religions as "pagan" was closely linked to the christology that held Jesus to be the unique Son of God and universal savior of all humanity. He was said to have given all power to his church to carry the redeeming message to all peoples. In the course of history the use of force for this purpose was legitimized. European peoples convinced themselves that they had a God-given responsibility to convert the rest of the world to Christianity, for otherwise these peoples would be condemned to eternal damnation.

I am proposing a hermeneutical principle: a theological teaching that despises, marginalizes, and discriminates against some persons cannot be from God who loves and cares for all humanity. It cannot also be from Jesus who was so kind and understanding to all.

If we say that the church was mistaken in such a presentation of its mission and role in salvation as to lead to genocide, then we can ask when and how is the church to be sure that it is not wrong in its theological teachings and activity.

The above is an argument from the negative impact of the teachings. A positive approach is that such a Christianity makes it difficult for Christians to be in frank, humble, and respectful dialogue with persons of other religions. Much as we may not desire it, this conviction of having the truth, of being the privileged offspring of God, tends to make Christians think they are superior in their religious thinking, or even better in their relationship to God. It tends to make them rather uncompromising, inflexible, and even arrogant in these matters — and with a conviction that they are holding on to a revealed faith out of loyalty to God. Christians become less open to see God in others and respect them for it.

Christian theology and Christians need a certain purification and humility in our approach toward other religions and relevant theological issues. Therefore, although we say that Jesus is divine, we cannot claim to know how and to what extent Jesus is God. We cannot affirm it in an exclusive sense. An inclusive sense, with openness to the divine in others, is an acceptable position. Then we would have to go further to find ways of considering how and to what extent any person is divine. In this process, both Christians and others will be prepared to see and acknowledge that the divine is in Jesus in a certain plenitude. We would at the same time be prepared to recognize the manifestations of the divine in others, according to certain criteria we may agree on.

The cosmic Christ, the uncreated Word, the Logos in St. John's term, the fullness, the beginning and end of all beings as in St. Paul, is beyond time and space, transcendent and universal. Christ in this sense is neither Greek nor Jew, neither male nor female — and, we might add, neither Christian nor Zoroastrian.

The cosmic Christ can be identified with the divine in such a way as to be understood as the divine principle all theists acknowledge. Such a Christ is beyond all religions and can be the principle of the widest human communion or ecumenism. Identified with all humanity and the whole universe, while transcending it, this cosmic Christ can be the inspiration for the care of nature and of Mother Earth — the source and term of all life in the world.

Christ thus understood is present to all, is the source of all inspirations, the Eternal Word, the Light of Lights. This divine truth is the source of all religions, all motivations for good, of liberative movements, ideologies, and processes for human betterment.

This cosmic Christ is then identical with the supreme being in other religions understood as life and light — and with Yahweh, Allah, Atman-Brahman, the Tao, and in a sense Nirvana or Moksha. Those who are not Christians may then see the cosmic Christ as God who is not a particularist diety, a monopoly of Christians and their churches. Liberated from captivity to Christians, Christ would be seen as the God whom all theists accept, and the bliss all seek — Satchit Ananda, the source of a just and peaceful world.

Concerning Christ in us, there are many statements that can be understood as identifying Christ and his disciples. St. Paul speaks often of it. "I live, not I, Christ lives in me." In St. John, Jesus says, "When that day comes, you will know that I am in my father and that you are in me, just as I am in you." All these can be understood as indicating a close relationship between the disciples of Jesus and God. But we cannot conclude that they *are* God, which would be totally unbelievable. The texts speak of divinity and association with Christ, not in a philosophical and exclusive sense, but in a spiritual and even mystical union with God.

Concerning Jesus we can acknowledge him as divine in a manner we cannot define and that is nonexclusive. What is more important is to see how Jesus lived, what he taught and why he was treated as he was by the people of his time. It is more important to see the life and death of Jesus as it is actually portrayed in the Gospels. The so-called descending theology has done immense damage to Jesus, Christianity, and the world by giving us a theology that did not bear witness to the real human life of Jesus, and on the contrary made him so divine, and Christians so much in control of him, that they felt superior and acted arrogantly and intolerantly.

Jesus needs to be liberated from such a theology. The church too has to liberate itself to follow more closely the teaching of Jesus as we know from the lifework of Jesus rather than from later theological elaborations.

The life that Jesus' example can give to the world is one based on the belief that all human beings are sisters and brothers. For each of us, personal and collective fulfillment lie in self-giving for others. Jesus chastised formal and legalistic religion and opposed the evil doing of the rich and powerful. What he wanted was justice in economic and social relationships, and the sharing of possessions was a way of life among his first disciples. For living and speaking as he did, he was killed by religious leaders and political rulers.

The *historical Jesus* gave a message and a witness that can be the life of the world if Christians live as he calls them to. Christ as the cosmic Lord is the universal motivator of all beings—to truth, harmony, and oneness in the divine. How, then, is Jesus of Nazareth, the founder of Christianity, related to the cosmic Christ of biblical revelation? Jesus of Nazareth is the Christ in the sense of being the Messiah expected by the Jews, the anointed one of God. He is also spoken of as Jesus Christ, meaning the divine Christ. How the historical Jesus is related to the transcendent Christ is part of the mystery of the incarnation, which we cannot comprehend or explain fully. But the fact that the historical Jesus is Christ does not prevent God from manifesting the divine in and through other persons in human history. The cosmic Christ present in all beings is the reality whom Jesus calls us to recognize.

Jesus Christ, as a historical person intimately related to God, can, as the cosmic Christ, objectively be the life of the world. And as Jesus who, faithful to his convictions, gave his life for his people, he can be the way, the truth, and the life for meaningful human fulfillment in holiness.

Today we need contextual theologies that relate to the circumstances of different peoples and their struggles for personal and social liberation and fulfillment. These can be understood in relation to both Jesus of Nazareth and the cosmic Christ. But merely contextual theologies are inadequate for understanding Jesus the Christ as the life of the world or for motivating the churches in their witness and mission.

The elements of a more universal planetary theology need to be delineated, taking into account the life and teaching of Jesus, the cosmic significance of Christ, the human search for meaning in personal life, and the oneness and interdependence of the world today.

Such a theology can be evolved by correlating the more universal truths of the biblical revelation—for example, the oneness of God, creation, the unity of the human race, salvation and liberation in Jesus the Christ, the demands for justice, the care of the earth, and peace. A theology like this will be universal—human and global—not the justification of domination by any race, sex, class, or religion.

Churches in the years ahead will have to sharpen their abilities to analyze both local and global situations, and encourage options and strategies relevant to different levels of action. They can also articulate a thinking that interrelates the different struggles of today: of race, of class, of age, or sex, of North/South and East/West. Recognizing what is valid and authentic in each struggle, the churches can help correlate them in a perspective of integrated human liberation.

The theology of the kingdom of God can be helpful here. It can link the Christian mission of inner personal liberation with liberation in society. It can articulate how Christian communities must be built in and through service to the world. Were that to happen, Christian commitment to justice and peace would be both socially prophetic and an act of worshiping the God who wants the fullness of human life.

Internally, the churches would become more participatory: externally, they would be more open to each other and to the wider human community. And the Spirit of Jesus would animate Christians to grow in the service of the cosmic Christ who is present and seeking full realization to all persons and in the whole world until the end of time.

Thus can Jesus Christ be the life of the world.

Here I am proposing only an insight that needs to be further developed. The liberation of theology in this direction can make Jesus more presentable, especially in our Asian context. It will also challenge Christians to be more committed to live what Jesus taught. His message is primarily one of love and self-giving for others. Theology made it too much a matter of redemption from some guilt that humanity was alleged to have incurred. The overcoming of selfishness is important, but it has to be proposed in the context of God's great love for all human beings of all times and places.

This approach will give us a missiology that is more sincerely respectful of others of all faiths and persuasions. Ecclesiology will have to be rethought more profoundly, without the exclusive claims to truth, grace, and power that the church has asserted for centuries. This is a phase of liberation of theology that would seem to be required in the coming years. In going forward in this direction, Christians and Christanity can open up to the presence of the divine in all humanity, and humbly come forward to transform this unjust and cruel world to be more akin to the kingdom of God that Jesus preached and gave his life for. I hope Gustavo Gutiérrez and our friends in Latin America will contribute to such a growth of theology and life in the coming decades as they have done in the past twenty years in several other valuable dimensions.

38

Martin Luther King, Jr., and the Third World

JAMES H. CONE

When Martin Luther King, Jr., achieved international fame as the leader of the Montgomery bus boycott in 1955–56, no African country below the Sahara had achieved political independence from the colonial regimes of Europe. When he was assassinated twelve years later in Memphis, Tennessee, the great majority of African countries had gained their independence. Since 1968 Africans have continued their "stride toward freedom," overcoming the political domination of Europeans in every country, except South Africa. Today black South Africans and their supporters, under the leadership of Archbishop Desmond Tutu, Alan Boesak, Nelson and Winnie Mandela, and a host of others in the African National Congress and similar organizations are currently engaged in a protracted life and death struggle against apartheid.

As with Africa, similar struggles for freedom happened in Asia and Latin America. The struggles of the poor in all societies remind us that the fires of freedom are burning and nothing short of justice for all will establish peace and tranquility in the world.

As we reflect upon the significance of the life and thought of Martin Luther King, Jr., for Americans, it is important to remember that the meaning of his life is not bound by race, nationality, or creed. Speaking of the international significance of his son, Daddy King was correct when he said: "He did not belong to us, he belonged to the world."[1] I would add that Martin Luther King, Jr., belonged particularly to the Third World, the world of the poor, the disinherited. It is therefore important to ask about his significance for the peoples of Africa, Asia, and Latin America and of their significance for him. What impact did the liberation movements in the Third World (particularly in Africa) have upon the actions and ideas of Martin Luther King, Jr.? What influence did his life and thought have upon Third World persons struggling for freedom? In this essay, I will limit my analysis to the impact of Third World liberation movements upon the development of Martin King's theology.

Martin King's thinking on this and other questions falls into two periods.[2] The first begins with the Montgomery bus boycott in December 1955 and ends with the enactment of the Voting Rights Bill in August 1965. The second period commences in the fall of 1965 as King begins to analyze more deeply the interrelationship of racism, poverty, and militarism in the policies of the United States government. In both periods his ideas are defined by his faith in the God of justice, love, and hope. The difference between the two periods is the shifting emphasis among these attributes as he seeks to develop a nonviolent philosophy of social change that will eliminate racial and economic exploitation and establish peace in America and the world.

During the first period, King's thinking is defined by an optimistic belief that justice can be achieved through love, which he identified with nonviolence. The place of the Third World liberation movements in his thinking was to reinforce his liberal optimism regarding the certainty of the rise of a new world order of freedom and equality. In the early months of the Montgomery bus boycott, King began to interpret the black struggle for justice in America as "a part of [an] overall movement in the world in which oppressed people are revolting against . . . imperialism and colonialism."[3] He believed that black persons' fight against segregation in America was identical with the spirit that led Africans, Asians, and Latin Americans to revolt against their European colonizers. Both revolts (blacks in America and the poor in the Third World), according to King, signify "the birth of a new age." Using that phrase for the title of an address to the Alpha Phi Alpha Fraternity (August 1956), he said: Third World persons have "lived for years and centuries under the yoke of foreign power, and they were dominated politically, exploited economically, segregated and humiliated."[4]

Because King saw little difference between colonialism in Africa and segregation in America, he employed the same language to describe both experiences. Speaking about the impatience of black and Third World peoples with oppression, King often said:

> There comes a time when people grow tired, when the throbbing desires of freedom begin to break forth. There comes a time when people get tired of being trampled over by the iron feet of the tramper. There comes a time when people get tired of being plunged across the abyss of exploitation, where they have experienced the bleakness and madness of despair. There comes a time when people get tired of being pushed out of the glittering sunlight of life's July and left standing in the pitying state of an Alpine November.[5]

With this and many statements like it, King's point was to emphasize that black and Third World persons became fed up with segregation and colonialism. "In the midst of their tiredness," something happened to them. They began to reevaluate themselves, and as a result, they "decided to rise up in protest against injustice."[6] The protests of the oppressed throughout the world, King believed, were nothing but a signal that "the time for freedom has come."[7] No resistance from the oppressors can abort freedom's birth because, as King often said (quoting Victor Hugo), "there is no greater power on earth than an idea whose time has come."[8] King's travel to the independence celebration of Ghana (1957), the rapid achievement of the independence of other Third World nations, and his study-tour of India (1959) deepened his optimism that freedom would soon be achieved.[9]

King's optimism regarding the prospect of freedom's achievement derived partly from the success of the civil rights movement in America and liberation movements in the Third World. The Montgomery bus boycott, sit-ins, and freedom rides, Birmingham, March on Washington, Selma March, and other less publicized civil rights victories throughout the South—all were linked with the success of anticolonialist movements in the Third World. King believed that freedom's time had come, because oppressed peoples all over the world were demonstrating that they will no longer accept passively their exclusion from the material riches of God's creation.

In King's view, segregation in America and colonialism in the Third World are nothing but the denial of the dignity and worth of human beings. Both the segregator and the colonialist are saying by their actions that blacks and other coloreds are inferior beings, incapable of governing themselves or living in a relationship of equality with white Americans and Europeans. As long as there was insufficient resistance from black and Third World peoples, the old order of segregation and colonialism remained unchanged. The new age of freedom began to break forth when a "New Negro" born in America and a "New Human Being" began to rise up from among the ragged and hungry masses of the world. Armed with a new sense of dignity and self-respect, both started to march together toward the promised land of freedom.

Of course, Martin King was aware that oppressors do not grant voluntarily freedom to the oppressed. He was also aware that white segregationists and European colonists had much more military power than their victims. Yet he contended that the coming of a new world order of freedom was inevitable. How could he be so sure? The answer is found in his faith in the biblical God of justice, love, and hope. No idea or strategy that King advocated can be understood correctly apart from his deep faith in the Christian God as defined by the black Baptist and liberal Protestant traditions. The new age is coming and cannot be stopped, because God, who is just and loving, wills that the oppressed be liberated. That is why King can say:

> Oppressed people cannot remain oppressed forever. The urge for freedom will eventually come. This is what happened to the American Negro. Something within has reminded him of his birthright of freedom; something without has reminded him that he can gain it. Consciously and unconsciously, he has been swept in by what the Germans call the *Zeitgeist*, and with his black brothers of Africa, and his brown and yellow brothers of Asia, South America, and the Caribbean, he is moving with a sense of cosmic urgency toward the promised land of racial justice.[10]

The German word *Zeitgeist* was employed often by King to refer to his belief that "the universe is under the control of a loving purpose, and that in the struggle for righteousness [we have] cosmic companionship."[11] This is what he had in mind when he said that Rosa Parks "had been tracked down by the *Zeitgeist*—the spirit of the times."[12]

The role of God in King's idea of the coming new age is reflected also in his use of the striking image of the "dream." Although he spoke often of the "American Dream," referring to the idea of equality in the Declaration of Independence, the Constitution, and the Jewish-Christian Scriptures, King's dream was not limited to racial equality in the United States, but was defined chiefly by its universality and eternality. To say that the dream is universal means that it is for all—blacks and whites, men and women, the peoples of Africa, Asia, Latin America, the United States, and Europe. To say that it is eternal means that equality is not a right conferred by the state; it is derived from God, the creator of all life.[13]

When King urges persons to "make the dream a reality" or to "face the challenge of a new age," he almost always tells them to "develop a world perspective." "All life is interrelated" because God is the creator of all. "No individual . . . [or] nation can live alone" because we are made for each other. No people can be who it ought to be until others are who they ought to be. "This is the way the world is made."[14]

When Martin King received the Nobel Peace Prize in 1964, it deepened his commitment to global justice and peace and reinforced his belief that God willed it. "I have the audacity to believe," he said in his acceptance speech, "that people everywhere can have three meals a day for their bodies, education and culture for their minds, and dignity, equality, and freedom for their spirits."[15] For King, the Nobel Prize was an "unutterable fulfillment,"[16] given in recognition of those fighting for freedom all over the world. His dream of a coming new age of freedom is eloquently expressed in his "Nobel Lecture":

> What we are seeing now is a freedom explosion. . . . The deep rumbling of discontent that we hear today is the thunder of disinherited masses, rising from dungeons of oppresion to the bright hills of freedom. . . . All over the world, like a fever, the freedom movement is spreading in the widest liberation in history. The great masses of people are determined to end the exploitation of their races and land. They are awake and moving toward their goal like a tidal wave. You can hear from rumbling in every village, street, on the docks, in the houses, among the students, in the churches and at political meetings.[17]

Because God is involved in the freedom struggles, King believed that it cannot be halted. Victory is inevitable. Success in the civil rights and Third World liberation movements combined with his deep faith in God's loving justice. It gave him an optimistic hope that freedom was not too far away.

Turning to the second period of King's thought, 1965–1968, I want to emphasize that certain bedrock ideas did *not* change. He did not change his mind regarding the basic principles of his faith or regarding the goal of freedom in the civil rights movement. In fact, his convictions regarding God's will to inaugurate a new age of freedom was deepened in the last years as he gave himself totally to the struggles for justice and peace in America and the world. His faith in nonviolence remained completely unshakable. What, then, was new or newly emphasized in the later period?

One thing was his great disappointment regarding the failure of the majority of white moderates in the North and South (in government, labor, church, business, and even the civil rights movement) to support the goal of genuine equality for blacks and other poor persons. For several years he thought that he could win the support of the decent "white majority" in America through a moral appeal to religion and the democratic traditions that they claimed to live by. But as early as his *Playboy* interview in January 1965 he acknowledged his great letdown regarding government officials and white moderates:

I have been dismayed at the degree to which abysmal ignorance seems to prevail among many state, city, and even federal officials on the whole question of racial justice and injustice. . . . But this white failure to comprehend the depth and dimension of the Negro problem is far from being peculiar to government officials. . . . It seems to be a malady even among those whites who like to regard themselves as "enlightened.". . . I wonder at [persons] who dare to feel that they have some paternalistic right to set the timetable for another [person's] liberation. Over the past several years, I must say, I have been gravely disappointed with such white "moderates." I am inclined to think that they are more of a stumbling block to the Negro's progress than the White Citizen's Counciler or the Ku Klux Klanner.[18]

When summer riots became a regular occurrence during the second half of the 1960s, King became impatient with whites who withdrew their support of the civil rights movement and began to say that "law and order" ought to be the highest priority of government. "I say to you," proclaimed King, "the riots are caused by nice, gentle, timid, white moderates who are more concerned about order than justice."[19]

Another disappointment for King was his failure to win the support of the majority of blacks to nonviolent direct action as the primary method for gaining their freedom. The Watts riot in August 1965 and others that followed in the urban centers (along with Black Power) revealed the great gap between King's optimism about nonviolence and the despair found in the random acts of violence in ghettos of American cities.

During the first ten years, Martin King and others in the southern-based civil rights movement had assumed that blacks of the North would benefit in a derivative fashion from the victories gained in the South.[20] The Watts riot and the subsequent rise of Black Power during the Meredith March in June 1966 showed that King badly miscalculated the self-esteem that northern blacks would receive from "straightened-up blacks" of the South. When he went to Watts, he was surprised that many blacks there had never heard of him, and even more astonished when he heard a group of young blacks boasting, "We won." "How can you say you won," King asked, "when thirty-four Negroes are dead, your community is destroyed, and whites are using the riots as an excuse for inaction?" "We won because we made them pay attention to us," they responded to him.[21] When King reflected on that response and the hostile reactions his message of nonviolence received from Chicago street gangs and young Black Power advocates during the Meredith March, he began to realize that the Civil Rights Act (1964) and the Voting Rights Bill (1965) did not affect significantly the problems of racism and poverty, especially among northern blacks.

King experienced a third disappointment. He expected the success of American blacks with nonviolence to help persuade the majority of the oppressed of Africa, Asia, and Latin America to adopt a similar method in their struggles for freedom. But instead of adopting the creative method of nonviolence, many Third World persons were openly advocating armed revolution. King was aware that even some theologians in Latin America were joining revolutionary groups in their efforts to overthrow oppressive governments.

All of this caused him to reevaluate, not the efficacy of nonviolence, but the depth of the problem of injustice in a global manner. When King began to analyze seriously global injustice, he concluded that the three evils of racism, poverty, and militarism were interrelated and deeply rooted, both in the socio-political life of America, and in the international economic order. King's focus on the global implications of racism in relation to poverty and war led him to the conclusion that the slums in American cities are a "system of internal colonialism"[22] not unlike the exploitation in the Third World by European nations.

King's global vision helped him to see that the socio-political freedom of blacks was closely tied to the liberation of their sisters and brothers in Africa, Asia, and Latin America. Token integration (that is, a few professionals moving into the existing mainstream of American society) was not true freedom. King wrote in *Where Do We Go From Here?*, "Let us not think of our movement as one that seeks to integrate the Negro into all the existing values of American society."[23]

The economic exploitation of Third World nations and the deepening poverty of the poor in the U.S.A. led King to the conclusion that there is something desperately wrong with America:

Why are there forty million poor people in a nation overflowing with such unbelievable affluence? Why has our nation placed itself in the position of being God's military agent on earth, and intervened recklessly in Vietnam and the Dominican Republic? Why have we substituted the arrogant undertaking of policing the whole world for the high task of putting our own house in order?[24]

These questions suggested to King the "need for a radical restructuring of the architecture of American society,"[25] so that it can serve the needs of humanity throughout the world.

The later years of Martin King's theology are also defined by a shift in emphasis and meaning regarding the themes of love, justice, and hope. Except for his great Holt Street address delivered in December 5, 1955, with its powerful focus on justice, the first period of King's spiritual and intellectual development is centered on love, with justice and hope being interpreted in its light.[26] But as a result of the bleak reflections just described, hope becomes the center of Martin King's thinking, with love and justice being interpreted in *its* light. The main difference between his early and later years regarding the idea of hope was this: in the early period, King's hope was similar to a naive optimism, because it was partly based on the progress of the freedom movement in America and the Third World, and the support it received from both the oppressed (by their active commitment to nonviolence) and the majority in the dominant classes (by their apparent commitment to formal equality). In contrast, King's hope, in the later years, was not based upon the backing he received from blacks and whites in the U.S.A. or from the international community. Rather, his hope was grounded almost exclusively upon his faith in the God of the biblical and black traditions who told him during the early months of the Montgomery bus boycott, "Stand up for righteousness. Stand up for justice. Stand up for truth. And lo, I will be with you, even until the end of the world."[27]

Instead of trusting human allies to produce a victory over the forces of organized evil, King's hope was now a transcendent one, focusing on the biblical God of the oppressed who "put down the mighty from their thrones, and exalted those of low degree" (Luke 1:52, RSV). This comes out in his critique of Vietnam, which he knew would alienate his former allies.

Nothing pained Martin King more than America's military involvement in Vietnam and the criticism he received from his white and black friends (in government, media, and the civil rights movement) for opposing it. America's escalation of the war in Vietnam, along with a deescalation of the war on poverty, and its indifference toward massive poverty in the Third World motivated King to become one of the most severe critics of the domestic and foreign policies of his government during the second half of the 1960s. He begins to speak like a prophet, standing before the day of judgment, proclaiming God's wrath and indignation upon a rich and powerful nation that was blind to justice at home and indifferent to world peace. Instead of speaking of the American dream as he had done so eloquently in the first half of the 1960s, he began to speak, over and over again, of an American nightmare, especially in Vietnam.[28]

Martin King did not enjoy criticizing his government. He loved America deeply, particularly its democratic and religious traditions of equality and justice as articulated in the Declaration of Independence, the Constitution, and the Jewish-Christian scriptures. But he could not overlook the great contradictions of racism, poverty, and militarism. For King there was no greater inconsistency between creed and deed than America's military adventures in Vietnam. He frequently referred to Vietnam as a small nation that quoted our Declaration of Independence in its own document of freedom when the people declared its independence from the French in 1945. "Yet," King said, "our government refused to recognize them. President Truman said they were not ready for independence. So we fell victim as a nation at that time of the same deadly arrogance that has poisoned the international situation for all these years."[29]

The arrogance that King was referring to was racism:

I don't believe we can have world peace until America has an "integrated" foreign policy. Our disastrous experiments in Vietnam and the Dominican Republic have been . . . a result of racist decision-making. Men of the white West . . . have grown up in a racist culture, and their thinking is colored by that fact. . . . They don't respect anyone who is not white.[30]

King also felt that the vehement criticisms he received from the white community regarding his opposition to the Vietnam war was motivated by racism. He spoke against his white allies in government and the media who supported his stand on nonviolence during the sit-ins and freedom rides, and in Birmingham and Selma, and then rejected his position on Vietnam:

They applauded us in the sit-in movement when we nonviolently decided to sit in at lunch counters. They applauded us on the freedom rides when we accepted blows without retaliation. They praised us in . . . Birmingham and Selma, Alabama. Oh, the press was so noble in its applause and . . . praise when I would say "Be nonviolent toward Bull Connor" . . . "Be nonviolent toward Jim Clark." There is something strangely inconsistent about a nation and a press that would praise you when you say, "Be nonviolent toward Jim

Clark," but will curse and damn you when you say, "Be nonviolent toward little brown Vietnamese children!"[31]

Martin King refused to accept the idea that being an American citizen obligated him to support his country in an unjust war. He refused to equate "dissent with disloyalty," as many of his critics did. On the contrary, he contended that he was the true patriot, because in his opposition to the war he was in reality defending America's tradition of freedom and democracy that was being violated in Vietnam. Furthermore, as a Nobel Laureate, King believed that he was obligated to transcend nationalism, and thereby to take a stand for world peace. But much more important than his obligation as an American citizen or of the world was his vocation as a minister of God. When persons queried him about the wisdom of mixing peace and civil rights, King responded:

> Before I was a civil rights leader, I answered a call, and when God speaks, who can but prophesy? I answered a call which left the spirit of the Lord upon me and anointed me to preach the Gospel. . . . I decided then that I was going to tell the truth as God revealed it to me. No matter how many people disagreed with me, I decided that I was going to tell the truth.[32]

For Martin King, telling the truth meant proclaiming God's judgment upon America for its failure to use its technological resources for the good of humanity. "Here we spend thirty-five billion dollars a year to fight this terrible war in Vietnam and just the other day the Congress refused to vote forty-four million to get rid of rats in the slums and the ghettoes of our country."[33] "The judgment of God is on America now,"[34] he said. He compared America to the rich man, Dives, who passed by the poor man, Lazarus, and never saw him. And like Dives who went to hell because he refused to use his wealth to bridge the gulf that separated him from Lazarus, "America," King said, "is going to hell, too, if she fails to bridge the gulf" that separates blacks from whites, the United States and Europe from the Third World.

Because Martin King believed that America's war in Vietnam violated its own democratic values and the moral principles of the universe, he could not keep silent. There comes a time "when silence is betrayal."[35] A nation that spends $500,000 to kill an enemy soldier in Vietnam and only $50 to get one of its citizens out of poverty is a nation that will be destroyed by its own moral contradictions.[36] "If something doesn't happen soon," King said, "I'm convinced that the curtain of doom is coming down on the U.S."[37]

Although King was often depressed about his government's refusal to stop the war in Vietnam and to eliminate poverty at home and in the Third World, he did not lose hope. In "A Christmas Sermon on Peace" he proclaimed that despite the nightmare of racism, poverty, and war, "I still have a dream, because . . . you can't give up on life. If you lose hope, . . . you lose that courage to be, that quality that helps you to go on in spite of all."[38]

It was King's hope that sustained him in the midst of controversy, enabling him to make solidarity with the victims of the world, even though he failed to achieve the justice for which he gave his life. King's hope was grounded in the saving power of the cross of Jesus Christ, and it enabled him to see the certainty of victory in the context of an apparent defeat:

> When you stand up for justice, you never fail. The forces that have the power to make concession to the forces of justice and truth . . . but refuse to do it . . . are the forces that fail. . . . If there is no response from the federal government, from the Congress, that's the failure, not those who are struggling for justice.[39]

It is difficult for persons who do not share Martin King's faith or his solidarity with the Third World to understand his meaning for the poor today. King's name is well-known and greatly admired in the Third World because his life and thought disclose profound insights about humanity that are relevant for all who are struggling for freedom.

"There is nothing in all the world greater than freedom."[40] Martin King gave his life for it. South African blacks, endowed with the same liberating spirit, are facing death daily, because they do not believe that whites have the right to determine the nature and the date of their freedom. The poor throughout the world are demonstrating with their bodies that one cannot begin to live until one is ready to die for freedom. Freedom is that quality of existence in which a people recognizes its dignity and worth by fighting against the socio-political conditions that limit its recognition in society.

Martin King's foremost contribution as a moral thinker was his penetrating insight into the meaning of justice during his time. No one understood justice with more depth or communicated it with greater clarity in the area of race relations in the U.S.A. and the world than Martin Luther King, Jr. Because of King, the world is not only more aware of the problem of racial injustice but equally aware of its interrelatedness with poverty and war. "Injustice anywhere is a threat to justice everywhere."[41]

The "anemic democracy" to which King pointed is still present in America and around the world. The dream is still unfulfilled. Whether we speak of the relations between nations or of the relations between persons within nations, the rich few are still getting richer and the poor who are many are getting poorer. To incorporate the true meaning of Martin Luther King, Jr., into America's national consciousness would mean using our technological resources to bridge the huge economic gap that separates the rich and poor nations.

King's greatest contribution was his ability to communicate a vision of hope in extreme situations of oppression. No matter how difficult the struggle for justice became, no matter how powerful were the opponents of justice, no matter how many persons turned against him, King refused absolutely to lose hope, because he believed that ultimately right will triumph over wrong. He communicated this hope to the masses throughout the world, enabling them to keep on struggling for freedom and justice even though the odds were against them:

> I am not going to stop singing "We shall overcome" because I know that "truth crushed to the earth shall rise again." I am not going to stop singing "We shall overcome," because I know the Bible is right, "you shall reap what you sow." I am not going to stop singing "We shall overcome," because I

know that one day the God of the universe will say to those who won't listen to him, "I'm not a playboy. Don't play with me. For I will rise up and break the backbone of your power." I'm not going to stop singing "We shall overcome," because "mine eyes have seen the glory of the coming of the Lord. He's trampling out the vintage where the grapes of wrath are stored. Glory hallelujah, his truth is marching on."[42]

NOTES

1. Cited in Coretta Scott King, *My Life with Martin Luther King, Jr.* (New York: Holt, Rinehart, & Winston, 1969), p. 294.

2. For the purpose of this essay, I will limit my analysis chiefly to two periods in King's thinking. However, it is important to note that I have found three periods in the development of his life and thought from the time of the Montgomery bus boycott (December 5, 1955) to his assassination (April 4, 1968). The first period is quite brief (early weeks of the boycott) and is defined by his primary focus on *justice*. The second period (early 1956 to the fall of 1965) focuses primarily on *love*. The third period (1966 to his assassination in 1968) focuses primarily on *hope*. The distinctions are not rigid, but rather a matter of emphasis in his thinking. In all periods the concern for justice, love, and hope are always present and intertwined. For an interpretation of the development of King's thinking in terms of the three periods, see my "The Theology of Martin Luther King, Jr.," *Union Seminary Quarterly Review*, 40/4 (1986) 21–39.

3. See Martin Luther King, Jr., "The Legitimacy of the Struggle in Montgomery," a one-page statement, May 4, 1956, Martin Luther King, Jr., Papers, Martin Luther King, Jr., Center for Nonviolent Social Change, Atlanta, Georgia, King Center Archives.

4. Martin Luther King, Jr., "The Birth of a New Age," August 7–11, 1956, p. 86, King Center Archives.

5. Ibid. King also used this statement in his first major address at Holt Street Baptist Church (December 5, 1955), and it was repeated in several addresses. A tape and printed copy are found at the King Center Archives.

6. Martin Luther King, Jr., "Facing the Challenge of a New Age," *Phylon*, 18 (April 1957) 26. This is essentially the same address that he delivered at the Alpha Phi Alpha convention in August of the same year.

7. See Martin Luther King, Jr., "The Time for Freedom Has Come," *New York Times Magazine* (September 10, 1961) 25, 118–19.

8. Ibid., p. 25. This quotation was frequently used in King's addresses.

9. For King's interpretation of the impact of the independence celebration of Ghana upon him, see especially his "Birth of a New Nation," a 22–page address delivered at Dexter Avenue Baptist Church, April 1957; see also Homer Jack, "Conversation in Ghana," *Christian Century* (April 10, 1957) 446–48. For King's interpretation of his trip to India, see "My Trip to the Land of Gandhi," *Ebony*, 14 (July 1959) 84–92; "Sermon on Gandhi," March 22, 1959, an 11–page address, King Center Archives. See also Swami Vishwananda, "With the Kings in India," a souvenir of Dr. Martin Luther King's visit to India, February-March 1959 (New

Delhi: Gandhi National Memorial Fund); "Farewell Statement" upon his departure from New Delhi, India, March 9, 1959, a one-page statement; "Statement of Dr. King upon landing at New York City," March 18, 1959, a one-page statement; King Center Archives.

10. "Letter from Birmingham City Jail," *The New Leader*, June 24, 1963, p. 8.

11. Martin Luther King, Jr., *Strength to Love* (Philadelphia, 1981), p. 154.

12. *Stride Toward Freedom* (New York: Harper, 1958), p. 44.

13. See especially his commencement address at Lincoln University, "The American Dream," June 6, 1961, published in the *Negro History Bulletin*, May 1968, pp. 10–15. This address was presented in Lynchburg, Virginia, March 12, 1961, available on tape at the King Center Gift Shop, Atlanta.

14. Ibid.

15. "The Acceptance Speech of Martin Luther King, Jr., of the Nobel Prize on December 10, 1964," in the *Negro History Bulletin,* 31 (May 1968) 21.

16. See his 27-page Nobel Lecture, "The Quest for Peace and Justice," Nobel Academy, December 11, 1964, Oslo, Norway, p. 1, King Center Archives.

17. Ibid., p. 5.

18. "Playboy Interview: Martin Luther King," a reprint of the January 1965 issue of *Playboy*.

19. "Transforming a Neighborhood into a Brotherhood," a 16-page address recorded by the Federal Bureau of Investigation, August 10, 1967, for the National Association of Real Estate Brokers, San Francisco, p. 9, King Center Archives.

20. See "Next Stop: The North," *Saturday Review* (November 13, 1965).

21. See Martin Luther King, Jr., *Where Do We Go From Here: Chaos or Community?* (Boston: Beacon Press, 1968), p. 112.

22. James Bevel, one of King's aides, spoke often of the Chicago slums as a "system of internal colonialism." King also adopted the same description for his addresses. See the "Chicago Plan," a statement by King, January 7, 1966, p. 3, King Center Archives; speech by King, "European Tour," March 1966, p. 8, King Center Archives.

23. King, *Where Do We Go From Here: Chaos or Community*, p. 133.

24. Ibid.

25. Ibid.

26. See note 2 above.

27. See his 14-page sermon, "Thou Fool," preached at Mt. Pisgah Baptist Church, August 27, 1967, Chicago, p. 14, King Center Archives. This sermon includes King's account of his deep crisis of fear during the Montgomery bus boycott, which led to his appropriation of the faith of his early childhood. I think this is the most critical turning point in King's life. Although I have always maintained that King's faith, as defined by the black church, was indispensable for understanding his life and thought, David Garrow was the first person to identify the "kitchen experience" (as it might be called) as the decisive experience in defining his faith. See especially his essay on this issue and his definitive text, *Bearing the Cross: Martin Luther King, Jr., and the Southern Christian Leadership Conference, 1955–1968* (New York, 1986). My interpretation of the experience is found in Cone, "Theology of Martin Luther King, Jr.," *Union Seminary Quarterly Review*, 40/4 (1986) 26f.

28. For an account of the development of King's position on Vietnam, see Adam Fairclough, "Martin Luther King, Jr., and the War in Vietnam," *Phylon*, 45/1 (1984);

see also Russell E. Dowdy, "Nonviolence vs. Nonexistence: The Vietnam War and Martin Luther King, Jr.," M.A. thesis, North Carolina State University, Raleigh, 1983. For King's reference to his dream being turned into a nightmare, see especially Martin Luther King, Jr., *The Trumpet of Conscience* (New York: Harper & Row, 1968), pp. 75f.

29. "Why I Am Opposed to the War in Vietnam," a sermon preached at Ebenezer Baptist Church, April 30, 1967, p. 8.

30. "A Testament of Hope," reprinted from *Playboy*, January 1969, p. 4.

31. "Why I Am Opposed . . . ," p. 6.

32. Ibid., pp. 3, 4.

33. "Standing By the Best in an Evil Time," sermon preached at Ebenezer, August 6, 1967, pp. 7–8, King Center Archives.

34. Ibid., p. 6.

35. "Martin Luther King, Jr.: Beyond Vietnam," April 4, 1967, Riverside Church, a pamphlet of Clergy and Laity Concerned, New York, with responses by Robert M. Brown, Vincent Harding, Anne Braden, and C. T. Vivian (1962), p. 1, King Center Archives.

36. This was a point that King repeatedly made.

37. An address at a rally of the "Pre-Washington Campaign," Albany, Georgia, March 22, 1968, p. 7, King Center Archives.

38. King, *The Trumpet of Conscience*, p. 76.

39. "The Other America," address at Local 1199, Hunter College, March 10, 1968, p. 11, King Center Archives.

40. "Facing the Challenge of a New Age," p. 34.

41. Cited in Pat Watters, *Down to Now: Reflections on the Southern Civil Rights Movement* (New York, 1971), p. 366.

42. "To Minister to the Valley," an address at the "Ministers' Leadership Training Program," Pre-Washington Campaign, Miami, Florida, February 23, 1968, p. 21, King Center Archives.

39

Mestizaje as a Locus
of Theological Reflection

VIRGIL ELIZONDO

From the perspective of the millions of Hispanics in the United States, two great events took place in 1971 which have had a tremendous impact on Hispanic ministry in the United States: the birth of the Mexican-American Cultural Center (MACC) and the first publication in Lima, Peru, of Gustavo Gutiérrez's *Teología de Liberación*. Since then, Gustavo and the work of MACC have been intimately interrelated. Both emerge out of the same situation: the need for the church to see the suffering of the poor, to hear their cries, and to enter into their quest for liberation! In a way there was nothing new. Moses had already started the way, Jesus had died for it, and others in time have dedicated their lives to it.

What was radically new about MACC and Gustavo was that in a time when the institutions of the church had generally speaking ignored the cries of the poor or at best had sought to feed them, clothe them, and give them minimal medical aid, this new way was beginning with the poor themselves becoming the active agents of the salvation of all! It was not for the church to go out to the poor to be of service, but for the poor themselves, in response to God's word, to become church and work for the betterment of their own situation. As long as we did it "for the poor," we would maintain them poor! But to empower them so that out of their own poverty they would dare to dream and begin something really new, would indeed be an act of the all-powerful creative Spirit of God.

It has been my privilege to know Gustavo well since 1971. I have been his student, close friend, and collaborator. He has come to MACC every summer. It was here that he learned English and was able to experience the complexities of the U.S. way of life. He formed close friendships with MACC's team, especially our scripture scholars John Linskens and Juan Alfaro, both of whom are continually feeding him good scriptural interpretations and works that can further the biblical understanding of liberation. Everyone at MACC and in the archdiocese of San Antonio loves him and believes in him.

Whether eating, exchanging jokes, discussing scripture, exploring new theological insights or church practices, swimming, or speaking about the issues of the poor in Latin America, the U.S.A., or anywhere in the world, being with Gustavo has always been a memorable experience. Padric O'Hare, formerly of Boston College, says that Gustavo is the only person he has ever met who seems to consciously live in the presence of God every moment of his life. I would certainly concur with that opinion. In the summer of 1985, Archbishop Flores introduced Gustavo to an auditorium full of expectant listeners saying: "The two people I most admire and respect in this world are Mother Theresa and Father Gustavo for they have both chosen to do the greatest work of all: dedicate their lives to the service of the poor."

THE MACC CHALLENGE

The Hispanic Catholics of the United States have experienced a long history of neglect and oppression not only by society at large, but by the very church that is supposed to be our mother. We had somewhat been ministered to but we had never been invited to be active ministers in our own church. The church was so foreign to us that many felt priests were born Irish or Spanish, but it was unthinkable that we would become a priest or a religious.

Quite often we were scolded because we were not what the foreign missioners expected us to be as measured by the standards of the Catholicism of their place of origin. But hardly ever were we confirmed in our faith and helped to grow and develop in our pilgrimage of faith. Yet it was the deep faith and simple home practices of our *abuelitas* and *abuelitos* (grandparents) that sustained us in the faith and maintained us loyal to the Catholic tradition.

Church institutions had been so oppressive to us that when the radical Chicano movements started in the 1960s, the leaders often told priests and religious who tried to join them to get lost. They felt that the only way to help Hispanics get ahead was to get rid of Catholicism. It was painful to hear their insults, but as painful as their accusations were, we had to admit that they were true—if not totally, at least 95 percent of what they were saying against the church was correct. The church had kept us out and had witnessed and by its silence approved the ongoing exploitation and oppression of the Hispanics in the country.

The Chicano movements gave inspiration to the Chicano clergy and later on to all the Hispanic clergy in this country. We began to organize and to work for change within our own church. It was quickly evident that it was not sufficient to simply use Spanish in the liturgy, create our own music, and get more people involved in the work of the church. Much more was needed. We needed both practical know-how so that we could make the structures of our society work in favor of our people and we needed to create a new knowledge about ourselves, our social situation, and our religious beliefs. Until now, others had been telling us who we were. Nobody had bothered to ask us "Who are you?" Until now, all kinds of people had studied us, but no one had even sought to enter into conversation with us so that they might truly understand who we see ourselves to be. This was the very root of our oppressions. We were not allowed to be who we were. We were never allowed to simply say: "I AM."

It was at this moment of the struggle that we met Gustavo and his method of doing theology. It was God-sent! He was conceptualizing and expressing perfectly what we felt had to be done but had no idea of how to do it or even that we were on the right track. From the documents of Vatican II and our own experience of exclusion, we pretty well sensed what had to be done, but it was not yet clear.

Reading Gustavo's work was like turning on the light-switch.

The first thing we learned from Gustavo was that theology is so important that we cannot leave it to the theologians alone ... and much less to theologians who are foreigners. Theology cannot be imported and neither can it be developed in isolation from the believing and practicing community. It is a joint enterprise of the believing community, which is seeking the meaning of its faith and the direction of its journey of hope lived in the context of charity. Great theologies were coming out of other parts of the world, but no one could do our theologizing for us. We had both the privilege and the responsibility! What follows is an attempt to do our own interpretation of our Christian existence.

THE HUMAN SITUATION OF MEXICAN-AMERICANS

The ancestors of today's Mexican-Americans have been living in the present-day U.S.A. since the early 1700s. Our group did not cross the border to come to the U.S.A., rather the U.S.A. expanded its borders and we found ourselves to be a part of the U.S.A. Since the early beginnings, many generations have crossed the Rio Grande to come over to the other side of the family lands. Yet we have always been treated as foreigners in our own countryside—exiles who never felt at home. The Mexican-Americans are a people twice conquered, twice colonized, and twice mestized. This is our socio-historical reality!

Mestizaje: The Undefined Identity and Consequent Margination

Mestizaje is simply the mixture of human groups of different makeup determining the color and shape of the eyes, skin pigmentation, and makeup of the bone structure. It is the most common phenomenon in the evolution of the human species. Scientists state that there are few, if any, truly "pure" human groups left in the world and they are the weakest because their genetic pool has been gradually drained. Through mixture, new human groups emerge and the genetic makeup is strengthened. Biologically speaking, *mestizaje* appears to be quite easy and natural, but culturally it is usually feared and threatening. It is so feared, that laws and taboos try to prevent it from taking place for it appears as the ultimate threat to the survival of the species itself.

Mestizaje could certainly come in various ways, but it is a fact of history that massive *mestizaje* giving rise to a new people usually takes place through conquest and colonization. This has certainly been the case of the Mexican and the Mexican-American *mestizaje*. The first one came through the Spanish conquest of Mexico beginning in 1519 and the second one started with the Anglo-American invasion of the Mexican northwest beginning in the 1830s. The French biologist Ruffie states that, since the birth of Europe 35,000 years ago, when the invading Cro-Magnons mated with the native Neanderthals, no other event of similar magnitude had taken place until the birth of European-Mexico less than five hundred years ago. I would add that a similar event of equal magnitude is presently taking place in the southwest of the United States—an area larger than Western Europe and populated by several million persons.

Conquest comes through military force and is motivated by economic reasons.

Yet, once it has taken place, the conquest is totalitarian. It imposes not only the institutions of the powerful, but also a new worldvision in conflict with the existing one. This imposition disrupts the worldvision of the conquered in such a way that nothing makes sense anymore. In many ways, the ideas, the logic, the wisdom, the art, the customs, the language, and even the religion of the powerful are forced into the life of the conquered. Although the conquered try to resist, the ways and worldvision of the powerful begin to penetrate their minds so that, even if political and economic independence come about, the native culture can never simply return to its preconquest ways.

Yet there is not only the obvious violence of the physical conquest, but the deeper violence of the disruption and attempts to destroy the conquered's inner worldvision, which gives cohesion and meaning to existence. The conquered's fundamental core religious symbols provide the ultimate root of the group's identity because they mediate the absolute. They are the final tangible expressions of the absolute. There is nothing beyond them that can put us in contact with God. They are the ultimate justification of the worldvision of the group and the force that cements all the elements of the life of the group into a cohesive, meaningful, and tangible world order. When such symbols are discredited or destroyed, nothing makes sense anymore. The worldvision moves from order into chaos, from significant mystery into a meaningless confusion.

Hence, the ushering in of new religious symbols, especially when they are symbols of the dominant group, are in effect the ultimate conquest. In a nonviolent way, missioners were the agents of a deeper violence. They attempted to destroy that which even the physical violence of the conquerors could not touch—the soul of the native people. In spite of the missionary's conscious opposition to the cruel and bloody ways of the conquistador, the nonviolent introduction of religious symbols of the Spanish immigrant in effect affirmed and justified the way of the powerful, and discredited and tried to destroy the way of the powerless. This same process has taken place with the predominantly Irish-German clergy and religious, who have ministered to Mexican-American Catholics.

The most devastating thing about the conquest is that it established a relationship so concrete and so permanent that it took on the nature of a metaphysical reality. In many ways, it determines the behavior and the characteristics of the members of each group. It even influences the theological reflection as the members of the conquistador group will appeal to scripture and theology to explain and legitimate the relationship. Martin Marty in his classical book, *The Righteous Empire*, gives an excellent exposition of how theology and biblical studies can be used to legitimize oppression. The powerful now establish their own version of truth as objective truth for everyone and impose it through their various means of power.

The image of the conquistador as "superior" and of the conquered as "inferior" will be imposed and interiorized by all the media of communications: dress, food, manners, language, modes of thinking, art, music, bodily gestures, mannerisms, entertainment, and all the institutions of society, such as the family, economics, school system, politics, and church, and most of all by the religious imagery and mythology. It is now the gods of the powerful who preside over the new world order. The totalitarian image that colonizing Europe established and implanted in the colonized peoples as the universal model for everyone continues to have a determining influence around the world. This "normative image" of Western civilization continues to be reinforced and projected through television and movies, books, periodicals, universities, and the European/U.S.A.-controlled religions. Only the white Western way appears as the truly human way of life; all others continue to be relegated to an inferior status. This is not necessarily a conscious effort, but it takes place all the time.

Yet, in spite of the difficult situation of inequality, the very seeds for the destruction of this dichotomy of colonizer-superior vs. colonized-inferior are physically implanted by the conquistador himself. Through his very bodily intercourse with the women of the conquered group, a new biological-cultural race is born, a race that will be both conquistador and conquered, superior and inferior, at one and the same time: he or she will be a real blood sister/brother of both, without being exclusively either. Furthermore, because the mother is the fundamental transmitter of deep cultural traits, it is the culture of the conquered that will gradually triumph over the culture of the conquistador in providing the dominant and deepest personality characteristics of the new group.

Mestizos are born out of two histories and in them begins a new history. The symbolic and mental structures of both histories begin to intermingle so that out of the new story which begins in the mestizo, new meanings, myths, and symbols will equally emerge. They will be meaningful to the mestizo as the firstborn of a new creation, but will remain incomprehensible to persons who try to understand them through the meanings, mythologies, and symbols of either of the previous histories alone. Yet from birth to maturity, there is a long period of painful search.

The deepest suffering of the mestizo comes from what we might call an "unfinished" identity or better yet an undefined one. One of the core needs of human beings is the existential knowledge that regardless of who I am socially or morally, I AM. The knowledge of fundamental belonging—that is, to be French, American, Mexican, English—is in the present world order one of the deepest needs of persons. When this need is met, it is not even thought about as a need, but when it is missing, it is so confusing and painful that we find it difficult to even conceptualize it or speak about it. We strive "to be like" but we are not sure just which one we should be like. As Mexican-Americans, we strive to find our belonging in Mexico or in the United States—only to discover that we are considered foreign by both. Our Spanish is too anglicized for the Mexicans and our English is too mexicanized for the Anglos.

In the case of Mexico, it was the mestizo image of our Lady of Guadalupe who provided the beginning of the new socio-cultural synthesis. It was not merely an apparition, but the perfect synthesis of the religious iconography of the Iberian peoples with that of native Mexicans into one coherent image. This marks the cultural birth of a new people. Both the parents and the child now have one common symbol of ultimate belonging. For the first time, they can begin to say "we are." As the physical birth of Mexicans had come through the conquest, the cultural birth came through the apparition. It is only after the apparition that those who had wanted to die now wanted to live and to celebrate life. In and through her, new meanings, myths and symbols will begin to emerge that will be truly representative and characteristic of Mexico.

Struggles for Accepting and Belonging

In the first stages of the struggle to belong, the mestizo will try desperately to become like the dominant group, for only they appear to be fully civilized and human. This struggle includes every aspect of life because the whole world structure of the dominant will have been assimilated and made normative for human existence. It equally involves a violent rejection of the way of the conquered because that now appears to be inferior. Only the scholars of the dominant group will appear as credible, only their universities as prestigious, their language as civilized, their medical practices as scientific, and their religion as true religion. The dominated will sometimes attempt to keep some of their original folklore, but, in every other way, they try to become like the dominant.

Some of the well-intentioned and kind of the dominant group will help the brighter and more promising ones (according to their own standard of judgment) to better themselves by "becoming like us." They will privilege them with scholarships to the best universities in Europe or the United States, and help them to learn the European or American way of life and language.

Some of the marginated will make it into the world of the dominant society only to discover that they will never be allowed to belong fully, and furthermore that down deep inside they are still somewhat "other." Yet it is this very pain of not being able to belong fully that also marks the beginning of a new search.

In the first stages of the search, the ones who choose not to join the struggle to become like the dominant ones will tend to reject the world of the dominant in a total way: absolutely nothing good can come out of it. They will not only reject it but will hate it passionately. The only way to treat the dominant ones is to get rid of them. They are the ones who are guilty not only of the individual sin of homicide, but of the collective sin of ethnocide.

Throughout all these struggles, there is something radically new beginning to emerge. Even though the seeds are planted from the very beginning, and biologically this new life begins from the very start, it will take time for the cultural identity to emerge as a distinct identity of its own. This new identity does not try to become like someone else, but it struggles to form its own unique individuality. It accepts from both parent cultures without seeking to be a replica of either. It is like the maturing child who no longer tries to be like the mother or like the father, nor to simply reject both of them, but is simply himself or herself. Through the pains and frustrations of trying to be what we are not, the uniqueness of our own proper identity begins to emerge. It is an exciting moment of the process and usually the most creative stage of the life of the group.

It is at this moment that the quest to know ourselves begins to emerge in a serious way. In the beginning, knowledge of ourselves will be confused because we see ourselves through a type of double image—that is, through the eyes of the two parent groups. As the group develops, its own proper image will begin to emerge and it will be easy to study ourselves more critically. It is this new and more clearly defined self-image of who we are as Mexican-Americans that is presently beginning to take shape. As usual, it is the poets, the artists, and the musicians who are beginning to paint and to sing and to suggest the new identity. It is now the critical thinkers who are coming in and beginning to deepen, to conceptualize, to verbalize, and to communicate the reality of our identity. And it is only now that for the first time we begin to ask ourselves about our Christian identity, about our church and about our religion—What does it really mean? Who are we as Mexican-American Christians?

The Human Situation: Divisions and Collective Self-Protection

When one looks at the history of humanity, then wars, divisions, and family fights appear more natural than do peace, unity, and harmony. This is evident from the global level down to the family cell. It appears more natural for brothers and sisters to fight one another than to love one another. We struggle to protect ourselves against each other and to conquer others before they conquer us. We prepare for peace by preparing for war. Only violent means appear to be able to control or curb violence. Might makes right because power establishes its views as objective truth so as to justify its own position of privilege. The survival of the fittest appears to be the first law of individuals and of society—the survival of the powerful at the cost of the weak.

From this struggle for survival at the cost of others, certain anthropologico-sociological characteristics and behavioral laws appear. The members of the dominant group in power will see themselves as pure, superior, dignified, well-developed, beautiful, and civilized. They see themselves as the model for all others. They see their natural greatness as the source of their great achievements. Even the least among them consider themselves superior to the best of the dominated group.

On the other hand, they look upon the conquered and colonized as impure, inferior, undignified, underdeveloped, ugly, uncivilized, conservative, backward. Their ways are considered childish and their wisdom is looked upon as superstition. Because might is subconsciously assumed to be right, everything about the weak is considered to be wrong and unworthy of being considered human. The conquered are told that they must forget their backward ways if they are to advance and become human. Acculturation to the ways of the dominant, in every respect whatsoever, is equated with human development and liberation.

Even the best among the dominant group find it very difficult to truly accept the other as other: to enjoy their foods, learn from their wisdom, speak their language, dress in their styles, appreciate their art and their music, interpret life through their philosophies, live in their ways, and even worship through their forms of cult. Even though many go out, even heroically, to be of service to the poor and the oppressed, and really love them, there is still an inner fear and rejection of their otherness. The way of the powerful as the normative human way for all persons is so deeply ingrained that it literally takes a dying to oneself to be able to break through the cultural enslavements that keep the dominant from appreciating the inner beauty, the values, the worth, and the dignity of the ways of the conquered.

Because of the image imposed upon them about themselves, some of the conquered will begin to think of themselves as inferior and good for nothing. This develops a type of domesticated, happy-go-lucky, subservient attitude in relation to the dominant. It is a very dehumanizing existence, but the powerless have no choice—either conform to the status assigned by the powerful or be eliminated physically. Law and order, policy and justice, work in favor of the rich against the poor. Whereas the rich tend to be considered innocent until proven guilty, the poor are usually considered guilty until proven innocent. They are blamed for all the problems of society and are considered to be the source of all evil and crime. Thus, the very victims of the institutionalized violence of power are labeled by the establishment as the causes of this violence! The powerful can define the image and status of the oppressed as "guilty of all evil" and force them to live accordingly. The poor and the oppressed thus serve as the scapegoats of the crimes of the establishment, which can continue to think of itself as pure and immaculate. However, as long as the traditions of the oppressed continue, especially their deepest religious traditions, they may be forced to live as dirt, but they cannot be forced to perceive themselves as such. Through their traditions, perfectly understood by them but incomprehensible to foreigners, they continue to perceive themselves as they truly are: free human beings with full human dignity who, although dominated through external powers, nevertheless remain free and independent in the innermost core of their being.

The in-group will defend tradition, law, and order because they are the privileged ones of the establishment. National and personal security will be among the top priorities of this group as it strives to maintain the status quo. For the powerful, tradition protects their position of privilege; for the powerless, their own traditions are the ultimate rejection of the status quo of the dominant—their bodies might be dominated but not their souls.

Tradition functions in a diametrically opposed way for the powerful and for the powerless. For the powerless, tradition is the affirmation of inner freedom, independence, and self-worth. It is the power for the radical transformation of the existing order. For the moment, it might appear as a tranquilizer, but we cannot underestimate its power in keeping a people alive as a people. As long as their traditions are alive, they are assured of life and ultimate liberation. If their traditions disappear, they will no longer have to work for integral liberation, because they will have ceased to exist as a people.

In attempting to analyze the dynamics between the oppressor in-group and the oppressed out-group, three constants seem to function as anthropological laws of human behavior.

When one studies the human story across the ages, the tendency of group inclusion/exclusion—that is, to protect our own by keeping others out—appears to be one of the most consistent and fundamental anthropological laws of nature. Dominant groups will struggle to maintain outside influences in a multiplicity of ways, and weaker or dominated ones will likewise fear and resist any type of intrusion. The purity of the group must be maintained. Human barriers of race, class, language, family name, education, economic status, social position, and religion are regularly used as signals to distinguish "our own" from "the others."

The second tendency that appears as an anthropological law of nature is: others can be used and enjoyed, but a social distance must be maintained. Deep friendships might develop and even strong love relationships, but the social barriers are so deeply interiorized and assimilated that they are very difficult to do away with. There are not just laws that keep peoples apart, but the relationship of superior-inferior that is established, projected, transmitted, assimilated, and even sacralized by religion. This keeps persons from truly appreciating each other as fully equal and from seeing the true human dignity of one another. Even the best among the dominant group tend to see and treat the others as inferior and "different." We can even do good things for the lesser others, but they remain lesser. They can be exploited legitimately because the culture and the laws of the dominant sanction the superior-inferior relationship. This gives the "master" the right and the obligation to use and "protect" the lesser ones.

This law of social distance is probably the hardest one to break through because it is not only enforced by external laws and the economic-political mechanisms of the land, but it is interiorized in a multiplicity of ways. For example, in ordinary commercials, we see blacks waiting on whites, but I have never seen a commercial with a white serving a black. Blacks, but never racially mixed families, appear in commercials. Brown-skins do not even appear at all. Social barriers of separability are drilled into a people through all the media of communication and education. Even religious education material and religious images in our churches exhibit a definite racial preference, thus indirectly telling the others that they cannot be reflected in the sacred.

Finally, the third constant that appears as an anthropological law of nature is: anyone who threatens to destroy or annul the barriers of separation will be an outcast—an impure untouchable who must be eliminated.

As should be evident by now, *mestizaje* is feared by established groups because it is the deepest threat to all the humanly made barriers of separation that consecrate oppression and exploitation. It is a threat to the security of ultimate human belonging—that is, to the inherited national/cultural identity that clearly and ultimately defines who I am to myself and to the world. It is even a deeper threat to established societies because the mestizo cannot be named with clarity and precision. So much is in the mystery of a name! I am comfortable when I can name you, for, in many ways, it indicates that I am somewhat in control of the situation. I may not like what I know, but at least I have the comfort of knowing what it is. But there is a nervousness when I do not know who you are—your name and your cultural nationality are so important, for they tell me who you are personally and fundamentally. They give me your immediate and ultimate human identity.

Because of the hyphenated identity, mestizos cannot be named adequately by the categories of analysis of either group. They do not fit into the single history set of norms for testing and identifying persons. This is threatening to both groups—we can name them and even study them, but they cannot name us or even figure out how to really study us. It is threatening for anyone to be in the presence of one who knows us very well even in our innermost being, but we do not know who they are. To be an outside-insider, as the mestizo is, is to have both intimacy and objective distance at one and the same time, for, insofar as we are in Mexico, we are outside the United States; but insofar as we are in the United States, we are distant from Mexico. As such we can see and appreciate the aspects of both, which neither sees of themselves or each other. In this very in-out existence lies the potential for our creativity: to pool the cultural genes and the chromosomes of both so as to create a new one!

The potential for newness will not be actualized automatically. The mestizo can simply become like one of the parent groups and continue to do unto others as they have done unto us. However, they can equally, although with more hidden difficulties than anyone suspects, choose to live out the radical meaning of their new being. This is exciting but difficult because, even though the dominant way may be rejected totally and explicitly, subconsciously the oppressed will strive to become like the oppressor, for they have already assimilated many of the characteristics of the dominant group. Will the group simply obtain power and acceptance by reverting to the ways of the parent group or will they initiate new life? That is the key question.

As a Mexican-American Christian, I am convinced that the full potential of *mestizaje* will be actualized only in and through the way of the Lord, which brings order out of chaos and new life out of death. It is in the Lord's way that the salvific and liberating role of our human mestizo way finds its ultimate identity, meaning, direction, and challenge.

THE CONCRETE-HISTORICAL MEANING OF GOD'S SAVING WAY

The Human Identity of the Savior

The racial-cultural identity of a person is the very first and immediate revelation of who one is. We all have stereotype prejudices about certain colors, accents, languages, features, regions, and religions. There is a natural tendency to categorize persons according to our sterotypes of them and to prejudge them as to their human worth and potential even before they have said or done anything. Looks are all-important and they are the first revelation, according to the standards of the world, of the worth and dignity of the person. Persons from the outer regions of any country are usually looked down upon as rustics, whereas those from urban centers look upon themselves as sophisticated.

What was the racial-cultural identity of Jesus? What did others think of when they first saw or heard of him ... before they even heard him speak or saw his actions? These are all-important questions, for we know from the New Testament itself that it is in the human face and heart of Jesus that God has been self-revealed to us. It is through the full humanity of Jesus that God has allowed us to see God in a human way.

There is no doubt that, during his lifetime, Jesus was regularly known as a Galilean, that most of his disciples were from Galilee, and that most of the things we remember best of his activity took place in Galilee. There is no doubt that Galilee plays a key role in the life and mission of Jesus as presented in the Gospels.

The full human signification of the kenosis of the Son of God becomes evident when we look at the image of Galilee in Jesus' time. First of all, if it had not been for Jesus, Galilee would probably remain an unknown region of the world. Jerusalem, Greece, and Rome were all important with or without Jesus, but not Galilee. It was an outer region, far from the center of Judaism in Jerusalem of Judea and a crossroads of the great caravan routes of the world. It was a region of mixed peoples and languages. In Galilee the Jews were looked down upon and despised by the others as they were in the rest of the world. They were considered to be stubborn, backward, superstitious, clannish, and all the negative stereotypes one could think of. Furthermore, the Jews of Judea looked down upon the Galilean Jews, for they considered them ignorant of the law and the rules of the temple, contaminated in many ways by their daily contacts with pagans, not capable of speaking correct Greek, for their language was being corrupted by admixture with the other languages of the region. In short, their own Jewish relatives despised them as inferior and impure. Because of their mixture with others, they were marginated by their own people. There were not doubts about the cultural *mestizaje* that was taking place and, knowing the ordinary situation of human beings, a certain amount of biological *mestizaje* was equally taking place. Culturally and linguistically speaking, Jesus was certainly a mestizo between Judaism and the other cultures that flourished throughout Galilee. And we know from the early Jewish charges that tried to discredit Jesus that he was even accused of being the bastard son of a Roman soldier named Pantera, which could also be a colloquial term for simply meaning "a Roman," which could have made of him a biological mestizo as well. I am, of course, in no way denying or even questioning that Jesus was conceived by the Holy Spirit. What I am saying is that in his human appearance, as viewed by those who knew him only in a worldly way and not through the eyes of faith, he certainly appeared to be of mixed origins. The New Testament itself gives clear evidence that nothing good was expected to come out of Galilee.

The point of bringing out all this is to appreciate the human beginnings of God's mission. God becomes not just a human being, but the marginated, shamed, and rejected of the world. He comes to initiate a new human unity, but the all-important starting point is among the most segregated and impure of the world. Among those whom the world has thrown out, God will begin the way to final unity. It is among those whom the world labels as "impure" that a new criteria for real purity will emerge.

Because the world expected nothing good to come out of Galilee, God chose it to be the starting point of God's human presence among us. The principle behind the cultural image of the Galilean identity is that God chooses what the world rejects. What is marginal to the world is central to God. It is through those whom the world has made nothing that God will reduce to nothing the power and wisdom of the world. It is through the poor and nonpersons of the world that God continues to reveal God's face and heart in a human way and among them—the Galilees and Galileans of today—salvation continues to begin for all the peoples of the world.

The Cultural Function of His Mission

The mission of Jesus is not some sort of esoteric or aesthetic truth. He comes to live out and proclaim the supreme truth about humanity, which will have immediate and long-term implications in everyday life and in the history of humanity. Those who hear his word and are converted to his way will see themselves and will equally see all others in a radically new way. This new image of self and of others will allow everyone to relate with each other as never before.

Because of his concrete human identity, Jesus had personally suffered the pains of margination and dehumanizing insults. He was concerned with the pains of hunger, sickness, bad reputation, rejection, shame, class struggles, loneliness, and all the real sufferings of humanity. His concern was not abstract, but real and immediate. He spoke with the Samaritan woman, ate with the rich, the tax collectors, and sinners alike. He did not feel repelled by the leper; he enjoyed the company of women and little children. Jesus was truly at home with everyone and it is evident that everyone felt at home with him. This is nowhere more evident than in his ability to enjoy himself at the common table fellowship with everyone without exception.

Out of the cultural suffering of rejection, Jesus offers a new understanding of the kingdom. He did not come to restore the kingdom of David for the Jewish people, but to initiate the reign of God who is the Father of everyone. The innermost identity of Jesus was his life of intimacy with God-Father. It is this living relationship with the Absolute that cuts through and relativizes all human images of importance or nonimportance, dignified or undignified. When we know the ultimate origins of a person—that he is really the son of the king—the superficial appearances are no longer important. It is the ultimate origins and name of a person that give us his true worth. It is precisely this intimacy with God-Father which is the basis of the innermost identity of Jesus, which he offers to all others. It is not the labels that the world places on persons that count, but one's own innermost identity and image of oneself as reflective of the likeness of God. By discovering that God is our real Father we begin to see everything in a new way. No longer will I see others as superior or inferior to me, but as brothers and sisters of the same Father. In this realization is the basis for a totally new value system for humanity. In fidelity to God, Jesus refuses to conform to any human law or tradition that will dehumanize and make appear as inferior any human being whatsoever. The truth of Jesus will upset humankind's criteria of judgment. Because one is, one is a child of God. But precisely because everyone can now belong, those who have set up and guarded the multiple barriers of separation, which allow them to enjoy the privileges of being "in" at the cost of keeping the so-called inferior ones "out," will not only refuse the invitation but will discredit the new way and try to prevent it from coming into existence.

But it is not sufficient to invite the rejected into the kingdom. It is not sufficient to tell the exploited and marginated of society that they are truly free human beings who are equal to all others. One must go to the roots of the human mechanisms, both to the external and the internal structures of society, to make known the segregating and dehumanizing evil that has been institutionalized and is now hidden in the various structures of the group. Jesus makes known that he must go to Jerusalem, the route of the sufferings of his people. Truth in the service of love must bring out clearly the evil hidden in human structures, which passes as good. Such a confusion allows the evils of power to appear as the good of society, to even appear as the sufferings of the marginated, as the causes of all evil. Criminals appear as good; victims appear as criminals. This is the on-going confusion of Babel, which continues to mask and confuse both the evil and the good of the world.

Jesus appears in the New Testament as the aggressive prophet of nonviolent love who refuses to conform to the violence of the structures in full loyalty to the tradition of the God of his people, of the God who sees the suffering, who hears the cries of affliction, and who wills to save. He questions the human traditions that oppress or destroy a people. Jesus must go to Jerusalem because that is the center of institutionalized power. When he arrives he goes to the very core of Judaism: the temple. In Jerusalem we see Jesus who does not hesitate to question the very legitimacy of the structures that were enslaving the masses of the people. The house of the God of compassion and justice had become the place that now legitimized and covered up the evil ways of the establishment. The same story is found in all human institutions. We need institutions in order to live in an orderly and peaceful way. Yet, all institutions have the tendency to become self-serving to the benefit of those in control. They are set up to serve persons, but persons end up serving them. It is this very tendency to absolutize that must be confronted and made known. As institutions, customs, and traditions become absolutized, they function as the idols of the group. Whether we call them God or not, they function as the real gods of the group. To question them is the same as questioning God. And when we challenge them, we will be accused of blasphemy. Yet to the degree that these ways dehumanize or reject any human being, they must be questioned in the name of God. But Jesus does not confront the power of the world with a power of the same order. He does not give in to the ways of humanity. He confronts the power of the world and human violence with a power of an entirely different order: the power of unlimited love, which will not give in to violence to eliminate violence.

The nonviolent way of Jesus worked in a diametrically opposed way to the nonviolent way of the missioners of the power countries. First of all, he begins by assuming the way, the language, and the world vision of the Galileans—the nonpersons of the world. The all-powerful God, in becoming a Galilean, converts so as to become the marginated, the rejected, and the nonperson of the world. Secondly, he does not only denounce the accepted practices of the powerful, as good missioners often do, but unlike the average traditional missioner, he even denounces and desacralizes their ultimate authority as enshrined in their religious symbols, for it is the religious symbols of the powerful that ultimately legitimize their way as God's way. Thirdly, the radical difference between the missionary activity of Jesus and that of missioners who are culturally and nationally members of the powerful countries is apparent in the response of the officials.

Official Judaism condemned Jesus and got rid of him. His accusers disowned him to the Romans because he questioned their ultimate authority and the ultimate legitimacy of their structures. The officials of mission-sending countries support and reinforce the missionary endeavor because it in effect affirms and perpetuates the legitimacy of their own world order. In supporting the missions, they affirm their own ultimate authority and the divine legitimacy of their ways. Let me be clear on this point; this is not necessarily done in an intentional or malicious way; in fact, I would say that quite often it is done with the best of intentions; however, the final result remains the same. The Spanish missioners did not hesitate to chastise openly and consistently the crimes and abuses of the conquest; however, they legitimized the way of the conquerors by affirming their ultimate symbol as superior and true in relation to the symbols of ultimate reality of captured peoples.

The way of Jesus to Jerusalem and the cross is the challenging task of those who are on the margins of society. Their temptation will always be to become simply the powerful themselves, as even the disciples wanted to do. But the challenge is to be willing to die so that a new way will truly be ushered in. The authorities kill Jesus but they cannot destroy him. He remains faithful to his way to the very end. He came to reject every type of human rejection and, even when all appear to have rejected him, even his God, he rejects no one. He dies in perfect communion with his people and his God. He came to tear down barriers of separation; and no matter what humanity tried to do to stop him, they were not able to break him down. As he lived his life in communion with everyone—so he died. All had rejected him, but he rejects no one.

God's love in and through Jesus triumphs over all the divisive hatreds and consequent violence of humanity. Jesus passes through death to life. In resurrecting him, God rejects the rejection of humanity, destroys all the charges of illegitimacy and demolishes the idolized structures. In the resurrection, God ratified the entire way and message of Jesus. It is from the resurrection that the entire way of Jesus and every aspect of his life takes on a liberating and salvific signification.

It is in the resurrection that the new life initiated and offered to everyone by Jesus is now fully and definitively present. No human power will be able to destroy it or slow it down. Jesus is the firstborn of the new creation, and in his followers a new human group now begins. It is definitely a new human alternative now present in the history of humanity.

First of all, those who had nothing to offer now have the best thing to offer to everyone: new life. It is the rejected and marginated Galileans who have received the Spirit and, without ceasing to be Galileans, now see themselves in a new way as they begin to initiate the new humanity. Everyone is invited, but it is the very ones who had been excluded who are now doing the inviting. It is obvious from the history of the early church how quickly the new way spread to *all peoples*. It crossed all boundaries of separation. Persons, without ceasing to be who they were culturally, nevertheless saw themselves in such a new way that the ordinary human barriers were no longer obstacles to the new fellowship. It is equally evident that the crossing of cultural boundaries was not easy, for each group had its own unsuspected idols, yet the miracle is that it took place. Cultural-national groups, which had been totally separated, now can come together—no longer Jew or gentile, master or slave, male or female, but all one in Christ. They continued to be who they were, but they lived their nationality and religion in a radically new way. Their identity was affirmed but their exclusiveness was destroyed. This openness led them to discover new values and criteria of judgment . . . from competition to cooperation, from divisions to unity, from strangers to a common family, from a superior or inferior status to common friends and all children of the same father.

The radical all-inclusive way of Christianity started among the rejected and lowly of society. This is the ongoing starting point. In the Spirit, they struggle to build new human alternatives so that others will not have to suffer what they have had to suffer. It is they who first hear the invitation to the new universal family of God, and it is the converted poor and suffering of the world, who see themselves in a new way, who now go out to invite—by deeds and words—all others into the new society. God continues to begin where humanity would never suspect. Out of the Nazareths and Galilees of today, salvation continues to come to the entire world.

THE GOD-MEANING OF OUR MEXICAN-AMERICAN IDENTITY AND MISSION

"God chose those whom the world considers absurd to shame the wise"
(1 Cor. 1:28)

It is in the light of our faith that we discover our ultimate identity as God's chosen people. It is in the very cultural identity of Jesus the Galilean and in his way from Galilee to Jerusalem that the real ultimate meaning of our own cultural identity and mission to society become clear.

For those who ordinarily have a good sense of belonging, the idea of being chosen is nothing special. But for one who has been consistently ignored or rejected, the idea of being noticed, accepted, and especially chosen is not only good news, but new life. For in being chosen, what was nothing now becomes something, and what was dead now comes to life. In the light of the Judeo-Christian tradition, our experience of rejection and margination is converted from human curse to the very sign of divine predilection. It is evident from the scriptures that God chooses the outcasts of the world not exclusively but definitely in a preferential way. Those whom the world ignores, God loves in a special way. But God does not choose the poor and the lowly just to keep them down and make them feel good in their misery. Such an election would be the very opposite of good news and it would truly be the opium to keep the poor quiet and domesticated. God chooses the poor and the marginated of the world to be the agents of the new creation.

The experience of being wanted *as one is*, of being needed and of being chosen, is a real and profound rebirth. Those who had been made to consider themselves as nothing or as inferior will now begin to appreciate the full stature of being human beings. Out of the new self-image, new powers will be released, which have always been there but have not been able to surface. Through this experience, the sufferings of the past are healed though not forgotten, and they should not be forgotten. For it is precisely out of the condition of suffering that the people are chosen so as to initiate a new way of life where others will not have to suffer what the poor have suffered in the past. When one forgets the experience of suffering, as has happened to many of our migrant groups in this country, such as the Irish in Boston, then they simply inflict the same insults upon others that had previously been inflicted upon them. The greater the suffering and the more vivid the memory of it, the greater the challenge will be to initiate changes so as to eliminate the root causes of the evils which cause the suffering. It is the wounded healer who has not forgotten the pain of the wounds who can be the greatest healer of the illnesses of society.

It is in our very margination from the centers of the various establishments that we live the Galilean identity today. Because we are inside-outsiders, we appreciate more clearly the best of the traditions of both groups, while equally appreciating the worst of the situation of both. It is precisely in this double identity that we in effect have something of unique value to offer both. The very reasons for the margination are the bases of our liberating and salvific potential not only for ourselves but for the others as well. In a privileged way, God is present in the marginated, for distance from the powers of the world is closeness to God. It is consistently in the frontier regions of human belonging that God begins the new creation. The established centers seek stability, but the frontier regions can risk to be pioneers. It is the frontier people who will be the trailblazers of the new societies. "The stone which the builders rejected has become the keystone of the structures. It is the Lord who did this and we find it marvelous to behold" (Matt. 21:42).

"I Have Chosen You To Go and Bear Much Fruit" (John 15:16)

God chooses people not just to make them feel good, but for a mission. "I have chosen you to go out and bear much fruit" (John 15:16). To accept God's election is not empty privilege, but a challenging mission. It is a call to be prophetic both in deeds and in words. It is a call to live a new alternative in the world, to invite others into it, and to challenge with the power of truth the structures of the world that keep the new alternative from becoming a reality.

Our Mexican-American Christian challenge in the world today is not to try to become like someone else—Mexicans or Americans—but to combine both into a new way. It is through the very mechanisms of forging a new and more cosmopolitan identity that new life begins to emerge. It must be worked at critically, persistently, and creatively, for the temptation will always be there to become simply one or the other of the previous models. The temptation will always be there to restore the kingdom rather than to usher in the kingdom of God. In our present powerlessness we may think that this is stupid, but, in our faith, we know that we must take the risks and begin to initiate new ways of life that will eliminate some of the dehumanizing elements of the present one. We know that we will not eliminate them all, nor will this come about easily and without much effort, organization, and frustration, but nevertheless the efforts must be made to introduce new forms and new institutions that will continue some of the best of the past while eliminating some of the worst. We will not build the perfect society, but we must do our part to at least build a better one. We must begin with the grass roots, but we must equally go to the very roots of the problems.

This is our "divine must"! We, too, must harden our faces and go to Jerusalem. We must go to the established centers of power, whether political, economic, educational, or religious, to confront their sacred idols which prevent them from truly serving all the people. It is the idols of society which function in favor of the rich and the powerful, and against the poor and powerless. It is they which mass the hidden viciousness and manipulations of the wise of the world who find many ways of exploiting the poor and the simple of the world.

We really do not have a choice if we want to be disciples following Jesus on his way to the cross. It is this road from Galilee to Jerusalem which has to be continued if evil is to be destroyed, not with new forms of evil, but with the power of truth in the service of love. We have no choice but to speak the truth which brings to light clearly the evil of the world, knowing fully well that the powers of darkness will not stop at anything in order to put out the light.

"Your Grief Will Be Turned to Joy" (John 16:20)

It is in our fiestas that our legitimate identity and destiny is experienced. They are not just parties; in fact they are the very opposite. They are the joyful, spontaneous, and collective celebrations of what has already begun in us even if it is not recognized by others or verbalized even by ourselves. It is the celebration of the beginning of the ultimate eschatological identity where there will be differences but not division. It is the celebration of what has already begun in germ but is yet to be totally fulfilled. Yet the fiesta is a foretaste and experience, even if for a brief moment, of the ultimate accomplishment. It is a result of who we are and a cause of what is yet to become. For just as it is true that the celebrations of the people can be used to drug the people and keep them in their misery, it is equally true that the fiestas can be used as rallying moments that not only give the people an experience of togetherness, but can also nourish the movements of liberation. In the fiestas, we rise above our daily living experiences of death to experience life beyond death. They are the moments of life that enable us to survive, to come together, to rally, and to begin anew. The spirit not only to survive but to bring about a new existence can be enkindled in the fiestas so as to ignite the people to action.

Fiestas without prophetic action easily degenerate into empty parties, drunken brawls, or the opium to keep the people in their misery. But prophetic action without festive celebration is equally reduced to dehumanizing hardness. Prophecy is the basis of fiesta, but the fiesta is the spirit of prophecy. It is in the combination of the two that the tradition of faith is both kept alive and transmitted to newcomers. It is through the two of them that the God of history who acts on our behalf, on behalf of the poor and the lowly, continues to be present among us bringing the project of history to completion.

Thus it is precisely through our *fiestas* that we are kept together as a people. It is through them that we have continued to maintain our identity and sense of belonging. They are the deepest celebrations of our existence—meaningful to those who belong and incomprehensible and folkloric to outsiders. They are the lifeline of our tradition and the life sources of our new existence.

40

Critical Thought and Messianic Trust: Reflections on a Jewish Theology of Liberation

MARC H. ELLIS

In a fascinating and important book, *Against the Apocalypse: Response to Catastrophe in Modern Jewish Culture*, David Roskies examines the history of the Jewish people through its various responses to destruction. What Roskies finds is a people with a remarkable ability to reclaim ancient Jewish archetypes and therefore create meaning within suffering and death. "The greater the catastrophe, the more the Jews have recalled the ancient archetypes," Roskies writes. And so in the ghettos of Eastern Europe the archetypes of destruction were alive in the minds of the common people and intellectuals alike: "The burning of the Temple (the sacred center), the death of the martyr (the sacred person), and the pogrom (the destruction of the Holy Community)." The walls and barbed wire that separated Jews from the non-Jewish population paradoxically helped to bring some of the internal boundaries down:

The elite were brought closer to the masses, the assimilated closer to the committed, the secular closer to the religious, Yiddish closer to Hebrew. The Modernists became, despite their long battles against it, part of the literature of consolation. With the ghetto's intellectuals moving closer to the people, the writers could use the polylingualism of Jewish Eastern Europe to restore conceptually and socially the idea of a Jewish nation that was the penultimate consolation for the ultimate destruction. And a literature that was for centuries retrospective (including "prophecies after the fact") became increasingly prophetic—so that, in fact, analogies could be used at last not for consolation but for action, including uprisings.[1]

The scribes of the ghetto wrote as an act of faith and, in fact, participated in and transformed the "liturgy of destruction," which the Jewish people had articulated over the millennia. Though overwhelmingly secular in background and outlook, the ghetto writings continually referred to religious themes. Yitzhak Katzenelson, a secular poet, organized a public reading of the Bible on the day the Warsaw ghetto was sealed, though this was to demonstrate a continuity of history as a people rather than belief in God. However when it came to the Psalms, Katzenelson rejected them as too placid a form of response to catastrophe. At the same time Hillel Zeitlin, for years a modern religious existentialist, began translating the Psalms into Yiddish and when his ghetto tenement was blockaded, Zeitlin arrived at the roundup point for deportation dressed in prayer shawl and tefillin.[2]

We have here, in its most difficult articulation, memory as a form of resistance: the refusal to cut oneself from one's own people while speaking to the world in cries of anguish. Roskies concludes that to understand the collective response of the Jewish people one must look to the writers "who because they shared the same fate and were intimately involved in all facets of the people's Armageddon, were able to transmute the screams into a new and terrible scripture."[3]

Today, forty-five years after the Warsaw ghetto uprising and its subsequent liquidation, these archetypes of destruction take on new form in a recently empowered Jewish people. It is not too much to say that the liturgy of destruction has come to legitimate that which it originally resisted: occupation and intervention, expropriation and statelessness, torture and murder. Memory as a form of resistance – the religious existentialist translating the Psalms and arriving for deportation with prayer shawl and tefillin – is replaced with memory as a form of oppression – scripture read to justify settlements in occupied territories and armed invasions in Lebanon. This "new and terrible scripture" continues to be written now with the blood of others.[4]

The liturgy of destruction, articulated in many ways, is known and felt by the Jewish people around the world and especially in the two most powerful Jewish communities, North America and Israel. But that part of the liturgy, oppression as it has developed since the Six Day War in October 1967, is unspoken or denied. To speak of it is to face grave consequences, including the threat of excommunication and, still worse, the charge that one is creating the context for another holocaust. Yet honesty demands an accounting because the archetypes of the temple, the martyr, and the pogrom, are being played out in an arena where the persecuted are no longer powerless Jews, rather Palestinians and others who exist on the other side of Israeli power.

HOLOCAUST THEOLOGY

The liturgy of destruction gave birth after the war to a powerful and radical theology, Holocaust theology. Coming from the periphery of Jewish life, this theology challenged Jewish religious and secular perspectives by claiming the Holocaust as the formative event of contemporary Jewish life. To be a Jew is to stand within the event of Holocaust, to see this as the orienting event of our lives. The Holocaust calls for a renewed commitment to being Jewish even as it shatters the previous categories within which modern Jews live. The nineteenth-century categories of Orthodox and Reform Judaism, with their understanding of Torah and the prophetic, as well as secular liberal and radical ideologies, with their optimistic understanding of progress and universalism, must all be rethought in light of the

Holocaust. Thus Holocaust theology challenges the entire religious and secular structure of Jewish life with its entrenched institutions, interests, and assumptions. That which stood at the center previous to the Holocaust—the synagogue, liberalism, radical politics—ultimately recedes to secondary positions. According to Holocaust theology, the future of the Jewish people is found in remembrance and self-empowerment rather than prayer or politics.[5]

Though Holocaust theologians are known and celebrated today—Elie Wiesel, Emil Fackenheim, and Richard Rubenstein, for example—their initial works were met as much with derision and conflict as enthusiasm and gratitude. The reasons for this reception involve the religious questions they raise as well as the new institutions they call for to pursue empowerment; both challenge Jewish leadership and sensibilities. To overcome these obstacles and create a norm for the Jewish community today, Holocaust theology simply speaks to the depths of Jewish historical experience and thus to the Jewish people.

Despite differing perspectives within Holocaust theology, its aspect of remembrance and empowerment assumes a religious significance. Holocaust theologians surface the dialectic of holocaust and empowerment that is the command of the Holocaust victims to survive and flourish as a people in a hostile world, the major expression of which is found in the state of Israel and a politically active Jewish community in the United States. Yet that command is shadowed by the haunting cries of the ghetto scribes: the Holocaust event critiques all unjust use of power, even if that power is wielded by Jews. Though empowerment is mandated, the Holocaust calls for an ethic tried in the death camps of Auschwitz and Treblinka. The cry "never again" represents a demand to the world on behalf of the Jewish people as well as a hope that no people in the future shall suffer as the Jews have.[6]

From the beginning this dialectic of Holocaust and empowerment was couched in symbolic language, and as the years passed political and military realities often superseded the radical, indeed prophetic, statements of earlier years. Holocaust theology meant something quite different before the 1967 Six Day War than after, before the 1973 Yom Kippur War than after, before the 1982 Lebanese War than after, before the 1987 uprising in the occupied territories than after. Critical to these changes is the increasingly militaristic and annexationist policies of Israel in the Middle East, the new global role of arms merchant and counterinsurgency expert played by Israel, and the expanded role of the U.S.A. as Israel's guarantor and funding agency. In fact Holocaust theology did change to meet these changing historical realities by downplaying that side of the dialectic which critiqued unjust power and emphasizing the importance of empowerment in a hostile world. Thus by the 1980s the Jewish community faced an intriguing and dangerous paradox: a radical theology that is politically neoconservative. Despite the protests and the public anguish expressed by some of the Holocaust theologians over certain Israeli and U.S. policies, it is fair to characterize the three most known theologians— Wiesel, Fackenheim, and Rubenstein—and hosts of other intellectuals, theologians or not, as political neoconservatives. In this way they mirror a shift in the Jewish community at large, even as they provide theological legitimation for this movement.[7]

Nowhere is this shift more evident than in the progressive theologian and activist Irving Greenberg. In an important and radical analysis of the Holocaust and its implications, published in 1974, Greenberg wrote that after the Holocaust "no

statement theological or otherwise can be made that is not credible in the presence
of the burning children," and that the victims of the Holocaust ask us above all
else "not to allow the creation of another matrix of values that might sustain another
attempt at genocide." Greenberg affirmed empowerment as an essential aspect of
fidelity to the victims of the Holocaust, although he added the proviso that to
remember suffering propels the Jewish community to refuse to create other victims.

The Holocaust cannot be used for triumphalism. Its moral challenge must also
be applied to Jews. Those Jews who feel no guilt for the Holocaust are also tempted
to moral apathy. Religious Jews who use the Holocaust to morally impugn every
other religious group but their own are the ones who are tempted thereby into
indifference at the Holocaust of others (cf. the general policy of the American
Orthodox rabbinate on U.S. policy in Vietnam). Those Israelis who place as much
distance as possible between the weak, passive diaspora victims and the "mighty
Sabras" are tempted to use Israeli strength indiscriminately (i.e., beyond what is
absolutely inescapable for self-defense and survival), which is to risk turning other
persons into victims of the Jews. Neither faith nor morality can function without
serious twisting of perspective, even to the point of becoming demonic, unless they
are illuminated by the fires of Auschwitz and Treblinka.[8]

By the 1980s Greenberg's understanding of the Holocaust as critique is overshadowed by the difficult task of empowerment. He comments favorably on the
reemergence of American power, applauding Reagan's arms buildup, the stationing
of medium-range missiles in Europe, the development of the Strategic Defense
Initiative, supporting rebel forces in Angola, the withdrawal of the United States
from UNESCO, and the continued funding of the Contras in Nicaragua. Greenberg's emphasis on empowerment allows him to take the high road when analyzing
Ronald Reagan's trip to Bitburg in May 1985.

> Overall Ronald Reagan's record in commemorating the Holocaust has been
> very good. He serves as honorary chairman of the campaign to create a
> national memorial. He has held commemorations of the Holocaust in the
> White House and spoken passionately of the need to remember. His support
> for Israel—the single most powerful Jewish commitment that a Holocaust
> shall not recur, the haven where most of the survivors built their new lives—
> is exemplary. Our criticism of this particular callous misjudgment must not
> be allowed to falsify the total overall picture, which is a good one. And we
> shall have to work with him again.[9]

In a revealing theological and political transformation, the ultimate danger has
become the prophetic critique of empowerment.[10] When empowerment suffices in
and of itself, religious language, already chastened by the event of mass death, takes
on a form that Jews have rarely experienced in the last two thousand years. Empowerment becomes like a god. More specifically, and especially in the diaspora,
the state of Israel assumes a deified existence. Of course, Israel as God has many
ramifications, not the least of which is the diminution of critical thought. How can
we understand the history that gave birth to Israel and the history it is now creating
if we place Israel above history—as if it transcends critical analysis? Could we say
that Holocaust theology, born amid a harrowing and challenging epoch as a creative
response to destruction, no longer provides the tools of analysis that enable us to

understand the concrete history that we as a people are creating? It should not surprise us that Holocaust theologians speak more often about Palestinian terrorism and less about continuing Israeli repression in the occupied territories; most often about the importance of Israel as a strategic ally of the United States than Israel's support of repressive regimes in South Africa, Central America, and other regions around the globe.[11]

TOWARD A JEWISH THEOLOGY OF LIBERATION

Today we need a new Jewish theology that speaks of the horrors of the Holocaust and the need for empowerment, yet seeks empowerment defined by an ethical path. It needs to articulate our situation as it is rather than as we hoped it would be. A new Jewish theology speaks of a renaissance of Jewish life as well as its cost: Israel as an occupying power, expropriator of land, torturer of prisoners, and arms exporter. The return to Israel may be our ideology; a new Jewish theology faces the fact that 75 percent of the Jewish people do not and will not live in Israel and that now more Israelis leave Israel each year than emigrate to it. The fastest growing diaspora community in the world today is made up of Israelis who leave Israel. A new Jewish theology must further critically evaluate our success and power in North America and its consequences: single issue politics; uncritical support of U.S. foreign policy; alliance with economic classes and religious communities that are conservative and traditionally anti-Semitic. In short, a new Jewish theology begins by highlighting that which Holocaust theology has been unable to articulate—the cost of our empowerment.[12]

Though difficult and dangerous as it might seem, by emphasizing the cost of empowerment the difference between empowerment and liberation comes into focus. A dialectical tension, once found in Holocaust theology, reemerges and thus theology's critical edge can come to the fore. Empowerment is critiqued by its cost and is seen less as an end in itself. Instead it becomes a necessary and flawed step along the path toward a more comprehensive and fulfilling liberation. We have boldly proclaimed that the world cannot claim liberation without our own; so too we face the reality that we are not liberated until all are, even those we may name as enemy.

A Jewish theology that broadens the contours of empowerment to liberation is born and named as a Jewish theology of liberation. It states unequivocally that solidarity with our own people and the ethical values that form the center of our tradition, and solidarity with all peoples who are struggling for justice, including the Palestinian people, are at the center of the personal and communal life of the Jewish people. However, solidarity, like empowerment, cannot remain on the level of principle or high-minded phraseology. Rather our concrete solidarity, or lack thereof, needs to be stated in detail, politically and religiously. For example, the continuing Israeli relationship with South Africa demonstrates a lack of solidarity with the struggle of the South African people and thus critiques our empowerment. A religiosity that makes biblical claims for the land for a people without a land and justifies the expulsion of those who have lived on the land is a critique of the religious foundations of our empowerment.[13]

Resources for such a theology of liberation are surfacing within the Jewish com-

munity today, though they are not without their own contradictions. Arthur Waskow's neoorthodox theology attempts to articulate a justice agenda, though he
retains a safe distance from the critical question of Israel and proffers too heavy a
dose of unreflective mysticism. Organizations like New Jewish Agenda bring together secular and religious Jews around a common ethical pursuit, but they remain
on the fringe of the larger community. Movements in Israel like Oz veShalom,
Religious Zionists for Strength and Peace, address the increasingly militaristic religious community, while remaining small in number and ineffectual. Jewish feminists continue to address the patriarchal qualities of Jewish organization, learning,
and ritual in important ways, though a broader political agenda is in need of exploration. The new journal *Tikkun*, formed in response to the neoconservative journal *Commentary*, seeks to address the political and religious issues in a different
key; whether it can escape a concern for legitimacy within the Jewish community
leaves the outcome of this endeavor in doubt. However, despite their various limitations, these remain prophetic attempts on the periphery of established Jewish
power.[14]

Yet the plain and bold language needed at this juncture of our history is somehow missing. The critical issue of power and oppression—the breakthrough point—
is talked around, or submerged in slogans and ritual claims of loyalty to the community. The suffering continues, even escalates, at the same time that our theology
and activity become more refined. We are in a state of paralysis as our affluence
and power grows. Even the progressive movements within Jewish life remain in the
dialectic of Holocaust and empowerment, unable to move toward liberation, for to
enter the terrain of liberation is to call into question at a radical level the structures
and perspectives of the Jewish community now built upon the foundations of Holocaust theology.

To say that these voices are missing within the Jewish community is a sad and
lamentable fact, yet there are Jewish voices speaking in the language of liberation.
For many who have spoken in the past, and many who speak today, are ostracized
from the community and even in some cases excommunicated. They, like the ghetto
scribes, are mostly secular, meticulously analyzing the history we are creating. Together they comprise a hidden tradition that calls the Jewish community to a difficult
fidelity. In doing this they help lay the groundwork for a Jewish theology of liberation.[15]

RECOVERING THE HIDDEN TRADITION

The "hidden tradition" was first analyzed by Hannah Arendt, a German Jewish
philosopher who emigrated to France after Hitler's rise to power in 1933 and then
to the United States in 1941. Though her two greatest works, *The Origins of Total-
itarianism* and *The Human Condition*, established her reputation as a political philosopher, her book *Eichmann in Jerusalem* is the best known to the general public
because of the controversy it caused and the vehement condemnation she received
by the Jewish press. The tone of criticism, often heard today, is best summed up
by a letter the great Jewish scholar Gershom Scholem wrote Arendt in 1963: "In
the Jewish tradition there is a concept, hard to define and yet concrete enough,
which we know as *Ahabath Israel*: 'Love of the Jewish people. . . .' In you, dear

Hannah, as in so many intellectuals who came from the German Left, I find little trace of this."[16]

Yet it was Arendt's independence and critical thought that rankled the Jewish community rather than the substance of her philosophy. In fact it was her recovery and transformation of the hidden tradition of recent Jewish history that allowed her the space to think through the difficulties of our age and interweave the particular plight of the Jewish people with the broader contours of Western history. She was, in Russel Jacoby's terminology, a public intellectual, deeply Jewish though free of Jewish institutional pressure and power.[17]

According to Arendt, the hidden tradition began almost two hundred years ago with the Enlightenment and Jewish emancipation in Western Europe. This gave rise to greater participation of Jews in society even as they remained outsiders in the social and political realms. This outcast status gave rise to two particular types of Jews in society: the "conscious pariahs" who transcended the bounds of nationality to "weave the strands of their Jewish genius into the general texture of European life," and the "parvenus" who tried to achieve status by raising themselves above their fellow Jews into the respectable world of the gentiles. Arendt chose to place herself as a conscious pariah and thus endured a dual difficulty that all conscious pariahs shared, becoming marginal in relation to European society and to the Jewish community as well. As Ron Feldman analyzes the situation, conscious pariahs were "neither parochially Jewish, like their Eastern European cousins, nor were they part of the wealthy Jewish upper class of bankers and merchants that controlled Jewish-Gentile relations." The conscious pariah constituted a hidden tradition because there were few links between those who affirmed their pariah status—for example, Heinrich Heine, Sholam Aleichem, Franz Kafka, and Walter Benjamin—or ties with the rest of the Jewish community. Standing exclusively neither inside nor outside their Jewish or European heritage, conscious pariahs used both as platforms from which to gain insight into the other.[18]

Amid the tumult of the twentieth century, with its reign of mass dislocation and mass death, particularly seen in the Jewish Holocaust, the pariah could no longer afford the role as simply outsider: the pariah had to become political, and thus Arendt recognized the creation of a Jewish homeland in Palestine as essential to the future of the Jewish people. However, Arendt's Zionism was from the beginning critical and nonstatist. Though chastised and hidden from view today, Arendt's support for and warnings about the Zionist experiment are relevant in the present.[19]

Just months after the partition of Palestine and the establishment of a Jewish state in 1948, Arendt wrote a perceptive and troubling essay, "To Save the Jewish Homeland: There Is Still Time." According to Arendt the declaration of statehood had polarized positions on both sides: non-Zionist Jews were now diehard enthusiasts and moderate Palestinian Arabs were being forced to choose sides. Palestinian Jews and American Jews were essentially in agreement on the following propositions, propositions Arendt felt were detrimental to the possibility of peace:

The moment has now come to get everything or nothing, victory for death; Arab and Jewish claims are irreconcilable and only a military decision can settle the issue; the Arabs—all Arabs—are our enemies and we accept this fact; only outmoded liberals believe in compromises, only philistines believe in justice, and only shlemiels prefer truth and negotiation to propaganda and

machine guns; Jewish experience in the last decades—or over the last centuries, or over the last two thousand years—has finally awakened us and
taught us to look out for ourselves; this alone is reality, everything else is
stupid sentimentality; everybody is against us, Great Britain is anti-Semitic,
the United States is imperialist—but Russia might be our ally for a certain
period because her interests happen to coincide with ours; yet in the final
analysis we count upon nobody except ourselves; in sum—we are ready to go
down fighting, and we will consider anybody who stands in our way a traitor
and anything done to hinder us a stab in the back.[20]

Arendt saw this unanimity of opinion as ominous, though characteristic of our
modern mass age. It tended to dissuade discussion and reduce social relationships
to those of an "ant heap": "A unanimous public opinion tends to eliminate bodily
those who differ, for mass unanimity is not the result of agreement, but an expression of fanaticism and hysteria. In contrast to agreement, unanimity does not stop
at certain well-defined objects, but spreads like an infection into every related
issue." The loyal opposition, so important to critical thought and politics was in the
process of being eliminated.

For Arendt, the two great contributions of Jewish settlement, the Kibbutz movement and Hebrew University, as well as the great precedent of cooperation between
a European people and a colonized people were in danger of collapse. The advantage of the Jewish people in having no imperialist past to live down was also threatened, and thus its ability to act as a vanguard in international relationships on a
"small but valid scale" was being lost. Even if the Jews won the war and affirmed
their claim to statehood, the unique possibilities and achievements of Zionism in
Palestine would be destroyed:

The land that would come into being would be something quite other than
the dream of world Jewry, Zionist and non-Zionist. The "victorious" Jews
would live surrounded by an entirely hostile Arab population, secluded inside
ever-threatened borders, absorbed with physical self-defense to a degree that
would submerge all other interests and activities. The growth of a Jewish
culture would cease to be the concern of the whole people; social experiments
would have to be discarded as impractical luxuries; political thought would
center around military strategy; economic development would be determined
exclusively by the needs of war. And all this would be the fate of a nation
that—no matter how many immigrants it could still absorb and how far it
extended its boundaries (the whole of Palestine and Transjordan is the insane
Revisionist demand)—would still remain a very small people greatly outnum-
bered by hostile neighbors.[21]

The ends of such an endeavor were clear to Arendt: degeneration into a warrior
state with the political initiative in terrorist hands. The Jewish state could only be
erected at the price of a Jewish homeland.[22] Arendt closed her essay with the
following proposition and hope:

1. The real goal of the Jews in Palestine is the building up of a Jewish
homeland. This goal must never be sacrificed to the pseudosovereignty of a
Jewish state.

2. The independence of Palestine can be achieved only on a solid basis of Jewish-Arab cooperation. As long as Jewish and Arab leaders both claim that there is "no bridge" between Jews and Arabs (as Moshe Shertok has put it), the territory cannot be left to the political wisdom of its own inhabitants.

3. Elimination of all terrorist groups (and not agreements with them) and swift punishment of all terrorist deeds (and not merely protests against them) will be the only valid proof that the Jewish people in Palestine has recovered its sense of political reality and that Zionist leadership is again responsible enough to be trusted with the destinies of the Yishuv.

4. Immigration to Palestine, limited in numbers and in time, is the only "irreducible minimum" in Jewish politics.

5. Local self-government and mixed Jewish-Arab municipal and rural councils, on a small scale and as numerous as possible, are the only realistic political measures that can eventually lead to the political emancipation of Palestine. It is still not too late.[23]

Two years later Arendt wrote of the nonnationalist tradition in Zionism and the danger of nationalism for small nations relating to military and economic dependency. To continue support from abroad Israel might find itself in the "unenviable position of being forced to create emergencies, that is, forced into a policy of aggressiveness and expansion." Arendt concluded: "The birth of a nation in the midst of our century may be a great event; it certainly is a dangerous event."[24]

There are, of course, many other facets of Arendt's thought that bear analysis and she herself became so discouraged about the state of Jewish discussion that she virtually ceased writing on Jewish topics in 1966. Like most Jews, though, when catastrophe threatened she rallied behind Israel. Celebrating the victory in the Six Day War of June 1967 she wrote to Mary McCarthy, "Any real catastrophe in Israel would affect me more deeply than almost anything else." In the Yom Kippur War in October 1973 Arendt feared that Israel might this time be destroyed and she offered financial and moral assistance. Arendt the nonnationalist was in the same boat with other dissenting Jews in fearing another holocaust. What Arendt did not know was the extent of destruction possible, for Israel had compelled the United States to provide a "massive shipment of conventional weapons" to Israel by threatening to use nuclear weapons against their adversaries in the Middle East.[25]

With her death in 1975, she was also spared knowledge of the inevitable consequences of an occupation that has now entered its third decade: consistent violations of human rights, including torture and murder. Just ten years after her death some Israeli writers heralded the arrival of Israel as a leading global arms exporter, the thought of which would have horrified Arendt. To be sure Arendt's critical analysis continues today in such writers as Noam Chomsky and Jane Hunter, though the opposition and its power are even more concentrated now than they were in Arendt's time. Forty years after her most powerful essay on the critical issues of Jewish life, Arendt's judgments seem more than accurate; they were and are prophetic.[26]

SOLIDARITY AND THEOLOGICAL CRITIQUE

Though Arendt was thoroughly secular in her outlook, others in the hidden tradition struggled toward a religious vision in literary and philosophical frameworks. This is true of two figures about whom Arendt wrote, Franz Kafka and Walter Benjamin. We might say that from the beginning of the hidden tradition there was a dialectical tension between secular and religious critique most exemplified in Walter Benjamin's "Treatise on History." Here he suggests the possible interplay of political revolution and theology, as in his statement: "Our experience forbids us to conceive history in fundamentally atheological terms, however little one ought to try to write it in theological terms." This tension of politics and theology allowed Jewish intellectuals of the hidden tradition to investigate the world beyond the confines of Jewish particularity without absolutizing the secular. In retrospect, this search bore great fruit in both realms though often at great emotional and physical cost. The loneliness and isolation of Kafka and Benjamin, of Hannah Arendt herself, testifies to the difficulty of living between two worlds, at home in neither.[27]

The experience of Holocaust has brought this sense of isolation and abandonment to a deeper level, and the dialectic of secular and religious critique has collapsed into a militancy, both secular and religious, that reinforces the isolation which it hoped to end. Empowered, the Jewish people feel more embattled than generations previous to the Holocaust. Though Israel is one of the most formidable military powers in the world, the Jewish perception is that it is continually on the brink of holocaust. This accounts for the curious, one might even say blasphemous, comparison of Adolf Hitler and Yasir Arafat, one a genocidal murderer of the Jewish people, the other considered by those outside the Jewish community as a moderate in the Middle East. The liturgy of destruction rehearsed by Holocaust theologians again plays a major role here; it does not help us to understand the history we are creating today and thus distorts the question of what it means to be faithful as a Jew within empowerment.[28]

Movements of renewal within the Jewish community speaking in identifiable religious language as well as a revived and transformed hidden tradition are crucial to challenge the dominance of Holocaust theology. The hidden tradition, especially, needs to maintain its link with secular language and critique as it begins to explore religious language and activity in a new light. That which was latent in Kafka, Benjamin, and Arendt comes to the fore in a dialectical tension responding to changed circumstances and historical configurations.

There is little question that the major transformation of religious language and activity in the West and around the world since the Holocaust is found in Christian political and liberation theology with its emphasis on critical thought and solidarity in the struggle for justice. It is here that a multitude of images and possibilities opens to the Jewish people. Such an exploration is difficult because of the history we have been through together, but political and liberation theology, especially, provide an opening to understand the struggles and suffering of those around the world. For they take seriously the question of suffering and often express it in a conceptual framework—exodus, prophecy, idolatry—bequeathed to the world by the Jewish people. This allows us to see our own history in another, less isolationist perspective. At the same time, it calls forth a critical understanding of our own empowerment. The issue of solidarity raised by political and liberation theology forces us to move beyond a theology that no longer describes the history we are creating.[29]

For both Jew and Christian the question of solidarity begins with the Jewish experience of suffering in the Holocaust and the Christian response. Johann Baptist Metz's essay, "Christians and Jews after Auschwitz," is crucial here. Metz, a German Catholic theologian, sees Auschwitz as a turning point rather than an end point in Christian-Jewish relationships. He asks Christians, "Will we actually allow it to be the end point, the disruption which it really was, the catastrophe of our history, out of which we can find a way only through a radical change of direction achieved via new standards of action? Or will we see it only as a monstrous accident within history but not affecting history's course?" Clearly for Metz the Holocaust is the turning point in Christian history and Christian-Jewish relationships. To the question of whether a Christian can pray after Auschwitz, Metz responds in the affirmative because Jews prayed in Auschwitz.[30]

The root of Jewish-Christian ecumenism comes into focus as a common journey forged in suffering: "We Christians can never again go back behind Auschwitz: to go beyond Auschwitz, if we see clearly, is impossible for us of ourselves. It is possible only together with the victims of Auschwitz." Even theodicy is challenged: Metz considers as blasphemy Christian belief structures that are "initiated outside this catastrophe or on some level above it." Again the reference is to Jewish suffering. Meaning can be invoked only as it was within Auschwitz and in dialogue with the heirs of Auschwitz.[31]

For Metz, forging an alliance with the victims of Auschwitz means in the first place the end of persecution of Jews by Christians. But it also means something else:

If any persecution were to take place in the future, it could only be a persecution of both together, of Jews *and* Christians — *as it was in the beginning.* It is well known that the early persecutions of Christians were also persecutions of Jews. Because both groups refused to recognize the Roman Emperor as God, thus calling into question the foundation of Rome's political religion, they were together branded as atheists and haters of the human race and were persecuted unto death.[32]

Thus Metz accomplishes the important task of placing the Jewish victims at the center of Christian consciousness and resistance as well as inviting contemporary Jews and Christians to accompany one another in the difficult project of social critique and transformation.

Gustavo Gutiérrez, the Peruvian theologian of liberation, citing the work of Metz in relation to Europe and North America asks the Jewish people to take the next step: to accompany others in their suffering in the present. In the conclusion of his book, *On Job: God-Talk and the Suffering of the Innocent,* Gutiérrez writes of the Holocaust as an "inescapable challenge to Christian conscience and an inexcusable reproach to the silence of many Christians in the face of that dreadful event." The question of human suffering and God's presence is an essential one, but for Latin Americans the question is not "How are we to do theology after Auschwitz?":

The reason is that in Latin America we are still experiencing every day the violation of human rights, murder, and the torture that we find so blameworthy in the Jewish holocaust of World War II. Our task here is to find the words with which to talk about God in the midst of the starvation of millions, the humiliation of races regarded as inferior, discrimination against women, especially women who are poor, systematic social injustice, a persistent high rate of infant mortality, those who simply "disappear" or are deprived of their freedom, the sufferings of peoples who are struggling for their right to live, the exiles and the refugees, terrorism of every kind, and the corpse-filled common graves of *Ayacucho*. What we must deal with is not the past but, unfortunately, a cruel present and a dark tunnel with no apparent end.[33]

Rather, the question asked in Latin America is "How are we to do theology *while Ayacucho lasts*? How are we to speak of the God of life when cruel murder on a massive scale goes on in "the corner of the dead?"[34]

Metz and Gutiérrez suggest the way to lessen Jewish isolation and preoccupation with Jewish suffering through accompaniment and activity on behalf of those who suffer today. Could it be that our particularity would once again lend depth to the struggles of others as well as be rewoven into a broader texture of human struggle and hope? Still, if Christians cannot move into the future without the victims of Auschwitz, and if the theological question today revolves around the corner of the dead, then the ecumenical project has a critical edge for Jews as well as Christians. For we are contributing to the corner of the dead and Jews cannot move forward without the very victims we are creating. To paraphrase Metz, the challenge might be stated thus: "We Jews can never go back behind empowerment: to go beyond empowerment, if we see clearly, is impossible for us by ourselves. It is possible only with the victims of our empowerment."

These are hard words for Jews to hear and to speak; they suggest a culpability in the liturgy of destruction that the ghetto scribes could hardly imagine. A new and terrible scripture it is which bears recitation to our children. However, the hidden tradition of critical thought as well as a newfound solidarity with those who once oppressed us may also allow us to transform our empowerment into the path of liberation. In this light, the central questions facing the Jewish community are: How are we to do theology in the face of the Jewish Holocaust while *Ayacucho* continues? How are we contributing to the corner of the dead? How can we move beyond complicity into a solidarity that is confessional, transformative, and actively engaged in the pursuit of justice? As in any movement outward toward those who are suffering, it is at the same moment a movement toward the deepest themes of Jewish community life: ethics, the prophetic, and the refusal of idolatry. Hence, the task of a Jewish theology of liberation: to join with others in the ongoing struggle for human dignity and justice with the hope that we can become what we are called to be.

NOTES

1. David G. Roskies, *Against the Apocalypse: Responses to Catastrophe in Modern Jewish Culture* (Cambridge: Harvard University Press, 1984), p. 198. Also see p. 197.
2. Ibid., p. 212.
3. Ibid., p. 202.
4. See Marc H. Ellis, *Toward a Jewish Theology of Liberation* (Maryknoll, N.Y.:

Orbis, 1987), pp. 45–46. Today the Palestinian refugee camps/ghettos serve as the locus for memory as a form of resistance. For a discussion of the recent uprisings in the West Bank, see John Kifrea, "The 'Uprising' Fires Palestinian Pride," *New York Times,* Jan. 1, 1988, p. 3.

5. Ellis, *Jewish Theology,* pp. 7–24, 28–37.

6. Ibid., pp. 20–22.

7. For Richard Rubenstein's confession that his own analysis of the Holocaust leads him to a conservative position, see *The Cunning History: Mass Death and the American Future* (New York: Harper and Row, 1975), pp. 95–97.

8. Irving Greenberg, "Cloud of Smoke, Pillar of Fire: Judaism, Christianity, and Modernity after the Holocaust," in *Auschwitz: Beginning of a New Era?* Eva Fleischner, ed. (New York: KTAV, 1977), p. 22. Also see pp. 27, 28, 29.

9. Irving Greenberg, "Some Lessons from Bitburg," *Perspectives* (New York: National Jewish Resource Center, May 1985), p. 4. Also see idem, "On the Third Era in Jewish History: Power and Politics," *Perspectives* (1980), p. 6, and idem, "Power and Peace," *Perspectives* (Dec. 1985), pp. 3, 5. Elie Wiesel did little better in his much publicized rebuke to President Reagan as he accepted the Congressional Medal of Achievement. See Wiesel's response in *Bitburg and Beyond: Encounters in American, German, and Jewish History,* Ilya Levkov, ed. (New York: Shapolsky Publishers, 1987), pp. 42–44.

10. Greenberg writes: "There is a danger that those who have not grasped the full significance of the shift in the Jewish condition will judge Israel by the ideal standards of the state of powerlessness, thereby not only misjudging but unintentionally collaborating with attempted genocide" (see Greenberg, "The Third Great Cycle in Jewish History," *Perspectives* [New York: National Jewish Resource Center, 1981], p. 25).

11. For a discussion of these relationships, see Jane Hunter, *Undercutting Sanctions: Israel, the U.S. and South Africa* (Washington, D.C.: Washington Middle East Associates, 1986), and idem, *No Simple Proxy: Israel in Central America* (Washington, D.C.: Washington Middle East Associates, 1987).

12. For a more in-depth discussion of this theme, see Ellis, *Jewish Theology,* pp. 25–46. Neoconservatives emphasize instead the "new antisemitism" that has emerged in our empowerment. See Nathan Perlmutter and Ruth Ann Perlmutter, *The Real Anti-Semitism in America* (New York: Arbor House, 1982).

13. Perlmutter, *Anti-Semitism,* p. 116. Also see Roberta Strauss Feuerlicht, *The Fate of the Jews: A People Torn Between Israeli Power and Jewish Ethics* (New York: Time Books, 1983), pp. 219–88.

14. For my initial analysis of Arthur Waskow, New Jewish Agenda, Oz ve-Shalom, and Jewish feminism, see Ellis, *Jewish Theology,* pp. 47–65. Today my analysis would emphasize the limits of these approaches, especially neoorthodox theology.

15. An example of a person who is ostracized—even vilified—for his opposition to certain Jewish leadership positions is Noam Chomsky. You would think from the treatment he receives that Chomsky refuses the legitimacy of the state of Israel, the excommunicable sin. That he accepts the legitimacy of Israel *and* Palestine but documents Israeli domestic and foreign policy in detail makes him even more dangerous. See his book *The Fateful Triangle: The United States, Israel, and the Palestinians* (Boston: South End Press, 1983). As Roberta Strauss Feuerlicht writes,

"Today criticism of Israel is grounds for excommunication from the Jewish community" (*Fate of the Jews*, pp. 281–82).

16. Gershom Scholem, "Eichmann in Jerusalem," in *Hannah Arendt; The Jew as Pariah: Jewish Identity and Politics in the Modern Age*, Ron H. Feldman, ed. (New York: Grove Press, 1978), p. 241. For an account of Arendt's life, see Elisabeth Young-Bruehl, *Hannah Arendt: For Love of the World* (New Haven: Yale University Press, 1982). For Arendt's response to Scholem, see Arendt, *Pariah*, pp. 245–51.

17. Arendt, *Pariah*, pp. 67–91. For the demise of the public intellectuals, see Russell Jacoby, *The Last Intellectuals: American Culture in the Age of Academe* (New York: Basic Books, 1987).

18. See Feldman's introduction to Arendt, *Pariah*, pp. 18–19.

19. In 1948 Arendt wrote: "The real goal of the Jews in Palestine is the building up of a Jewish homeland. This goal must never be sacrificed to the pseudo-sovereignty of a Jewish State" (*Pariah*, p. 192). Arendt was not alone in this understanding; see Martin Buber, "The Meaning of Zionism" in *A Land of Two Peoples: Martin Buber on Jews and Arabs*, Paul R. Mendes-Flohr, ed. (New York: Oxford University Press, 1983), pp. 179–84.

20. Arendt, *Pariah*, p. 181. It is from these understandings that certain myths regarding the birth of Israel came into being. For a lifelong Zionist's investigation of these myths, see Simha Flapan, *The Birth of Israel: Myths and Realities* (New York: Pantheon, 1987).

21. Arendt, *Pariah*, p. 187.

22. Ibid., pp. 182, 184, 186, 188, 189.

23. Ibid., p. 192.

24. Ibid., pp. 221–22.

25. For Arendt's reaction, see Young-Bruehl, *Love of the World*, pp. 454–55. For the threatened use of nuclear arms, see Chomsky, *Fateful Triangle*, p. 466.

26. The power of Jewish organizations is documented in Paul Findley, *They Dare to Speak Out: People and Institutions Confront Israel's Lobby* (Westport, Conn.: Lawrence Hill, 1985), and in Edward Tivnan, *The Lobby: Jewish Political Power and American Foreign Policy* (New York: Simon and Schuster, 1987).

27. For Benjamin's understanding of the dialectic of secular and religious, see Walter Benjamin, "Theses on the Philosophy of History," in *Illuminations*, Hannah Arendt, ed. (New York: Schocken, 1978), pp. 255–76. For his importance to a Jewish theology of liberation, see Ellis, *Jewish Theology*, pp. 94–95. For a fascinating study of Kafka and his Jewishness, see Marthe Robert, *As Lonely As Franz Kafka* (New York: Schocken, 1986).

28. For an analysis of Arafat as a moderate, see Alan Hart, *Arafat: Terrorist or Peacemaker* (London: Sidguick and Jackson, 1984). On the question of contemporary Jewish history and fidelity, see Ellis, *Jewish Theology*, pp. 1–4, 121–22. My point here is that theology's central task is to nurture the questions that we need to ask about the history we are participating in and creating. The reason that Holocaust theology became normative in the Jewish community is that it did precisely that. By being unable to do this in the present, Holocaust theology helps produce a sense of isolation and distortion. That is why we need a new theology.

29. For a lengthy discussion of the dialectical relationship between Jewish contact with Christian liberation theology and the question of solidarity, see Ellis, *Jewish Theology*, pp. 67–90. I conclude: "Is this not the place of meeting that demands an

opening to other struggles, an opening that at the same time calls us to the depths of our own history?"

30. Johann Baptist Metz, *The Emergent Church: The Future of Christianity in a Postbourgeois World* (New York: Crossroad, 1981), pp. 18, 19. Metz also explores the difficulty Christians have had in taking Auschwitz and thus contemporary Jews seriously: "Have we really listened attentively during the last decades? Do we really know more today about the Jews and their religion? Have we become more attentive to the prophecy of their history of suffering? Or is the exploitation not beginning again, this time in a more sublime fashion because of being placed under the banner of friendliness toward the Jews?"

31. Ibid., p. 19.

32. Ibid., p. 20.

33. Gustavo Gutiérrez, *On Job: God-Talk and the Suffering of the Innocent* (Maryknoll, N.Y.: Orbis, 1987), p. 102.

34. Ibid., pp. 101, 102.

41

Pakistani Women: Yearning for Liberation

MARIAM FRANCIS

Just one month ago, Azra, a very lively staff nurse, who had always been pampered and very well taken care of by her parents and five brothers, came back to her paternal house with a smashed nose.[1] With great pain she told her story:

> In all honesty I have served my husband wholeheartedly, but he is never happy. I am a staff nurse, work eight hours, and back home do everything as every Punjabi woman does. He scolds me and blames me for not having children [after two years of married life]. The day he broke my nose he said he wanted to have freshly cooked vegetables for breakfast. I prepared the breakfast, but as it was time for duty hurriedly changed into my uniform and asked Christopher to help himself to breakfast. He became angry for not being served at table and, picking up the nearest implement, beat me and smashed my nose.

Azra said that she was tired of being treated so badly and could no longer fulfill what was said at her marriage: "you enter it in a bridal suit, and will emerge only in your coffin."

This is not an unusual account of a middle-class woman. There are even more atrocities going on in the lower-middle class—indeed, at every level—in Pakistan. Almost every home, almost every woman, has the same kind of story to tell when sharing intimately—though in public each will boast about being the luckiest one.[2]

I taught in La Salle School, Faisalabad, for five years. Besides teaching, my favorite work was visiting mothers of the students. They were all well off with very few problems about money, but there were even fewer who did not have serious problems with their husbands. At that time, ten years ago, I was the outcome of a rigid formation, with convent school education and an Italian novitiate background. I felt pity for my friends, tried to give them suggestions now and then. In fact two of them were on the verge of divorce, but with my help as a teacher, things were rehabilitated and the women are living happily in their homes. But all this I was doing from a teacher's point of view: to know the families of my students in order to know why they behaved in a certain way. I never thought "women" could be an issue for me.

I joined the Pastoral Institute staff in 1979. And here, for the first time in my life, I began to be aware of real problems and issues. In 1983 a seminar in liberation theology opened my eyes to see new horizons in a more human way.[3] And here I am today, a woman seeing with different eyes the problems of 1974–79. That I never tried to understand then was not because I did not want to, but because I could not. These issues are now in front of me as a priority to be considered and dealt with.

WHO IS A PAKISTANI WOMAN?

Can any woman penetrate her real self? I think one can lift the veil and may find a great deal about herself, but in spite of these efforts it is hard to reach the core of her authenticity. The Pakistani woman does not know who she is. She leads, in the majority, a highly cloistered life, cut off even from herself. No matter where she is, a Pakistani woman, whether in a tribal, feudal, or urban environment, whether highly qualified and professional or a self-sufficient peasant toiling alongside her menfolk, she disappears within her class and becomes a nonentity.[4] The quality and mode of difference ranges from province to province.

The harsh laws governing the conduct of Baluch and Pathan women make them the least visible in society. They are invisible in having no share in any field and are ignored by statistics and scholars alike. Custom covers their head at the age of six. Education is out of the question for them, thus diminishing the possibility of change for them in the future. Punjab and Sind have a greater number of urban centers than do the tribal provinces. Educational facilities are available to a greater number of women, who are less oppressed by tribal or family laws and have many chances to develop themselves. A few of them are prominent figures with high posts, but they are exceptions to the rule.

The majority of educated Pakistani women belong to the silent and unmentioned world; 80 percent of our sisters are in the rural areas or in industrial centers doing cheap labor, increasing the wealth of some *wadera*, "landlord." Women are a poor and virtually illiterate majority who lead an anonymous life of hardship and toil involving long hours of tedious chores for which there is ridiculously low compensation, or, most of the time, neither compensation nor recognition. Many of these women, like Azra, bear the double burden of housework and outside work. They are the first to rise, clean the house, prepare breakfast, and then awake their children and husbands; they are the last to sleep, having first washed dishes and ironed clothes for the next morning. Not only do women have longer days than the rest of the family, they are the last to eat and probably eat what remains. Thus they suffer from malnutrition and anemia.[5]

A Pakistani woman in whatever sphere she is, whatever title she may have or may boast of having, as emancipated from all sorts of laws and customs, is still governed by the immutable rules of patriarchy: "she is a woman after all and a woman has to abide by certain rules."

THE BURDEN OF CULTURE

Last April, there was a drama on television called "Anarkali."[6] This was not the Anarkali of the Moghul period who was walled up by the great King Akbar because

Sheikhu his son fell in love with her (she was a mere maid and it was against royal custom and Indian culture for a low-class woman to seduce a prince). The television drama described an Anarkali of 1988 who was sacrificed at the altar of culture. Married to a covetous mill owner whose only desire is to make money, she is used by him as a means of access to the rich and powerful, in order to live in high society. He always wants her to be in her best dress and jewelry. He surrounds her with his wealth and is astonished, angry, and out of control when she points out that what she really wants is to be free. She wants to do gardening, cooking, painting, and writing. He refers continuously to their class culture in which rich women do not do gardening, do not talk to commoners, do not go to workers' houses because they must maintain their social status. Cattle often have nose rings, the easier to control them; the nose rings of these women are gold, but the purpose is the same. They have no decision-making power of their own, and worse than that, no will or desire—for there is nothing to live for when every day offers nothing but dying.

In my experience, past and present, I have seen poverty in upper and upper-middle-class women—the more painful because it is unacknowledged. They have no aim in life, yet neither do they complain about life "because it simply is like this." This is the culture of a rich society that has given up thinking of alternatives. Many times these ladies (*begums*) remind one of a poultry farm where hens are force-fed. Everything is thrown in front of them so they might not fly the coop.

What about other women under cultural pressure? Working women must bear insults because certain areas within their category are culturally prohibited to them. What woman can pass a bazaar without being pinched or hearing lewd comments?

In this culture, even innocence is suspect. Shabbo was standing at the outer door of her house talking to her friend. She had no *dopatta* (veil) on her head, and they were joking and laughing. She clapped her hands when she laughed and the boys passing the road watched them. Surely, they felt, the girls were doing this to attract their attention: "probably she is a hot girl, dying to get married." Good girls, in that culture, are those who are obedient, are well-covered, never raise their eyes toward their elders or the other sex, never laugh loudly, do not have great expectations from life, do not have needs except to have nice clothes and good food, never talk in front of their fathers, and never say a word of like or dislike in the matter of their marriage companion. The Pakistani woman has accepted all this without question: all these rules and regulations are her fate. God wanted all this from her when she was created woman, at least the way God has been presented to us.

ECONOMIC AND FINANCIAL BURDEN

Like most Third World women, the Pakistani woman is subject to harsh economic problems. Pakistan, as an agricultural country, has most of its population in the rural area. Here 70–80 percent of the work, in what are recognized as economically productive tasks, is done by women—although the data do not reflect their presence, for all agricultural production is considered the result of male labor. The women have been marginalized even in this. Rural women work an average of 14–16 hours a day.[7] They assume all responsibiliy for food, cleanliness, and the general welfare of the family. In addition she has to collect fuel, repair her primitive mud stove, repair the mud walls of her home, and look after any domestic animal her family owns. She takes food to the fields for her menfolk and while they are eating and resting she cuts fodder, digs vegetables, and washes clothes on the hand pump. She participates in the agricultural cycle, harvesting wheat and picking cotton. After all this, the credit goes to menfolk and she does not get even the satisfaction of being recognized. She has done everything except plowing and watering the fields at night.[8]

She is accountable for the money from sales and is often blamed and beaten for carelessness or any shortcoming. After men and women have worked equally in the field, the men take their *huqqa* (water pipe) and go to gossip in the village, leaving the women to start the evening duties.

What is there to say about the women employed in factories, notably in textiles, pharmaceuticals, and packaging?[9] Women are preferred in this employment because they are considered more servile, cheaper, more efficient, and thus more productive than men.

There is also an invisible "army" working within the confines of their homes. These women belong to a bit more elevated class than those hired in factories. These are those helpless women who, to make an extra rupee or two, lead monotonous lives in very cheap labor. Our markets are decorated with their skilled work, such as *zarri* work (gold embroidery) on clothes and shoes, ready-made dresses, all sorts of designs in different stitches on *dopatta* and *kurta*. There are thousands and thousands of home industries like this. The rich trader or entrepreneur buys their work cheaply and banks his profit in Switzerland. They have used the sweat of these illiterates, further isolating them from others, and exploiting their need (very often, the men of these houses are a prey to drugs and gambling).[10]

SOCIAL BURDEN

Cultural abuses have a great impact on social life. Nizambdin is a radio comedian. In a recent broadcast,[11] he was betting who could tell the biggest lie. His biggest lie: "This morning I saw two women sitting on a bench and they were quiet." This was greeted with predictable laughter. It is quite painful to women to listen to and read these kinds of jokes. They are not simple jokes to humor men, but indicate, rather, the reality of life. Society does not respect women as women. They are considered insensitive objects owned by men. As a person, the woman is denied an identity of her own. She is a commodity, a "visitor" in her father's family to be kept in trust until claimed. Her father's house is not hers. Her husband can divorce her at any time and in old age she is at the mercy of her sons. It is a curse for a mother to die in her daughter's house. From beginning to end, she is never secure and does not know where she belongs.

At times younger persons have been asked to make an analysis and study of the origin of Punjabi *gali* (verbal abuse). The worst results point always to mothers and sisters. It has become such a part of our life that even women very easily use such language against themselves as if they have absorbed this attitude from their mothers' wombs. The dignity of women within all these structures is problematic and this not only in civil society. The church, too, is influenced by it. It is enough to hear the jokes of seminarians and priests to realize that the menfolk of the church feel women to be less human than themselves.

RELIGIOUS AND POLITICAL BURDEN

Pakistan as an Islamic country cannot be separated from its politics. They are linked together. In a particular way the islamization of 1979 began by controlling women in the name of religion. In more concrete terms, this control is achieved by denying them access to social, political, and religious power. Men decide for them who they should be and how they should act. The Qur'ān is so interpreted to curtail women's rights. Instead of dealing with the many serious and urgent issues, like poverty, illiteracy, public health, and sewerage, the authorities, together with *maulanas* and *maulvis*, discuss the position of women and their status in society.

Islamization has made the Pakistani women unique from among all the rest of the women in the world. Nowhere in the world will one hear that a lady was slapped by a total stranger (in his zeal for Islam) in a bakery for not having her head covered.[12] Another *maulvi* was angry to see women without the *burqa* (long veil) and he gave a lecture on the loudspeaker, putting all these women in eternal fire because they were indecent and a temptation for men.

In the beginning, when there had been a great craze for the restoration of Islam, many strange things happened. Women bore the brunt of this zeal because it seemed as if everyone had a license to pass judgment and be the guardian of women's morality. The tragedy continued with the promulgation of the Hadood Ordinance. This ordinance treated punishment and the manner in which punishment was to be executed. Its victims were mostly women, for adultery, fornication, rape, and prostitution; all are reduced to the same level. The ordinance did not differentiate between adultery and rape. The "how" of punishment was essentially the same for both except for some minimal changes. This and other laws, such as the law of evidence, "the witness of two women is equal to one male," provoked women a great deal. The indignation and frustration led them to take an aggressive step in the prophetic movement, WAF (Women's Action Forum). This is a non-structured, informal, free-floating group of activists, feminists concerned with many specific issues.

In the beginning WAF contained only upper-class women because they were the ones wounded and criticized, but very soon, like fire in a forest, the middle class joined them. There is a new identity among them, grounded in a new self-awareness, a more critical self-knowledge. This new self-confidence and self-assurance, joined together in WAF, made them aware they had emerged from their small world: they came to know and realize their own great potential. They experienced an active determination to shape their own selves and the world in which they live. Instead of passively conforming to a centuries-old predetermined role, they made a resolution to decide for themselves what to be and what to do.

This Spirit of God, who inspires where it wants and wherever it sees it is time, blew among the Pakistani oppressed. For the oppressed have become conscious of their degrading situation: they have awakened for their transformation, for liberation and salvation. This transformation has come, in themselves and others, in a newly found independence. Thus, the "new woman" will reach a "new earth"[13] just as the Israelites reached the promised land when commanded by the Lord. "Why are you crying out for help? Tell the people to move forward" (Exod. 14:15). Yes, liberation and salvation—for transformation—is not to rest but to continually move forward, and women have understood this.

The issue of women rises out of one of those sinful situations of socio-historical development. Men cannot acclaim their friendship with God unless they accept the wholeness of humanity as the work of God. "Accepting this, the collective dimensions of sins are rediscovered," says Gutiérrez.[14] For sin is not an act, it is an attitude toward malice, toward wrong: sin exists in the "hamartisphere" (Greek, *hamartia* = sin). It is not enough for WAF and other women's movements to dedicate themselves to discover and restore their womanhood: they must also devise strategies for the conversion of men to the building of a new society.

Jesus, the radical liberator, restored women as the work of God's hand. In this, he liberated men from their own ideological slavery, those who thought that they were the privileged. Jesus said, "I tell you, tax collectors and prostitutes are going into the kingdom of God ahead of you" (Matt. 21:31). In *A Theology of Liberation*, Gustavo Gutiérrez deals with three levels of liberation: political liberation, the liberation of man-woman throughout history, and liberation from sin and admission to communion with God.[15] For the Pakistani women yearning for liberation, the three are linked together and have to be realized at the same time.

The threefold hamartisphere (the sphere of sin) has taken centuries to become rooted and both men and women have made the world we live in. It is not women's struggle and effort alone that will break through this structure. Men and women together and the Pakistani church and Christian women will have to snatch salvation from its present rigid political and historical context. Only in Christ does the all-comprehensiveness of the liberating process reach its fullest sense.

Pakistani women have a great task in front of them. They have remained far behind in human history, but Muslim and Christian women have come to discover that the God under whose label they have lost their full rights is a God fashioned by maleness. They will move forward together with their brothers in a great hope. Like Paul, everybody on the road of freedom can say, "To get this done I toil and struggle, using the mighty strength that Christ supplies, which is at work with me" (Col. 1:29).

NOTES

1. This essay is based, mostly, upon my personal experience and contact with all kinds of women. There is very little of fruit from reading. In a very simple way, I have tried to speak of the Pakistani woman's inner world, believing, like Leonardo and Clodovis Boff, that "more knowledge is gained in practice than from theory ... [that] it is easier to experience than to think out. Therefore, on this level, wisdom and prudence are more useful than is analytical reasoning. And in this, ordinary persons are often way ahead of the learned" (*Introducing Liberation Theology* [Maryknoll, N.Y.: Orbis, 1987], p. 41).

2. This is borne out by the experience of over three years of monthly meetings with women in the Pastoral Institute, Multan.

3. "Seminar on Liberation Theology," sponsored by the Justice and Peace Commission of the Conference of Religious Superiors, in Faisalabad, 1984.

4. *Women of Pakistan: Two Steps Forward, One Step Back?*, by Khawar Mumtaz and Farida Shaheed (Lahore: Vanguard Press, 1988), p. 21.

5. "Women and Work," by Najma Sadeque, *Focus* (1987), p. 42.

6. Pakistan Television, "Drama 88," April 26, 1988.

7. *Women of Pakistan*, p. 24.

8. Ibid., p. 25.

9. "Women and Work," pp. 46–47.

10. Ibid., p. 50.

11. Pakistan Radio Broadcast, Lahore, May 29, 1988.

12. *Women of Pakistan*, p. 71.

13. Cf. *New Woman, New Earth: Sexist Ideologies and Human Liberation*, by Rosemary Radford Ruether (New York: Seabury Press, 1975).

14. *Gustavo Gutiérrez, A Theology of Liberation* (Maryknoll, N.Y.: Orbis, 1973), p. 175.

15. Ibid., pp. 21–36.

42

Doing Theology in a Counterrevolutionary Situation

CARTER HEYWARD

In June 1985, twelve Christians from the United States joined a number of Cuban theologians in a conference on our work as Christian educators. We met for a week in El Seminario Evangélico, a school of theology founded by Episcopalians, Presbyterians, and Methodists. The seminary sits on a hill overlooking the town of Matanzas, about a hundred kilometers from Havana, and serves often as a gathering place for Christians who are committed to the work of justice.

We went to Cuba well versed in liberation theology. Our expectation was that we would find there among sister and brother Christians a well-cultivated theology of liberation. What we discovered, however, was a deeply committed Christian people not in need of a "theology of liberation" in the way we in the United States are. Liberation theology is born in situations of gross economic oppression, and Cubans are citizens of a nation in which poverty has been eliminated. Where the state has assumed the work of economic justice as basic to its own purpose, the religious community is freed to discover dimensions of its own "thirst after righteousness," which move it beyond the work of resistance to forces of greed and hunger.

Yet, a revolution is never really won. No society is perfect. Cuban Christians have their work cut out for them. But much of Cuba's revolutionary work has been done. In areas of poverty, illiteracy, health care, and social philosophy, the revolution's achievements over the last twenty-six years have been almost miraculous. However, because Cuba still has far to go—especially in matters of gender and sexuality, and to some lesser degree in terms of race—it would be inaccurate to suppose that Cuba is a postrevolutionary society. Cuba might be described more accurately as a prorevolutionary nation. The leaders of the Cuban revolution look toward rather than away from social change as vital to the well-being of the Cuban people. It seems clear to Fidel Castro, and to many (not all) other leaders in both the Communist Party and the Christian church, that the massive overhauling of oppressive structures has not been finished. What *has* been accomplished is the restructuring of the society's economy. There is literally no poverty in Cuba. In this way, the Cuban island can serve as a light to other Caribbean and Latin American

397

nations in which a large majority of persons remains captive to forces of economic exploitation.

Relative to Cuba, the United States is a counterrevolutionary society. On a global pendulum of pervasive economic injustice, we sit close to one end, with Cuba at the other. Thus, in contrast to Cuba's revolutionary church, Christians in the United States who believe that the elimination of poverty should be a priority of the church are postured in adversary relationship to a counterrevolutionary state.

Moreover, unlike Christians throughout Latin America and the Caribbean, mainstream religious persons in the United States are not attempting radically to transform, much less overthrow, our government. Not since 1776 has there been a broad-based effort in this direction. There have been significant social movements directed against the government, but every major attempt has been to correct or reinterpret, not restructure, the Constitution; to ameliorate, not seriously transform, the inequities of the economic underpinnings of our society. Even the Civil Rights movement fell short of constituting a revolution that would transform the prevailing economic institutions of the nation, such as family, education, religion, and business. Unlike many Latin Americans, the majority of U.S. citizens neither understands nor acknowledges economic class realities as existing. Our national consciousness is cemented historically in broadly libertarian ideals of individual "rights" and the "freedom" of each "man" (white propertied male) to shape his own fortune. Such "freedom" means more than justice to most U.S. citizens. Those in this nation who see that until the economic basis upon which this nation stands is transformed, injustices of all forms will prevail, are disregarded as "un-American."

The proudly counterrevolutionary Reagan administration recognized that such persons have begun again to coalesce in efforts as apparently diverse as the pro-creative choice and sanctuary movements. Feminism and Central American solidarity commitments have some common roots in a growing awareness among many of their adherents that patriarchy, imperialism, racism, and advanced capitalism make dangerous bedfellows. For most revolutionaries in the United States, the economy is not—and cannot be, in a complex First World situation—the only "issue." Racism, sexism, heterosexism, anti-Semitism, imperialism, ageism, environmental hazards, and other forces of contempt toward creation demand serious attention. In this complex matrix, increasing numbers of U.S. citizens, including Christians, are troubled by the extent to which economic exploitation is, in a concrete, daily sense, the fiber that holds together the oppressive texture of our society.

In this essay, I hope to disentangle some of the diverse threads that may give a theology of liberation its particular shape. The trip to Cuba and earlier visits in Nicaragua have helped clarify for a number of liberation theologians in the United States how different our religious missions may be depending upon the politics and social structures of the nation in which we live and work. As noted earlier, economic enslavement is not the only form of socio/spiritual bondage. Genuinely revolutionary efforts do not cease with the elimination of poverty. The work of justice-making must take seriously the struggle of the poor and all who are marginalized, trivialized, or disregarded by those who hold authority in the nation and its institutions. A theology of liberation must reflect an awareness of connections between economic exploitation and such other forms of social oppression as white racial supremacy, male gender hegemony, compulsory heterosexuality, cultural and religious imperialism.

After assessing briefly some differences between the political situations of the revolutionary—justice-making—churches in the United States, Cuba, and Nicaragua, I will turn my attention specifically to revolutionary Christianity in the United States and to how the United States—especially those of us who are white, middle-strata women and men—might envision our work in this nation at this moment in history.

CHURCH-STATE RELATIONS: A CRITICAL FACTOR IN SHAPING REVOLUTIONARY CHRISTIANITY

The structures of economic justice in the United States and Cuba are diametrically opposite, but the shape of Christianity in these two nations has been similar. Both are modern secular societies, in which the modern church, prior to televangelism, has not assumed a central role in public policy. In both the U.S.A. and Cuba, most twentieth-century Christians have presumed a split between the "spiritual" mission of the church and the "political" work of the state. In Cuba, the state has been the moving force for economic justice and the revolutionary church has assisted in this work. In the United States, the state has perpetuated structures of poverty and the progressive church has been merely a prod to the state and a caretaker of those who suffer the wounds of class: rich and poor, black and white, male and female.

The revolutionary church in Nicaragua stands in bold relief to its counterparts in Cuba and the United States. Nicaragua is a deeply Christian *and* revolutionary society. The nation that only nine years ago overthrew the Somoza tyranny has had to resume its revolutionary struggle, this time against the counterrevolutionaries (Contras) who, like Somoza, are sustained by American economic interests. As in Cuba, the bottom line of the Nicaraguan revolution has been the peoples' movement toward the elimination of poverty in a society in which, prior to 1979, the Somoza family owned 42 percent of all arable land and in which one out of three children did not reach the age of one. In contrast to Cuba, Christians in Nicaragua have been revolutionary leaders since the earliest days of the movement to overthrow the Somozas. Christians and non-Christians alike in Nicaragua cite the invaluable leadership of the *comunidades de base cristiano*—Christian base communities—in galvanizing the nation for the struggle against Somoza in the mid-70s and, today, in the struggle against the Contras. Ernesto Cardenal, priest and minister of culture, speaks for many Nicaraguan Christians when he says, as he did to a group of us last year, "I became a revolutionary because I was a Christian, and I am able today honestly to call myself a Christian because I am a revolutionary." This is the voice that greets the traveler in Nicaragua. Christians and political revolutionaries are not merely "in dialogue" or "in cooperation." They are, in many cases, the *same*: to love God is indeed to side with the poor.

As in Cuba and the United States, the revolutionary church in Nicaragua is beset by a counterrevolutionary form of Christianity. In Nicaragua and Cuba, it takes the form of that part of the organized church that opposes socialization of national resources and espouses publicly the separation of the "spiritual" arena of the individual's life from the "political" arena of the nation's aims and struggles. Unlike the reactionary church in the United States, the churches in Cuba and Nicaragua, which propagate a "doctrine of anticommunism," are unable to collude with their national governments in maintaining the economic structures of poverty.

What we may recognize among these three countries is a church-state variable that shapes the mission of the revolutionary church. In Nicaragua, where the revolutionary church and state overlap—sharing not only the same vision but also many of the same persons as leaders—the church is like the leaven in the loaf. The explicitly spiritual character of Christian witness, such as in Defense Minister Miguel d'Escoto's fasting for peace, brings a dimension of pastoral care into even the most hard-edged business of the revolutionary government. We learned in Cuba that Fidel Castro has been impressed by the extent of revolutionary Christian commitment in Nicaragua and sees it as a model for future church-state relations in Cuba.

In Cuba, where the revolutionary church and state do not overlap in terms of leadership but rather share a common goal, the church is more like a junior partner in an organization committed to a single task: the work of justice. Through dialogue, cooperation, and critique, the church is able to join in the work—which could not be done as well without it. The government is the senior partner, in that it retains the authority to determine what concrete shape justice-making will take in Cuba.

In the United States, where the revolutionary church and the counterrevolutionary state share neither leaders nor vision, the justice-seeking church is more like a fly in the ointment than the leaven in the loaf, or like a lesbian feminist whom the firm fires rather than the junior partner. This adversarial stance is evidenced in current U.S. government campaigns against the sanctuary movement, Puerto Ricans who seek independence, abortion rights, and virtually all advocacy programs for the poor and for black and other racial/ethnic minority persons.

When our Cuban *compañeros/as* pointed out to us that they do not espouse a theology of liberation because, unlike other Latin American and Caribbean countries and unlike the United States, they do not need liberation, they are signaling the critical role played by the actual social situation in which theology is done. These progressive Cuban Christians acknowledge the imperfections—and injustices—in both their society and their church. But they wanted us to be as clear as they are that Cuban is distinctively Cuban—not Nicaraguan, North American, Russian, or even "Cuban" in the sense in which it is portrayed in so-called free-world propaganda.

Let us turn now to some of the distinctions that characterize the work of revolutionary Christians in Nicaragua, Cuba, and the United States.

Nicaragua: A Theology of Revolution

Because a large number of Nicaraguan Christians are involved in the Nicaraguan government and because the "people's church" has never been perceived by non-Christian revolutionaries as a threat or a counterrevolutionary force, the revolutionary church in Nicaragua is able to be about what it understands its faithful mission to be: feeding the hungry, clothing the naked, teaching the illiterate to read and write, providing health care to the sick, and struggling against the United States' well-financed efforts to undo work in these areas. In a real, historical sense, *los yanquis* represent today to the revolutionary church and state in Nicaragua what the Somoza family represented for forty years: the United States is the enemy of the people who comprise the church and state, the enemy of justice, and the enemy of a God of justice.

Therefore, the people's church has a fourfold mission: (1) to participate in building and staffing health clinics, schools, food cooperatives, and other agencies that serve the daily needs of the poor; (2) to participate in the armed, as well as the educational, struggle against *yanqui imperialismo*, which is shorthand for those forces bent upon maintaining the gap between rich and poor; (3) to embody an evangelical spirit within the Christian church so as to convert counterrevolutionaries to the radical faith-claims of justice; and (4) to provide informed critiques of government and church where either fails to honor its pledge to respect and serve all citizens. An example of the revolutionary church's critique of the government has been in the largely successful efforts of such Christian leaders as Moravian pastor Norman Bent's insistence that the Sandinistas take seriously the plight of the Miskito Amerindians and other non-Hispanic peoples on the east coast.

The mission of justice-making Christians in Nicaragua is simultaneously one of pastoral care, political and military struggle, evangelism, and prophetic advocacy. In this church, "spiritual" needs—prayer life, personal growth in the Spirit, and individual needs for healing, forgiveness, and hope—are attended within the context of the Christian community's collective commitment to justice for all. Nicaraguans minister to their neighbors, whether in the form of adopting orphans, extending the family to include those who are homeless, grieving with one another, or celebrating together occasions of thanksgiving and joy. Throughout the United States today are formerly cynical Christians who "went to Nicaragua" and there witnessed the Body of Christ, broken for us—and resurrected in a hope that restored our faith.

Nicaragua libre is as vibrant an example as one is likely to find anywhere in the world—along with South Africa—of a revolutionary situation in which a theology of revolution—an activist, urgent theology of liberation—is an organic consequence of the peoples' faith in a God who casts down the mighty from their throne and does not send the poor empty away.

Cuba: A Theology of Affirmation and Critique

Like Nicaragua, Cuba had to spend the early years of its revolution contending against Yankee imperialism. Unlike Nicaragua, Cuba had the occasion, at the Bay of Pigs, to stem the tide of U.S. aggression and thereby to undercut the possibility of a protracted drain of its resources in defense of its national independence.

Throughout the first decade of the young revolutionary Cuban society, the church fared neither as well as it has in Nicaragua nor as poorly as the United States government would have us believe. Christians were not lined up and slaughtered "for their faith" but there was among the Communist Party considerable antagonism toward Christians. We learned from Cuba's progressive church-people that the "reeducation" camps, which the party instituted in 1965 and dismantled three years later, were a means of attempting to reeducate "undesirable"—counterrevolutionary—Cuban citizens. Along with actual political adversaries to Fidel Castro and the party, such groups as known homosexuals and vocal Christian leaders were interred in these camps. The camps were modeled (in purpose) after China's Maoist "reeducation" program but apparently resembled (in effect) the United States internment of Japanese-American citizens during World War II.

On the basis of what we saw and heard, the contemporary Cuban government is far less repressive than tales of the "reeducation" camps would lead us to fear. Fidel Castro admitted long ago that the camps were a mistake. He and other party members have become increasingly less orthodox in their Marxism. To cite Cuba simplistically as a "Marxist-Leninist" state is to miss entirely the fact that, whereas Cuba is indeed a Marxist country, Cuban Marxism is distinctly Cuban.

In terms of daily energy, the revolutionary church in Cuba is not as sorely taxed as its Nicaraguan counterpart. This is because the Cuban revolution is twenty years ahead of the Nicaraguan and, moreover, is spared the onslaught of U.S. military subterfuge against its people. For most of the last twenty-nine years, Cuba has been able to work with a startling measure of success in transforming the structures and institutions of its society that had contributed to poverty. The spiritual value of this accomplishment is not lost on Cuba's revolutionary Christian community. As a 91-year-old Episcopal parishioner said to me after church one Sunday, "No, I'm not a communist—but there used to be children lying dead of hunger in our streets, and they are no longer there. Is this not a miracle? Is it not the will of God? Can you say to me that you do not believe our nation is doing what Jesus would have us do?" In such a context, the church can relax a bit. For no longer is the people of God suffering under the yoke of starvation, disease, illiteracy, torture, and other forms of unjust death. As in Nicaragua, Cuban Christians are involved in building and staffing clinics, schools, and other public service agencies, but this justice-work does not carry the immediate urgency of a life-or-death situation for children who once lay dying in the streets.

Cuba's revolutionary Christians, then, have a four-fold mission, which parallels but does not replicate the work of the Nicaraguan church. (1) Cuban Christians are involved at all levels (except party membership) in the justice-making work that must be done as the nation continues to be shaped as a home for all. This is where the "junior partner" analogy is apt. The government has made economic justice its primary aim, and the progressive church moves along with the government toward meeting this goal. (2) The church participates in the government's resistance against imperialistic claims that would threaten the Cuban character of society. Whether the threat comes from Moscow, as the United States has contended all along, or from Washington, as the continuation of the U.S. economic sanctions against Cuba would suggest, the revolutionary church understands that no extraneous power can be allowed to set the agenda for Cuban society. (3) The justice-making church has an impressive evangelical task in relation to those Cuban Christians who are more upset that their country is run by communists than they are grateful that poverty has been eliminated. The Episcopal bishop of Cuba, Emilio Hernandez said to me, "Our problem when it comes to ordaining priests is not who has a vocation to the priesthood, but who has a vocation to remain in Cuba." Behind Emilio Hernandez' words lay a recognition that many, if not most, Cuban Christians are unhappy with the Cuban government. Revolutionary Christians lament the rise within the church of the "spirituality" that bifurcates justice from the love of God. These church members understand that their primary mission must include evangelism within and to the Christian community, teaching the work of justice as the work of God and, in so doing, affirming fundamental aims and efforts of the Cuban state. (4) The justice-making church in Cuba has an important role to play in critiquing and challenging not only the counterrevolutionary church but also the Cuban government, whether the specific issue is the ongoing exclusion of Christians from certain "high-risk security" jobs; the perpetuation of racist assumptions among Hispanics in relation to Afro-Cubans; or the Cuban government's unwillingness to treat heterosexism—hence, sexism as well—as a structure of oppression. This is an evident failure of Cuba's Communist Party, as also of Nicaragua's Sandinistas, and the government of the United States. The Cuban revolutionary church's prophetic advocacy role in challenging the effects of traditional Christian and Marxist ideology constitutes a critical dimension of its mission. Again and again, we heard Cuban Christians say that the church must combat dogmatism: any rigid, unchanging policy or teaching of either church or state.

By Cuba's revolutionary Christian people we were told that the church is to some degree responsible for the prevailing counterrevolutionary attitudes that many Cubans still harbor toward women's liberation, gay and lesbian sexuality, and Hispanic supremacy over Afro-Cubans. Several Christian theologians lamented this in our presence, noting that where the Communist Party has failed to make major inroads in the work of justice, it has been in part to pacify attitudes that have been cemented historically in Hispanic culture and secured by Christian teachings. Sexually repressive religious sensibilities, for example, have been reinforced by strains of orthodox Marxism. Many progressive Christian and communist leaders see that sexist/heterosexist attitudes are problematic in dogmatic currents of *both* Christian and Marxist traditions. For this reason, Cuba's most genuinely revolutionary Christians are at least as concerned about the state's failure to complete the revolution by assuring that all women and men will be treated with dignity and respect.

In assuring us that women's ordination would "surely pass" (as it did) in the Cuban Episcopal Church's July 1985 convention, which was being convened specifically for this vote, Bishop Emilio Hernandez smiled as he remarked, "The fact that we live in a progressive nation makes it easier for the church to do what is just." Hardly a typical "radical," the soft-spoken and rather traditional prelate echoed the sense we got from conversations with Christians and communists, professional theologians and local parishioners, seminarians and shopkeepers throughout our Cuban *encuentro*: the justice-seeking church in Cuba is planted in the fertile soil of a basically prorevolutionary society, which is not closed to challenge or change. As "partners" who are not always on the best of terms, and whose "partnership" is rather new and still marked by mutual suspicion, the revolutionary church and state in Cuba are embarking on a significant relational journey. The greatest antagonists to this cooperation continue to be those communists and Christians who do not "believe" that these two "philosophies" can be compatible. Cuba's revolutionary Christian community has learned during the last three decades that not only can this happen—it has taken place already in a common solidarity with the poor.

United States: A Theology of Resistance

In a counterrevolutionary situation, the most realistic aim of revolutionary Christians may be to keep the worst from happening. As such, the mission of the justice-seeking church in the United States is at variance with its counterparts in revolutionary societies. Ours is necessarily a *defensive* posture against the destructive powers of the injustices maintained by the state. Rather than being able to embody the fourfold mission of the churches in either Cuba or Nicaragua, the progressive Christian community in the U.S.A. must be an arena of resistance to the complex of structural dynamics that govern our civil and religious lives. Keeping the worst from happening is no small or superficial vocation. In a counterrevolutionary society—be it Germany in the 1930s or the United States in the 1980s—*organized resistance to oppression is revolutionary work*—more revolutionary in fact than the fantasy of overthrowing the configuration of racist, sexist/heterosexist, classist, and imperialistic forces that hold in place the unjust power relationships in which the shape of our nation is secured.

What this means is that the justice-making church in the United States cannot envision itself (1) as a partner or leader in government efforts to build a just society—because our government is not attempting to do this—nor (2) as an agency of resistance primarily to imperialistic assaults by other nations against our own—although this is exactly what conservative churches suggest, in their doctrine of anticommunism, is their primary aim. Moreover, (3) because the state is not on the side of the poor and marginalized in the United States, our evangelical work with the Christian church is beset sorely by a reactionary civil religion. Thus, we cannot simply evangelize—preach a commitment to justice within the Christian community—because such Christian education is continually undermined by the state's admonitions against such "demons" as "communism," "unfair burdens on tax payers," lack of patriotism, "antifamily movements," and the like. Contrary to what Christian liberals have tended to believe, in a counterrevolutionary society neither Christian education nor a cumulative mass of well-educated Christian individuals moves mountains. The forces of social oppression are too deeply entrenched in our religious and civil traditions and their effects too devastating to support individualistic, "spiritual," and "inner-directed" approaches to our prophetic mission. (4) The revolutionary church cannot simply criticize or challenge the unjust practices of either church or state. In the revolutionary societies of Nicaragua and Cuba, such dialogue can have substance, because leaders of both state and church appreciate the justice-oriented goals of both state and church. In the United States by contrast, progressive Christians cannot expect to be able merely to dialogue with either civil or religious authorities about such injustices as the deportation of Central American refugees, the economically exploitive character of capitalism, the setbacks in civil rights for black and other racial/ethnic minorities as well as for women, and the denial of civil and ecclesial affirmation of gay/lesbian persons.

Talk is cheap only for the rich and those who are perched at the top of the dialogical pyramid. For the poor, racial/ethnic minorities, women, and gay/lesbian persons, talk becomes quickly an expensive drain on important creative energies. Study commisions, task forces constituted to examine injustices, committee reports, and even "democratic" processes of voting and "majority rule" can easily become synonymous with denial, procrastination, and finally broken promises to those postured historically on the bottom of power relationships. Revolutionary U.S. Christians should not spend themselves in attempting to persuade the leaders of our churches and government through those authorized channels of study, dialogue, critique, and challenge in which we have no power to effect concrete changes in social or ecclesial policy on our own terms and timetables. Rather, we must be actively involved together in doing everything we can to impede the smooth operations of injustice—whether we encounter them in the church, beyond the church in the larger society, or most often in both church and state.

How, then, might U.S. Christians envision our work of resistance? I suggest here *nine* basic elements of such a mission, which are interdependent and should not be read in order of priority. Together, these might provide a clue as to what a theology of liberation might look like in our counterrevolutionary situation.

1. *Vision.* We must be clear among ourselves that we envision a world (which Jesus referred to as "the kingdom of God") in which all persons and other living creatures can enjoy our life together, and that the world we envision is not simply "heaven" but rather is a way of being in relation to one another here on this earth. In God's realm there is no line of demarcation between "church" and "world," "religion" and "politics," "theological" work and whatever work benefits the people and other creatures of the earth. For this reason, we cannot accept the arbitrary distinction between what the church should be about and what the rest of the world (including our national government) should be doing. Nor can we accept any structure of justice or injustice as disconnected from others. Our vision is broadly ecumenical, unabashedly political, profoundly spiritual, and essentially moral. It is also indisputably biblical, both Hebrew and Greek in character, in that we are persuaded by faith that one God of history is the God of all creation and that, in both exodus and passion narratives, this God whose name is love is known to us as an Advocate, a Liberator from the oppressive forces in history that imprison our bodies, our souls, and our capacities to imagine ourselves as loved and loving persons.

2. *Analysis.* Our "God-talk" wears thin unless we are able to say specifically to what or to whom we are referring when we make such faith-claims that "God lives at the margins of society"; "God loves the poor"; "Blessed are those who thirst after righteousness"; or "We believe that this is what God requires." In order to be able to substantiate our faith, we must be able to think well and clearly—not necessarily academically, but intelligently—about the society and world in which we live and how we understand the work and will of God to be related to our own. This clarity of reason requires an analysis of how the pieces fit together in this world; of what the basic themes in human life seem to be; and of how we envision our work as God's people in a situation in which we walk with others a narrow path between hope and despair. We must begin to make the connections between battered women, cuts in food stamps, the MX missile, the Krugerrand, capital punishment, swastikas on synagogues, hungry kids in Harlem and Appalachia, refugees in New Mexico, the so-called Right to Life movement, Harvey Milk's murder and Dan White's suicide, "Rambo" and Ronald Reagan's popularity, "Star Wars," and what our seminaries are teaching, and what our priests and pastors are preaching.

For such an analysis we need more than traditional religious creeds, systematic theology, psychotherapy, spiritual direction, or prayers—as helpful, even vital, as these resources may be. We must teach one another the lessons we have not learned in our schools or churches. We must find and share the resources we need to learn to feel more deeply, to think more clearly, to be more fully *common* people. We Christians must help one another become more honest and intelligent as a body of faithful women, men, and children. Our spiritual mandate is not to become more intellectual but rather to step into the mainstream of human life and struggle with open minds and probing hearts.

3. *Expectations.* As an idealistic people, fundamentally Greek in philosophical heritage, Christians have expected traditionally either too much or too little from ourselves. Trapped in a dualistic conception of the cosmos, we have known neither (1) how to raise up our sense of ourselves as human without putting down God, nor (2) how to experience ourselves as not isolated spiritual monads but rather as one body, one family, with one responsibility that we share. We have not understood experientially or theologically (and the Christian religious tradition has been at fault here) that together we are an empowered body. Augustine observed that we are a *massa damnata* — a damned species. No astute observer/participant in the late twentieth century could disagree with him about this. But whereas Augustine saw the extent to which we human beings have only ourselves to blame for this mess, he failed to perceive the possibility that we share a responsibility for undoing the damage we have done — and that we can do it. Together we are not a morally or politically impotent body.

Thanks to the Augustinian legacy of self-deprecation, we Christians have historically tended to expect too little rather than too much of ourselves. Modern Christian liberalism seemed for a while to reverse this direction, however, and a large corpus of theological materials composed in the nineteenth and twentieth centuries would lead us to believe that what the world needs is a growing number of reasonable, caring, intelligent, white men to set everything straight. A theology of resistance in the late twentieth century cannot afford to buy into such fundamentally flawed theological assumptions. On the basis of our vision of ourselves as one body, we must come more and more into our power to act with God as co-creators of a just world, and at the same time we must learn to think small. We cannot play hero to the world. We cannot do everything that needs to be done, and we cannot do everything at once. Wherever we can actually effect justice, we must — and we must not wallow in either guilt or anxiety about all the many, infinitely varied, demands or occasions that we cannot meet.

4. *Leadership.* When do we follow and when do we lead? How do we know whom to follow and how do we know when we ourselves must lead? These questions, which often confounded us, have a quite simple answer: in a given situation, we follow those who have the least social power, those who are on the bottom. In situations in which we ourselves are among those at the bottom, we lead. And we must be clear about what we mean by "leadership." Our vision is not basically about heroes, experts, supermen, or superwomen; nor about presidents, chairpersons, bishops, priests, or others who "hold authority." We are talking about *power* as a quality of personal commitment — about being empowered/empowering others to make a creative difference in the world/church. Seldom, if we look to the bottom, will such empowered/empowering leaders hold elected or appointed offices. Insofar as we ourselves are such leaders, seldom will we hold authority in civil or ecclesial institutions. Our leadership must come not only from the bottom of the historical social arrangement — for example, between whites and blacks, or between men and women. It must come moreover from the margins of the bottom itself. We are not likely to find creative leadership from those racial/ethnic minority persons — or white women — who have evidently "made it" in the dominant institutions of our society. To the extent that any of us has made it, we need always to look beyond our-

selves—our authority, credentials, and respectability—for leadership, bearing in mind that our best work for justice will always happen in spite of our having accrued some measure of institutional authority.

5. *Strategy.* "Strategy" is the concrete basis upon which we are moving toward the accomplishment of our goal. It undergirds our whole mission, not just separate pieces of our efforts. We need to realize that the most formidable strategy of effective resistance to injustice is in acting our way into public debate and dialogue, rather than attempting to persuade those who govern the church and state to change their ways so that we can act morally. Civil or ecclesial disobedience is a primary strategic form of resistance. Nowhere could this be clearer in our contemporary nation than in the work of the sanctuary movement. In the world in which we live, the important moral configuration of disobedience to unjust law and acceptance of the consequences will never be outdated. It is virtually a key to revolutionary Christianity in the United States.

6. *Community.* "Community" is an overworked word among Christians in the United States. It is less so in Cuba and especially in Nicaragua because it carries powerful historical meaning in the recent histories of these nations in which revolutionary Christianity has been, in fact, a communal phenomenon. Our vision in the U.S.A. may be of ourselves together in community, but our actual experiences tend to reinforce the ideology of ourselves as individuals who choose to come together in parishes, schools, work places, families, and other organizations. We are often least aware of being in community in the very institutions in which members talk the most about it—the Christian church.

Much has been presented in the United States about the *comunidades de base cristiano* in Latin America. Those of us who have participated in these communities have seen what the church can be—an inclusive, nonauthoritarian, body of interdependent members whose lives literally are bound up one in another and who share a common commitment to justice. If these communities were dependent upon a bishop, a priest, a "father," a "mother," or one particular lay leader to tell them what to do—or that they should do it—they would not be communities in anything but name. The power of community is sparked among the persons who come together and is embodied in mutual engagement. The vitality of community is rooted in the shared realization that, like the early church, they hold all things in common. No one's individual needs or demands is given precedence over any other's; paradoxically, each individual person is taken seriously.

Our white middle-class distinction in the United States between "task" and "process" would be unintelligible in the *comunidades de base,* because they do not accept a distinction between what is being done and how it is happening. Task and process are the same. To attend to one is to meet the other. And so it is that revolutionary Christianity is a deeply listening, pastoral, passionate, angry, and active community. This is what we in the United States can look forward to and help create wherever we are working. The possibility of such community is neither utopic nor illusory. It can happen anywhere, and it can happen now. But it will not happen unless we create it, and we cannot create it as long as we are looking to either the institutional church or the government for permission, answers, or affirmation.

7. *Education.* First, we need to realize that we have as much to learn as to teach about justice. Secondly, we must look to those at the bottom to teach us. Thirdly, we must begin to see that genuinely Christian education is a communal undertaking

in which truth is born out of, and in the midst of, human experience. It does not come from one person or from one group of persons. It does not come simply from the Bible, the Christian tradition, or our capacity for reason. It comes in the context of engagement and struggle with these resources only inasmuch as we are aware that there will always be other voices, from the margins of the bottom, to stretch our securities and sensibilities. Just when we think we have it, truth gets blown apart by those who are bumping up against us. A basic rubric of Christian education should instruct us to be as mindful of what we don't know as of what we do. Christian dogmatics and apologetics have been all but useless in teaching us this critical truth.

8. *Worship.* It has become increasingly difficult for many revolutionary U.S. Christians to go to church. When justice-seekers are met by ministers who interpret their vocation as that of bringing others to a god whom they themselves have been privileged to find, justice-seekers are in serious trouble. The trouble may be even more serious if our suspicion is confirmed that the minister finds God primarily in a prayer book—its history, theology, rubrics, order, esthetics. It is hard to imagine a more counterrevolutionary symbol than a prayer book that has become an icon of divine order.

Liturgy is the work of the people—contemporary people as well as our ancestors. If the work of the people is rooted in a commitment to justice, the people's liturgy should reflect above all this commitment. Worshiping for justice requires an appreciation of our common past and heritage. But worshiping for justice requires also fresh imagination and the courage to envision that which our ancestors did not; time and space to struggle with one another about vision and expectations; leadership from the bottom and from the margins; action-based liturgical praxis; genuine community-building; for an honest, open-ended desire to discover and share whatever may be true for our lives today in the world of God.

9. *Feminism.* Among the twelve Christians who went to Cuba, nine were feminist women theologians; three were male theologians who are friendly to feminism and joined in presenting a feminist perspective at the conference. Perhaps the most valuable offering we twelve were able to take to our Cuban *compañeros/as* was our feminist commitment—an advocacy of gender and sexual justice as connected systematically to all forms of oppression. Speaking on behalf of Cuban women, especially Christian women, Dora Valentín and a handful of other Cuban feminists told us that our presence *as feminists* was a special gift to the women of Cuba. Cuban feminists paid tribute to their nation's efforts to secure women's liberation against formidable resistance from traditional church teachings as well as traditional attitudes among both Hispanics and Afro-Cubans. Most of the revolutionary Cuban Christian men with whom we met were less clear than the women that sexism is still a problem for the state—or that it ever has been for the church. Our group from the United States observed that the trivialization of women and fear of homosexuals among Cuba's revolutionary Christians made us feel very much at home!

At the end of the week's meeting, however, the Cuban Christians stated emphatically that our "nonbourgeois" understanding of feminism as a thoroughgoing commitment to justice for all persons—and especially women in a sexist society—had been enormously important for them. They proposed ongoing collaboration on *feminism* between Christian feminists from the United States and Cuba's revolutionary Christian community.

U.S. feminists have received a similar message, though in more muted form, from Nicaraguan feminists, given their necessary preoccupation with survival in the context of daily bombing, torture, and death. As in both the United States and Cuba, we saw in Nicaragua the effects of patriarchy as an ideology so deeply entrenched that it can be routed out only over generations and then only in a situation of relative social stability. Only in a society in which men and women do not have to stand guard twenty-four hours a day, lest they lose their lives or their children to such violent forces as the Contras, can the historical effects of sexual and gender injustice be recognized as problematic for the whole society, rather than merely for individuals who cannot "adjust" to hatred of males or females. This does not mean that sexism/heterosexism is less important than other structures of oppression, but rather that it is so tightly fastened in the texture of patriarchy that it may well be the last-noticed impediment to a fully just society, indeed the stuff of the "final revolution."

Not only does feminism provide a socio-political analysis of the linkage among all forms of injustice, it determines also a critical praxis in which to do the daily work of resistance in a counterrevolutionary state like the United States whose leaders have targeted feminism as the enemy of the people. We pointed out to our friends in Cuba and Nicaragua that, in the United States, "feminism" has become a code word among counterrevolutionaries for "communism," "atheism," and "evil" — in short, a synonym for persons who are sympathetic to places like Nicaragua and Cuba; and that far from being a bourgeois obsession, the advocacy of women and of gay men and lesbians across race and class lines in the United States has become a vital dimension of the revolutionary work that must be done in and beyond the church in this country at this time.

Our Cuban and Nicaraguan pilgrimages confirmed our commitment to feminism as essential to the mission of revolutionary Christianity in the United States, and moreover seemed to strengthen the resolve of members of Cuban and Nicaraguan Christians to embody a feminist commitment in their own work.

However revolutionary Christians choose to participate or not in the traditional theological and liturgical contexts of our denominations, we are discovering together ways of worshiping a God of justice who may be represented by *Christa* — the female Christ — whom many of us image as black and as more than one solitary female. Several years ago the sculpture *Christa* by Edwina Sandys was put on display in New York's Cathedral of Saint John the Divine. She caused considerable panic, as well she might, because she is a powerful symbol of revolutionary Christianity in this counterrevolutionary situation.

43

Mujeristas: A Name of Our Own

ADA MARÍA ISASI-DÍAZ

To be able to name oneself is one of the most powerful acts any human person can do. A name is not just a word by which one is identified. A name also provides the conceptual framework, the mental constructs that are used in thinking, understanding, and relating to a person. For almost fifteen years now, Hispanic women in the U.S.A., who struggle against ethnic prejudice, sexism, and in many cases, classism, have been at a loss as to what to call ourselves. The majority of Hispanic women have simply called themselves *cubanas*, *chicanas*, or *puertorriqueñas*, and most probably will continue to do so. Some of us have called ourselves *feministas hispanas*. Though *feminista hispana* has been an appellation riddled with difficulties, we have felt the need for a name that would indicate primarily the struggle against sexism that is part of our daily bread while also helping us identify one another in the trenches as we fight for our survival within Hispanic communities and U.S. society at large. But using *feminista hispana* has meant giving long explanations of what such a phrase does not mean.[1]

Feministas hispanas have been consistently marginalized in the Anglo feminist community because of our critique of its ethnic/racial prejudice and lack of class analysis. At the same time, when we have insisted on calling ourselves *feministas*, we have been rejected by many in the Hispanic community because they consider feminism a preoccupation of Anglo women. Yet Hispanic women widely agree with an analysis of sexism as an evil within our communities, an evil that plays into the hands of the dominant forces of society and helps to repress and exploit us in such a way that we constitute the largest number of those at the lowest economic stratum. Likewise, Hispanic women widely agree that, though we make up the vast majority of those who participate actively in the churches, we do the work but do not participate in deciding what work is to be done; we do the praying but our understanding of the God to whom we pray is ignored.

As Hispanic women we, therefore, continue to search for a name that will call us together, that will help us to understand our oppression, that will identify the specificity of our struggle without separating us from our own communities. And in our search we turn to our music—an intrinsic part of the soul of our culture. In love songs as well as in protest songs we are simply called *mujer*—woman. "Yo soy mujer en busca de igualdad, no aguantaré abuso ni maldad. Yo soy mujer y tengo dignidad, y pronto la justicia será una realidad,"[2] proclaims a song composed by women in the South Bronx. "Mujer, tú eres mujer, porque supiste ver, la realidad de tu poder,"[3] sings Rosie Sanchez. "Hoy canto al Dios del Pueblo en mi guitarra, un canto de mujer que se libera,"[4] sings Rosa Marta Zárate. She continues, "God listened to the cry of our people, made an alliance with the poor and the exploited, and frees woman from the chains imposed on her with cruelty for centuries." And the song ends by repeating time and again, "la mujer, la mujer, la mujer."

Yes, we are *mujeres*, and those of us who make a preferential option for *mujeres* are *mujeristas*.[5] As Rosa Marta's song says so clearly, a *mujerista* is one who struggles to liberate herself, who is consecrated by God as proclaimer of the hope of her people. *Mujerista* is one who knows how to be faithful to the task of making justice and peace flourish, who opts for God's cause and the law of love. In the *mujerista* God revindicates the divine image and likeness of women. The *mujerista* is called to gestate new women and men: a strong people. *Mujeristas* are anointed by God as servants, prophets, and witnesses of redemption. *Mujeristas* will echo God's reconciling love; their song will be a two-edged sword, and they will proclaim the gospel of liberation.[6]

At the same time that we name ourselves *mujeristas*, we want to rename our theological enterprise. What we called up to now Hispanic women's liberation theology will henceforth be called *mujerista* theology. *Mujerista* theology, a concept which is beginning to be articulated, is part of the daily voice of *mujeristas*, for Christianity is an intrinsic element of Hispanic culture. *Mujerista* theology articulates religious understandings of Hispanic women. It always uses a liberative lens, which requires placing oneself radically at the core of our own struggling pueblo. *Mujerista* theology brings together elements of feminist theology, Latin American liberation theology, and cultural theology, three perspectives that intertwine to form a whole. These three perspectives critique and challenge each other, they inform each other, giving birth to new elements, to a new reality.

Like other liberation theologies, *mujerista* theology is indebted to the generative theological work of Gustavo Gutiérrez. This essay, which is a further development of the articulation of *mujerista* theology that I have already published,[7] deals with two *mujerista* understandings that engage specific themes of Gutiérrez's theological writings. I here further develop the *mujerista* position that the real theologian is the community and not exclusively those of us with academic training. I will demonstrate that this is firmly rooted in the epistemological privilege of those who are oppressed and in the fact that all liberation theologies are about "doing theology," which cannot be done but as a member of a community. Secondly, after suggesting a nonoppressive way of using the Bible, I will propose the story of Shiphrah and Puah at the beginning of the Book of Exodus as a biblical interpretive key to the *mujerista* struggle. A third theme this article deals with has not been explicitly addressed by Gutiérrez but is a must for *mujerista* theology because of the twofold and at times threefold oppression Hispanic women suffer. It is the issue of power.

HACER TEOLOGÍA — A COMMUNAL TASK

Mujeristas are increasingly aware of how false and evil is any attempt to separate action from reflection. The physical participation of Hispanic women in programs and action is often sought, but they are seldom asked to be involved in deciding or designing content. Hispanic women are seldom invited to reflect on the reasons and motivations for their actions. But *mujeristas* will always insist on the need to be actively involved in the reflective moment of praxis. Without reflection there is no critical awareness, no conscientization and, therefore, no possibility of self-definition and liberation.

One of the most pervasive themes of *mujerista* theology is the preferential option for the poor and oppressed. This preferential option is based on the epistemological privilege of the poor because they can see and understand what the rich and privileged cannot. It is not that the poor and oppressed are morally superior or that they can see better. No, their epistemological privilege is based on the fact that, because their point of view is not distorted by power and riches, they can see differently:

> The point of view of the poor . . . pierced by suffering and attracted by hope, allows them, in their struggles, to conceive another reality. Because the poor suffer the weight of alienation, they can conceive a different project of hope and provide dynamism to a new way of organizing human life *for all*.[8]

The epistemological privilege of the poor should be operative in a very special way in the theological enterprise. It is the understandings of the divine, the way of grappling with questions of ultimate meaning in the daily lives of grassroots Hispanic women which constitute *mujerista* theology. Theological reflection cannot be separated from theological action in the doing of theology. Therefore *mujerista* theology is a praxis which consists of two interlinked moments: action and reflection. *Mujerista* theology is a doing theology, which does not place reflection and articulation above action. Neither does *mujerista* theology see the theological enterprise as a second moment following the praxis, for all action, at the moment that it is taking place, has a reflective quality. Because *mujerista* theology is a praxis, it is, therefore, the community as a whole that engages in the theological enterprise.

Among liberation theologians who are academically trained, there seems to be concern about their role and title. If the community as a whole is the one that does theology, what is the task of those of us who call ourselves theologians? I believe there is no way of averting this identity crisis once the epistemological privilege of the poor is recognized and theology is understood as a praxis, a doing theology. The only way for academically trained theologians to resolve their dilemma is to participate fully in a community of struggle and to do theology as members of that community. The gifts of the academically trained theologian who is part of a community of struggle will not be wasted. The theological community needs some of its members to be enablers and facilitators during the reflective moment of praxis — which does not happen only when one is sitting down! Those who are trained academically can well put their gifts at the service of the community at this time. They can indeed be very instrumental in enabling the community to understand that its daily struggle for existence is not separate from its religious understandings, sentiments, beliefs. They can take responsibility for gathering what the community is saying and writing it down so the community can benefit from it in the future, so that it may be shared with other communities of struggle, and so that one day those voices may be an intrinsic element of the societal norm.

Elsewhere, following the lead of Carlos Abesamis, I have proposed calling the enablers/writers of the theological reflection of the community "theological technicians."[9] Several of my colleagues have objected to such a title. Maybe we are not ready to name ourselves. But what *mujerista* theology insists on saying is that the community of struggle is the one that does theology, and not individuals who are not intrinsic members of the community. Those of us who are academically trained and are intrinsic members of a community of struggle must do theology with our community and not as separate individuals. The theological articulations we write, therefore, should always be birthed by the community, discussed in the community, understandable to the community. Because the theological articulations we write are but a moment in the praxis of the community, such an articulation must always be open, in flux. It must always welcome revision and be evolving.[10]

SÉFORA Y FUÁ – AN INTERPRETIVE KEY

For *mujeristas* the primary role of the Bible is to influence the "horizon or ultimate way in which the Christian looks at reality."[11] This biblical influence mainly yields an ethical model of relationality and responsibility that is/can be/should be operative in the struggle for liberation. The way liberation theologies have used the Bible up to now, however, will not effectively contribute to building a model of relationality and responsibility. Most liberation theologies' use of the Bible is limited to a "simple learning."[12] What liberation theologies have promoted are "certain exemplary themes such as exodus, prophetic criticism of society . . . Jesus' confrontation with authorities,"[13] Jesus as a member of a marginated group—the Galileans,[14] and so forth. Or liberation theologies have also reworded biblical stories using popular terminology in order to make them relevant to different situations of struggle in the world today.[15]

Instead, the Bible should be used to promote a critical consciousness, to trigger suspicion, which is the starting point of the process of conscientization. The Bible should be used to learn how to learn—"to involve the people in an unending process of acquiring new . . . information that multiplies the previous store of information."[16] This new information becomes a source that can be consulted "in order to solve new problems the people have not faced before."[17] The Bible must not be directly applied to a problem—it does not offer a solution to any given problem. Instead the Bible must become a resource for learning what questions to ask in order to deal appropriately with the problem at hand.

This way of using the Bible liberates the Bible—frees it from becoming a mere guidebook about the correct thing to do. The Bible cannot be the only tool, nor is it always the main tool, which *mujeristas* use to reflect on who we are, what are our "attitudes, dispositions, goals, values, norms, and decisions."[18] The Bible should always be seen as only *one* of the traditions through which the community can remember its past, its roots, the source of its values, customs, and practices. Any and all sources that help "to nurture and reform the community's self-identity as well as the personal character of its members,"[19] must be seriously engaged by *mujeristas*. Furthermore, the Bible as well as any other text to which the community of Hispanic women gives authority should be used only as an integral part of a process that helps Hispanic women to be self-determining. This way of using the Bible makes it clear that each person has to decide how she is to participate in the struggle for liberation.

Specific biblical stories can and should serve as interpretive keys in the struggle for liberation of Hispanic women. In looking at specific biblical passages as interpretive keys, I intend for us to use them to help us understand the questions we need to ask, questions that shed light on the oppressive situations we *mujeristas* face today. An interpretive key does not demand compliance to a given archetype or prototype, but rather helps us to be critical about the situation at hand. An interpretive key helps us ask questions instead of insisting that it can provide answers. When we use the Bible in this way we claim that the starting point is always the situation at hand and not the Bible. As an interpretive key, no biblical passage can be *the* deciding factor in our lives. Seeing certain passages of the Bible as an interpretive key allows *mujeristas* to be self-determining—to be the ones that decide what to do and how to do it.[20]

Shiphrah and Puah stand at the beginning of the most formidable and formative event for the Hebrew people, the exodus event. And yet, little attention has been paid to them. The action of these two women is indeed an interpretive key for *mujeristas* today and it needs to be explored at length. Their story in Exodus 1:15–22 helps raise questions about what should be our role as *mujeristas* in the struggle for our own liberation and the liberation of our *pueblo*.

Exodus 1:15–22[21] starts with an order from the pharaoh: Shiphrah and Puah[22] are to kill sons born to Hebrew women. Though a man, the pharaoh, stands at the beginning of the narrative, it is not his action but rather the actions of these women that are of primary concern.[23] The pharaoh attempts to deal with the growing number of Hebrews.[24] However, had he been able to foresee the persistence of the women in thwarting his decree, he might have been more successful in his attempt to check the Hebrew population growth by ordering all female infants to be killed![25]

Were these two midwives Egyptian or Hebrew? The Massoretic text reads, "Hebrew midwives."[26] But a minor variation in the grammatical forms yields "midwives of the Hebrews," which is the way the Septuagint and the Vulgate read.[27] The ambiguity of the text introduced by the variation can be seen as a way of moving "beyond nationalistic concerns to bear witness to the power of faith to transcend ethnic boundaries."[28] Uncertainty, then, about the midwives' nationality allows us to suggest that the main moving force and motivating principle of their action was the fear of God.

Fear in this text is not fear of punishment. The fear of God that Shiphrah and Puah felt was generated by a sense of *mysterium tremendum*, "a mystery in divine holiness which produces . . . a sense of terror."[29] This sense of terror is not merely negative but is also an expression of faith, trust, love, and communion, based on God's unmerited, gratuitous, and unearned love. The defiant act of Shiphrah and Puah makes life for the Hebrews possible, and their risky, clever answer to the pharaoh, which puts them in immediate danger, is born out of their own relationship with God. Their fear of God "becomes the principle of human behavior and the beginning of wisdom,"[30] making them mothers, life-givers of the Hebrew people.

A literary analysis of this pericope further strengthens the image of the midwives as life-givers. The pericope portrays the pharaoh as the source of death. In contrast, the midwives are portrayed as the source of life. Between the role of the pharaoh and that of Shiphrah and Puah "stands the fear of God as a motivating factor (v. 17) and as an attitude of faith which reaps its reward (v. 21a)."[31] This reward, though there is no clear way of reading verses 20–21, is a reward that corresponds to Shiphrah's and Puah's deed.[32] They are blessed with a progeny. Furthermore, Shiphrah and Puah, as v. 20 seems to indicate, "are credited with building up the house of Israel."[33]

The story of Shiphrah and Puah foreshadows the exodus event. Their defiant attitude toward the pharaoh foreshadows the attitude of Moses and Aaron. Like the pharaoh with whom Moses and Aaron will have to deal, this pharaoh becomes increasingly stubborn. The midwives' brave stance forces the pharaoh to escalate his strategy. His attempt to finish with the Hebrews will "force God's hand." Remembering the covenant made with the Israelites, God will intervene in their behalf. The exodus movement has started. Secondly, Shiphrah and Puah save the Israelites. Their actions make the exodus possible. No liberation is possible without life; these women are indeed givers of life. No liberation is possible without courage to act and willingness to risk; these women are indeed risk-takers, agents of their own history and of the history of their people.

As an interpretive key which can be used by *mujeristas*, the story of Shiphrah and Puah raises many questions that we apply to our situation today. Often caught against our will between the oppressor and the oppressed, how can we, Hispanic women, be self-determining? How can we be about liberation, no matter what our role in life is? When we do not have power or strategic advantage, do we give in or do we find a way to resist? Can we sacrifice one for the sake of many? Can a few be liberated at the expense of others? What is the critical lens that *mujeristas* must use all the time: Hispanicness or liberation? How does the God of *mujeristas* differ from the God of the pharaohs of our days, or the God who the pharaohs of our world believe themselves to be? How do we as oppressed persons remain faithful to our God?

Each *mujerista* must allow Shiphrah and Puah to ask her many different questions. These questions will produce not jarring pieces but rather elements that will come together to form a tapestry of the whole. Such a weaving will depict a vision of justice that is not possible without liberation, and this is precisely the task of *mujeristas* today: to be about the task of liberation.

PODER MUJERISTA — REINVENTING POWER

One of the most important and at the same time most difficult understandings to keep in the forefront of *mujerista* theology is the difference between equality and liberation. Equality has to do with participation by the oppressed in the structures that exist today. Liberation, on the other hand, is about radical change of the oppressive societal structures. To think that equality for all is possible within the present structures of society is a mistake. The structures of society today, all of them linked and controlled or at least heavily influenced by patriarchy, necessitate someone at the bottom, someone to be oppressed, someone from whom others can benefit. Those in control, those who benefit from present societal structures, wish to maintain those structures at all cost. Therefore, though they may not like it, they are willing to allow the marginated of society to gain equality—to participate in the structures that the powerful control—but they will oppose liberation with all their might.

Liberation demands that we bring about a new order of relationship among

415

persons, whether that relationship is a personal or a business relationship. The powerful of today cannot hold on to their power with one hand and extend an invitation to the poor and oppressed with the other. Liberation, therefore, is most threatening to the powers that are because by insisting on redefining power, liberation does away with their privileged position. But those who insist on liberation must understand that a redefinition of power also challenges the way the poor and the oppressed themselves structure and participate in the struggle of liberation. The way we carry out our struggle will be an integral part of the outcome. Therefore, we must move away from authoritarian, hierarchical structures of power in our communities of struggle. We must work to operate out of a circular model of leadership and use a consensual process when the community has to make decisions.

For us *mujeristas* power is the ability to enable all persons to become the most they themselves can be. It must be clearly understood that in the Hispanic culture persons can become fully themselves only in relation to the community and not as isolated individuals who look out only for themselves. Our understanding of power demands that we work incessantly to create the political, economic, and social conditions needed for the self-realization of all persons. It also requires establishing relational structures and operational modes in all spheres of life which facilitate and promote the self-realization of all persons. Finally, our understanding of power requires promotion of the creativity of all persons so they can contribute efficaciously to the common good.[34]

Mujerista theology struggles to bring up the question of power in every single moment of the doing of theology. Furthermore, *mujerista* theology challenges all liberation theologies to place the question of power at the heart of their theological enterprise. The focus might be different but the questions about power must always be asked. For example, what do we mean when we say that God is all-powerful? Is our God an enabling God or a controlling God made to the image and likeness of the males who control the society in which we live? If power as understood today in our society is good, then it should be shared by all. Then why has Mary been portrayed exclusively as a submissive woman and why is this submissive Mary proposed as the main example for Roman Catholic women? What would reinventing power mean for the "power of orders" so very central to the present understanding of priesthood in the Roman Catholic Church? What would priestly ministry entail if power is understood as enablement and fostering creativity instead of control and domination? What happens to our ethics and morality if we raise the question of power when making decisions? In conclusion, how do our theological discourse and the structures of our churches bless and sanctify the understanding of power as control and domination?

The struggle for liberation of Hispanic women is being carried out in many different ways by many different *mujeristas* all around the U.S.A. *Mujerista* theology is one of the voices of such a struggle—a struggle which is life for us because we have learned from our grandmothers and mothers that *la vida es la lucha*.

NOTES

1. Ada María Isasi-Díaz, "Toward an Understanding of *Feminismo Hispano* in the U.S.A.," in *Women's Consciousness, Women's Conscience*, Barbara H. Andolsen,

Christine E. Gudorf, and Mary D. Pellauer, eds. (New York: Winston, 1985), pp. 51–61.

2. "I am a woman searching for equality; I will not put up with abuse and wickedness. I am a woman and I have dignity, and justice will soon be a reality." Words by Maria del Valle and Mildred Bonilla.

3. "Women, you are women, because you have known how to recognize the fact that you are powerful."

4. "Today I sing to the God of my people with my guitar; I sing a song of a woman who liberates herself."

5. I am much indebted to the work of black feminists who have preceded us in this struggle to name ourselves. Their use of the term "womanist" has influenced me immensely. I am particularly grateful to Katie Cannon, Joan Martin, and Delores Williams with whom I have had the privilege of sharing much. See especially Delores S. Williams, "Womanist Theology: Black Women's Voices," in *Christianity and Crisis* (March 2, 1987) 66–70.

6.   Cántico de Mujer
                  Rosa Martha Zárate Macías

1. Hoy canto al Dios del Pueblo en mi guitarra	Lucas 1:46–55
un canto de mujer que se libera,	
Dios se solidariza con mi causa,	
me consagra portavoz de la esperanza.	
Dios escuchó el clamor de nuestro pueblo	Judit 8:21–28
se alió al empobrecido y explotado	
y a la mujer libera de cadenas	
impuestas con crueldad por tantos siglos.	
¡DICHOSA MUJER LA QUE SABE SER FIEL	Judit 13:20
AL QUEHACER DE IMPLANTAR	14:9–10
LA JUSTICIA Y LA PAZ!	
¡BENDITA SERA LA MUJER QUE HACE	
OPCION	Lucas 8:1–3
POR LA CAUSA DE DIOS,	Nican Mopohua
POR LA LEY DEL AMOR!	
2. Harás justicia a todas las mujeres	
que firmes no cayeron ante el yugo	
nos das la libertad y reivindicas	Génesis 1:27
¡Oh, Dios, tu semejanza originaria!	
Al mal pastor que causa tanto daño	
al gobernante infiel que vende al pueblo,	
a todo quien oprime tú destruyes	
sin piedad del poder tú los derrumbas.	
3. Nos llamas a gestar en nuestro vientre	
mujeres y hombres nuevos, pueblo fuerte	
Nos unges servidoras, profetisas,	Mateo 27:55–56
testigos de tu amor que nos redime	
Has puesto en mi cantar una esperanza	Marcos 16:1–8
Seré eco de tu amor que reconcilia	
Espada de dos filos sea mi canto	Judit 9:10–14

pregón de un Evangelio libertario.
(used with permission)

7. Ada María Isasi-Díaz and Yolando Tarango, *Hispanic Women: Prophetic Voice in the Church* (San Francisco: Harper and Row, 1988).

8. José Míguez Bonino, "Nuevas Tendencias en Teología," *Pasos* (1985) 22.

9. Isasi-Díaz and Tarango, *Hispanic Women*, pp. 105–6.

10. I want to thank María Antonietta Berriozabal and Yolanda Tarango with whom I discussed at length using *mujerista* as our "name." I also want to thank many Hispanic sisters who never allowed me to rest comfortably under the name "feminist."

11. Charles Curran, *Catholic Moral Theology in Dialogue* (Notre Dame, Ind.: Fides, 1972), p. 53.

12. Juan Luis Segundo, *The Liberation of Theology* (Maryknoll; N.Y.: Orbis Books, 1982), p. 118.

13. Norman K. Gottwald, "Socio-Historical Precision in the Biblical Grounding of Liberation Theologies" (unpublished address to the Catholic Biblical Association of America, San Francisco, August 1985), p. 11.

14. Virgilio Elizando, *Galilean Journey* (Maryknoll, N.Y.: Orbis Books, 1983).

15. The best known examples of this are the four volumes of *The Gospel of Solentiname* (Maryknoll, N.Y.: Orbis Books).

16. Segundo, *Liberation*, p. 121.

17. Ibid., p. 119.

18. Curran, *Moral Theology*, p. 64.

19. Stanley Hauerwas, "The Moral Authority of Scripture: The Politics and Ethics of Remembering," in *The Use of Scripture in Moral Theology*, Charles E. Curran and Richard A. McCormick, eds. (New York: Paulist Press, 1984), p. 245.

20. Dianne Bergant, "Exodus as a Paradigm in Feminist Theology," in *Exodus — A Lasting Paradigm*, Bas van Iersel and Anton Weiler, eds. (*Concilium*; Edinburgh: Clark, 1987), pp. 100–106.

21. Much of the material in Exodus comes from the J source. P provides a framework for the J material, while E has been used to supplement J. The core of the material of the pericopes here examined comes from the supplementary source, E. Supplemental material has to have some significance, whether literary, historical, or theological, for it to be considered worth adding. That the compilers/editors of the present text added this pericope would indicate that in some way it is intrinsic to the history, the theme, the theological understanding of the exodus.

22. "The two midwives have apparently Semitic names. Puah may mean 'splendid one' or perhaps 'girl'.... Shiphrah appears ... on a list of Egyptian slaves and means 'fair one'" (Brevard S. Childs, *The Book of Exodus* [Philadelphia: Westminster, 1974], pp. 8–12).

23. J. Cheryl Exum, " 'You Shall Let Every Daughter Live': A Study of Exodus 1:8–2:10," *Semeia*, 28 (1983) 3–82.

24. "The attribute *Hebrew* applied here to the midwives represents the first use in Exodus of this term, which is due to recur a number of times in the continuation of the Book.... The word in question signifies in general people who were aliens in their environment, and were mostly employed as servants or slaves. In Egyptian texts, the aforementioned Egyptian term refers to enslaved people, who were compelled to do forced labour in the service of the pharoah. In the Bible the children

of Israel, or their ancestors, are called *Hebrews* particularly when the writer has in mind the relationship to the foreign environment in which they find themselves. . . . Here, in Exodus, whilst the children of Israel are still free men [sic], they are called by their honoured designation, *children of Israel*, even when pharoah speaks of them (v. 9). But after the commencement of their servitude, they are usually referred to as *Hebrews*" (U. Cassuto, *A Commentary on the Book of Exodus* [Jerusalem: The Magnum Press, The Hebrew University, 1967], p. 13).

25. "Depatriarchalizing in Biblical Interpretation," *JAAR*, 41 (1973) 34.

26. Childs, *Exodus*, p. 16.

27. Exum, "You Shall Let," p. 72.

28. Ibid.

29. Samuel Terrien, "Fear," in *The Interpreter's Dictionary of the Bible*, vol. 2, Emory Stevens Bucke, ed. (New York: Abingdon, 1962), p. 257.

30. Ibid., pp. 258–59.

31. Verses 18–19 relate the confrontation between the pharaoh and the midwives. Pharaoh had ordered them directly and, therefore, he is the one to whom they have to report. Because they have defied his direct order, their defiance is a direct action against him. But their defiance in the form of noncompliance is so clever that the best the pharaoh can do is to reword his order and impose it in general upon everyone. Therefore, from now on the pharaoh will find it all the more impossible to hold anyone accountable for not following his orders.

32. Ibid., p. 74.

33. Ibid.

34. Isabel Allende, *The House of the Spirits* (New York: Knopf, 1985), pp. 358–68; Charlotte Bunch, *Passionate Politics* (New York: St. Martin's Press, 1987); Nancy Hartsoch, *Money, Sex and Power* (Boston: Northeastern University Press, 1985); and Carter Heyward, *The Redemption of God* (Washington, D.C.: University of America Press, 1984).

44

Theological Perspectives of a Religious Woman Today

MARY JOHN MANANZAN, OSB

To be a Christian today in a land where injustice and oppression abide is a challenge. To be a religious woman in such a situation is doubly so. It calls for a radical rethinking of the meaning of being a Christian and of the imperative of religious commitment. It precipitates a spiritual crisis. It demands a consequent revision of one's way of life—a true conversion, a *metanoia*.

This essay will not be a theoretical speculation of what could be the challenges of being a religious woman today, but is a sharing of actual experiences and ongoing reflection on them. Some of these reflections have already been put in writing so I will quote extensively from my own writing.

SOCIETAL CONTEXT AND PERSONAL COMMITMENT

One of the most valuable insights of liberation theology is the contextualization of theological reflection and the necessity of the analysis of society as its starting point. It is likewise the characteristic of this way of theologizing to regard one's involvement in the process of societal liberation as the substance of its reflection. This first section will therefore be devoted to these two important points.

Characteristics of Philippine Society

I am a religious woman living in a Third World country, the Philippines. My country is known as the only Christian country in the Far East, having been christianized by the Spanish colonization in the sixteenth century. It remained a Spanish colony for roughly three and a half centuries and then fell into the hands of the United States in 1898, becoming its colony for the next fifty years. It was occupied by the Japanese for three years during the Second World War. It became independent in 1946 and was put under martial law in 1972, suffering twenty years of one-man rule, which ended in the famous Edsa Event of February 1986.

But this event, impressive as it was, did not end the misery of the people. There was a change in the head of the nation but there was no change in the class of those who rule. The oppressive political machinery and its armed component remain. The orientation of the country's economic development model continues. In other words, there was no social revolution. Thus the fundamental problems of the people still prevail—namely, the grossly inequitable distribution of resources (2% of its 56 million inhabitants owning and controlling 75% of its land and capital); and the foreign control of its economy through transnational corporations and through the debt link to the IMF and World Bank. U.S. interventions into its economic and political life have in fact become more overt. These core problems have been responsible for the massive poverty existing in the land, causing 75 percent of the population to live below the poverty line with dire consequences such as malnutrition, brain-damaged children, unemployment and underemployment, brain and muscle drain, chronic insurgency, and intensifying militarization that has cost so many Filipino lives.

Baptism of Fire

It was the same situation of crisis, oppression, and injustice that made me respond to a telephone brigade in 1975 asking nuns, seminarians, and priests to come to the rescue of six hundred striking workers in a wine factory, La Tondeña. It was the first strike attempted after the strike ban issued following the declaration of martial law in September 1972.

I had just come from a six-year study leave in Germany and Rome, and I was teaching contemporary philosophy in the Jesuit Loyola University. I joined a group called "Interfaith Theological Circle," which aimed at evolving a "Filipino theology" in the air-conditioned library of the university. Needless to say we came under critique for doing "intellectual gymnastics" in spite of producing what appeared to us as extremely erudite papers on the subject. After a period of defensiveness, we realized that it was indeed futile to evolve such a theology without getting involved in the struggle of the people. This was what made me respond to the invitation of the Tondeña workers. There I had my first encounter with military brutality and experienced helplessness before the reality of force and institutional violence. That was where we established the "Friends of the Workers."

The Tondeña strike inspired a hundred more strikes in a period of three months as we went from one factory to the other, gaining valuable learning experiences from persons, getting an insight into the root causes of their problems. Helping workers immersed us in the problems of slum dwellers, for the workers lived in slums. We joined human barricades to stop demolitions. We formed composite groups that spearheaded rallies and marches. We were recruited into negotiating teams to face the military in mass actions. And inevitably we got involved in the fate of political detainees who were arrested in marches, rallies, and pickets and snatched from their houses in midnight raids.

The Anguish of Awareness

This initiation into the struggles of the people shook the framework of my Christian and religious existence. I quote at length an article I wrote at the time describing this experience:

Social awareness can mean real anguish. Exposures even on a minor scale to the miseries of our people and a serious reflection on these experiences can confront us with facts that would question our former values. And yet it takes time to adopt and synthesize a new set of values one is beginning to perceive. One is back to zero, during this period. One is barren. One stops giving talks or writing articles, because one feels empty, one needs to be reeducated. This awareness gives one a sense of urgency that may seem fanatic to those who either do not see or who confine social consciousness to community assemblies. Here is where one can make a mistake in strategy, become overzealous, and turn off people. But there is indeed a constriction of the heart, which one feels when one talks with persons who see no further than the four protective walls of their houses or convents. Here is where awareness can cause real loneliness. All of a sudden one is on a different plane when talking with one's family, one's closest friends and colleagues. Not to be able to share values can be a painful form of isolation and the slow, painstaking trial and error attempts to share these new values and new imperatives without turning people off can bring one to a point of helplessness and frustration further aggravated by one's clearer and closer perception of the magnitude of the problem and the uncertainty, tasks, and corresponding magnitude of the proposed solutions. To confront in others time and time again one's own prejudice, one's own blind spots, one's own doubts, is to relive time and time again one's own metanoia without the sense of relief at the thought that the decision and choice lies within one's power. But perhaps the greatest anguish is the yawning gap between one's insight and one's generosity. Insight brings with it imperatives to action that may mean crucial decisions, and to perceive and yet not to have the courage or moral energy to act is a real agony. To conscientize is truly a serious business, because the price of awareness is anguish.[1]

To take stock of things and understand what was happening to themselves, thirty priests and sisters initiated an alternative retreat, which they called *Hakbang* (step forward). These were five days of sharing in-depth experiences of how they got involved, a sharing of anxieties, doubts, apprehensions, fears, hopes, engaging in an analysis both of the society and the church, and formulating visions for both a transformed society and a renewed church. Every day was climaxed by a creative liturgy that recapitulated the sharing during the day. This alternative retreat was repeated for other groups. The result was a leveling of consciousness, a greater clarity of vision, a renewed courage born out of common experiences of personal liberation, and a greater motivation to go forward.

Intensified Involvement in the Struggle of the Oppressed

One important insight that emerged from the *Hakbang* was the need to analyze reality and a greater systematization of commitment. Tools of analysis were learned, adapted, systematized, applied, and shared. Focusing of one's energies brought about a sort of division of labor.

I became chairperson of the Task Force Orientation of Church Personnel of the

422

Association of Major Religious Superiors. My team and I designed modules for conscientization seminars, which we gave to religious, priests, teachers, school administrators, and church workers all over the country and even at times to certain other parts of Asia. The modules consisted of a biblical perspective, church history, analysis of society, institutional analysis (of religious congregations, schools, or groups), formulation of common thrusts, and systematic planning. We likewise organized rank-and-file sisters into the National Organization of Religious Women in the Philippines (NOW-RP).

As dean of college of a school for women, I worked out with my faculty a reorientation of the school toward an education for social transformation. We renewed the school's mission statement and the objectives of the school and different departments. A Third World perspective was adopted in the revision of the curriculum. We formed a team to give conscientization seminars both to the faculty and students. Later on the cocurricular activities were likewise reoriented. Behavioral objectives for the kind of students we wanted to educate were formulated. Criteria for evaluation of what a socially oriented school should concretely manifest were likewise clearly described. Innovative method such as exposure programs, panel discussions with grassroots leaders, tent fora, discussion groups, and the like, were devised. Administration, faculty, and students met each other at rallies, demonstrations, pickets, and other forms of mass actions. Themes on different aspects of an education for justice were focused on each year: social awareness, commitment, involvement, community building. Periodic evaluation and departmental audits were made to ensure understanding and implementation of the orientation. Through years of trial and error, small advances and setbacks, an outside accrediting team could write in 1987, twelve years after the reorientation was launched, the following observation:

> One very prominent characteristic of the school is the stress on Christian commitment manifesting itself in social justice and social responsibility especially toward the poor, the marginalized, and the oppressed. This feature is visible not only in the activities especially oriented toward community involvement. It seems to pervade the whole atmosphere and life of the school.[2]

In 1978, when a series of oil price hikes were decided without consultation of the people, a group of twelve persons founded the Citizens' Alliance for Consumer Protection, of which I became the secretary general up to this day. This organization tackled consumer issues, such as price hikes, junk foods, banned drugs, breastfeeding, nuclear energy, fertilizers and pesticides, taxes, in the context of the national economy. It grew into a federation of organizations that could mobilize rallies, demonstrations, boycotts, and marches. It launched consumer education through lectures, seminars, radio programs, and a mobile theater.

The energy desk of this association was formed when the government of President Marcos started to resist the Bataan Nuclear Free Philippines Coalition. This and other antinuclear organizations such as NO NUKES succeeded in putting a stop to the nuclear plant. They also successfully lobbied for a nuclear weapons–free provision in the constitution and are at present lobbying for the removal of U.S. bases in the Philippines.

Commitment to Women's Concerns

The feminist movement is new in the Philippines. Although concerned with prostitution in the Philippines, I did not get involved in the feminist movement until 1978 when I was invited to a World Council of Churches Conference in Venice on human rights and women. When I returned to the Philippines I cofounded with three other women the *Filipina*, which can be considered the first organization of women with a conscious and expressly feminist orientation. With another woman I established the Center for Women Resources. This latter took the initiative in 1984 to call a conference of all women's organizations that mushroomed at the time. In this conference, the federation of women's organization, GABRIELA, was born. It is now the most extensive federation of women in the Philippines, counting a hundred member organizations and about forty thousand individual members. In 1986 I was elected its national chairperson and in 1987 reelected for a period of two years.

GABRIELA has clearly defined the orientation of the women's movement in a Third World country like the Philippines. It sees women's liberation within the context of the economic, political, and cultural transformation of society. This is the necessary though not sufficient condition of women's liberation. There is no total human liberation without the liberation of women in society. And this is not an automatic consequence of either economic development or political revolution. In other words, the women's movement is an essential aspect of the very process of societal liberation.

GABRIELA makes use of seven main strategies to achieve its goal. The most important strategy is organization, because oppressed groups are empowered by organization. GABRIELA is organized according to sectors, regions, and areas of interest. GABRIELA members are mobilized along national issues, such as foreign bases, foreign debts, consumer issues. It also initiates campaigns on specifically women's concerns such as prostitution, mail-order brides, and domestic violence. The third strategy is education, both formal and informal, institutional and non-institutional. It is of utmost importance to awaken the awareness of women to their situation because the great majority of women have internalized their oppression. The fifth strategy, feminist scholarship, differs from education by its emphasis on the development of the women's perspective in the different academic disciplines — for example, psychology, theology, history. The legal strategy achieved a major victory when the women's campaign on women's rights resulted in the inclusion of the equal rights provision in the newly ratified Philippine Constitution. For women who are victims of violence, crisis centers are being established for legal, medical, and psychological aid. The urban poor women in slum areas have been helped by livelihood projects, day care centers, and primary health care clinics. These constitute the welfare strategy. Finally, the women believe in an international solidarity strategy because the women's cause is a universal cause. Every year the international desk of GABRIELA organizes a WISAP (Women International Solidarity Affair Philippines) conference attended by women from different parts of the world.

The Cost of Commitment

In the preceding pages, the anguish of awareness has been shared. This is preliminary to the cost of commitment. In the thirteen years that I have been involved in the struggle of the poor and the oppressed in the Philippines, I have witnessed the tremendous cost of commitment of persons I knew and worked with, ranging from black propaganda, disappearances, arbitrary arrests, torture, political detention, and rape, to massacre, assassinations, and "salvaging."

I have been labeled a "communist" subversive, and have been served a subpoena for speaking at a rally on the oil price hike, which was considered "agitation for rebellion." Not only is one harassed by the military and by the conservative press, one is likewise subject to the suspicions of church officials who feel "disturbed" and "threatened." There is also the alienation of former friends and relatives who cannot understand one's commitment and involvement.

THEOLOGICAL REFLECTION

With a group of theologically trained persons called THRUST and a wider interdisciplinary group called FIDES, theological reflection on the continuous struggle is being undertaken. Lately, the group has published its first volume, *Religion and Society—Towards a Theology of Struggle*. I would like to discuss this work by sharing our efforts and insights in three ongoing endeavors: reflecting on a theology of struggle, developing a feminist theology of liberation in Asia, and evolving a new spirituality.

Towards a Theology of Struggle

It was only after years of being involved in the struggle that the groups who hesitated to put down anything in writing, because it seemed difficult to write something while one is still undergoing a process, decided to make tentative written reflections about what they were experiencing. The term "theology of struggle" emerged from the reflections although there was no claim of forming a theological school. As Fely Carino puts it: "There were no pretensions here of making or developing a new dogmatic theology or of laying claim to a new theological discovery that could be included in the ever-expanding index of theological constructs." Rather:

> What was foremost in their minds and what was the focus of their attention was the sharpening of the Philippine struggle itself and how Christians can participate and contribute fully in that struggle. More important to these are questions of equipment and empowerment, and the usefulness and service-ability of the Christian tradition in theological, liturgical, and symbolic expression to make Christians more effective in the struggle to bring about transformed Philippine society and an equally transformed Philippine church.[3]

It is therefore clear that this theology is not about "struggle," but it is first and foremost theology "in" and "of" the struggle.

One of the first exponents of this theologizing is Carlos Abesamis, SJ. His scriptural work of twenty-five years has provided it with a biblical perspective. Fr. Abesamis, using the creedal statements of the Bible, has developed a theology of total and concrete salvation, which traces this concept through the different periods of the Old and New Testaments and the early church. Salvation, as experienced by our foreparents of the faith, Abesamis writes, "was not salvation of the soul from sin but the bestowing of the blessing that affects the totality of life of an Israelite and of the Israelitic nation."[4] It is total because it affects the whole person, not only the soul, and also because it is not only for the individual but for society as a whole. It is concrete, because it is a liberation from concrete evils such as poverty, slavery, injustice, oppression, sin; and because it means the working out of concrete blessings, which, though these cannot be perfected in this world, begin here and now.

On this biblical foundation I built my own reflections on church history. The dichotomies of matter/spirit, heaven/earth, body/soul came into Christianity not from its Hebrew tradition but from its hellenization. In an article entitled "The Religious Today and Integral Evangelization," I explained:

In its early years of growth, Christianity found itself flourishing in the Hellenistic culture of the Greco-Roman world. It is understandable that the early Fathers of the Church steeped in this culture explained and spread the teachings of Christianity in the conceptual framework in which they found themselves. They use the categories of Greek philosophy especially that of Plato in their explanation and exposition of Christianity. It is not strange therefore that platonic dualism would now more and more influence Christian thought. Platonic dualism took three forms: *metaphysical*, the dualism of two worlds — the "real world" of ideas and the phenomenal world of senses; *epistemological* — the dualism of two forms of knowledge, the real innate knowledge of the world of ideas and opinion or sense knowledge; and the *psychological* — the dualism of body and soul.[5]

This accounted for the development of the other-worldly concept of salvation, its exclusive focus on the soul, and the suspicious outlook on the body and alienation from the world (*fuga mundi*). In the institutionalization of Christianity, systems of doctrine, morality, ritual were developed and were protected by a wall of orthodoxy. I realized the role of the "heretics" such as Galileo Galilei, Giordano Bruno, Meister Eckhardt, and Teilhard de Chardin in the survival of the church. They refused to be confined within the walls of orthodoxy and insisted at the cost of their reputations or even of their lives to rethink and rephrase theological concepts.

Vatican II made a breakthrough in tearing down the walls of orthodoxy and in the freer atmosphere of theological thought. Dichotomies were healed; the world began to be taken seriously as the only arena for salvation. This taking seriously of the world meant taking seriously its problems, the greatest of which is poverty. The Synod on Justice in 1972 added the insight that the deeper reality of poverty is injustice. Its document, *Justice in the World*, made the programmatic statement: "Action in behalf of justice and participation in the transformation of the world fully appears to us as a constitutive dimension of preaching the gospel."[6] This, I believe, formed the basis of all contextualized "theology of struggle" in the Philippine experience, because "justice" and "transformation of the world" would have remained abstract concepts if not taken in the concrete context of a particular place and time. The locus becomes the struggles for justice by oppressed peoples of particular countries in the world.

This change of theological perspective could not but exert an influence in the understanding of religious life. My own reflection on the matter appears in the same article cited previously. I wrote then:

> But even while turning her attention to these actions for justice, the religious has likewise to rethink her religious life, her vows, her spirituality, and lifestyle according to the insight that justice is a constituent dimension of her being a Christian and religious.
>
> The vow of poverty takes on more flesh and blood than the usual econo-mizing or asking of permission. Poverty today must be truly experienced in the surrendering of vested interests, in true simple living, if possible, in "pitch-ing one's tent" among the poor. At the very least it would demand an un-reserved sharing of one's resources with the poor and the oppressed.
>
> Celibacy takes on a more positive meaning in the freedom of heart that is needed to be truly available to the many. . . .
>
> Obedience can take on a new dimension in letting one's role be defined by the needs of the people. The *vox populi, vox Dei* adage takes on a new reality. One begins to listen with the ear of one's heart to people instead of dictating to them or taking the leading role. Just as there is a personal and communal poverty, there is likewise a personal and communal obedience. Congregations and religious communities have to learn to obey the signs of the times. They learn to insert themselves meaningfully into the local church where they find themselves.[7]

Developing an Asian Feminist Theology

As a religious woman, my commitment to the oppressed which started with political militancy, developed into a commitment for the struggle of women against gender oppression. Again being a religious woman brought my attention to the religious roots of women's oppression. Together with Asian women coming from different religious and cultural backgrounds, we came to the insight that all religions have oppressive as well as liberating elements, which could serve for or against women; so far, more of the oppressive factors have been used to rationalize and justify the continued subordination of women.

The starting point of this Asian effort at theologizing from the women's per-spective is the particular struggle of Asian women. The statement of the Asian Women's Consultation in Manila in November 1985 summarizes this in its first paragraph:

> In all spheres of Asian society women are dominated, dehumanized, they are discriminated against, exploited, harassed, sexually used, abused, and re-garded as inferior beings who must always subordinate themselves to the so-called male supremacy. In the home, church, education, and media, women have been treated with bias and condescension. In Asia and all over the world, the myth of the subservient, servile Asian woman is blatantly peddled to reenforce the dominant male stereotype image.[8]

The document then focused on the particular oppression of the different Asian women. Regarding Filipino women, it pinpoints the following oppressive factors:

Filipinas, like many of their Asian sisters, are subjected to job discrimination and are exposed to health hazards in factories, multinational companies, and export processing zones. Because of the severe economic crisis and with the advent of sex tourism, and the presence of U.S. bases, many leave home to become migrant workers in hostile alien lands. Furthermore, many are raped, tortured, imprisoned, and killed for their political beliefs.[9]

This situation of Asian women was condemned as a "sinful situation."

An ecumenical group called AWIT (Association of Women in Theology) is engaged in reinterpreting biblical pericopes from the woman's point of view. These women realize that the Bible is often used to justify the subordination and discrimination of women, especially the creation story and the Epistles of St. Paul. They denounce the misogynistic writings of the fathers and doctors of the church. They expose the introduction of the norms and practices of the patriarchal society in Philippine society. They criticize the domesticating role of theological concepts. Sr. Virginia Fabella, for example, makes the following critique of the way Mary has been taught and how the emerging feminist theology tries to correct it:

One of the ways Catholicism has contributed to the subordination of women, especially in the church, is by its portrayal of Mary. Through the ages Mary has been depicted as silent, sweet, self-effacing, docile, passive, submissive, a *Mater Dolorosa*. Actually this portrayal of Mary is a masculine perception of idealized femininity, which has been inflicted on us and which many of us in turn have tried hard to internalize. In recent times, however, women have begun to appropriate the Bible for themselves without the mediation of male interpreters, and realize how Mary has been misrepresented. They see Mary of the gospel, especially of the Magnificat, as a woman of faith and intelligence, who is gentle and attentive, yet decisive and responsive, a woman of deep compassion but also of great courage, who is able to take the initiative and make great sacrifices and is willing to risk in order to accomplish God's word and will. This is, to a growing number of women, and should be to us, the true Mary, who is proto-disciple, yes, but above all, *woman*.[10]

Feminist liberation theology is still in its infancy in the Philippines and in Asia, but it has delineated for itself the following all-encompassing agenda:

The agenda of renewal must include all aspects of theology from the reinterpretation of scriptures, to a historico-critical reflection of church doctrines from the women's point of view to the rediscovery of the great women of church history, to the fundamental questioning of the church's hierarchical structure, its constricting prescriptions, its discriminating practices, and the sexist language of its liturgy. It likewise includes the critical analysis of the particular culture in order to distinguish the liberative elements from oppressive forces that affect women.

These will lead to the stripping away of the false consciousness of women and free her to discover herself and her potentialities and to come to her full blossoming. In the running over of this bliss, she together with all peoples of God will use this energy toward the transformation of society into a "new heaven and a new earth."[11]

The Emerging Spirituality

Involvement in human struggles brings one to a spiritual crisis. I have described the anguish that comes with initial awareness and the costly consequences of commitment. One goes into a kind of dark night of the soul (*noche oscura*) and when one emerges, one experiences a shake-up in one's spirituality, which may result either in "giving up one's faith" (some of my friends have made this option) or one undergoes a real *metanoia*.

The emerging spirituality, in my experience, shows four trends. It is a spirituality that is liberational, integral, feminist, and oriental.

During the *Hakbang* or alternative retreat of the religious and priests mentioned in the beginning of this paper, each one shared their journey to commitment. The remarkable consensus was that each one experienced an inner liberation. Christ, the fully liberated person, became the inspiration. The involvement with oppressed persons helps one into a better self-knowledge and self-acceptance, which become the basis of an inner liberation manifesting itself in a growing freedom from fear, from idols, and from bitterness and resentment. Freedom from fear does not consist in not feeling fear but in the ability to distinguish between groundless fear and substantiated fear, and to act in spite of such a substantiated fear. One becomes less worried about what the "anonymous they" might be thinking or criticizing. Besides being free from this "negative idol," one also experiences a freedom from legalism and from sacralizing law or from being enslaved to positive idols that one had put on pedestals during one's life. Although acknowledging the bitterness and resentment in one's negative experiences, one begins to transcend them into a creative and positive resolution of one's problems.

There is also a remarkable simplifying of one's faith and one's practices. There is an integration of the vertical and horizontal dimensions of one's religious life. To elaborate:

> It is understandable that one's spirituality will be influenced by this new thrust or else there will be a painful dichotomy. One's life of prayer will be "invaded" by the anguish of people. The psalms take on a relevance in confrontation with new pharaohs and a new Egypt or the need for a new Exodus and a new Promised Land. Liturgy will have to echo the crying aspirations of the oppressed as much as the joy of every step toward their liberation. The asceticism of the religious committed to justice need not be contrived. It will be imposed on her by the difficult situations that will inevitably arise; the demands of people that cannot be put on a rigidly controlled timetable or calendar; in the expected persecution from the rich and powerful whose vested interests will be endangered; and in the misunderstandings of friends and loved ones who would be threatened by one's radicality.[12]

The feminist perspective to spirituality developed as women started to reflect on their experiences as women, both personal and social, as well as on their common struggle against their manifold oppression. This spirituality is nourished by their growing understanding of their self-image which has been obscured by the roles that have been assigned to them by a patriarchal society. This in turn influences their interpersonal relationships and touches the collective consciousness that is growing among them as they struggle against exploitation and discrimination. It is shaped by the victories, small or big, which they have achieved in their struggle. Women's emerging spirituality is therefore not just a vertical relationship with God but an integral one. It is shaped not only by prayer but by relational experience and struggle, personal, interpersonal, and societal.

The release of creative energy and the new insights in the women's struggle have likewise affected a new focus and new expressions of spirituality. It is creation-centered rather than sin- and redemption-centered. It is holistic rather than dualistic. It is risk rather than security. It is a spirituality that is joyful rather than austere, active rather than passive, expansive rather than limiting. It celebrates more than it fasts; it lets go rather than holds back. It is an Easter rather than a Good Friday spirituality. It is vibrant, liberating, and colorful.

The holistic aspect that feminist influence has exerted on spirituality has likewise given rise to a phenomenon newly observed among activists in the Philippines, and that is the reclaiming of the contemplative heritage of Asia's great religions. More and more social activists in the Philippines are taking up the practice of Zen, which they undertake with great enthusiasm. Ruben Habito explains that the term "spirituality" equates with the Greek *pneuma* (spirit), which in turn equates with the Hebrew *ruah*, the breath of God. Throughout the Old and New Testaments, the breath of God plays a key role in all the events of salvation history from creation to the incarnation. Habito then shows the relationship between Zen practice and social militancy:

Paying attention to one's breathing in Zen is seen not simply as a physical exercise that keeps one concentrated on one point, but as the very abandonment of one's total being to this Breath of God, here and now. It is letting one's whole self be possessed by the Spirit of God, to be vivified, guided, inspired, and fulfilled in it.

And as one is "overshadowed" by the Spirit, one's whole being is offered for God's dynamic liberating action in history, to preach the good news to the poor. To proclaim release to the captives. To set at liberty those who are oppressed.[13]

In another way of expressing this, Sister Elaine MacInnes writes of the socially significant effect of Zen practice:

Our dissipated energies gradually become more unified and we start to gain some control over our superactive mind. Tensions are released, nerves are relaxed, and physical health generally improves. Emotions are sensitized. We begin to experience a kind of inner balance and gradually dryness, rigidity, hang-ups, prejudice, egoism melt and give way to compassion, serenity, ego-lessness, and social concern.[14]

The koan method presents the Zen student with "riddles," which the intellect will repel but which is grasped by the self-nature in an intuitive response. The student soon comes to see that everyday life is a koan, which invites response. As Sister Elaine further writes: "when we see someone thirsty, we give a drink. When we are confronted with injustice, we cannot remain unmoved."[15]

This recourse to oriental mysticism for social activists closes the full circle of action/contemplation action.

CONCLUSION

Being a religious woman today is more difficult, less simple, more demanding, but definitely more challenging. When I hear a young woman answer the question "Why do you want to enter the convent?" with "because I want to have peace and quiet," I just smile.

The religious life has come a long way from the *fuga mundi* principle of the early days of monasticism. Religious women who were particularly the objects of enclosure laws of canon law because they were not only *religious* but *women*, have emerged from this constraint and have become involved in the burning issues of society and in some cases have been on the forefront of militant causes.

Personally, I find being a religious woman today in a Third World country a dangerous but challenging and meaningful existence. It forces one to go back to the original meaning of the core of the Christian message. Impelled by a sense of urgency because of the lived experience of suffering and oppression, religious women are inspired to a consequent living out of this Christian imperative in the concrete struggles of their world. This in turn gives them an experiential insight into the meaning of the paradox of committed freedom. The religious woman committed to justice becomes truly convinced that to seek her life is to lose it and to lose her life is to gain it, not only for herself but for others—for those who will perhaps see the fulfillment of her vision of a better world, something she will probably not see in her own lifetime.

NOTES

1. Sr. Mary John Mananzan, editorial in *Conversatio*, September 1975.

2. Report of PAASCU Accrediting Team, August 1987, p. 1.

3. F. Carino, *Religion and Society* (Manila, Fides, 1988), p. 11.

4. Carlos Abesamis, "Total Salvation, Key to Understanding the Mission of the Church in Asia Today" (unpublished manuscript), p. 3.

5. Mary John Mananzan, "The Religious Today and Integral Evangelization," *Lumen Vitae*, 31/3 (1976) 316–17.

6. Introduction, *Justice in the World*.

7. Mananzan, "Religious Today," pp. 321–22.

8. Statement of the Asian Women's Consultation in *Voice from the Third World*, 8/2 (December 1985) 32–33.

9. Ibid.

10. Virginia Fabella, "Mission of Women in the Church in Asia: Role and Position," in Mary John Mananzan, ed., *Essays on Women*, (Manila: St. Scholastica's College, 1987), p. 144.

11. Mary John Mananzan, "Woman and Religion," in Carino, *Religion and Society*, p. 119.

12. Ibid.

13. Ruben Habito, "Zen Spirituality: Attuning to the Breath of God," in *Total Liberation* (Maryknoll, N.Y.: Orbis, 1989), p. 105.

14. Sr. Elaine MacInnes, "What Is Oriental Spirituality?" in *Asia's Gift to a Total Christian Spirituality*, p. 5.

15. Ibid.

45

Theology in a Prophetic Mode

ALBERT NOLAN, OP

It is not without reason that Gustavo Gutiérrez has been hailed throughout the world as a modern-day prophet. The theology of liberation has been described as theology in a prophetic mode. In South Africa we have tried to develop this particular aspect of the theology of liberation. What does it mean to do theology in a prophetic mode?

It would be foolhardy to attempt a comprehensive outline of prophetic theology in this brief essay. However, there is a fundamental characteristic of this mode in theology that underlies everything else and that distinguishes it from every other theology or mode of theology. And this is the characteristic of being time-bound. All prophecy and prophetic theology speaks of, and speaks to, a particular time in a particular place about a particular situation. This is the characteristic of theology in a prophetic mode that I would like to examine in this essay.

The Kairos Document has drawn our attention quite recently to the theological significance of a particular moment in history, a crisis, a *kairos*. And it has nailed it down to the particular crisis in which South Africa finds itself today. This alone would make the theology of the Kairos Document prophetic in character or mode. But unfortunately the document devotes no more than a page and a half to this all-important notion of a *kairos* or moment of truth. Much more needs to be said if theology in a prophetic mode is to be taken up and developed fully, effectively, and powerfully in South Africa. Moreover, it is no mere coincidence that this path of investigation would also be one of the ways of liberating ourselves from the dominant Western world that still imprisons and entombs our theology in South Africa.

Western theology is singularly unprophetic because it understands all truth to be timeless and universal. This understanding, among other things, became a very convenient tool for colonizing the minds of much of the human race and for excluding all possibility of prophetic thinking. The biblical prophets were far removed from our Western intellectuals in many ways, including the fact that their message was not timeless and universal.

Gerhard von Rad, after many years of research on "the message" of the prophets, draws this conclusion:

> It is all-important not to read this message as if it consisted of timeless ideas, but to understand it as the particular word relevant to a particular hour in

history, which therefore cannot be replaced by any other word. The prophetic word never tries to climb into the realm of general religious truth, but instead uses even the most suspect means to tie the listening partner down to his [sic] particular time and place in order to make him understand his own situation before God.[1]

There is a typically non-Western way of conceiving time that is not only Hebrew and biblical but also, in at least some ways, African. The Western concept of time, however, has been part and parcel of our education in South Africa as elsewhere. And it has its uses. But it would not be possible to speak theologically and prophetically about a particular moment of time without going beyond the Western concept of chronological time.

The simplest and briefest way of making this clear and of developing a basis for a prophetic theology in South Africa today would be to make a clear distinction between three kinds of time. The three kinds of time might best be designated by the three Greek words *chronos*, *kairos*, and *eschaton*.

CHRONOS

This is the typically Western concept of time. *Chronos* means time as a measurement. It is the time of measured hours and dates, the time that is recorded on clocks and calendars. A historical epoch in this way of thinking is something that is identified by the date when it began and the date when it ended. Time is conceived of as a measured and numbered empty space that can be filled with events of greater or lesser importance. It is what one might call quantified time.

This is what comes to mind immediately and almost exclusively in Western thinking when the word "time" is mentioned. A quantified measurement. However, this is not the way the Bible thinks of time. In the words of von Rad, "Today one of the few things of which we can be quite sure is that this concept of absolute time, independent of events, and, like blanks on a questionnaire, only headings to be filled up with data which will give it [time] content, was unknown to Israel."[2]

KAIROS

This word, on the other hand, refers to time as a quality. A particular *kairos* is the particular quality or mood of an event. This is clearly and succinctly expressed in the famous passage from Ecclesiastes (3:1–8):

> There is a time for everything;
> a time for giving birth,
> a time for dying,
> a time for planting,
> a time for uprooting,
> a time for killing,
> a time for healing,
> a time for knocking down,
> a time for building,

a time for tears,
a time for laughter,
a time for mourning,
a time for dancing. . . .
a time for loving,
a time for hating;
a time for war,
a time for peace.

For the Hebrew, to know the time was not a matter of knowing the hour or the date; it was a matter of knowing what kind of time it was. Was it a time for tears or a time for laughter, a time for war or a time for peace? To misjudge the time in which one was living might be disastrous. To continue to mourn and fast during a time of blessing would be like sowing during harvest time (see Zech. 7:1–3). Time here is the quality or mood of events.

This concept of time is not entirely foreign to us. It is particularly meaningful to those who inherit an African culture and even more meaningful when we are involved in an intensified struggle to change the times. We know about times of mourning that make it inappropriate to celebrate a joyful Christmas. We have discussed about whether it is a time for boycotting or a time for returning to school. There is a time for conflict and confrontation and a time for reconciliation and peace but, unfortunately, we do not relate each different *kairos* to God as easily and as naturally as the persons of the Bible did. This indeed is where prophetic theology comes in and where we have much to learn from the Bible.

In the Bible the prophet was someone who could tell the time. He (or she) could see what kind of time it was and what kind of action would be appropriate now. The prophets could read the signs of the times, which means they could interpret the *kairos*, interpret the signs that would indicate what kind of time it was (compare Matt. 16:3 with Luke 12:56).

Prophecy, however, was not just a matter of knowing one's *kairos*; it was also a matter of finding God in it. For the prophets, God determined the different times and therefore it is God who speaks to us and challenges us through our particular *kairos*. Revelation has a tremendous immediacy here. God is directly involved in the changing times. God speaks loudly and clearly through this crisis or that conflict or some victory over the forces of evil. Theology in a prophetic mode is a theology that can find and experience God as alive and active in the excitement or the sadness or the suffering of our present *kairos*. This is not to say that every moment of chronological time is equally important or significant, and that God can be found equally in every and any event. Not every event in history is a *kairos*. A divine *kairos* is a very special and significant time. There are lulls in history when nothing of significance happens. For the Bible such chronological times are simply not history. History is the succession of God-inspired events. The gift of the prophet is the ability to recognize such events, such critical times, and to spell them out as moments of truth, as challenges, as opportunities, as times for decision and action. A *kairos* is a privileged time that not everyone is called to witness or participate in. Such was, of course, the time of Jesus and that is why he could say to his disciples: "Happy the eyes that see what you see, for I tell you that many prophets and kings wanted to see what you see and never saw it" (Luke 10:23–24). The time of Jesus was of course a unique and unrepeatable *kairos*. But that does not mean that there can be no other specially privileged times. Today in South Africa, according to the prophetic theology of the Kairos Document, is indeed for us an unprecedented *kairos*.

It is at times like these that God visits the people, that God walks down our streets and enters right into our homes. Everyday life is turned upside down and inside out, and nothing will ever be the same again. These are the favorable times, the times of grace when God offers us the kind of opportunity that our predecessors might have longed to see but never saw. And woe betide us if we do not rise to the challenge.

But even this is not all. The real specialness and seriousness of a prophetic *kairos* is determined by its relationship to another kind of time: the *eschaton*.

ESCHATON

Eschatological time or the *eschaton* is a notoriously difficult concept. Biblical scholars crack their heads over it and come up with a whole range of different theories from realized eschatology to consistent eschatology and existential eschatology. I have no intention of delving into these theories, because I think that the present crisis in South Africa can provide us with a simple and practical appreciation of what the prophets had in mind.

Put quite simply, an *eschaton* is an event of the near future, an act of God that determines the quality, the mood, and the seriousness of our present time—that is to say, it turns the present moment into a particular kind of *kairos*. This way of thinking about God and time requires some unpacking.

A very important characteristic of all prophetic thinking is that it turns the attention of the people from the past to the future. Prophets are called prophets precisely because they speak about the future. Instead of trying to understand the present in terms of the events of the past (for example, exodus, Mount Sinai, or King David), the prophets ask the people to think of the present time in terms of a future act of God. They challenge the people to break with the past and to look forward to something new: "Remember not the former things," says God in Isaiah, "I am going to do a new thing" (43:18–19).

An *eschaton* is a qualitatively and radically new event. It is interesting to notice how often the prophets use the word "new": the new covenant, the new age, a new heart, a new spirit, the new heaven and new earth, the new Jerusalem, or simply the fact that God is going to do a new thing. They looked forward to a future in which new and unprecedented things would happen, and even when they looked back to the past and the traditions of the past they would interpret them anew in view of the new future. Thus the covenant makes them think of the new covenant to come, the exodus turns their attention to the new exodus, and Jerusalem to the new Jerusalem, and so forth.

The prophets did not use the Greek word *eschaton*. When they spoke of the new future they called it "the day of Yahweh," "the day of vengeance," or "the latter days," or "the days that are coming," or simply "the day." At a later stage the *eschaton* was referred to as "the coming of the new age" and Jesus is making use of the same idea when he speaks of "the coming of the kingdom of God."

The first and most important thing that all the prophets, and Jesus, have to say about this new future or *eschaton* is that it is "near," "at hand," "coming soon." The prophets stand up to make the momentous announcement that "the day of Yahweh is near" (see, for example, Isa. 13:6,9; Jer. 46:10; Ezek. 7:7, 12; 30:3; Joel 1:15; 4:14; Zeph. 1:7, 14; Zech. 14:1) and Jesus comes to proclaim that "the kingdom of God is near" (Matt 4:17 and par.). Of course they are not all referring to the same day nor are they all speaking about the last day. The *eschaton* is a new saving act of God that was imminent or near for them at that time.

The new saving act of God that will happen on the day of Yahweh is an act of judgment and salvation. Not that they have in mind what we call the last judgment or eternal salvation. They have in mind a particular day or time when God will punish those who are presently doing evil and save or vindicate or liberate those who are now enslaved or in exile or suffering oppression. The Hebrew verb "to judge" means literally "to put right what is wrong." We can say then that the *eschaton* is an event of the near future in which God is going to put right all that is presently wrong. That will mean punishment for those who are doing wrong and salvation for those who are being wronged.

In the minds of the Old Testament prophets this future event will take the form of a mighty war[3] in which the forces of evil will be destroyed so that peace and justice may reign on earth. Many of the prophets give vivid and terrifying descriptions of this mighty war of liberation. For but a few examples, one can read about the imminent destruction of Babylon and Edom in Isaiah 13 and 34 and the terrifying massacre of the Egyptians by the Babylonians in Jer. 46:1–24 and Ezekiel 30, not to mention the many descriptions of the slaughter of the Jewish ruling class in Jerusalem on the day of Yahweh because of all their sins (see, for example, Joel 21:1–11 and Ezek. 37).

The prophets found no pleasure in describing all this horrific bloodshed. They trembled and shuddered at the very thought of it and they describe the fear and suffering of so many of the people with great compassion. Theirs is not a dispassionate and objective description of a war, but a prophetic warning about a world-shaking event that will be experienced as a cosmic upheaval: "The earth quakes, the skies tremble, sun and moon grow dark, the stars lose their brilliance" (Joel 2:10).

We know this apocalyptic-type description of a cosmic upheaval and we come across it again in the Gospels (for example, Mark 13:24–25). It is fundamentally the experience of a terrible war that changes the face of the earth and is a turning point in human history. It is an *eschaton*.

But the day of Yahweh is not only a day of vengeance, a time of gloom and doom. The prophets were in no doubt about the terrifying seriousness of what was going to happen, the awful seriousness of God's anger. But they never lost hope. On the contrary, the peace, the salvation, the justice, and the equality that they were always hoping for would be the outcome of these very wars and upheavals. They have equally vivid descriptions of the peace and happiness that God will bring: when the lion lies down with the lamb (Isa. 11:6–9; 65:25) and swords are melted into plowshares (Isa. 2:2–5); (Mic. 4:1–5) when there will be nothing more to fear (Zeph. 3:13) and peace and justice will reign supreme (Isa. 32:16–17) because the law will be written in the hearts of the people (Jer. 31:33) and the spirit of God will be in them (Ezek. 36:26). On that day God will put right all that is now wrong.

Oppressors will be destroyed or converted and the poor and oppressed will live in peace (Zech. 3).[4]

This same idea of an *eschaton* appears in the New Testament when Jesus speaks about the coming of wars and rumors of wars (Mark 13:7) and the destruction of Jerusalem (Luke 19:43–44; 21:20–23:28). This he speaks of as the birth pangs of God's kingdom (Mark 13:8).

However, for Jesus and the prophets the destructive side of the *eschaton*, the bloodshed, is not inevitable and absolutely unavoidable. As far as the Jewish prophets were concerned, there was probably very little, if anything, that they could do about the massacre of the Egyptians by the Babylonians or later of the Babylonians by the Medes except to see that it would be to the advantage of Israel. But when the Israelites themselves, or at least their ruling class, are the oppressors, then at least the prophets can appeal to them in the name of Yahweh to change their ways before they are destroyed. This is where Jesus' and the prophets' oft repeated call to repentance and conversion comes in, the element of *metanoia*. And this is what constitutes their present moment as a special divine *kairos*, a moment of truth.

A *kairos* is a moment of grace, a unique opportunity precisely because the *eschaton* or day of reckoning is near. It is a time for decision and action, a time for oppressors and wrong-doers to be converted. And at the same time, the *kairos* is a time for rejoicing and for hope because the *eschaton* as the day of liberation is near at hand—whether the oppressor is converted or not, whether there will be bloodshed or not. The element of hopefulness and expectancy in any genuine *kairos* should not be overlooked. It is indeed one of the constitutive elements of a divine *kairos*.

The fundamental insight of prophetic theology, then, is the recognition that an *eschaton* or day of reckoning and liberation is near. It is this that turns the present moment into a *kairos* and everything else in prophetic theology follows from here. But one may well ask how anyone can be sure that an eschatological event is close at hand or how the prophets themselves could have known when their *eschaton* would occur.

Here again we would first need to be reminded that the nearness of an *eschaton* is not a matter of *chronos* or measured time. In other words, a prophet would not be able to tell you the day or the hour when all these things will happen. Jesus makes this quite clear when he says that nobody, not even he himself, knows the day or the hour (Mark 13:32 and par.). But the impossibility of pinning the *eschaton* down to a chronological date did not make Jesus or the prophets any less certain about the central truth that their *eschaton* was near. What they are speaking about, then, is another kind of time relationship, the extremely close relationship between the present *kairos* and a future *eschaton*. In fact, qualitatively speaking, the two events are so bound up together that they are almost contemporaneous. The *eschaton* is the event that determines and qualifies, or should determine and qualify, the whole mood and atmosphere of the present time.[5] If we believe that war, revolution, liberation, or any other total upheaval is imminent, this will color our whole understanding of our present reality. Once we realize that something totally new is about to happen, we are already living in a new time. Or if we come to believe that the day of reckoning is upon us, we are forced to decide to make our choices and take sides immediately. It is the approaching *eschaton* that turns our present crisis into a make-or-break *kairos*.

But that still leaves us with the question of how one is to know that there is an *eschaton* on the horizon. The answer is quite simply that we discover this, as the prophets did, by reading the signs of the time. If one interprets one's own time correctly and especially if one can see the events of one's time with the eyes of God, then one sees clearly what all the signs are pointing to. One can foresee what is going to happen sometime in the near future, even if one cannot calculate the exact day or the hour. Prophetic theology begins with some such insight or foresight.

SOUTH AFRICA TODAY

The Kairos theologians have drawn the conclusion that the present moment in South Africa is a *kairos*, but they have not spelt out very clearly and in a truly prophetic manner why this particular moment should be regarded as a divine *kairos*. Reference is made to the conflict between oppressor and oppressed, and to the division in the church which claims the loyalty of both the oppressor and the oppressed. That indeed is a crisis and does indeed raise some serious questions about the meaning of Christianity but in and by itself it does not make our present time a *kairos*.

What is not explicit in the Kairos Document, although it is implied throughout the document, is that what we are now facing is an *eschaton*. What all the signs are now pointing to is that one way or another the day of liberation is near. Apartheid's days are numbered. In the near future this whole oppressive system is going to be utterly destroyed and a totally new, liberated, and peaceful society will be built up in its place. The people are determined to do this and to do it soon and all the signs indicate that this drive toward liberation and peace through justice is now unstoppable. Of course, it will be resisted, violently resisted, but it can no longer be stopped. This means that we must expect, unfortunately, more violence, more conflict and possibly more bloodshed before our society can be turned completely upside down to become a land of justice and peace.

In religious or theological terms, this is our *eschaton*. The day of Yahweh is at hand. The day of reckoning, when God will put right what is wrong in our country is now very near. The terrifying seriousness of God's anger and love, of God's justice and mercy, are about to descend upon us in a manner that might well make what the Old Testament prophets were talking about look like child's play. God is no less involved in our present crisis and in the upheaval that is about to take place here, than God was in the crisis and in the upheavals of the history of Israel.

That is what makes our present time in South Africa a truly prophetic *kairos*. A time of judgment and salvation. A time for real fear and trembling. A time when everything is at stake. A time for taking a clear stand. A time of tears and sadness that is nevertheless fraught with hope and joyful anticipation.

But it is also a time for us to act in the name of God, as the prophets did, to minimize the bloodshed. It is the sort of time when we should drop everything to proclaim from the rooftops that the day of reckoning is upon us and that the day of liberation has dawned. It is a time to appeal for immediate repentance and radical change; a time to call upon all in the world who can still hear the voice of God to do everything in their power, and at whatever cost to themselves, to hasten the downfall of the apartheid regime and so bring the violence of oppression to a speedy end. Now is the time. God is near.

439

NOTES

1. Gerhard von Rad, *The Message of the Prophets* (London: SCM, 1968), p. 100.

2. Ibid., p. 77.

3. Ibid., pp. 95ff.

4. Norbert Lohfink, "Zefaunia und das Israel der Armen," in *Bibel und Kirche* 3/3 (1984) 100–108, summarized in *Theology Digest*, 32/2 (1985) 113–24.

5. Albert Nolan, *Jesus Before Christianity* (Maryknoll, N.Y.: Orbis, 1976), p. 141.

46

Christian Feminism
and African Culture:
The "Hearth" of the Matter

MERCY AMBA ODUYOYE

THE MATTER

There is a "Nairobi 85" poster that reads "appropriate technology: if it is not appropriate for women, it is not appropriate." My contention is that any element in African culture that is not liberating for women will not liberate all the energy required for Africa's well-being. Whatever is deemed appropriate for Africa must first pass the test of being appropriate for the daughters of Africa.

In a theological circle, the complexities of the issue of "Christ and culture" is evident, so this essay presents another perspective on a difficult problem. For an African woman who names herself a Christian and a student of the Christian religion, Christ and culture comprises more than an academic study. It is a crucial issue of life if life is to be lived with any degree of integrity, wholeness, and wholesomeness.

The women who are named Christian feminists are those of the global sisterhood who have refused to give up the church and who are putting up resistance to the male takeover of the religion of Jesus of Nazareth. I have in mind all women who are rereading and retelling the manifestation of God in human experience and who continue in the struggle to keep the church faithful to the vision of Jesus of Nazareth as a community that lives before God. I am referring to the women who are drawing the curtains of half-truths off the Christian story, so that we might all come to an appreciation of the real demands of the gospel.

An African who is a Christian and who feels herself part of the global sisterhood has to cope not only with all that Western Christian women have to contend with, but in addition there are elements of African culture even more deeply rooted than Christianity that militate against her image of herself as a genuine and full member of those who see themselves as created in the image of God.

In Africa, where a Christianity captured by Western culture seeks to present itself as the only authentic expression of the Christian religion, the situation becomes grave indeed. Western norms in general have operated and continue to

operate in Africa as being superior perspectives on human living. In our search for
fullness, we have treated Western magic pots and canes with equal respect, expecting them to yield only that which is life-giving. We never learned the whole
secret of technology.[1] Now we have come to realize that a theology appropriate for
Europe is not necessarily appropriate for Africa. Similarly, the theology deemed
appropriate for African men is not always appropriate for women. An Akan proverb
says *Nea oda ne gya na onim senea ehyehye fa* ("it is the person sleeping by the fire
who knows the intensity of the heat"). So, do not let African men tell you that
African women do not need to speak of oppression, nor allow them to define what
is the real source of oppression for African women. By the same token, the voices
of women from one stratum of African women's experience do not constitute the
African women's voice! There is no idealistic "African woman," but there are broad
influences in Africa that condition women's lives with varying degrees of success.

With African culture, Islamic norms, Western civilization, and the church's traditional antifeminism piled upon the African woman, the world has been led to see
African women as not more than the quintessence of the status called "the oppressed." African men protest against this portrait. African women, unable to reach
the world media, act out their reaction to oppression in their local situations, un-
heralded and unrecorded by television cameras, either in public or individually. I
am one such individual, but I do belong to a growing community of African women
in the theological field who are committed to the ethos of Christian feminism and
the effectiveness of Christianity in Africa.

MOTHER-CENTEREDNESS VS. PATRIARCHY

Born and brought up among the Akan, a people with a mother-centered culture,
I grew up with a clear sense of being needed. Without the women, there is no *abusa*
(clan). The integrity, wholeness, the very existence of the *abusa* depends upon its
women. Its property and insignia of authority pass down the line of women. You
are, because your mother is!

I grew up with an ego that nothing was going to repress. Accepting the responsibilities that go with being the first child, and even more important, the first daughter, and making the sacrifices necessary for and on behalf of the unit, was identical
with being myself. The integrity of the *abusa,* and specifically of my mother's line,
is what guarantees the self that I claim and am proud to be. Without the *abusa,*
and its principle of the irreplaceable nature of the role of mothering in a society,
I become nothing.

That was precisely how I began to feel among the patriarchal and patrilineal
Yoruba, my affined family, and in the westernized sector of life in Africa, the
church, the university, jurisprudence, and to some extent, the economy. All con-
spired to tell me that the Akan view of life and its organization of human society
was a dying one. But I refused to bow to this conspiracy, and still do so wholeheartedly. I felt invisible, but I was being asked to wear the Yoruba *etu* (deep navy
blue, and very expensive), I who stepped out resplendent in the multicolored and
multipatterned *kente.* I was being cast in the mode of breeder and housekeeper, I
whose ancestors were rulers and goddesses. Patriarchy, it was said, was a superior
structure.

Why do these so-called more developed social structures continue to expect motherhood from all women, take the mothering provided by women for granted, and *then* place fathers at the centers of affairs? I sensed injustice, for where no power of policy-making is available, the powerless should not be held accountable for the failure of the system. All around me was evidence of a system that enjoined obedience on women, assigned them the blame for all that went wrong, but excluded them from making decisions. My Akan blood proved an effective insulation against patriarchal domination and gave me energy to be myself.

I was convinced that I did not owe the patriarchal system the same self-abnegation I owe the *abusa,* for whereas the *abusa* affirms my being, the patriarchal system took my "mothering" of situations and events for granted. I was convinced that "dying to self" in this alien culture cannot promote inner harmony or enable me to nurture a self I can live with. I asked myself again and again, "Amba, are you willing to live up to the expectations of the systemic patriarchy that is eating up all other forms of relationships in Africa?" My soul always answered with a clear no! My answer to the patriarchalization of African society remains no! I cannot speak for other African women; I can only tell you why I refuse. I know there are other African women who have refused to comply, and there have always been. Further, I am convinced that there is a growing number of African women who refuse to bow the knee to the Baal lord called patriarchy and that there shall always be. I, therefore, refuse to gloss over the oppressive aspects of African culture.

OPPRESSION VIA RELIGION

Socio-political and even economic participation is governed by religious beliefs of the primal religion of Africa. Being an integral part of the culture, Africa's religion affects Christians and Muslims alike. Social practices and values are governed by religious rituals and taboos. A couple of illustrations are apposite. When the Akan hear of a birth, the first question is "Which is it?" The Akan expect more girls than boys, for it is through its women that the departed return to this dimension of human existence. The mother-centered Akan prefer girls, yet a religious principle of the male as "spirit-protector" puts women under the discipline of men and undermines their image as decision-makers and the bearers of authority. Where did the Akan get the notion that only the male can provide spiritual sustenance to the human race? "Without the women the lineage ceases to exist," the Akan declare, yet for public performance most lineages are represented by men.

Why has the Akan woman chosen or assented to be the power behind the throne? The "hearth" of the matter is that a male intangible principle has crept into the system to assume control over the female principle in order to control the return of the ancestors. This rule of the male is symbolized in the Akan culture by exclusive arrogation of the prerogative of "naming" to fathers. It is interesting that the patriarchal Yoruba, sure of the control of the father, do not insist on an exclusive right to naming for fathers. The so-called family name, passed on from father through sons, is a European imposition for several African peoples and has had the effect of accenting the role of patriarchy.

ON THE STRUCTURING OF RELATIONSHIPS

One could rationalize the Akan naming system by saying it is evidence of co-operation and complementarity, a system in which a man enables a woman to bring her forebears back to life in return for enabling him to keep the names of his forebears alive. As the male complements the female in procreation, so in societal organization there is a bifocal system that operates on role-differentiation by age and sex. This is said to be devoid of the element of hierarchy. But it is at this point that contact with Western patriarchy has had its worst effect. From horizontal relations and roles of equal value, a dominant structure that operates hierarchically has been imposed. Needless to say, because it suited the Akan men, not only did they not inform the West of what the Akan culture demands, they collaborated and proceeded to enjoy the new power thrust upon them and were only too happy to operate these alien structures of domination. The process continues today.

West African market women are the only ones who have been able to effectively use the traditional all-women's structures, before which the patriarchal armor of Westernized governments cracks. Christian women simply begin their own churches or play it the men's way as Western women have done for centuries—using coping tactics that are particularly African. Women are not involved in policy-making, but they are known to render policies unworkable. Where it hurts is that "woman power" becomes labeled as having nothing but a nuisance value. Her right to join in deciding what is right is not recognized.

QUESTIONS OF BELIEF

Politically, with the growth of the male principle in religion, mother-centeredness was losing its hold. Westernization simply accelerated the process. On the familial scene it held out when in personal relationships even the most rabid misogynist African man remained attached to the breasts that fed him. The belief that a mother's displeasure was the most inauspicious influence in the life of a man kept men respectful of mother's wishes.

On the other hand, religious beliefs worked what I consider negative influence in the lives of women, Christians included. Is the African woman who is a Christian in a position to ignore cultural demands that stem from primal religious beliefs? For instance, is she prepared to test the threat that a girl whose "bride service" is not fulfilled will die at childbirth? Is she ready to test out the belief that unconfessed adultery brings about difficult births and that a girl whose puberty rites have not been performed dares not become pregnant? How does one apply the hermeneutic of suspicion, under the threat of death, especially that of one's child? Perhaps with one's own life one could experiment, but with another's one has no right. That life belongs to the whole *abusa*. The mother is the link in the chain and dares not break it.

It is clear that female sexuality is a pretext for the exclusion of women of child-bearing age from rituals of African religion, but does anyone dare to undertake a feminist critique of this primal religion? When religious beliefs hedge the woman-spirit in with the threat of death, where is she the lifegiver? The question "Why is this?" is a natural one. My reading of the situation is that the deep sense of awe surrounding childbearing places a distinction between men and women that is irksome to men. A means of appropriating this awesomeness had to be found. It is at this stage that a male-centered interpretation was invented with the aid of religion.

An illustration from the Yoruba religion might prove instructive.

444

THE IFA ORACLE

Looking at women and religion, one cannot but turn to what diviners have had to say about women. Ifa says:

> Women are liars,
> Women are traitors,
> Let no man open his mind to women.

Male fears of the female, couched in religious language, are put in the mouth of divine beings who are themselves male figures. These fears abound in African myths as in lewd, male jokes. Osa perpetuates it, telling those who consult Orunmila, "Oya is more dangerous than Sango" (the wife is more dangerous than the husband).[2] "Meji," a poem, which on the surface is about how the silk-cotton tree survives all the machinations of her enemies, is seen by Judith Gleason as referring to aggressiveness[3] and how the female power is manifested in magic and the use of witchcraft. The Yoruba word for a witch is said to mean "mother eats," reflecting the power of Yemoga, mother of all the divinities save Oduduwa and Obatola, and who is also mother of all witches.

It seems, however, that this potential for witchery is passed down the women's line! It is an attribute of women, derived from a myth announcing the destinies of three divinities: Ogun, the warlord, Obatala, the molder of human beings, and Yemoja, our mother. In eisegesis of the myth, Orunmila, the divinity of the Ifa Oracle, is said to explain to women through divines that "God's power to women" is given "to sustain the world." Thus women are warned not to exaggerate but to exercize their "prerogative with discretion." The oracle continues: "Alas, our Mother is a violent woman." Explaining the difference in how men and women use their aggressiveness, the oracle says:

> Women kill men
> Or do nothing else against them;
> but men kill, beat, rape, and enslave women.

This, the oracle explains, is the result of the test of aggressiveness between Yemoja and Obatala, in which Yemoja was the loser.[4]

When I read the poems, I see how the persistence, faith, foresight, and sheer determination to perpetuate life propels the cotton plant to survival. What is called magic here, I choose to call God's grace. The tricks played on death by Esu in the parallel poem "Ogunda Meji" enables Orunmila to appropriate death's wife. To me, this reads like the contrived manipulation of religio-cultural traditions to get what one wants. The triumph of technology over magic/religion may be a positive development, but I doubt that the manipulation of religion by men is positive:

> "How can you eat a man's food and turn around to kill him?' asked Esu. . . .
> When death did not know what else to do, he said, "Tell Orunmila that he can keep the women."

We may not agree with Gleason's interpretation,[5] but the fact of the double standards by which we judge aggressiveness in women and men is instructive.

The Ifa explanation of the division between male and female falls far short of the theory of complementarity. It legitimates a state of antagonism, and sacralizes men's manipulation of the instruments of divination, to dictate who women are and what is expected of them. What strikes me most is this: men, unable to fathom the reason for the resilience of women-spirit, have chosen to *imagine* her quality of understanding of life and her strength of spirit as emanating from magical sources. It is something of an irony, a life-denying irony, that men's manipulation of the spirit world should be called *religion*, whereas women's spirituality is disparaged as sustained by *magic* and therefore needing to be controlled. Men's fear of women, their counterpart, is a source of pain.

WOMEN'S RELIGION

I continue to struggle with what holds women to religion when male-manipulated religion consigns women to a situation of submission and alienation. Reading Flora Nwapa's *Efuru*[6] and her *Never Again*,[7] it dawned on me that the spirit of religion, to which women and some men are bound, is the spirit of life. If to create and preserve life is the core of women-being, why do African women, whose lives are centered on childbearing, become devotees of a childless goddess, Uhamiri, who demands the same status of them? So asks Nwapa at the end of *Efuru*.

A white American ex-nun responded to this goddess with a poem in which she saw Uhamiri, living a rich, benevolent, and caring life uncontrolled by a male partner, choosing only childless women as her agents. Perhaps this needs to be wheeled to the center stage of African women's lives to change minds and attitudes. She ends the poem with the words:

> I look to you Uhamiri.
> I look to you for courage in my life
> And I promise it's not just
> Foolish idolatory that makes
> Me gaze at you in wonder and love.

She names the piece "Uhamiri, the Holy Near." She was convinced that Uhamiri, the goddess of the lake, is an authentic manifestation of the Akan insight concerning woman as the foundation of life. Will the contemporary fascination with the goddess free the woman-spirit? African women have never been without goddesses, but they have sought life from divinities both female and male. The question is this: What does one do with the aspects of this religion-based culture that require women to "mother" life and leave men with the spiritual duty of "managing" this life, and give men the power of determining what constitutes the well-being of the whole community?

African women, working, living, and independent of men, are still committed to the welfare of others. The hearth of the matter here is that the divine is made in the image of the male by men, for worship by women who are denied access to the means of ascertaining the will of the divine except through men, for even the diviners of the will of Uhamiri are men.

African culture has the power to circulate religious concepts with consequences that make women resist change, avoid risks, and seek stable, secure structures within which to have and to hold their children. (The category "children" includes husbands!) They crave for a calm atmosphere within which to promote the integrity and welfare of the community they have risked their individual lives to engender, build up, and sustain.

The Yoruba proverb says:

> However narrow the entrance,
> A layer will get to her eggs.

These self-fulfilling proverbs from nature and myths of antiquity are the real indicators of the prioritizing of African women's self-image.

I am at the verge of labeling religion the most subtle and the most dangerous male technique invented to co-opt women to collaborate in the suppression of their own powers, that power calumnized as magic. I hesitate when I ask myself, "What is Uhamiri's role in African culture? What shall I say about her?" She, who protected whole villages, women and men, and kept them safe from the ravages of war, what does one say of the goddesses of the lake whose closest associates are women who mother, but are not mothers? What does one say of Uhamiri the thunder, who is also Uhamiri the kind? The hearth of the matter is the manipulative use of religion.

Rituals that use sexuality to divest women of power and enthrone men for the same reason, are found in African religion as in Christianity, making the African Christian woman a creature that has little hope of being defined by anything but gender. Women who seek leadership in a mixed group of men and women may find themselves being told to see themselves as "the supreme head" of all the women in that group. This, they will be told, is the "high honor that any reasonable worker in the Lord's vineyard should gladly accept." Men do not find it sufficient to be "supreme head" of the men—they cannot afford to have women who are not under the control of men. If this should not hurt, I do not know what should.

COMPLEMENTARITY

Complementarity, the final African argument for discounting contemporary women's self-naming, appears a rare gem and a most exquisite jewel, until one tries to wear it. My sisters, be not deceived, for it is nothing but a soap-bubble shimmering at the edge of a child's blowpipe. Touch it and it is no more. That is the hearth of the matter. African women hurt, because, although accepting the mothering of the community, their well-being as persons is treated as secondary, if it is considered at all. Women hurt when the mode and extent of complementary tasks are determined by the gender and not by qualities and skills within the individual persons.

African women hurt when their brothers use the final argument, *"after all you are a woman!"* To begin to deal with this final solution to the threat of women's liberation, as one who is an African and a Christian, I call on all my brothers, African or whatever, black and white, to preface all their authoritative statements about women with: "When the woman is human."

When the woman is human, then, complementarity will work and a life-venerating culture will grow; how and to what extent each person complements the other will be determined by negotiation. An Akan proverb says, *Wannkasa nam ho a woma wo dompe*. The nearest I have seen in the English language is "The limit of the tyrant is in the endurance of the oppressed." So my contribution to the building up of true community is to make known where the hearth of the matter is and to advocate "negotiated participation."

APPENDIX

Anansesem: Appropriate Technology

Once there was a great famine. Everybody was starving and so was Kweku Ananse, his wife Aso, and their four children, Ntikuma, Big Head, Shiny Stomach, and Twiggy Legs. Kweku, Aso, and Ntikuma did all they could, but not so much as the other three. Big Head's head got bigger. You could shave or put on makeup, comb your hair or beard quite accurately, standing before Shiny Stomach's shining stomach, and Twiggy Legs could have won a leggies' competition against the mosquito. Farms were dried up. So everyone roamed the forests to see what could be found to eat. Oh, it was really bad!

One day Kweku was roaming to search for food. He found a beautiful black pot. He exclaimed, "What a gorgeous pot!" The pot retorted, "I am not called Gorgeous." "Oh, what, then, is your name?" asked Ananse. The pot replied, "My name is Fill-up-Let's-Eat." So Ananse said, "Fill up, let's eat." Immediately all the good things he had missed because of the famine appeared. Ananse ate his fill and hid the pot. So he went every day and had his meals while others starved. It did not take long before Ntikuma discovered the secret of Father Ananse and took the other children along. They had a feast, washed the pot, and put it where they had found it. Now, the pot did not like to be washed!

The next day Kweku Ananse went to "The Feast of the Pot." He was really hungry, for he had waited long to make sure no one was following. He took the pot from its hiding place, knelt before it, and intoned, "What a beautiful pot." No reply. "Oh pot, you are truly gorgeous." Not a sound. What's gone wrong? Well, before the divine being, requests must be stated three times, so Kweku in his most humble but insistent voice repeated, "Oh, Pot! I say you are really beautiful." Deep silence greeted the third and final supplication. There must be something wrong. He took a closer look. The pot had been washed!

Angry and hungry, Ananse went off deeper into the forest to look for something to eat, just as everybody else was doing. He came to a stream and there among the reeds he saw a very beautiful cane. He could not help but exclaim, "This is undoubtedly the most beautiful cane I have ever seen." The cane was offended. "I am not called Beautiful," it said. "What, then, is your name?" queried Ananse, all expectation. "My name is *Wonim ye a Yebi ma memhwe*—meaning 'If you know how to do it, go ahead and let's see.'" The cane put on a performance such as only canes know how to do. Ananse was getting the worst beating of his life. A bird watching from a branch could no longer keep "The Secret of the Cane." She whistled to Ananse, "If you were wise, you would say 'cool it.'" Kweku amidst painful screams barely managed to say "Cool it," and the beautiful cane went back to its hiding place.

There is the perfect revenge for all who used the pot without understanding. He paid periodic visits and made sure he appeared well fed. Ntikuma discovered the secret, took the other children along, and the cane did only what canes know best. That is why the ancients say, "If you see someone doing something, do not do the same thing, for you will not know all the taboos involved." And that is why I say: like appropriate technology, if an African theology is not appropriate for women, it is not appropriate for Africa.

NOTES

1. See the Akan folktale in the Appendix. Told to explain why naughty children are caned, it carries other messages, such as the self-centeredness of the male principle as exhibited by Ananse in contrast to the solidarity of youth and the other-directedness of women.

2. Wande Abimbola, "Oyeku Meji," in *Sixteen Great Poems of Ifa* (New York: UNESCO, 1975), pp. 105–8, lines 159-61.

3. Wande Abimbola, *Ifa Divination Poetry* (New York: NOK Publishers, 1977).

4. Wande Abimbola, "Oyeku Meji." It seems to me that his interpretation of Osa Meji's referring to "victory over one's enemies, and freedom from death and illness" would be close to the ordinary use of the poem. Abimbola studied to be a diviner. See also, his *Ifa, An Exposition of Literary Corpus* (Ibadan: Oxford University Press, 1976).

5. Judith Gleason (with Aworinda and Ogundipe), *A Recitation of Ifa, Oracle of the Yoruba* (New York: Grossman Publishers, 1973), pp. 12–13 and 136–37.

6. Flora Mwapa, *Efuru* (Hienemann, Africa Writers Series).

7. Flora Mwapa, *Never Again* (Oslo, Norway: West Africa Book Venture).

47

Wrestling in the Night

SAMUEL RAYAN, SJ

Reading Gustavo Gutiérrez's fine work *On Job*,[1] I became aware that several of its leading themes and emphases were, time and again, meeting, mingling, and parting in my mind with kindred concerns and accents of two other cherished works: the Bhagavadgítá (= Gítá)[2] and the *Poems of Gítánjali* (= *Poems*)[3]. The Gítá is a sacred text, a poem, a dialogue, like the book of Job, and quite ancient too; it is Job's near contemporary, being probably younger than Job by a century or two. The *Poems*, however, are quite recent and are not particularly sacred or religious though deeply human and spiritual. The author of the *Poems* was a schoolgirl who died of cancer soon after her sixteenth birthday; the authors of the other two poetic colloquies were, we may surmise, women or men of mature years, skilled in all the sophistication of philosophical theories and theological debates. The cultural and religious differences among the three works are deep. All the more remarkable is the overlapping of so many of their stresses, the coincidence of the spirit they breathe, and the convergence of their ultimate thrust.

WORD OF GOD

All three works represent our pursuit of God and God's pursuit of us through the tangled web of our painful, conflict-ridden, historical existence. Not only pursuit but struggle and wrestling of the human and the divine: wrestling in the night, wrestling with nameless, unnameable mystery, which in the end leaves us "dislocated," renamed, blessed, and equipped to face the world and build a future (see Gen. 32). All three works open on a scene of perplexity and pain with which it is hard to come to terms. Job is full of lament and rebellion; Arjuna of the Gítá raises questions and breaks down in anguish; Gítánjali too has some sharp whys, though she clothes her protests and laments in gentle trust. In all three works the sufferer finally stands face to face with God and finds peace or meaning or the strength to act and to endure, not in intellectual and reasoned answers to questions posed by the critical mind, but in direct spiritual experience that we can only describe as mystical. In each case the encounter is mediated by nothing but the clarity of intense innocent suffering or of dawning conversion. In each case, the new experience tends to subvert traditional positions in theology and piety.

In Job God speaks from the heart of the storm; God speaks only in response to

Job's demands—and that, at the close of a lengthy debate among friends. In the Gítá God (Krishna) takes the initiative and sustains the dialogue from start to finish. The use of dialogue to express and convey a spiritual experience is itself highly significant. Dialogue is not only a literary form, but responds to the inner structure of spiritual experience, which at its higher reaches is interpersonal exchange, the weaving of a relationship in partnership between God and human beings. In the *Poems* it is only the young poet who sings her sad songs, but many a line is prayer directed to God or to loved ones; and it is not hard to discern behind the songs, within the songs, the answering, the prompting, the enabling voice of God.

Common to all three is a sense of the overwhelming gratuitousness of God's love and the call to respond, or actual response, in selfless concern for God, for God's project for the world, for God's people, for God's earth and ours. In each case disinterested faith and love are shown as correlates of God's gracious love made manifest in creation and, mysteriously, in history—even in the history of painful reeducation and testing by fire. There is in every case a distinct journey from despondency to joyful living or dying; from preoccupation with the ego to other-centeredness; from dharma (righteousness) as traditional way of life to dharma as innovative collaboration with God's love-designs and best wishes for our world; and from narrow individual or group interest to concern for the welfare of the world as a whole and of every created reality.

We cannot but take the three testimonies together. The voice of the great sufferers and questioners of ancient Israel has become our inheritance within the movement stemming from a unique Israelite, Jesus of Nazareth. The testimony also of the seekers, seers, and fighters of old who originated and molded India's culture and spirituality holds and nourishes some of the deepest roots of our life. And the witness of our simple and strong sisters and brothers like Gítánjali releases into the strife and confusion of our history a clarity and hope and faith from which we are able to live. The three words belong together, and become God's word addressed to us and our community here and now, judging and gracing us, and challenging us to be creative and free for one another.

JOB

Believing for Nothing

Gutiérrez starts his reflections from the wager on which, from a literary standpoint, the Book of Job rests. The wager concerns the reality, even the possibility, of disinterested faith in God and love for God. The position of the satan is that religion is mercenary. Persons believe because believing pays, and not because they view God as worthy *in se* of love and following. In human eyes God's worth lies in the wealth and welfare God can and does bestow. God is "buying" devotees and so gaining a foothold in human history. Should the flow of wealth and well-being cease, God would begin to be discarded and religion to wither away. Such is the satan's estimate of human beings and of God.

God's estimate of human beings is different. Even God can be proud of human beings. They have in them enough of nobility and greatness to be able to "believe for nothing," to love disinterestedly, to live sacrificially, to be faithful to God and neighbor even in the midst of dispossession, ruin, and pain. Of this, Job is illustration and proof. God made the bet with the satan, and in Job human beings won it for God. There is a proud revelation of the human in that "the satan has lost his wager . . . for Job continues to cling to the Lord in his suffering even when he comes close to despair."[4] Gutiérrez concurs with the revolutionary conclusion of the author of Job that there is something shallow, debasing, demonic about a utilitarian religion in which faith and behavior hinge on expectation of reward. In self-seeking religion all the relationships are vitiated; there is in it the construction of an idol instead of an encounter with God.[5] It leads to "contempt for human beings and a distorted understanding of God."[6] This point, debated in the subsequent dialogue in Job, will be treated at length with great subtlety in the Bhagavadgítá.

Job's painful journey, traced through the dialogues, lands him and us on a host of problems and many discoveries. Suffering of the innocent raises the problem of justice, which is basically a problem of God and of faith in God. Instead of rejecting God as torturer of the innocent, Job challenges the foundations of the prevailing theology of retribution. Eventually he comes to see that "if justice is to be understood in its full meaning and scope, it must be set in the context of God's overall plan for history."[7] This is a perspective to which careful attention and elaboration are accorded in the Gítá. When Job found that his experience at once of innocence and of suffering contradicted the doctrine of retribution, "he had the courage to face up to this contradiction and to proclaim it for all to hear." He rejected both the traditionally and officially upheld moral order and the God who was alleged to be its ground and guarantor.[8] His cry and quest is for a new image of God and a new language. Our cry and quest today is no different.

Shifts

In the process a number of mental and spiritual shifts occur.

1. Job moves "from an ethic centered on personal rewards" to "another focused on the needs (and, we may add, the further possibilities) of one's neighbor."[9]

2. Along with that goes widening of concern and an expansion of the spirit when attention shifts from personal pain to the wretched condition of the vast masses of the oppressed of the land.

3. As a result the conviction deepens that "real belief in God entails solidarity with the poor so as to ease their undeserved suffering by establishing 'uprightness and judgment.' " To go out of oneself, laying aside one's own problem and pain, in order to liberate and lift up other sufferers is "to find a way to God" and to a new language about God.[10] Gustavo makes the significant point that "vision of God . . . and defense of the poor . . . are combined in the experience of Job as a man of justice. They are two aspects of a single gift from the Lord and a single road that leads to the Lord."[11]

4. Once the truth is grasped that the suffering of the poor is not caused by God but by the wicked, the rich, and the exploiter, the whole argument takes a new turn. God is no longer the accused; God is seen as the challenger of the wicked rich, as the friend of the poor and as an imperative of justice for the oppressed.

5. With that Job is able to transcend "a penal view of history," and finds himself enfolded in a world of grace. There unfolds a surpriseful awareness that the mean-

ing of justice overflows its legal and prophetic definitions. Justice is far richer and profounder than retribution. Justice must be seen as situated within the framework of God's gratuitous love. May we hold, then, that it is love and not justice that has the final say?[12] We must be careful not to suggest a dichotomy and distance between love and justice. Justice remains crucial because it is love's basic form and prime imperative. In a situation of oppression, God cannot be revealed except as a call for and practice of justice, and a clear option for the oppressed.

6. Perception of this unbreakable link between justice and love is a step toward recognition of the utter freedom of God who cannot be shackled by anything, not even by our ethics and theologies of justice,[13] but can be encountered only within the practice of justice and loving relationships. That means concern for justice will unfold into contemplation of God's gratuitous love and abounding tenderness, which provide justice with its true horizons, reference points, and depths of meaning. The justice of God is God's love that gives and forgives endlessly. Among such gifts are opportunities and challenges, at times painful and mysterious, to grow to the Everest possibilities of the human heart—opportunities of the kind offered to Job and to Jesus.

7. One aspect of this growth is the insight that there is more to creation and God's ways than to serve human utility; not everything is for direct human use and control. Much in creation is God's freedom, God's joy, God's *leela* or play, as we would say in India. Nature is not all consumer goods or merchandise. Much of it is art and its meaning is contemplation through which nature becomes we and we become it.[14]

8. There is, then, the experience of growth from lament and bitter questioning to an attitude of wonder, worship, silence, and surrender. In the end is Job renouncing his "lamentations and dejected outlook" rather than repenting of his rash questioning, as Gutiérrez suggests?[15] Why does his encounter with God not culminate in an ecstatic song of joy and praise as Arjuna's encounter does in the Bhagavadgítá?

9. That song is perhaps implied in Job's passage from a faith based on hearsay, dogmatic traditions, and external authorities to a faith based on direct engagement with the mystery of the divine. The passage from ideas of God and pieties gathered from conventions and fashioned in times of well-being to others springing from new spaces in the soul carved out by suffering, is big surely with songs of joy yet unsung.

Method

As we listen to Job and his friends, "it becomes clear that we are in the presence of two types of theological reasoning." Job's friends "take certain principles as their starting point and try to apply them to Job's case." Their method is a priori, doctrinal, abstract. Job, on the other hand, starts from the concrete reality of his experience, which he finds subversive of abstract principles. Gutiérrez emphasizes:

> Job's words are a criticism of every theology that lacks human compassion and contact with reality; the one-directional movement from theological principles to life really goes nowhere. A quest for understanding that is based on human and religious experience gives a glimpse of other ways of speaking (and keeping silent) about God.[16]

Within the experience-based approach itself two phases may be distinguished. They mark Job's theological journey. The first phase raises questions, seeks to criticize and to unravel, to speak and to formulate. It then deepens into the second phase, which is one of contemplation, adoration, and silence. At this stage we live gently with questions to which no answers are available; the questions are no longer experienced as painful, nagging, or imperious, because they have become reset within a larger horizon of mystery, which is best approached in worship and wonder, and expressed in the language of doxology rather than that of dogma. The questions have become cherished symbols of our creaturely finiteness, the frontiers where we are unceasingly loved into being. We are happy that the God we adore is greater than our heart, our theology, and our church. We are glad we can sit in silence and joy over the unspeakable pressure of the real upon our heart. Apophatic theology is welcome back. Our ancestors, the Seers and *Rishis*, faced with the real beyond name and form, kept repeating *Neti Neti* (*na iti, na iti*), "Not thus, Not thus," but always other and greater, and greater still.

Job wrestled with himself and with unmerited suffering. He wrestled with his own theological convictions and their God as these were being undermined by his personal experience and the history of the oppressed masses. He wrestled with the God of his faith until, beyond the conventional conceptions of justice, he came to see the truth of the wonder of God's freedom and capacity for love—a love that is not shallow or sentimental but strong enough to put God's friends and God's children through tests like those that Job and Jesus underwent in order to foster and bring out what is most human and noble in them, what is unconditionally faithful and selfless. For God what matters is not painlessness but the making great of those God loves: fuller, richer, deeper being for women and men and things.

THE BHAGAVADGÍTÁ

The Thrust

This is a different kind of poem, a different drama. There is no explicit wager here as in Job. Nevertheless the central concern is identical. Is the human being, suffering from massive deprivation, humiliation, and despondency, capable of listening to God and working with God for the defeat of *adharama* (injustice) and the establishment of dharma (justice), not to gain anything for oneself but for the good of the world and the welfare of all creatures? The Gítá affirms the possibility and the necessity, and thus rejoins Job.

Being a dialogue between Krishna and Arjuna, the Gítá would correspond structurally to the last section of Job where God addresses the sufferer after the latter had raised a point and taken a stand. In the course of the dialogue themes are discussed that exhibit close affinity to themes in Job: God's graciousness, the gratuitousness of God's love, the position of that love as the ultimate source of reality; concern for human persons and respect for their limited freedom; being partial to the poor and taking sides with the victims; revelation in nature and the call to contemplation; the framing of nature within the horizons of history; challenge to conventional theologies and practices; encountering God in the midst of history's conflicts; and a deepening awareness of the divine as unspeakable mystery. The

Gítá opens as does Job with a scene of crisis and pain. The turning point comes with a vision of the divine, issuing into ecstasy and surrender. But the decisive factor that commits Arjuna to the historical tasks named by the Lord is the revelation of and encounter with the Lord's unconditional love.

The Setting

The Bhagavadgítá, a poem that proposes to probe deeply into "the verities of a life of integrity,"[17] stands in the *Bhíshma-parvan* (Bhíshma canto) of the massive Indian epic, *Mahabharata*. Though critics are divided in their view of the relationship between the epic story and the doctrinal elaborations of the Gítá, the reading of the Gítá is greatly helped by memory of its literary setting. The poem is a long dialogue between Arjuna, a warrior, and Krishna, his charioteer, the manifestation of the supreme person, in the battlefield of Kurukshetra. Arjuna is one of the five Pándava princes, of whom the eldest, Yudhishthira, was noted for his passion for justice and fair play. War broke out between the Pándavas and their hundred half brothers, the Kauravas, the eldest of whom, Duryodhana, was an evil man. Yudhishthira became king, established suzerainty over all neighboring kingdoms, and celebrated the occasion with extravagant show of wealth and power. Envy, fanned by this success and hatred provoked by the behavior of the Pándava prince Bhíma, a blustering giant and bully, led Duryodhana to plot the destruction of the Pándavas by fraud and arson. The scheme failed. Duryodhana then invited Yudhishthira to a fraudulent dice contest. The Pándava king lost, forfeiting all that he had. The blind father of the hundred brothers had the penalties canceled, and got a new capital built for the Pándavas. Yudhishthira let himself be coaxed into a second dice contest in which he staked and lost everything again, including his freedom, his brothers, and their common wife, Draupadi. Draupadi was publicly insulted and humiliated by the Kaurava side. By the terms of the contest, the Pándavas had to live in exile in the forest for twelve years, and incognito for an additional year.

Duryodhana's attempts to kill them or incriminate them having miscarried, and the thirteen years having elapsed, the Pándavas come back demanding the return of their authority and kingdom. Entrenched in power, Duryodhana refuses. All efforts at conciliation and a peaceful settlement founder; all the efforts of Krishna and others to mediate were thwarted by the Kaurava chief. To avoid war and spare the people, the Pándavas offer to forgo their royal rights and be satisfied with five villages. Even this was denied. War was what Duryodhana wanted and war was the one last resort left to the Pándavas to secure a minimum of justice and to curb fraud, crowned and enthroned in insolence. Both sides approached Krishna for help. This Yadava king would join one side as a noncombatant ally while his army would support the other side. The Kauravas chose Krishna's troops, and the Pándavas were happy to have Krishna with them as Arjuna's charioteer.

Arjuna's Grief

At zero hour, as the battle was about to begin, Arjuna, redoubtable archer who had never known defeat, suddenly broke down at the prospect of having to kill so many of his revered and beloved brothers, elders, teachers, and friends. He was overcome with compassion and sadness; his limbs quailed; his body shook, his mouth went dry, his skin burned all over; he felt unsteady, his mind began to reel, and the great bow slipped from his hand. His spirit overpowered by sorrow, he sank down on the seat of the chariot. Tears filled his troubled eyes. Stricken with weakness and bewildered about his duty, Arjuna resolved not to fight and became silent (G 1:28–30, 47; 2:1–11). It was as if the great archer had been struck down by invisible arms before the battle began—struck down like Job whose determination to seek and find a way of speaking correctly about God led him, says Gutiérrez, "through a battlefield in which . . . the shots came at him from every side."[18]

Was this the shock of a crisis of conscience? Or the anguish of being caught in "the *dharmic* dilemma of a war, which was both just and pernicious?"[19] Or was it a failure of nerve and "a momentary collapse of morale?" Was the claim to a sudden flood of compassion a species of rationalization? Was Arjuna dismayed in reality by the fate that confronted him as he stood facing his own masters like Drona and Bhíshma, in the art of war? Was he retreating from the arena of history because the action he had to perform was painful?[20] It was at any rate "a swing into inaction, a virtual death of the spirit."[21] It was the dark night of the soul.[22] Arjuna is not, as Job was, struck down with malignant ulcers. He is afflicted with something far deeper, far more excruciating: doubt and despondency; the bitter memory of injuries heaped gratis on him and his brothers; the searing memory of Draupadi's humiliation. The Kurukshetra scene is the arrival point of a long history of fraud, frustration, and suffering, and of pride trampled underfoot. It was for Arjuna a galling moment and a crucifying dilemma. The question of innocent suffering is not raised; but it could be. Not that the Pándavas are faultless, but that this particular conjunction of events and the enormity of the situation are the result of evil Kaurava machinations.

Three other questions are raised and discussed. They concern (1) the traditional theology of withdrawal and inaction versus the new call to committed historical involvement; (2) the secret or open desire-driven, self-centered activity versus the ideal of self-denying, other-centered commitment; and (3) the realization of the interrelatedness of human beings and the universe of realities, together with their rootedness in God who comprehends and permeates everything, holding them together and accompanying their evolutionary and conflictual journey toward completion.

Retreat versus Involvement

Krishna finds Arjuna's way of resolving the crisis simplistic and unacceptable. He would urge action: "cast off thy petty faintheartedness and arise." Do not falter, but resolve on battle for that is every Kshatriya's duty (G 2:3,31,33,37). If action is seen as tightening of ties to the unreality of "phenomenal," ephemeral existence, know that abstention from work will not make you free from action; there is no actionless existence. Do thou then thy alloted work (G 3:3,4,5,8). There are reasons for this injunction: work is your contribution to the turning of the wheel of the world. Not to make a contribution, though benefiting from the world process, is to be evil like the wicked who cook food for themselves alone; "verily they eat sin" (G 3:13,16). Act in order to set an example to one another: What would happen if everyone abstained from work? God is ever engaged in work lest the world fall in ruin (G 3:30–34; 4:15). The world is of worth to God; it is no illusion; it is God's project. So precious is it to God that God labors unceasingly for its progress, and accepts responsibility for being a model to human beings.[23]

We may not choose to drift passively down the streams of historical processes. We must choose action to affirm ourselves and accept responsibility for ourselves, for each other, for the earth. The war in which Arjuna is engaged is, we are told, a just war. What is one to do with those who care nothing for justice and, like the Kauravas, violate all dharma with impunity? Paul Mundschenk observes:

> There is a clear implication here that it is incumbent upon us to stand up and resist others when their actions are clear expressions of insolence or injustice . . . with violence or without, we are to live by dharma, righteousness, which includes standing up to every measure of evil that comes our way. Not to do so becomes our own violation of dharma, and undermines our own inner journey, our sense of reconciliation.[24]

To withdraw is to leave the world as it is in its injustice, fraud, and conceit, and to decline responsibility for its redemption and transformation.

An old theology or ideology of flight from the world is rejected. It is in action that the self affirms, remakes, and realizes itself and the world. Are we not defined by what we have done, and still more by what we can yet do? Does not even physical science tell us that "action rather than matter is basic?"[25] In an earlier scene in the epic, during a debate with her husbands, Draupadi had passionately affirmed that life was action and no man of integrity and justice could abdicate action.[26] Conventional theology and spirituality bade Arjuna turn back from action on grounds that Krishna would subsequently show to be inauthentic and questionable because they fail to take into account the whole realm of reality, the complexity of historical situations, and above all, the world of God's grace and love, which must be the ultimate reference point in all matters whatever.

Mundschenk invites us to reflect that Arjuna represents us, "the variegated, protean community called humankind." We, too, start out confused. Arjuna's predicament, like ours, "arises from an elemental characteristic of human action in the world. . . . Human action must frequently be carried out within the context of moral uncertainty." Mundschenk adds that the uncertainty is "more poignantly felt in the context of modern capitalist society where competition is the fuel which feeds the social machinery."[27]

Nishkámakarma: Disinterested Action

Action is unavoidable: it is life. But action could spring from self-centered desire and greed or from a detached heart bent on doing what is right and what would benefit the whole community and the entire world. The denunciation of selfishness and greed, which is a major theme of the Gítá (1:38,45; 2:5,8,60,62,70; 3:37, etc.), receives the most poignant expression as the battle draws to a close with the Kauravas slain and Bhíshma, the patriarch of the clan, laid low. At that point one of the victorious Pándavas declares that selfishness is death, the desire to possess is death. Bhíshma concurs: selfishness is the basic factor that destroys the inner integrity of a people. The survivors realize that the real war has only begun: the war to be waged by the soul within the soul against greed.[28] Krishna advises Yudhishthira to recognize the enemy within and to prepare for the new war. The mind of the epic is that the total carnage in which the war ends is the bitter fruit of unmitigated greed, treachery and egotism: of the Kauravas, obviously, but also of the Pándavas. The epic probes their hidden greed and pride. They had obtained suzerainty through conquest; they had indulged in empire-building activity. This and the subsequent exhibition of pomp and power lie at the root of the catastrophe.

It is made clear that Yudhishthira accepts the challenge to the dice contest in the hope of acquiring Duryodhana's land and wealth. He persisted in the game despite heavy losses and the evidence of cheating, because of the "competitive frenzy of the excited gambler." The Pándavas practiced trickery and unfair means to kill Drona, Karna, and Duryodhana. Even the great Bhíshma was led by self-interest to equivocal and noncommitted answers when Draupadi raised the question of Yudhishthira's right to stake her in the contest after he had forfeited his own freedom. It was the clash of unbridled greed on both sides that led to the tragedy of total death.[29] Krishna Chaitanya states the message pointedly when he notes that "the world cannot survive if every man is predatory."[30] The alienation and disruption we experience today at the core of our personal and societal life stand in direct line with and direct proportion to the loyalty with which we have followed Adam Smith's capitalist doctrine of self-interest—that ultimate ground on which greed has been organized on world scale.

The Gítá, therefore, is pointing another way; a way of life instead of one of death, a way of being and acting in partnership with God for the re-creation and completion of the world. What saves our humanity is neither flight from the world nor immersion in it, but discerning commitment. What matters is neither inaction nor action but "disinterested action," other-centered work, sacrificial living (G 3:3–10). "The world is in the bonds of action, unless the action is consecration" (G 3:9, J. Mascaro's version). For Arjuna renunciation *of* action was the only solution, but for Krishna the real solution consists in renunciation *in* action.[31] Gítá teaches not the abandonment of work but the conversion of all works into *nishkámakarma*, desireless action.[32] We have a right to action, not to its ultimate outcome; let not fruits of action, reward, and gain be our motive. He who hugs desires attains no peace; the path to peace is action free of desires and longings, without any sense of I and mine (G 2:47,55,56,70,71; 3:19; 4:20,21; 5:2,10; 6:24; 18:6,9,10,23,26,49,54). It is the Yogin who goes beyond the fruits of meritorious deeds assigned to the study of the Vedas, austerities, and almsgiving who attains the supreme and final status. (G 8:28). The best sacrifice, penance, or gift is that which proceeds from a sense of duty and faith, without the expectation of reward or return (G 17:11,17–25).

Significantly, the last prayer Arjuna makes in the Gítá is for the knowledge of the true nature of renunciation and surrender (G 18:1). More significantly, Arjuna is told in the end to leave all duty and religion behind and care only for Krishna and the welfare of the world (G 18:66; see 54–66). Commercial religion and mercenary ethics, which hinge on hope of retribution and reward, are as firmly transcended here as in the book of Job.

Going beyond this negative teaching on renunciation, the Gítá demands that work is oriented toward the noblest, altruistic goals. The goal is *lokasamgraha*, the maintenance of world order, the unity of the cosmos, and the interconnectedness of society. The goal is to become *sarvabhutahite ratah*, taking intense delight in the good and well-being of all creatures (G 3:20,25; 5:25; 12:4).[33] In disinterested action there is passionate interest, but it is other-centered, centered on God's purposes for the world, centered on God. As we have seen, work must be done as a sacrifice. The world arose from God's sacrifice. Sacrifice is the source of other-centered existence and life as community. And ultimately life is consecration to God (G 3:7–10; 9:27–34; 12:20; 18:54–65).

The conclusion is that renunciation of fruit and reward, and the surpassing of mercenary religion, is but the negative side of something profoundly positive: a way of attaching ourselves to God and God's program for the world. Going to the Lord and being with the Lord in the company of all creatures is the final fruit of life. Paradoxically, then, nonattachment is shown as yielding the highest reward, the inner fruit of other-centered action. The fruit of love is love and life. The fruition of disinterested devotion and service is "deepened being."[34]

Centering in God

Getting involved in history and striving for the unity and welfare of creation in its entirety, Arjuna is to seek and find God in all realities. As he makes progress, his transformation deepens. He is helped by Krishna to center himself and the cosmos on Krishna's person. Already in 2:61, a pointed reference to Krishna instructs Arjuna to "remain firm in Yoga, intent on me." From then on Krishna is presented both as the Absolute and as the Incarnate in history. He is the origin and the end, the ultimate resting place of the universe. The world holds together in him. He dwells in the heart of every creature. Those who know his birth and work "will come home" and will know no separation. Therefore, "resign all works to Me; take refuge in Me; see all existence in Me; see Me in everything and everything in Me" (G 3:30–32; 4:8–10,35; 7:1–7,13–20; 6:30–31,47). Krishna's wonder, beauty, and saving power are presented in many colors and accents (8:4–7,13–15; 9:4–7,16,19,22,26; 10:4–8), until the call sounds to total surrender:

> Give Me thy mind, give Me thy heart,
> Give Me thy offering and thy adoration;
> And thus with thy soul in harmony,
>   and making Me thy supreme goal,
>   thou shalt in truth come to Me.
> [9:34 = 18:65, Mascaro's version].
> He who works for Me, who loves Me,
> whose End Supreme I am,
>   free from all things, and with love for all creation
>   he in truth comes to Me [11:55].

The whole of chapter 12 is devoted to urging us to focus on Krishna, to fix our minds on him with worshipful faith, to lay all our actions on him, to set our thoughts on him, to make his service the supreme aim of life, and to perform actions solely for his sake. Those who do so "come to Me; in Me shall they live hereafter; they are dear to Me; and exceedingly dear are those who, with faith and love, hear and heed this life-giving word of Mine" (chap. 12; see also 13:2,10,18,28; 18:54–58,63–70).

The first outcome of this focusing on Krishna is a confession of faith on the part of Arjuna: Krishna is proclaimed the Supreme Brahman and all his words are accepted as true (10:12–18). Arjuna has been brought to the point where he now wants to meditate—center himself—on Krishna. How may he do it? He is instructed to think of whatever is the very best, the highest, the most excellent in any sphere or line of being or activity, and to see it as a symbol suggestive of something of the unutterable mystery that is Krishna:

> I am the Self seated in the heart of all things . . .
> Of the lights, I am the radiant sun . . .
> Of the senses, I am mind and of beings I am consciousness . . .
> Of weapons, I am the thunderbolt . . .
> Of creations, I am the beginning . . .
> Of Feminine beings, I am Fame and Prosperity, Speech,
>   Memory, Intelligence, Constancy, and patient Forgiveness . . .
> I am the Beauty of all things beautiful . . .
> I am the Goodness of all who are good . . .
> I am the silence of all hidden mysteries . . .
> And of the knowers of wisdom, I am the Wisdom
>   [10:19–40].

In sum, then,

> Know that whatever is beautiful and good,
> whatever has glory and power,
> is only a portion of my own radiance. . . .
> Know that with one single fraction of my Being,
> I pervade and support the universe [10: 41–42].

A revelation of the mystery in a riot of symbols; and a direct experience of the mystery given in a discourse (chap. 9 and 10). We are far from the din and horror of the battlefield, and Arjuna is waking from his trauma. "My bewilderment is gone from me, says he, because I have been granted the grace of a Word concerning the Self, the Supreme Mystery" (11:1).

However, he does not yet commit himself to action on behalf of justice. That final conversion takes place only at the very end when Arjuna will stand ready to do Krishna's word (18:70). It comes as the result of a further revelation, a deeper experience, given not in symbolic discourse but in direct vision, though that, too, is and cannot but be made up of symbols. From spiritual trauma and paralysis there is no exit via reasoning and argument. It is not his friends' theology nor his own outraged logic that transforms Job from a lamenting and debating sufferer into a contemplative capable of placing pain meaningfully within a world enveloped in God's gratuitous love. Job's conversion occurs within a transit from hearsay to vision. The same pattern is realized in the Gítá. It is as the *Kena Upanishad* says:

he is known in the ecstasy of an awakening (Kena II.4).

That ecstasy is the content of chapter 11. The discourse-revelations already given bring Arjuna to prayer for vision (11:3–4). The vision is granted together with a new eye, an eye of faith and love, with which to perceive the vision (G 11:8). At the sight of Krishna's cosmic form, resplendent with the light of a thousand suns, with many mouths, eyes, ornaments, and weapons, with face turned everywhere, carrying all creation in his body, wonderful and terrible, Arjuna is overcome with astonishment, terror, and rapture. He is transported with devotion, praise, and prayer:

> I bow before thee, I prostrate in adoration,
>   and I beg thy grace, O gracious Lord!
> As a father to his son, as a friend to his friend,
>   as a lover to his beloved,
> Thou, O Lord, should bear with me [11:44].

The chapter closes with renewed accent on unconditional love as the only authentic relationship between God and human beings. It is not by Vedic studies or austerities or almsgiving but by unswerving devotion alone can Krishna be truly seen and entered into (G 11:52–54).

Both Job and Arjuna had profound spiritual experiences that came to them in the hour of darkness and changed them. To Job God spoke of the mystery of creation; to Arjuna God gave a vision of the divine in its cosmic dimensions. To the one, God spoke from the heart of the storm; the other was spoken to while a tempest of doubt and dismay was lashing his soul. Job was rendered speechless by a volley of questions from the Lord of the storm; Arjuna is enriched with words of joyous praise. Both are reestablished in freedom, and enabled to walk in love, and work for the liberation of the victims of greed and of self-regarding religion, which uses God for private gain. Both Job and the Gítá bear witness to the truth of God's liberating presence in the midst of life's struggles and history's vicissitudes: a presence that does not tranquilize us but challenges and urges us to act against *adharma* and create a new world that could reflect and respond to the world of grace, which is God's best wishes for us.

Paul Mundschenk, struck by chapter 11 and the cosmic vision, muses that what Arjuna learns, or does not, and indeed cannot, learn, is more telling than what he sees. For "is it not the case that Krishna is another name for Ultimate Mystery? The Gítá then amazingly explores the psychology of the sensitive, caring human being at a loss as to what to do in a world whose ultimate origin and meaning remain the mystery of mysteries. As then, now Arjuna is dazzled but he never really gets a straight answer." Neither does Job, who also is dazzled into silence. But there is more than dazzle. There is insight. The heart has had a fresh touch and taste of the divine. And the heart has its experiences of which the head may know little (as Paschal reminds us).

Mundschenk is right when he points out that "a free and candid response to the immense cosmic mystery can only be an expression of deep elemental gratitude and appreciation—the sense of thankful goodwill that brings praise, benediction. One feels blessed. One overflows with the same goodness and thanksgiving at the very fact of being itself and one's own being in the world."[35] Historically expressed, gratitude and appreciation would spell collaboration with the mystery to uproot *adharma*, to enhance life, and to shape a world of freedom and love within the range of the possible, which keeps expanding.

Of such "deep elemental gratitude and appreciation," the *Poems of Gítánjali* is a telling instance.

POEMS

Gítánjali

She was born in Meerut on June 12, 1961. She died, of cancer, in Bombay on August 11, 1977. For months she lived a lingering death, her frail body racked by pain, in her home or at the hospital, between which she journeyed every few days as her body broke down or recovered from time to time. A blurb on the jacket of the *Poems* says:

> Gítánjali's line of life ascends to the agonies of early disease, then rises to wrestle with her fate. In the ultimate suffering her faith is confirmed: nothing is without purpose. She dies into the earth to be miraculously reborn in the message of her poetry.

Gítánjali loved to write, paint, and watch the sea outside her window. Her suffering and loneliness found expression in her poems. Every piece she wrote was carefully hidden away "in little corners of her room; behind books and sofa seats or toys in the *almirah*; inside books, and cushion covers, or the pockets of old discarded skirts."[36] They were found by her mother and published through the miraculous collaboration of many persons whom they had touched and moved to tears.

Voice of suffering, the poems are nevertheless free of despair and self-pity and the horror of death. They are songs of beauty and innocence, full of wisdom and "the quiet dignity of one who had learned to live with hurt." They are witnesses to a beautiful child's simplicity, love of life, ear for the music of words, and implicit faith in God.[37] In the *Poems* we do not first have a scene of suffering, dilemmas, and traumatic experiences as in Job or the Gítá, followed then by long discussions, and culminating finally in fresh spiritual insights that enable one to face life with courage on a new level of awareness beyond agonizing questions. This structural pattern, common to Job and the Gítá, is realized in the *Poems* in almost every piece. Each poem depicts the entire journey from death to life; each voices the perplexity and the courage; each reflects the pain and the faith. Nearly every poem is the whole story in miniature: each encompasses the crucifixion as well as the resurrection.

There is no word from God. God never speaks to Gítánjali as God does finally to Job and throughout to Arjuna. And yet who could doubt that what the child writes is a response to some word she has heard? No more penetrating and purifying word could there be than her pain, her suffering, her sense of the nearness of death. In the depths of pain, in the depths of her shattered soul, the girl has heard and felt. Therefore, there are times when she requests us, "please, be silent, let me hear the whisper of God."[38] There is no awe-inspiring vision here of cosmic mystery as there is in the Gítá; no passage as in Job from hearsay to sight. Yet, who can miss the inner vision from which Gítánjali's simple words take on their poignancy and their power?

Pain

Gítánjali's is an experience comparable to Job's; perhaps more tragic and hurting than his. A child is being handed over to death, and she knows it. Everything is being taken from her: the life she loves, her beloved mother and father, her friends, her pets, her dreams, her childhood. She is on the cross all the time we see her. Job was there for a while, and Arjuna for a short spell. But this child is to remain nailed till the end. And yet she would not be extinguished. She would live: she has learned to love. Gítánjali knows how to turn her complete undoing into a song with wings of praise and thanks. To turn her little life into a thing of beauty forever, enshrined in a faith that suffering only deepens and illumines.

She prays in the night for mercy upon her wounded heart. She tries not to weep, but it is not easy to hide her grief or bring the aching heart to rest. Her heart, stung with the bitter truth of death's closeness, bleeds. It is a heart at the center of which waves of sorrow follow upon sorrow's waves. Gítánjali sees herself as a harp in the hand of God: now God caresses it tenderly, now God strikes it sharply, so her heartstrings quiver with pain—heartstrings already worn out and torn with the "stress and strain" of conflicting emotions overpowering. She had been a girl full of life, and fun-loving, who could laugh and cry at the same time. Now life for her has shrunk to medicine time and dreary nights. All that's left now is a handful of memories, bittersweet. "How beautiful life was!" The memory makes her "feel overwhelmed for all that she has lost." She sees herself as a wounded bird, paralyzed and helpless; her heart sinks when the sun goes down; her spirit is in turmoil, and a dark, sinister feeling creeps up her soul: and "bruised and crushed lies my trust, faith, and soul."[39]

Death waits to claim her. She is not afraid; she will welcome death "with open arms." Gítánjali knows that death does not come on her own but on orders from the Lord. The girl's concern is that she has no costly gifts with which to receive the guest. All she has is some tears and "my wasted form." Of that form the young girl is tragically, pathetically conscious. She has nothing in all the world to claim as her own but "my distorted form." She recalls or imagines a visit to her school during an interval of recovery, and is stunned by the shocked, silent stare of friends at her shrunken form. For surely "Gítánjali is not unaware of her beauty shorn." Death was a great and welcome guest, yet at the thought of it a shudder passed through the child and she swayed.[40]

There were times when she felt utterly miserable, past tears, "in the very gates of hell." Times when she saw her world crash at her feet. Times when she wished her heart could freeze and cease to be sensitive to hurt; when she felt her store of endurance had run out; when she feared her faith might fail, and she might go mad. Before that should happen, please God, take me away. Even nature seemed to her to seek for ways of adding to her suffering. An angry night wind tore off the top of the beautiful tree she loved to watch from her window, "the only soothing sight" for her "fast dimming eyes." That, too, was taken away.[41]

Questioning and Trusting

Is Gítánjali, then, on the dung-hill with Job? The child would probably reject the metaphor. "Illness, too, is a gift of God, and Gítánjali accepts it with grace." "Nothing is unimportant, not even death."[42] That does not prevent Gítánjali from raising questions, Joblike. "What have I done to deserve this?" she asks God. "What have I done to deserve this?" she asks happiness, which once loved to be where she was. Where are the happy days gone, O lord, and why? She tells God face-to-face that God has betrayed her trust and refused her all she yearned for. She speaks as Jeremiah spoke, and cries as Jesus cried on the cross. The child has many questions, which nobody cares to answer. "Perhaps there are no answers." The answer perhaps is silence. But "the sound of silence is overbearing her feeble heart," and "gnawing at her day and night." It is "deafening." The questions and the silences "bounce back and hit her hard." But when she thinks of God's kindness in the years gone by, she feels ashamed of herself for having asked, "Why, God, why?"[43]

Trust is Gítánjali's basic and abiding stance. It is what she deliberately cultivates. Trust and faith and gratitude with a joyful conviction of being loved by God and fellow humans—not trust that health would be restored or life spared, but the act of giving herself into God's keeping even as she saw her life ebbing fast and death standing by to claim her. In the cold and stormy night a lamp burns steadily in her heart, guiding her through the dark to her destination. Gítánjali has given God all her trust and faith. She trusts God despite the clamor of sorrows, despite God's betrayal of her trust:

> I trust Thee.
> Yet,
> Though you have
> Betrayed my trust
> And refused me,
> All I yearn for . . . .
> But dear God . . .
> Isn't it amazing
> For I trust you
> Still?

To Job God spoke from the heart of the storm; to us Gítánjali speaks from the heart of the storm that has gathered around her and is going "to gather her like dust." The child is afraid, "but yet I trust in God." "God alone knows what is best." As her desire to live burns bright and yet her hope wavers and her dreams slip away, she decides, "with a trust most rare," to follow the beacon God has sent and let God steer her life's boat to where God wishes. When the awareness first dawned on her that only a short while was left for her on this earth, it hurt; but soon she mastered the moment and "placed myself and my trust in the palm of His hand."[44]

Your Will Is Best

Gítánjali's faith is not propped up by hope of reward, nor by fear of punishment. She is not afraid: "I have not sinned or wronged any living soul." She is both afraid of death and not afraid of it. She prays for mercy, health, and life, and yet she has "long stopped begging for mercy." Her prayer to her dear God is for strength to accept his will and for faith to know that "your will is best." "Oh please, help me to trust you not from fear but because of love and faith." There is nothing this child seeks "save the truth." And in you, God, "lies the truth, and therefore, I seek you."[45]

She seeks God everywhere and in all things: in the rising sun, in eventide, in her pain, in her mother and father and their tenderness. She seeks God at all times: when she dreams and drifts, when God takes her pain away and rare moments of laughter come. She will seek God most when the hour of death descends. At that hour, "dear God, be by my side, hold my hand, take me where you want."[46] Gítánjali knows that God cares, "Oh, God does care." "People can let you down, God will not." She could, therefore, say in the tradition of Job that, when "sorrow, grief, and pain are near," and we lose "someone most dear," it is time "to reach out for God's hand." For God alone knows what is right. "Trust God and leave all else aside."[47] With death's shadow already falling on her and grief gripping her soul, she still has the clarity and the courage to say with Job and with Jesus: "if that's how you wish, thy will be done." Her prayer for her loved ones is that when the time of parting comes they should just be near, hold her hand, and "with utter trust give in to God" and let her die with dignity.[48] Nights may be dark for her soul, too, but when day breaks "my heart sings glory to you, oh God," for the gift of another day. Praise to God, for why should Gítánjali be sad "if flowers can die, which are so young and lovely to behold?"[49] We have in the poems many such resonances of the concluding part of Job and of the nature-contemplation in the Gítá.

The Welfare of All

What is most remarkable about Gítánjali is her ability to forget herself and become genuinely concerned with others, the courage and clarity of a wholly selfless spirituality. Herself dying daily, dying inch by inch, wrenched by pain, with death at her door, Gítánjali is not preoccupied with herself but anxious for others. There is evidence of a sustained struggle against the onslaught of self-pity. Even as her "tears flow silent, fast and free" she makes the brave promise "never to indulge in self-pity again." She prays for help "not to rail in self-pity," not to be swept away in its torrents.[50]

When her own heart breaks and her tears make "a permanent track" down her cheeks "like a shortcut through the lawn," her thoughts go to those who were caring for her, keeping watch, and trying to cheer her with songs. She does everything possible to lessen their suffering: she would act brave, control her tears, suppress her cry. She asks God to break her heart, break it, if necessary, but please be just, and do it "in such a way that no one should get hurt." Her own pain she can bear; what she cannot bear is the pain in the eyes of those who love her. In the stillness of the night she pleads with God: "wipe out the scars in the hearts of those who loved me."[51]

Naturally, the child's first concern is for her parents: those "two loving souls who held her close to their heart" on "the night of the storm," when their eyes held no promise and avoided meeting their child's. She recalls the agony and tenderness of her father, the source of her faith and strength.[52] Her mother is special; very special, dear and divine. To that brave woman her heart goes out. Her mother is the one Gítánjali most mentions next perhaps only to God. Her greatest pain is that her mother suffers in silence. May she not think unkindly of God, may she be there "when I meet my end," may she be thankful that her baby is at rest at last.[53] The girl makes adoring mention of her granny, affectionately names her brother, and remembers her friends with joy. May none of them suffer but take her departure in peace.[54]

Gítánjali's heart reaches out far beyond the circle of her relatives and friends. She seeks strength from God not only for herself and her loved ones to be able to bear the anguish day by day, but the grace to be merciful to all who hurt her, or need her; the grace to spread whatever happiness she can. Her days are numbered but she has so many tasks to fulfill. Her days are numbered and she has so many dreams to bring to blossom: "to feed the down and the poor, and wipe their tears with my hands to see them happy."

As she turns to God, Gítánjali realizes that she is not the only afflicted person in this wide world. Therefore, before asking for mercy for herself and for the gift of a little sleep in the night, she would pray for all those "who like her are ill and cannot sleep for pain," and for all "who are poor and friendless, sad and lonely."[55]

Her sympathy extends to animals and all of nature. Once again she is at one with the Gítá in the ideal of joy, in the welfare of all beings. Micky and Judy, her pet dogs, are puzzled why their frolicsome friend is now so quiet. "They look upon me so dolefully, and it breaks my heart; these dumb friends are better than many human beings" who have no heart, who say they love but never serve. Oscar the lame crow was a friend for whom Gítánjali used to wait with a breakfast of crumbs. A bird song lingers in her thoughts and—was it a sad song or a song of joy?— teaches her not to stop singing "just because I am unwell." From her hospital bed of pain Gítánjali's thoughts fly back home to Moti the stray dog she had befriended and cared for. She misses him. She thinks of him each time she sees a loaf of bread. She asks others to see to it that Moti is fed. Is Moti shivering with lack of love, or has someone given him a rug? She remembers the paw he extended to her as she sat in the car to be driven to the hospital. "I care for you in a very special way, which you would never know, anyway." Her heart whispers a prayer for Moti: "May you find a friend to take care of you."[56] Bruce Allsopp finds *Moti My Friend* the most touching of Gítánjali's poems. It is "a crystalline expression of the anguish of a being prevented by illness from serving a fellow being who has become dependent."[57]

This girl's soul vibrated with all nature. Every evening with a sinking heart she watched the sun set, not knowing if she would see the glory of the rising sun again. The moon shining in a little puddle reflects the lamp of faith that burns in the temple of her heart, guiding her to her destination. The prospect of a visit home suddenly bathes the world in sunshine, and in the dazzling brilliance of her joy the rising sun looked dim. Gítánjali grieved over a tree broken and flowers scattered by a night wind. She contemplates the flowers standing by her bed and realizes that these young and lovely things too will die and be discarded "just as I will be." Why should I be sad in such company? "Praise to you, O God." Much of the nature with which her heart chimed is reflected in a presentation of a valley and dew-kissed grass and chirping birds, and treetops, cows, sheep, horses, and stray dogs as well as stagnant pools, clear springs, and sunrise greeting the world with warmth, till it sets and lets the stars shine; the sun sets "leaving behind the radiance of love."[58] And in the silent, painful nights that follow, the moon strangely bathes the girl's aching heart and brings gushing endless childhood memories.[59]

Such is Gítánjali: wrestling with pain, with death and life, and with God. And growing through it all in faith and love; surpassing herself and meeting the mystery—of life, of her own heart, and of her God in the purity and transparency of childhood, in the intense fire of suffering. Gítánjali is another wager won. All clever cerebral criticism of religion and all pretentious and verbose theologies have been silenced and bidden to simple faith and a song of praise. Gítánjali is the song of the Third World. With this young and broken mystic symbol God has challenged us. Does not God too feel challenged and pressed to repentance? How could God have the heart to test so frail a flower so utterly and cruelly? To confound what modern satan and what intractable cynicism did God make this bet? "Why, we ask with Pritish Nandy, should such unbearable agony come upon those who have never hurt anyone? Is sorrow our ultimate destiny in this imperfect universe?" I do not know, we answer with Pritish Nandy; "all I know is this: these poems have hurt me by an awareness. The miracle of pain that opens up worlds we never knew existed."[60]

Now that Gítánjali lives and has won the wager for God, God can be proud of her, as God is proud of Job, and Krishna of Arjuna. We are proud of her, too. Though the memory of her brings the tide rising in our eyes, we can see her a revelation of what God can achieve, of what we can become, of what we are. A disclosure of human nobility and human possibility: the pure love and pure suffering of which the heart is capable. The wonder and the beauty of what God is able to create and nurture on this earth, beyond commodity culture, cold calculations, and the arrogance of power. We are called on to thrill with joy and thank God with Jesus for revealing these things to little ones.

Gítánjali means there is hope for humankind. She means we can "believe for nothing." Her meaning is that God is great, and is bent on making us great, too. The meaning of this gentlest, frailest, fading, never-fading flower of a girl is that it is good to be a human being and live on this earth, even if the earth is soaked in our own tears. It is good to share life with persons and animals and trees and earth and sky. The message of her life is that it is good to believe and to adore. Gítánjali means God is here. It is good to love God "for nothing." God is so worthy, so precious.

That is what Job and Arjuna and Gítánjali are telling us.

NOTES

1. Gustavo Gutiérrez, *On Job* (Maryknoll, N.Y.: Orbis Books, 1987). Original title: *Hablar de Dios desde el sufrimiento del inocente* (Lima: C.E.P., 1986).

2. See S. Radhakrishnan, *The Bhagavadgita* (London: George Allen and Unwin, 1948/1967); J. Mascaro, *The Bhagavad Gítá* (Hamondsworth: Penguin, 1962); R.C. Zaehner, *The Bhagavad Gítá* (Oxford, 1969). The title means "the Lord's song."

3. Published by Oriel Press, London, 1982, with an Introduction by Pritish Nandy. "Gítánjali" = a song-offering (from the title of a collection of Tagore's songs).

4. *On Job*, p. 11.

5. Ibid., pp. 4–5.

6. Ibid., p. 30.

7. Ibid., pp. 30, 57, 67.

8. Ibid., pp. 82, 84.

9. Ibid., p. 31.

10. Ibid., p. 48, 88.

11. Ibid., p. 96.

12. Ibid., pp. 88–89.

13. Ibid., pp. 70–72, 77–79.

14. Ibid., p. 69.

15. Ibid., pp. 86–87.

16. Ibid., pp. 30, 27–29.

17. K. Chaitanya, *The Mahabharata. A Literary Study* (New Delhi: Clarion Books, 1985), pp. 206–7.

18. *On Job*, p. 93.

19. J. A. B. Van Buitenan, *The Bhagavadgita in the Mahabharata* (Chicago: University of Chicago Press, 1981), p. 5.

20. Chaitanya, *Mahabharata*, pp. 279–352.

21. R. A. Malagi, "Dying into Life: The Prologue Scenes in the Bhagavadgita and La Divina Comedia," in *New Essays in the Bhagavadgita*, compiled by Arvind Sharma (New Delhi: Books and Books, 1987), p. 191.

22. Chaitanya, *Mahabharata*, p. 249 (see Gítá 2:7 [Mascaro]).

23. Ibid., pp. 252–53.

24. P. Mundschenk, "The Psychology of the Bhagavadgita," in *New Essays* (n. 21), p. 23.

25. Chaitanya, *Mahabharata*, p. 255, where reference is made to S. Petrement's *Simone Weil* (1976), to Arthur M. Young's *The Reflexive Universe* (1976), and to B. L. Atreya's *The Philosophy of Yogavasishtha* (1936).

26. *Mahabharata, vana-parvan* (forest canto), chap. 32.

27. Mundschenk, "Psychology," p. 17.

28. *Mahabharata, shanti-parvan* (peace canto) chap. 13, 16, 58.

29. Ibid., *vana-parvan* (forest canto), chap. 34. See Chaitanya, *Mahabharata*, pp. 190–95.

30. Chaitanya, *Mahabharata*, p. 275.

31. S. Gopalan, "The Concept of Duty in the Bhagavadgita: An Analysis," in *New Essays* (n. 21), p. 8.

32. Radhakrishnan, *Bhagavadgita*, p. 352, ad 18:2.

33. Ibid., p. 139.

34. Chaitanya, *Mahabharata*, p. 200.

35. Mundschenk, "Psychology," p. 22.

36. Nandy, Introduction to *Poems of Gítánjali*, pp. xv, xvii.

37. Ibid., pp. xv, xvi, xviii; Bruce Allsopp, Foreword, p. xii.

38. *Poems*, p. 89.

39. Ibid., pp. 6, 7, 11, 19, 26, 38, 39, 44, 70, 84, 145, 146.

40. Ibid., pp. 9, 26, 27, 59.

41. Ibid., pp. 48, 54, 60, 150.

42. Ibid., pp. 27, 154.

43. Ibid., pp. 6, 40, 58, 56, 67; Jeremiah 20:7–13; Mark 15:34.
44. Ibid., pp. 39, 41, 56, 58, 82, 97, 98, 127.
45. Ibid., pp. 5, 6, 11, 20, 54, 68.
46. Ibid., pp. 3, 12–13.
47. Ibid., pp. 45, 50, 89, 147.
48. Ibid., pp. 20, 56, 84, 122.
49. Ibid., pp. 38, 64.
50. Ibid., pp. 11, 52, 54.
51. Ibid., pp. 137, 147.
52. Ibid., pp. 4–5, 28–29, 42–43, 63–64, 83, 130–31.
53. Ibid., pp. 32, 35, 42, 53, 77, 91, 104, 122, 125–26, 138.
54. Ibid., pp. 65–66, 32–33, 113–14, 120, 153.
55. Ibid., pp. 61, 81, 103, 110.
56. Ibid., pp. 14, 22–23, 28, 100, 115–16.
57. Allsopp, Preface to *Poems*, p. xii.
58. *Poems*, pp. 123, 124.
59. Ibid., pp. 2, 41, 57, 63–64, 79.
60. Ibid., pp. xvi, xvii.

PART VI

LOOKING
TOWARD
THE FUTURE

48

Women in the Future
of the Theology of Liberation

MARÍA CLARA BINGEMER

> I believe that ... to explore the spiritual
> journey of women is also to explore the
> spiritual journey of human beings. ... I
> think that if women are valued and make
> tenderness attractive, they will liberate
> many men who refuse to recognize that
> they have this experience in their lives too,
> and must have it.
> —Gustavo Gutiérrez

It is audit time in Latin America. The theology of liberation is coming up to its twentieth birthday. It is time to look back to the past in order to be able to distinguish the present, and having distinguished it, to be able to desire and construct the future. It is time to ask some questions. After these twenty years of laborious construction and slow consolidation, what does the theology of liberation look like? What is its future?

To answer these questions we have to look at the faces of those who have the leading roles in this theology, those without whom the theologians themselves and even Latin American theology would not exist—the poor and oppressed. It was their shouting that caused a disturbance and ended up echoing round the church until there was no escaping it—their passion and their imprisonment, their indestructible hope, the fire of their desire for liberation, conceived and brought into the world a new language for talking about the ancient and eternal truths of the Christian faith.

Today, however, the faces of these poor and oppressed look different. Out of the mass of faces of the great poor majority of Latin America three types in particular are emerging and attracting attention, presenting new challenges to church and society. They are the blacks, Amerindians, and women. These groups, oppressed for centuries by their color, race, and sex, are now essential for an evaluation of the theology of liberation and for any attempt to glimpse its future, because they bring into theology new issues, a new method, and a new language.

Women in particular interest us most closely here. Their state of double oppression—by their socio-economic situation and by their sex—calls for the attention of society and the church.[1] Their presence in the development of Latin American theology has recently been felt with increasing weight and frequency. Their ideas and their language have already been recognized as among the most serious and solid products of Latin American theology. This presence enjoyed by women in the theology of liberation enables us to hope for a bright and joyful future. From the mouths and hearts of these once silent and invisible workers for the kingdom there is now coming a message of jubilation that says, "Rejoice!" The half of humankind that thought of itself as absent from theology's discourse—and in particular from the theology of liberation—has now made itself present and is speaking. And this widens the horizon and helps us to see with more clarity the Absolute Future that goes out to meet those who wait in hope.

Women are active producers of theology, just as they are an object of theological reflection. They bring their own method and a particular perspective with which to conceive and express the traditional topics of the faith within the process of Latin American liberation. In all this they are emerging and finding their place. Because of this all those men and women who are committed to the same service and enlightened by the same hope, and give their lives daily so that imprisonment may end and the kingdom come, are exclaiming jubilantly, "Rejoice!" The new event is taking place and the Spirit is blowing. The female presence in the theology of liberation is growing and becoming visible, tempering struggle with festivity, force with tenderness, and rigor with desire. God's kingdom is in its advent—more than that, it is in our midst.

WOMEN AS PRACTITIONERS AND SUBJECTS OF THEOLOGY

Women's past in the world of theology was largely silence and invisibility. Though present in the church—and even with a numerically stronger presence than men—their faces were not seen or their voices heard in any "shouting from the housetops," when any audible and recognized statement had to be produced and uttered.

In the case of theology, and more specifically, theological production, the silence and the absence were particularly marked. Women as subjects did not appear with any prominence in theology treatises, courses, or books. Subsumed in the treatise on "theological anthropology," where human beings were considered in their status as the image and likeness of God, women, diluted and forgotten even in language, were at the most allowed to be included in the ambiguously androcentric term "man."[2] The category "man" sought to designate the human being as a whole, man and woman, but insensibly the form influenced the content and the object of consideration came to be in fact male humankind, rather than the totality of humankind, man and woman. The specificity, the differentness, of women, their characteristics, their ways of feeling, their particular way of being the image of God, were obliterated in the dark night of time in a diffuse anthropologico-theological category that did not do justice to the richness of their being.

Similarly, in theological production, the past for women was marked by centuries of absence as practitioners, and by a deep silence. Until recently there were in the history of theology no books or articles written by women, no chairs occupied by women, no courses run by women. No one even bothered to specify the sex of the authors of theological texts or of professors of theology. It was "obvious" that such work was a male prerogative.[3] For all this time women's ways of thinking and talking did not enrich theology with their own characteristics, did not shape it with their way of feeling and thinking, did not color it with their own different accents. As a result, theology, the church, and humankind were the poorer. And women suffered like the woman in the parable of Luke 15:8–10, who searched tirelessly and persistently for the lost coin whose existence she knew of with unshakeable certainty, and which she was unwilling to give up her claim to any longer.

Today, therefore, we are witnessing the awakening of women in the church and in theology. And although it is an awakening inevitably marked by the signs of the breaking of an age-old silence, the dazzle of a sight suddenly seen from the depths of an endless tunnel, it still shows signs of promise that hint at what it has still to disclose, in addition to what it has so far revealed. It is like the tip of an iceberg that makes us suspect a whole vast transparency still submerged, and desire its full and rapid emergence.

What women are saying is making itself strongly heard in the world of theology.[4] It is making itself heard as a message distinct in kind. Women's ideas and language are no longer the insecure stammering of a person whose tongue has recently been loosed, nor is the torrent of talk that has made verbal diarrhea a female characteristic in popular opinion. It is a new and different theological message, a deliberate decision to speak. The message is systematic and ordered, and contains a distinct style all its own, visible in everything from the selection of topics for systematic investigation, the emphasis given to biblical texts, and the way they are approached and explained, to the premises and structure of arguments, the framework of theological discourse.

Women's theological message in the present, which gestated in the long night of absence and silence, shines a new light on all theology, the same light that shone from the face of the woman in the parable of Luke 15:8–10 when she found the coin that had always been hers, after she had lost it and searched for it.[5] This coin was the currency of mystery, of God's truth and word, the currency of the secret of life in abundance, revealed to her from the beginning and now rediscovered as something to be revered, pondered on, and proclaimed.

From their long experience of silence, women have acquired the wisdom, ancient and always new, that speaks the word and silence, in a harmonious combination of gestures, prophecies, lamentations, and counsels, able to express—though never exhaust—the mystery of the presence of the divine in the human. Understanding life and the slowness of its processes, women apply this knowledge in their theologizing. For a woman, bringing into being theology is like bringing into being a life, a new creature. It means carrying it in her womb, giving birth to it after many months, feeding it, and protecting it with her body, defending it, and watching it grow. It means thinking about, pondering on, and talking about the revealed word with power and courage, but also with patience—doing, building, and talking, but also being silent, waiting, hoping, and celebrating. And besides all this, more important than all this, with the transparent and pure happiness of someone who has found what she was looking for and now cannot celebrate alone, she *has to* call her "friends and neighbors" and say, "Rejoice with me, for I have found the coin I had lost!" For a woman, doing theology means finding a way into a new solidarity, into a theology that cannot be done in isolation, but only in solidarity, in community, in the church.

It is at this point that a new future in the theology of liberation opens up for women. One of the fundamental features of the Latin American theological venture known as the theology of liberation is that it is a collective theological enterprise. The theologian of liberation no longer regards herself as someone who thinks, ponders, writes, and speaks in isolation, out of her individual experience, about the reading she has done on her own, or her own brilliant reasoning. She sees herself as the spokeswoman for the great mass of oppressed persons who have recently woken from centuries of the most bitter oppression of all kinds, are standing up, and rediscovering themselves as responsible and active initiators. They are eager to rewrite history from their own point of view, to reinterpret the liberating message of God's covenant with the people and Jesus Christ's liberating act in terms of their own situation of captivity, in order to turn them into a source of strength, insight, and strategy to live and suffer in their struggle. Theology comes into this process as an ally and a spokesperson. Through sharing in the aspirations, the organization, and the faith-lives of these oppressed persons, the theologian finds her raw material, which she then returns to them in the form of a worked out, systematic argument; for they have helped to bring it to birth and, along with her, are creators and theologians.

This is what is happening as women enter the domain of theology. Their awakening and their speaking are not the sum of isolated experiences, but are the sign of a new, fascinating, and indestructible solidarity with their comrades from poor communities who, beneath the surface of history, are weaving the threads and sewing the stitches of the liberation of the poor on the Latin American framework. With the word of God and the gospel of Jesus as their only wealth, the women of the Latin American poor are taking over the leadership and the administration of the great majority of the increasing number of biblical groups and basic ecclesial communities, giving the church a new look and a new vigor. In the farthest corners of Latin America, they are there, catechists taking responsibility for education in the faith and the deeper assimilation of the gospel, ministers and servants of communities organizing to struggle and celebrate. In rural areas, in *favelas*, in the poor communities on the edges of the big cities, they are organizing in groups around their common work, inspired by their faith in the Lord and their love for the people of which they are a part. Mothers' clubs, community gardens and kitchens, and a variety of other women's organizations are springing up everywhere, organizing the struggle, strengthening faith, defending life, consolidating courage and unity, celebrating the feast.[6]

It is these women whom the woman theologian today accompanies and speaks for. Her theological message is called to reflect, organize, and make audible the unsystematic message that comes, in the raw state, from the rough and experienced lips of poor women. Prompted by the experience of faith, these women from poor communities are taking responsibility for practical struggles on behalf of their people. The woman who does theology, one more among them, a sister and companion, receives from their calloused and affectionate hands, still warm from hard labor for the building of the kingdom, her mission and the stuff of her reflection. Within this greater collective struggle, she is called on to develop her argument and reflection in order to return it as a humble and willing contribution to the continuing process of liberation.

Women's future in the theology of liberation is thus the future of the liberation of all human beings, men and women, who, from the depths of their oppression, desire and call out for the God of life, who brings liberation—socio-economic, political, cultural, racial, ethnic, sexual—from every type of death.

Theological Method

Theology's past is heavily imprinted with the primacy of the rational. Ever since it divorced itself from spirituality, which gave it flexibility, beauty, and movement, theology ran the serious risk of becoming stiff—of treating reason as the one universal mediator of its thought and language. In this way it often became circumspect and cold, not allowing for all the other fundamental elements of human life and also, therefore, of the divine life that is theology's source and model: sensitivity, gratuitousness, experience, desire. Theology's past, therefore, is imprinted with this almost absolute primacy of rationality, and this had much to do with the fact that theology was done almost exclusively by men.[7]

The theology done in the past was, in addition, marked by an abstract language and style in its presentation of the life and truths of the faith. Theological language has often fallen into the temptation of divorcing itself from reality, the hard ground of experience, and of spinning complicated and esoteric theories unrelated to real life, unrelated to the detail of everyday concerns, unrelated to the questions brewing in the minds of the faithful, unrelated to the burning desire in their hearts. The result of this was a theology distant even from the detail of church life, foreign to the deepest aspirations of the people of God, remote from the sufferings and anguish of all sorts of poor and oppressed who longed, from the depths of their imprisonment, for light and a word of guidance. Theological concepts and theories ran the risk of becoming empty words if they could not name the distant spring they flowed from, what deep existential reality, what vital aspiration and desire they expressed; if they could not turn themselves into intelligible communication with the people of God they were meant to serve.

Women's entry into the domain of theology brings with it a new way, a new method, of conceiving and expressing this 2,000-year-old theology. Entering into the domain of theological reflection with their specific and different bodiliness, open to ever-new and innovative messages, available for invasion and creative fecundation, destined to be host and protector of life, women are revolutionizing the very rigor and system of theological method.[8] Their present irruption into the circumspect and rational male theological world of the past is as disconcerting and new as that of the woman in John's Gospel (12:1–8) who invaded the meal taking place within the very strict social and ritual norms of Judaism with her presence and her perfume.[9] Breaching expectations and regulations and following the impulse of the desire that overflowed from her heart, the woman filled the space with a new scent, which none could avoid smelling and breathing in.

The presence of women in theology brings with it this same air of the new and unexpected. Today we are witnessing women's theological message being uttered and heard amid the formerly monolithic and impregnable structure of male theology. And, even though the first impression that emerges is one of a foreign body and the nonintegration of a foreign body, not properly assimilated into the system, the female way of doing theology is finding its place and gaining ground. The courage to pour out the perfume at someone else's party is followed by the moment at which the perfume poured out struggles and collides with the ancient scents that have traditionally formed the environment. The present is made up of this plurality of scents, sometimes apparently incompatible, and often in conflict.

The future of the female way of doing theology is therefore inseparably linked with desire.[10] The primacy of rationality must be replaced by the primacy of desire, the cold circumspection of purely scientific inquiry must give way to a new sort of systematics springing from the impulse of desire that dwells at the deepest level of human existence and combines sensitivity and rationality, gratuitousness and effectiveness, experience and reflection, desire and rigor. "God is love" (1 John 4:8). If this is so, God can only be, in the beginning, the object of desire; not of necessity, not of rationality. Theology—which seeks to be reflection and talk about God and God's word—therefore cannot but be moved and permeated throughout its whole extent by the flame of desire. At a particular point in its theological articulation, reason, science, and systematic rigor have their role and their place, but they can never suffocate the greater desire, never tame the divine pathos, which, from all eternity, has broken silence and become a loving and calling word, kindling in its turn in the hearts of humankind an irresistible and insatiable desire. Theology is called—humbly—to bear witness to and give an account of this burning desire. Born of desire, theology exists as theology only if it is upheld and supported by desire, in the direction of the desire that is its goal and its horizon.[11]

The presence of women in the world of theology brings back to the front line, to the front of the stage of the church's life, that primacy of desire for which purely rational concepts do not allow.[12] A woman finds it unthinkable to divide her own being into watertight compartments and treat theological work as a purely rational activity. Moved by desire, a totalizing force, she does theology with her body, her heart and hands, as much as with her head, and the ripe fruit that she begins to make available is the result of slow and patient pondering of experiences lived deeply and intensely, confronted with the tradition of the past and with the normative landmarks of the journey of the people of Israel and the church.

In this way the Spirit, the motor and origin of desire, poured out on history and humanity, finds good and fertile ground for creative imagination. As well as referring back constantly and faithfully to the Jesus of the past as the ultimate and definite norm, it opens the future to infinite possibilities of inventiveness and newness in expressing the Christian mystery. At the center of theological reflection and discourse, which remain open to a future still not fully explored, the Spirit reinstates the rights of the poetic and symbolic as literary genres, the only ones able to reach the heart of the matter and touch the hem of the Spirit and of Beauty.[13]

Everything I have just said about theology done by women with their whole selves is particularly true, and indeed characteristic, of the theology of liberation. Talking of desire is not to talk of an aseptic impulse that obeys sterile and preserved esthetic rules. When we talk about desire we are talking about human beings at their deepest level, in their deepest and ultimate truth, in their vital force,[14] and therefore in their most authentic and legitimate aspirations. We are talking about what makes our bodies quiver and tremble with pleasure, about our noble and threatened vulnerability, our greatness, which depends on our fragility. When a human being's most basic and vital needs are denied, when he or she is deprived of the essential elements that make up and sustain life at its most fundamental, it is human desire itself, the person's deepest core, the truest and most basic impulse, that is attacked and violated.[15]

From this point of view Latin America has been systematically attacked in its vital desire. The poor, who make up the vast majority of the population, daily experience the weight of domination. Bending and wasting their bodiliness, imprisoning them in remorseless deprivation and oppression, also bends and wastes their ability to desire and know themselves desired, and so their ability to live and express themselves fully as human beings. The process of liberation begins to take place when the poor become conscious of the desire repressed within themselves and let it emerge, release it as a cry, and feel it at the same time to be the energy for the struggle. It is in this liberation of desire that theology is called to give its message, and specifically in our case, theology done by women.[16]

Women's future in the theology of liberation, then, means for them to place their integrated and integrating approach at the heart of this struggle and this process. To be a woman means to be able to combine experience and action, to be able to grapple with oppression and liberation, to be able, in the midst of disaster, to glimpse the superabundance of grace. It is an ability, in a situation filled with vast and profound contradictions, to integrate and see the unity in contrasts and differences, to be able to discern and contemplate in the disfigurement of the cross the breath of hope and the weight of the glory already starting to shine. It is the ability not to lose the thread of the desire that, from the depths of a disfigured world, groans with unspeakable groans to proclaim the birth of the new creation, already visible. Women have received this ability as a gift, and women in poor communities in Latin America exercise it every day.

A challenging and promising future lies in store for a woman doing theology in the context of the theology of liberation. The challenge is to *restore the primacy of desire within theological discourse.* The promise is that she will be enlightened and led by that desire toward the kingdom where liberation will be a full reality. In the midst of the hopeful and stubborn struggle, which consists of the pain and joy of her sisters from poor communities, she is called to place her reflection and her arguments, not only at the service of the struggle, but also as decorations at the celebration. With her theological message uttered in favor of life and light, denouncing the forces of darkness and death, she is called to inaugurate new ways of listening to revelation, of expressing the experience of faith, of reading and interpreting the word of God, of thinking about and unfolding the great themes and chapters of theology. And all the while she allows herself to be possessed by the desire that inflames and summons, that keeps alight, not consumed, the flame of love in the face of everything that threatens to extinguish it.

The Great Themes of Theology from a Woman's Viewpoint

The theology of liberation is not a different theology from that which grew out of the experience of the people of Israel, of Jesus of Nazareth and the apostles. It is the same faith-experience, the same desire, the same love made flesh, now reflected on in conjunction with the sufferings and hopes for liberation of the oppressed.[17] Consequently it does not deal with different topics, but the same topics as in the great line of the church's theology, which are studied from a new point of view in the theology of liberation.[18] What Christian faith is able to say about itself in this new and different perspective will reveal the relationship it has with the real questions raised by the human beings of today in their various struggles as they develop out of their historical activity.[19] The content of a theology from a woman's perspective is determined by the same principle. It will tackle the same themes, reflect on the key tenets of Christian theology, taking into account women's views and methods.

One of the constants of theology in general—and the theology of liberation is no exception to this generalization—is that it has always been done by men. This does not deprive it of value or of the status of true theology—that is, inspired and systematic reflection, a metalanguage related to revelation and faith—but it necessarily limits its scope and vision. It is not possible for only one of the sexes of humankind to encompass and do justice to the whole mystery of being human, and therefore still less to that of the revelation of the divine in the human. Theological reflection has lacked the desire, the heart, the body, and the head of a woman to enable it to be more fully itself, to enable new treasures to be discovered and brought to birth out of the womb of God's word, so that the image of God—man and woman—could be more perfectly revealed and made known.

This is beginning to happen, at a steadily increasing rate. However, whereas in the First World there is already a considerable volume of theology produced by women, with a large number of books and articles published,[20] in the Third World the process of theological production by women is taking place in a different way. It is more collective, less "visible," in terms of large, impressive publications, more of an antlike infiltration, coming gradually up from the base of church life and gradually penetrating theological production as a whole.

Specifically, women's theological production in Latin America regards itself as part of the larger body of the theology of liberation, as a humble and modest contribution to the process of the total redemption of all classes of oppressed. In bringing out their theological message, Latin American women are not trying to engage in a power struggle with men, still less to replace the male model of theological reflection by the female one. They are looking and working for "a new synthesis in which the dialectic present in human existence can really take effect, without destroying any of the vital components."[21]

If the past was silence and absence of a female perspective on the content of theology, the present is marked by increasing visibility, gently exerting its influence. In the Latin American theological community, the female touch is gradually becoming apparent, a woman's approach to problems, a woman's feeling in raising certain issues. The first publications are beginning to appear, the slowly ripened fruit of contact with the base, along with the women from poor communities who make the church exist in history at the day-to-day level. Meetings are being organized at local, regional, and national levels. The Ecumenical Association of Third World Theologians (EATWOT) is encouraging dialogue between women theologians from Africa, Asia, and Latin America, and from minority groups in North America. These meetings, dialogues, and interchanges produce conclusions that take forward women's contributions within the general framework of theological reflection committed to the process of liberation.[22] There are also topics that appear and become dominant when studied in this new light. They are gradually opening up a path for the future of women's theological thinking.

The woman who does theology in today's Latin America, in solidarity with the poor and from the depth of their oppression, has every day the experience of *seeing the Lord*, as Mary Magdalen, on the first day of the week, beside the tomb, *saw* the light of the new life and heard her name spoken by the mouth of the risen Lord: "Mary!" (John 20:16). And she did not keep the experience to herself, but went to talk about the things the Lord had told her (John 20:18). This is what is happening to women who do theology. Having seen the Lord and heard new things from his lips, they go and reflect on them, assimilate them, and communicate them in their words and in their way.

So now we are able to witness a new way of approaching the Bible and the sacred texts, a way devised by women, a new reflection on Jesus Christ, on Mary, on the church; a new experience and a new understanding of the living God who is the center from which all theology emanates and on which it all converges. There is a new way of understanding and celebrating the eucharist and the other sacraments. These topics and others not yet broached are gradually forming and filling out the new and original fabric of Latin American theology.[23]

Women and the Bible

Women and the poor in Latin America rediscovered the Bible at the same time. When those who had been kept out of the way, outside the word of God, once again discovered the entrance to the book that was theirs, which spoke of their struggles, their hopes, their desires, and their covenant of love with a compassionate and loving God, women were present. The great movement of study and reading of the Bible that sprang up throughout Latin America—with biblical circles, basic ecclesial communities, and short courses of biblical formation for pastoral workers from poor communities—shook consciences and challenged other parts of the church. The poor were rediscovering holy scripture, the word of God; were once more taking possession of and establishing residence on ground that was their own.

Despite all this, women with a certain level of feminist consciousness began to ask a number of questions about the Bible. They felt deeply involved and identified with the great accounts of liberation contained in scripture, and Jesus' treatment of them as described by the Gospels proclaimed to them the good news of the kingdom as a discipleship of equals.[24] On the other hand, in their reading of the Bible they came up against the problem of the clear and explicit marginalization of women in various passages of scripture, in both Old and New Testaments. This fact drew the attention of women who were becoming aware of their situation, and in particular of women theologians specializing in holy scripture.

The work of these new biblical scholars revealed something new: there is a difference between reading the Bible from the point of view of the poor and reading it from a woman's point of view. Whereas a poor man may find himself affirmed and defended by the mouth of the living God throughout the holy scriptures, the poor woman, in contrast, as a woman, while feeling the company and the presence of the holy Spirit in her life and history, does not know how to deal with the texts that seem to marginalize her and treat her as an inferior human being.[25] This problem is all the greater in that the poor communities where this explosion of biblical renewal is taking place are particularly marked by patriarchal and male-supremacist ideologies. In this context reading biblical texts that seem to reaffirm female segregation may help to confirm women still further in the oppression that crushes them, and this time with the very authority of the word of God.

Because of this, Latin American women biblical scholars are working particularly with women from poor communities for a deeper understanding of the nature of biblical texts. They present the text as the testimony of a people and a faith-community with particular cultures, within which divine revelation is transmitted — God's word *in* human words — as a saving word always supporting the lowest and the oppressed, who include women. The spirit of the revealed text, which is profoundly liberative, relativizes the antifeminism of a patriarchal culture that may give a negative tone to some parts of the Bible.

In addition they are attempting to recover the origins of Christianity from a woman's perspective. In so doing they bring to light and emphasize the figures of the women who appear to be builders of the history of salvation, whom a traditional interpretation often forgets or relegates to a secondary plane. Examples are the Egyptian midwives of Exodus 1, the subversives Tamara and Agar, who felt completely free to question the Jewish law, and finally the whole legion of women who can be found in the Gospels and the Acts of the Apostles playing an active part in the early stages of the church.

Latin American interpretation of the Bible from a woman's viewpoint is thus taking place in a process of distancing and approach.[26] The distancing means putting aside the more current interpretations, which are already implicit in our reading. It means recovering the capacity for awe and terror, to see new things never seen before in texts read and heard so many times. The other side is an attempt to get closer to the Bible, linked to daily life, with its experiences of pain, joy, happiness, hope, hunger, repression, celebration, and, lastly, struggle. In this way women's reading of the Bible, through this dialectic of distancing and coming closer, will advance, not as a theoretical or abstract intellectual exercise, but as a desire to find meaning for their present, to discern the desire and will of God in the detail of their own history. In the process women in Latin America are creating a new look for exegesis, and a new way of understanding the principle of biblical authority.[27]

MARY OF NAZARETH, TRAVELING COMPANION

Speaking about women from a Christian point of view inevitably means speaking about Mary of Nazareth, the mother of Jesus. Presented and venerated from the beginning by Christianity as the perfect woman, she who carried in her womb God made flesh, Mary was, and has continued to be, presented to women as the model to be followed, imitated, and inwardly assimilated. However, traditional Mariology has often presented an image of Mary that instead of promoting and liberating women, has confirmed and confined them in their ancient oppression. Submissive and passive, entirely absorbed in domestic activities, idealized and exalted for her individualistic virtues, Mary of Nazareth was, in the eyes of women who were beginning to become aware of their situation and wanting to take responsibility for their lives, a source of perplexity rather than inspiration and motivation for the struggle.

The theology of liberation set out to recover the figure of Mary in its liberating and prophetic potential. Stressing above all the text of the Magnificat (Luke 1:46–55), this theology gave to the poor women of Latin America, to the women who lead the basic ecclesial communities, a Mary whose face was no longer only that of Our Lady, glorious queen of heaven, but also and primarily an elder sister and traveling companion.[28] In Latin America this prophetic and liberating Mary takes on many loving faces: the Morenita of Guadelupe who appeared to the Amerindian Juan Diego in Mexico, the black Aparecida who allowed herself to be found in the waters of the river Paraiba in Brazil, Nicaragua's Purisima, Cuba's Virgin of Charity, and so on. In all these, Mary, the valiant and prophetic daughter of Sion, committed to justice, faithful to her God and to her people, inspires and strengthens women's unity and struggle, redeeming and ennobling them in their own eyes.

But there was still a need for women themselves to get down to the task of developing a reflection on the mother of the redeemer. Alongside many other female figures in the Bible and the history of the church, Mary emerges as the prototype, the one who says most clearly to every woman who she is and who she is called to be. There was a need for her figure and symbol not only to speak to women, but —much more important—to speak to the whole people of God *through the mouths of women.* This is now happening in Latin America. The first essays in Mariology by women are beginning to appear, introducing a female way of seeing the figure of Mary.[29]

What is new about this work is that it reveals a Mary no longer considered individualistically, in terms of a model of ascetic virtues to be imitated, but as a collective symbol, a type of the faithful people within which the holy Spirit of God finds fertile ground to raise up the new people, the seed of the kingdom, which will inaugurate the new creation. This new approach leads in turn to a reconsideration and reinterpretation of the traditional Mariological themes, the Marian dogmas and the church itself, which Mary symbolizes. A church like that in Latin America, which seeks to be a church of the poor and of the people, will find in this Mariology produced by the wombs and heads of women a new and rich source of inspiration for working out its identity.

THE THREEFOLD GOD IN A FEMALE PERSPECTIVE

For some time now theology has begun to see the need to conceive and speak of God in the feminine, to believe in, invoke, and proclaim God in the feminine. It is no longer adequate to reflect on the divine mystery that creates, saves, and sanctifies us as identifying primarily with one of the two sexes, rather than integrating and harmonizing the two sexes, without suppressing their enriching differences—at the same time as it transcends them. To achieve this, theology has to go beyond the traditional theological conception, which sees a woman as God's image only in her rational soul and not in her sexed female body, and therefore sees God as andromorphic, conceived and understood in male terms, which, in considering God's covenant with humankind, identifies the divine party (God) as male and the human party (Israel, the church) as female.

Christology developed from a woman's viewpoint has sought to be a way into this new conception of God. The form this has taken in Latin America has been to search for the key that the liberative approach has used throughout its study of the Gospels: an analysis of Jesus' egalitarian behavior as revealed by his encounters and relations with women.[30] Among the ways in which Jesus broke with tradition, one of the clearest has to do with women. His behavior toward the women marginalized by Jewish society was not only new, but even shocking, surprising even his own disciples (John 4:27). Women were singled out as beneficiaries of his miracles (Luke 8:2; Mark 1:29-31; 5:25-34; 7:24-30) and were active participants in the assembly of the kingdom (Luke 10:38-42), leading figures in and recipients of the good news he brought.

As well as breaking the taboo that marginalized them, Jesus redeemed their bodiliness, which had been humiliated and proscribed by Jewish Law. In curing the woman with the hemorrhage, who was impure to the Jews, he exposed himself to the risk of making himself impure by touching her (Matt. 9:20-22). In allowing his feet to be touched, kissed, and anointed by a known public sinner, he led his Pharisee host to cast doubt on his prophetic status (Luke 7:36-50). And not only that: Jesus also allowed women to question and influence him. His encounters with them changed not just them, but him too. The Gospels show us Jesus learning from women and giving way to their requests. He did so with his mother Mary, who advanced his "hour" in Cana (John 2:1ff.). He did so with the Canaanite woman, who "dragged out of him" the miracle she wanted with much pleading, so setting in train the process of the proclamation of the good news to the gentiles (Matt. 15:21-28: Mark 7:24-30).

Jesus' incarnation and messianic consciousness is an exchange, in which the God-man both gives and receives, proclaims and listens, loves and is loved. In this reciprocity women have an important place. And this man of flesh and blood, who treated women like this and was loved and known by them, who proclaimed their full dignity as daughters of God and citizens of the kingdom and was proclaimed by them God's Messiah, is the same man who had his way confirmed by the Father in the resurrection and is now Kyrios, the glorious Lord seated at the right hand of God.[31] Christology is thus—today as ever, and more than ever—the good news of salvation for all the oppressed, and among them for women who are looking for their place in world and church.

Nevertheless, it is not so much in christology as in the doctrine of the Trinity, in the mystery of the communion of the three divine persons, the unquestionable center of the Christian faith, that the main road to a concept of God in women's terms is being sought. To say that God is Father, Son, and Holy Spirit is not, and cannot be, in any way equivalent to saying that the divine community is composed of three persons identified as male. The thinking being done by women theologians in Latin America today seeks to recover the biblical root of the experience of God, which uses the word *rahamin*, "womb," female entrails, to refer to God's love.[32] Countless Old Testament texts, especially in the prophets, refer to God by this part of the female body. The effect of this is that in theology—feminist or not—God the Father is being called also Mother or, better, Maternal Father or Paternal Mother.[33] These divine female entrails, pregnant with gestation and birth, which have been identified in the Father, also appear in the incarnate Son, who in the Gospels is driven to cry out in frustrated maternal desire to gather under his wings the scattered and rebellious "chickens of Jerusalem" (Luke 13:34). They appear in the Spirit, the divine *ruach,* who in the labor of creation "hatches" the cosmos, which is to burst forth from the primitive chaos, who is sent like a loving mother to console the children left orphaned by Jesus' departure (John 14:18,26) and to teach them patiently to pronounce the Father's name, Abba (Rom. 8:15).

A rich future is in store for the theology of liberation in the female dimension of God. The poor who are discovering themselves as active makers of history and are organizing for liberation are experiencing God as the God of life, as embodying the very fulness of life, as the only source from which it is possible to derive hope and promise in the situation of death they live every day. God's female entrails— maternal *rahamin,* fertile, in labor and compassionate—enable this liberation to come about with force and firmness, but also with creativity and gentleness, without violence. Once God is experienced, not only as Father, Lord, strong warrior, but also as Mother, protection, greater love, struggle is tempered with festivity and celebration of life, permanent and gentle firmness ensures the ability "to be tough without losing tenderness," and uncompromising resistance can be carried on with joy, without excessive tension and sterile strain. God's compassion, flowing from female and maternal entrails, takes on itself the hurts and wounds of all the oppressed, and a woman who does theology is called to bear witness to this God with her body, her actions, her life.[34]

THE EUCHARIST CELEBRATED AND SYMBOLIZED BY THE FEMALE BODY

The theology of the sacraments is something that as yet has received little attention from women theologians. Nonetheless there exists a whole body of women's experience of sacramental life—in its significance and in its liturgical celebration— that promises to be a rich seam for the future of women in theology, and specifically in Latin American theology.

Everywhere at the base of the Latin American church, and in a very special way in the basic ecclesial communities, the liturgy has a predominant place. It is the place for festivity, for the celebration of life in its purest truth and transparency, where the experience of faith is expressed not only with the mouth and in words, but with all the body's resources, singing, gestures, and dance, and in which tangible material symbols signify deeper and definitively transcendent realities.

In this celebration of faith and life, women have an important role. With their integrated and unified selves and attitudes, they are able to express cheerfully and happily in the community celebrations even the hardest and most painful struggles, which are part of the community's life. As they live the gospel joy, which is not necessarily happiness, and which therefore may exist alongside pain and even make it the raw material of its hope, the women of the poor communities find in the liturgy a privileged space to show the work and the struggle they carry on—in the unions, in the mothers' clubs, in the neighborhood associations, community gardens, and canteens, and in various other forms of popular community organization. The eucharist celebrated where women are active participants and organizers, as well as being the subversive memory of the Lord's death and resurrection, is the joyful distribution and sharing of bread among all, with joyful and generous hearts, just as the Acts of the Apostles describes the agape of the New Testament church (Luke 2:46).

But there is also another dimension in which women find themselves and identify themselves with the sacrament of the eucharist. This is the strict significance of the sacrament as the transubstantiation and real presence of the body and blood of the Lord, which, under the species of bread and wine, are given to the faithful as food. Feeding others with one's own body is the supreme way God chose to be definitively and sensibly present in the midst of the people. The bread that we break and eat, and that we profess to be the body of Jesus Christ, refers us back to the greater mystery of his incarnation, death, and resurrection. It is his person given as food; it is his very life made bodily a source of life for Christians. But it is women who possess in their bodiliness the physical possibility of performing the divine eucharistic action. In the whole process of gestation, childbirth, protection, and nourishing of a new life, we have the sacrament of the eucharist, the divine act, happening anew.

Throughout Latin America, in the rural areas and the poor districts on the edges of cities, there are millions of women conceiving, bearing, and suckling new children of the common people. Sometimes they do it with difficulty, pain, and suffering, sometimes with the last trickle of life left in them.[35] This female body, which is extensive and multiplies in other lives, which gives itself as food and nourishes with its flesh and blood the lives it has conceived, is the same body that wastes away and dies tilling the earth, working in factories and homes, stirring pans and sweeping floors, spinning thread and washing clothes, organizing meetings, leading struggles, chairing meetings, and starting singing. It is the woman's body, eucharistically given to the struggle for liberation, really and physically distributed, eaten and drunk by those who will—as men and women of tomorrow—continue the same struggle of patience and resistance, pain and courage, joy and pleasure. Breaking the bread and distributing it, having communion in the body and blood of the Lord until he comes again, means for women today reproducing and symbolizing in the midst of the community the divine act of surrender and love, so that the people may grow and the victory come, which is celebrated in the feast of true and final liberation.

Women who do theology in Latin America and who share with their sisters from the poorest environments the same sacramental vocation, the same eucharistic destiny, are called to open, with their reflection and discourse, a new path, a possible future, so that this sacramental act may become more and more present, recognized, and believed in in Latin America's journey toward liberation.

"THERE IS NEITHER MALE NOR FEMALE ... YOU ARE ALL ONE IN CHRIST JESUS" (GAL. 3:28)

There is a future on the horizon of the theology of liberation. After twenty years of movement, life, and suffering, along a road composed not just of light but also of darkness and uncertainties, we can look back with gratitude and note the ground covered and the achievements won. However, we can and should equally look forward with hope and attempt to discern what remains to be done and where the road leads.

There is a future on the horizon of the theology of liberation. The poor who have arisen and awoken to take on the task of building their own history, and whose shouts provoked the theology, are joining together in community bases and growing stronger in their organization. In turn, the process of liberation they are leading is becoming more complex and developing new facets. New groups begin their own struggles, denouncing more clearly the different forms of oppression from which the peoples of Latin America suffer. We do not hear now only of socio-economic and political oppression. Oppression is also cultural, sexual, racial, and ethnic. The one captivity has various names, and alongside the disfigured faces of the categories of poor listed by the Puebla documents (peasants, workers, old persons, etc.),[36] the faces of the victims of other forms of oppression are emerging, as they take their place in the fight for liberation: women, blacks, Amerindians.

Among these women, after challenging society and church life, some have entered the domain of theology. The history of salvation is beginning to be reinterpreted from their perspective, theological reflection is beginning to accept them as practitioners, as an issue and subject matter, welcoming into its discourse the enriching difference of their language, their experience, and their methods. Desire, brought by their hands, once more has full civil rights in theology's domain, spiritual experience and liturgical celebration mix with scientific rigor in joyous and rich combination. Theological study and argument are beginning to be carried out, not just with the intellect, but with all that material life provides: pain and happiness, anguish and hope, body, hands, heart. Poetry is once more a literary form suitable for expressing the mystery of God.

This present is an opening and a guarantee for a future that is opening up and coming to meet all Latin Americans. Worked eschatologically from within, pregnant with the presence of the one who, already risen and victorious, still remains crucified in the passion and death of the poor and oppressed of Latin America, this future can be seen to be full of women's presence. This is cause for happiness and rejoicing for women, and for all those who through them will receive the good news of the proclamation of the gospel of liberation. "Rejoice!" says the voice of the woman who has found the coin lost for so long, and which had been given to her by God from the beginning. And today, at this point in the history of Latin America, this voice repeats, in tones of joy, "Rejoice!" The Latin America of today is pregnant with the kingdom of tomorrow. In that kingdom differences will be integrated in a differentiated communion in which there will in future be "neither Jew nor Greek, neither slave nor free, neither male nor female," but all will be "one in Christ Jesus" (Gal. 3:28).

—translated from the Portuguese by Francis McDonagh

NOTES

1. It is a fact that someone who is poor in socio-economic terms, and also a woman, suffers twice over. See Gustavo Gutiérrez's remarks on this in his interview with Elsa Tamez: "That's what we said from a theology of liberation perspective, a phrase which is now very well known: 'doubly marginalized and doubly oppressed,' which we got into the Puebla document. (Unfortunately in the published version they moved it into a note, whereas in the version approved at Puebla it was in the

body of the text, but it's there [para. 1134n.].) And I think that it's true that women are doubly marginalized and oppressed, as poor persons and as women" (*Teólogos de la liberación hablan sobre la mujer* [San José, Costa Rica: DEI, 1986] p. 52; Eng. trans. *Against Machismo* [Oak Park, Ill.: Meyer-Stone Books, 1987, p. 40].)

2. Sexism still persists in theological language, as in language in general, despite the deliberate efforts being made today to overcome it. Efforts are still not sufficient, if they do not reflect an underlying change of attitude, which might eventually make such care with language unnecessary.

3. Cf. I. Gebara, "A mulher faz teologia. Um ensaio para reflexão," in I. Gebara and M. C. L. Bingemer, *A mulher faz teologia* (Petrópolis: Vozes, 1986), p. 9.

4. I realize that theology is not the only area in which women's voices are being heard. This is happening in all areas of society. But a complete study of the phenomenon would go beyond the limits of this chapter.

5. I realize that Luke's Gospel uses the image of the coin in a different context, that of God's mercy for sinners, but I have taken the liberty of using it in a different way.

6. I should like to mention in particular here the new outlook of the pastoral program for marginalized women. Instead of taking women out of prostitution and then working with them, this new program establishes itself within the women's own environment and forms groups, communities, and Bible classes there, in an attempt to bring the word of God and the good news of the gospel into this whole situation, which is the object of discrimination and marginalization on the part of the dominant sectors of society. See H. de'Ans, "Pastoral da mulher marginalizada—13 anos de caminhada libertadora," *Revista Eclesiástica Brasileira,* 47/187 (1987) 651–54.

7. I do not mean to claim that sensitivity, the sense of gratuitousness, and desire are exclusive attributes of women. The way in which our civilization has separated male and female into watertight compartments, isolating both in opposing and even irreconcilable characteristics, has left men for a long time trapped in "the rational," repressing their emotions and not allowing them to make "concessions" to their sensitive and affective side. The remark, "Men don't cry," which mothers and fathers make to boys, is significant here. See Gustavo Gutiérrez's remarks in *Teólogos de la liberación hablan sobre la mujer,* pp. 56–57.

8. On woman as this open structure, permeated by and host to life, see I. Gebara and M.C. Bingemer, *Maria Mãe de Deus e mãe dos pobres* (Petrópolis: Vozes, 1987), pp. 117–26; Eng. trans. *Mary: Mother of God, Mother of the Poor* (Theology and Liberation Series) Maryknoll, N.Y.: Orbis, 1989.

9. Parallels in Matt. 26:6–13; Mark 14:3–9; Luke 7:36–50.

10. See Alves, *What Is Religion?* (Maryknoll, N.Y.: Orbis, 1984), p. 63. "We are our desire." The author goes on to define religion as a message of desire, an expression of nostalgia, and a hope of pleasure.

11. Here we give the name desire even to God. If God is love, we have to say also that God is desire. Love desires and moves, comes toward the object of its desire, arousing in it desire in turn. Where there is desire, there is a chance of having more passionate and dedicated work, giving to the other, love. If desire is extinguished, all that remains is need, which, once satiated, disappears. Rationalism does not allow for this dynamism of desire, inherent in human beings. Desire only survives in a climate of gratuitousness, not in one of immediate needs. Theology—

like any other experience and action to do with the sphere of religion—is an activity involving desire and an object of desire. The excessive rationalism that has dominated Western theological thinking has overshadowed this dimension.

12. See Gebara, "A mulher faz teologia," p. 22.

13. See ibid.: "this procedure is the giving back to theology of the poetic dimension of human existence, for the most profound aspects of human nature can be expressed only by analogy, mystery can be expressed only in poetry, and gratuitousness can be expressed only through symbols." The psalms and wisdom literature are sources where this primacy of desire can be verified.

14. For a phenomenology of desire, see D. Vasse, *Le temps du désir* (Paris: Seuil, 1968).

15. See E. Dussel, *La producción teórica de Marx. Un comentario a los Grundrisse* (Mexico City: Siglo XXI, 1985), p. 340.

16. See R. Alves, *What Is Religion?*, p. 79: "But martyrs have appeared—Gandhi, Martin Luther King, Oscar Romero, and many others. Religious leaders are intimidated, persecuted, threatened, expelled, arrested.... This would not happen if they were in alliance with power. They are witnesses to the political significance of prophetic religion, an expression of the hurts and hopes of the powerless. Opium of the people? Maybe, but not here. In the midst of the martyrs and prophets, God is protest and the power of the oppressed."

17. See Gebara, "A mulher faz teologia," p. 24.

18. See L. Boff and C. Boff, *Introducing Liberation Theology* (Maryknoll, N.Y.: Orbis, and London: Burns & Oates, 1987) p. 43.

19. See G. Gutiérrez, *A Theology of Liberation* (Maryknoll, N.Y. : Orbis, 1973, and London: SCM, 1974), pp. 133ff., referring to the new perspectives of theology arising from the facts of underdevelopment and dependency, and historical action in support of the oppressed.

20. Notably E. Schüssler Fiorenza, L. Russel, R. R. Ruether, and others in the U.S.A., K. E. Borressen, C. Halkes, D. Sölle, and others, in Europe.

21. Gebara, "A mulher faz teologia," p. 27.

22. For example, in 1988 Brazil held its third national meeting of women theologians on the theme "Women, Theology, and Land." The Ecumenical Association of Third World Theologians (EATWOT) has a specific project on women and theology. Meetings have already been held on the three continents and a dialogue between women theologians of the First and Third Worlds is now in preparation, as is a larger and broader dialogue between men and women theologians.

23. I have selected only a few of the themes. It would be impossible to deal with all of them here.

24. On this see A. M. Tepedino, *"Mulheres discípulas nos Evangelhos—discipulado de iguais,"* doctoral thesis presented in the Pontifical University of Rio de Janeiro in April 1987.

25. See. E. Tamez, *Mujer y Bíblia,* mimeographed text presented at the Intercontinental Consultation on Third World Theology from a Woman's Perspective, Oaxtepec, Mexico, December 7–14, 1986.

26. See Tamez, *Mujer y Bíblia,* pp. 9–10.

27. Ibid.

28. See the article by L. Boff, "Maria, mulher profética e libertadora—a piedade mariana na teologia da libertação," *Revista Eclesiástica Brasileira,* 38/149 (March

1978) 39–56. See also my article, "Maria, a que soube dizer não," *Grande Sinal*, 40/4 (May 1986) 245–56.

29. See, e.g., *Concilium*, 168 (1983) *Mary in the Churches*, and the May 1985 issue of *Grande Sinal*, both written by women. See also the recent book, Gebara and Bingemer, *Mary: Mother of God, Mother of the Poor* (Theology and Liberation Series) (Maryknoll, N.Y.: Orbis, 1989).

30. On this see N. Ritchie, "Mulher e Cristologia," contribution to the meeting of Latin American women theologians, Buenos Aires, October 1985, published in *Revista Eclesiástica Brasileira*, 46/181 (1986) 60–72.

31. See also M. C. L. Bingemer, "Jesucristo y la salvación de la mujer," paper presented to the Intercontinental Consultation on Third World Theology from a Women's Perspective, pp. 15–16.

32. On this see M. C. L. Bingemer, "A Trindade a partir da perspectiva da mulher," in Gebara and Bingemer, *A mulher faz teologia*, pp. 31–79.

33. See L. Boff, *O rostro materno de Deus* (Petrópolis: Vozes, 1979); idem, *Trinity and Society* (Maryknoll, N.Y.: Orbis, 1988).

34. See the remarks on this aspect of the female character by L. C. Susin, "O Negrinho do Pastoreio—leitura teológica de uma lenda," *Revista Eclesiástica Brasileira*, 48/189 (1988) 49: "The drama of expiation, first and foremost, welcomes maternally the suffering provoked by others. Like the mother with child who carries and puts up with her child, she is stomach, lap, shoulders, body support, platform of a world. She is a store and laboratory of mercy, in which the human is welcomed in its impurity and perversion, put right and sanctified in order to be returned to its proper form, without the tortuousness of violence. To accept violence and respond with its opposite demands a resistance that is already divine because it is a supportive resistance that unconditionally bears evils and violence and breaks the vicious circle of their ever-more sophisticated violations, absorbing and 'digesting' in itself, without releasing them, but, by a metabolism and synthesis of mercy, gives back expiation. This is the supreme service—sacrifice, 'making sacred'—to another, restoring the other's humanity and the new creation."

35. See the true story told by Clodovis Boff in L. Boff and C. Boff, *Introducing Liberation Theology*, pp. 1–2: "One day, in the arid region of northeastern Brazil, one of the most famine-stricken parts of the world, I met a bishop going into his house; he was shaking. 'Bishop, what's the matter?' I asked. He replied that he had just seen a terrible sight: in front of the cathedral was a woman with three small children and a baby clinging to her neck. He saw that they were fainting from hunger. The baby seemed to be dead. He said, 'Give the baby some milk, woman!' 'I can't, my lord,' she answered. The bishop went on insisting that she should, and she that she could not. Finally, because of his insistence, she opened her blouse. Her breast was bleeding; the baby sucked violently at it. And sucked blood. The mother who had given it life was feeding it, like the pelican, with her own blood, her own life."

36. See paragraphs 28–73.

49

Reflections of a North American: The Future of Liberation Theology

ROBERT McAFEE BROWN

> Among the things Billy Pilgrim could not change were the past, the present, and the future.
> —Kurt Vonnegut, *Slaughterhouse Five*

Persons writing about the future had better invoke Kurt Vonnegut's help. We do not control the future absolutely, with the significant exception of our ability to destroy it absolutely. But we do control it to some extent. The reason we do so is that we all have pasts that condition our lives in the present, and thus either enlarge or diminish our ability to lend some measure of direction to the future. To talk about the future, therefore, is also to talk, however briefly, about the past and present. Herewith:

THE PAST: BEING INVITED TO LEARN

My own initial exposure to liberation theology was cerebral. I had been asked by Philip Scharper to do a blurb for the dust jacket of a new book by a theologian of whom I had then never heard, Gustavo Gutiérrez, on a topic of which I was equally innocent, *A Theology of Liberation*. I will never forget the experience of turning over page after page of galley sheets in the summer of 1972 and thinking, "If this is right, I have to start my theological life all over again." The impact was sufficient for me to risk commenting in the blurb that Gutiérrez's book "may well be the most important book . . . of the decade." This uncharacteristic prescience has, I think, been vindicated and then some: fifteen years down the line *A Theology of Liberation* remains the basic interpretation of liberation theology.

The cerebral exposure began to take on more flesh and blood a year later when our daughter, fresh out of high school, spent a year in Chile, beginning just three months after the coup that established the Pinochet regime in power, and she shared with us what she was experiencing of both the brutality of dictatorship and the extraordinary courage of "ordinary" Christians who were living (and dying) for liberation. Shortly after that, I was fortunate enough to attend the first "Theology in the Americas" conference at Detroit in 1975, when theologians from Latin America and North America met face to face. My own conscienticizing took a quantum leap after a comment of Gonzalo Arroyo, a Chilean Jesuit, who at one point addressed the North Americans with the query, "Tell me, why is it that when you speak of *our* theology you call it 'Latin American theology,' but when you speak of *your* theology you call it 'theology'?" I realized, quite suddenly, that with the best will in the world, we North Americans were still identifying *our* point of view as normative, and *their* point of view as culturally-conditioned and thus in need of periodic reexamination and correction by reference to the norm. Another decade of theological existence down the drain.[1]

But liberation theology cannot truly be communicated through books or secondhand experiences or conferences. It can be communicated only through human lives, and a subsequent trip to South America after the above events, two later trips to Cuba, and three still later trips to Nicaragua, have provided me with whatever inklings I now have of the power of liberation theology. I see it as truly a "theology of the people" rather than of professional theologians, rising out of the cries of the distressed, refined in the experience of those who may not even be able to read or write, clarified in the thousands of *comunidades de base*, and embodied in lives that risk everything in order to be faithful to the good news of a God who hears their cry, who consequently sides with them in their distress, and who works with them for liberation—a liberation in which they play a central role even while recognizing that the ultimate attainment of liberation will be God's gift.

So there is a new reality in the life of the people of God today, a reality embodied in the lives of those who struggle and suffer and often die, and in so doing reacquaint the rest of us with an understanding of the gospel so demanding that most of the time we would prefer to avoid it, until those struggles and sufferings and deaths become witnesses too powerful for us to shut out.

THE PRESENT: BEING INVITED TO RESPOND

What are we to do with all of this in North America? I suggest three ways in which we need to respond.

1. Our first obligation is simply *to hear and to hear correctly*. We must make sure that we do not distort, caricature, or willfully misrepresent the claims to which those lives and deaths bear both militant and silent witness.

Unfortunately, our North American track record is not enviable in this regard. Because liberation theology represents a threat to much of the ease and comfort we have, many who ought to know better distort its message in order to discredit it. Let one example suffice. Ernest Lefever, whose nomination by President Reagan to become assistant secretary of state for human rights was rejected by Congress, feels that liberation theology has been accorded more attention than it deserves, chiefly by those whom he gratuitously characterizes as eager "to embrace novelty and the radical chic shibboleths of the past two decades."[2] Against "a disquieting tendency to take it too seriously," Lefever feels that "a posture of benign neglect" would be more appropriate. He defines liberation theology "as a utopian heresy because it sanctified class violence," and utopianism as "an escape from responsibility." So much for hundreds of martyrs in the liberation struggle.

He complains that attention to a "preferential option for the poor" negates "concern for every man, woman, and child," for we are "all in need of liberation and redemption." Even the most cursory examination of the literature will make clear, as Gutiérrez notes time and again, that a "preferential" option does not mean an "exclusive" option but a starting point: if the needs of the poor begin to be attended to, then some of the injustices of society will begin to be overcome.[3] The Roman Catholic bishops at Puebla in 1979 furthermore coupled their message about a preferential option for the poor with "a preferential option for youth," indicating another priority for the church, and making clear that the two go hand in hand.[4]

Lefever compounds the above misunderstanding by claiming further that a preferential option for the poor "pits class against class and encourages enmity." This is only a fresh version of the perennial canard that liberation theologians exalt violence. Actually, the notion of "class struggle" is a *description* of what is taking place in many Third World countries. There *is* a powerful minority, and there *is* a powerless majority, and there *is* a "struggle" between them, because the few with most of the goods refuse to share them, and the many with few of the goods demand a larger share. Liberation theology is not trying to foment class struggle, *pace* Lefever, but to overcome it by a gospel that not only talks about justice but points out existing injustices. Lefever argues that "it stresses novelty at the expense of the tried and true." No one but a North American "intellectual" could make such a callous statement, for "the tried and true" has been responsible for centuries of Third World oppression.

Lefever also accuses liberation theology of fostering "economic determinism." Further, "it sponsors a new materialism." Liberation theologians are accused of promising to remove social ills "by a more equal distribution of material goods," and of suggesting (along with Karl Marx) that freedom, culture, music, love, and so forth, are all "economically determined."

Such charges are so far off the mark that they do not deserve serious comment, and I have devoted more space to Mr. Lefever's irresponsible accusations than they deserve simply to make the point that if persons like him, who ought to know better, can present such insensitive critiques, there are many more who will fall prey to such simplistic and erroneous reductionism. The task of ensuring that liberation theology gains a fair hearing will be ongoing.

2. A second obligation is to try to see the role of the United States in the Third World through the eyes of those committed to liberation. Here the shoe really begins to pinch, for we are told by those who perceive themselves as oppressed that they perceive persons like us, and the social systems we uphold, as their oppressors.

My experience has been that when North Americans are confronted by such a claim, the first reaction is one of incredulity ("How can they talk that way when we send them so much aid?"), usually followed by anger ("If that's the way they feel about us, so much the worse for them"). There may also be pain and wistfulness ("We certainly don't intend to hurt them; we are really trying to help, and maybe we can send more food and clothing to make up for past mistakes").

As soon as the analysis gets more refined, the Achilles' heel in the posture of injured feelings begins to surface ("It sounds as though they are attacking capitalism"). The truth of the matter, of course, is that they are, and the further truth of the matter is that this often offends North Americans more than anything else, because the very core of their belief-system is being challenged.

Some of the Latin American analysis is quite sophisticated, engaged in by Third World thinkers who can hold their own in a serious debate with economic counterparts from the First World. Some of it is also descriptive and indeed poignantly so, and it must be heard by us. We are invited to look at lives destroyed, villages bombed, children starving, human hopes receding, and sooner or later the question must be faced: Who is responsible for this? And while it is too simplistic to charge that it is only U.S. corporations, or U.S. banks, or U.S. right-wing politicians, it is nevertheless clear that high among the real contributors to the ongoing misery are all of the above.

Where do the North American chuches and theological community fit into this? We are part of it to the extent that both our message and our mission are complicit in support of the injustices of our society, and the moment of truth comes for us (as we will presently examine) when we realize that a choice between the gospel and the "powers that be" is forced upon us, and that if we say yes to the first we must say no to the second. So we are called upon to assess, preferably at first hand, some of the consequences of what happens when a watered-down faith turns out to be in lockstep with U.S. foreign policy and U.S. corporations exploiting those overseas.

We cannot have the luxury of assuming that what is happening in Latin America or Africa or Asia is really not our concern, either as citizens of the United States of America, or as members of the kingdom of God. We bear a major responsibility for the upheaval and distress of the world, and that assessment must surface in our consciousness if we are to begin to act as responsible global beings.

3. If we are willing (1) to hear the liberation message clearly on its own terms, and (2) hear its assessment of our responsibility for much of the world's oppression, this must (3) challenge us *to rethink and re-create our own message*. The task is not to decide that Latin American liberation theology is the way of the future, and seek to import it. The task is rather to discover where our own areas of need for liberation are located, and begin to create a liberation theology for North America. This will call for the most exacting kind of honesty, confession, struggle, and rebuilding.

Fortunately, this process has already begun, not with the creation of a single North American theology of liberation, but with the creation of a number of indigenous North American theologies of liberation. Let us take brief account of this important fact.

The initial liberation theology to be spawned on North American soil is surely black theology, which has grown directly out of the U.S. black experience of oppression, victimization, marginalization, and powerlessness.[5] In one of those curious acts of prescience of which he was frequently capable, Dietrich Bonhoeffer prophesied back in 1931 that it might be the black churches that would save America.[6] And it is indeed the case that to the degree that there has been a new sense of concern for justice in the United States and in the American churches, that concern has sprung in significant measure from black theology and the black churches.

A second indigenous North American liberation theology is feminist theology. Feminist movements have, to be sure, spread worldwide, but the articulation of a way of doing theology from a feminist perspective had important origins in the United States. Once again this has grown out of the experience of a group of human beings who, like blacks, have undergone oppression, victimization, marginalization,

494

and powerlessness. It is encouraging to see how quickly links with women from other parts of the globe have been established by North American feminist theology, as local realizations of outrage have been replicated globally.[7]

Nor are these the only liberation theologies that have sprung from North American soil. Particularly distinctive has been the concern among Amerindians to create a theology springing from their situation of oppression. This theology, which has distinctively American geographical and cultural roots, clearly shares affinities with the black South African situation, where government treatment discloses disturbing parallels to the treatment Amerindians have received (and continue to receive) in the United States.[8]

A fourth distinctive North American liberation theology has grown out of gay and lesbian oppression. While this issue is by no means a uniquely North American one, the most significant articulations of the shape of such a theology have again come from the United States.[9] And the list can continue: Puerto Rican theology, Hispanic theology, theology for Philippine-Americans, and so on.

These positions, all of which have distinctive emphases that must not be artificially conflated, nevertheless do share the common characteristic that they are the products of groups who have experienced oppression, victimization, marginalization, and powerlessness. They have needed time and space to work out their own distinctive emphases and develop both self-awareness and a sense of self-worth ("Black is beautiful," "The Lord's my shepherd and he knows I'm gay," "Christ in a poncho," and so forth). It is now clear, however, at least to this observer, that these varied theologies will increasingly draw closer to one another, not only by significant overlapping of their concerns, but also by the realization that together they can wield a power they can never hope to wield separately.

THE FUTURE: BEING INVITED TO ACT

I referred to myself in the above paragraph as an "observer" rather than a participant. What kind of cop-out is this?

The truth of the matter is that in relation to the groups just described, I *am* an observer; I am not black, female, Amerindian, gay, Puerto Rican, Hispanic, or Filipino. I am (in terms that are descriptive to some and pejorative to others) a white male North American. This is at best a dubious category in which to be cast, for it is a historical fact that with whatever separates all the liberation viewpoints cited above from each other, they agree that the main architects of their oppression have been and continue to be members of the white male North American establishment.

In the light of this fact, how can we white, male North Americans relate to the liberation struggle? Is there a liberation message for us as well? Can there be a liberation message from us as well? It is these themes that I propose to examine for the balance of this essay.

I shall not attempt anything so grandiose as a full-blown "liberation theology for white male North Americans," particularly in ten pages.[10] My more modest agenda will be to try to identify some of the issues we must confront realistically, if we are to come within hailing distance of a meeting place between ourselves and the liberation struggles of others. Out of a massive potential agenda, I arbitrarily choose five themes:

1. *On being an "oppressor."* As indicated above, there is a widespread consensus among oppressed peoples that we are the ones most responsible for their misery. When confronting us with this estimate, they sometimes add, in an act of generosity, "Of course, I don't mean you personally...," which mitigates the sting a bit, but only a bit. Who wants to be tagged an "oppressor," even if it is only guilt by association?

We have to deal with the fact, however, that the charge has substance, and that much of the structural violence in the world today can be laid at the door of white males, even if not all of them are North Americans. I do not consider it creative to respond by saturating ourselves with guilt, however, for guilt is not only an unsatisfactory motivation for change, but also tends so to immobilize its advocates that they are effectively exempt from doing anything beyond wallowing in self-depreciation.

Since those who most truly work for liberation are those who *need* liberation, is there any meaningful way in which we can claim that we, denominated as "oppressors," are also among the "oppressed," and must work for our own liberation as well as the liberation of others?

This is a tricky proposal because it immediately sounds self-saving, but I have long been impressed by the remark of Basil Moore, writing out of the South African struggle:

> I am prepared to trust and stand alongside a man who is fighting *for himself and his own freedom* if I know that his freedom is bound up with mine. I cannot wholeheartedly trust a man who is fighting *for me*, for I fear that sooner or later he will tire of the struggle.[11]

So a recognition that all of us occupy some territory on both sides of the hyphen in the "oppressor-oppressed" contrast may be a creative act. I know of no one who has made this point of view clearer, from within the feminist struggle, than Karen Lebacqz. In *Justice in an Unjust World* (Minneapolis: Augsburg, 1987), she acknowledges that "by virtue of skin color, solvency, education, religious background, and nationality," she has advantages denied to most women. She is part of a group that rules... and oppresses. She has not, and cannot, experience the oppression that Jews have felt, or the desperately poor and disenfranchised, the wheelchair occupant, the black woman. And yet, she is a woman, "and even in white, solvent, well-educated Christian America, women are oppressed" (p. 14). This fact is then catalogued in some detail. So she can "speak both as an oppressor and as oppressed," and this posture, rather than being the basis for a cop-out, helps Professor Lebacqz "to temper my oppressor mentality by remembering my own experiences of oppression and by attending to the voices of the oppressed" (p. 15).

In addition to this kind of recognition, to the degree that we could identify the source of our own oppression, we might be able to work collaboratively with others in the liberation theology.

What, then, is the source of our own oppression? Unless we can "name" it, we will remain caught in its thrall, for we will not even be aware of its hold over us. I suggest that our oppressor is not a group within our social-economic system so much as it is the very socio-economic system itself. We are the inheritors of, and have been conditioned to accept uncritically, a whole series of "virtues" that are

meant to be self-evident and self-validating. They include such things as the necessity of upward mobility, both personally and professionally; the willingness to
compete, by fair means or foul, against those who threaten our success or our job
or our nation; a commitment to "looking out for Number One," for no one else
will; a conviction that the payoff for hard work is material comfort of an increasingly
lavish sort; a willingness to put our jobs ahead of our families; a belief that it is
both appropriate and necessary to check our moral values at the entrance to the
work place, for the bottom line is always profit, and nothing must interfere with
that.

If the above sounds like a caricature, I submit that that is simply an indirect
indication of its accuracy, for few of us are ready to believe that we have gotten
locked into a social structure in which greed and exploitation are two sides of the
same coin. At all events, I propose that one of our first jobs is to examine these
and other criteria of success in the marketplace, and ponder the degree to which
we have been oppressed by such structures without knowing it. I am not sanguine
that a revolution of the ruling class is about to sweep through our society. But I
am convinced that if there are to be significant changes in our society to "liberate
the oppressed" (as Jesus said so well), they will come only to the extent that we
properly "name" the oppressor and begin to find ways to challenge its sovereignty.

2. *On being a "traitor to one's class."* The cost for doing so can be great. If it is
our initial plight to be categorized by the left as sell-outs, it will be our increasing
plight, should we press these issues, to be categorized by the right as traitors. "You
have inherited a wonderful situation," we will be told, "the benefits of which are
due to market capitalism, and you are not only ungracious to seek to bite the hand
that feeds you so well, but disloyal to suggest that we should seek 'a more excellent
way.' " Concern for the social good will be presented as betrayal of the values of
"individual initiative," and concern for the poor will be linked (as in the baleful
example of Mr. Lefever) with fomenting violence or espousing economic determinism, and thus betray the ultimate apostasy that we are really communists at heart.

Let us be honest. Such charges may not threaten us in the abstract, but when
they are pronounced by friends, colleagues, and (maybe the bottom line if we are
really honest) those who hold control over our jobs and livelihoods, the pressures
to keep quiet and conform are great.

For some of us, the tensions will be exacerbated by the fact that cries of treason
(though clothed in more genteel theological garb) will come from members of our
churches, who will see even an implicit attack on middle-class values as an attack
on themselves, and indeed on the church, to the degree (a high degree) that the
church is a reflection of, and support for, middle-class values.

For all of us, the bottom line is going to be more than simply fending off personal
attacks, however; it is going to have something to do with lifestyles—that is, not
just how we think, but how we live. With a few notable exceptions like Richard
Shaull (see his *Heralds of a New Reformation* [Maryknoll, N.Y.: Orbis, 1984], esp.
chap. 6, "Changing Values and Changing Sides"), most of us who live within the
"establishment" have found it convenient not to face this issue. When push comes
to shove, we are inclined to settle for reform tactics rather than revolutionary
commitment, choosing gradual change rather than significant confrontation. I have
no personal heroics to report on this front, but I am increasingly convinced that
those of us who are mainstream must face more directly the liberation challenge

as it affects us personally and as it colors what we do within our churches.

3. *On working within church structures.* But the church is not solely a repository of middle-class values. It has a history, usually submerged but occasionally breaking out above the surface, of siding with victims, calling rulers to account, and discovering, often to its surprise, that without human contrivance fresh resources in the heritage reassert themselves in times of crisis.

There are two reasons why it is important to try to carry on the liberation theology struggle within the churches. First of all, the churches themselves need to hear a liberation message that can deliver them from excessive co-optation by the principalities and powers of this world. If we really believed in *ecclesia semper reformanda* (the church always to be reformed), then the breath of the Holy Spirit that is blowing today in some parts of the church (notably in the Third World) could fan new flames of ardor and commitment in our own lives. The second reason for relating the liberation struggle to the churches is that there is no other vehicle in society that has more potential for keeping the struggle alive and well, and overcoming the burnout factor that hamstrings so many other social groups. The recuperative power of the gospel can keep churches from being subservient to any ideology—in a world where all sorts of ideologies, particularly those of the right wing, trap or subsume liberation concerns within their own very different agendas.

To be sure, organized churches move with maddening slowness when issues of justice and liberation are involved, and those who work within them will need involvement with other groups in society as well, in order to avoid the erosion of personal engagement by institutional timidity. But there can be a healthy dialectic here, with institutional and personal cross-fertilization helping to enhance the life of both groups.

There is another point to be made. Within the churches today there is an increasingly widespread discussion that has important implications for liberation concerns: are the churches moving into a new "confessional situation" (what has historically been called a *status confessionis*) in which, on certain issues we have to say something like the following: "Until now, it has been possible to be a Christian and hold either side of the argument; but we have now reached a place where our understanding of the Christian message is *so clear* that taking exception to it is no longer possible. Those who now dissent removed themselves from the company of believers." The situation came to a head in the Confessing Church in Germany after the rise of Hitler, and the conclusion was reached: to say yes to Jesus Christ means to say no to Hitler. A similar conclusion has been reached by many of the churches of South Africa: to say yes to Jesus Christ means to say no to apartheid.[12] And increasing numbers of Christians today, particularly in the United States, are reaching the conclusion that to say yes to Jesus Christ may have to mean saying no to nuclear weapons.[13] There is also beginning to be some discussion within the churches about the impossibility of a simultaneous yes to Jesus Christ and to market capitalism.[14]

These are important movements, and it may be that part of our engagement in the liberation struggle will be to forward such discussion within the churches and find ways to act upon it.

4. *On "speaking truth to power."* If the declaration of a *status confessionis* is the extreme situation, representing an all-out frontal attack on an otherwise accepted

position, there are many points short of that in which we have an obligation to "speak truth to power."

It can be questioned whether "middle-class" persons have any significant power in a world dominated by a power elite and corporate structures whose effective control is in the possession of a tiny handful; our illusion of power (the ballot, "shareholder resolutions," dissent in public life, and so on) may be greater than its actuality. And yet as long as there are structures within a society that provide any access to the molding of public opinion, we have an obligation to use them.

One of the ways of "speaking truth to power" will be to concentrate on the very issue of power itself, and this has the added virtue in the present essay of providing an example of how North American and South American liberation concerns, though focusing on the issue of power, may need to say and do different things in their different contexts. In most Third World countries, although the internal power of a dictator may be inordinate, the power of these countries in terms of international leverage is virtually nil. They have no real control over their own destinies; they cannot decide what crops to grow if shareholders in a multinational corporation rule otherwise; they cannot control access to world markets for their exports save as First World nations allow; and they are saddled with debts so massive that there is no way they can ever expect to be free of stultifying indebtedness. In such situations, obviously, the Christian message must be related to liberation *from* such dependency, and liberation *for* a significant measure of control over their lives. They must pray for, act for, struggle for, power.

In North America, however, the situation is different and the liberating message must consequently be different. If Third World peoples are those who scarcely know the taste of power, First World nations like ours are drunk with it. If Third World nations have too little power, First World nations have too much, and with awesome consistency use it destructively. The task of liberation theology in our situation, therefore, is "to speak truth to power" in an effort to show (1) that rather than clutching more and more power to ourselves, we must share it; and (2) that the legacy of our remaining power must begin to be used creatively rather than destructively. Stated so baldly, these sound like either platitudes or irrelevant nonsense, but the truth of the matter is (1) that if we do not begin to share power, it will finally be taken from us, and (2) that to the degree that we continue to use it destructively, we will be sowing the seeds of a whirlwind that will finally engulf and destroy us. Instances of our nation's abuse of power can be documented in relation to almost any country with which we have had economic relations. We have had an almost unerring instinct to back forces of injustice, shore up dictators, and finance rebellions against countries that want to give "people's" democracy a chance to work. The names of Chile and the Philippines spring unaided to the mind. As I write, the notorious instance is Nicaragua, where for over a century we have imposed our will on a tiny and desperately poor country, usually by military intervention—a policy the Reagan administration has been obsessively desirous of pursuing yet again, determined to topple a regime whose chief sin is its refusal to "say uncle" to Uncle Sam. I am persuaded that one of the reasons the Reagan administration did not long ago invade Nicaragua is because, throughout the land, groups of Christians, working with other citizens, have attempted to "speak truth to power" by denouncing the administration's policy of intimidation and destruction.

5. *On broadening the base.* I noted earlier that in the case of burgeoning indig-

enous liberation theologies—black, feminist, Amerindian, gay/lesbian, Puerto Rican, Hispanic, and Filipino—an initial need for separateness, in order to refine their individual agendas, is beginning to be replaced by a desire to work together, not only for mutual self-enrichment, but because only together can they be effective instruments for social change. There is nothing the principalities and powers would like more than to have political protest groups continue fighting among themselves.

I doubt that such groups are enchanted, at least yet, by the notion of joining forces with white male North Americans, and it is also likely that many white male North Americans still feel ill at ease in the company of those with whom past associations have often been conflictual. But as many doors as possible must be set ajar now so that later they can more easily be opened wide. If the liberation struggle is going to move beyond a series of discrete, private, and unconnected dreams, the base must be broadened to be as inclusive as possible of all these theological commitments. And the base must be broadened as well beyond the strictly theological community. The experience noted in the previous section—that church groups and other citizens joined forces to create a stronger voice in combatting U.S. policy in Nicaragua—must become a model for other issues as well. The resultant theologies must include large doses of social analysis, "doing theology" must become more communal and less dependent on theological superstars, and new vocabularies must be developed that avoid the sexism, racism, and classism of so much traditional theology.[15] What must happen, in other words, is that persons be liberated to join the human race, rather than continuing to live in enclaves.

CONCLUSION

In an essay in a book honoring Gustavo Gutiérrez, it may seem strange not to have given more explicit attention to his writings, but I am gambling on the hunch that this is one of the best ways to "honor" him. Our theological task is not to become clones of Gustavo, but, having learned from him, to make use of the various resources with which he reacquaints us (scripture, tradition, social analysis, and personal engagement, for example) as we struggle to be faithful to the gospel in our situations, just as he has tried to be faithful to it in his.

There is, of course, another resource still—Gustavo's own writings. We need them as anchors to keep us moored to reality. Part of our own hope for the theological future is the promise that he will keep writing, and the assurance that from each new book we will learn new things. (How long, let us ask proddingly, until the promised volume on Las Casas appears?) Most of all, however, to those fortunate enough to know him, the total congruence between what he writes and what he lives remains his supreme contribution to the rest of us.

Better perhaps to leave it there. We should not, after all, further embarrass one who is already a little embarrassed at being the subject of a festschrift.

NOTES

1. For an account of the conference, see S. Torres and J. Eagleson, eds., *Theology in the Americas*, (Maryknoll, N.Y.: Orbis, 1976).
2. See "Liberation Theology as a Utopian Heresy," in *Face to Face, an Interreligious Bulletin* (Winter 1987) 18–20.

3. See G. Gutiérrez, *The Power of the Poor in History* (Maryknoll, N.Y.: Orbis, 1983), pp. 126ff., 136–142, 149; *We Drink from Our Own Wells* (Maryknoll, N.Y.: Orbis, 1984), p. 101; "El Evangelio del Trabajo," in Gutiérrez et al., *Sobre el Trabajo Humano* (Lima: CEP, 1982), pp. 43–57, and many others.

4. See J. Eagleson and P. Scharper, eds., *Puebla and Beyond* (Maryknoll, N.Y.: Orbis, 1979), pp. 267–72. I have commented on the Puebla treatment of this matter in ibid., pp. 341–43, and more fully in W. Tabb, ed., *Churches in Struggle* "The Preferential Option for the Poor' and the Renewal of Faith," (New York: Monthly 'Review Press, 1986), pp. 7–17.

5. The literature is extensive. See esp. J. Cone, *For My People: Black Theology and the Black Church* (Maryknoll, N.Y.: Orbis, 1984); G. Wilmore, *Black Religion and Black Radicalism*, 2nd ed. (Maryknoll, N.Y.: Orbis, 1983); C. West, *Prophesy Deliverance* (Philadelphia: Westminster, 1982).

6. D. Bonhoeffer, *No Rusty Swords* (New York: Harper and Row, 1985), "Protestantism Without Reformation," pp. 92–118.

7. Here, too, the literature is extensive. See inter alia R. Ruether, *Sexism and God-Talk*, (Boston: Beacon, 1983); C. Heyward, *The Redemption of God* (Washington: University of America Press, 1982); M. Katoppo, *Compassionate and Free: An Asian Woman's Theology* (Maryknoll, N.Y.: Orbis, 1980); L. Russell, ed., *Feminist Interpretation of the Bible* (Philadelphia: Westminster, 1985).

8. See V. Deloria, *God is Red* (New York: Delta, 1973), and the interpretive material in Reist, *Theology in Red, White, and Black* (Philadelphia: Westminster, 1975).

9. Cf. G. Edwards, *Gay/Liberation: A Biblical Perspective* (New York: Pilgrim Press, 1984); R. Scroggs, *The New Testament and Homosexuality* (Philadelphia: Fortress Press, 1983); Glaser, *Uncommon Calling* (New York: Harper and Row, 1988).

10. Because the term "white male North American" fails to yield a satisfactory acronym, no matter how the letters are arranged, I shall henceforth identify this breed simply by the pronoun "we."

11. Moore, *The Challenge of Black Theology in South Africa* (Atlanta: John Knox, 1974), p. 5, italics added.

12. See J. De Gruchy and C. Villa-Vicencio, *Apartheid is a Heresy* (Grand Rapids: Eerdmans, 1983).

13. I have dealt with these issues in *Saying Yes and Saying No: On Rendering to God and Caesar* (Philadelphia: Westminster, 1986), esp. chap. 1 and 2. See also the important article by G. Hunsinger, "Barth, Barmen, and the Confessing Church Today," *Katallagete* (Summer 1985) 14–27, and the extended responses in ibid. (Fall 1987) 1–108. This material deserves the widest possible circulation.

14. U. Durchrow, *Global Economy: A Confessional Issue for the Churches?* (Geneva: World Council of Churches, 1987). I have a brief commentary, "Global Realities, Local Theologies," in *Christianity and Crisis*, Feb. 15, 1988, pp. 15–16.

15. Writings that begin these tasks are R. Shaull, *Heralds of a New Reformation* (Maryknoll, N.Y.: Orbis, 1984); M. Lamb, *Solidarity with Victims: Toward a Social Transformation* (New York: Crossroad, 1982); W. Tabb, ed., *Churches in Struggle: Liberation Theologies and Social Change in North America* (New York: Monthly Review Press, 1986); J. Nelson-Pallmeyer, *The Politics of Compassion: Hunger, the Arms Race, and U.S. Policy in Central America* (Maryknoll, N.Y.: Orbis, 1987).

50

Liberation Theology:
A Difficult but Possible Future

PABLO RICHARD

It is interesting that for this celebration of twenty years of liberation theology and the sixtieth birthday of our dear master and friend Gustavo Gutiérrez, we all start thinking not about the past but also the future. We are all convinced not only that liberation theology has a *future* but that it is theology's *only future*. We are also well aware that this future will be difficult. If liberation theology wants to remain faithful to its past and keep its identity, it will have to face an increasingly difficult future. However, the lives of poor Latin American Christians have been and go on being even more difficult, and so has the renewal of the church through the ecclesial base communities. But difficult does not mean impossible, providing that we find the right way and the necessary strength to keep to it.

I find it extraordinarily appropriate to reflect thus on the future of liberation theology in solidarity with Gustavo Gutiérrez. I do not want to go into personal details here, but it is obvious to me that over the last twenty years Gustavo has been an inspiration to us; he has taught us ways of seeing and what constitutes the tap root of liberation theology. Whenever we have felt bewildered or discouraged, it has been Gustavo who has given us fresh insight and heart. I have written this article with special gratitude to him and with a strong hope for the future of liberation theology.

In this article I shall try to develop, very briefly, the seven fields in which I think liberation theology has been most fruitful and in which I think it will find its strength in the future. I shall try to answer the fundamental question: *Where does our strength lie*? If we know where our strength really is, then we know where we should grow and where we should concentrate our work and hope.

1. SPIRITUALITY AND LIBERATION THEOLOGY

God lives and bestows self-revelation in the world of the poor and their struggles for liberation. This special presence and revelation of God in the heart of the people is liberation's theology deep root, whence it draws its strength and future.

Liberating spirituality is the capacity to live, experience, discern, and express God's presence among the oppressed. Liberation theology reflects in a systematic and critical way the God who appears in spirituality. If liberation theology comes to be broken off from its root in spirituality, it loses its purpose and dies as theology. Liberation theology can develop only from its root in the spiritual world of the poor: their silence, prayer, and joy.

It has often been said, and rightly, that what destroys our spirituality is not atheism but idolatry. Idolatry is the "spirituality of death," which invades everything today and radically perverts the meaning of God in our society. The fruit of idolatry is death; the root of social sin is idolatry. An important task of liberation theology is to distinguish between liberating spirituality and destructive idolatry: between the God of life and the idols of death. Liberation theology has power and a future to the extent that it succeeds in this discernment. Liberation theology is capable of this discernment only in the light of the spiritual experience of the poor. Liberation theology must elaborate theological criteria for this discernment.

Traditional theology is a theology that becomes more repetitive every day. It is empty, feeble, lacking in significance and—why not say so?—boring. It is a science cultivated in closed elitist academies. The world is not interested in this theology, and neither is this theology interested in the world. The cause of its sterility is that *the dominant theology has no spirituality, no God, and does not communicate God's word.* It is a theology confused by idolatry. Often it is a theology of death. Liberation theology can maintain its power and originality only if it is a theology of the God of the poor and a theology capable of hearing and transmitting God's word revealed to the poor. This is its strength and its future.

2. POPULAR RELIGIOUS AWARENESS AND LIBERATION THEOLOGY

The religious awareness of the people is a combination of many things: popular religiosity, indigenous religions, Afro-American religions, animistic traditions, magic. . . . The religious world of the people is an ocean too vast for anthropologists, sociologists, and theologians to plumb. For us it bears two important characteristics: it is an *alternative* religious awareness and in a certain sense it is an awareness *informed by the gospel* and *asserting the gospel.*

First, it is an alternative awareness to the predominant religion, and often an alternative to the religious predominance of a church of Christendom. It is a "popular" as opposed to "official" religious awareness. Secondly, it is an awareness to some degree colored by the preaching of the gospel. In spite of five centuries of conquest and spiritual manipulation, many seeds and germs of the gospel have penetrated the soul of popular culture and religion. Moreover, it is an awareness informed by the mysterious presence and revelation of God in the world of the poor. And the church of the poor's gospel-preaching work, from Bartolomé de Las Casas to Archbishop Romero, has had a real impact on popular religious awareness.

Liberation theology can have power and a future only if it succeeds in taking root in this alternative and evangelical religious awareness of the people. If it fails to take root here, liberation theology will be merely another elitist, intellectualist, and sterile theology. Only through the religious awareness of the people can we come *historically* to the God of the poor and discover the power of God's liberating presence and word. Liberation theology has its historical roots in popular culture and religion. It will never become a popular alternative to the religious system of domination, it will never have evangelizing power if it gives up its roots in popular religious awareness. Liberation theology has not let itself be carried away by the liberal, fundamentalist, "charismatic" trends that have tried to preach the gospel to the people in a way that is outside and against all their own cultural and religious tradition. Liberation theology maintains the relationship between faith and religion, faith and culture, faith and people. This is the necessary condition for it to develop, keep its identity, and have a future.

3. ECONOMICS AND LIBERATION THEOLOGY

By *economics* I mean here the safeguarding and continuation of everyone's life, but especially *the lives of the poor and oppressed*. Fundamentally life means: work, land, food, health, housing, education, environment, rest, and celebration (festival). Here I am not talking about a dialogue between theology and economics, or a theological reflection on economics. I am saying that life, especially the lives of the poor, must be taken as theology's rationale. I am not talking about the meaning of life or an economic or political program, but about *life* as a criterion for discerning what is *rational* and what is *irrational*; as the criterion for discerning *true* from *false*, *good* from *evil*, the *beautiful* from the *ugly*. What is rational, logical, true, good, and beautiful is that all, especially the poor, should have life. What is irrational, illogical, false, evil, and ugly is that the poor should not have life. Hunger, unemployment, malnutrition, illiteracy, and the destruction of nature is irrational, illogical, evil, and ugly. When we speak about economics and theology, we mean the epistemological problem of our criteria of rationality and truth. The great challenge for liberation theology is the life of the poor as the criterion of theological rationality. Real life is not just a problem of economic, political, or cultural reality; it is also a spiritual and theological reality.

Saint Irenaeus put it succinctly: *gloria dei vivens homo* (God's glory is the living human being). God's own glory and credibility are at stake in the lives of the poor. This epistemological option, this option for life as a criterion of rationality, truth, goodness, and beauty, is what makes liberation theology, at its deepest level, liberating. And its liberating power is what makes it theology, because God's glory is revealed in the lives of the poor. We are not talking about a purely sociological problem, but about the very nature of liberation theology as *theology* and as theology of *liberation*.

4. ECCLESIAL BASE COMMUNITIES AND LIBERATION THEOLOGY

The three previous points—spirituality, popular religious awareness, and the lives of the poor as the criterion of rationality—took us to the root of liberation theology. They are the *radical,* original, and originating elements of liberation theology; they are its spiritual, historical, and epistemological foundation.

But now we must pass from the root to the trunk—to keep the tree metaphor. The root is invisible because it is underground, but the trunk is what makes this root visible and gives it body. Liberation theology's trunk consists of the ecclesial base communities (EBCs). These EBCs keep liberation theology alive and liberation theology develops through them.

Here I do not want to define the EBCs. Neither am I assuming that they have a single or universal model. I am merely talking about a presence of the *church,* experienced in a *communal* way and firmly established at the *base.* The EBCs are not an ecclesial movement or simply a pastoral model. They are the church itself, the life of the church at the base, among the people. Whenever we have an ecclesial presence, of a communal type, established at the base, then we have EBCs, whatever their form or organization. By base, of course, I mean the human, geographical, social, political, ethnic, and racial base of the church. From its beginning, liberation theology has been identified with this historical expression of the church. This is where it was born and for whose sake it lives. The presence of Christians in popular movements and the reconstruction of the church in terms of popular faith have been the major events giving rise to liberation theology. Therefore, liberation theology is not just an intellectual or theological trend. It is a work of critical and systematic reflection within the church.

In what way have the EBCs marked the very essence and development of liberation theology? Let us recall first the specific way in which EBCs work and then let us see how this dynamic has put its stamp on liberation theology. The specific key strategic element of the EBCs is *participation* — the participation of the poor and oppressed as active subjects, doers, makers of history within the church. The poor were always passive objects in the church of Christendom: objects of gospel-preaching, pastoral attention, objects of charity. Under Christendom, participation was always almost impossible. It was very difficult even for the middle, and upper classes, impossible for the poor, especially the most marginalized among them: indigenous populations, peasants, blacks, women.

Today the poor are irrupting into the church and they are doing so mainly through the EBCs. The poor participate now as active subjects and doers in the church. This has been possible because of the political, social, cultural, and religious awakening of the Latin American peoples over the last few decades, but also because of the church's own preferential option for the poor. It is the result of the church's liberating spirituality lived out in the world of the poor. It is the result of the evangelization of popular religious awareness and of the church's entering the world of the poor and oppressed, and taking their lives as its criterion of rationality and truth. Not only do the poor participate as active subjects in the church, their participation is creative. The poor participate by creating a new language, a new symbolism, a new "rhythm," new liturgical forms, new prayers, a new reading of the Bible, new ministries, and a new theological reflection.

This creative participation of the people in the church, which has begun only recently, is a creative participation from these oppressed groups' own cultural, religious, ethnic, racial, and human standpoints. This movement of creative participation by the people as subjects in the church has had a profound effect on liberation theology. Now there is a new doer, a new maker of history, in the church, and this new active subject is doing theology or at least inspiring new theological reflection in the church. The emergence of this new active subject, forgotten for centuries in the church, perhaps since the first century, is what is crucial about the EBCs and what is giving rise to liberation theology. From here liberation theology draws its power and its future. If one day liberation theology became separated, cut off from, this new historical subject in the church, it would wither and possibly die as liberation theology.

5. BIBLICAL HERMENEUTICS AND LIBERATION THEOLOGY

The most profound and important work done by the EBCs is what we call *popular Bible reading*. Poor Christians are appropriating the Bible and stamping it with their own spirituality and culture. This practice is as old as the history of the EBCs but only in the last few years have we been reflecting critically on it and doing consciously organized and biblical work in terms of popular Bible reading. From this practice a *hermeneutics of liberation* is also arising. This is just the theoretical expression of the practice of Bible reading in the communities. Let us look now at the essential elements of this biblical practice and theory, and draw a few conclusions for the future of liberation theology.

We can distinguish three moments in the hermeneutics of liberation: the political, the spiritual, and the hermeneutic properly speaking. In the *political* the poor emerge as new historical subjects: it is they who actively pursue the hermeneutic process. The poor are reading the Bible and interpreting it from their own point of view. These persons who are now actively engaged in the hermeneutic process, are the same historical subjects—the poor—as those at the base and root of the production process of this same Bible.

Today we repeat enthusiastically that the Bible is the historical memory of the poor—and it really is. But for centuries this was forgotten and the voice of the poor was not heard. The Bible became the property of clerics and intellectuals. Today the Bible has been restored to its rightful owners. The poor take possession of the Bible today and read it from the point of view of their own culture, awareness, and history.

In the *spiritual*—the second moment of the hermeneutic process—what appears is a new experience of God in the world of the poor and oppressed. Liberating spirituality is making a strong impression on biblical hermeneutics. There is an experience of God and God's word that precedes the hermeneutic process and is more important than all biblical interpretation. The Bible is read to discern this presence of God and God's living word today in our history. God is greater than the Bible. The absolute in history is God's word. The Bible is an instrument in the service of God's word. The greater the experience of God and God's word in the world of the poor, the better and clearer is their biblical interpretation.

Finally, we have the *hermeneutic* moment properly so called. Here there is a struggle between different readings of the Bible. The Bible comes to a people already interpreted, but the interpretation given is normally alien to their awareness, culture, and spirituality. It is necessary to regain the text and the history of this biblical text from the viewpoint of the poor. Every moment of the hermeneutic process is conflictive and so we can say that in the hermeneutics of liberation a political, spiritual, and hermeneutic rupture takes place. First there is a political rupture with the dominant system, ideology, and culture. Then there is a spiritual rupture with the dominant idolatry, the idolatrous spiritualism of a system of death. Finally, and most specifically, there is a hermeneutic rupture with an already given dominant reading and interpretation of the Bible. There is no doubt whatever that we are seeing this triple rupture in the hermeneutics of liberation. What distinguishes us is not a particular hermeneutical line but this rupture, which is explicitly political, spiritual, and hermeneutic.

If we assume the distinction between the literal, historical, and spiritual meaning of the biblical text, we can say that the greatest creativity in popular Bible reading is taking place in the spiritual. There is a production of meaning that is affecting the biblical text itself and the history behind the biblical text. When the EBCs read the Bible to discern and express the word of God in our own historical reality, biblical history and the text itself acquire new meaning. Over the last few years poor Christian persons in Latin America have read Exodus, the Prophets, Psalms, Gospels, Apocalypse. All these texts today have a new, liberating meaning for the people. They have become living texts, capable of reading our history and trans- forming our communities so that they become prophetic. This new spiritual meaning of the Bible is not arbitrary, because, on the one hand, it is rooted in the experience of God in the world of the poor, and it is also "controlled" by exegetic work that discovers the literal meaning and the historical meaning of the text. Likewise we are accompanied by the sense of faith in the church as people of God and the magisterial authority of our pastors.

Liberation theology finds strength and renewal in popular Bible reading. There is an unlimited field for its development here. In the future, liberating hermeneutics will be the main activity of liberation theology and will give it even deeper roots in the political and spiritual lives of poor Latin American Christians. In the near future the main literary production of liberation theology will be in the biblical field and here it will find a new impetus and development.

6. THE THIRD WORLD AND LIBERATION THEOLOGY

The world population in the year 1900 was 1,600 million. Today, there are 5,000 million of us. At the end of the century the earth will have 6,350 million inhabitants. Between 1988 and the year 2000 humanity will increase by 1,350 million. This is about the same increase as that since the time of Jesus until 1900. In this century there has been a demographic explosion never before seen in human history. But the most significant thing is that this growth has been mainly in the Third World— that is to say, in poor countries and among the poor in all countries. In the year 2000, twenty percent of humanity will live in the so-called developed world and eighty percent in underdeveloped countries (including China). Today, three out of every four inhabitants of the earth live in the Third World. By the end of the century, four out of five will live in the Third World. But the Third World is not just a numerical reality, it is also a human, religious, and cultural reality. The great religions with a written tradition (Islam, Judaism, Buddhism, Hinduism . . .) are Third World religions. In the Third World we also have the greatest wealth of indigenous culture, as well as immense riches in human values and qualities. The Third World is poor, but rich in humanity, religion, and culture.

The twenty-first century (and why not say the whole of the third millennium) will certainly be the century (and millennium) of the Third World. Humanity will be concentrated there numerically and also there will be the greatest human, cul- tural and religious wealth of the world in the future. Christianity can have a future and power only if it succeeds in taking root in this Third World. Christianity was born in Galilee and Palestine, which was the Third World of the Roman empire. Later, it grew among the poorest and most marginalized peoples. But from the sixteenth century onward, it spread to Latin America, Africa, and Asia with the expansion of Western colonialism. This did not prevent the gospel from being preached up to a point in many regions and groups in the Third World—with relative success in some places and disasters in others. But sociologically speaking, Christianity has a Western colonial past, and this stamp remains on it today. The churches of Asia were the ones that suffered most from this past and this stamping, and so they are the ones that most clearly denounce the dominant Western colonial character of Christianity. Latin America, as part of the Third World, is also becoming aware of its indigenous and Afro-American roots, and discovering Christianity's Western colonial character.

The Catholic Church will never be able to take root in the Third World unless it gets away from this Western colonial past and form. It is not a question of radically breaking with the West but of dialectically moving beyond this colonial past, so that Christianity can become indigenized and take root in the Third World. Christianity must get back to its origins and recover its identity in Third World terms, in terms of the world's poor countries and the poor in all the world. The church can have a future only if it succeeds in defining its place and mission in the Third World, where the majority of human beings live and where humanity's greatest human, cultural, and religious wealth is to be found. If the church ignores the Third World today and does not manage to take root there, it could be due to a Western colonial memory of the past. The decolonializing of the church and its "going native" in the Third World means looking at its universality or catholicity from a new point of view. The axis of Catholicity does not pass through New York, London, Paris, Moscow, Tokyo, but through the heart of the Third World countries with all their human, cultural, and religious wealth.

If we take the Third World as Catholicity's new horizon and the place where the church, most importantly, ought to be, we also take up the fundamental contradiction experienced by the Third World today. This fundamental contradiction is between the power centers basically situated in the developed world and the poor oppressed masses of the Third World. This is usually called the North-South contradiction. It is a contradiction between life and death, between the Third World masses struggling for their lives, and the financial, technological, political, cultural, and ideological centers of death situated in the developed world. The contradiction is not with the inhabitants of the industrialized world, but with the centers of power and death situated in that world. At world level the church must increasingly become the spiritual force of the poor and poor countries in their struggle for life against the centers of power and death.

As well as the North-South contradiction, there is the East-West contradiction, but this is not the more significant one for the Third World. On the contrary, the East-West contradiction has been used to cover up the Third World's problems and justify domination of it. It forces us into a kind of geopolitical fatalism, in which opting for the West necessarily means being in contradiction to the East, and vice versa. The world struggle is presented as the confrontation of "democracy" (West) and "communism" (East). We are forced to enter this confrontation and thus we are made to forget the tremendous reality of death in the Third World. In the Third World we opt for life and we want to have the freedom to use what is best in both West and East for the sake of life in the Third World. Our struggle in the Third World is not against communism, but against poverty and wretchedness.

Liberation theology is perhaps the most mature product of the process of de-colonialization and de-Westernization in the church. Liberation theology's future is also linked to this process. However difficult, one of liberation theology's fundamental tasks will continue to be dialogue with Asian and African theologies, and also with other non-Christian Third World religions, as well as the indigenous traditions of Latin America. Liberation theology must grow in the Third World; this is its own natural and "supernatural" cultural and religious space.

7. LIBERATION THEOLOGY AS "PROFESSIONAL" THEOLOGY

Liberation theology has its root in the spirituality and life of the people. Its organic development is in the base communities. But this is not enough. Liberation theology must also have a "professional" development. The word "professional" is not really very appropriate, but it would be worse still to use the word "academic." By professional development I mean that liberation theology should be pursued in a professional way by persons who devote themselves entirely to this task. This professional work must be completely rooted in spirituality, and its organic trunk will be the base communities. The spirituality of the people and the base communities must give life and strength to liberation theology, and liberation theology must draw sustenance from them. In this way, it differs from traditional academic theology, which is sustained and fed by an intellectual life cut off from the people and the ecclesial community. Liberation theology consciously tries to overcome the dualism between intellectuals and the people. We believe in the people's intellectual capacity on the one hand, and on the other we believe that all intellectual activity cut off from the people is sterile.

As a professional theology, liberation theology must fulfill various tasks:

1. *Systemization of the work that has been done*:

From time to time it is necessary to create a vision of the whole, which will allow us to communicate our theology to others, so that it can be studied systematically by those who study theology in a professional manner. This work of systemization is required for the sake of universal communication and dialogue. What is new is that this work is now being done collectively. It is not a *summa theologica* composed by one author.

2. *Dialogue with other, non-theological disciplines*:

In the social and economic sciences as well as in art and literature, a liberating movement is taking place, which is very similar to liberation theology. In former times dialogue was carried on almost exclusively with philosophy. Today we must extend it to other disciplines, and this requires a lot of time and hard work.

3. *Insertion of liberation theology into the church's history and tradition*:

It is necessary to study, critically and systematically, all theological traditions from the viewpoint of liberation theology. Biblical exegesis, church history, the history of spirituality and theology, and many other traditional theological fields must be deepened by liberation theologians—and this also requires a lot of time and hard work.

CONCLUSION

Liberation theology's future is difficult but possible. Liberation theology is the only possible theology *in the Third World* and the only possible future for *theology*.

All this is clear, but it is also a challenge to us. Our certainty in saying this does not come from ourselves but from God and poor, believing Latin Americans. Liberation theology has been given to us; it is a free and transcendent gift of God to our Afro-Indian oppressed America.

In this article I have tried to answer the question: Where lies our strength? This is a fundamental question to prevent us from making mistakes and growing weak in the future. I hope that this article has given a humble and tentative answer to this question. At any rate it represents my deepest conviction and is the result of many years' reflection and experience.

To conclude in a few lines, we can say that liberation theology's future lies in its spirituality, its root in the cultural and religious life of the poor, its commitment to liberation in Latin America. It is the experience of the God of the poor, the freely giving, transcendent God who comes to meet us in the world of the oppressed, who obliges us to do theology, liberation theology. Here fundamentally lies our strength and our intelligence. Furthermore liberation theology's future lies in the EBCs and the rise of a new church model in Latin America. Our theology has always developed in the church, and in the reconstruction of our church as a church of the poor lies our strength and our future. I have also pointed out popular Bible readings and liberation hermeneutics as a fruitful area for growth and development of liberation theology. In the immediate and also the distant future, liberation theology will be above all a biblical theology of liberation. By appropriating the Bible on behalf of oppressed Christianity, liberation theology will discover new strength. The future and power of liberation theology also lie in its capacity for dialogue with Third World theologies, especially with African and Asian theologies of liberation; and with the great Third World non-Christian religions. This is the scope for liberation theology's universal growth. Finally, liberation theology must affirm its future as a professional theology, in dialogue with all the disciplines of liberation.

—translated from the Spanish by Dinah Livingstone

Contributors

LUISE AHRENS is a Maryknoll sister with a master's degree and doctorate in English literature from Fordham University. She served in Bandung, Indonesia, as a professor in the master of arts program at the Provincial University of West Java, taught technology and English at the Bandung Institute of Technology, and was on the staff at the Bandung Catholic Seminary. She returned from Indonesia to serve on the central governing board of the Maryknoll Sisters in March 1983, and was elected president of the congregation in 1984. She is a member of the Global Awareness Committee of the Leadership Conference of Women Religious and on the Board of the U.S. Catholic Mission Association. In 1986 she was awarded the honorary title of doctor of humane letters by Manhattanville College.

ANA FLORA ANDERSON is professor of New Testament studies at the Theological Institute, Nossa Senhora da Assunção (archdiocese of São Paulo), where she teaches in the undergraduate and graduate schools of theology. She is the coordinator of the department of biblical studies in the graduate school of theology and editor of the Jerusalem Bible (in Portuguese). She is author of biblical commentaries on the Gospels of Mark, Matthew, and Luke, and the Apocalypse. During the last twenty years, she has worked in courses of evangelization for basic christian communities.

PAULO EVARISTO ARNS is archbishop of São Paulo, Brazil. He is an active journalist and the author of many books and articles. He is a member of the United Nations Independent Commission on International Humanitarian Issues, Pax Christi International, and the Peace and Justice Service in Latin America. Among the honors he has received are the Nansen Prize from the United Nations High Commissioner for Refugees and France's highest honor, the degree of *Commandeur* in the National Order of the Legion of Honor.

TISSA BALASURIYA, is director of the Centre for Society and Religion in Colombo, Sri Lanka. His books include *Jesus Christ and Human Liberation*; *Eucharist and Human Liberation*; *Planetary Theology*; and *World Churches and Integral Liberation*. He is an editor of *Logos, Quest, Social Justice*, and *Voices of Third World Theology*, and a founding member of the Ecumenical Association of Third World Theologians (EATWOT).

GREGORY BAUM holds a master's degree in mathematics and a doctorate in theology. During the Vatican Council he was a *peritus* at the Secretariat for Promoting Christian Unity. From 1959 to 1986 he taught theology and religious studies at St. Michael's College in the University of Toronto. Since 1986 he has taught at McGill University in Montreal. He is the editor of *The Ecumenist* and a member of the editorial committee of *Concilium*. His most recent book is *Theology and*

Society. Over the last decade or so his main interests have been political theology and social theory. He is an active member of the New Democratic Party, the Canadian equivalent of the British Labor Party.

FREI BETTO (Carlos Alberto Libanio Christo) is a Brazilian Dominican brother who works with ecclesial base communities and pastoral agents. He has studied journalism, philosophy, and theology. He was a political prisoner of the military dictatorship of Brazil between 1969-1973. His books include *Against Principalities and Powers* and *Fidel and Religion.*

ANA MARÍA BIDEGAIN, born in Uruguay, is now a citizen of Colombia. She is a lay Catholic historian of the church. She holds a doctorate in history from the Catholic University of Louvain. She currently teaches at the University of the Andes (Bogotá, Colombia) and Duke University. She has published three books: *Nacionalismo, Militarismo y Dominación en América Latina; Iglesia, Pueblo y Política;* and *Asíactuaron los cristianos en la historia de América Latina.*

MARÍA CLARA BINGEMER, a Brazilian lay Catholic theologian, is a professor of theology at the Pontifical Catholic University of Rio de Janeiro, and the Santa Ursula University. She is presently finishing her doctoral dissertation in systematic theology at the Gregorian University. She is regional coordinator of EATWOT for Latin America and is co-author, with J. B. Libanio, of *Christian Eschatology,* and, with Yvonne Gebara, of *Mary: Mother of God, Mother of the Poor.*

LEONARDO BOFF is a Franciscan priest, educated in his native Brazil and Munich, Germany. A professor of theology in Petrópolis, Brazil, Boff also serves as advisor to the Brazilian Conference of Bishops and the Latin American Conference of Religious. One of the major champions of the theology of liberation, Boff is author of *Ecclesiogenesis*: *Jesus Christ Liberator*; *Church: Charism and Power*; and (with Clodovis Boff) *Introducing Liberation Theology.*

WILLIAM BOTELER is a Maryknoll priest who served fourteen years in Bolivia as a pastor, director of the Family Life Center, and superior of the Maryknoll Bolivian Region. He received a master's degree in theology from the Maryknoll Seminary and a master's degree in pastoral counseling from Loyola College in Baltimore. Presently he is superior general of the Maryknoll Fathers, Brothers, and Lay Missioners.

ROBERT McAFEE BROWN is professor emeritus of theology and ethics at Pacific School of Religion in Berkeley, California. He also taught at Macalester College, Union Theological Seminary, and Stanford University. His first encounter with the thought of Gustavo Gutiérrez came in 1972 when he was asked to write a blurb for the dust jacket of *A Theology of Liberation,* an experience described in his contribution to this volume. Since then, he has tried to interpret Third World theological concerns to North Americans, in such volumes as *Theology in a New Key: Responding to Liberation Themes; Gustavo Gutiérrez; Unexpected News: Reading the Bible with Third World Eyes; Saying Yes and Saying No: On Rendering to God and Caesar;* and *Spirituality and Liberation: Overcoming the Great Fallacy.* In all these works the influence of Gutiérrez is evident. Professor Brown has a Ph.D. from Columbia University, where he studied with Reinhold Niebuhr and John Bennett, and is an ordained Presbyterian minister.

CURT CADORETTE is an associate professor at the Maryknoll School of Theology. He received his doctorate from St. Michael's College in the University of Toronto, where he specialized in the relationship between theology and the social sciences. From 1974 until 1981 he worked in the altiplano of Peru where he did research on indigenous Peruvian cultures. He has published *From the Heart of the People: The Theology of Gustavo Gutiérrez.*

JAMES H. CONE is Charles A. Briggs Professor of Systematic Theology at Union Theological Seminary, New York. His numerous publications include *Black Theology and Black Power; A Black Theology of Liberation; The Spirituals and the Blues; God of the Oppressed;* and *Black Theology: A Documentary History* (with Gayraud Wilmore).

HARVEY COX is Victor S. Thomas Professor of Divinity at Harvard Divinity School. His many books include *The Secular City; Seduction of the Spirit; Religion in the Secular City,* and most recently, *The Silencing of Leonardo Boff: The Vatican and the Future of World Christianity.*

ENRIQUE DUSSEL has doctorates in philosophy, history, and theology. He is professor at the National Autonomous University of Mexico (UNAM) and president of the Commission for the Study of History of the Church in Latin America (CEHILA), coordinator of the same commission in EATWOT, and a member of the Executive Committee of IAMS. His numerous books include *History of the Church in Latin America* and *Philosophy of Liberation.*

VIRGIL ELIZONDO is a native of San Antonio, Texas, who theologizes out of the living faith experience of his own people—the Mexican-Americans. He is the founder and president of the Mexican-American Cultural Center in San Antonio. His pastoral ministry as parish priest and religious educator, his wide experience as teacher, writer, and lecturer, and his doctoral studies in Manila and Paris provide a unique background for his works. Currently he is on the board of *Concilium* and a member of EATWOT. Author of *Galilean Journey: The Mexican-American Promise,* Elizondo is recognized as the major theologian of the Mexican-American faith community.

MARC H. ELLIS received his doctorate from Marquette University and is professor of religion, culture, and society studies at the Maryknoll School of Theology, where he directs the Justice and Peace program. He has written four books, *A Year at the Catholic Worker; Peter Maurin: Prophet in the Twentieth Century; Faithfulness in an Age of Holocaust;* and *Toward a Jewish Theology of Liberation.* Dr. Ellis has been a visiting lecturer at Heythrop College, University of London, and has traveled and lectured extensively in North America, Europe, Latin America, Asia, and the Middle East.

MARIAM FRANCIS has studied in Pakistan, obtaining her M.A. from the University of the Punjab, and in Rome earning a diploma in theology. Currently on the staff of the Pastoral Institute in Multan, Pakistan, she has written extensively for vernacular magazines, especially *Achucha Charwaha,* and for the English periodical *Focus.* Involved principally with the formation of laity, she is actively engaged in interfaith dialogue on women's issues. Her concerns in these last two areas have earned her invitations to consultations of the Federation of Asian Bishops' Conference on Dialogue, in Varanasi in 1983, and of the Christian Conference of Asia in Lahore, Manila, and Singapore.

MARIE J. GIBLIN received her Ph.D. in Christian ethics from Union Theological Seminary in New York City. She is presently assistant professor of theological studies at the Maryknoll School of Theology. She worked for nine years in Tanzania and continues research on Africa with emphasis on U.S.A.-Africa policies.

GILBERTO DA SILVA GORGULHO, a Dominican priest, is professor of Old Testament studies at the Theological Institute, Nossa Senhora da Assunção (archdiocese of São Paulo), where he teaches in the undergraduate and graduate schools of theology. He is coordinator of the department of sacred scripture and president of CESAP (Ecumenical Center of Services in Evangelization and Popular Education). He is editor of the Jerusalem Bible (in Portuguese) and author of biblical commentaries on the Gospels of Mark, Matthew, and Luke, the Apocalypse, and Zechariah. For fifteen years, he has been coordinator of the archdiocesan program on Basic Christian Communities.

NORMAN K. GOTTWALD is Wilbert Webster White Professor of Biblical Studies at New York Theological Seminary. He has pioneered socio-critical study of the Hebrew Bible with the controversial *The Tribes of Yahweh,* and is also the author of *The Hebrew Bible: A Socio-Literary Introduction* and the editor of *The Bible and Liberation.*

ROGER HAIGHT, a Jesuit, is professor of systematic and historical theology at Regis College in the Toronto School of Theology. He received his Ph.D. from the University of Chicago in 1973. Since then he has lived and taught in Asia, Africa, and Latin America. His writings include *An Alternative Vision: An Interpretation of Liberation Theology.*

BARBARA HENDRICKS, a Maryknoll sister, has a B.Ed. and a master's in theological studies. She has twenty-two years of mission experience in Peru and Bolivia. In 1970 she was elected President of the Maryknoll Sisters Congregation and served in this capacity until 1978. During this time she was an active member of the Global Ministry Committee of the Leadership Conference of Women Religious and the U.S. Catholic Mission Council. She recently finished a term of five years as director of orientation for new missioners in the Cochabamba Language Institute in Bolivia, and is presently a member of the staff of the communications department of the Maryknoll Sisters in Maryknoll, N.Y.

CARTER HEYWARD, an Episcopal priest, received her doctorate from Union Theological Seminary, New York. Active in women's and gay/lesbian movements, she is the author of *The Redemption of God: A Theology of Mutual Relation* and *Revolutionary Forgiveness: Feminist Reflections on Nicaragua.* She supports civil rights and antiwar movements, works in solidarity with Central American peoples, and promotes Jewish-Christian feminist endeavors.

FRANÇOIS HOUTART received his doctorate in sociology from Louvain University where he is professor and director of the Center for Socio-Religious Research. He has done extensive research in Asia and Latin America and has published a number of books, including *The Church and Revolution; Genesis and Institutionalization of Indian Catholicism;* and *Church and Revolution in Latin America.*

ADA MARÍA ISASI-DÍAZ, a Cuban-born feminist, activist, and theologian, is a frequent lecturer and writer on Hispanic women and women and the Church. She is the author of *Hispanic Women: Prophetic Voices in the Church.*

CÉSAR JEREZ, a Jesuit, was born in Guatemala. He has a B.A. in classical humanities, M.A. in philosophy from Quito (Ecuador), M.A. in theology from Frankfurt (Germany), M.A. in social sciences and Ph.D. in political science from Chicago, and several honorary doctorates. He was provincial of the Jesuits in Central America (1976–1982) and president of the Provincials' Conference of Northern

Latin America (1979–1982). He is at present rector of the Central American University (UCA) in Managua, Nicaragua, and professor of political science there and at the Landivar University, Guatemala. He has published many articles and books, including *El Salvador, Año Político, 1972; Decisiones Políticas e Integración Centroamericana; Christians and Development.*

ALOYSIUS JIN LUXIAN, a Jesuit father and former rector of the Catholic seminary in Shanghai, who was imprisoned for eighteen years by the communists, was ordained Chinese-appointed auxiliary bishop of the Shanghai diocese in 1985.

STEPHEN JUDD is a Maryknoll missioner from Butte, Montana, with twelve years of pastoral experience in southern Peru among the Aymara and Quechua peoples. Presently he occupies the position of executive director of the *Instituto de Pastoral Andina* in Sicuani near Cusco. Prior to entering Maryknoll in 1972 he received his B.A. and M.A. degrees in Spanish and Latin American literature from the Universities of Montana and New Mexico, respectively. His master's degree in divinity was granted by the Maryknoll School of Theology in 1978. In October 1987 he received his Ph.D., with a specialization in the sociology of religion, from the Graduate Theological Union in Berkeley, California. His dissertation was entitled "The Emergent Andean Church: Inculturation and Liberation in Southern Peru, 1968–1986." In addition he has published articles in *Concilium, Missiology,* and journals in Peru.

STEPHEN KIM is the archbishop of Seoul, South Korea. Cardinal Kim is president of the Bishop's Conference of Korea and has been awarded honorary doctorate degrees at Sogang University in Korea and the University of Notre Dame. He became a cardinal in 1969.

NICHOLAS LASH, a Roman Catholic born in India in 1934, has been Norris-Hulse Professor of Divinity at the University of Cambridge, England, since 1978. His publications include: *His Presence in the World; Change in Focus; Newman on Development; Voices of Authority; Theology on Dover Beach; A Matter of Hope: A Theologian's Reflections on the Thought of Karl Marx; Theology on the Way to Emmaus; Easter in Ordinary: Reflections on Human Experience and the Knowledge of God.* He is a fellow of Clare Hall (Cambridge), a member of the theology committee of the Episcopal Conference of England and Wales, and of the editorial directorate of *Concilium.*

PENNY LERNOUX is a prize-winning American journalist who has worked in Latin America since 1961. She is the Latin American correspondent for the *National Catholic Reporter* and *The Nation,* and contributes to many other publications including *Maryknoll Magazine.* Her books include *Cry of the People,* on the changing role of the Latin American Catholic Church; *In Banks We Trust;* and *People of God: The Struggle for World Catholicism.* She is currently working on the history of the Maryknoll Sisters.

ARTHUR F. McGOVERN, a Jesuit, is currently a professor of philosophy at the University of Detroit. He holds a doctorate from the University of Paris and a licentiate in theology. He has published numerous articles on Marxism and Catholic social teaching. The author of *Marxism: An American Christian Perspective* and co-author of *Ethical Dilemmas in the Modern Corporation,* he is currently completing a work on liberation theology and its critics.

OTTO MADURO was born in Venezuela where he studied at the Central University of Venezuela and at Louvain, from which he obtained his M.A. in religious sociology and his Ph.D. in philosophy magna cum laude. He has held academic posts in his own country and in the United States, where he is a visiting professor at the Maryknoll School of Theology. He has published four books on the general subject of religion and liberation, among them *Religion and Social Conflict,* as well as more than sixty articles and reviews in America and Europe.

MARY JOHN MANANZAN, a Missionary Benedictine sister from the Philippines, has a doctorate degree in linguistic philosophy with a minor in systematic theology and missiology from Wilhelms Universität, Münster, Germany, and the Gregorian University in Rome. She is currently Dean of College of St. Scholastica's College, Manila, and directress of the Institute of Women's Studies. She is active both in the nationalist and women's struggle in the Philippines. She is chairperson of GABRIELA, a national federation of women's organizations, and co-foundress and secretary general of Citizens' Alliance for Consumer Protection. She has edited the Integral Evangelization Series and the Women's Studies series. Her latest publications are *Essays on Women* and *Women and Religion.*

JOHANN BAPTIST METZ is professor of Catholic theology and director of the Institute for Fundamental Theology at the University of Münster. He is a member of the Board of Foundation of the University of Bielefeld and its Center for Interdisciplinary Studies (including the projects of an Ecumenical Research Center). His many books include *Theology of the World; Faith in History and Society; The Emergent Church; Poverty of Spirit; Followers of Christ; The Courage to Pray* (with K. Rahner); *Religion and Political Society* (with J. Moltmann); *Our Hope: A Confession of Faith for this Time,* and *Toward Vatican III* (with Tracy and Küng).

JOSÉ MÍGUEZ BONINO was born in Argentina in 1924. He has a licentiate in theology from the Facultad Evangélica de Teología in Buenos Aires and a Ph.D. in systematic theology. He has held parishes in Bolivia and Argentina, and taught systematic theology and ethics at the Facultad Evangélica de Teología (later ISEDET) since 1954. He has also taught as visiting professor in Italy, France, Great Britain, the U.S.A., Costa Rica, and Chile. He has been active in the ecumenical movement as observer at the Second Vatican Council and member of the Faith and Order and the Presidium of the U.C.C. He was one of the founders of the multiparty and multisectorial Permanent Assembly for Human Rights in Argentina in 1975, during the military regime. He has published numerous articles within the stream of Latin American liberation theology. His latest books are *Room to Be People* and *Toward a Christian Political Ethics.*

MARIE AUGUSTA NEAL is a Sister of Notre Dame de Namur and a professor of sociology at Emmanuel College in Boston. She has been visiting professor of sociology at the University of California at Berkeley, 1968, and at Harvard Divinity School, 1973–75. She is author of *Values and Interests in Social Change; A Socio-theology of Letting Go; Catholic Sisters in Transition;* and *The Just Demands of the Poor.* She has published numerous articles and is a past president of the Association for Sociology of Religion, 1971–72, and of the Society for the Scientific Study of Religion, 1982–84.

ALBERT NOLAN was born in South Africa in 1934. He entered the Dominican Order in 1954 and studied in South Africa and Rome. Since then he has lectured in seminaries and theological schools, has been engaged for some time in pastoral work among the poor, and was for many years a university chaplain. Until recently he was the national chaplain to Catholic students in South Africa and is now provincial of the Dominican Order in Southern Africa.

MERCY AMBA ODUYOYE, a native of Ghana, holds degrees in religion and theology from the University of Ghana and Cambridge University, respectively. She has worked and traveled extensively for several ecumenical organizations, including EATWOT, the World Student Christian Federation, the All Africa Conference of Churches, and the World Council of Churches, and has served as visiting lecturer at Selly Oak Colleges, England, and Harvard University. Author of *Hearing and Knowing*, she is presently Deputy General Secretary of the World Council of Churches in Geneva.

TERESA OKURE, a Roman Catholic sister from Nigeria with a Ph.D. in Scripture from Fordham University, is professor at the Catholic Institute of West Africa in Port Harcourt. She is executive secretary of EATWOT.

ALOYSIUS PIERIS, a Jesuit, founder and director of the Tulana Research Centre in Kelaniya, Sri Lanka, earned the first doctorate in Buddhist studies ever awarded a non-Buddhist by the University of Sri Lanka. He also holds degrees from London University and Pontificia Facoltà di Teologia, Naples. Pieris has taught at Cambridge University, Gregorian University, the Graduate Theological Union, Washington Theological Union, and Union Theological Seminary. An editor of the journal *Dialogue* and a member of EATWOT, he is the author of *Love Meets Wisdom: A Christian Experience of Buddhism* and *An Asian Theology of Liberation*.

SAMUEL RAYAN, an Indian Jesuit, has a B.A. in literature, a licentiate in philosophy, and a doctorate in theology. For some twelve years he served as chaplain to university students. Since 1972 he was professor of theology in the Vidyajyoti Institute of Religious Studies, Delhi. More recently he accepted appointment as principal of the new Indian School of Ecumenical Theology, Bangalore. He is active in ecumenism—serving as a Catholic member of the WCC commission on Faith and Order, 1968–1983—and in the cause of Third World and liberation theologies, as a member of the Indian Theological Association and EATWOT. He co-edits *Jeevadhara,* a journal of Christian interpretation, and numerous articles of his on theological and spiritual topics have appeared in periodicals and books in India and abroad. His published books are: *The Holy Spirit: Heart of the Gospel and Christian Hope*; *The Anger of God*; and *In Christ: The Power of Women*.

PABLO RICHARD was born in Chile in 1939. He has a degree in theology from the Catholic University of Chile, a degree in Holy Scriptures from the Pontifical Biblical Institute, Rome, a doctorate in the sociology of religion from the Sorbonne, Paris, and an honorary doctorate in theology from the Free Faculty of Protestant Theology in Paris. At present he lives in Costa Rica and is titular professor of theology at the National University and a member of DEI (Ecumenical Department of Research). He trains pastoral workers for Ecclesial Base Communities in Central America. His most recent works are: *La Iglesia Latinoamericana entre el temor y la esperanza*; *Morte das Cristiandades e Nascimento de Igreja (Death of Christendoms, Birth of the Church)*; *La fuerza espiritual de la Iglesia de los pobres*.

PETER A. ROSAZZA is regional bishop of the southern region of the archdiocese of Hartford with residence in New Haven. Bishop Rosazza is a member of the National Catholic Bishops' Conference Committee for Latin America and Advisor to the New England Catholic Collegiate Association. He helped to draft the

Catholic Bishops' Pastoral Letter on the United States Economy, and Catholic Social Teaching and the National Pastoral Plan for Hispanic Ministry.

ROSEMARY RADFORD RUETHER is Georgia Harkness Professor at Garrett-Evangelical Seminary. She is contributing editor to *Christianity and Crisis, The Ecumenist,* and *Theology Today.* Her books include: *Faith and Fratricide; Sexism and God-Talk;* and *Contemporary Roman Catholicism: Crisis and Challenges.*

EDWARD SCHILLEBEECKX was born at Antwerp, Belgium, and was ordained in 1941. He studied at Louvain, Le Saulchoir, Paris, the Ecole des Hautes Etudes, and the Sorbonne. He became doctor of theology in 1951 and magister in 1959. Since 1958 he has been teaching systematic theology and hermeneutics at the University of Nijmegen, the Netherlands. He has received several honorary doctoral degrees and, in 1982, the European Erasmus prize for theology. He has authored many books, among them *Jesus, an Experiment in Christology,* and *On Christian Faith, the Spiritual, Ethical, and Political Dimensions.*

ELISABETH SCHÜSSLER FIORENZA is Krister Stendahl Professor of New Testament Studies at Harvard Divinity School. A past president of the Society of Biblical Literature, she is the author of many books on New Testament studies and feminist hermeneutics, including *In Memory of Her* and *Bread Not Stone.*

JON SOBRINO, a Jesuit, is professor of systematic theology at the José Simeón Cañas University of Central America in San Salvador and co-director of *Revista Latinoamericana de Teología* at the same university. He has published numerous articles and books, including *Christology at the Crossroads; The True Church and the Poor; Jesus in Latin America*; and *Spirituality of Liberation.*

DOROTHEE SÖLLE was born in Cologne, Germany. She holds graduate degrees from the universities of Göttingen and Cologne, and has taught philosophy, literature, and theology in several German universities. At present, she divides her year between New York City, where she is a professor at Union Theological Seminary, and Hamburg. Her published works include *Revolutionary Patience* and *Of War and Love.*

SERGIO TORRES was born in Chile and ordained there in 1955. After studying social sciences at the Gregorian University in Rome, he returned to Chile, was named pastoral secretary of the diocese of Talca, and became vicar general under Bishop Manuel Larrío. Between 1973 and 1980 he lived in New York, working in a parish of Spanish-speaking immigrants and participating in the programs of "Theology in the Americas" and of EATWOT. He is the editor of *Theology in the Americas,* and co-editor of *The Emergent Gospel: Doing Theology in a Divided World* and *The Challenge of Basic Christian Communities.* He lives today in Chile, where he is pastor of the parish of San Lucas in the prefecture of Santiago, and teaches systematic theology in the Alfonsín Institute of Pastoral Theology.

DESMOND M. TUTU is a South African bishop and general secretary of the South African Council of Churches. He is the author of *Crying in the Wilderness* and *Hope and Suffering.* Bishop Tutu was awarded the 1984 Nobel Peace Prize.

ELIE WIESEL, winner of the 1986 Nobel Peace Prize, is Andrew W. Mellon Professor in Humanities at Boston University and chairman of the U.S. Holocaust Memorial Commission. His many books include *Night, A Beggar in Jerusalem,* and *Souls on Fire.*